Network and Traffic Engineering in Emerging Distributed Computing Applications

Jemal H. Abawajy
Deakin University, Australia

Mukaddim Pathan
Telstra Corporation Limited, Australia

Mustafizur Rahman
IBM, Australia

Al-Sakib Khan Pathan
International Islamic University, Malaysia

Mustafa Mat Deris
Universiti Tun Hussein Onn, Malaysia

Managing Director: Lindsay Johnston
Senior Editorial Director: Heather A. Probst
Book Production Manager: Sean Woznicki
Development Manager: Joel Gamon
Development Editor: Hannah Abelbeck
Assistant Acquisitions Editor: Kayla Wolfe
Typesetter: Adrienne Freeland
Cover Design: Nick Newcomer

Published in the United States of America by
    Information Science Reference (an imprint of IGI Global)
    701 E. Chocolate Avenue
    Hershey PA 17033
    Tel: 717-533-8845
    Fax: 717-533-8661
    E-mail: cust@igi-global.com
    Web site: http://www.igi-global.com

Library of Congress Cataloging-in-Publication Data

Network and traffic engineering in emerging distributed computing applications / Jemal H. Abawajy [...et al.], editors.
     p. cm.
  Includes bibliographical references and index.
  Summary: "This book focuses on network management and traffic engineering for Internet and distributed computing technologies, as well as present emerging technology trends and advanced platforms"--Provided by publisher.
   ISBN 978-1-4666-1888-6 (hardcover) -- ISBN 978-1-4666-1889-3 (ebook) -- ISBN 978-1-4666-1890-9 (print & perpetual access) 1. Computer networks--Management. 2. Electronic data processing--Distributed processing. 3. Internet. I. Abawajy, Jemal H., 1982-
   TK5105.5.N4648 2013
   621.39'8--dc23
                              2012004761

British Cataloguing in Publication Data
A Cataloguing in Publication record for this book is available from the British Library.

All work contributed to this book is new, previously-unpublished material. The views expressed in this book are those of the authors, but not necessarily of the publisher.

To my lovely wife Maliha Omar and my children – Jemal

To my lovely wife Ziyuan for her warmth, patience, and understanding during the hours of late night when I was busy editing this book. This book would not have come to light without her continuous support – Mukaddim

To my parents – Mustafiz

To my family; parents and all others – Sakib

To my parents, wife and children – Mustafa

Table of Contents

Section 1
Network Management and Traffic Engineering

Yang Hong, Carleton University, Canada
Changcheng Huang, Carleton University, Canada
James Yan, Carleton University, Canada

Mohd Farhan Md Fudzee, Tun Hussein Onn University, Malaysia
Jemal Abawajy, Deakin University, Australia

Raja Al-Jaljouli, Deakin University, Australia
Jemal Abawajy, Deakin University, Australia

Jorge Bernal Bernabé, University of Murcia, Spain
Juan M. Marín Pérez, University of Murcia, Spain
Jose M. Alcaraz Calero, Cloud and Security Lab Hewlett-Packard Laboratories, UK
Jesús D. Jiménez Re, University of Murcia, Spain
Félix J. García Clemente, University of Murcia, Spain
Gregorio Martínez Pérez, University of Murcia, Spain
Antonio F. Gómez Skarmeta, University of Murcia, Spain

Section 2
Emerging Technologies and Advanced Platforms

Detailed Table of Contents

Section 1
Network Management and Traffic Engineering

Chapter 1

Yang Hong, Carleton University, Canada

Changcheng Huang, Carleton University, Canada

James Yan, Carleton University, Canada

This chapter focuses on mechanisms for preventing widespread SIP network failure effectively, by presenting a systematic investigation of current state-of-the-art overload control algorithms. This chapter first reviews two basic mechanisms of SIP, and summarizes numerous experiment results reported in the literatures which demonstrate the impact of overload on SIP networks. After surveying the approaches for modeling the dynamic behaviour of SIP networks experiencing overload, the chapter presents a comparison and assessment of different types of SIP overload control solutions. Finally it outlines some research opportunities for managing SIP overload control.

Chapter 2

Mohd Farhan Md Fudzee, Tun Hussein Onn University, Malaysia

Jemal Abawajy, Deakin University, Australia

This chapter provides coverage of service-oriented content adaptation schemes that have emerged to address content-device mismatch problem. In this scheme, content adaptation functions are provided as services by third-party providers. Clients pay for the consumed services and thus demand service quality. As such, negotiating for the QoS offers, assuring negotiated QoS levels and accuracy of adapted content version are essential. Any non-compliance should be handled and reported in real time. These issues elevate the management of service level agreement (SLA) as an important problem. This chapter presents prior work, important challenges, and a framework for managing SLA for service-oriented content adaptation platform.

Chapter 3

Raja Al-Jaljouli, Deakin University, Australia

Jemal Abawajy, Deakin University, Australia

This chapter discusses the e-negotiation system and its components with particular emphasis on negotiation strategies. A negotiation strategy defines strategic tactics, which advise on the proper action to select from a set of possible actions that optimizes negotiation outcomes. Usually, a fixed strategy is implemented during the course of negotiation regardless of significant decision-making factors including market status, opponent's profile, or eagerness for a negotiated goods/service. This chapter presents the main negotiation strategies and outlines the different decision-making factors that should be considered. It also presents different utility functions in existing literature.

Chapter 4

Jorge Bernal Bernabé, University of Murcia, Spain

Juan M. Marín Pérez, University of Murcia, Spain

Jose M. Alcaraz Calero, Cloud and Security Lab Hewlett-Packard Laboratories, UK

Jesús D. Jiménez Re, University of Murcia, Spain

Félix J. García Clemente, University of Murcia, Spain

Gregorio Martínez Pérez, University of Murcia, Spain

Antonio F. Gómez Skarmeta, University of Murcia, Spain

This chapter presents a proposal for describing high-level security policies and for carrying out the policy refinement process for which low level policies and configurations are achieved. Firstly, an analysis of different research works related to the specification of security policy is provided. Then, a detailed description of the information model used for describing the information systems and the policies is described. After that, the language designed for specifying high level security policies is explained as well as the low level language based on the common information model. Finally, some aspect about the policy refinement process done in the policy-based system in order to achieve low-level policies from the high-level security policies is outlined together with a description of the tools which can assist in the definition of the security policies and in the process refinement process.

Chapter 5

Laiping Zhao, Kyushu University, Japan

Kouichi Sakurai, Kyushu University, Japan

This chapter presents processing and routing techniques for a wireless sensor network that is green aware. While wireless sensor networking plays a critical role in many important applications, it also contributes to the energy footprint - which continues to increase with the proliferation of wireless devices and networks worldwide. Energy-efficiency becomes a major concern in the development of next generation sensor systems and networks. This chapter discusses data management techniques from energy efficiency point of view for green wireless sensor networks.

Chapter 6

This chapter focuses on the next generation networks that must support mobility for ubiquitous communication between any two nodes irrespective of their locations. The process of registration in Mobile IP protocol requires large number of location updates, excessive signaling traffic and service delay. This problem is solved by Hierarchical Mobile IP (HMIP) using the concept of hierarchy of Foreign Agent (FA) and the Gateway Foreign Agent (GFA), Mobility Anchor Point (MAP) to localize the registration information. The performance depends upon the selection of GFA or MAP and some key parameters. This chapter discusses several HMIP based mobility management schemes with a comparative analysis of those protocols and proposes an efficient mobility management scheme.

Section 2
Emerging Technologies and Advanced Platforms

Chapter 7

This chapter provides coverage on autonomous management where the elements of the managed system display individualistic proactive behavior to maintain operations within specific bounds. To this end, dynamically adaptable protocol stack offer a systemic capacity for change during runtime according to current operational requirements, thus providing an essential framework feature of autonomic systems. This chapter presents design blueprints for self-configuration and self-optimization capacities on the basis of protocol frameworks offering dynamic adaptation features.

Chapter 8

This chapter discusses the motivation, challenges, and solutions for network and Internet quality of service management. It outlines real-world scenarios to analyze both the requirements and the related research challenges, discuss the limitations of existing solutions, and goes into the details of practitioners' current best practices, promising research results, and the upcoming paradigm of service level management aware network connections. Special emphasis is put on the presentation of the various facets of the quality assurance problem and of the alternative solutions elaborated with respect to the technical heterogeneity, restrictive information sharing policies, and legal obligations that are encountered in international service provider cooperation.

This chapter presents a computation migration scheme that can achieve dynamic load balancing, improve data access locality, and serve as the enabling mechanism for auto-provisioning of cloud computing resources. This chapter provides a study of concepts behind computation migration and its performance in a multi-instance cloud platform. It introduces a handful of migration techniques working at diverse granularities for use in cloud computing. In particular, it highlights an innovative idea termed stack-on-demand (SOD), which enables ultra-lightweight computation migrations and delivers a flexible execution model for mobile cloud applications.

Chapter 10

This chapter talks about privacy schemes in participatory sensing, which is a revolutionary new paradigm where ordinary citizens voluntarily sense their environment using readily available sensor devices such as mobile phones and systematically study, reflect on, and share this information using existing wireless networks. The potential lack of privacy of the participants in such system makes it harder to ensure their voluntary contribution. Thus preserving privacy of the individuals contributing data has introduced a key challenge in this area. On the other hand, data integrity is desired imperatively to make the service trustworthy and user-friendly. This chapter describes different interesting approaches have been proposed so far to protect privacy that will encourage participation of the owners of data sources in turn.

Chapter 11

This chapter presents a survey of related works on the combination field of workflow scheduling and fault tolerance technologies. Generally, these works are classified into six categories corresponding to the six fault tolerance technologies: workflow scheduling with primary/backup, primary/backup with multiple backups, checkpoint, rescheduling, active replication, and active replication with dynamic replicas. An in-depth study on these six topics illustrates the challenge issues explored so far, e.g. overloading conditions, tradeoffs among scheduling criteria, et cetera, and some future research directions are also identified.

    Yacine Rebahi, Fraunhofer Fokus, Germany
    Reinhard Ruppelt, Fraunhofer Fokus, Germany
    Mohamed Nassar, INRIA Research Center Nancy – Grand Est, France
    Olivier Festor, INRIA Research Center Nancy – Grand Est, France

This chapter highlights that fact that the current shift towards Voice-over-IP (VoIP) networks increases to exposure to fraud due to the lack of strong built-in security mechanisms and the full usage of the open Internet. It discusses an anti-fraud framework within the SCAMSTOP project. Although a short description of the framework is provided, the focus of this chapter is mainly on the methods used to detect fraudulent activity. In particular, this chapter focuses on unsupervised methods including signature and clustering based techniques. Preliminary testing results are also discussed.

Preface

A distributed system consists of several autonomous computers that communicate through a computer network. Usually there is a common goal that all these networked computers try to achieve. The same definition could be rewritten by considering different types of computing devices instead of only computers in traditional sense. Examples of distributed computing systems include wireless sensor networks, Internet, World Wide Web (WWW), Peer-to-Peer (P2P) networks, multiplayer online games network and virtual reality network, distributed database network, distributed information processing network (e.g. airline ticket reservation system), aircraft control system, industrial control system, clustered, and grid systems. As these technology paradigms are very diverse and vast, many types of network management issues are prevalent in present day Internet and distributed computing systems.

Network management and traffic engineering are among the perpetual research issues for any kind of network infrastructure. Any type of wired or wireless network needs proper management of routing, Quality of Service (QoS), fairness, scheduling, security, and similar issues. Some general network management policies could be applied to any kind of network in general, while some schemes work only in a specific network setting. Traffic engineering is a more specific term intended to analyze the traffic pattern, packet movement, and packet handling within the network of devices. Traffic engineering basically deals with the statistical techniques used in telecommunications. Both network management and traffic engineering are needed for Internet and distributed computing environments to ensure proper policies are enacted depending on the requirements at hand. Also, it is important to ensure guaranteed traffic flow among the network entities so that the entire network remains healthy and well functioning.

While management issues may deal more or less with the known issues, the authors and editors envisage a huge expansion of the directions of network related research issues in the coming days. Cloud computing, grid computing, next-generation internet, next-generation network, future internet, green communication, and networking, and other similar terms are becoming more common day-by-day. All these new platforms and settings of networks could offer new research issues that might not have been thought before. Multi-faceted research topics could demand more thought processing and more solutions to the unknown problems and issues. Hence, this book includes chapters that cover some of the futuristic views and emerging trends that are beneficial for the readers.

This book focuses on network management and traffic engineering for Internet and distributed computing technologies, as well as present emerging technology trends and advanced platforms. It puts together some of the critical aspects of Internet and Distributed Systems. This book is expected to serve as a premier reference source for the academics, students, researchers, readers, and knowledge seekers in the related fields. The book focused on including chapters that can easily explain a particular topic, sometimes even a complex issue. In this book, 12 chapters are included after a rigorous review process.

The reviewers and editors who handled the review processes are the experts in the relevant fields. The 12 chapters of this book are divided into 2 sections: (i) Network Management and Traffic Engineering, and (ii) Emerging Technologies and Advanced Platforms.

The first section of the book deals with Network Management and Traffic Engineering issues. The first chapter in this section, by Hong et al., is titled "*A Comparative Study of SIP Overload Control Algorithms.*" This chapter focuses on mechanisms for preventing widespread SIP network failure effectively, by presenting a systematic investigation of current state-of-the-art overload control algorithms. This chapter first reviews two basic mechanisms of SIP, and summarizes numerous experiment results reported in the literatures which demonstrate the impact of overload on SIP networks. After surveying the approaches for modeling the dynamic behaviour of SIP networks experiencing overload, the chapter presents a comparison and assessment of different types of SIP overload control solutions. Finally it outlines some research opportunities for managing SIP overload control.

Fudzee and Abawajy, in chapter 2, "*Management of Service Level Agreement for Service-Oriented Content Adaptation Platform*" provide coverage of service-oriented content adaptation schemes that have emerged to address content-device mismatch problem. In this scheme, content adaptation functions are provided as services by third-party providers. Clients pay for the consumed services and thus demand service quality. As such, negotiating for the QoS offers, assuring negotiated QoS levels, and accuracy of adapted content version are essential. Any non-compliance should be handled and reported in real time. These issues elevate the management of service level agreement (SLA) as an important problem. This chapter presents prior work, important challenges, and a framework for managing SLA for service-oriented content adaptation platform.

Then, Al-Jaljouli and Abawajy present "*Strategies for Mobile Agent-based Negotiation in e-Trade,*" which discusses the e-negotiation system and its components with particular emphasis on negotiation strategies. A negotiation strategy defines strategic tactics, which advise on the proper action to select from a set of possible actions that optimizes negotiation outcomes. Usually, a fixed strategy is implemented during the course of negotiation regardless of significant decision-making factors including market status, opponent's profile, or eagerness for a negotiated goods/service. This chapter presents the main negotiation strategies and outlines the different decision-making factors that should be considered. It also presents different utility functions in existing literature.

Chapter 4, "*Security Policy Specification*" by Bernabé et al. presents a proposal for describing high-level security policies and for carrying out the policy refinement process for which low level policies and configurations are achieved. Firstly, an analysis of different research works related to the specification of security policy is provided. Then, a detailed description of the information model used for describing the information systems and the policies is described. After that, the language designed for specifying high level security policies is explained as well as the low level language based on the Common Information Model. Finally, some aspect about the policy refinement process done in the policy-based system in order to achieve low-level policies from the high-level security policies is outlined together with a description of the tools which can assist in the definition of the security policies and in the process refinement process.

The chapter, "*Workflow Scheduling with Fault Tolerance*" by Zhao and Sakurai presents a survey of related works on the combination field of workflow scheduling and fault tolerance technologies. Generally, these works are classified into six categories corresponding to the six fault tolerance technologies: workflow scheduling with primary/backup, primary/backup with multiple backups, checkpoint, rescheduling, active replication, and active replication with dynamic replicas. An in-depth study on these six topics illustrates the challenge issues explored so far, e.g. overloading conditions, tradeoffs among scheduling criteria, et cetera. Some future research directions are also identified.

Chapter 6, "*Privacy in Participatory Sensing Systems*" concludes this section. In this chapter, the authors, Sabrina and Murshed talk about privacy schemes in participatory sensing, which is a revolutionary new paradigm where ordinary citizens voluntarily sense their environment using readily available sensor devices such as mobile phones and systematically study, reflect on, and share this information using existing wireless networks. The potential lack of privacy of the participants in such system makes it harder to ensure their voluntary contribution. Thus preserving privacy of the individuals contributing data has introduced a key challenge in this area. On the other hand, data integrity is desired imperatively to make the service trustworthy and user-friendly. This chapter describes different interesting approaches have been proposed so far to protect privacy that will encourage participation of the owners of data sources in turn.

The second and final section of the book presents Emerging Technologies and Advanced Platforms to the readers. Wang et al., in "*A Computation Migration Approach to Elasticity of Cloud Computing,*" present a computation migration scheme that can achieve dynamic load balancing, improve data access locality, and serve as the enabling mechanism for auto-provisioning of cloud computing resources. This chapter provides a study of concepts behind computation migration and its performance in a multi-instance cloud platform. It introduces a handful of migration techniques working at diverse granularities for use in cloud computing. In particular, it highlights an innovative idea termed *stack-on-demand (SOD)*, which enables ultra-lightweight computation migrations and delivers a flexible execution model for mobile cloud applications.

"*Managing Network Quality of Service in Current and Future Internet,*" by Yampolskiy et al., discusses the motivation, challenges, and solutions for network and Internet quality of service management. It outlines real-world scenarios to analyze both the requirements and the related research challenges, discuss the limitations of existing solutions, and goes into the details of practitioners' current best practices, promising research results, and the upcoming paradigm of service level management aware network connections. Special emphasis is put on the presentation of the various facets of the quality assurance problem and of the alternative solutions elaborated with respect to the technical heterogeneity, restrictive information sharing policies, and legal obligations that are encountered in international service provider cooperation.

Then, in "*Enabling Frameworks for Autonomic Adaptation of Networking Capacities in Future Internet Systems,*" Gazis et al. provide coverage on autonomous management where the elements of the managed system display individualistic proactive behavior to maintain operations within specific bounds. To this end, dynamically adaptable protocol stack offer a systemic capacity for change during runtime according to current operational requirements, thus providing an essential framework feature of autonomic systems. This chapter presents design blueprints for self-configuration and self-optimization capacities on the basis of protocol frameworks offering dynamic adaptation features.

Chapter 10, "*Mobility Management Issues for Next Generation Wireless Networks*" by Saha and Mukhopadhyay, focuses on the next generation networks that must support mobility for ubiquitous communication between any two nodes irrespective of their locations. The process of registration in Mobile IP protocol requires large number of location updates, excessive signaling traffic and service delay. This problem is solved by Hierarchical Mobile IP (HMIP) using the concept of hierarchy of Foreign Agent (FA) and the Gateway Foreign Agent (GFA), Mobility Anchor Point (MAP) to localize the registration information. The performance depends upon the selection of GFA or MAP and some key parameters.

This chapter discusses several HMIP based mobility management schemes with a comparative analysis of those protocols and proposes an efficient mobility management scheme.

Then, in *"Energy Efficient Data Query, Processing and Routing Techniques for Green Wireless Sensor Networks"* Behzadan and Anpalagan present processing and routing techniques for a wireless sensor network that is green aware. While wireless sensor networking plays a critical role in many important applications, it also contributes to the energy footprint, which continues to increase with the proliferation of wireless devices and networks worldwide. Energy-efficiency becomes a major concern in the development of next generation sensor systems and networks. This chapter discusses data management techniques from energy efficiency point of view for green wireless sensor networks.

"SCAMSTOP: A Platform for Mitigating Fraud in VoIP Environments," by Rebahi et al., is placed as the last chapter of the book that highlights that fact that the current shift towards Voice-over-IP (VoIP) networks increases to exposure to fraud due to the lack of strong built-in security mechanisms and the full usage of the open Internet. It discusses an anti-fraud framework within the SCAMSTOP project. Although a short description of the framework is provided, the focus of this chapter is mainly on the methods used to detect fraudulent activity. In particular, this chapter focuses on unsupervised methods including signature and clustering based techniques. Preliminary testing results are also discussed.

Prior technical sources are acknowledged citing them at appropriate places in the book. In case of any error, the editors would like to receive feedback so that it could be taken into consideration in the next edition. They hope that this book will serve as a valuable text for students especially at graduate level and reference for researchers and practitioners working in the Internet and distributed computing systems and its emerging consumer applications.

Best Regards,
The Editors

Jemal Abawajy
Deakin University, Australia

Mukaddim Pathan
Telstra Corporation Limited, Australia

Mustafizur Rahman
IBM, Australia

Al-Sakib Khan Pathan
International Islamic University, Malaysia

Mustafa Mat Deris
Universiti Tun Hussein Onn, Malaysia

Acknowledgment

The book came into light due to the direct and indirect involvement of many researchers, academicians, developers, designers, and industry practitioners. Therefore, we acknowledge and thank the contributing authors, research institutions, and companies whose papers, reports, articles, notes, Web sites, study materials have been referred to in this book. Furthermore, many of the authors have acknowledged their respective funding agencies and co-researchers, who made significant influence in carrying out research. Throughout the working period of the book, its organization, selection of chapters for specific sections, we were constantly involved in discussion to fine tune our work. We have directed the authors to provide high quality manuscripts with minimal errors within the texts.

With the contributions from authors, we have tried to make this book as rich as possible within our capacity. We thank the Almighty to allow us to complete this work within the given schedule. Alongside the valuable time and efforts from the editors of this book, the authors contributed significantly with their valuable works and opinions during the book editing phase. Because of the rigorous review process and selection policy enforced by the editorial board, we could not include all the submitted chapters. However, we also thank those authors whose contributions could not be selected for the final book. Besides these, we are very thankful to Kristin M. Klinger, Director of Editorial Content and Erika Carter, Acquisition Editor of IGI Global for accepting our book proposal and giving us the opportunity to work on this book project. Last but not the least, we are thankful to the editorial assistant from IGI Global, Hannah Abelbeck, for the continuous support and cordial assistance during our work on the book to keep it in line with the publisher's policies and key dates.

Best Regards,
The Editors

Jemal Abawajy
Deakin University, Australia

Mukaddim Pathan
Telstra Corporation Limited, Australia

Mustafizur Rahman
IBM, Australia

Al-Sakib Khan Pathan
International Islamic University, Malaysia

Mustafa Mat Deris
Universiti Tun Hussein Onn, Malaysia

Section 1
Network Management and Traffic Engineering

Chapter 1
A Comparative Study of SIP Overload Control Algorithms

Yang Hong
Carleton University, Canada

Changcheng Huang
Carleton University, Canada

James Yan
Carleton University, Canada

ABSTRACT

Recent collapses of SIP servers in the carrier networks indicates two potential problems of SIP: (1) the current SIP design does not easily scale up to large network sizes, and (2) the built-in SIP overload control mechanism cannot handle overload conditions effectively. In order to help carriers prevent widespread SIP network failure effectively, this chapter presents a systematic investigation of current state-of-the-art overload control algorithms. To achieve this goal, this chapter first reviews two basic mechanisms of SIP, and summarizes numerous experiment results reported in the literatures which demonstrate the impact of overload on SIP networks. After surveying the approaches for modeling the dynamic behaviour of SIP networks experiencing overload, the chapter presents a comparison and assessment of different types of SIP overload control solutions. Finally it outlines some research opportunities for managing SIP overload control.

INTRODUCTION

Internet telephony is experiencing rapidly growing deployment due to its lower-cost telecommunications solutions for both consumer and business services. Session Initiation Protocol (SIP) (Rosenberg et al., 2002) has become the main

DOI: 10.4018/978-1-4666-1888-6.ch001

signaling protocol to manage multimedia sessions for numerous Internet telephony applications such as Voice-over-Internet Protocol (IP), instant messaging and video conferencing. 3rd Generation Partnership Project (3GPP) has adopted SIP as the basis of its IP Multimedia Subsystem (IMS) architecture (3GPP WG, 2011). With the 3G (3rd Generation) wireless technology being adopted by more and more carriers, most cellular phones and other mobile devices are starting to use or are in the process of supporting SIP for multimedia session establishment (Faccin, Lalwaney, & Patil, 2004).

Figure 1 illustrates a simplified architecture of a SIP network. A SIP network consists of two types of basic elements: User Agent (UA) and Proxy Server (P-Server) (Rosenberg et al., 2002). A user agent can act as a user agent client (UAC) or as a user agent server (UAS). A P-server not only acts as the contact point with UA for core network service access but also provides routing for the signaling messages. SIP is responsible for establishing, modifying and terminating sessions for multimedia communication among multiple UAs.

RFC 5390 (Rosenberg, 2008) identifies the various reasons that may cause server overload in a SIP network. These include but are not limited to poor capacity planning, dependency failures, component failures, avalanche restart, flash crowds, denial of service attacks, etc. In general, anything that may trigger a demand burst or a server slowdown can cause server overload and lead to overload propagation and server crash, thus bringing down the whole SIP network.

The objective of this chapter is to present a systematic investigation of current state-of-the-art SIP overload control algorithms which aim at preventing server crashes in carrier networks. In order to provide a better knowledge of the major

cause of SIP network collapse, the next section reviews two basic mechanisms of SIP, and describes the existing works on the performance study of the SIP overload. The third section surveys the related SIP modeling and analysis which can help network planners, operators, and researchers to understand how server overloading and widespread SIP network failure may happen under short-term demand bursts or server slowdowns. The forth section makes a comparative study of different types of SIP overload control solutions, thus helping carriers choose the appropriate solutions to avoid potential SIP network collapse (e.g., Skype outage (Ando, 2010) or VoIP outages in British Telecom, Vonage and Wanadoo (Materna, 2006)) in different overload situations. Finally, some future works for the SIP overload control are discussed.

SIP OVERVIEW

SIP works in the application-layer for session establishment. Figure 2 depicts a typical procedure of a session establishment. To set up a call, a UAC sends an "Invite" request to a UAS via the two proxy servers. The proxy server or the UAS returns a provisional "100Trying" response to confirm the receipt of the "Invite" request. The UAS returns an "180Ring" response after

Figure 1. Simplified architecture of a SIP network

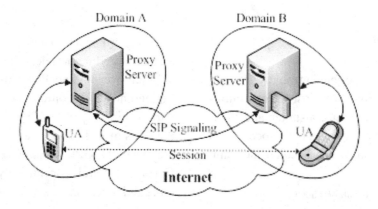

confirming that the parameters are appropriate. It also evicts a "200OK" message to answer the call. The UAC sends an "ACK" response to the UAS after receiving the "200OK" message. Finally the call session is established and the media communication is created between the UAC and the UAS through the SIP session. The "Bye" request is generated to finish the session, thus terminating the communication.

SIP Retransmission Mechanism

SIP works independently of the underlying transport layer where Transmission Control Protocol (TCP) and User Datagram Protocol (UDP) may be deployed. SIP introduces a retransmission mechanism to maintain its reliability (Govind, Sundaragopalan, Binu, & Saha, 2003; Rosenberg et al., 2002). In practice, a SIP sender uses timeout to detect message losses. One or more retransmissions would be triggered if the corresponding reply message is not received in predetermined time intervals.

SIP RFC 3261 (Rosenberg et al., 2002) suggests that the SIP retransmission mechanism should be disabled for hop-by-hop transaction when running SIP over TCP to avoid redundant retransmissions at both SIP and TCP layer (Rosenberg et al., 2002). However, recent experimental evaluation on SIP-over-TCP overload behaviour by Shen & Schulzrinne (2010) demonstrates that TCP flow control mechanism cannot prevent SIP overload collapse for time-critical session-based applications due to lack of application context awareness at the transport layer. Nahum, Tracey, & Wright (2007) claim that using TCP to deliver SIP messages degrades server performance from 43% (under stateful proxy with authentication) to 65% (under stateless proxy without authentication) when compared with using UDP.

Nearly all vendors choose to run SIP over UDP instead of TCP for the following reasons (Hilt & Widjaja, 2008; Hong, Yang, & Huang, 2004; Noel & Johnson, 2007; Shen & Schulz-

Figure 2. A typical procedure of session establishment

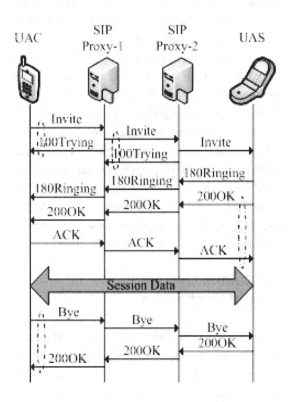

rinne, 2010; Stevens, 1994): (1) The overhead of state management such as three-way handshake prevents TCP from real time application which is a critical requirement for SIP protocol; (2) SIP works at application layer while TCP works at transport layer. Even if TCP can provide reliability at transport layer, SIP messages can still be dropped or corrupted at the application layer; (3) Designed for preventing congestion caused by bandwidth exhaustion, the complex TCP congestion control mechanism provides little help for SIP overload which is caused by CPU constraint.

In order to provide the reliable recovery of the message loss, SIP has two types of message retransmission: (a) a sender starts the first retransmission of the original message at T_1 seconds, the time interval doubling after every retransmission (exponential backoff), if the corresponding reply message is not received. The last retransmission is sent out at the maximum time interval $64 \times T_1$ seconds. Thus there is a maximum of 6 retransmissions. Default value of T_1 is 0.5s. The hop-by-hop "Invite"-"Trying" transaction shown in Figure 2 follows this rule (Rosenberg et al., 2002); (b) a sender starts the first retransmission of the original message at T_1 seconds, the time interval doubling after every retransmission but capping off at T_2 seconds, if the corresponding reply message is not received. The last retransmission is sent out at the maximum time interval $64 \times T_1$ seconds. Thus there is a maximum of 10 retransmissions. Default value of T_2 is 4s. The end-to-end "OK"-"ACK" and "Bye"-"OK" transactions shown in Figure 2 follows this rule (Rosenberg et al., 2002).

SIP Built-in Overload Control Mechanism

When the message arrival rate exceeds the message processing capacity at a SIP server, overload occurs and the queue increases, which may result in a long queuing delay and trigger unnecessary message retransmissions from its upstream servers. Such redundant retransmissions increase the CPU loads of both the overloaded server and its upstream servers. In this way, overload may propagate from server to server in a network, and eventually bring down the entire network (Hilt & Widjaja, 2008).

The SIP protocol provides a basic overload control mechanism through a 503 (Service Unavailable) response (Rosenberg et al., 2002). When a temporary overload occurs at a SIP downstream receiving server, it can decline to forward any request by sending a 503 response to its corresponding upstream sending server. The overloaded downstream server can insert a Retry-After header into the 503 response message, which specifies the duration during which the upstream server should not send any further requests to amplify the overload. After the duration expires, the upstream server can attempt to forward the requests to detect whether the overload is can-

celled at the downstream server or not. Without a Retry-After header, a 503 response only rejects the current request, while all other requests can still be forwarded to the overloaded downstream server. This will amplify the overload by making the overloaded server continue spending CPU resources to reply with further 503s. After receiving a 503 response, the upstream server can try to re-route the request to other alternate server.

Experimental Results of the Impact of SIP Overload

In IP-telephony converged networks, customers expect timely responses to their service requests. Therefore, all the signaling elements must meet the requirements of a session setup, which means that SIP servers should process messages within real-time constraints. The main processing requirements of SIP elements were discussed and a number of performance metrics were described by Cortes, Ensor, & Esteban (2004). Performance measurement based on four different implementations demonstrates that parsing, string handling, memory allocation, and thread architecture have a significant impact on SIP elements (Cortes, Ensor, & Esteban, 2004). Noel & Johnson (2007) have investigated the impact of the overload on a reference SIP-based VoIP network through numerous simulations. Under the two cases of no controls and

Figure 3. Simplest SIP network topology where all user agents are communicating via single proxy server

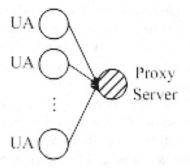

applying 503 Retry overload control mechanism, the comparison of the message goodput and call blocking probability demonstrates that the built-in 503 retry control can increase the message goodput from 32% to 56% (Noel & Johnson, 2007).

Figure 3 depicts the simplest network topology of a SIP system, where all user agents are communicating via a single proxy server. Using the topology shown by Figure 3, Hilt & Widjaja (2008) made performance evaluation of an overloaded SIP server, and their experimental results were shown by Figure 4. In their experiment, the proxy server has a capacity of about 160 calls per second (cps); all associated timer firing intervals use the default values specified in SIP RFC 3261 (Rosenberg et al., 2002); the buffer size of the proxy server is set to be B=1000 messages. Goodput is defined as the effective message throughput, which can

be regarded as the original message rate for setting up the calls.

Figure 4 shows how an overload brings a goodput collapse to a SIP server. During the time period of the initial 1000s, the server has sufficient capacity to process the offered load which mainly consists of the original request messages and corresponding response messages. Thus the server utilization is less than unity, as shown by Figure 4(c). After a calling hold time, the goodput approaches the offered load at about 150 cps, as shown by Figure 4(a). When the offered load increases to exceed the server capacity at time t=1000s, the overload occurs, and the queue builds up to cause buffer overflow. Then the server has to drop messages and triggers retransmission timers and corresponding retransmissions from the user agents, as shown by Figure 4(b). In the mean time, the long queuing delay also triggers

Figure 4. Dynamic behaviour of a SIP server upon an overload

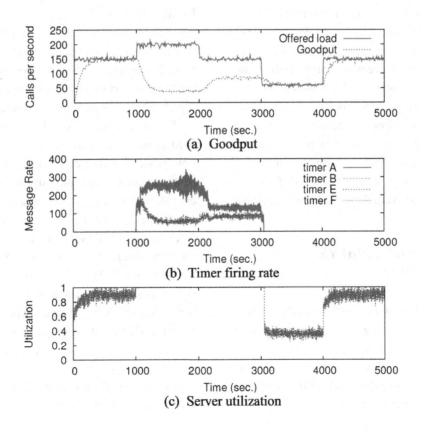

(a) Goodput

(b) Timer firing rate

(c) Server utilization

redundant retransmissions. The retransmissions amplify the offered load significantly, and lead to a low goodput which indicates overload collapse, as shown by Figure 4(a). At time t=2000s, the offered load decreases to 150 cps (i.e., below the server capacity), the server still exhibits a low goodput, indicating the persistent overload collapse. Only after the offered load decreases dramatically at time t=3000s, the server can clear retransmission timers eventually, thus cancelling the overload finally, as shown by Figure 4.

In summary, without additional overload control mechanisms applied, the comprehensive study of SIP overload performance by Hilt & Widjaja (2008) demonstrates the two facts: (1) the servers using the current SIP protocol are vulnerable to overload and overload collapse, when SIP servers are deployed in different domains on a large scale (e.g., different types of session control functions in IMS); (2) a significant drop in goodput can be observed, if the server capacity is reached, when SIP runs over TCP and hop-by-hop retransmission is disabled. In addition, Linux experimental result provided by Nahum, Tracey, & Wright (2007) shows that when overload occurs at a SIP server, the response time increases sharply rather than linearly in proportion to the load, thus deteriorating the performance very quickly.

All these experimental results indicate the potential collapse of a SIP network due to the overload, which has already happened in the real carrier networks (e.g., VoIP outages in British Telecom, Vonage and Wanadoo, see Materna, 2006).

MODELING AND ANALYSIS OF SIP OVERLOAD

Modeling has become an efficient approach to study the properties of a signalling protocol. In order to find the root cause of SIP overload collapse, different analytical models and fluid models have been proposed to analyze the statistical characteristic or dynamic behaviour of SIP.

Analytical Models for Stable Signaling Systems

Prior to SIP becoming the dominant signaling protocol in the Internet, modeling and analysis of general signaling protocols have been done in the past. Ji, Ge, Kurose, & Towsley (2007) compared soft-state and hard-state signaling protocols based on the probabilities of inconsistent states among different servers along a signaling path. The states of a signaling protocol were modelled as a Markov chain under the assumptions: (a) there is no sudden signaling demand surge; (b) both arrival rate and service rate are Poisson process; (c) the signaling network is stable (Ji, Ge, Kurose, & Towsley, 2007). Instead of providing a model for a specific signaling protocol such as SIP, Ji, Ge, Kurose, & Towsley (2007) described five different signaling approaches that incorporate various hard-state and soft-state mechanisms, and qualitatively discussed the factors that influence system performance. All signaling protocols can be classified into five categories: pure soft-state signaling (SS), soft-state signaling with explicit removal (SS+ER), soft-state signaling with reliable trigger messages (SS+RT), soft-state signaling with reliable trigger/removal message (SS+RTR, e.g., SIP), and hard-state signaling (HS).

Ji, Ge, Kurose, & Towsley (2007) uses Figure 5 to describe a general continuous time Markov model for five different types of signaling protocols in a single-hop signaling system. The events, which can occur during a basic signaling operation for a sender/receiver pair (e.g., UAC/UAS pair in a SIP system), can be classified into four signaling categories: (1) **State setup**. When a sender (e.g., UAC) initializes its local state for a signaling session, it transmits a signaling message containing the state to a receiver (e.g., UAS). After a channel delay τ, the message reaches the receiver, enabling the receiver to achieve a consistent state as the sender; (2) **State update**. When a sender updates its local state, it needs to send the new state value to its receiver so that the state update can propagate to the receiver successfully; (3) **State removal**. When a session is terminated, the sender removes its state, and informs the receiver to remove the corresponding state; (4) **False state removal**. A receiver incorrectly removes the state, but its sender still maintains the state. This would terminate the session unexpectedly.

Each state of the Markov model shown by Figure 5 consists of a pair of values (α, β), where α and β are the states of the sender and receiver respectively: (1) Model state $(*,-)$ indicates that a state has been installed at the sender but not at the receiver, representing the initial stage of a session; (2) Model state $(-,*)$ indicates that the sender has removed the state, but the receiver still maintains the state; (3) Model state $(=)$ indicates that both sender and receiver have consistent state; (4) Model state $(\neq)$ indicates that both sender and receiver have different state (i.e., both have installed state, but the state values are different); (5) Model state $(-,-)$ indicates that the state is

removed from both the sender and the receiver, and the system stays at an absorbing state. In addition, every inconsistent state (i.e., $(*,-)$, $(-,*)$ or $(\neq)$) is divided into two separate Markov substates denoted by subscripts 1 and 2.

Figure 5 illustrates the transitions among the Markov states and uses different line styles to indicate four different events (i.e., state setup, state update, state removal, and false state removal) that trigger state transitions, where λ_u is state update rate, λ_d is state removal rate of a sender, and λ_f is false state removal rate of a receiver. Each of five different types of signaling protocols can be modeled using the model (shown by Figure 5) with different transition rates.

In order to provide a better understanding of the Markov model for different types of signaling protocols, we describe the model transitions (shown by Figure 5) for SIP (i.e., SS+RTR protocol) in the following four signaling categories.

Figure 5. Continuous time Markov model for different signaling protocols in single-hop signaling system

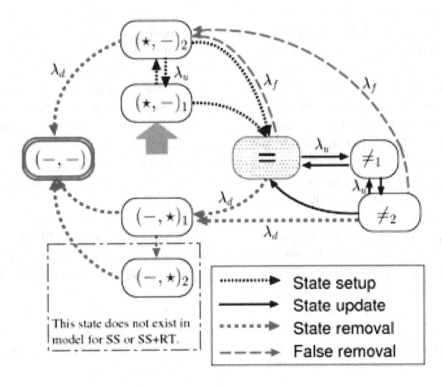

- **State setup:** A sender (or UAC) initializes a new signaling state, corresponding to the initial state $(*,-)_1$ of the model. Then the sender transmits a message to install the consistent state in a receiver (or UAS), followed by one of two events: (1) After a channel delay τ, the message can reach the receiver successfully with a probability $(1-p_l)$, where p_l is channel loss rate. This event is modeled by the transition from state $(*,-)_1$ to state $(=)$ with a rate $(1-p_l)/\tau$; (2) The message is lost with a probability p_l during the transmission. This event is modeled by the transition from state $(*,-)_1$ to state $(*,-)_2$ with a rate p_l/τ. A refresh message will be sent every refresh interval T_F and corresponding retransmitted refresh message will be triggered after a retransmission timer T_R expires. Each refresh message can reach the receiver successfully with a probability $(1-p_l)$. This event is modeled by the transition from state $(*,-)_2$ to state $(=)$ with a rate $(1/T_F+1/T_R)(1-p_l)$.

- **State update:** After a session is established, the Markov chain is in state $(=)$, i.e., the sender (or UAC) and the receiver (or UAS) have consistent state. The event that the sender updates its state with a rate λ_u, is modeled by the transition from state $(=)$ to state $(\neq_1)$ with a rate λ_u, and followed by two events: (1) The state update message reaches the receiver successfully with a probability $(1-p_l)$ after a channel delay τ. The event is modeled by the transition from state $(\neq_1)$ to state $(=)$ with a rate $(1-p_l)/\tau$; (2) The state update message is lost with a probability p_l during the transmission. The event is modeled by the transition from state $(\neq_1)$ to state $(\neq_2)$ with a rate p_l/τ. A refresh message will be sent every refresh interval T_F and corresponding retransmitted refresh message will be triggered after a retransmission timer T_R

expires. Each refresh message can reach the receiver successfully with a probability $(1-p_l)$. This event is modeled by the transition from state $(\neq_2)$ to state $(=)$ with a rate $(1/T_F+1/T_R)(1-p_l)$.

- **State removal:** A sender (or UAC) has a mean state removal rate λ_d, indicating that the mean period of a session is $1/\lambda_d$. If the sender removes its state before the receiver obtain the consistent state, the Markov chain simply transits from state $(*,-)_2$ to state $(-,-)$ with a rate λ_d. If the receiver has the consistent state or inconsistent state, the Markov chain would transit from the corresponding state $(=)$ or $(\neq_2)$ to state $(-,*)_1$ with a rate λ_d. Since a refresh message will be sent every refresh interval T_F and corresponding retransmitted refresh message will be triggered after a retransmission timer T_R expires, the receiver would removes its state if it does not receive refresh message after a state-timeout timer T_X expires, or it receives explicit removal message, or it receives retransmitted explicit removal message after a retransmission timer T_R expires. The event is modeled by the transition from state $(-,*)_1$ to state $(-,-)$ with a rate $1/T_X+(1-p_l)/T_R$.

- **False state removal:** The loss of the refresh message sent by a sender would cause the false state removal at its receiver after the state-timeout timer T_X expires. The event is modeled by the transition from state $(=)$ or $(\neq_2)$ to state $(*,-)_2$ with a rate λ_f.

Based on the same assumptions made by Ji, Ge, Kurose, & Towsley (2007), some models have been created for signaling protocols (e.g., Lui, Misra, & Rubenstein, 2004; May, Bolot, Jean-Marie, & Diot, 1999; Raman & McCanne, 1999; Zaim et al., 2003). Raman & McCanne (1999) presented an analytical model for soft-state protocol and defined an associated consistency metric to evaluate the tradeoffs and performance of soft state communication. Queuing analysis and simulation were performed to study the data consistency and performance tradeoffs under a range of workloads and link loss rates (Raman & McCanne, 1999).

Lui, Misra, & Rubenstein (2004) developed three analytical models to evaluate the robustness of soft/hard state protocols under three network conditions: denial of service attacks, correlated lossy feedback channel, and implosion under multicast services. Simulation results demonstrated that hard state protocols can be optimized to outperform their soft state counterparts under the stable network conditions, but their performance degrades at a much faster rate than that of soft state protocols. Soft state protocols are much more resilient to varying network conditions due to unanticipated fluctuations of call demands in the real signaling network (Lui, Misra, & Rubenstein, 2004).

Hong, Huang, & Yan (2010a) created a Markov-Modulated Poisson Process (MMPP) model to analyze the queuing mechanism of SIP server under two typical service states. The MMPP model can be used to predict the probability of SIP retransmissions, because the theoretical retransmission probability calculated by MMPP model is located within the confidence interval of the real retransmission probability obtained from numerous simulation replications (Hong, Huang, & Yan, 2010a). High retransmission probability caused by short demand surge or reduced server processing capacity during maintenance period may overload and crash a SIP server.

All the above analytical models are useful for studying the statistical performance and predicting the overload probability of a SIP network.

Fluid Model for Overloaded SIP System

As the retransmission mechanism would amplify the SIP overload and make an overloaded SIP

server unstable, the analytical models created for a stable SIP system (e.g., Ji, Ge, Kurose, & Towsley, 2007; Lui, Misra, & Rubenstein, 2004; May, Bolot, Jean-Marie, & Diot, 1999; Raman & McCanne, 1999; Zaim et al., 2003) cannot effectively analyze and evaluate the dynamic performance of an overloaded server.

Hong, Huang, & Yan (2010b) developed a fluid model to capture the dynamic behaviour of SIP retransmission mechanism of a single server with infinite buffer. A related study of a tandem server gives the guidance on how to extend the innovative approach to model an arbitrary SIP network (Hong, Huang, & Yan, 2010b). The fluid model can help researchers speed up the performance evaluation using the fluid-based simulation, when extremely high message arrival rate and service capacity of a SIP network are well beyond the computational capabilities of current event-driven simulators (Liu et al., 2003). Numerous simulation results demonstrate that (1) SIP server behaviour is sensitive to the parameters of signaling demands and initial conditions, a characteristic of chaotic systems; (2) overload at a downstream server can propagate to its upstream servers and therefore cause widespread collapse across a SIP network (Hong, Huang, & Yan, 2010b).

On the other hand, the finite buffer would drop messages when a transient overload cause buffer overflow. Retransmission for message loss recovery is non-redundant, while retransmission trigger by long overload delay is redundant. Another novel strategy was introduced to classify different types of retransmission messages so that a fluid model was created for an overloaded SIP tandem server with finite buffer (Hong, Huang, & Yan, 2011a). The impact of finite buffer size on SIP retransmission mechanism was studied in case of the overload. A small buffer size can be a simple overload control mechanism with a cost of arbitrarily high call blocking rate (Hong, Huang, & Yan, 2011a).

SIP OVERLOAD CONTROL

Recent collapses of SIP servers due to emergency induced call volume or "American Idol" flash crowd in real carrier networks have attracted great research attention and motivated different types of strategies to address SIP server overload problem (Hilt & Widjaja, 2008; Noel & Johnson, 2007; Shen & Schulzrinne, 2010). In order to help researchers gain a comprehensive picture of current proposed SIP overload control solutions, we identify two broad classes of SIP overload control mechanisms: load balancing approach and load reducing approach. Figure 6 depicts the classification for the existing SIP overload control schemes. Load balancing approach aims to avoid the overload by distributing the traffic load equally among the local SIP servers (e.g., Jiang et al., 2009; Warabino, Kishi, & Yokota, 2009), while load reducing approach tries to prevent the overload collapse by reducing the traffic load in the whole SIP network (e.g., Hilt & Widjaja, 2008; Hong, Huang, & Yan, 2010c; Noel & Johnson, 2007; Ohta, 2006a; Shen, Schulzrinne, & Nahum, 2008).

Load Balancing

The load balancing strategy distributes the newly incoming traffic to each local server based on its available processing capacity, thus reducing the probability that overload happens at a specific server. As a default part of numerous operating systems, SIP Express Router (SER) provides a load balancing module to mitigate the overload caused by large subscriber populations or abnormal operational conditions (IP Telecommunications Portal, 2011). Dacosta, Balasubramaniyan, Ahamad, & Traynor (2009) analyzed the relationship between the latency of message delivery and call throughput in a network configuration where SIP proxies are distributed but the database servers are centralized. Request batching was combined with parallel execution to balance the demands for bandwidth and the call failure rates of a SIP proxy, thus improving call throughput and reduce call failure rate significantly (Dacosta, Balasubramaniyan, Ahamad, & Traynor, 2009).

Jiang et al. (2009) proposed three novel algorithms for balancing load across cluster-based SIP servers. Each algorithm estimates the server load dynamically and performs session-aware request assignment. Call-Join-Shortest-Queue algorithm tracks the number of SIP calls allocated to each back-end server and routes a new incoming call to the server with the least number of active calls; Transaction-Join-Shortest-Queue algorithm routes a new incoming call to the server with fewest active transactions, rather than with the fewest calls; Transaction-Least-Work-Left algorithm routes a new incoming call to the server with the least load, given that different type of transaction consume different cost and the work load is determined by the aggregated estimated cost of the total transactions. All three algorithms

Figure 6. The classification for the existing SIP overload control schemes

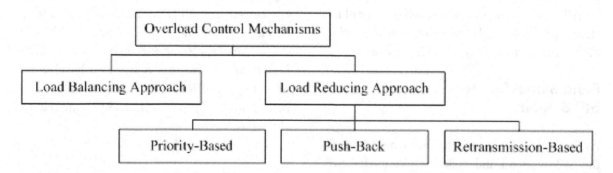

exhibit short response time by distributing requests across the cluster more fairly, thus minimizing occupancy and the corresponding waiting time for a particular request behind others for service (Jiang et al., 2009).

Peer-to-Peer network technology was integrated with SIP to balance the traffic load. Warabino, Kishi, & Yokota (2009) proposed session control architecture "Minimum Core", where the core network cooperates with overlay networks to keep the call-setup time as short as possible, while minimizing processing and traffic load on the core network. In the "Minimum Core", small base stations realize autonomous SIP session control using peer-to-peer technology (Warabino, Kishi, & Yokota, 2009). Huang (2009) applied peer-to-peer technology for locating and discovering interested SIP peers. The peers are virtually grouped by classifying their interested topics into n-tuple overlay virtual hierarchical tree in the overlay network. Caching the addresses of peers can prevent the overload of SIP traffic in tree structure (Huang, 2009).

To achieve fixed-mobile convergence (FMC) and ease the integration with the Internet, IMS aids the access of multimedia and voice applications from wireless and wired terminals. Figure 7 illustrates a simplified architecture of the IMS

control layer. The main elements of the layer are: the Home Subscriber Servers (HSS) and different types of Call/Session Control Function (CSCF) servers with different purposes. The control layer connects to the Application Server (AS) in the application layer and to the User Equipment (UE) through transport layer (3GPP WG, 2011). A Proxy-CSCF (P-CSCF) acts as the contact point for UE to access the core network service; an Interrogating-CSCF (I-CSCF) provides routing for the signaling messages; and a Serving-CSCF (S-CSCF) takes full responsibility for UE registration, session control, and service routing with AS. An IMS core network provides services for individual end users through a complete set of signaling procedures. The main procedures include UE registration and de-registration, P-CSCF discovery, S-CSCF assignment, session establishment and termination, QoS negotiation and home network directing (3GPP WG, 2006). Due to the stochastic nature of signaling traffic, demand burst can potentially overload certain servers and degrade server performance significantly, which may result in the unrecoverable server collapse (Planat & Kara, 2006). When signaling traffic surge overloads an IMS server which can be S-CSCF or P-CSCF or I-CSCF server, load balancing can mitigate the overload by transfer-

Figure 7. Simplified IMS control layer overview

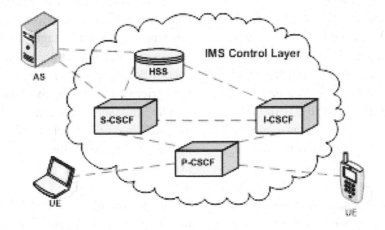

ring part of the load to other servers within the same domain.

S-CSCF load balancing – As each S-CSCF server virtually handles all major tasks and processes the majority of signaling traffic, it is vulnerable to overload (3GPP WG, 2011). To subscribe IMS service, each UE initials the registration to associate with a specific S-CSCF. For administrative purpose, each UE is required to perform re-registration periodically. Experimental data analysis by Xu, Huang, Yan, & Drwiega (2009) demonstrates that the increased percentage in registration/de-registration traffic can only slightly affect the overall load distribution over different IMS elements, thus the changes in registration and de-registration rate may affect the consequent total network traffic load, but have limited impact in the general load distribution. In order to avoid further overload at potentially over-utilized S-CSCF, Xu, Huang, Yan, & Drwiega (2009) proposed de-registration based load balancing scheme to re-directs consequent SIP traffic from the over-utilized S-CSCF to the other under-utilized ones. An AS is deployed in the application layer to communicate with S-CSCFs from the core network, and acts as the load-balancing decision maker. By periodically collecting status information (e.g., server utilization) from each S-CSCF, the AS evaluates the S-CSCF load condition and initiates de-registration requests to the overloaded S-CSCF (Xu, Huang, Yan, & Drwiega, 2009).

P-CSCF load balancing – Each P-CSCF routes the SIP requests between the UE and the other S-CSCF/I-CSCF, and establishes a security association with the UE. Once a UE is registered with a specific S-CSCF, the P-CSCF memorizes the SCSCF for the UE (3GPP WG, 2011). Maintaining the periodic registration for a large number of UEs would consume a large amount of computing and memory resources of SIP nodes (Kitatsuji, Noishiki, Itou, & Yokota, 2010). A UE registration scheme proposed by Kitatsuji, Noishiki, Itou, & Yokota (2010) not only balances the workload

over multiple P-CSCF nodes, but also reduces the required P-CSCF nodes up to 40% from the standard session initialization procedure of IMS.

I-CSCF load balancing – Each I-CSCF stores a routing table and decides the message routing to S-CSCFs. In order to serve a large number of requests as efficient as possible, the I-CSCF has to route SIP messages with minimal state information. A SIP message overload transfer scheme proposed by Geng, Wang, Zhao, & Wang (2006) not only provides efficient SIP message routing in high volume I-CSCF servers to balance the load to different S-CSCF servers, but also leverages redundant servers to reduce the message disruption in cases of server failures.

However, load balancing tries to avoid SIP network failures by reducing the utilization of those servers that may become overloaded. When the total message arrival rate exceeds the aggregated processing capacities of all local servers, load balancing schemes cannot prevent the overload collapse.

Priority-Based Overload Control

When all the local servers are experiencing heavy load, priority-based control approaches aim at mitigating the overload by rejecting the calls with low priority.

A priority enqueuing scheme provides differentiate service for different types of SIP messages in every SIP proxy server, where "INVITE" messages are placed into low priority queue and other types of SIP messages are placed into the high priority (Ohta, 2006a). Each proxy server checks both queues alternately. Only when the high priority queue is empty, the server processes "Invite" messages in the low priority queue. Once the proxy server is overloaded, every "INVITE" message would be hardly forwarded to its destination, thus reducing the traffic load by forbidding the successive non-INVITE transactions (Ohta, 2006a). Instead of holding "INVITE" messages in the low priority queue, two thresholds are created for the low priority queue. When the overload drifts the low priority queue over the lower threshold, the proxy server starts to reject the calls with a certain probability (Garroppo, Giordano, Spagna, & Niccolini, 2009).

Amooee & Falahati (2009) leveraged priority queue to overcome the overload problem of an IMS system by blocking non-priority calls. Similar to the priority scheme, Dacosta & Traynor (2010) developed a novel authentication protocol to reduce the load on the centralized authentication database dramatically, while improving the overall security of a carrier-scale VoIP network.

Push-Back Overload Control

Since the CPU cost of rejecting a session is usually comparable to the CPU cost of serving a session (Shen, Schulzrinne, & Nahum, 2008), cancelling "INVITE" transaction using priority queuing scheme is not very cost effective. Therefore, numerous push-back solutions have been proposed to reduce the traffic loads of an overloaded receiving server by advertising its upstream sending servers to decrease their sending rates.

Local overload control mechanism suggests an overloaded SIP server to reject SIP requests locally by sending 503 responses to its upstream servers without Retry-After header (Hilt & Widjaja, 2008). The 503 response code with no Retry-After header would suppress retransmissions of the rejected requests. In bang-bang control algorithm, each server works at underload and overload states alternately: underload state turns to overload state when message queue size exceeds a high threshold; overload state turns to underload state when message queue size falls below a low threshold. All messages are accepted in underload state, while all new arrival INVITE requests are rejected in overload state (Hilt & Widjaja, 2008). In occupancy algorithm, every new arrival INVITE request is rejected with a probability p, where the probability is regulated dynamically to clamp the processor occupancy

(or utilization) below a given target value (Hilt & Widjaja, 2008). Rejecting a request consumes less processing resources than fully processing it, however, an overloaded SIP server still needs to utilize most of its processing capacity to reject requests if the newly offered workload is very high. In distributed overload control, an overloaded downstream server informs its overload information explicitly to its upstream sending servers, so that each upstream server can reduce the message sending rate to cancel the overload at the downstream server (Hilt & Widjaja, 2008).

A new retry-after control scheme determines the retry-after timer based on the overloaded proxy load so that the overloaded proxy can drain its input queue to a low level more quickly and significant goodput improvement can be achieved (Noel & Johnson, 2009). For processor occupancy control scheme, an overloaded downstream server calculates a target call rate based on its processor occupancy, and then broadcasts the rate to all its upstream servers (Noel & Johnson, 2009). Similarly, queue delay control scheme performs overload control by calculating a target call rate based on the queuing delay of the overloaded server (Noel & Johnson, 2009). Window-based control scheme allows the edge proxy to forward a new call to a core proxy if and only if the number of outstanding call requests for the core Proxy is strictly less than the corresponding window size. Otherwise the edge proxy rejects the respective call of UAC (Noel & Johnson, 2009).

Three window-based feedback control algorithms proposed by Shen, Schulzrinne, & Nahum (2008) make each downstream receiving server dynamically calculate a window size for its upstream servers based on the overload status. Rate control algorithms implemented by Shen, Schulzrinne, & Nahum (2008) attempt to clamp the message queuing delay or the processor occupancy below a target value. In addition, many other push-back solutions have been proposed to improve the goodput of an overloaded server (e.g., Abdelal & Matragi, 2010; Homayouni, Jahanbakhsh, Azhari, & Akbari, 2010; Montagna & Pignolo, 2010; Ohta, 2006b; Shen & Schulzrinne, 2010; Sun, Tian, Hu, & Yang, 2009; Wang, 2010; Yang, Huang, & Gou, 2009).

The main idea of the push-back control solutions is to cancel the overload of a server by reducing the sending rate of its upstream servers. This would increase the queuing delays of newly arrival original messages at the upstream servers, which in turn cause overload at the upstream servers. Overload may thus propagate server-by-server to sources. Unlike a source in TCP typically generates large amount of data, a UA in SIP only generates very few signalling messages. This leads to rejections of a large number of calls which means revenue loss for carriers. However, it may be unnecessary to reject calls when temporary overload only lasts a short period of time.

Retransmission Rate-Based Overload Control

When retransmissions are caused by the overload rather than the message loss, they will bring extra overhead instead of reliability to the network and exacerbate the overload (Sun, Tian, Hu, & Yang, 2009). Through the analysis on the queuing dynamics of two neighboring servers, Hong, Huang,

& Yan (2010c) discovered the root cause of the overload propagation which had been verified by numerous experiments (e.g., Hilt & Widjaja, 2008; Noel & Johnson, 2007). Figure 8 depicts the queuing dynamics of two neighboring servers where the initial overload occurs at the downstream Server 2 due to server slowdown (Hong, Huang, & Yan, 2010c). There are two queues at each server: one to store the messages and the other to store the retransmission timers (Hilt & Widjaja, 2008; Shen, Schulzrinne, & Nahum, 2008). The queuing dynamics for the message queue of the downstream Server 2 can be obtained as

$$\dot{q}_2(t) = \lambda_2(t) + r_2(t) + v_2(t) - \mu_2(t), \qquad (1)$$

where $q_2(t)$ is the queue size and $q_2(t) \geq 0$; $\lambda_2(t)$ is original message rate; $r_2(t)$ is retransmission message rate; $v_2(t)$ is response message rate; $\mu_2(t)$ is the message service rate.

Like Equation (1), we can obtain the queuing dynamics for the message queue of the Server 1 as

$$\dot{q}_1(t) = \lambda_1(t) + r_1(t) + r_2'(t) + v_1(t) - \mu_1(t), \qquad (2)$$

Figure 8. Queuing dynamics of an overloaded server and its upstream server

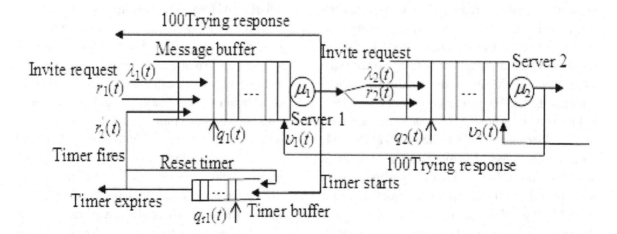

where $q_1(t)$ is the queue size and $q_1(t) \geq 0$; $\lambda_1(t)$ is original message rate; $r_1(t)$ is retransmission message rate corresponding to $\lambda_1(t)$; $r'_2(t)$ is retransmission message rate generated by Server 1 for $\lambda_2(t)$; $v_1(t)$ is response message rate corresponding to $\lambda_1(t)$, and the response messages will remove the corresponding retransmission timers from timer queue q_{r1}; $\mu_1(t)$ is the message service rate. When Server 2 performs its routine maintenance and reduces its service capacity for signaling messages, the original message rate $\lambda_2(t)$ is larger than the service rate $\mu_2(t)$, the queue size $q_2(t)$ tends to increase according to Equation (1) (i.e., $\dot{q}_2(t) > 0$). After a short period, the queuing delay of Server 2 is long enough to trigger the retransmissions $r'_2(t)$ which enter the queue of Server 1. If the total new message arrival rate of $\lambda_1(t)$, $v_1(t)$ and $r'_2(t)$ is larger than the service rate $\mu_1(t)$, the queue size q_1 would increase (i.e., $\dot{q}_1(t) > 0$, as indicated by Equation (2)) and may trigger the retransmissions $r_1(t)$ to bring the overload to Server 1. This indicates the overload propagation from the downstream Server 2 to its upstream Server 1. After queuing and processing delay at Server 1, the retransmitted messages $r'_2(t)$ enter Server 2 as $r_2(t)$ to increase the queue size $q_2(t)$ more quickly (as described by Equation (1)), thus making the overload at Server 2 worse.

Therefore, while other existing load reducing approaches aim at reducing the original message sending rate of the upstream servers, reducing the retransmission rate can mitigate the overload while maintaining the original message sending rate. The advantages of keeping the original sending rate are less blocked calls and more revenue for the carriers. The key to the retransmission-based solution is to detect overload reliably so that overload can be differentiated from the occasional message loss.

A solution for the differentiation is as follows. A copy of each original message is placed into a retransmission timer queue at an upstream sending server after it is transmitted to a downstream re-

ceiving server. A corresponding response message disables the retransmission timer by removing the original message from the retransmission timer queue. Otherwise, a retransmission would be triggered to recover the potential message loss. When the overload at the downstream receiving server delays the processing of the original message thus the corresponding response, the retransmission timer queue builds up and unnecessary retransmissions are stimulated. Therefore, the queue size of retransmission timer queue was used to detect the overload and a heuristic Retransmission Timer Queue Control (RTQC) algorithm was proposed by Hong, Huang, & Yan (2011b) to mitigate the overload by controlling retransmission rate. When the overload is anticipated at a downstream server, its upstream servers retransmit the messages with a probability based on the instantaneous retransmission timer queue size. Figure 9 depicts the relationship between retransmission probability and retransmission timer queue size. Maximum queue threshold q_{rmax} and minimum queue threshold q_{rmin} are chosen to calculate retransmission probability p. Both queue thresholds are adaptively tuned by the average original message departure rate of the upstream server (Hong, Huang, & Yan, 2011b). The packet loss over the Internet causes the message loss directly. Global packet-loss index provided by The Internet Traffic Report (ITR, 2010) indicates that current global packet loss statistic averaged $\zeta = 8\%$ packet loss. A minimum retransmission probability p_{min} is maintained to achieve a low call blocking probability in case of the overload (Hong, Huang, & Yan, 2011b). The main advantage of the heuristic control algorithm is its simple implementation structure. However, when sporadic bandwidth congestion at the TCP layer causes arbitrarily high message loss thus creating a long retransmission timer queue at the SIP layer, the minimum retransmission probability would lead to sluggish message loss recovery.

Only a retransmitted message for message loss recovery is a non-redundant request message as well as an original message, while a retransmis-

Figure 9. Retransmission probability vs. retransmission timer queue size in case of SIP overload

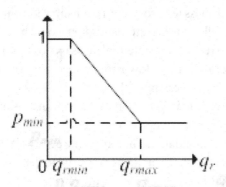

sion caused by the overload delay is redundant. Correspondingly, a response message corresponding to a redundant retransmitted message is redundant. Thus the redundant retransmission ratio was adopted as the overload indicator (Hong, Huang, & Yan, 2010c). Using a control-theoretic approach, the interaction of an overloaded downstream server with its upstream server was modelled as a feedback control system in Hong, Huang, & Yan (2010c). They proposed the Redundant Retransmission Ratio Control (RRRC) algorithm to keep the redundant retransmission ratio to an acceptable level by controlling the retransmission message rate of its upstream servers, thus mitigating the overload at the downstream server. Since redundant retransmission messages can only be detected after its corresponding response messages are received, such delay might lead to sluggish reaction and potential throughput loss.

As the queuing delay has been well accepted as a more reliable indicator of overload, some existing push-back solutions (e.g., Noel & Johnson, 2007; Shen, Schulzrinne, & Nahum, 2008) attempt to clamp the bottleneck queuing delay below a predefined target queuing delay by reducing the original message rate. The impact of the retransmission rate on the queuing delay of an overloaded server was studied. For the round trip delay between an overloaded server and its

upstream server, the queuing delay is dominant, while transmission and propagation delay are negligible (Shen, Schulzrinne, & Nahum, 2008). The upstream server can estimate the round trip delay as the queuing delay of its overloaded downstream server. Hong, Huang, & Yan (2011c) developed the Round Trip Delay Control (RTDC) algorithm to clamp the queuing delay of the overloaded downstream server below a desirable target delay.

Without the modification of the SIP header, the three retransmission-based control solutions (i.e., RTQC, RRRC and RTDC) locate the control algorithm in each upstream server and detect the overload in the downstream server implicitly. In case of short-term overload, the retransmission-based control mechanism can mitigate the overload effectively without rejecting calls or reducing network utilization, thus avoiding the disadvantages of other types of overload control solutions.

Standards on SIP Overload Control

Gurbani, Hilt, & Schulzrinne (2011) have proposed The Internet Engineering Task Force (IETF) Request for Comments (RFC) draft recently to provide the design guideline for SIP overload control mechanism. The Internet-draft defines new parameters for the SIP via header for overload control. These parameters are used to convey overload control information between SIP entities (Gurbani, Hilt, & Schulzrinne, 2011). Different types of the overload control approaches summarized above can be the candidates of future SIP overload control mechanism for potential large scale deployment in the carrier networks.

CONCLUSION AND RESEARCH OPPORTUNITIES

This chapter has briefly reviewed the signaling mechanism of SIP, the dominant signaling protocol in the Internet. The retransmission mechanism for maintaining SIP reliability and the built-in overload control mechanism with limited efficiency have been introduced. Then the chapter has reviewed two main modeling approaches to help researchers understand the root cause of the SIP overload collapse through analyzing theoretically the statistical characteristics and dynamic behaviour of a SIP system. Finally current proposed SIP overload control solutions have been classified into four different types and discussed in details.

Load balancing mechanism and SIP built-in overload control mechanism have been deployed in the carrier networks. Other three types of load reducing approaches are still in the stage of research proposals. Unlike load balancing, priority-based and retransmission-based control approaches, most existing push-back control solutions recommended by SIP overload control RFC (Gurbani, Hilt, & Schulzrinne, 2011) require the modification of the SIP message header in order to explicitly exchange the overload information between neighbouring servers. However, changing the SIP message header requires a time-consuming standardization process and the cooperation among different carriers in different countries. Considering a large scale deployment of SIP servers in the current Internet, new overload control schemes must be incrementally deployable, and slight increases in complexity or cost may be strongly resisted by the carriers. The solutions without modifying protocol header may lure more interests from the carriers due to the ease of quick implementation.

Resource over-provisioning can reduce the overload probability significantly, but such passive action would cause low average capacity utilization and increase the capital costs. Rejecting calls can mitigate the overload quickly, but it would reduce the revenue and decrease user satisfaction index. It may be unnecessary to reject calls upon a short-term overload.

In the future work, carriers and researchers can cooperate to evaluate the efficiency of different SIP overload control approaches by performing field test in the carrier networks. To achieve a good trade-off between the revenue and the response time to cancel the overload in different overload scenarios (e.g., short-term overload and long-term overload), more research is needed to determine how to choose and combine different types of overload control approaches to avoid the potential SIP overload collapse.

REFERENCES

Abdelal, A., & Matragi, W. (2010). Signal-based overload control for SIP servers. In *Proceedings of IEEE CCNC*, Las Vegas, NV.

Amooee, A. M., & Falahati, A. (2009). Overcoming overload in IMS by employment of multiserver nodes and priority queues. In *Proceedings of International Conference on Signal Processing Systems*, (pp. 348-352).

Ando, R. (2010, December 22). Internet phone and video service Skype went down in a global service outage. *Reuters News*. Retrieved from http://www.reuters.com/article/idUSTRE6BL47520101222

Cortes, M., Ensor, J. R., & Esteban, J. O. (2004). On SIP performance. *Bell Labs Technical Journal*, *9*(3), 155–172. doi:10.1002/bltj.20048

Dacosta, I., Balasubramaniyan, V., Ahamad, M., & Traynor, P. (2009). Improving authentication performance of distributed SIP proxies. In *Proceedings of IPTComm*, Atlanta, GA.

Dacosta, I., & Traynor, P. (2010). Proxychain: Developing a robust and efficient authentication infrastructure for carrier-scale VoIP networks. In *Proceedings of the USENIX Annual Technical Conference*, Boston, MA.

Ejzak, R. P., Florkey, C. K., & Hemmeter, R. W. (2004). Network overload and congestion: A comparison of ISUP and SIP. *Bell Labs Technical Journal*, *9*(3), 173–182. doi:10.1002/bltj.20049

Faccin, S. M., Lalwaney, P., & Patil, B. (2004). IP multimedia services: Analysis of mobile IP and SIP interactions in 3G networks. *IEEE Communications Magazine, 42*(1), 113–120. doi:10.1109/MCOM.2004.1262170

Garroppo, R. G., Giordano, S., Spagna, S., & Niccolini, S. (2009). Queueing strategies for local overload control in SIP server. In *Proceedings of IEEE Globecom*, Honolulu, Hawaii.

Geng, F., Wang, J., Zhao, L., & Wang, G. (2006). A SIP message overload transfer scheme. In *Proceedings of ChinaCom*.

Govind, M., Sundaragopalan, S., Binu, K. S., & Saha, S. (2003). Retransmission in SIP over UDP - Traffic engineering issues. In *Proceedings of International Conference on Communication and Broadband Networking*, Bangalore, India.

3GPP WG. (2006). *IP multimedia subsystem Cx and Dx interfaces: Signaling flows and message contents*. 3GPP TS 29.228, Release 7, v7.6.0.

3GPP WG. (2011). *3rd generation partnership project*. Retrieved from http://www.3gpp.org

Gurbani, V., Hilt, V., & Schulzrinne, H. (2011). *Session initiation protocol (SIP) overload control*. IETF Internet-Draft, draft-ietf-soc-overload-control-02.

Hilt, V., & Widjaja, I. (2008). Controlling overload in networks of SIP servers. In *Proceedings of IEEE ICNP*, Orlando, Florida, (pp. 83-93).

Homayouni, M., Jahanbakhsh, M., Azhari, V., & Akbari, A. (2010). Controlling overload in SIP proxies: An adaptive window based approach using no explicit feedback. In *Proceedings of IEEE Globecom*, Miami, FL, USA.

Hong, Y., Huang, C., & Yan, J. (2010a). Analysis of SIP retransmission probability using a Markov-modulated Poisson process model. In *Proceedings of IEEE/IFIP Network Operations and Management Symposium*, Osaka, Japan, (pp. 179–186).

Hong, Y., Huang, C., & Yan, J. (2010b). Modeling chaotic behaviour of SIP retransmission mechanism. *International Journal of Parallel, Emergent and Distributed Systems*, iFirst. doi:10.1080/17445760.2011.647912

Hong, Y., Huang, C., & Yan, J. (2010c). Mitigating SIP overload using a control-theoretic approach. In *Proceedings of IEEE Globecom*, Miami, FL, U.S.A.

Hong, Y., Huang, C., & Yan, J. (2011a). Modeling and simulation of SIP tandem server with finite buffer. *ACM Transactions on Modeling and Computer Simulation, 21*(2). doi:10.1145/1899396.1899399

Hong, Y., Huang, C., & Yan, J. (2011b). Controlling retransmission rate for mitigating SIP overload. In *Proceedings of IEEE ICC*, Kyoto, Japan.

Hong, Y., Huang, C., & Yan, J. (2011c). Design of a PI rate controller for mitigating SIP overload. In *Proceedings of IEEE ICC*, Kyoto, Japan.

Hong, Y., Huang, C., & Yan, J. (2012). Applying control theoretic approach to mitigate SIP overload. *Telecommunication Systems Journal*, in press.

Hong, Y., Yang, O. W. W., & Huang, C. (2004). Self-tuning PI TCP flow controller for AQM routers with interval gain and phase margin assignment. In *Proceedings of IEEE Globecom*, Dallas, TX, US, (pp. 1324-1328).

Huang, L. (2009). Locating interested subsets of peers for P2PSIP. In *Proceedings of International Conference on New Trends in Information and Service Science*, (pp. 1408-1413).

ITR. (2010). *Internet traffic report*. Retrieved from http://www.internettrafficreport.com/

Ji, P., Ge, Z., Kurose, J., & Towsley, D. (2007). A comparison of hard-state and soft-state signaling protocols. *IEEE/ACM Transactions on Networking, 15*(2), 281–294. doi:10.1109/TNET.2007.892849

Jiang, H., Iyengar, A., Nahum, E., Segmuller, W., Tantawi, A., & Wright, C. (2009). Load balancing for SIP server clusters. In *Proceedings of IEEE INFOCOM*, (pp. 2286-2294).

Kitatsuji, Y., Noishiki, Y., Itou, M., & Yokota, H. (2010). Service initiation procedure with on-demand UE registration for scalable IMS services. In *Proceedings of the Fifth International Conference on Mobile Computing and Ubiquitous Networking*, Seattle, WA.

Liu, Y., Presti, F. L., Misra, V., Towsley, D. F., & Gu, Y. (2003). Scalable fluid models and simulations for large-scale IP networks. In *Proceedings of ACM SIGMETRICS*, (pp. 91-101).

Lui, J. C., Misra, V., & Rubenstein, D. (2004). On the robustness of soft-state protocols. In *Proceedings of IEEE ICNP*, Berlin, Germany, (pp. 50–60).

Materna, B. (2006). Threat mitigation for VoIP. In *Proceedings of Third Annual VoIP Security Workshop*, Berlin, Germany.

May, M., Bolot, J. C., Jean-Marie, A., & Diot, C. (1999). Simple performance models of differentiated service schemes for the Internet. In *Proceedings of IEEE INFOCOM*, (pp. 1385–1394).

Montagna, S., & Pignolo, M. (2010). Comparison between two approaches to overload control in a real server: "Local" or "hybrid" solutions? In *Proceedings of IEEE MELECON*, (pp. 845-849).

Nahum, E. M., Tracey, J., & Wright, C. P. (2007). Evaluating SIP server performance. In *Proceedings of ACM SIGMETRICS*, San Diego, CA, US, (pp. 349–350).

Noel, E., & Johnson, C. R. (2007). Initial simulation results that analyze SIP based VoIP networks under overload. In *Proceedings of 20th International Teletraffic Congress*, Ottawa, Canada, 2007.

Noel, E., & Johnson, C. R. (2009). Novel overload controls for SIP networks. In *Proceedings of 21st International Teletraffic Congress*, 2009.

Ohta, M. (2006a). Overload protection in a SIP signaling network. In *Proceedings of International Conference on Internet Surveillance and Protection*.

Ohta, M. (2006b). Overload control in a SIP signaling network. In *Proceeding of World Academy of Science* (pp. 205–210). Vienna, Austria: Engineering and Technology.

Planat, V., & Kara, N. (2006). SIP signaling retransmission analysis over 3G network. In *Proceedings of MoMM2006*, Yogyakarta, Indonesia.

Raman, S., & McCanne, S. (1999). A model, analysis, and protocol framework for soft state-based communication. In *Proceedings of ACM SIGCOMM*, Boston, MA, US.

Rosenberg, J. (2008). *Requirements for management of overload in the session initiation protocol*. IETF RFC 5390.

Rosenberg, J., et al. (2002). SIP: Session initiation protocol. *IETF RFC 3261*.

Shen, C., & Schulzrinne, H. (2010). On TCP-based SIP server overload control. In *Proceedings of IPTComm*, Munich, Germany.

Shen, C., Schulzrinne, H., & Nahum, E. (2008). SIP server overload control: Design and evaluation. In *Proceedings of IPTComm*, Heidelberg, Germany.

Stevens, W. R. (1994). *TCP/IP illustrated (Vol. 1)*. Boston, MA: Addison-Wesley.

Sun, J., Tian, R., Hu, J., & Yang, B. (2009). Rate-based SIP flow management for SLA satisfaction. In *Proceedings of IEEE* (pp. 125–128). New York, USA: IFIP IM.

Telecommunications Portal, I. P. (2011). *SIP express router*. Retrieved from http://www.iptel.org/ser/

Wang, Y. G. (2010). SIP overload control: A backpressure-based approach. *ACM SIGCOMM Computer Communications Review*, *40*(4), 399–400.

Warabino, T., Kishi, Y., & Yokota, H. (2009). Session control cooperating core and overlay networks for "minimum core" architecture. In *Proceedings of IEEE Globecom*, Honolulu, Hawaii.

Xu, L., Huang, C., Yan, J., & Drwiega, T. (2009). De-registration based S-CSCF load balancing in IMS core network. In *Proceedings of IEEE ICC*, Dresden, Germany.

Yang, J., Huang, F., & Gou, S. Z. (2009). An optimized algorithm for overload control of SIP signaling network. In *Proceedings of 5th International Conference on Wireless Communications, Networking and Mobile Computing*.

Zaim, A. H. (2003). JumpStart just-in-time signaling protocol: A formal description using extended finite state machines. *Optical Engineering (Redondo Beach, Calif.)*, *42*(2), 568–585. doi:10.1117/1.1533795

KEY TERMS AND DEFINITIONS

Hard-State Signaling Protocol: In hard-state signaling protocol, a receiver holds the installed state until it receives a state teardown message from its sender which explicitly requests to remove the installed state.

Session Initiation Protocol (SIP): SIP is the main signaling protocol to manage multimedia sessions for numerous Internet telephony applications such as Voice-over-IP, instant messaging and video conferencing. 3rd Generation Partnership Project (3GPP) has adopted SIP as a basic signaling protocol of its IP Multimedia Subsystem (IMS) architecture for IP-based streaming multimedia services in wireless systems.

SIP Overload: SIP overload occurs when a signaling element, such as a SIP user agent or proxy, has insufficient resources to process all the arrival messages successfully. Resources represent the total capabilities which a signaling element can use to process a message. Resources not only include internal resources such as CPU processing, memory, input/output, or disk resources, but also include external resources such as a database or DNS server, where CPU processing, memory, input/output, and disk resources of those servers are effectively part of the logical element processing the message.

Soft-State Signaling Protocol: In soft-state signaling protocol, the state of a receiver should be removed automatically when its time-out timer expires. In order to maintain a session for a service, the sender that initially installed the state should periodically sends a refresh signaling message to keep the corresponding state in its receiver. SIP is a soft-state signaling protocol.

Chapter 2
Management of Service Level Agreement for Service-Oriented Content Adaptation Platform

Mohd Farhan Md Fudzee
Tun Hussein Onn University, Malaysia

Jemal Abawajy
Deakin University, Australia

ABSTRACT

It is paramount to provide seamless and ubiquitous access to rich contents available online to interested users via a wide range of devices with varied characteristics. Recently, a service-oriented content adaptation scheme has emerged to address this content-device mismatch problem. In this scheme, content adaptation functions are provided as services by third-party providers. Clients pay for the consumed services and thus demand service quality. As such, negotiating for the QoS offers, assuring negotiated QoS levels and accuracy of adapted content version are essential. Any non-compliance should be handled and reported in real time. These issues elevate the management of service level agreement (SLA) as an important problem. This chapter presents prior work, important challenges, and a framework for managing SLA for service-oriented content adaptation platform.

INTRODUCTION

Recently, Gantz and Reinsel (2010) reported that the current amount of digital content available online is 487 billion gigabytes (GB) and is expected to increase rapidly. Most of these existing contents however, are originally designed for display on desktop computers. With the proliferation of client devices varied in their sizes and capabilities (e.g., processing power, input and output facilities), it is becoming increasingly difficult for direct content delivery to varying devices without layout adjustment (Mohan et. al, 1999). Moreover, not every device can play all media types or formats. For

DOI: 10.4018/978-1-4666-1888-6.ch002

example, a non-multimedia mobile phone cannot play continuous video clips, while only H.264, MPEG-4 and M-JPEG formats are currently supported for iPhone video playback. As such, certain widely employed video formats such as MKV and FLV will require format conversion or additional player before they can be played on iPhone. To address this problem, a service-oriented content adaptation platform that provides content adaptation functions as services to clients has recently emerged as an efficient, flexible, and scalable paradigm (Berhe et.al, 2005; Nordin et.al, 2007; Shahidi et.al, 2008; Liu et.al, 2008; Tonnies et.al, 2009). Example of content adaptation functions are format conversion, transcoding, distillation and media translation (Mohan et. al, 1999; Lum and Lau, 2003; Hsiao et.al, 2008).

The service-oriented content adaptation is distributed and totally open platform. Three major requirements for a service-oriented content adaptation system are performance, availability and security. Performance requirements imply the capability of coping with different workload intensity, adapting rich content to various adaptation requirements and assuring service quality. Availability and security requirements suggest that the system must always ready to serve clients requests, and capable to withstand attacks and failure (Park et.al, 2001). In this chapter, we focus on service quality assurance. This is achieved through service level agreement (SLA).

A client's content request is composed of multiple content objects which require a series of content adaptation tasks (Shahidi et.al, 2008). In the service-oriented content adaptation scheme, each task is performed by a particular content adaptation function that potentially be provided by multiple services located across the wide-area network. Clients pay for the consumed content adaptation services, thus demand service quality. As such, appropriate services are selected based on QoS levels tailored to specific adaptation requirements. Commitment negotiated upon by both clients and providers is officially documented through the

SLA. During service delivery, negotiated SLAs require real-time verification (Zhou et.al, 2005). This makes the monitoring and measurement of SLA an important issue. If violation occurs, appropriate action (e.g., penalty, conflict resolution) should be taken. As such, a mechanism to handle SLA compliancy is required. On the other hand, when an SLA is likely to be violated, the corresponding service provider can take proactive action that includes outsourcing the task to the similar service provider (Park et.al, 2001; Pathan and Buyya, 2009a). These issues necessitate an effective management of the SLA.

In this chapter, our main contribution is a framework of SLA management for service-oriented content adaptation. The assurance of QoS in service-oriented systems is becoming increasingly important for both clients and service providers (Park et.al, 2001). This necessitates the requirement for SLA. However, SLA is being neglected in existing service-oriented content adaptation systems (Berhe et.al, 2005; Nordin et.al, 2007; Merat et.al, 2008; Tonnies et.al, 2009). Moreover, unlike other Internet services (e.g., VoIP, content delivery network) that focus solely on monitoring network and throughput QoS levels (Menasce, 2002; Prokkola, 2007), SLA for service-oriented content adaptation should take into account content adaptation accuracy-related QoS (e.g., translation accuracy, conversion accuracy). We have incorporated these issues in constructing the framework.

The work presented in this chapter will provide readers the background knowledge of SLA management for service-oriented content adaptation systems.

BACKGROUND

In recent years, the challenge of service-oriented content adaptation is shifting from a focus on enabling content adaptation performed by a set of services (i.e., composite services), to a focus on assuring accurate adapted content version delivered within promised QoS levels. As more clients start to use content adaptation as a service discovered in a real time manner, and as the number of competing services with similar adaptation function increases, QoS is becoming a differentiating factor; thus SLA management will become more important. In this section, we describe the motivational example and related research issues.

Motivational Example

To motivate the necessity of SLA for service-oriented content adaptation, consider this:

Zack went to visit his relative at Royal Women's hospital in Melbourne. Zack learns that his relative has been diagnosed with a heart complication. To get more information on the heart complication that his relative diagnosed with, Zack decided to browse, using his web-enabled mobile phone, the e-health server at the hospital. Confronted with medical jargons received from the e-health server and to make sense of it all, Zack decided to browse an e-learning server. Zack prefers a summary of the heart condition explanation in French text. However, the content on the e-learning server consists of several inter-related pages of heart and blood vessels information and each contains a long English text with some related graphics.

Suppose Zack is a subscriber of ABC system that provides content adaptation as a service. As a client, Zack logs into the system to facilitate his request. During previous registration, he ticked time and cost QoS types in the client QoS requirement checkbox. The system analyses Zack's content adaptation requirements using a built-in adaptation decision-taking engine and realizes that two content adaptation tasks are required (i.e., (a) t_1: English to French text translation, and (b) t_2: French text summarization) to achieve the desired content form (i.e., a summarized French text for each Web page). The system looks up at a participant business registry r to find suitable services that is capable of performing these two tasks. Further suppose that the potential providers have been discovered.

Let us say t_1 and t_2 can be performed by services s_1 and s_2 respectively. Providers of services t_1 and t_2 advertise 'one for all' QoS level offers for both cost and time QoS. Assume both services are free (i.e., cost $= 0$) via trial version. Adaptation time offered by s_1 and s_2 are 13000 and 9500 milliseconds respectively. Then, providers of services s_1 and s_2 are contacted to perform related tasks. When the adapted content version is ready, it is sent back to Zack's mobile device.

To motivate the need for SLA, a basic experiment is conducted to measure the actual QoS delivery for this content adaptation scenario. It is used to demonstrate if non-compliance (e.g., violation) can occur. In this experiment, the monitoring apparatus only monitors the adaptation time QoS. The cost QoS is not monitored as it is freely provided to the client. Assume the required content object level for both tasks t_1 and t_2 have been delivered accordingly. The experiment is run for two requesting devices with different capability. The first client device is a mobile (i.e., iPhone 3GS) using 3G wireless HSPDA 7.2Mbps network, while the second device is a desktop PC running on 100Mbps network. Desktop device is used as a comparison in order to study the impact of QoS levels (i.e., execution time) on different device capabilities. In this experiment, adaptation time is measured when the task is initiated until the adapted content is displayed at client displays (Hsiao et.al, 2008). s_1 and s_2 are provided by Babelfish Yahoo! (http://babelfish.yahoo.com/) and ExtractorLive (http://www.extractorlive.com/on_line_demo.html), respectively. The content object files (http://www.uri.edu/e-health/index.php) size varies from 15,000 to 30,000 bytes and mainly made up of text and some images.

Figure 1 captured the adaptation time QoS. The result has revealed that the adaptation time for the same task and file size is varied between two different requesting devices. For instance, a client requesting content using a mobile device experience longer time to receive the adapted content version. Please note however, the accuracy of measured value is influenced by network bandwidth.

The implication of the experiment is threefold. First, on the client standpoint, the QoS offers being delivered can be violated. This necessitates a mechanism to monitor and assure actual QoS levels are tailored with the promised QoS levels. Second, on the service provider standpoint, 'all for one' QoS offer (i.e., fixed SLA) has impact on business (e.g., marketing). Take waiting time QoS for example - the provider may advertise waiting time QoS based on a certain server load. For instance, if the offered QoS is for the worst case scenario (e.g., heavy load), they may lose business to others that offer better QoS levels. On the other hand, if the offered QoS is for the best

case scenario (e.g., fair load), it may easily lead to violation and get penalized when experiencing flash crowds. This suggests that providers should negotiate QoS offers with clients based on individual adaptation requirements. Alternatively, providers can advertise separate QoS levels for different set of client device or preference groups. This is also aligned with the claim made by Park et al (2001) that QoS expectations are driving clients to negotiate specific QoS levels with their providers. Third, on the administration standpoint, non-compliance of QoS level is not necessarily being a violation. It can be resulted from other parties, such as network or natural disaster. In this light, certain non-compliance should be considered as conflict that requires resolution rather than penalty. This necessitates the requirement for SLA management. In this context, the central problem is how to provide quality management that beneficial for both clients and service providers.

Figure 1. Monitoring adaptation execution against varied file sizes for desktop and mobile devices

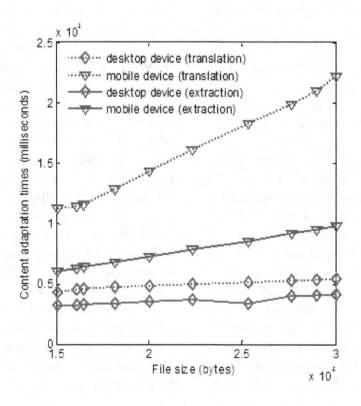

Research Issues of SLA Management

A service level agreement (SLA) is a formal contract negotiated between a service provider and the client for the service. It outlines the relationship between parties to understand each other's needs, preferences and expectations. It should include how to perform future service delivery including QoS levels required, performance-tracking techniques, performance reports, managing problems and conflicts, security and termination (Triennekens et.al, 2004). The management of SLAs is a new challenge and of an important issue in service-oriented content adaptation. Here, we highlight some of the main research issues on SLA management. It can be divided into:

- **SLA definition and performance QoS:** It deals with standard for service level (QoS) performance parameters in Internet services: what they are and how their value are derived or computed for the SLAs. However, some SLAs are made of non-standardized QoS metrics and attributes, especially when the QoS specifications are provided by different providers. This is due to a different perception of the same concept and different type of system reading for the same metric (i.e., different associated units [minutes versus seconds] thus implying different associated value [1 versus 60] respectively) (Brandic et.al, 2009). As a result, it arouses the problem of inferring equivalence on two QoS metrics. Moreover, unlike other Internet services, it is important to have a standard to specify the accuracy of adapted content object in service-oriented content adaptation platform.
- **SLA negotiation:** In practice, existing service providers advertise 'one for all' QoS offer for their published services. The offered QoS are accepted directly without further negotiation, which render this approach (i.e., fixed SLA) violation-prone (Menasche, 2002). Due to the heterogeneity of adaptation requirements (i.e., client devices and preference, network bandwidth and variation of amount of content requested) and current adaptation server load, a mechanism for negotiating QoS levels is of important requirement. Negotiation enables QoS being negotiated for specific adaptation requirements before agreement between clients and providers is finalized.
- **SLA measurement and monitoring:** This issue deals with how to accurately measure the QoS being delivered to the client. Each service QoS levels should able to be measured accordingly (Kritikos and Plexousakis, 2009). Client should receive exact adapted content version. This necessitates accurate measurement tool for each adaptation function. A standard and cost effective monitoring apparatus should serve as the basis for effective SLA management. This issue includes the placement of monitoring apparatus.
- **SLA compliance management:** This issue deals with how to manage and control QoS levels delivered to comply with negotiated SLAs. A non-compliance of SLA is not necessarily a violation. It can be caused by a conflict as well. As such, a mechanism to determine the type and the corresponding action of an SLA non-compliance case requires urgent attention. This includes reporting mechanism to deal with clients who demand real-time reporting of SLA compliance (Park et.al, 2001). The report is used to confirm that clients are receiving QoS levels and the adapted content version they were promised.
- **Service outsourcing:** Selected service providers may not been able to meet the QoS demand by clients. One way to deal

with this is by rejecting future requests, however, this action may increase clients' frustration and decrease service providers' reputation (Xu et.al, 2007). On the other hand, there are many services that provide the same adaptation function. In this case, an over-committed service provider can outsource tasks to others in order to guarantee negotiated QoS levels. A new SLA is negotiated between the new client (i.e., the provider who outsources the task) and service provider (i.e., the peer provider that undertakes the outsourced task). This necessitates an efficient management for service outsourcing.

Noticeably, QoS is the key factor that relates the agreement within an SLA between the client and the service provider. There are several views of quality that can be implemented in managing SLA for service-oriented content adaptation platform (Kritikos and Plexousakis, 2009; Pathan and Buyya, 2009b). *Quality as functionality* is measured by considering the amount of functionality that a service can offer to its clients. One service is considered better than others in one of these two cases: it provides a function (or additional function) that is not provided by other, or/and secondly it provides a better value for the same function across providers. *Quality as conformance* is a view of comparing the actual QoS delivery with the promise. A good service means that it delivers no less than the stated promise. *Quality as reputation* depends on clients expectation and experience from the service. It is built collectively over the time of the service existence from clients' feedback (Xu et.al, 2007). A service with good reputation means that it consistently provided specific functionality with specific performance over the time. Most of existing Internet services (e.g., Park et.al, 2001; Pathan and Buyya, 2009b) based their QoS monitoring using *quality as conformance* view.

Much research work has been done on service's quality definition and description for Internet and Web services (Zhou et.al, 2005; Kritikos and Plexousakis, 2009). Efforts such as WSML (Sahai et.al, 2002), WSLA (Ludwig et.al, 2003), DAML-QoS (Zhou et.al, 2004) and OWL-Q (Zhou et.al, 2005) are trying to make QoS description more flexible to describe and present the formal description of a service. To address non-standardized QoS metrics and attributes, a mechanism for mapping SLAs is studied in Brandic et. al 2009. However, to the best of our knowledge, there is no attention given on describing content adaptation performance QoS in service-oriented content adaptation.

SLA monitoring also has received a considerable attention. Monitoring is performed on performance QoS metrics. Prokkola (2007) classifies QoS into two: objective and subjective. Objective QoS is concrete and quantitative. It can be measured directly (e.g., throughput, packet loss ratio, packet delay, packet jitter). Subjective QoS, on the other hand, corresponds to the service quality from the user perspective or experience i.e., how does the user feel about the quality. It is much more difficult to be measured. Mean opinion score (MOS) tests are often used in actual measurements (Prokkola, 2007). Existing monitoring apparatus such in Pathan and Buyya (2009b) can be used to monitor objective QoS such as waiting time. Additionally, a suitable mechanism and tool to measure adaptation performance QoS is also required for service-oriented content adaptation.

To date, few frameworks (Park et.al, 2001; Bhoj et.al, 2001; Zhou et.al, 2005; Brandic et.al, 2009) for managing SLA exists but it does not fit well with service-oriented content adaptation. This is due to the different requirements of SLA for service-oriented content adaptation scheme. For example, adapted content version requires accuracy assurance in addition to QoS levels. Thus, what is required is a framework for managing SLA that is tailored for service-oriented content adaptation.

A MANAGEMENT FRAMEWORK FOR SERVICE LEVEL AGREEMENT

In this section, we will give a brief description of the management framework of SLA for the service-oriented content adaptation platform. This includes the outline of essential components required for managing SLA.

Conceptual Framework

SLA is a powerful mechanism for expressing all commitments, expectations and restrictions in a business transaction (Balakrishnan and Somasundaram, 2011). It formally identifies what guarantees are being offered to the client. The main objectives of SLA in service-oriented content adaptation are (a) to facilitate two-way communication between negotiating parties that includes understanding of need, priorities, and specifications, (b) to protect against expectation creep that includes the identification and negotiation of service levels, (c) to have mutually agreed standard, and (d) to gauge service effectiveness that includes the basis for performing assessment.

In this framework, brokers and providers have the mechanism to establish SLA. A broker, on behalf of the client, negotiates SLA with service providers. These newly created SLA clearly express the required QoS to be maintained till the end of services execution, the required content object level to be delivered, the penalties in case of failure to provide the offered QoS and the resolution actions in case of a conflict. Interaction between participating parties is bound by reference policies. After the successful creation of SLAs, providers are tasked to perform adaptation. These services execution are monitored to ensure offered QoS levels and required content adaptation are obeyed. In case of any violation against these offered levels, or any conflict; either decided or reported by the client, there should be an enforcement mechanism to penalize the provider or to resolve the conflict, respectively. Figure 2 depicted the SLA framework for service-oriented content adaptation scheme.

The framework serves a workflow to manage SLA. It is composed of three inter-related phases: (a) creation, (b) monitoring, and (c) enforcement. A service-oriented content adaptation platform spans across multiple stakeholders, i.e., clients, service providers and brokers. To enable transparent interaction between stakeholders and serve as the system's guidelines, reference policies are required.

Figure 2. SLA framework for service-oriented content adaptation

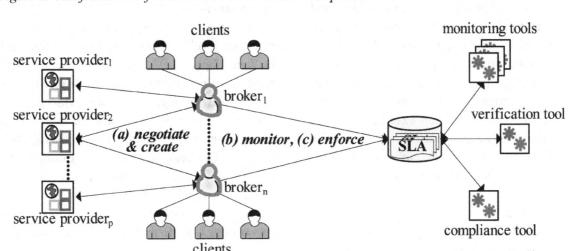

Reference Policies

Reference policies are created by the administrator. These policies can be modified, added or deleted. Stakeholders are obligated to these policies while dealing with one another through the system. For example, each broker must refer to broker policy before initiating negotiation with service providers. Four policies are defined as the following:

- **Broker policy:** The broker policy specifies (a) how the broker interacts with the client when a content request is initiated, (b) how the broker plays the roles in order to decide the adaptation decision and to delegate the tasks for serving the request, (c) how broker determines the content object level required, (d) how broker coordinates with other components (i.e., negotiation, compliance manager, and monitoring apparatus) in the framework, (e) how to manage and cope with changing circumstances (e.g., service failure) in order to enforce the SLA, and (f) how to manage the client's complaint.
- **SLA policy:** The SLA policy specifies (a) the stakeholders of a given SLA, (b) SLA definition, (c) how SLA is defined through assertions, (d) where SLAs are stored (e) how SLA compliance is monitored, (f) how SLA is negotiated between providers and clients, and (g) how SLAs are terminated.
- **Services execution policy:** This policy specifies (a) the interaction requirement for the participating service providers, (b) how service chain is formed and communication is invoked to execute tasks, (c) what are the protocols for service chaining, (d) how to handle violations and conflicts detected during execution, (e) how to terminate the service chain when the client is served, (f) how to rearrange the service chain when recovery operation is required or outsourcing operation is activated, and

(g) how to finalize payment to the services in the service chain when termination is successful.
- **Bypassing policy:** The bypassing policy specifies (a) the bypassing conditions (e.g., content server failure, natural disaster, theft, etc.), and (b) the necessary actions when a bypassing condition is declared or detected. This includes adequate provision for disaster recovery and business continuity planning to protect the continuity of the services being delivered.

Creation Phase

Creation phase is responsible for creating negotiated SLA of each service required to perform a given task. Negotiation occurs in either one of these two scenarios: (a) between the provider and the broker, or (b) between one provider with another (in case of service outsourcing or peering). In this chapter, we focus on the former case. The motivation for negotiation in the first scenario is due to the fact that existing service providers advertise 'one for all' QoS offer for their published services. The offered QoS levels are accepted directly without further negotiation i.e., fixed SLA. However, due to the heterogeneity of adaptation requirements (e.g., requests' size), network bandwidth and providers' server load, this approach is shown to be violation-prone.

Also, a particular provider may not be able to meet QoS levels; either demanded by or promised to clients. Specifically, this can be due to several reasons such as: (a) the provider realized that its current load is heavy; and (b) the provider realizes that the current requests being served will free up some resources in a short time, thus QoS adaptation (i.e., new QoS) can be offered. For example, if a provider realizes that it cannot deliver within the offered QoS (e.g., waiting time) due to heavy load, the potential requests being can be offered with a new waiting time. In this sense, the response time (i.e., adaptation time + waiting time) for the client to get the adapted content version is being revised.

SLA creation stores essential information. This information includes service definition and specification, client's adaptation requirement, performance metrics (i.e., QoS), QoS measurement and reporting, non-compliance management (i.e., penalties and conflict resolution), and bypassing conditions. Table 1 and 2 show some examples of common QoS and specific performance QoS. Standard QoS description and ontology is stored in the QoS ontology database. QoS ontology is important to define standard description and specification between stakeholders. It can be developed in a manner similar to Dastjerdi et al (2010).

Negotiation

Figure 3 illustrates the negotiation process including the interaction sequence. Service providers advertise services in a participating business registry. A broker, on behalf of the client discovers available services from the registry. A particular discovery technique such in Pathan and Buyya (2009a) can be used to filter the candidate services. When suitable services are selected, the broker initiates negotiation with providers for new QoS levels to customize with the specific adaptation requirement (e.g., how much c cost and t times it takes to perform a task of s size) and to consider current load, until a final agreement is achieved. For instance, a service provider advertises one base

cost c_b and time t_b for serving a request of s size. The broker can internally determine the request size and estimate the actual cost and time based on the given advertisement. At the provider's end, it performs the same cost and time calculation. If both parties agree with the new calculated adaptation time and cost QoS, SLA can be settled.

Also, the provider might need to anticipate the current load to evaluate whether the offered waiting time QoS is within delivery or not. If the provider realized that its current load is heavy, it rejects the incoming requests. Alternatively, it internally calculates the expected waiting time and negotiates for QoS adaptation with the broker of the request. If both parties agree with the new calculated adaptation time, cost and waiting time QoS, SLA is settled and the request is queued into the buffer, waiting to be served. During negotiation, both parties refer to the QoS ontology and related reference policies as guideline, so that the same QoS specifications are used.

Negotiation can be classified into three: one-to-one, one-to-many and many-to-many. Administrator decides which approach to be implemented, as long as it can maximize clients' utility. A study by Kersten and Lai (2007) provides an insight on existing negotiation approaches and strategies. In our context, one-to-one approach is used for its simplicity of bargaining (Fatima et. al, 2006). For each task, the broker negotiates with the potential provider for the best QoS offer. This is performed for all tasks, simultaneously or in sequence. The

Table 1. Example of common QoS for a service

QoS	QoS category	QoS description	Example of QoS metric	Example of SLA
Adaptation time	Objective	Time required to perform the adaptation function	millisecond, second, minute	Service must be delivered ≤ (110% of negotiated time)
Waiting time	Objective	Waiting time before the request is being served	millisecond, second, minute, time unit	Waiting time ≤ (promised waiting time)
Cost	Objective	Cost charged to perform the adaptation function	cent, dollar	Cost charged ≤ negotiated cost
Rating	Subjective	Denote the rating of service delivery	Likert scale	not available

Table 2. Example of adaptation functions including related objective QoS and SLA

Adaptation functions	Function description	Objective QoS	Example of SLA
Filter	Remove information, content	Accuracy	100% of required information is removed
Annotate	Add information to content	Accuracy Completeness	>90% of subtitles annotation is accurate >95% of the movie file is annotated with subtitles
Transcode	Change to different format (within the same content type)	Accuracy	Transcoded content format must be readable and contain > 95% of the original object
Translate	Change to different content language	Accuracy Completeness	95% of English translation is accurate 95% of English text is translated
Convert	Change to different content type	Accuracy Completeness	The converted version is semantically tailored with the original version The converted version must 100% be in the new content type required
Extract	Extract keyword/ summarize from content	Accuracy	>80% of the summarized text is accurate, readable (i.e., in the same language of the original version) and error free.

final deal must tailor at both ends when deadline is met. In future, we plan to explore one-to-many approach. The negotiation component enables providers to engage in QoS negotiation with the broker, while at the same time, providers in negotiation maintain a reference table of QoS commitments made to others. In practice, QoS negotiation is done at session level which is in sequence of service requests. Also, different QoS metrics or unit between negotiating parties can be mapped in real time, in a manner similar to Brandic et al (2009). When the negotiation process is suc-

cessful, the negotiated SLA is stored in the SLAs repository and is achieved during verification.

SLA Schema

A generic SLA schema is used to document the negotiated SLA for each service. The WS-agreement acts as wrapper around this schema (Balakrishnan and Somasundaram, 2011). The schema consists of one root element called *SLA* tag. It consists of five core child elements: *SLAID, ServiceID, Expiration, Service Level Objective (SLO),* and *Non-compliance* tags. The *SLAID* tag specifies the

Figure 3. Negotiation in creation phase

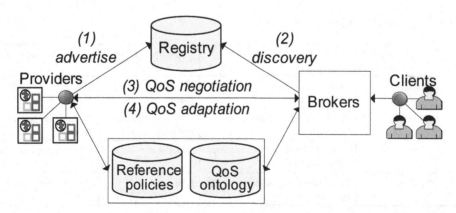

Table 3. Example of an SLA tags property

SLA ID	Service ID	Expiration	Service level objectives	Non-compliance
$001.s_m$	s_m	(dd/mm/yyyy)	QoS levels:- Q_1^p , cost: [type: cost]; [offer value:50]; [unit: cents]. Q_2^p , transcoding accuracy: [type: accuracy];[offer value: > 90]; [unit: %]. Q_3^p , waiting time: [type: time];[offer value: 200]; [unit: millisecond]. Content required:- Q_4^p , output required: [file type: movie]; [unit format: AVI]; [unit fps: 25fps]; [unit res.: 800*480].	Violation [penalty]; Q_1^p : [receipt adjustment]. Q_2^p and Q_4^p : [p_1: 50% cost reduction], [p_2: re-adaptation] Q_4^p : [30% cost reduction]. Conflict resolution [action]; Q_1^p , Q_2^p , Q_3^p and Q_3^p : [notice of conflict] Bypassing conditions: [ISP failure, disaster] [Action: terminate SLA]

SLA id while the *Service ID* tag specifies the service id for which this SLA is created. The expiration time of this SLA is specified in the *Expiration* tag. *SLO* tag contains *QoS Type* with corresponding *Offered QoS*, and *Content object level Required* child elements. For each QoS $\in \{1...n\}$, descriptions containing the negotiated QoS type (e.g., cost, rating and adaptation time) is specified in *QoS Type*, whereas the negotiated QoS level is specified in *Offered QoS* tag. *Content object level Required* specifies the required adaptation level of the content object. The *SLO* tag will be later used during verification process. Suppose any non-compliance of SLO caused by the provider or reported by the client, the *non-compliance* tag is referred. It stored the consequences of violation or conflict. If a violation is decided, the penalty specified in *Violation* tag is referred, whereas if a conflict is decided, the resolution action specified in the *Conflict* tag is referred. Table 3 depicts the example of an SLA tags property.

To formally describe the SLO within an SLA, assertion is used. This formalization provides a feasible solution for SLO monitoring, measurement and compliance management. Each assertion

a_n is an atomic statement, and reflects the obligation of a service through the relationship that constraints the agreed variables according to the SLO. Table 4 describes the commonly used notions.

From operational standpoint, statement in an assertion made up of logical predicates to relate between values (Bhoj et.al, 2001). A logical predicate is composed using variable and logical operators (e.g., constraints $\{\leq, \geq, =, \neq, >, <\}$) that are imposed on those variables. Variables must reflect the operation or measurement of a service. In our context, assertion is used for the verifica-

Table 4. List of commonly used notation

Notation	Description
A_s	A set of assertions for service S_{ij}
S_{ij}	Service j for task i
Q_k^p	A set of offered Q_s levels and required adaptation level for the service S_{ij}
Q_k^d	A set of actual Q_s and Q_c being delivered for the service S_{ij}
SC	SLA compliancy of A for a particular S_{ij}

tion purpose between the offered QoS with the actual QoS and the required content object's level with the delivered version. For instance, suppose a service is required to provide a specific content object's level of images with a certain QoS levels. When the system notifies the provider to perform the particular task, the provider must agree to provide the service with the required content object's level and within offered QoS. In this case, the agreed terms are the QoS and content object's level and relationships are the obligations of QoS and content object's level, respectively. In our context of SLA monitoring, we adopted the *quality as conformance* view to evaluate the QoS and content object's level. That is, offered QoS or required content object's level for delivering service s is denoted as Q_k^p while Q_k^d is the actual QoS or content object's level delivered by the provider. Then the assertion for the service s_{ij} is given by;

$$SLA_{s_{ij}} : a_k = f\left(Q_k^p, Q_k^d\right) \tag{1}$$

where f is the function that measures the conformance between Q_k^p and Q_k^d of service s_{ij} and $k \in \left\{1, \ldots, b-1, b, b+1, \ldots c-1, c\right\}$ is the total number of QoS (denoted by b) and content object's level (denoted by c). Each SLA is made up of one service id and consists of a set of assertions. Each assertion within a service is unique, i.e., no assertion created in an SLA is identical.

The total number of assertions to be created, for a given content request is bounded by Equation (2), where q is the total of QoS and content object level with 1 and k are the lower and upper bounds respectively, and s_q is the number of services having a particular q.

$$A\left(p\right) = \sum_{q=1}^{k} q \times s_q . \tag{2}$$

Assume we have 3 tasks served by 3 services, with service to q mapping of 2. As per Equation (2), we have: $(1 \times 0) + (2 \times 3) = 6$ assertions are created.

For time complexity analysis, we focus on SLAs initialization time. We followed the analysis methodology descibed in Yunhua et.al, 2008. Let S be the total number of services and A is the total number of assertion for each service. The analysis assumes that there is constant number of A for each service. The time complexity for initialization services is $O(S)$ and for initialization assertions is $O(A)$. Thus, $O(SA)$ is the time complexity for the SLAs initialization.

The next step is to verify each assertion using the monitoring apparatus during the service execution.

Monitoring Phase

Every service must be capable of being measured and the result being analyzed and reported. Monitoring is a formal phase to verify whether the actual QoS and content object's level are delivered within the negotiated SLA during service execution. The monitoring apparatus can be placed at the broker (or at a third party location) and the monitored QoS and content object's level are updated to the corresponding service's assertions for verification or auditing process. Unlike others Internet services (e.g., VoIP service), which focus on network based performance QoS parameters such as throughput, packet loss ratio and packet delay (Zhou et.al, 2005), SLA parameters for service-oriented content adaptation focus on adaptation-related parameters. Examples of these parameters are presented in Table 2. Figure 4 depicts the example of monitoring apparatus that measure QoS and content object level during service delivery.

Verification

The monitored QoS levels are compared with assertions created. An assertion can be either

Figure 4. Monitoring phase

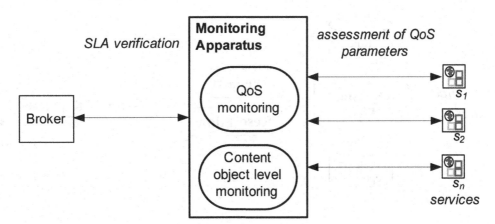

TRUE or FALSE. It depends on the obligation of the QoS or content object's level during verification. For positive monotonic QoS (e.g., accuracy), the assertion's obligation to be met is that the actual QoS must be equal or greater than (i.e., $\geq$) the promised QoS, whereas for negative monotonic QoS, the actual QoS must be equal or less than (i.e., $\leq$) the promised QoS. For positive monotonic QoS, if $a_i = \left\{ Q_k^p \leq Q_k^d \right\}$ is met, then the assertion is TRUE, vice versa. On the other hand, for negative monotonic QoS (e.g., time and cost), if $a_i = \left\{ Q_k^p \geq Q_k^d \right\}$ is met, then the assertion is TRUE, vice versa. For content object's level, the assertion's obligation to be met is that the actual content object's level must be equal with (i.e. =), the required content object's level, and if $a_i = \left\{ Q_k^d = Q_k^p \right\}$ is met, then the assertion is TRUE, vice versa. TRUE assertion is equal to 1 while FALSE assertion is 0. An SLA compliancy SC for a given service s_{ij} is denotes as following:

$$SC_{s_{ij}} = \prod_{k=1}^{K} a_k \qquad (3)$$

where $\forall k \in \left\{ 1,...,K \right\}$, 1 and K are the lower and upper bounds for a as in (1).

If all the assertions for the service s_{ij} are TRUE, the SLA is in compliance, while the SLA is in non-compliance form if any of the assertion is FALSE, i.e., $SC = 0$. When a non-compliance case detected, the broker invokes the enforcement phase. This phase determines the non-compliance type and the corresponding action. A non-compliance case may also be the result of reported cases received from clients. For example, a client can report a case if the adapted content version received at his end is not as expected.

Enforcement Phase

The enforcement phase is used to (a) decide whether a non-compliance case is a direct violation, a conflict or a result from bypassing conditions, (b) to enforce the necessary action and (c) to provide a real-time compliance reporting to clients. When violation is decided, it determines the corresponding penalty to its producer. On the other hand, when a conflict is decided, the corresponding resolution action is taken. Decision engine can be used to determine the non-compliance case. Figure 5 illustrates the enforcement phase.

Decision Engine

Decision engine utilizes the decision logic to produce non-compliance decision. The input to

Figure 5. Enforcement phase

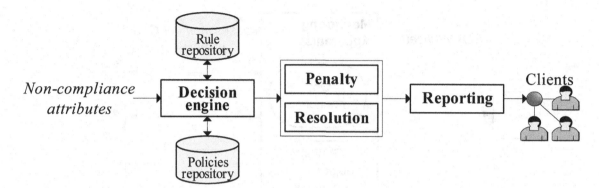

the engine is non-compliance attributes, i.e., "v", "w" and "x". "v" represents the form of the non-compliance; either detected during verification or complained by the client when the adapted content is received at the client end. This provides the client a way to submit complain. "w" denotes the aspect of non-compliance (i.e., QoS level, required content object or both), while "x" denotes the source (i.e., SLO, bypassing condition, external). Bypassing conditions are retrieved from the bypassing policy stored in the policies repository. These attributes are gathered or determined by the broker in real-time. Then, the engine uses the decision logic to decide whether a violation or conflict has occurred, before assigning the corresponding penalty or resolution action. For example, a conflict can occur due to bypassing condition.

The decision logic utilizes a rule-based technique as the reasoning engine to identify non-compliance type and the corresponding act to be taken. Expert knowledge is used to model rules in a manner similar to He et al (2007) and e HeTong et al (2009). The rule engine helps the system to achieve better automation (Zhou et.al, 2005; Yang and Shao, 2007). The rule takes a form as shown below:

Rule n: IF (case == v && w && x) THEN y;

$$(4)$$

where "n" is the particular predefined rule to be identified, and "y" is the non-compliance type (i.e., violation, conflict, bypass). The number of "v", "w", and "x" must be at least one. Rules can be added, deleted or modified, and is managed in offline mode. It is stored in the rules repository. Table 5 presents some examples of the non-compliance attributes.

For example, suppose we have a non-compliance detected during verification, e.g., the QoS level of text translation accuracy is below the negotiated level. The broker identified the case as *detected*, the aspect of non-compliance is QoS level and the source is SLO of accuracy QoS. These attributes are submitted to the decision logic and represented using Equation (3), as the following:

v = detected, w = QoS level, x = SLO of accuracy QoS

Using this information, the broker searches for the corresponding rule n stored in the rule repository where "v", "w" and "x" hold. The resulted rule n classifies the non-compliance type. When the non-compliance type has been identified, it is submitted to either one of these services: the violation enforcement service or the conflict resolution service. The violation enforcement service get invokes when it gets the violation notification. Based on the SLA id, it refers to the

Table 5. Example of non-compliance attributes

form v	aspect w	source x	resulting y
detected	QoS level	SLO of QoS q	violation
complain	content object level	external	conflict
		bypass	

penalty specified in the violation tag and invokes the appropriate penalty mechanism. In practice, a violation is penalizes in term of monetary. Other consequences of SLA violation are disbanding the services from service chain and re-selecting services. On the other hand, the conflict resolution service get invokes when it gets the conflict notification. Based on the SLA id, it refers to the resolution action specified in the conflict tag and invokes the resolution mechanism.

Reporting

Finally, the broker sends a real time report to the client. The report includes compliance status. As the enforcement phase and content adaptation execution are run concurrently, the compliance processing does not affect the overall time for the client to receive the adapted content form. In the case where a particular service failed, the broker notifies the discovery and selection mechanisms to re-execute, and resend the content segment together with the adaptation control information to the re-selected provider. The failed service is handled according to the SLA. In this chapter, the exploitation of the recovery mechanism is left for future work.

Example of Using the SLA Framework

In this subsection, we present an example of SLA management using the presented SLA framework. It is used to demonstrate how the framework can be applied systematically and to show a clear view of the advantages that the framework brings. The

example scenario used (Tonnies et. al, 2009) is given below:

Suppose Adam subscribed to a Video-on-Demand content provider who offers latest movies. Adam wants to watch a new English movie 'Sanctum 3D' on his Macbook Air. Assume that the suitable format of the movie to be streamed should be in a resolution of 800*480 and encoded in MPEG4 with 25 frames per second (fps). Further suppose Adam would prefer to watch the movie with English subtitles. However, the original video is without subtitle and in AVI format. The video content provider does not have the capability to personalize the content. To start streaming the movie, Adam contacts his content adaptation service providers via a Web service call (i.e., logging into the system).

Getting Adaptation Requirements

Adam preferred to minimize the service cost and waiting time but requires acceptable level of adaptation accuracy. So, he ticks cost and accuracy in the client QoS requirement checkbox. First, the system's broker analyses Adam's content adaptation requirements using a third party adaptation decision-taking engine similar to Tong et al (2010) and produced the adaptation decision. To achieve the desired content form (i.e., a transcoded movie file with English subtitles), the broker realizes that two tasks are required: (a) video transcoding (i.e., format conversion and resolution resizing), and (b) English title annotation. Assume that t_1 is the predecessor of t_2 and must be performed

Table 6. Example of adaptation requirements

Task	Source file	Adaptation requirements, ar_n	Adapted file
t_1	Media type: Movie Format: AVI Audio: English Stereo Length: 90 minutes Resolution: 1024*768 fps: 25 subtitle: No	$ar_1 \rightarrow$Convert: AVI to MPEG4 $ar_2 \rightarrow$Resize: 1024*765 to 800*480 QoS: Cost and transcoding accuracy	Media type: Movie Format: MPEG4 Audio: English Stereo Length: 90 minutes Resolution: 800*480 fps: 25 subtitle: No
t_2	Media type: Movie Format: MPEG4 Audio: English Stereo Length: 90 minutes Resolution: 800*480 fps: 25 subtitle: No	$ar_3 \rightarrow$Annotate: English subtitles QoS: Cost and annotation accuracy	Media type: Movie Format: MPEG4 Audio: English Stereo Length: 90 minutes Resolution: 800*480 fps: 25 subtitle: English

in sequential. Example of detailed adaptation requirements are given in Table 6.

The system's broker looks up at the local business registry to find suitable services that capable of performing these two tasks. The broker aims to select providers that minimize cost and waiting time but guarantee the adaptation accuracy > 80%. Further suppose that available providers have been discovered. Each task can potentially be performed by two services. For instance, t_1 can be performed by two services $\{s_{11}, s_{12}\}$ and t_2 can be performed by two services $\{s_{21}, s_{22}\}$. Providers advertise their offered QoS, as given in Table 7.

Negotiating SLAs

Based on Table 7, the broker decided to select service s_{12} and s_{21}. The broker invokes the negotiation mechanism to negotiate with service providers of s_{12} and s_{21}. The negotiation is performed to finalize the offers with the specific adaptation requirements stated in Table 6. s_{12} provider agreed with the same QoS offers but s_{21} provider increases cost to 65 cents for 90 minutes annotation duration. Also, the provider of s_{21} realized that its current load is heavy, thus offering a new waiting time of 150ms. Then, both the broker and providers came into agreement. The broker also realizes that QoS performance measurement tools are required. The broker is capable of measuring t_1 compliance using a built in tracking tool (i.e., tool to check the movie format and resolution setting). However, there is no in-house measurement tool for t_2, so it will be outsourced. Final service cost charged can be verified with electronic receipts. Assume the broker found a third party measurement tool (trial version) that capable of analyzing the accuracy of subtitles annotation. The broker builds the SLAs reference table that includes essential information, as in Table 8.

Negotiated offered QoS levels and required content object level of each service are transformed into SLA containing necessary assertions. The general assertion form for this case is denoted as the following:

$$SLA_{S_{12}} : a_1 = f\left(Q_1^p, Q_1^d\right),$$
$$a_2 = f\left(Q_2^p, Q_2^d\right),$$
$$a_3 = f\left(Q_3^p, Q_3^d\right),$$
$$a_3 = f\left(Q_4^p, Q_4^d\right).$$

$$SLA_{S_{21}} : a_1 = f\left(Q_1^p, Q_1^d\right),$$
$$a_2 = f\left(Q_2^p, Q_2^d\right),$$
$$a_3 = f\left(Q_3^p, Q_3^d\right),$$
$$a_3 = f\left(Q_4^p, Q_4^d\right).$$

Table 7. Offered QoS levels

Task	Service	Cost (cent)	Waiting time (millisecond)	Adaptation accuracy
t_1	s_{11}	90	100	>95%
	s_{12}	40	110	>80%
t_2	s_{21}	50	120	>95%
	s_{22}	50	110	>85%

Table 8. Example of essential information in the SLA reference table

SLA	Adaptation requirement	QoS levels / SLO	Measurement tools	Penalties & Resolution
s_1	ar_1 and ar_2	Q_1^p , cost: 40 cents Q_2^p , transcoding accuracy > 80% Q_3^p , waiting time > 110ms Q_4^p , output required: English movie in AVI format, 25fps, in 800*480	Cost: receipt Accuracy: format check, resolution check, fps check Waiting time: time check Derived from accuracy	Penalties: Q_1^p violation; receipt adjustment. Q_2^p to Q_4^p violation; p_1: 50% cost reduction, p_2: re-adaptation Conflict resolution: Q_1^p to Q_4^p : notice of conflict Termination condition: Standard bypassing
s_2	ar_3	Q_1^p , cost: 85 cents Q_2^p , annotation accuracy > 95% Q_3^p , waiting time > 150ms Q_4^p , output required: English movie with English subtitles	Cost: receipt Accuracy: English audio must be annotated with correct English subtitles Waiting time: time check Derived from accuracy	Penalties: Q_1^p violation; receipt adjustment. Q_2^p to Q_4^p violation; p_1: 40% cost reduction, p_2: re-adaptation Conflict resolution: Q_1^p to Q_4^p : notice of conflict Termination condition: Standard bypassing

The specific assertions including the operation to be verified are given as follows:

$$SLA_{S_{12}} : a_1 = \left\{ 40 \geq Q_1^d \right\},$$
$$a_2 = \left\{ 80\% \leq Q_2^d \right\},$$
$$a_3 = \left\{ 110 \geq Q_3^d \right\},$$
$$a_4 = \left\{ transcoded\ file = Q_4^d \right\}.$$

$$SLA_{S_{21}} : a_1 = \left\{ 85 \geq Q_1^d \right\},$$
$$a_2 = \left\{ 95\% \leq Q_2^d \right\},$$
$$a_3 = \left\{ 150 \geq Q_3^d \right\},$$
$$a_4 = \left\{ annotated\ file = Q_4^d \right\}.$$

Monitoring SLAs

Three different purpose monitoring apparatus are required to be arranged. The broker monitors the actual QoS of transcoding and evaluates the transcoding accuracy using apparatus 1, and checks if electronic receipts posted by providers are correct using apparatus 2. The third party apparatus (i.e., apparatus 3) monitors and evaluates the annotation accuracy. The broker also checks the output of both services (i.e., derived from accuracy measurements of apparatus 2 and 3). The result of monitoring for each service s_{12} and s_{21} and sends it to the verifier.

The verifier runs the corresponding conformance verifications for SC_{s12} and SC_{s21}. Assume that the actual transcoding and annotation accuracy for both s_{12} and s_{21} are 100% and 96%, respectively. Electronic receipts received by the broker denoted that s_{12} is charging extra 10 cent, while cost for s_{21} remains constant. First, the value is updated into corresponding assertion of s_{12} and s_{21} SLA, as the following:

$$SLA_{S_{12}} : a_1 = \{40 \geq 50\},$$
$$a_2 = \{80\% \leq 100\%\},$$
$$a_3 = \{110 \geq 109\},$$
$$a_4 = \{transcoded\ file = true\}.$$

$$SLA_{S_{21}} : a_1 = \{85 \geq 85\},$$
$$a_2 = \{95\% \leq 96\%\},$$
$$a_3 = \{150 \geq 145\},$$
$$a_4 = \{annotated\ file = true\}.$$

The verifier performs Equation (3) for both $SC_{s12} : 0 \times 1 \times 1 \times 1 = 0\ (FALSE)$ and $SC_{s21} : 1 \times 1 \times 1 \times 1 = 0\ (TRUE)$. It detects and submits a non-compliance case of s_{12} (including the specific information of the SLA id and what

QoS being non-compliance) to the compliance management.

Managing Non Compliance and Reporting

The broker identifies the non-compliance attributes. This includes the non-compliance aspect (i.e., cost QoS level) and the source (i.e., SLO - provider of s_{12} has made an extra charge). Then it uses the decision-making logic to determine the non-compliance type. The input to the decision logic is as the following:

v = detected, w = QoS level, x = SLO of cost QoS

Then, the decision-making mechanism found that rule 7 holds for the given non-compliance case:

Rule 7: IF case == (detected && QoS level && SLO of cost QoS) THEN cost violation

The broker looks up at the violation tag in the given SLA and found out that the action to be taken for cost QoS violation as per Table 8. It issues a notice to the provider for a corrected version of the receipt. The provider receives the violation notice and submits the corrected receipt. The broker reports (via email) the adaptation and compliance status, and attaches the final receipt to the client.

Advantages of the Framework

The SLA framework can benefit users in many ways. The given example shows a clear view of the framework's advantages as the following:

- **Organized SLA management:** The framework provides an organization of SLAs lifecycle that includes creation, monitoring and enforcement phases. This framework can be applied by Internet services similar to content adaptation services. Each phase of the framework can be customized to tailor with the specific application.

- **Avoiding potential violation or conflict:** Each SLA has to be negotiated before being settled. From the example given, by anticipating the current server load into the waiting time, the s_{21} provider can avoid potential SLA violation. Also, by taking into account the request size, an actual cost can be estimated, thus avoiding potential conflict between the broker and provider.

- **Systematic non-compliance management:** The framework enables rule-based non-compliance decision making. In this way, both brokers and providers have a clear view of violations or conflicts occurrences and can take necessary actions to solve it. The reporting mechanism provides the clients with the essential status.

FUTURE RESEARCH DIRECTIONS

Service level agreement framework for service-oriented content adaptation is an important initial step in the service-oriented content adaptation research. In order for the framework to be fully implemented, there are several technical challenges lie ahead. Objective performance metrics for content adaptation services should be standardized. Each of these metrics should be able to be measured and analyzed. Therefore, development of QoS monitoring and measurement methods require urgent attention. This should include a mechanism to evaluate the accuracy of the adapted content version. The development of the decision engine for the non-compliance management also is of exciting topic. An interesting aspect to explore is how the framework operates in cases where there are multiple users demanding content adaptation services and they have to be served with different QoS because of for example-constraint on

resources. Alternatively, the QoS can be assured if outsourcing or peering is possible, especially when a particular provider is experiencing heavy load.

CONCLUSION

There is a widespread use of wireless and mobile devices - mobile phones, PDAs, Pocket PCs, handheld PCs, car navigation systems, and notebook PCs – however, with different capabilities due to varying processors, screen sizes, input methods, software libraries, and more. And with this variety of device capabilities, certain device-content mismatches (e.g., improper content layout, unable to view certain content object) arise for users who want to browse the Web. Recently, a service-oriented content adaptation scheme has emerged to address the content-device mismatch problem. As clients pay for the consumed adaptation services, assuring negotiated QoS levels and adapted content version through SLA is vital. This chapter builds on and contributes to the work in service-oriented content adaptation, with the aim of deriving a framework for managing SLA. To the best of our knowledge, there is no prior work done for managing SLA that is tailored to the service-oriented content adaptation platform. The framework is made of three core phases: creation, monitoring and enforcement. The creation phase includes QoS negotiation and a generic schema of an SLA tag. The monitoring phase specifies how SLA is validated and discusses essential monitoring apparatus. Compliance management in the enforcement phase includes the decision logic to determine non compliance type and the corresponding action. We also provide a working example on how the SLA management framework is applied with a given scenario. The workflow includes getting adaptation requirements, negotiating SLAs, monitoring SLAs, managing non-compliance and reporting.

REFERENCES

Balakrishnan, P., & Somasundaram, T. (2011). SLA enabled CARE resource broker. *Future Generation Computer Systems*, *27*(3), 265–279. doi:10.1016/j.future.2010.09.006

Berhe, G., Brunie, L., & Pierson, J.-M. (2005). Content adaptation in distributed multimedia systems. *Journal of Digital Information Management: Special Issue on Distributed Data Management*, *3*(2), 96–100.

Bhoj, P., Singhal, S., & Chutani, S. (2001). SLA management in federated environment. *Journal of Computer Networks*, *35*, 5–24. doi:10.1016/S1389-1286(00)00149-3

Brandic, I., Music, D., Leitner, P., & Dustdar, S. (2009). VieSLAF framework: enabling adaptive and versatile SLA-management. *Lecture Notes on Computer System*, *5745*, 60–73. doi:10.1007/978-3-642-03864-8_5

Buyukkokten, O. (2002). Efficient web browsing on handheld devices using page and form summarization. *ACM Transactions on Information Systems*, *20*(1), 82–115. doi:10.1145/503104.503109

Dastjerdi, A., Tabatabaei, S., & Buyya, R. (2010). An effective architecture for automated appliance management system applying ontology-based cloud discovery. *10th IEEE/ACM International Conference on Cluster, Cloud and Grid Computing* (pp.104-112). New York, NY: IEEE Press.

Fatima, S., Woolridge, M., & Jennings, N. (2006). Multi issue negotiation with deadlines. *Journal of Artificial Intelligence Research*, *6*, 381–417.

Fawaz, Y., Berhe, G., Brunie, L., Scuturici, V.-M., & Coquil, D. (2008). Efficient execution of service composition for content adaptation in pervasive computing. *International Journal of Digital Multimedia Broadcasting*, *2008*, 1–10. doi:10.1155/2008/851628

Gantz, J., & Reinsel, D. (2010). *The digital universe decade- Are you ready?* IDC Digital Universe Report May 2010. Retrieved Mac 21, 2011, from http://www.emc.com/digital_universe

He, J., Gao, T., Hao, W., Yen, I., & Bastani, F. (2007). A flexible content adaptation system using a rule-based approach. *IEEE Transactions on Knowledge and Data Engineering*, *19*(1), 127–140. doi:10.1109/TKDE.2007.250590

Hsiao, J., Hung, H., & Chen, M. (2008). Versatile transcoding proxy for Internet content adaptation. *IEEE Transactions on Multimedia*, *10*(4), 646–658. doi:10.1109/TMM.2008.921852

Keller, A., & Ludwig, H. (2003). The WSLA framework: Specifying and monitoring service level agreements for web services. *Journal of Network and Systems Management*, *11*(1), 57–81. doi:10.1023/A:1022445108617

Kersten, G., & Lai, H. (2007). Satisfiability and completeness of protocols for electronic negotiations. *European Journal of Operational Research*, *180*(2), 922–937. doi:10.1016/j.ejor.2005.04.056

Kritikos, K., & Plexousakis, D. (2009). Requirements for QoS-based web service description and discovery. *IEEE Transactions on Service Computing*, *2*(4), 320–327. doi:10.1109/TSC.2009.26

Liu, S.-H., Cao, Y., Li, M., Kilaru, P., Smith, T., & Toner, S. (2008). A semantics- and data-driven SOA for biomedical multimedia systems. *10th IEEE International Symposium on Multimedia* (pp. 553-558). New York, NY: IEEE Press.

Lum, W., & Lau, F. (2003). User-centric content negotiation for effective adaptation service in mobile computing. *IEEE Transactions on Software Engineering*, *29*(12), 1100–1111. doi:10.1109/TSE.2003.1265524

Menasce, D. (2002). QoS issues in web services. *IEEE Internet Computing*, *6*(6), 72–75. doi:10.1109/MIC.2002.1067740

Mohan, R., John, S., & Li, C.-S. (1999). Adapting multimedia Internet content for universal access. *IEEE Transactions on Multimedia, 1*(1), 104–114. doi:10.1109/6046.748175

Moore, B., Ellesson, E., Strassner, J., & Westerinen, A. (2001). Policy core information model – Version 1 specification. *IETF RFC 3060*. Retrieved October 13, 2010, from http://tools.ietf.org/html/rfc3060

Nordin, N. A., Shin, W. H., Ghauth, K. I., & Mohd, M. I. (2007). Using service-based content adaptation platform to enhance mobile user experience. *Proceeding of the 4th International Conference on Mobile Technology and Applications* (pp. 552-557). New York, NY: ACM Press.

Park, J., Baek, J., & Hong, J. (2001). Management of service level agreements for multimedia Internet service using a utility model. *IEEE Communications Magazine, 39*(5), 100–106. doi:10.1109/35.920863

Pathan, M., & Buyya, R. (2009a). Resource discovery and request-redirection for dynamic load sharing in multi-provider peering content delivery networks. *Journal of Network and Computer Applications, 32*(5), 976–990. doi:10.1016/j.jnca.2009.03.003

Pathan, M., & Buyya, R. (2009b). Architecture and performance models for QoS-driven effective peering of content delivery network. *Multiagent and Grid System, 5*(2), 1574–1702.

Prokkola, J. (2007, July). *QoS measurement methods and tools*. Paper presented at the Easy Wireless Workshop of 16th IST Mobile and Wireless Communications Summit, Budapest, Hungary.

Sahai, A., Durante, A., & Machiraju, V. (2002). *Towards automated SLA management for web services*. Technical Report HPL-2001-310, Hewlett-Parkard Labs, Palo-Alto, CA.

Shahidi, M., Attouk, A., & Aghvami, H. (2008). Content adaptation: Requirements and architecture. *Proceedings of the 10th International Conference on Information Integration and Web-based Applications and Services* (pp. 626-629). New York, NY: ACM Press.

Song, X., & Dou, W. (2011). A workflow framework for intelligent service composition. *Future Generation Computer Systems, 27*(5), 627–636. doi:10.1016/j.future.2010.06.008

Tong, M., Yang, Z., & Liu, Q. (2010). A novel model of adaptation decision-taking engine in multimedia adaptation. *Journal of Network and Computer Applications, 33*(1), 43–49. doi:10.1016/j.jnca.2009.06.004

Tonnies, S., Kohncke, B., Hennig, P., & Balke, W.-T. (2009). A service oriented architecture for personalized rich media delivery. *IEEE International Conference on Service Computing* (pp. 340-347). New York, NY: IEEE Press.

Trienekens, J., Bouman, J., & Zwan, M. (2004). Specification of service level agreements: Problems, principles and practices. *Software Quality Journal, 12*, 43–57. doi:10.1023/B:SQJO.0000013358.61395.96

Xu, Z., Martin, P., Powley, W., & Zulkernine, F. (2007). Reputation-enhanced QoS-based web services discovery. *IEEE international Conference on Web Services* (pp. 249-256). New York, NY: IEEE Press.

Yang, S., & Shao, N. (2007). Enhancing pervasive web accessibility with rule-based adaptation strategy. *Journal of Expert Systems with Applications, 32*, 1154–1167. doi:10.1016/j.eswa.2006.02.008

Yunhua, K., Danfeng, Y., & Bertino, E. (2008). Efficient and secure content processing by co-operative intermediaries. *IEEE Transactions on Parallel and Distributed Systems, 19*(5), 615–626. doi:10.1109/TPDS.2007.70758

Zhou, C., Chia, L., & Lee, B. (2004). DAML-QoS ontology for web services. *Proceeding of IEEE International Conference on Web Services* (pp. 472-479). New York, NY: IEEE Press.

Zhou, C., Chia, L., & Lee, B. (2005). Semantics in service discovery and QoS measurement. *IEEE IT Professional*, 7(2), 29–34. doi:10.1109/MITP.2005.41

ADDITIONAL READING

Masri, E. A., & Mahmoud, Q. H. (2007). Crawling multiple UDDI business registries. *Proceedings of 16th International World Wide Web Conference* (pp. 1257-1258). New York, NY: IEEE Press.

Md Fudzee, M., & Abawajy, J. (2011). QoS-based adaptation service selection broker. *Future Generation Computer Systems*, 27(3), 256–264. doi:10.1016/j.future.2010.09.005

Md Fudzee, M. F., & Abawajy, J. H. (2008). A classification for content adaptation systems. *Proceedings of the 10th International Conference on Information Integration and Web-based Applications and Services* (pp. 426-429). New York, NY: ACM Press.

Md Fudzee, M. F., & Abawajy, J. H. (2010). Request-driven cross-media content adaptation technique. In K. Ragab, T. Helmy & A. Hassanien (Ed.), *Developing advanced web services through P2P computing and autonomous agents* (pp. 91-113). Hershey, PA: Information Science Publishing.

Menasce, D. (2004a). QoS-aware software components. *IEEE Internet Computing*, 8(2), 91–93. doi:10.1109/MIC.2004.1273492

Menasce, D. (2004b). Mapping service level agreements in distributed applications. *IEEE Internet Computing*, 8(5), 100–102. doi:10.1109/MIC.2004.47

Prangl, M., Szkalicki, T., & Hellwagner, H. (2007). A framework for utility-based multimedia adaptation. *IEEE Transactions on Circuits and Systems for Video Technology*, 17(6), 719–728. doi:10.1109/TCSVT.2007.896650

Rosario, S., Benveniste, A., Haar, S., & Jard, C. (2008). Probabilistic QoS and soft contracts for transaction-based web services orhestrations. *IEEE Transactions on Service Computing*, 1(4), 187–200. doi:10.1109/TSC.2008.17

Rosen, K. H. (2007). *Discrete mathematics and its applications* (6th ed.). New York, NY: McGraw Hill Press.

KEY TERMS AND DEFINITIONS

Assertion: An atomic statement, and reflects the obligation of a service through the relationship that constraints the agreed variables according to the service level objective (SLO).

Content Adaptation: An automatic mean to tailor content to a specific context, e.g., device or user preferences.

Content Adaptation Service: A service provided by a service provider that is capable of performing a certain content adaptation function.

Monitoring Apparatus: A tool to monitor and/or to verify the SLA for compliancy.

Non-Compliance: An action occurs when the SLA is not being delivered accordingly.

Quality of Service: A qualitative/quantitative offer of a certain service's criteria. It is a key factor that relates the agreement within an SLA between the client and the service provider.

Service Level Agreement: A formal contract negotiated between a service provider and the client for the service.

Service-Oriented Content Adaptation: A platform that provides content adaptation functions as services to clients.

Chapter 3
Strategies for Agent–Based Negotiation in E–Trade

Raja Al-Jaljouli
Deakin University, Australia

Jemal Abawajy
Deakin University, Australia

ABSTRACT

E-negotiation handles negotiation over the Internet without human supervision and has shown effectiveness in concluding verifiable and more favorable agreements in a reasonably short time. In this chapter, the authors discuss the negotiation system and its components with particular emphasis on negotiation strategies. A negotiation strategy defines strategic tactics, which advise on the proper action to select from a set of possible actions that optimizes negotiation outcomes. A strategy should integrate negotiation goals and reactive attitudes. Usually, a fixed strategy is implemented during the course of negotiation regardless of significant decision-making factors including market status, opponent's profile, or eagerness for a negotiated goods/service. The chapter presents the main negotiation strategies and outlines the different decision-making factors that should be considered. A strategy uses a utility function to evaluate the offer of an opponent and advises on the generation of a counter offer or the best interaction. The authors finally discuss different utility functions presented in the literature.

INTRODUCTION

Negotiation is a process in which two or more parties have conflicting requirements in terms of goals and demands and try to reach mutual agreement through concession or change in re-

quirements (Pruitt, 1981). E-negotiation refers to negotiation conducted over the Internet and has been proposed to facilitate negotiation and generate better outcomes. It is an automated process that tries to optimize utilities of negotiating entities through iteration. It facilitates negotiation

DOI: 10.4018/978-1-4666-1888-6.ch003

through the Internet as being free from place and time constraints. It also saves negotiators time and effort they usually spend in trying to reach an agreement.

E-negotiation is a hot research topic and represents a strategic stage in e-commerce (Sandholm, 1999). It manages beliefs and goals of interacting parties, and tries to resolve conflicts through concessions and search for affordable and acceptable alternatives (Calisti, 2002). It overcomes limitations of human negotiation that suffers from emotional, rational, or superficial responses. It also keeps a record of negotiation traces for later verification or jury cases. Moreover, it offers much broader market search and results in error-free calculations that promote customer satisfaction and trust in E-negotiation.

E-negotiation can be fully automated through the deployment of software intelligent agents. Agents can autonomously carry out negotiation on behalf of negotiating entities. Agents can be stationary or mobile. Agent-mediated negotiation has recently received much attention (Faratin et al., 1998; Kraus & Lehmann, 1995; Fatima et al., 2002, 2004; Luo et al., 2003; Li & Tesauro, 2003; Sandholm, 1999). The implementation of mobile agents in E-negotiation has shown that they are more efficient than stationary agents as they exhibit distinctive characteristics (Chen et al, 2008): (1) ability to reduce network loads; (2) dynamic adaptation to changes in the environment; (3) ability to overcome network latency; (4) asynchronous and autonomous execution. Hence, mobile agents have been recommended for E-negotiation (Faratin et al., 1998; Kraus & Lehmann, 1995).

Negotiation is a vital component of electronic trading. It is the key decision-making approach used to reach consensus between trading partners. Mobile agents have recently been proposed for negotiation in electronic trading applications. Agents are deployed to act on behalf of consumers and vendors roaming the Internet, negotiating their particular requests with various service providers,

and making decisions autonomously. They have shown effectiveness in automating human decisions such as concluding verifiable agreements, facilitating global trading, and optimizing clients' utilities. Moreover, they ensure timely delivery of services/resources, and less resources allocation.

Negotiation can be classified based on the number of participants as one-to-one, one-to-many, or many-to-many. They can negotiate a single issue or multiple issues. Also, they may negotiate multi-attributes of a particular issue. Negotiation can be bilateral or unilateral. During the course of negotiation, mobile agents are expected to receive offers from service providers and would accordingly respond with counter offers based on a predefined set of rules referred to as negotiation strategy. The strategy makes decisions based on preferences, constraints the negotiating entity has initially set. Preferences can be such as a non-stop route flight, and constraints can be such as price limit, warranty period, or bid deadline. Negotiation strategies vary from patient, desperate, to partially patient strategies. Negotiation strategies have a significant effect on the outcomes of negotiation and, thus, mobile agents seek negotiation strategies that optimize the utility of a negotiating entity.

In this chapter, we address agent-based negotiation strategies in e-Trade. We first present a background on E-negotiation and its real applications, interaction styles, and characteristics. We then describe E-negotiation system and related components including negotiation models and negotiation procedures. We then describe the different architectures of E-negotiation system. Next, we outline the different E-negotiation parameters including issues, attributes, preferences, and constraints with particular focus on temporal constraints. We then discuss different negotiation strategies and the two implemented tactics including the concession tactic and the search for alternatives tactic. We also discuss the different approaches for selecting a negotiation strategy. Finally, we present utility functions for multi-issue price-based negotiation and multiple constraints negotiation. Various factors that have effect on utility are discussed including time discount factor, cost of delay factor, offer expiry time, bid deadline, vendor's profile, and market status.

The chapter focuses on a very recent mobile agent-based E-negotiation strategy (Al-Jaljouli & Abawajy, 2010) that optimizes entity's utility while shortening negotiation time. The strategy considers the effect of various temporal constraints including offer expiry time, communication delays, processing queues, and transportation times. It ensures satisfactory market search, avoids loss of best utility offer that would expire before bid deadline, and avoids early bid settlement that would result in overpriced bids.

BACKGROUND

E-Negotiation Applications

E-Negotiation has significant applications in a broad range of areas including economics, politics, manufacturing, business, commerce, military, etc. We discuss the following applications of E-negotiation.

- Negotiating business transaction
- Negotiating resource allocation
- Negotiating tasks allocation/obligation distribution
- Negotiating corporation establishment
- Negotiating service level agreement
- Negotiating resolution of group conflicts
- Negotiating personnel acquisition

Negotiating Business Transaction

Two parties negotiate the attributes of goods of interest e.g. price, warranty period, etc. It takes place in business-to-business, business-to-consumer, and business-to-government transactions.

Negotiating Resource Allocation

Two or more parties negotiate the split of shared facility or resource, e.g. meeting room, printer or scanner at business premises to ensure fair resource distribution and avoid disputes or collisions.

Negotiating Task Allocation/Obligation Distribution and Scheduling

In organizations, managers and leaders employ automated negotiation to effectively distribute obligations/tasks among employees based on their expertise and qualifications. A contractor may distribute tasks among sub-contractors and schedule tasks accordingly.

Negotiating Corporation Establishment

Partners negotiate terms of contract for the formation of a corporation inclusive taxation liability, management responsibilities, allocation of business profits and losses, and personal liability for lawsuits.

Negotiating Service Level Agreement

A service consumer negotiates with a service provider the quality of service of interest.

Negotiating Resolution of Group Conflicts

Law firms may negotiate issues of conflict and analyze common preferences and interests of disputed entities in a group to arrive at grounds of settlement. Negotiation can also take place between politicians, philosophers, and linguistics.

Negotiating Personnel Acquisition

Employers can deploy negotiating agents to continuously search marketplaces on their behalf for personnel of specific qualifications and experience till a nearly match or a match is captured. Moreover, agents can negotiate contractual terms (Kurbel, 2005).

Negotiating a Service Quotation

A client may search for quotations from several service providers for building a network and can then negotiate quotations (Faratin & Rodriguez, 2005).

Negotiating Supply-Chain Process

Negotiation takes place between individual supply chain partners as regards the different phases of transforming raw material into products to be delivered to the customer. For example, manufacturers negotiate with suppliers for raw material; wholesalers negotiate with manufactures for manufacturing capacity; manufactures negotiate with logistics channels for distribution; retailers negotiate with logistics channels for delivery services (Wong, 2004).

Negotiation Interaction Styles

There are different types of interaction between entities involved in negotiation. They can be classified as follows (Rubinstein, 1985; Kraus et al., 1995).

- Cooperative interaction
  - Symmetric
  - Asymmetric
- Symmetric competitive interaction
- Conflict interaction

Symmetric cooperative interaction: Negotiating entities gain from negotiation and try to reach mutually favored agreement. They try to maximize the sum of all their utilities/gains even if their individual utilities are low in negotiation outcome and, hence are referred to as devoted entities. In multi-attribute negotiation, agents have differ-

ent preferences, but are cooperative and need to reach a compromise agreement. They can reach Win-Win agreement on attributes of preference by conceding on attributes of less importance and exploiting the less favored attributes of their opponents.

Asymmetric cooperative interaction: one negotiating entity gains while the other entity loses at the conclusion of an agreement. They try to maximize the sum of all their utilities/gains even if their individual utilities are low in negotiation outcome and, hence are referred to as devoted entities. In single attribute negotiation, negotiating entities have different preferences, but are cooperative and need to reach an acceptable agreement. One entity has to concede till the other entity reach Win-Lose agreement on the negotiated issue.

Symmetric competitive interaction: negotiating entities take actions that are rational for themselves irrespective of other entities benefits. They make compromises throughout negotiation till an agreement is concluded. They try to satisfy preferences and maximize utilities/gains of their own. They do not cooperate with each other and, hence are referred to as self-interested entities. They do not trust each other and try to hide their preferences during negotiation to limit any exploitation actions the opponent may take that might lower their utilities (Hindriks & Tykhonov, 2008). Entities would have incomplete information about opponents and, thus are subject to limited-rationality as they cannot be sure of the best action to take. They need time to learn and build knowledge through negotiation about opponent's attitudes and intensions. They may not surely reach maximum utility.

Conflict interaction: all negotiating entities are not willing to make any compromise and, hence negotiation aborts.

Negotiation Characteristics

Entities can negotiate a *single issue* (e.g. an airline ticket) or *multiple issues* (e.g. a holiday deal that consists of airline tickets, car hire, and accommodation). The negotiation might be *single-constraint* negotiation (e.g. purely price-based) or *multi-constraint* negotiation (e.g. price, warranty period, and delivery options). Multi-constraint negotiation involves complex decisions that take into account multiple factors. Also, negotiation can be *bilateral* or *unilateral*. In bilateral negotiation, negotiating entities exchange offers and counter offers, whereas in unilateral negotiation offers flow in one direction. Auction is an example of unilateral negotiation as buyers send offers to a bidding agent. Negotiating entities can be *patient* or *impatient*. The impatient entity tries to end the negotiation the soonest possible and once an acceptable offer is available, while the patient entity tries to extend the negotiation as long as possible to improve its individual utility. Negotiation can be scheduled as a *single-round* negotiation or *multi-round* negotiation (Al-Jaljouli & Abawajy, 2007).

NEGOTIATION SYSTEM

Negotiation Models

Negotiation can be classified based on the number of negotiating entities into three models: one-to-one, one-to-many, or many-to-many negotiation. The three models of one-to-many negotiation are discussed below.

One-to-One E-Negotiation Model

One-to-one bilateral negotiation is used in bargaining systems, where agents carry out bilateral negotiations exchanging offers and counter offers (kfir-dahav et al., 2000). The price-based negotiation is an example where both buyer and seller try to maximize their own utilities. The buyer negotiates for the least possible pay and the seller negotiates for the most possible gain. They have conflicting goals and different negotiation deadlines. They have incomplete information about each other

and bargaining is under time constraints in terms of negotiation deadlines. They have deadlines as private information and the negotiating entity with an earlier deadline has a weak bargaining power. They can jointly reach an agreement that meets their acceptable and most possible utilities. At a bargaining equilibrium, a negotiating entity cannot be better off without causing a drop in the utility of its opponent.

A buyer who has interest in multiple goods/services represents one-to-one bilateral multi-issue negotiation model (Lomuscio et al., 2003). For example, the buyer may need to buy a desktop, scanner, and printer from a particular seller. He may also negotiate multiple constraints as regards the goods/service to buy. He may negotiate three constraints: a price limit of 850 AUS$ for a laptop; warranty period of two years; and installment plan of 18 months from a particular seller.

One-to-Many E-Negotiation Model

The one-to-many negotiation can be bilateral or unilateral. The unilateral negotiation is implemented in auctions such as Vickery, English, and Dutch (Sandholm, 1996), whereas, the bilateral negotiation is implemented in bargaining. The unilateral negotiation is based on the use of centralized complex agent that carries simultaneous negotiations with multiple sellers. The information flows in one direction in form of offers from the sellers to the buyer. The buyer tries to maximize its utility and imposes a deadline for negotiation. The buyer agent would reject any offer that is received after the bid closes (bid deadline). The drawbacks of the model are: (1) It does not allow interactive negotiation with bilateral flow of information in form of offers and counter offers; (2) The buyer agent can only implement a single negotiation strategy during the course of negotiation; (3) It suffers from scalability problem as the agent conducts tremendous number of simultaneous negotiations; (4) Buyer agent is expected to be able to store the simultaneous negotiations at once in its state; (5) It represents a one-point-failure model that results in negotiation failure whenever the agent is captured or destroyed.

There are three different setups for the bilateral negotiation and as follows.

- Setup (a) is based on a *single stationary agent* that carries out concurrent one-to-one negotiations (Hamed Kebriaei & Majid, 2008).
- Setup (b) is based on a *stationary agent that assigns stationary sub-agents* to individually carry out one-to-one negotiations (Neumann et al., 2003).
- Setup (c) is based on *mobile agents* (*MA*) that migrate to e-marketplaces negotiating potential vendors on behalf of clients. They autonomously carry out negotiation and execute client's request.

The three setups are depicted in Figure 1. Setups (a) and (b) would result in excessive communication loads and costs. Whereas, setup (c) overcomes the problems of the other two models as the mobile agent moves to marketplaces and directly collects offers saving time and cost and reducing exchanged messages.

Negotiation is under two time constraints: bid deadline and expiry time of offers. In auctions, the bid deadline is known to vendors engaged in negotiation. Usually, advantageous offers have limited-time validity and might expire before bid deadline. There is a risk that these offers would be missed out and, hence clients may not reach maximum utility. On the other hand, a malicious vendor might be able to speculate that the bid task is critical and would then set a short validity time of its offer forcing the bidding agent to reason early and award the bid before waiting for more valuable offers that might be forthcoming. It would result in limited search space and awarding over-priced bids.

Many-to-One E-Negotiation Model

Many-to-one bilateral multi-constraint negotiation takes place when a group of participants on one side negotiate a deal/contract with one participant on the other side (Fershtman, 2000). Participants in the group may have conflicting preferences

Figure 1. One-to-many negotiation setup models

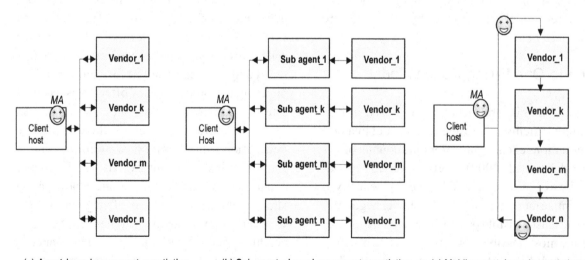

(a) Agent-based concurrent negotiation   (b) Sub agents-based concurrent negotiation   (c) Mobile agent-based negotiation

and priorities as regards the negotiation agenda. An example is a couple interested in home mortgage where the husband is concerned about the first payment and the wife is concerned about the installment plan. They should firstly agree on a negotiation agenda and can negotiate the constraints of concern sequentially or simultaneously with the seller.

Negotiation Procedures

A negotiating entity having interest in multi-issues has to decide on the sequence in which issues are negotiated. A negotiation procedure defines a particular sequence in which issues can be negotiated. There are three key procedures: (1) Package deal procedure (Fatima et al., 2006; Keeney & Raiffa, 1976); (2) Simultaneous procedure (Fershtman, 2000); (3) Sequential procedure (Busch & Horstmann, 1997). All issues are bundled together and negotiated in the package deal procedure, whereas, the issues are negotiated simultaneously but independently of each other in the simultaneous procedure. The issues are discussed one after another in the sequential procedure. The three procedures lead to different outcomes (Fershtman, 2000). The package deal produces the Pareto optimal outcomes (Fatima et al., 2006), which maximizes an agent's individual utility. There is an agenda for selecting a negotiation procedure (Fatima et al., 2004). The negotiating entity can select from two agendas: (a) exogenous, and (b) endogenous. The exogenous agenda defines a negotiation procedure before the start of negotiation, whereas, the endogenous agenda allows negotiating entities to decide on the order in which issues are negotiated during the course of negotiation.

SYSTEM ARCHITECTURE

Negotiation is represented by five negotiation models (Robinson & Volkov, 1998; Kersten &

Noronha, 1999; Li, 2001; Zhuang et al., 2008, Gutman & Maes, 1998; Gil Iranzo, 2005; Al-Jaljouli & Abawajy, 2007, 2010). Robinson and Volkov have defined a negotiation model of three phases: analysis, interaction design, and negotiation implementation. Kersten and Noronha have defined a negotiation model of three phases: pre-negotiation, conduct of negotiation, and post settlement. Li has defined a negotiation model of four phases: analysis, design, execution, and post-negotiation analysis. Zhuang et al. have extended Li's negotiation model to include an evaluation and ranking phase before the execution phase. The additional phase makes use of experience and history of negotiations, client's preferences, and vendors' profiles. Gutman and Maes have defined a negotiation model of six phases: need identification, product brokering, merchant brokering, negotiation, purchase and delivery, service and evaluation. Gil Iranzo has defined a negotiation model of five phases: user interaction, search, negotiation, outcomes, and control. The first three models do not make use of experience, knowledge, and negotiation history in the current negotiation. Furthermore, they only consider a single thread in multi-lateral negotiation. Zhuang model does not include the purchase and delivery phase. Gil Iranzo model employs a stationary agent that communicates with a directory of services to locate a meta-search agent that advises on a set of service providers registered for the service of interest. It calls for offers and exchanges offers and counter offers with service providers. Negotiation continues till an agreement is reached or negotiation is aborted. The model does not include ranking phase.

Al-Jaljouli and Abawajy have defined multi-bilateral negotiation model of five phases and deploys mobile agents in negotiation as shown in Figure 2. In *phase 1*, a client places a request with a mobile agent and provides its requirement profile. The profile includes: attributes such as description of service/goods of interest, and number of items; constraints such as price limit, expected delivery time (T_{ED}), or warranty period; preferences such as a particular delivery method. The phase is referred to as *planning and analysis phase*. In *phase 2*, the client agent plans the bid, estimates a utility limit, and locates potential vendors in e-marketplaces to negotiate with based on experience, knowledge, and past negotiation records. It then traverses the Internet and collects offers from the potential vendors until bid deadline T_{EB}. Usually, negotiation models schedule offer evaluation at a time later than the bid deadline. The model instantly verifies and evaluates a collected offer. The phase is referred to as *bidding phase*. In *phase 3*, the client agent migrates to a trusted host (TS), where it can securely carry out final verification and evaluation of the collected offers. It then ranks offers and short-lists competitive offers. Next, it selects particular constraints and preferences to negotiate with competitive vendors that would maximize client's utility. The phase is referred

to as *evaluation and ranking phase*. In *Phase 4*, the client agent migrates to short-listed vendors and collects amendments to their original offers, if any exists. The client agent then returns to the trusted host (TS) where it evaluates the outcomes of negotiation. If the client requirements are not satisfied and utility is not yet maximized, then it starts a second round of negotiation represented in phases 3 and 4. Negotiation rounds continue until the satisfaction of client requirements or bid deadline. The phase is referred to as *negotiation phase*. In *phase 5*, the client agent determines the winning vendor that best meets client's requirements and maximizes client's utility and then settles an agreement with the respective vendor; otherwise it aborts negotiation without reaching an agreement (Shiraz & Barfouroush, 2008; Si et al., 2007).

The client agent sends a purchase order to the winning vendor and sends reject messages to

Figure 2. Negotiation phases of one-to-many bilateral agent-based negotiation

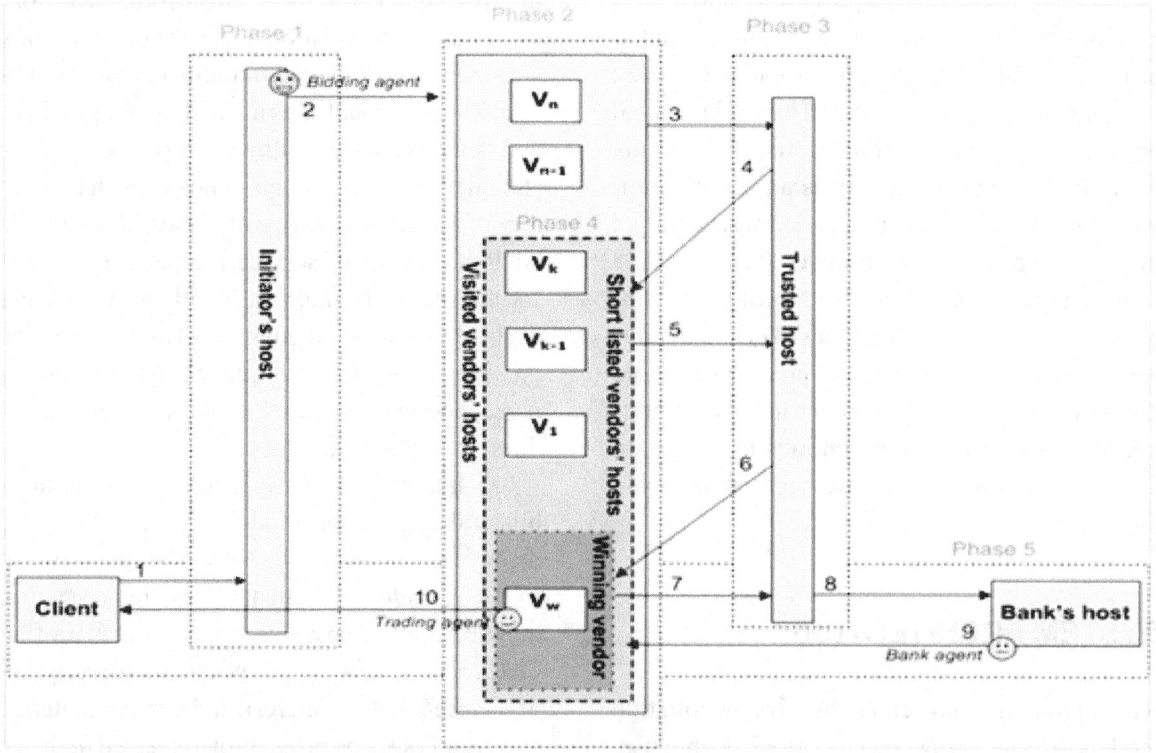

other vendors. It waits for an acceptance message and then makes a payment order to client's bank to process a payment for the winning vendor. Upon receipt of payment, the winning vendor delivers service/goods to the client. The service/goods should be delivered to the client not later than the expected delivery time T_{ED} the client initially sets. Finally, the client sends an acknowledgement to the winner agent on receipt of service/goods. The phase is referred to as *settlement and delivery phase*.

NEGOTIATION PARAMETERS

Clients should firstly verbalize their requirements into negotiation parameters that include the following:

- Issues
- Attributes
- Preferences
- Constraints

A client may be interested in a holiday package that includes multiple issues: airline ticket, care hire, and accommodation. Attributes can be destination, travel dates, and number of travelers. Constraints can be price limit (upper and/or lower) or booking confirmation deadline. Preferences can be non-stop route or particular carrier. The negotiation problem can be considered as constraint satisfaction problem CSP and the negotiation process can be modeled as constraint based reasoning (Kumar, 1992; Sycara et al., 1991; Yokoo, 2001).

Preferences are set as variables with associated domains. Constraints can be on the domains of variables and should remain private during negotiation. A negotiating agent may deduce some information about the constraints of its opponent from offers and accept-reject decisions the opponent makes. Negotiating agents try to reach a mutual agreement through search for alternatives.

A client agent needs to set temporal constraints that define the time needed to complete each of the negotiation phases. The temporal constraints have effect on the negotiation agenda and are listed in Table 1. They can be defined based on knowledge of similar past negotiation episodes or can be dynamically allocated according to changes in the environment. Normally, temporal constraints do not overlap as depicted in Figure 3. There is a time slot (Δt) between every two successive negotiation phases that accommodates for the time the client agent incurs due to its transportation across the Internet, communication delays and processing queues at visited hosts. The client agent may start offer evaluation before the bid deadline, particularly if an advantageous offer has an expiry time earlier than bid deadline.

The client agent should maintain the privacy of temporal constraints, particularly, End_time of bid (T_{EB}) and End_time of negotiation (T_{EN}). It should not disclose temporal constraints to any negotiated vendor. A seller agent that learns a temporal constraint, e.g. T_{EB} would maliciously delay its offer to limit market search or negotiation. It may also try to capture the client agent for a while so the agent would not have enough time for an adequate market search or negotiation, and thus the seller agent would have better chances to win the request.

At initiation, the client agent sets a deadline (T_{EB}) for offers collection. The deadline should allow enough time for the completion of an adequate market search. It is expected that the longer the bid time is the broader is the search space. The negotiation deadline (T_{EN}) should also be earlier than the request's expected delivery time (T_{ED}), which the client has initially set. It should give enough time for settling an agreement with the winning vendor. It should also take into account: (1) communication delays; (2) processing queues; (3) transportation times. The client agent estimates the deadlines based on similar past negotiation episodes.

Table 1. Temporal constraints in E-negotiation

Notation	Time constraint
T_{SB}	Start_time of bid
T_{EB}	End_time of bid
T_{SE}	Start_time of evaluation
T_{EE}	End_time of evaluation
T_{SN}	Start_time of negotiation
T_{EN}	End_time of negotiation
T_{SS}	Start_time of settlement
T_{ES}	End_time of settlement

A seller agent might set a deadline for the offer it provides (T_{EV}), particularly for time-limited offers. It is recommended that the client agent completes the various negotiation phases before the deadline of the most advantageous time-limited offer and the request's expected delivery time (T_{ED}).

NEGOTIATION STRATEGIES

Mobile agent-based negotiation systems are defined by the negotiated issues, and the implemented negotiation protocol and strategy (Faratin et al., 1998). The implementation of a particular protocol or strategy is dependent on the goal of negotiation (Roussaki and Louta, 2003). The protocol defines rules that specify the possible actions for a negotiating entity. The negotiation strategy directs a negotiation entity on the best course of action to be taken at a certain negotiation stage in response to changes in the environment and which would result in an agreement that maximizes utilities of negotiating entities. Generally, strategies advise

a negotiating entity on how to generate an initial offer, how to interpret a received offer, and how to generate counter offers. A negotiation strategy can be represented as a trace of negotiation acts.

Negotiation strategies are classified into three major types based on simple decay functions (concession rates): linear, quadratic, and exponential, respectively (Ge & Dong, 2010). The strategies are as follows (Maes & Gutman, 1998).

- **Patient/frugal strategy:** there is a deadline for negotiation, but the negotiating entity seeks to reach an agreement before the deadline is reached.
- **Anxious strategy:** there is a deadline for negotiation, but the negotiating entity seeks to reach an agreement the soonest possible
- **Cool-headed strategy:** there is not a deadline to reach an agreement

Negotiation strategies try to reach a mutual agreement by implementing: (1) concession tactic; (2) search for alternatives tactic. We will discuss the two tactics in details in the next two sub-sections.

Concession Tactic

Usually, negotiating entities with conflicting goals/interests, engage in negotiation seeking somewhat midpoint that is agreeable to all parties. They may need to relax some bid constraints and preferences if they were not able to reach an agreement during negotiation. The magnitude of relaxation of constraints and preferences is referred to as

Figure 3. Negotiation temporal constraints

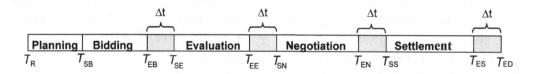

concession. It is assumed that negotiating entities are willing to make concessions during negotiation; however concessions may be overlooked, ignored, or unacknowledged. It is advisable that entities make fractional and contingent concessions so as to be appreciated and reciprocated by their opponents. They should avoid concession on high priority attributes and could make concession on low priority attributes, which might be of high priority to their opponents.

Negotiation strategies may advise on concession as regards its probability and level for each round of negotiation. They try to capture information about the negotiation strategies of opponents to learn their preferences and utility limit. Accordingly, they minimize concession levels in their own strategy (Wilkes, 2008; Hindriks & Tykhonov, 2008). The privacy of a negotiation strategy should be maintained during negotiation to limit the tendency of opponents trying to exploit the goodwill of a negotiating entity.

A negotiation strategy defines a set of negotiation tactics that can generate new values of negotiated variables to be used in preparing counter offers. It may use a combination of tactics during the course of negotiation. A tactic may recommend a negotiating entity to respond to an opponent's offer in different ways based on predefined concession rates. Assuming a price-based negotiation, a buyer agent can respond to a seller's offer as follows (Ge & Dong, 2010).

- **Conceder:** the buyer agent rapidly increases the price of an offer to the reserved price from the beginning of negotiation till the end. Conversely, the seller agent rapidly decreases the price of an offer to the reserved price from the beginning of negotiation till the end.
- **Boulware:** the buyer agent keeps the initial price of an offer almost till the negotiation deadline and then rapidly increases the price till the negotiation deadline is reached. Conversely, the seller agent keeps

the initial price of an offer almost till the negotiation deadline and then rapidly decreases the price till the negotiation deadline is reached.
- **Linear:** the buyer agent gradually increases the price of an offer during the course of negotiation. Conversely, the seller agent gradually decreases the price of an offer during the course of negotiation.

The different concession rates of a negotiating strategy are depicted in Figure 4. IP and RP represent buyer's initial price and reserved price, respectively. Whereas, TP and T_{EB} represent trading price and bid deadline, respectively.

Another tactic may recommend a negotiating entity to respond to an opponent's offer in different ways based on the style of interaction and as follows (Krovi et al., 1999).

- **Reciprocating:** the negotiating entity imitates the opponent.
- **Exploiting:** the negotiating entity makes less concession whenever opponents are competitive.
- **Cooperating:** the negotiating entity makes more concession whenever opponents are cooperative.

SEARCH FOR ALTERNATIVES TACTIC

It is designed for one-to-many bilateral negotiation that deploys mobile agents. A client agent migrates to marketplaces and collects offers from potential vendors. The implemented negotiation strategy tries to reach an agreement through search for alternatives rather than concession. There exists a risk that the client agent collects the most advantageous offer in last few minutes of its validity and before it completes a thorough market search. Usually, the agent continues on offer collection and might abort it few minutes

Figure 4. Negotiation concession rates

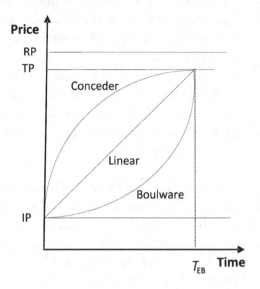

later than its validity. The most advantageous offer would be missed out and, hence, client's utility would not be maximized. The strategy presented in (Al-Jaljouli & Abawajy, 2010) takes into account the potential risk and does not delay the evaluation of offers till bid deadline. The strategy encourages early interruption of offer collection if there is a significant difference in price between the time-limited offer and other offers, whereas it does not if there is a marginal difference in price. It carries out prompt evaluation of each collected offer and verifies if the offer satisfies client's constraints and preferences. It then tests if a collected offer has the best utility and would expire earlier than bid deadline. If the offer passes the test, the strategy sets an alert and extends offer collection nearly till the expiry time of the offer. If the alert signals soon expiry of the offer, the strategy awards the bid to the respective vendor if it satisfies a constraint on minimum number of vendors to search and has the top utility among the so far collected offers.

The agent searches for the most similar need pattern to the client's pattern from the prefetched servers and then compares the current need pattern to previously recorded ones. Based on similarities between the two patterns (Zen, 2009), they advise on the minimum number of vendors to search before a decision can be made.

The strategy improves client's utility as it avoids loss of top utility offer that expires before bid deadline and avoids early bid award that would result in overpriced bids. Furthermore, it ensures adequacy of market search and possibly shortens offer collection time.

Strategy Selection

The outcomes of multi-issue bilateral negotiation are affected by the implemented negotiation strategy, in addition to the following factors (Fatima et al., 2003; Rahwan et al., 2002; Lomuscio et al., 2003):

- Negotiation protocol
- Participant preferences and constraints
- Attributes of the utility function
- Knowledge of opponent's information such as the reserve price or negotiation deadline
- Negotiation procedure and negotiation agenda

It is essential to select an appropriate negotiation strategy to optimize negotiation outcomes. The selection of a strategy is dependent on client's goals. A negotiating entity has different approaches for selecting of negotiation strategy. One approach implements a *non-adaptive strategy*, which the negotiating entity defines prior to negotiation. The approach has drawbacks: (1) the selection is not adaptive to changes in market status, and (2) A negotiating entity does not have enough knowledge and experience to make an appropriate selection of a negotiation strategy. A more efficient approach implements a *market-driven strategy*. The negotiation strategy can smoothly switch from one tactic to another during negotiation. It is adaptive to changes in: (a) entity's beliefs, (b) knowledge of the environment, and (c) attitudes (e.g. goals and obligations).

The following are the existing negotiation models that implement different approaches in selecting a negotiation strategy.

- Kasbah Model (Chavez et al., 1997)
- Case-based Model (Wong et al., 2000)
- Tete-a-Tete Model (Guttman et al., 1998)
- Market-driven Model (Sim & Wong, 2001)
- Adaptive Negotiation Agents (Krovi et al. 1999)

Kasbah Model

It is designed for bilateral price-based negotiation. Negotiating entities are competitive and negotiate between desired and reserved prices. They set a desired time for completing an agreement. The model assumes that the negotiating entity pre-defines a negotiation strategy before negotiation commences. A negotiating entity selects from the three negotiation strategies: patient/frugal, anxious, and cool-headed. The selected strategy defines a fixed rate of concession. It does not take into account changes in market status and does not place any restriction on negotiating entities such as allocation policies.

Case-Based Model

The negotiation model employs Experience Based Negotiation Agent (EBN) that captures formerly successful negotiation scenarios and dynamically generates adaptive negotiation strategies. It filters the best matched scenario, and uses it to recommend a concession level for generating an offer for the next negotiation round. If it did not find a matching episode, it selects from a set of predefined strategies. The negotiation agent encompasses a negotiation engine that advises on a concession level for generating a counter offer. It has access to data stored at the *Knowledge &*

Experience repository and carries out the following tasks:

- Retrieves relevant past negotiation scenarios.
- Assesses the similarity of retrieved negotiation scenarios to the current negotiation scenario. It tries to capture negotiation strategies with similar behavior/function and within client's budget.
- Concludes the most similar scenario to the current negotiation scenario.
- Uses the concluded scenario to recommend a concession level for generating a counter offer for the next negotiation round.

The knowledge & Experience repository consists of the following data types:

- Negotiation experiences
- Organizational data
- Similarity filters
- Adaptation guidelines

Negotiation experiences: It stores data about the current negotiation scenario. It consists of the following:

- Agent profile, counter offers, and concession
- Counter agent profile, offers, and concession
- Traded item
- Negotiation performance and outcomes

Organizational data: It stores hierarchy structure for organizing data of negotiation experiences. It facilitates search based on indexed negotiation experiences.

Similarity filters: It facilitates the capture of similar negotiation scenarios.

Adaptation guidelines: It has rules that assist the negotiation agent (EBN) in recommending a concession level for generating a counter offer in the next negotiation round.

Tete-a-Tete Model

It is designed for bilateral cooperative negotiation. Agents can negotiate multiple attributes including warranty period, payment method, installment options, service contracts, delivery time, etc. It employs the *Multi Attribute Utility Theory* (MAUT) (Schäfer, 2001) as a decision-making tool that evaluates offers as regards the multiple attributes of the bid. It does not place any restriction on agents such as allocation policies and does not suit competitive negotiation.

Market-Driven Model

It optimizes the selection of negotiation strategy by assessing the current market value, which is continuously changeable. The market value is estimated taking into account multiple factors: (1) remaining market time; (2) attractiveness of an agent's offer; (3) competition between trading agents.

Adaptive Negotiation Agents Model

It is based on automatic adoption of a negotiation strategy that takes into account: (1) information with regard to opponent's preferences and negotiation strategies; (2) cost of delay of agreement; (3) value of initial offers.

UTILITY FUNCTION

A negotiating strategy needs to evaluate an opponent's offer to decide on concession rate or to seek better offer. It evaluates offers based on values of client's constraints and preferences. In multi-criteria negotiation, the strategy takes into account weights of constraints and preferences. The value of a collected offer can be estimated

using a utility function, which can basically be defined as an entity's gain minus its cost (Sandholm, 1996). Nevertheless, there are important factors that should be taken into account in the utility function such as constant time discount factor and constant cost of delay factor. The constant time discount factor indicates that the desire of a buyer in goods declines with time due to inflation or goods are consumable. The constant cost of delay factor indicates that the negotiator bears a fixed cost of delay. A utility function has been presented for single-issue and multi-issue negotiation and considers the two factors (Fatima et al., 2003). The utility function is discussed in the following paragraphs.

Assuming two agents negotiate over the price of a single issue (i). Agent a acts on behalf on a particular client, while agent b acts on behalf of a particular vendor. They have distinct deadlines: T^a and T^b, and reserve price RP^a and RP^b respectively. The utilities of agents a and b are denoted as U^a and U^b respectively. The negotiation should end by the earlier deadline or the negotiation aborts. The time discount factor (δ) has an effect on individual's utility. In case of patient client, the utility increases with time ($\delta > 1$), whereas, it decreases in case of impatient client ($\delta < 1$). A particular tuple (RP, T, δ) is private to its agent. The price of the issue (i) is denoted as (p_i) at time (t_i). The time (t_i) is computed relative to the start time of negotiation. The utility function (U) for the two agents has been defined as in Equations (1) and (2).

$$U^a = (RP_i^a - p_i)(\delta_i^a)^{t_i} \tag{1}$$

$$U^b = (p_i - RP_i^b)(\delta_i^b)^{t_i} \tag{2}$$

Assuming the two agents negotiate over the price of multiple issues ($1 < i < n$), the utility function (U) has been defined as in Equations (3) and (4).

$$U^a = \sum_{i=1}^{n}(RP_i^a - p_i)(\delta_i^a)^{t_i} \qquad (3)$$

$$U^b = \sum_{i=1}^{n}(p_i - RP_i^b)(\delta_i^b)^{t_i} \qquad (4)$$

Assuming the time discount factor is the same for all negotiated issues, the utility function (*U*) has been defined as in Equations (5) and (6).

$$U^a = (\delta_i^a)^{t_i}\sum_{i=1}^{n}(RP_i^a - p_i) \qquad (5)$$

$$U^b = (\delta_i^b)^{t_i}\sum_{i=1}^{n}(p_i - RP_i^b) \qquad (6)$$

Assuming two agents negotiate multiple constraints and preferences $(1 \leq j \leq m)$ of a single issue, the utility function (*U*) has been defined in Equations (7) to (11) and is based on scoring functions (Volger et al., 1999). The client agent might negotiate two attributes: price of service and warranty period. The agent may also set upper and lower constraints $\left(min_j, max_j\right)$, for each negotiated attribute (*j*) for $(1 \leq j \leq m)$.

The value of an offer *S*(*X*) is calculated based on Equations (7) to (9).

$$S(X) = \sum_{1 \leq j \leq m} w_j.S_j(X) \qquad (7)$$

$$S_j(X) = \left| \left(\frac{X - min_j}{max_j - min_j}\right)^{\frac{1}{\beta}} \right| \qquad (8)$$

$$S_j(X) = \left| \left(\frac{max_j - X}{max_j - min_j}\right)^{\frac{1}{\beta}} \right| \qquad (9)$$

The parameter (*X*) represents the value of a negotiated attribute such as offer price. The parameter (β) defines the gradient of the scoring function. Equation (8) is used to evaluate small item values (*X*), while equation (9) is used to evaluate large item values (*X*).

Suppose the client only defines upper or lower limit of constraints of negotiated attributes, then the value of $S_j(X)$ is calculated based on equations (10) and (11). The strategy ranks the collected offers based on their values and deduces the best utility offer accordingly.

$$S_j(X) = \left| \left(\frac{X - min_j}{min_j}\right)^{\frac{1}{\beta}} \right| \qquad (10)$$

$$S_j(X) = \left| \left(\frac{max_j - X}{max_j}\right)^{\frac{1}{\beta}} \right| \qquad (11)$$

Attributes can be of discrete enumerated type (e.g. Boolean type) or numeral type. An enumerated attribute has a set of possible values and each value is associated with a rank that indicates the relative importance of a preference value to other values with respect to a particular criterion. The lower the rank is the higher is the attribute importance. In service-oriented negotiation, certain attributes can be of enumerated type and are imprecisely defined such as high quality, Ad hoc service, or short delivery. The negotiating agent can define values of enumerated attributes using FUZZY set theories that model conceptualization and process imprecise information (Bellman & Zadeh, 1970; Carvalho et al., 2005). The negotiating agent defines an appropriate preference value by selecting from a set of preference standards (Satty, 2008) predefined in the system as shown in Table 2.

Table 2. Preference predefined standards for discrete enumerated attributes

Importance level	Definition
1	Equal importance
2	Weak or slight importance
3	Moderate importance
4	Moderate plus importance
5	Strong importance
6	Strong plus importance
7	Very strong or demonstrated importance
8	Very, very strong
9	Extreme importance
Reciprocals of above	If activity *n* has one of the above numbers when compared to activity *m*, then *m* has the reciprocal value of *n* when compared with *n*

For example, a preference of high quality can be defined by selecting from a predefined standard given in Table 3. The rank lies within the interval of [1, 7]. The matching score of a preference (*X)* is FUZZY function that returns a number within [0, 1]. Assume the maximum rank number is *Max_rank*, the matching score of a given value of rank (*r*) is defined in (Zhuang et al., 2008) and as given in Equation (12).

$$x = \frac{Max\_rank - (r-1)}{Max\_rank} \qquad (12)$$

The parameter (w_j) is the normalized constraint weight (Zhuang et al., 2008) and indicates the relative importance of the constraint. The bigger the constraint weight is the more important is the constraint and the smaller is the concession (Zhuang et al., 2008). Agents can heuristically pre-define weights of constraints (Zen, 2009). They implement the Q-learning approach that combines decision functions and reinforcement learning algorithms (Braun et al., 2006). A learning agent that negotiates *m* constraints e.g. price, warranty period, delivery time, etc. defines a

matrix of weights of constraints (W) as given in Equation (13) for *n* negotiation tactics. The sum of weights conforms to Equation (14). It chooses the tactic that maximizes the expected utility.

$$W = \begin{bmatrix} w_{11} & w_{12} \cdots & w_{1n} \\ w_{21} & w_{22} \cdots & w_{2n} \\ \vdots & & \\ w_{m1} & w_{m2} \cdots & w_{mn} \end{bmatrix} \qquad (13)$$

$$\sum_{j=1 \dots m} w_j = 1 \text{ where } 0 < w_j < 1 \qquad (14)$$

A negotiating agent might collect multiple offers from vendors (V_i) for ($1 \leq i \leq$ n) and offers have expiry time T_{EV}^i. Assume the most advantageous offer has an expiry time that is earlier than the bid deadline, the utility function should take into account the effect of temporal constraints: offer expiry time T_{EV}^i and bid deadline T_{EB}. The utility function defined in (Al-Jaljouli & Abawajy, 2010) considers the factors and shows that the longer the expiry time of a time-limited advantageous offer is the better is the utility. The utility function is given in equations (15) and (16).

$$U = \left(\frac{P_{max} - P_{BP}^i}{P_{max}} \right) \qquad (15)$$

$$\text{Where} = \left(\frac{T_{EB}}{T_{EV}^i} \right), \text{ for } (T_{EV}^i < T_{EB}) \qquad (16)$$

In particular applications such as service-oriented negotiation, two phases of evaluation should be carried out. Firstly, vendors are evaluated based on vendor's profile and then offers are evaluated (Zhuang et al., 2008). The vendor's profile includes two factors: reputation and accumulated commercial credit. The reputation factor indicates the vendor's publicity level and ranges from zero to 1. Well-known vendors have

Table 3. Quality predefined standard

Quality level	Rank	Matching score
High	1	1
Very good	2	0.86
Good	3	0.71
Acceptable	4	0.57
Poor	5	0.43
Very poor	6	0.29
Unacceptable	7	0.14

higher reputation than unknown vendors. The accumulated commercial credit factor relates to past trade records. It sums the normalized number of past successful contracts the client had with the vendor and the average utility of all past contracts. The more contracts the vendor has the better is the accumulated commercial credit. If the client has never traded with the negotiated vendor, the vendor's profile would only include the reputation factor. The value of vendor's profile is defined in (Zhuang et al., 2008) and as given in Equations (17) and (18).

$$U^p = w^r\, U^r + w^{ac}\, U^{ac} \qquad (17)$$

Where U^p is the vendor's profile value; U^r is the reputation factor; U^{ac} is the accumulated commercial factor. w^r and w^{ac} denote weights of the two factors, respectively.

$$U^{ac} = w^{cn}\, U^{cn} + w^{au}\, U^{au} \qquad (18)$$

Where U^{ac} is the number of past successful contracts; U^{cn} is the average utility of past contracts; U^{au} is accumulated commercial factor. w^{cn} and w^{au} are weights of the two factors, respectively.

The evaluation of vendor's profile may include the following related issues (Wang et al., 2005):

- Reliability
- Security rank
- Delivery service

In complex negotiation, an additional phase may be carried out that evaluates the market based on multiple decision factors as listed below (Sim & Wong, 2001):

- Number of competitor suppliers
- Number of remaining items in stock
- Number of potential buyers
- Eagerness level to trade
- Remaining time for negotiation deadline
- Competition between suppliers

FUTURE RESEARCH DIRECTIONS

The future works of the discussed topic are to establish a framework for the selection of an appropriate negotiation strategy and to devise a utility function that incorporates the various decision-making factors including market status, supplier's profile, and eagerness for trading a negotiated goods/service, in addition to constraints and preferences the negotiating entity has initially set.

CONCLUSION

In this chapter, we looked at E-negotiation and the advantages it presents. We discussed several of its applications in fundamental tasks. We then presented the different interaction styles including symmetric/ asymmetric and cooperative/ competitive styles. Three negotiation models are described including: one-to-one negotiation model, one-to-many negotiation model, and many-to-one negotiation model. Also, real applications of negotiation models are presented. Negotiation can be over a single issue or multiple issues. There are three negotiation procedures that define the sequence in which multiple issues are negotiated. The different procedures are discussed and the architecture of a negotiation system is described in details with focus on multi-bilateral negotiation model.

A negotiating entity should carefully define the task to be negotiated and sets attributes, constraints, and preferences for negotiation. Temporal constraints such as offer expiry time or negotiation deadline control negotiation and have an effect on outcomes of negotiation. We discussed the interdependencies between different temporal constraints and the effect of advantageous time-limited offers on negotiation outcomes.

We outlined the different negotiation strategies and discussed the implemented tactics including concession tactic and search for alternatives tactic. The negotiation strategy can be fixed and predefined prior to negotiation or it can be dynamically adaptable according to changes in the environment. Several negotiation models that implement different negotiation strategies are outlined.

The negotiation strategy integrates goals and responsive attitudes and tries to reach an agreement through concession or search for alternatives. They advise on concession rate based on utility function that evaluates current offers. The key concession rates are discussed and utility functions are presented for different negotiation models. Offers are basically evaluated based on attributes, constraints, and preferences the negotiating entity predefines. There are significant factors that should be considered when evaluating an offer, including supplier's profile, market status, and eagerness for trading the negotiated goods/service.

E-negotiation aims for optimizing negotiation outcomes and negotiation strategies have a significant effect on negotiation outcomes. Hence, it is advisable to use dynamically adaptable strategies as negotiation environment is continually changeable. Moreover, strategies should not evaluate offers basically based on constraints and preferences the negotiating entity has initially set. Significant factors that have effect on negotiation outcomes such as market status should be considered.

REFERENCES

Al-Jaljouli, R., & Abawajy, J. (2007). *Electronic negotiation and security of exchanged information in e-commerce. Technical Report TR C07/12.* Deakin University, School of Engineering and Information Technology.

Al-Jaljouli, R., & Abawajy, J. (2007). Secure mobile agent-based e-negotiation for online trading. *Proceedings of the 7th IEEE International Symposium on Signal Processing and Information Technology (ISSPIT 2007)*, (pp. 610-615).

Al-Jaljouli, R., & Abawajy, J. (2010). *Negotiation strategy for agent-based E-negotiation. Proceedings of Principles and Practice of Multi-Agent Sytems*. PRIMA.

Bellman, R., & Zadeh, L. A. (1970). Decision making in fuzzy environment. *Journal of Management Science, 17*(4), 141–164. doi:10.1287/mnsc.17.4.B141

Braun, P., Brzostowski, J., Kersten, G., Kim, J., Kowalczyk, R., Strecker, S., & Vahidov, R. (2006). E-negotiation systems and software agents: methods, models, and applications. In Gupta, J. N. D., Forgionne, G. A., & Mora, M. (Eds.), *Intelligent decision-making support systems: Foundation, applications, and challenges*. Heidelberg, Germany: Springer Decision Engineering Series. doi:10.1007/1-84628-231-4_15

Busch, L., & Horstmann, I. (1997). A comment on issue-by-issue negotiation. *Journal of Games and Economic Behaviour, 19*, 144–148. doi:10.1006/game.1997.0543

Calisti, M. (2002). Constraint satisfaction techniques for negotiating agents. *Proceedings of AAMAS Workshop*.

Carvalho, M., Ekel, P., Martins, C., & Pereira, Jr. (2005). Fuzzy set-based multi objective allocation of resources: Solution algorithms and applications. *Invited talk from the 4th Congress of nonlinear analysis (WCNA 2004), 63*(5-7), 715-724.

Chavez, A., Dreilinger, D., Guttman, R., & Maes, P. (1997). A real-life experiment in creating an agent marketplace. *Software Agents and Soft Computing*, 160-179.

Chin, Y. Y., Lui, J. C., & Chen, S. (2008). A customer privacy protection protocol on agent-based electtronic commerce transaction. *Proceeding of 8th International Conference on Intelligent Systems Design and Applications (ISDA)*, Vol. 3, (pp. 6-10).

Faratin, P., & Rodríguez-Aguilar, J. (2005). Agent-mediated electronic commerce VI, theories for and engineering of distributed mechanisms and systems. *Proceedings of AMEC- Revised Selected Papers, LNCS 3435*. Springer.

Faratin, P., Sierra, C., & Jennings, N. R. (1998). Negotiation decision functions for autonomous agents. *Journal of Robotics and Autonomous Systems*, *24*(3-4), 159–182. doi:10.1016/S0921-8890(98)00029-3

Fatima, S., Wooldridge, M., & Jennings, N. (2002). Optimal negotiation strategies for agents with incomplete information. In J. J. Meyer & M. Tambe (Eds.), *Intelligent Agents VIII. Agent Theories, Architectures and Languages, Springer-Verlag, LNAI, Vol. 2333*, (pp. 377-392).

Fatima, S., Wooldridge, M., & Jennings, N. (2003). Optimal agendas for multi-issue negotiation. *Proceedings of the Second International Joint Conference on Autonomous Agents and Multi-agent Systems (AAMAS '03)*, (pp. 129-136).

Fatima, S., Wooldridge, M., & Jennings, N. (2004). An agenda based framework for multi-issue negotiation. *Journal of Artificial Intelligence*, *152*(1), 1–45. doi:10.1016/S0004-3702(03)00115-2

Fatima, S., Wooldridge, M., & Jennings, N. (2006). Multi-issue negotiation with deadlines. *Journal of Artificial Intelligence Research*, *6*, 381–417.

Fershtman, C. (2000). A note on multi-issue two-sided bargaining: Bilateral procedures. *Journal of Games and Economic Behavior*, *30*, 216–227. doi:10.1006/game.1999.0727

Ge, X., & Dong, S. (2010). Analysis and research of the negotiation strategies based on time constraint. *Proceedings of the 2nd International Workshop on Intelligent Systems and Applications (ISA)*, (pp. 1- 5).

Gil Iranzo, R. (2005). *Agents negotiating in semantic web architecture* (SWA). Ph.D. Thesis. Technology Department, University Pompeu Fabra.

Guttman, R., Moukas, A., & Maes, P. (1998). Agent-mediated electronic commerce: a survey.. *Journal of Knowledge Engineering Review*, *13*(3).

Hamed Kebriaei, H., & Majd, V. (2008). A simultaneous multi-attribute soft-bargaining design for bilateral contracts. *Journal of Expert Systems with Applications*, *36*(3).

Hindriks, K., & Tykhonov, D. (2008). Opponent modeling in automated multi-issue negotiation using Bayesian learning. *Proceedings of the 7th International Joint Conference on Autonomous Agents and Multi-Agent Systems, Vol. 1*, (pp. 331-338).

Keeney, R., & Raiffa, H. (1976). *Decisions with multiple objectives: Performances and value tradeoffs*. New York, NY: John Wiley.

Kersten, G., & Noronha, S. (1999). WWW-based negotiation support: Design, implementation.. *International Journal of Cooperative Information Systems*, *5*(2-3).

Kfir-Dahav, N., Monderer, D., & Tennenholtz, M. (2000). Mechanism design for resource bounded agents. *Proceedings of 4th International Conference on Multi-agent Systems (ICMAS)*, (pp. 309-315).

Kowalczyk, R., & Bui, V. (2001). Lecture Notes in Computer Science: *Vol. 2003. On constraint-based reasoning in e-negotiation agents. Agent-Mediated Electronic Commerce III* (pp. 31–46).

Kraus, S., Wilkenfeld, J., & Zlotkin, G. (1995). Multiagent negotiation under time constraints.. *Journal of Artificial Intelligence, 75*(2), 297–345. doi:10.1016/0004-3702(94)00021-R

Krovi, R., Graesser, A., & Pracht, W. (1999). Agent behaviors in virtual negotiation environments.. *IEEE Transactions on Systems, Man, and Cybernetics, 29*, 15–25. doi:10.1109/5326.740666

Kumar, V. (1992). Algorithms for constraint-satisfaction problems: A survey.. *AI Magazine, 32*–44.

Kurbel, K., & Loutchko, I. (2005). A model for multi-lateral negotiations on an agent-based job marketplace.. *Journal of Electronic Commerce Research and Applications, 4*(3), 87–203.

Li, H. (2001). *Automated e-business negotiation: Model, life cycle, and system architecture*. Ph.D. Thesis, Department of Computer and Information Science and Engineering, University of Florida.

Lomuscio, A., Wooldridge, M., & Jennings, N. (2003). A classification scheme for negotiation in electronic commerce. *International journal of Group Decision and Negotiation, 12*(1), 31-56.

Luo, X., Jennings, N., Shadbolt, N., Leung, H., & Lee, J. (2003). A fuzzy constraint based model for bilateral, multi-issue negotiations in semi-competitive environments.. *Journal of Artificial Intelligence, 148*, 53–102. doi:10.1016/S0004-3702(03)00041-9

McBurney, P., & Parsons, S. (2003). Dialogue game protocols.. *Journal of Communications in Multiagent Systems, LNCS, 2650*, 269–283. doi:10.1007/978-3-540-44972-0_15

Neumann, D., Benyoucef, M., Bassil, S., & Vachon, J. (2003). Applying the Montreal taxonomy to state of the art e-negotiation systems.. *Journal of Group Decision and Negotiation, 12*, 287–310. doi:10.1023/A:1024871921144

Pruitt, D. G. (1981). *Negotiation behavior*. Academic Press, Inc. Kowalczyk, R., & Bui, V. (2000). On fuzzy e-negotiation agents: Autonomous negotiation with incomplete and imprecise information (DEXA). *11th International Workshop on Database and Expert Systems Applications* (DEXA'00), Vol. 1034.

Rahwan, I., Kowalczyk, R., & Pham, H. (2002). Intelligent agents for automated one-to-many e-commerce negotiation. *Proceedings of the 25th Australian Conference on Computer Science*, (pp. 197-204). Australian Computer Society Press.

Robenstein, A., & Wolinsky, A. (1985). Equilibrium in market with sequential bargaining.. *Econometrica: Journal of the Econometric Society, 53*(5).

Robinson, W. N., & Volkov, V. (1998). Supporting the negotiation life cycle.. *Communications of the ACM, 41*(5), 95–102. doi:10.1145/274946.274962

Roussaki, I., & Louta, M. (2003). *Efficient negotiation framework and strategies for the next generation electronic marketplace*. MBA Thesis, National Technical University of Athens, Athens, Greece.

Saaty, T. (2008). Decision making with the analytic hierarchy process.. *International Journal of Services Sciences, 1*(1), 83–98. doi:10.1504/IJSSCI.2008.017590

Sandholm, T. (1996). Limitation of the Vickery auction in computational multi agent systems. *Proceedings of the Second International Conference on Multi-agent Systems (ICMAS-96)*, (pp. 299-306).

Sandholm, T., & Vulkan, N. (1999). Bargaining with deadlines. *Proceedings of the National Conference on Artificial Intelligence*. Retrieved from http://www.cs.wustl.edu/cs/techreports/1999/wucs-99-06.tr.ps.Z

Schäfer, R. (2001). Rules for using multi-attribute utility theory for estimating a user's interests. *Proceedings of Workshop on Adaptivity and User Modeling*.

Shiraz, M., & Barfouroush, A. (2008). Conceptual framework for modeling automated negotiation in multiagent systems..*Negotiation Journal, 24*(1), 45–70. doi:10.1111/j.1571-9979.2007.00166.x

Si, Y., Edmond, D., Dumas, M., & Hofstede, A. (2007). Specification and execution of composite trading activities..*Journal of Electronic Commerce Research, 7*(3-4), 221–263. doi:10.1007/s10660-007-9005-6

Sim, K., & Wong, E. (2001). Toward market-driven agents for electronic auction..*IEEE Transactions on Systems, Man, and Cybernetics, 3*(6), 474–484.

Sycara, K., Roth, S., Sadeh, N., & Fox, M. (1991). Distributed constraint heuristic Search..*IEEE Transactions on Systems, Man, and Cybernetics, 21*, 1446–1461. doi:10.1109/21.135688

Vogler, H., Spriestersbach, A., & Moschgath, M. (1999). *Protecting competitive negotiation of mobile agents*. IEEE Workshop on Future Trends of Distributed Computing Systems (FTDCS).

Wang, Y., Tan, K., & Ren, J. (2005). *Towards autonomous and automatic evaluation and negotiation in agent-mediated internet marketplaces* (*Vol. 5*, pp. 343–366). Kluwer Academic Publishers.

Wilkes, J. (2008). *Utility functions, prices, and negotiation*. HP Laboratories.

Wong, T., Fang, F., & Leung, D. (2004). Automating buyer-seller negotiation in supply chain management. *Proceedings of 5ᵗʰ Asia Pacific Industrial Engineering and Management System Conference*.

Wong, W., Zhang, D., & Kara-Ali, M. (2000). Negotiating with experience. *Proceedings of AAAI Workshop on Knowledge-Based Electronic Markets*, (pp. 85–90).

Yokoo, M. (2001). Distributed constraint satisfaction: Foundations of cooperation in multi-agent systems. Springer-Verlag. *IEEE Transactions on Knowledge and Data Engineering*, 143.

Zen, Z. (2009). An agent-based online shopping system in e-commerce..*Journal of Computer and Information Science, 2*(4), 14–19.

Zhuang, Y., Fong, S., & Shi, M. (2008). Knowledge-empowered automated negotiation for e-Commerce..*Journal of Knowledge Information Systems, 17*, 167–191. doi:10.1007/s10115-007-0119-x

ADDITIONAL READING

Bichler, M., Kersten, G., & Strecker, S. (2003). Towards a structured design of electronic negotiations..*Journal of Group Decision and Negotiation, 12*, 311–335. doi:10.1023/A:1024867820235

Collins, J., Jamison, S., Gini, M., & Mobasher, B. (1997(. Temporal strategies in multi-agent contracting protocol. *Proceedings of AAAI-97 Workshop on Using AI in Electronic Commerce, Virtual Organizations, Enterprise Knowledge Management to Re-engineer the Corporation*, (pp. 50-56).

Da-Jun, C., & Liang-Xian, X. (2002). A negotiation model of incomplete information under time constraints. *Proceedings of 1st International Joint Conference on Autonomous Agents and Multiagent Systems*, (pp. 128-134).

Dastani, M., Hulstijn, J., Toree, L., Boelelaan, D., & Amsterdam, H. (2000). Negotiation protocols and dialogue games. *Proceedings of Belgian-Dutch Conference on Artificial Intelligence (BNAIC)*, (pp. 13-20).

Davies, R., & Smith, R. (1983). Negotiation as a metaphor for distributed problem solving.. *Journal of Artificial Intelligence, 20*(1), 63–109. doi:10.1016/0004-3702(83)90015-2

Fershtman, C., & Seidmann, D. J. (1993). Deadline effects and inefficient delay in bargaining with endogenous commitment..*Journal of Economic Theory, 60*(2), 306–321. doi:10.1006/jeth.1993.1045

Filzmoser, M. (2010). *Simulation of automated negotiation* (1st ed.). doi:10.1007/978-3-7091-0133-9

Gatti, N., Giunta, F., & Marino, S. (2008). Alternating-offers bargaining with one-sided uncertain deadlines: An efficient algorithm..*Journal of Artificial Intelligence, 172*(8-9), 1119–1157. doi:10.1016/j.artint.2007.11.007

Giordano, G., Stoner, S., Brouer, R., & George, J. (2007). The influences of deception and computer-mediation on dyadic negotiations..*Journal of Computer-Mediated Communication, 12*(2). doi:10.1111/j.1083-6101.2007.00329.x

Jaiswal, A., Kim, Y., & Gini, M. (2004). Design and implementation of a secure multi-agent marketplace..*Journal of Electronic Commerce Research and Applications, 3*(4), 355–368. doi:10.1016/j.elerap.2004.06.005

Jennings, N., Faratin, P., Lomuscio, A., Sierra, C., & Wooldridge, M. (2001). Automated negotiation: Prospects, methods, and challenges..*Journal of Group Decision and Negotiation, 10*(2), 199–215. doi:10.1023/A:1008746126376

Jennings, N., Faratin, P., Norman, T., & O'Brien, P. (2000). Business process management system using ADEPT: A real-world case study..*International Journal of Applied Artificial Intelligence, 14*(5), 421–465. doi:10.1080/088395100403379

Kersten, G. E., & Lai, H. (2007). Satisfiability and completeness of protocols for electronic negotiations..*European Journal of Operational Research, 180*(2), 922–937. doi:10.1016/j.ejor.2005.04.056

Kersten, G. E., Strecker, S. E., & Law, K. P. (2004). Lecture Notes in Computer Science: *Vol. 3182. Protocols for electronic negotiation systems: theoretical foundations and design issues* (pp. 106–115). LNCS.

Kraus, S. (2001). *Strategic negotiation in multi-agent environment.* The MIT Press.

Kuwabara, K., & Lesser, V. (1989). Extended protocol for multi-stage negotiation. *Proceedings of the 9th Workshop on Distributed Artificial Intelligence.*

Lax, D., & Sebenius, J. (1986). *The manager as negotiator: Bargaining for cooperation and competitive gain.* The Free Press.

Lee, K. J., Chang, Y. S., & Lee, J. K. (2000). Time-bound negotiation framework for electronic commerce agents..*Journal of Decision Support Systems, 28*, 319–331. doi:10.1016/S0167-9236(99)00096-2

Levati, M. V., & Maciejovsky, B. (2001). Deadline effects in ultimatum bargaining: An experimental study of concession sniping with low or no costs of delay..*Journal Costs of Delay: International Game Theory Review, 7*, 117–135.

Linve, Z. (1979). *The role of time in negotiation.* Ph.D. Thesis, Massachusetts Institute of technology.

McBurney, P., & Parsons, S. (2003). Dialogue game protocols..*Journal of Communications in Multiagent Systems, LNCS, 2650*, 269–283. doi:10.1007/978-3-540-44972-0_15

Neumann, J., & Morgenstem, O. (1947). *Theory of games and electronic behavior.* Princeton, NJ: Princeton University Press.

Osborne, M., & Rubinstein, A. (1990). *Bargaining and markets*. San Diego, CA: Academic Press.

Ostwald, J. (1996). *Knowledge construction in software development: The evolving artifact approach*. Ph.D. Thesis, University of Colorado, USA. Retrieved from http://l3d.cs.colorado.edu/~ostwald/thesis/home.html

Rahwan, I., Kowalczyk, R., & Yang, Y. (2000). *Virtual enterprise design–BDI agents vs. objects. Journal of Recent Advances in Artificial Intelligence in e-Commerce, Lecture Notes in Artificial Intelligence*. Springer-Verlag.

Raiffa, H. (1982). *The art and science of negotiation*. Cambridge, MA: Harvard University Press.

Rosenschein, J. S., & Zlotkin, G. (1994). *Rules of encounter*. MIT Press.

Rubinstein, A. (1982). Perfect equilibrium in a bargaining model..*Journal of Econometrics, 50*, 97–110. doi:10.2307/1912531

Sandholm, T., & Lesser, V. (1995). Issues in automated negotiation and electronic commerce: Extending the contract net framework. In *Proceedings of the First International Conference on Multi-Agent System*, (pp. 328-335).

Ströbel, M., & Weinhardt, C. (2003). The Montreal taxonomy for electronic negotiations..*Journal of Group Decision and Negotiation, 12*(2), 143–164. doi:10.1023/A:1023072922126

Van Dinther, C., Conte, T., & Baust, G. (2008). Incentives and control for information revelation an empirical study..*Proceedings of the GDN, 1*, 41–42.

Wurman, P. (2001). Dynamic pricing in the virtual marketplace..*IEEE Internet Computing, 5*(2), 36–42. doi:10.1109/4236.914646

Yang, X. (2005). *Mobile agent computing in electronic business: Potentials, designs and challenges*. Ph.D. Thesis, Griffith University, Australia.

KEY TERMS AND DEFINITIONS

Cost of Delay Factor: Indicates that a negotiator bears a fixed cost of delay.

Market Status: Describes trading opportunities in the market in terms of number of competitor suppliers, number of remaining items in stock, number of potential buyers, and competition between suppliers.

Negotiation Procedure: Defines a particular sequence in which issues can be negotiated such as package deal procedure, simultaneous procedure or sequential procedure.

Negotiation Strategy: Advises a negotiating entity on the proper action to select for a set of possible actions that optimizes negotiation outcomes

Time Discount Factor: Indicates that the desire of a buyer in goods declines with time due to inflation or goods are consumable.

Utility Function: Estimates the value of an offer that serves as an indicator of the gains the offer provides to a negotiating entity.

Utility Limit: Defines the minimum acceptable utility a negotiating entity may accept.

66

Chapter 4
Security Policy Specification

Jorge Bernal Bernabé
University of Murcia, Spain

Jesús D. Jiménez Re
University of Murcia, Spain

Juan M. Marín Pérez
University of Murcia, Spain

Félix J. García Clemente
University of Murcia, Spain

Jose M. Alcaraz Calero
Cloud and Security Lab Hewlett-Packard Laboratories, UK

Gregorio Martínez Pérez
University of Murcia, Spain

Antonio F. Gómez Skarmeta
University of Murcia, Spain

ABSTRACT

Policy-based management of information systems enables the specification of high-level policies which need to be refined into lower level configurations suitable to be directly applied to services and final devices in order to achieve the high-level behavior previous specified. This chapter presents a proposal for describing high-level security policies and for carrying out the policy refinement process for which low level policies and configurations are achieved. Firstly, an analysis of different research works related to the specification of security policy is provided. Then, a detailed description of the information model used for describing the information systems and the policies is described. After that, the language designed for specifying high level security policies is explained as well as the low level language based on the Common Information Model. Finally, some aspect about the policy refinement process done in the policy-based system in order to achieve low-level policies from the high-level security policies is outlined together with a description of the tools which can assist in the definition of the security policies and in the process refinement process.

INTRODUCTION

Information systems are incredibly growing nowadays becoming more and more complex to be administrated. Managing huge systems is a very complex problem and this issue has been focused in several research works during the last years proposing alternatives to tackle different aspects of system management. An approach is the management of systems based on policies. It enables the specification of high level business policies which are refined into low-level policies suitable to be directly applied into final devices to achieve the high-level behavior previous specified.

DOI: 10.4018/978-1-4666-1888-6.ch004

Security is a key aspect to be controlled in information systems and policy-based systems can help to control it. To this end, security policies can be described by administrators using a language designed for this purpose which enables the description of high level security policies. Researchers have proposed multiple approaches for policy specification that range from formal policy languages that a computer can directly process and interpret, to rule-based policy notation using an if-then-else format. The definition and the usage of high level policy languages ease the process of policy specification reducing significantly errors therein. In fact, high-level policies require less effort to be written and maintained since a lot of details are hidden to writers. Note that this kind of policies does not need training or deep knowledge to be used even by (maybe not so skilled) administrators. This is especially suitable in security field in which any specification error potentially may cause a security hole in the information system.

In the policy definition process, the task of a policy manager is to transform the business policies into implementable policies using a formal language for this purpose. To do so, the manager uses a high level policy language that assures that the representation of security policies will be unambiguous and verifiable. Moreover, other important requirements of any policy language are:

- **Clear and well defined semantics:** The semantics of a policy language can be considered as well defined if the meaning of a policy written in this language is unambiguous at any time of its life-cycle.
- **Flexibility and extensibility:** A policy language has to be flexible enough to allow new policy information to be expressed, and extensible enough to allow new semantics to be added in future versions of this language.
- **Independent of the administrative domain:** where it will be used and, in particu-

lar, of manufacturers/providers of devices and services. A policy language is independent if a policy written in this language is independent of a specific deployment.
- **Readability:** A policy language must be easy to understand when read by the administrator.
- **Amenable to combining:** A policy language should include a way of grouping policies.

In addition, a policy language should facilitate the realization of functions related to policy framework. In this sense, other requirements are:

- **Access to policy information:** A policy representation oriented to facilitate queries about policy information.
- **Conflict detection:** A policy language which facilitates the process of conflict detection, either enabling a direct integration in conflict analysis tools, or having syntactic and semantics elements to facilitate the conflict analysis.
- **Policy distribution:** The policy representation may support of multiple bindings that is to be possible to convey policy instances in a number of different protocols.
- **Policy refinement:** A policy language may provide facilities or techniques to help in the policy translation process and to achieve policy and rules consistent at every level of abstraction.

This book chapter describes a proposal for describing high level security policies and for carrying out the policy refinement process for which low level policies are achieved, which can be directly applied over the final devices. First, an analysis of different research works related to the specification of security policy is provided in this chapter. Then, a detailed description of the information model used for describing the information systems and the policies is provided.

After that, the language designed for specifying high level security policies (SPL) is described, explaining how different security aspects can be modeled such as authentication, authorization, packet filtering and operational policies. Then, a low level language based on the Common Information Model (CIM) which could be directly enforced in current information systems is shown. Finally, some aspect about the policy refinement process done in the policy-based system in order to achieve low-level policies from the high-level security policies is commented together with a description of the tools which can assist in the definition of the security policies and in the process refinement process. The main intention of this chapter is to enable the reader to understand the basis related to policy-based management systems, languages for describing security policies and policy refinement processes.

BACKGROUND

A Critical Comparison of Policy Specification Approaches

There are various security policy models and policy specification languages in literature. We have selected as more representative, after a first analysis, Ponder (Damianou, Dulay, Lupu, & Sloman, 2001), XACML (OASIS, 2011) and the DMTF standards (Distributed Management Task Force, 2001) that we describe briefly below.

Ponder is a declarative, object-oriented language developed for specifying management and security policies. Ponder permits to express authorizations, obligations, information filtering, refrain policies, and delegation policies. Ponder can describe any rule to constrain the behavior of components, in a simple and declarative way.

The *eXtensible Access Control Markup Language (XACML)* describes both an access control policy language and a request/response protocol. The policy language provides a common means

to express subject-target-action-condition access control policies and the request/response protocol expresses queries about whether a particular access should be allowed and describes answers to those queries.

Common Information Model (CIM) is the main DMTF standard that provides a common definition of management-related information independent of any specification. In this sense, CIM model defines concepts for authorization, authentication, delegation, filtering, and obligation policies. However, for an information model to be useful, it has to be mapped into some specification. For that, DMTF defines two standards: Web-Based Enterprise Management (WBEM) uses an XML representation for CIM (CIM-XML), and WS-CIM provides a CIM mapping to WSDL and XML Schema.

From our perspective, some limitations are identified.

For Ponder:

- Limitations to express system descriptions using a standard way. Ponder lacks a information model for system and policy concepts;
- Limitations to extend the language to support new types of policies (e.g., confidentiality or security associations);
- Lack of interoperability with standard proposals with similar objectives (management and authorization policies), such as DMTF standards or XACML;
- Ponder policy representation is not suitable for Web services environments, although the new version Ponder2 (Imperial College London, 2011) overcomes this limitation.

For XACML:

- Limitations to express system descriptions using a standard way just the same as Ponder;

- Oriented to access control policies and it does not permit other types of policy (e.g., filtering or authentication);
- A policy generated with XACML is rather verbose and not really aimed for human interpretation;
- It is not clear if it is possible to express complex policies, although XACML provides the possibility for a policy document to refer to others.

For DMTF standards:

- CIM provides a wide support for management security policy and system concepts, but it must be extended to includes more concepts (e.g., related to routing);
- WS-CIM provides a representation more suitable than WBEM representation for tasks such as validation and semantic analysis, but WS-CIM representation is strong linked to Web services specifications and it makes complex.

The limitation to express system description and to support new types of policy avoids fulfilling requirements such as extensibility and flexibility. From our perspective, the lack of these requirements makes that Ponder and XACML are not suitable solutions whereas CIM Model is suitable to define a common format to represent any security policies and system description. Moreover, an advantage of the CIM-based approach to information management is that the model can be easily mapped to structured specifications such as XML, which can then be used for policy analysis as well as management of policies across networks.

The advantages of CIM Model have been identified by other works, e.g. the Polyander project (Sloman, Luk, Lupu, & Dulay, 2004) is partially addressing this issue for a management system where the objects to which policies apply are defined using the CIM information model, or the CIM Simplified Policy Language (CIM-SPL)

(DMTF Policy Working Group, 2009) is a proposed standard submitted by the DMTF Policy Working Group with the objective of providing a means for specifying if-condition-then-action style policy rules to manage computing resources using constructs defined by CIM.

CIM Information Model and its Representation

The Common Information Model (CIM) is an approach from the DMTF for providing consistent information models with well-defined associations that capture management content for applications, systems, networks, devices, and other technology-focused management domains. CIM models establish a common conceptual framework that enables both hardware and software providers to consistently represent management information across vendor boundaries.

CIM model is composed of a Core Model and Common Models, where the Core Model captures basic notions that are applicable to all areas of management and the Common Models are information models that capture notions that are common to particular management areas. The Common Models mainly considered in our work to represent security policies are:

- **CIM Policy Model:** The Policy Model provides a common framework for specifying system behaviors that are sufficiently abstract and scalable to configuring large complexes of computer systems, i.e. the Policy Model is a specific model for expressing policies in a general and scalable way.
- **CIM User and Security Model:** The objective of the User and Security Model is to provide a set of relationships between the various representations of users, their credentials, the managed elements that represent the resources, and the resource managers involved in system user administration.

The descriptions of CIM model are provided by the CIM Schema, but it is independent of any implementation or specific representation. However, for an information model to be useful, it has to be mapped into some encoding. In this sense, as Figure 1 shows, CIM can be mapped to (or represented as) several structured specifications.

CIM meta model provides a formal definition of the CIM models, i.e. it defines the terms used to express the models and its usage and semantics. Figure 2 shows the main elements of Meta Schema such as Schema that is a group of classes with a single owner, and Class that defines the properties and the methods common to a particular kind of object. The model also supports Indication that is the representation of the occurrence of an event, Association that represent relationships between two or more classes using references, and Qualifier that provides additional information about classes, associations, indications, methods, method parameters, properties or references.

Currently, CIM Schema is defined by the DMTF in MOF (Managed Object Format) format. However, MOF is not a valid representation for Web Services, being XML and WSDL examples of valid representations. According to our approach the XML specification is a good alternative for describing the CIM objects (i.e. classes, associations, properties, references and instances).

For mapping CIM objects using XML, there are two different alternatives: schema mapping and meta-schema mapping. The meta-schema mapping defines a DTD (Document Type Definition) to describe in a generic manner the notion of a CIM class or instance. CIM element names are mapped to XML attributes or element values, rather than to specific XML element names. On the contrary, the schema mapping defines an XML Schema to describe the CIM classes; in this approach CIM instances are mapped to valid XML documents for that schema. Essentially this means that each CIM class generates its own XSD fragment whose XML element names are the same that the corresponding CIM element names.

The meta-schema mapping was firstly adopted by the DMTF, as it only requires one standardized DTD for the whole CIM regardless the version of this information model used in one particular implementation. However, there are obvious benefits to employing a schema mapping (more validation power, and a slightly more intuitive representation of CIM in XML) and latter DMTF defined WS-CIM Mapping based on schema mapping.

From our perspective, the usage of a schema mapping facilitates the deployment of components of the Framework, and therefore we have adopted an internal format used for the low-level representation of policy rules based on CIM models using a schema mapping.

Figure 1. CIM modeling levels

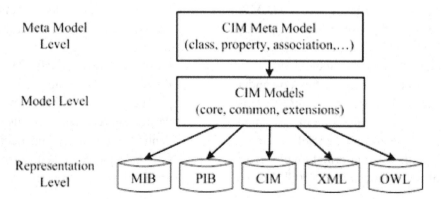

70

Figure 2. CIM meta schema (reduced)

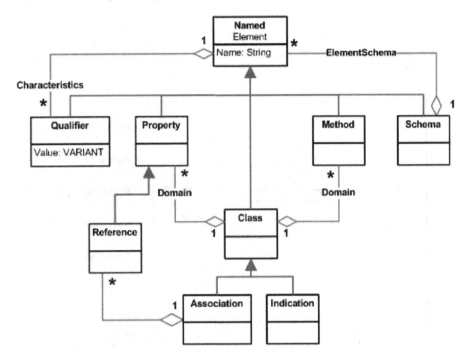

SPL: HIGH-LEVEL SECURITY POLICY LANGUAGE

The Security Policy Language (SPL) is the high-level language used by the security administrator to define the desired security behavior of the networked systems and applications. The description of these should have been created previously through a System Description Language (SDL). Both SDL and SPL are based on XML, due to the ease with which its syntax and semantics can be extended and the widespread support that it enjoys from all the main platform and tool vendors.

SPL supports different types of security policies and also allows grouping, priority and classification of these policies. Their syntaxes are defined by means of SPL Schema (see Figure 3). The SPL definitions are composed of a set of attributes and three groups of elements. The groups are the *CommonElements* group that represents common concepts, the *Policy* group that defines the set of security policies, and the PolicyGroups group that provides a mechanism to group and classify

policies. The relevant attributes are the *version* attribute that represents the current version of the document, the *schemaVersion* attribute represents the SPL Schema version, the *author* attribute represents the author of the SPL definitions, and the *description* attribute represents a textual description of the SPL instance.

CommonElements Group

The CommonElements group includes the Identities, Roles, Privileges, Security Levels, Filter Entries, and Privilege Constraints of the SPL definition.

Identities. The Identities element represents the security principals. For a given security context, an Identity imparts a level of trust, usually based on its credentials. The lifetime and validity of the Identity is dependent on the security policies.

Roles. The Roles element contains the set of roles that conforms the SPL. A Role is used to represent a position or set of responsibilities within a security context, and is filled by Identi-

Figure 3. P-SPL structure

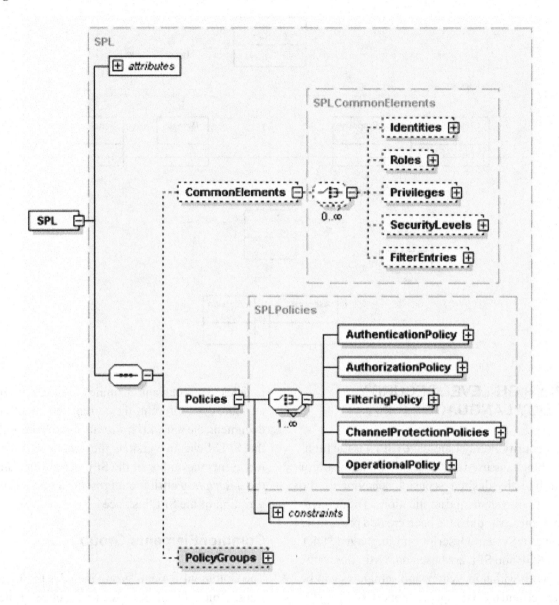

ties – i.e. the 'role occupants'. The position or set of responsibilities of a Role are represented as a set of rights defined by privileges.

Privileges. The Privileges element contains the set of Privileges, where a Privilege is the base for all types of activities which are granted or denied by a Role or an Identity. There are three different types of privileges: *GenericPrivilege* is used for general purposes, *ServicePrivilege* is used to represent the activities that are granted or

denied for a common Service, and *MailPrivilege* is used to represent the activities that are granted or denied for a Mail Service.

SecurityLevels. The SecurityLevels element represents a set of security level for policy classification. A simple example is to define security levels representing a low level as 'green', a medium level as 'yellow', a moderate level as 'orange', and a high level as 'red'.

FilterEntries. The FilterEntries elements contain the set of filters, where a FilterEntry is used by network devices to identify traffic and either forward it (with possibly further processing) to its destination, or to deny its forwarding.

Policy Group

The Policy group includes authentication, authorization, filtering, channel protection, and operational policies.

Authentication Policies (AuthenticationPolicy). Authentication policies are used to create rules defining the criteria for an identity (i.e. policy subject) to be authenticated in a network element (i.e. policy target). Some of the supported mechanisms are: shared secrets, basic authentication, biometric, networking identifier, Kerberos, certificates and Physical Credential.

Authorization Policies (AuthorizationPolicy). This type of policy allows to specify the authorization criteria based on privileges. The policy is defined by a *Target*, the network elements, a *Subject* the identities or/and roles, the *Privileges*, the activities granted or denied and the *Action*, i.e. grant or deny.

Filtering Policies (FilteringPolicy). This type of policies is used to create rules defining the filtering criteria used by a network element. Some of the types of conditions that can be applied: Source Address and Mask, Destination Address and Mask, Source port or source port range, destination port or destination port range, protocol type, DSCP, ToS Value, 802.1P Priority and other (extensible).

Channel Protection Policies (ChannelProtectionPolicies). They define the channel protection requirements based on security associations. Types of security associations are IPsec SA, IKE and SSL/TLS.

Operational Policies (OperationalPolicy). Operational policies allows describing the behavior of the network when any kind of event has been occurred. They implement the paradigm *"on-event-if-conditions-then-actions"*, although

the event does not explicitly specify to trigger the execution of the actions, it assumes an implicit event, such as a change of status. Many operational statuses are possible: unknown, OK, Error, Starting, Stopped, Lost communication and so on.

PolicyGroups Group. The PolicyGroups element provides a mechanism to group and classify policies. A policy group is an aggregation of Policy instances (PolicyGroups and/or Policy) that have the same decision strategy. When a large set of policies is managed, its usage is recommended.

Example

This section presents an example (see Figure 4) where the security policies are defined by administrator using SPL. The system elements of the example are a router, a radius server, a web server, and a mail server. These elements are defined by administrators using SDL. The policy elements of the example are composed of SecurityLevels, Identities, Roles, FilterEntries and Privileges.

The objective of this example is to define two security levels (i.e. Red and Green) corresponding to two different operational conditions of the network. For the first level, the network traffic is limited and service access is permitted to Golden User. And for the second level, service access is permitted to Silver User.

CommonElements

The example is composed of policies for two security levels, as shown in Box 1.

High security level is named by Red and Low security level is named by Green. Last common element is the filter entries used to represent UDP, IKE, TCP, and any traffic. This filter is used by the filtering policy.

User1 and User2 are the Identities that are classified by Roles. The Role Golden Users is filled by User1 and the Role Silver Users is filled by User2, as shown in Box 2.

Figure 4. Example P-SPL definitions

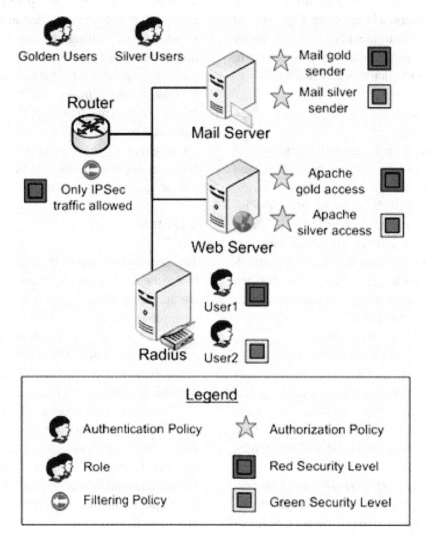

Box 1.

```
<SecurityLevels>
    <SecurityLevel>
        <Name>Red</Name>
        <Description>High security level</Description>
        <Level>1</Level>
    </SecurityLevel>
    <SecurityLevel>
        <Name>Green</Name>
        <Description>Low security level</Description>
        <Level>2</Level>
    </SecurityLevel>
</SecurityLevels>
```

The example in Box 3 is composed of privileges for mail access and web access. Mail gold access and web gold access are privileges to access without restrictions, whereas mail silver access and web silver access have a lower level.

Last common element is the filter entries used to represent UDP, IKE, TCP, and any traffic. This filter is used by the filtering policy presented in Box 4.

Security Policies

The example is composed of one filtering policy, two authentication policies, and four authorization policies. The policies are classified by security level.

The high security level implies four security policies that limit network traffic and service accesses. This is the filtering policy '*For Security*

Box 2.

```
<Roles>
    <Role>
        <Name>Golden Users</Name>
        <Description>Golden Users </Description>
        <Identities>
            <IdentityReferences type="Identity">User1</IdentityReferences>
        </Identities>
    </Role>
    <Role>
        <Name>Silver Users</Name>
        <Description>Silver Users</Description>
        <Identities>
            <IdentityReferences type="Identity">User2</IdentityReferences>
        </Identities>
    </Role>
</Roles>
```

Box 3.

```
<GenericPrivilege>
    <Name>Apache Silver Access</Name>
    <Description>Access privilege for clients</Description>
    <Granted>true</Granted>
    <Activities>
        <Activities>Read</Activities>
    </Activities>
    <Qualifiers>
        <Qualifier type="URL">http://umu.org/basic</Qualifier>
    </Qualifiers>
</GenericPrivilege>
>
```

Box 4.

```
<FilterEntry>
    <Name>UDP traffic</Name>
    <TrafficType>IPv4</TrafficType>
    <MatchCondition Type="Protocol Type">UDP</MatchCondition>
</FilterEntry>
```

Level Red, router permits only IPsec traffic allowed' that uses the filter entries above (see Box 5).

Another one is the authentication policy *'For Security Level Red, Identity User1 must authenticate as user1 in Radius Server'* that permits User1 authenticates (see Box 6).

And two authorization policies to gold access to web server and mail server, *'For Security Level Red, Role Golden Users has the privilege of Gold access to Web Server'* and *'For Security Level Red, Role Golden Users has the privilege of Gold access to Mail Server'*. The subjects for these policies are Golden User (see Box 7).

The low security level implies three security policies that limit service accesses to silver users. The authentication policy *'For Security Level Green, Identity User2 must authenticate as user2 in Radius Server'* that permits User2 authenticates. And two authorization policies to silver access to web server and mail server, *'For Security Level Green, Role Silver Users has the privilege of Silver access to Web Server'* and *'For Security Level Green, Role Silver Users has the privilege of Silver access to Mail Server'* (see Box 8).

INTERNAL FORMAT

The internal format is low level language for formal modeling and internally used by our framework to define the desired security behavior. The internal format is a de-facto standard for developers in our framework; it is based on the CIM Schema and represented using XML Schema technology.

CIM models try to cover a high range of aspects related to the information management.

CIM models are not suitable by itself, due to the huge amount of classes which is compound. To solve that inconvenient, we have defined both submodels: xCIM-SDL (xCIM System Description Language) and xCIM-SPL (xCIM Security Policy Language). The first one represents the medium level abstraction representation for System Description Language, whereas the second one represents the medium/low level abstraction representation for Security Policy Language.

The main features of the xCIM-SPL are the following ones:

- Based on the CIM Policy Model and CIM User-Security Model. The xCIM-SPL is based on CIM, including only relevant classes of the model as well as some extended classes.
- Filtering, authentication, authorization, channel protection and operational policies. Currently, xCIM-SPL supports these five policy types, but the language is easily extensible.
- Composed of an XML schema for each type of security policy. The xCIM-SPL is composed of five independent XML schemas (one for each policy type).
- Link to SDL elements described by the internal format. The link between xCIM-SPL and SDL elements is done using the internal format. Since both SPL and SDL instances are defined in internal format, this link is directly achieved using the internal format.

Box 5.

```xml
<FilteringPolicy securityLevel="Red">
    <Name>Only IPsec traffic allowed</Name>
    <Enabled>true</Enabled>
    <Filters>
        <Filter order="0">
            <Name>Allow IKE over UDP</Name>
            <Direction>Mirrored</Direction>
            <FilterEntries>
                <FilterEntry>IKE traffic</FilterEntry>
                <FilterEntry>UDP traffic</FilterEntry>
            </FilterEntries>
            <Action>Permit</Action>
        </Filter>
        <Filter order="1">
            <Name>Allow IKE over TCP</Name>
            <Direction>Mirrored</Direction>
            <FilterEntries>
                <FilterEntry>IKE traffic</FilterEntry>
                <FilterEntry>TCP traffic</FilterEntry>
            </FilterEntries>
            <Action>Permit</Action>
        </Filter>
        <Filter order="2">
            <Name>Deny all</Name>
            <Direction>Both</Direction>
            <FilterEntries>
                <FilterEntry>Any traffic</FilterEntry>
            </FilterEntries>
            <Action>Deny</Action>
        </Filter>
    </Filters>
    <Targets>
        <Target>
            <Type>CIM_ComputerSystem</Type>
            <Id name="CreationClassName">CIM_ComputerSystem</Id>
            <Id name="Name">umuNet.pix1</Id>
        </Target>
    </Targets>
</FilteringPolicy>
```

Box 6.

```
<AuthenticationPolicy securityLevel="Red">
    <Name>User 1 authentication</Name>
    <Enabled>true</Enabled>
    <Identities>
        <IdentityReferences type="Identity">User1</IdentityReferences>
    </Identities>
    <Credentials>
        <AccountCredential>
            <Name>User 1 account</Name>
            <AccountID>user1</AccountID>
            <AccountContext>umuNet.radius.umuNet.vo-radius
            </AccountContext>
        </AccountCredential>
    </Credentials>
    <Targets>
        <Target>
            <Type>CIM_SoftwareElement</Type>
            <Id name="Name"> umuNet.radius.umuNet.vo-radius</Id>
            <Id name="Version">1.1.6</Id>
            <Id name="SoftwareElementState">3</Id>
            <Id name="SoftwareElementID">umuNet.vo-radius</Id>
            <Id name="TargetOperatingSystem">0</Id>
        </Target>
    </Targets>
</AuthenticationPolicy>
```

Currently, the xCIM-SPL is based on CIM Schema v2.28 release, but future versions can include new types of policies and/or new classes, associations or properties. To build automatically the XML schema from any CIM version we designed an automatic transformation. The main design principles identified as part of this mapping process were:

- Every CIM class generates a new XML element;
- Every CIM generalization (inheritance) generates the declaration of a new XML extension element;

- Every CIM key property generates a new XML '<key>' (or '<unique>') element, which allows the unique identification of each XML element (i.e. CIM instance);
- Every CIM association is expressed in XML as entry references; this is the most suitable general-purpose mechanism currently available;
- A single XML database will host no more than one CIM implementation, and therefore the namespace is the same for all CIM instances stored in this database.

The Figure 5 shows the most relevant classes and associations of CIM Policy Model. The main

Box 7.

```
<AuthorizationPolicy securityLevel="Red">
    <Name>Apache Gold Access Policy</Name>
    <Enabled>true</Enabled>
    <Subjects>
        <Role>Golden Users</Role>
    </Subjects>
    <Privileges>
        <Privilege type="General">Apache Gold Access</Privilege>
    </Privileges>
    <Targets>
        <Target>
            <Type>CIM_SoftwareElement</Type>
            <Id name="Name">umuNet.web-mail.umuNet.vo-httpd</Id>
            <Id name="Version">1.3.27</Id>
            <Id name="SoftwareElementState">3</Id>
            <Id name="SoftwareElementID">umuNet.vo-httpd</Id>
            <Id name="TargetOperatingSystem">0</Id>
        </Target>
    </Targets>
</AuthorizationPolicy>
```

class is *PolicyRule* that is parent class and models any type of policy rule. The classes *PolicyGroup* and *PolicySet* are used to group policy rules and the class *SecurityLevel* determines a security level. The associations and aggregations establish the relations between them.

Regarding the associations:

- *PolicySetComponent* is an aggregation that collects instances of the subclasses of *PolicySet* (i.e. *PolicyGroups* and *PolicyRules*). Instances are collected in sets and they are prioritized relative to each other, within the set, using the property Priority of this aggregation.
- The *PolicyRuleInSystem* association makes explicit which *PolicyRules* are applied to a particular Element. This association permits to associate *PolicyRules* to *Systems* (e.g. *ComputerSystem*).

- The *PolicySetSecurityLevel* association assigns a particular *SecurityLevel* to *ManagedElement* which can be a *PolicyGroup* or *PolicySet*.
- *PolicySetValidityPeriod* is an aggregation that collects instances of *PolicyTimePeriodCondition*. These instances provide a means of representing the time periods during which a *PolicySet* is valid, (i.e. active).

The following sections provide the description of the classes, associations and properties relevant to each type of security policy, and xCIM-SPL examples of security policies.

Security Policies

Filtering rules. Basically, a Filtering rule (see Figure 6) is a rule representing filtering requirements

Box 8.

```
<AuthenticationPolicy securityLevel="Green">
    <Name>User 2 authentication</Name>
    <Enabled>true</Enabled>
    <Identities>
        <IdentityReferences type="Identity">User2</IdentityReferences>
    </Identities>
    <Credentials>
        <AccountCredential>
            <Name>User 2 account</Name>
            <AccountID>user2</AccountID>
            <AccountContext>umuNet.radius.umuNet.vo-radius
                </AccountContext>
        </AccountCredential>
    </Credentials>
    <Targets>
        <Target>
            <Type>CIM_SoftwareElement</Type>
            <Id name="Name">umuNet.radius.umuNet.vo-radius</Id>
            <Id name="Version">1.1.6</Id>
            <Id name="SoftwareElementState">3</Id>
            <Id name="SoftwareElementID">umuNet.vo-radius</Id>
            <Id name="TargetOperatingSystem">0</Id>
        </Target>
    </Targets>
</AuthenticationPolicy>
```

for a system. The class *PacketFilterCondition* specifies packet selection criteria (via association *FilterOfPacketCondition* to *FilterList*) for filtering policies. It is used as an anchor point to associate various types of filters with filtering rules (via association *PacketConditionInFilteringRule* to *FilteringRule*). A *FilterList* is used by network devices to identify traffic and either forward it (with possibly further processing) to its destination, or to deny its forwarding.

Authentication rules. Authentication rules (see Figure 7) define the authentication criteria used for an Identity in a network element. We can choose multiple authentications criteria like Biometrical authentication, Public and Private Keys,

Physical Credentials, etc. The class *AuthenticationCondition* determines the authentication criteria via the association *PolicyConditionInPolicyRule*.

Authorization rules. Authorization rules (see Figure 8) define the authorization criteria used in a network element for an Identity or Role based on privileges. For this purpose the class *AuthorizationRule* is associated to the following classes:

- The class *Identity* represents an element that acts as a security principal within the scope in which it is defined and authenticated.

Figure 5. Filtering policy classes and associations

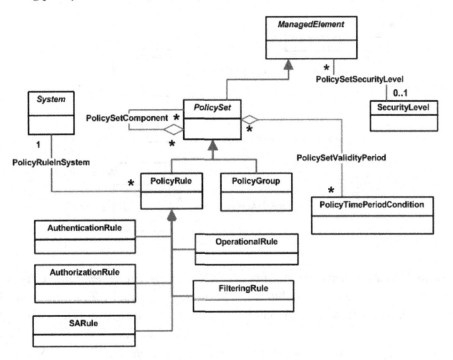

Figure 6. Filtering policy classes and associations

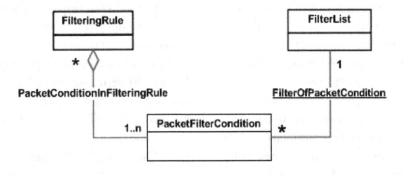

Figure 7. Authentication policy classes and associations

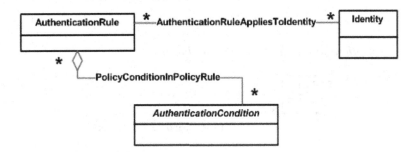

Figure 8. Authorization policy classes and associations

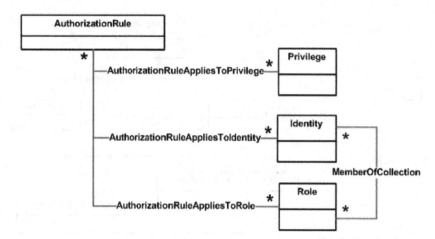

- The class *Role* is used to represent a position or set of responsibilities within an organization, organizational unit or other scope.
- The class *Privilege* is the base class for all types of activities which are granted or denied by a *Role* or an *Identity*. This class has a subclass called *ServicePrivilege* that specifies two types of service privileges; *MailPrivilege* for privileges related to mail, and *FileTransferPrivilege* for privileges related to transfer files.

An Identity can be associated to a Role via the association *MemberOfColletion*, and then this *Role* associated to an *AuthorizationRule*. It means the authorization criteria defined by *AuthorizationRule* is also applied to *Identity*.

Channel Protection rules. Channel Protection rules (see Figure 9) define the channel protection criteria used in a network element based on security associations. The class *SARule* and its subclasses (i.e. *IPsecRule*, *IKERule* and *SSLRule*) represent different types of channel protection rules. The class *PacketFilterCondition* is the same class that appears in filtering rules and specifies packet selection criteria (via association to *FilterList*) for channel protection rules.

Operational rules. Operational rules (see Figure 10) define an operational criteria used in a network element. The *OperationalRule* class is an aggregation of the following classes:

- The class *StatusCondition* represents the status of the monitored element. This status can be unknown, OK, error, starting, stopped, lost communication, etc.

Figure 9. Security association policy classes and associations

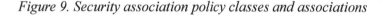
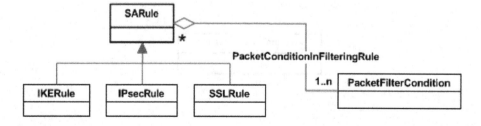

Figure 10. Operational policy classes and associations

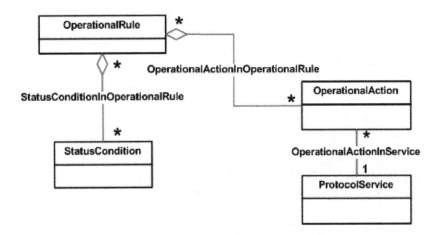

- The class *OperationalAction* specifies the action which should be executed if the monitored element reaches the status specified by the class *StatusCondition*. An *OperationalAction* is associated to a *ProtocolService*, which represents the service that implements the action.

Example

This section presents the security policies by xCIM-SPL of the example shown by Figure 4.

Since xCIM-SPL is very verbose, this section is focused on some elements of the security policies.

The Listing in Box 9 shows the instances of security levels. High security level is named by Red and Low security level is named by Green.

The Listing in Box 10 shows User1 and User2 are the identities that are classified by roles. Using the association MemberOfCollection, the Role Golden Users is associated to User1, and the Role Silver Users is associated to User1.

An example of security policy is shown in the listing below. This is the authorization policy to gold access to web server, '*For Security Level*

Box 9.

```
<xCIM_SecurityLevel>
    <Description>High security level</Description>
    <ElementName>Red</ElementName>
    <InstanceID>Red</InstanceID>
    <SecurityLevel>1</SecurityLevel>
</xCIM_SecurityLevel>
<xCIM_SecurityLevel>
    <Description>Low security level</Description>
    <ElementName>Green</ElementName>
    <InstanceID>Green</InstanceID>
    <SecurityLevel>2</SecurityLevel>
</xCIM_SecurityLevel>
```

Box 10.

```
<xCIM_MemberOfCollection>
    <Collection>
        CIM_Role.CreationClassName='CIM_Role',
        Name='Golden Users'
    </Collection>
    <Member>CIM_Identity.InstanceID='User1'</Member>
</xCIM_MemberOfCollection>
<xCIM_Role>
    <Description>Golden Users </Description>
    <CreationClassName>CIM_Role</CreationClassName>
    <Name>Golden Users</Name>
    <CommonName>Golden Users</CommonName>
</xCIM_Role>
<xCIM_MemberOfCollection>
    <Collection>
        CIM_Role.CreationClassName='CIM_Role',
        Name='Silver Users'
    </Collection>
    <Member>CIM_Identity.InstanceID='User2'</Member>
</xCIM_MemberOfCollection>
<xCIM_Role>
    <Description>Silver Users</Description>
    <CreationClassName>CIM_Role</CreationClassName>
    <Name>Silver Users</Name>
    <CommonName>Silver Users</CommonName>
</xCIM_Role>
```

Red, Role Golden Users has the privilege of Gold access to Web Server'. The association *PolicyRuleInSystem* associates the rule to the system target, the association *AuthorizationRuleAppliesToPrivilege associates* the rule to the privilege, the association *AuthorizationRuleAppliesToRole* associates the rule to the role, the association *AuthorizationRuleAppliesToTarget* associates the rule to the service target, and the association *PolicySetSecurityLevel* associates the rule to the security level, as presented in Box 11.

These examples show xCIM-SPL is very verbose, but it permits to correctly and fully represent CIM models.

TOOLS FOR POLICY REFINEMENT AND MANIPULATION

SPL to xCIM Translation

Since policy-based systems are naturally viewed at different levels of abstraction, it appears the need for the *"policy refinement"* is the task of passing from high-level specification to low-level device-oriented rules that fulfill the high-level requirements. Policy refinement or Policy translation is proved to be a complex problem, because policy and rules must be consistent at every level.

Box 11.

```
<xCIM_AuthorizationRule>
    <Enabled>1</Enabled>
    <SystemCreationClassName>CIM_ComputerSystem
        </SystemCreationClassName>
    <SystemName>sde.umu.org</SystemName>
    <CreationClassName>CIM_AuthorizationRule</CreationClassName>
    <PolicyRuleName>Apache Gold Access Policy</PolicyRuleName>
    <ConditionListType>1</ConditionListType>
    <SequencedActions>3</SequencedActions>
</xCIM_AuthorizationRule>

<xCIM_PolicyRuleInSystem>
    <Antecedent>
        CIM_ComputerSystem.CreationClassName='CIM_ComputerSystem',
        Name='sde.umu.org'
    </Antecedent>
    <Dependent>
        CIM_AuthorizationRule.SystemCreationClassName='CIM_ComputerSystem',
        SystemName='sde.umu.org',
        CreationClassName='CIM_AuthorizationRule',
        PolicyRuleName='Apache Gold Access Policy'
    </Dependent>
</xCIM_PolicyRuleInSystem>

<xCIM_AuthorizationRuleAppliesToPrivilege>
    <PolicySet>
        CIM_AuthorizationRule.SystemCreationClassName='CIM_ComputerSystem',
        SystemName='sde.umu.org',
        CreationClassName='CIM_AuthorizationRule',
        PolicyRuleName='Apache Gold Access Policy'
    </PolicySet>
    <ManagedElement>
        CIM_Privilege.InstanceID='Apache Golden Access'
    </ManagedElement>
</xCIM_AuthorizationRuleAppliesToPrivilege>

<xCIM_AuthorizationRuleAppliesToRole>
    <PolicySet>
        CIM_AuthorizationRule.SystemCreationClassName='CIM_ComputerSystem',
        SystemName='sde.umu.org',
        CreationClassName='CIM_AuthorizationRule',
        PolicyRuleName='Apache Gold Access Policy'
```

continued on following page

Box 11. Continued

```
    </PolicySet>
    <ManagedElement>
        CIM_Role.CreationClassName='CIM_Role',
        Name='Golden Users'
    </ManagedElement>
</xCIM_AuthorizationRuleAppliesToRole>

<xCIM_AuthorizationRuleAppliesToTarget>
    <PolicySet>
        CIM_AuthorizationRule.SystemCreationClassName='CIM_ComputerSystem',
        SystemName='sde.umu.org',
        CreationClassName='CIM_AuthorizationRule',
        PolicyRuleName='Apache Gold Access Policy'
    </PolicySet>
    <ManagedElement>
        CIM_SoftwareElement.Name='umuNet.web-mail.umuNet.vo-httpd',
        Version='1.3.27',
        SoftwareElementState='3',
        SoftwareElementID='umuNet.vo-httpd',
        TargetOperatingSystem='0'
    </ManagedElement>
</xCIM_AuthorizationRuleAppliesToTarget>

<xCIM_PolicySetSecurityLevel>
    <SecurityLevel>
        CIM_SecurityLevel.InstanceID='Red'
    </SecurityLevel>
    <PolicySet>
        CIM_AuthorizationRule.SystemCreationClassName='CIM_ComputerSystem',
        SystemName='sde.umu.org',
        CreationClassName='CIM_AuthorizationRule',
        PolicyRuleName='Apache Gold Access Policy'
    </PolicySet>
</xCIM_PolicySetSecurityLevel>
```

In fact, it is not possible, at present, to find the general solution.

In a context where conveying and deriving system information is tackled from the first steps of the designing phase, it is possible to obtain some usable results for policy refinement. In this sense, we define a high-level Security Policy Language (SPL) specifies rules classified in concrete five categories and a System Description Language (SDL) permits the possibility of assigning to specific instances information about the capabilities (that are also defined having the rules type in mind). The refinement consists in a translation from the high-level specification to low-level rules specified by a language based CIM-Policy Information Model (i.e. xCIM-SPL or internal format). The major benefit of specifying low-level rules in this way is that an organization can utilize a common information model that can be shared amongst services and service clients.

Our tools for policy refinement and manipulation provide Policy Console and Policy Translation Service that permits the definition and refinement of high-level rules. These tools reduce the errors and permit additional checks.

SPL allows to the administrator the definition of security policies using a friendly language, nearly to the spoken English, whereas internal format is a language for formal modeling and low level abstraction that is oriented to developers. So, we see the need of an automatic translation process (i.e. refinement) between SPL (friendly language) and internal format.

The translation process is based on the direct transformation the SPL elements to xCIM-SPL elements. However, policies in our proposal try to represent the administration requirements as closer to natural human concepts as it can. And so, human concepts are usually incomplete and ambiguous, assuming their lack of information to be filled by some external information taken from the context where the concepts are applied.

To reflect this human approach that uses context information, in the policies definition should also take into account some extra parameters that fill the lack of information of human concepts. These sets of extra parameters are defined by templates. The main functionality of the templates is to describe the parameters associated with the security levels that will be used in the system domain according to policy. The templates are created in order to simulate the behavior of the experts, only once.

The Figure 11 shows the translation process and how the templates complete the final xCIM-SPL description. The tasks Transform and Complete are deployed by XSL transformation because all documents (i.e. templates, xCIM-SPL definitions and SPL definition) are represented by XML.

To access of the information of these templates, we propose a Template Console that is make easy to work with templates, offering different operations with the templates like create, delete, update, get and check the templates definition.

Policy Console

The Policy Console is a graphical user interface which allows the administrator to easily manage SPL security policies. It deals with policies defined in the SPL and these policies are dynamically translated between the high level language SPL and the lower level language xCIM-SPL during the console usage.

Figure 11. SPL to xCIM translation process

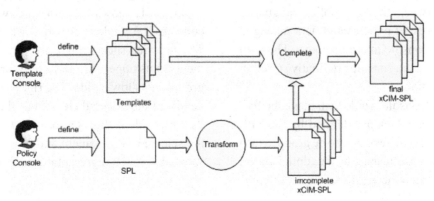

Figure 12. The policy administration window

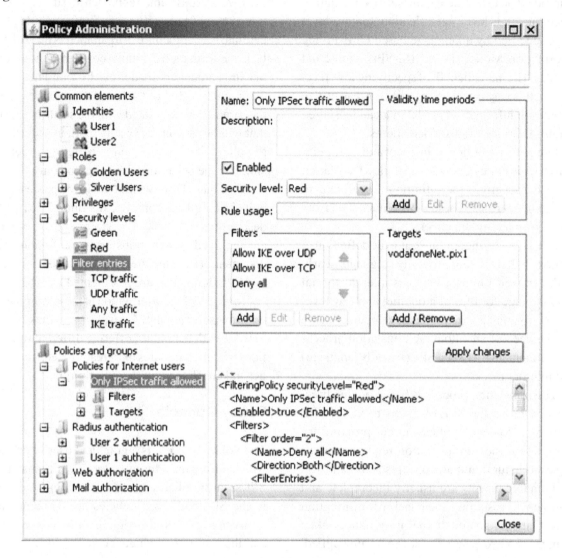

This graphical interface relies upon the framework which is in charge of making the dynamical translation between the two policy languages and also it stores all policies and data managed by the Policy Console into a database. Thus, all data managed by the console are finally stored in xCIM-SPL format.

The Policy Console is able to manage the five types of policies which are defined by the SPL language. These policies can also be grouped into policy groups to ease their use by the administrator. In addition to the policies, there is a set of common elements that are referenced by policies and that should be defined before creating the policy.

Figure 12 shows the main window of the policy console. The window is divided in two main areas. The left area shows a tree for the common elements in its upper side and a tree for policies and groups in its lower side. The right area shows the details of the selected element of the left area. In its upper side it shows a form with the details of the selected SPL element and in its lower side it shows the XML representation of such element.

FUTURE RESEARCH DIRECTIONS

Advanced Vision Based on Semantically-Rich Policies

The language xCIM-SPL and the language SPL cannot be arbitrarily combined with other specifications in a flexible manner and, with respect to more advanced operations, XML-encoded specifications do not embody the constructs for facilitating tasks like parsing, logical deduction or semantic interpretation. Semantically-rich policies introduce ontology based representation that permits such tasks.

The main ideas behind the specification of semantically-rich policies in the framework are the following ones.

Ontology based representation for information model. The CIM model is independent of any encoding and it can be mapped to multiple structured specifications. In this sense, CIM models are encoded by Ontology Web Language (OWL). An example of how CIM can be mapped to OWL is the following one:

- Class to owl:Class and its attributes to owl:DatatypeProperty.
- Association to owl:Class and its attributes to owl:ObjectProperty.
- Inheritance to rdfs:subclassOf and rdf:resource including the superclass name.
- Naming to URIs (Uniform Resource Identifier) in rdfs:about.
- If a qualifier has direct interpretation then it is used (e.g., Description direct to rdfs:Comment); otherwise, a specific owl:AnnotationProperty is created.

The OWL fragment presented in Box 12 shows the representation of the association MemberOf-Collection. This is represented using *owl:Class* and its two references using *owl:ObjectProperty*. The CIM names are mapped to the attributes *rdf:ID*. The attribute *rdf:domain* indicates the base class and the attribute *rdf:range* indicates the referenced class.

The OWL representation of an instance of this class is shown in the fragment presented in Box 13. The attribute *rdf:about* has the URI of the instance. The attributes *rdf:resource* indicate the instances taking part of the association.

The use of an ontology based representation of CIM model to describe a management system is a first, but significant step to achieve a solution that facilitates the management tasks and related reasoning processes about policies.

Policies like horn-like rules. Policies are defined by managers as if-then rules and they are encoded by Semantic Web Rule Language (SWRL) which extends the set of OWL axioms to include a high-level abstract syntax for Horn-like rules that can be combined with an OWL

Box 12.

```
<owl:Class rdf:ID='CIM_MemberOfCollection'/>
<owl:ObjectProperty rdf:ID='Collection'>
    <rdfs:domain rdf:resource='#CIM_MemberOfCollection'/>
    <rdfs:range rdf:resource='#CIM_Collection'/>
</owl:ObjectProperty>
<owl:ObjectProperty rdf:ID='Member'>
    <rdfs:domain rdf:resource='#CIM_MemberOfCollection'/>
    <rdfs:range rdf:resource='#CIM_ManagedElement'/>
</owl:ObjectProperty>
```

Box 13.

```
<memberofcollection:CIM_MemberOfCollection
 rdf:about='http://umu.org/cimowl/CIM_MemberOfCollection/User1OfGoldenUser'>
<memberofcollection:Collection
 rdf:resource='http://umu.org/cimowl/CIM_Role/GoldenUser'/>
<memberofcollection:Member
 rdf:resource='http://umu.org/cimowl/CIM_Identity/User1'/>
</memberofcollection:CIM_MemberOfCollection>
```

knowledge base. A useful restriction in the form of the rules is to limit antecedent and consequent atoms to be named classes, where the classes are defined purely in OWL.

SWRL defines a XML format and an abstract syntax to express rules informally. The fragment presented in Box 14 shows the association of Role *Golden Users* to the AuthorizationRule *Apache Gold Access Policy* in abstract syntax.

Adhering to this format makes it easier to translate rules to or from future or existing rule systems, including Prolog and Jena.

Reasoning capabilities. This CIM representation and its OWL encoding incorporate semantic expressiveness into the management information specifications to ease the tasks of validating and reasoning about the policies which definitely help in handling the security management complex tasks (e.g., conflict resolution). This is due to the fact that OWL is based on description logics. This simple and yet powerful kind of first order-like logic allows to perform reasoning tasks not only on individuals but also on the structure of the base information model which holds the instances, with efficient and sound algorithms.

Semantically-rich policies can be connected to the framework, but it implies the substitution of the internal format and therefore the change of other system components to take advantage of reasoning capabilities of this representation.

CONCLUSION

This chapter has presented the security policy languages used in our research project (University of Murcia, 2011), Security Policy Language and xCIM-SPL. Moreover, it has described some tools related to refinement and manipulation and complemented by an example where the reader can see the different abstraction levels of policy languages.

Security policy specification in our proposal contributes with innovative aspects. First the task of policy specification is separated of topological and functional description of the systems on which the policy should be applied, and so the process of policy definition is independent of the process of system definition, although both definitions meet the same internal format. Moreover, the internal

Box 14.

```
AuthorizationRule(A1?) ^ PolicyRuleName(A1?,'Apache Gold Access Policy') ^
            Role(R1?) ^ Name(R1?, 'Golden Users')
                        -->
            AuthorizationRuleAppliesToRole(ATR1?) ^
        PolicySet(ATR1?,A1?) ^ ManagedElement(ATR1?,R1?)
```

format is based on an information model accepted internationally that additionally provides basic requirements for a policy language such as well defined semantics, flexibility, extensibility, and independent of administrative domain. Finally, the tools associated to policy specification facilitate the tasks of administrator, and guarantee the process of specification.

REFERENCES

Damianou, N., Dulay, N., Lupu, E., & Sloman, M. (2001). The Ponder policy specification language. *International Workshop on Policies for Distributed Systems and Network, LNCS 1995*, (pp. 18-38).

Distributed Management Task Force. (2011). *DMTF standards*. Retrieved from http://www.dmtf.org/standards

DMTF Policy Working Group. (2009). *CIM simplified policy language (CIM-SPL), v1.0.0.0.* Retrieved from http://www.dmtf.org/sites/default/files/standards/documents/DSP0231_1.0.0.pdf

Imperial College London. (2011). *Ponder2 project*. Retrieved from http://ponder2.net

OASIS. (2011). *eXtensible access control markup language (XACML) version 3.0*. Retrieved from www.oasis-open.org/committees/xacml/

Sloman, M., Luk, W., Lupu, E., & Dulay, N. (2004). *Polyander project*. Retrieved from http://www-dse.doc.ic.ac.uk/Projects/polyander

University of Murcia. (2011). *Deresec project*. DEpendability and Security by Enhanced REConfigurability. Retrieved from http://www.deserec.eu/

ADDITIONAL READING

Adi, K. (2009). Typing for conflict detection in access control policies. *E-Technologies: Innovation in an Open World*, *26*(5), 212–226. doi:10.1007/978-3-642-01187-0_17

Aktuga, I. (2008). ConSpec – A formal language for policy specification. *Electronic Notes in Theoretical Computer Science*, 45–58. doi:10.1016/j.entcs.2007.10.013

Alcaraz Calero, J. M., et al. (2010). Towards an authorisation model for distributed systems based on the Semantic Web. *IET Information Security*, 1-11.

Alcaraz Calero, J. M. (2010). Detection of semantic conflicts in ontology and rule-based. *Data & Knowledge Engineering*, *69*, 1117–1137. doi:10.1016/j.datak.2010.07.004

Bauer, L. (2009). Composing expressive runtime security policies. *ACM Transactions on Software Engineering and Methodology*, *18*(9), 1–43. doi:10.1145/1525880.1525882

Becker, M. Y., et al. (2009). SecPAL: Design and semantics of a decentralized authorization language. *Journal of Computer Security*, 619-665. Craven, R., et al. (99). Security policy refinement using data integration: A position paper. *Proceedings of the 2nd ACM Workshop on Assurable and Usable Security Configuration*, (pp. 25-28).

Cuppens, F. (2007). High level conflict management strategies in advanced access control models. *Electronic Notes in Theoretical Computer Science*, *186*, 3–26. doi:10.1016/j.entcs.2007.01.064

Cuppens, F. (2010). Modeling contextual security policies. *International Journal of Information Security*, *7*(4), 285–305. doi:10.1007/s10207-007-0051-9

Davya, S. (2008). The policy continuum–Policy authoring and conflict analysis. *Computer Communications, 31*(13), 2981–2995. doi:10.1016/j.comcom.2008.04.018

Di Vimercati, S. (2007). Access control policies and languages. *International Journal of Computational Science and Engineering, 3*(2), 94–102.

Garcia Clemente, F. J. (2011). Semantic Web-based management of routing configurations. *Journal of Network and Systems Management, 19*(2), 209–229. doi:10.1007/s10922-010-9169-6

Hamed, H. (2006). Taxonomy of conflicts in network security policies. *IEEE Communications Magazine, 43*(3), 134–141. doi:10.1109/MCOM.2006.1607877

Hilty, M., et al. (2007). Policy language for distributed usage control. *LNCS Computer Security – ESORICS 2007, 4734,* (pp. 531-546).

Kandogana, E. (2011). On the roles of policies in computer systems management. *International Journal of Human-Computer Studies, 69*(6), 351–361. doi:10.1016/j.ijhcs.2011.01.004

Karat, J. (2009). Policy framework for security and privacy management. *IBM Journal of Research and Development, 53*(2), 1–1. doi:10.1147/JRD.2009.5429046

Kodeswaran, P. (2011). Enforcing security in semantics driven policy based networks. *Computer Standards & Interfaces, 33*(1), 2–12. doi:10.1016/j.csi.2010.03.010

Li, N. (2008). Beyond separation of duty: An algebra for specifying high-level security policies. *Journal of the ACM, 55*(3), 1–46. doi:10.1145/1379759.1379760

Marín Pérez, J. M. (2011). Semantic-based authorization architecture for Grid. *Future Generation Computer Systems, 27*(1), 40–55. doi:10.1016/j.future.2010.07.008

Martinelli, F. (2009). Idea: Action refinement for security properties enforcement. *Engineering Secure Software and Systems, LNCS, 5429,* 37–42. doi:10.1007/978-3-642-00199-4_4

Olmedilla, D. (2009). *Semantic Web policies for security, trust management and privacy in social networks.* Workshop on Privacy and Protection in Web-based Social Networks, Barcelona.

Peters, J. (2007). A holistic approach to security policies – Policy distribution with XACML over COPS. *Electronic Notes in Theoretical Computer Science, 168*(8), 143–157. doi:10.1016/j.entcs.2006.08.025

Qin, L. (2010). Semantics-aware security policy specification for the Semantic Web data. *International Journal of Information and Computer Security, 4*(1), 52–75. doi:10.1504/IJICS.2010.031859

Satoh, F., et al. (2007). Generic security policy transformation framework for WS-security. *IEEE International Conference on Web Services,* (pp. 513-520).

Swamy, N., et al. (2008). Fable: A language for enforcing user-defined security policies. *IEEE Symposium on Security and Privacy,* (pp. 369-383).

Yau, S. S. (2008). Security policy integration and conflict reconciliation for collaborations among organizations in ubiquitous computing environments. *LNCS Ubiquitous Intelligence and Computing, 5061,* 3–19. doi:10.1007/978-3-540-69293-5_3

Zhang, X., et al. (2008). Security enforcement model for distributed usage control. *IEEE International Conference on Sensor Networks, Ubiquitous, and Trustworthy Computing,* (pp. 10-18).

Zhou, J., & Alves-Foss, J. (2008). Security policy refinement and enforcement for the design of multi-level secure systems. *Journal of Computer Security, 16*(2), 107–131.

KEY TERMS AND DEFINITIONS

Policy Conflict: It occurs when two or more policies generate contradictory decisions.

Policy Console: The policy administrator defines and controls the policies of an administrative domain from a Policy Console.

Policy Language: It assures that the representation of policies will be unambiguous and verifiable.

Policy Model: A policy model provides a common framework for specifying system behaviors.

Policy Refinement: The policy refinement is the process to transform the specification of high level business policies into low level policies suitable to be directly applied into final devices.

Security Policy: A security policy is a set of rules describing how an organization manages, protects, and distributes sensitive information at several levels.

Semantically-Rich Policies: Semantically-rich policies introduce ontology based representation that facilitates tasks like parsing, logical deduction or semantic interpretation.

Chapter 5
Workflow Scheduling with Fault Tolerance

Laiping Zhao
Kyushu University, Japan

Kouichi Sakurai
Kyushu University, Japan

ABSTRACT

This chapter describes a study on workflow scheduling with fault tolerance. It starts with an understanding on workflow scheduling and fault tolerance technologies independently. Next, the chapter surveys the related works on the combination field of workflow scheduling and fault tolerance technologies. Generally, these works are classified into six categories corresponding to the six fault tolerance technologies: workflow scheduling with primary/backup, primary/backup with multiple backups, checkpoint, rescheduling, active replication, and active replication with dynamic replicas. An in-depth study on these six topics illustrates the challenge issues explored so far, e.g. overloading conditions, tradeoffs among scheduling criteria, et cetera, and some future research directions are also identified. As applications are increasingly complex, and failures become a severe problem in the large scale systems, the authors expect to provide a comprehensive review on the problem of workflow scheduling with fault tolerance through this work.

INTRODUCTION

As in the fields of high-energy physics, astronomy, aerospace sciences and bioinformatics, scientific applications are becoming quite complex and usually consist of large numbers of tasks. In such case,

workflow technologies are proposed to facilitate and automate the execution of these scientific applications. As discussed in the literature (Hu, Wu, Liu & Xie, 2007; Talukder, Kirley, Buyya & Tham, 2007; Wieczorek, Hoheisel & Prodan, 2009; Wu, Chi, Chen, Gu & Sun, 2009; Yu & Buyya, 2006a, 2006b; Zhao, Ren & Sakurai, 2011), a workflow, commonly represented by a directed

DOI: 10.4018/978-1-4666-1888-6.ch005

acyclic graph (DAG), can be seen as a collection of computational tasks that are processed in a well-defined order to accomplish a specific goal.

Many challenges have been addressed in the field of workflow scheduling. And a major one of them is that how to arrange the schedule to satisfy a requested criteria, which could be execution time, reliability, monetary cost or tradeoffs among them. While the scheduling performance on execution time has been studied for years since 2002 (Topcuoglu, Hariri & Wu, 2002), fault tolerance recently attracts a great attention for two main reasons: (1) System scale is growing fast, and failures are consequently becoming popular within large-scale clusters. One example is, according to the failure data from Los Alamos National Laboratory (LANL), annually more than 1,000 number of failures occur at system No. 7, which consists of 2014 nodes in total (Schroeder B. & Gibson G.A., 2006). Assuming some processors, whose MTBF is five years, then a cluster with two thousand such kind of processors, will produce more than one failure per day on average. (2) Heterogeneous systems, which are associated with many flexible and various hardware configurations, increase the complexity of system management, and perform more failures than the homogeneous system. Grid computing, for example, aims to combine together all volunteer machines of the world, presents a significant challenge for resource management. Given this context, fault tolerance technologies, e.g. primary/backup, active replication scheme, have been proposed. And they employ either time redundancy or resource redundancy to ensure the automatic execution of applications. However, most of the existing works, either on workflow scheduling or on fault tolerance, cover the alternative area. And only a few of them considered both sides together. Furthermore, most practical systems, e.g. Hadoop, Condor, have not yet applied a combining consideration into their implementations.

In this study, we have a combining consideration on the workflow scheduling and fault toler-ance problem. The rest of this chapter is organized as following. Firstly, we give a brief introduction on the workflow scheduling and fault tolerance problem in section II and section III, respectively. Then, Section IV surveys the proposed fault tolerant workflow scheduling algorithms, which apply the primary/backup into scheduling. Section V presents the related works on rollback-recovery or rescheduling. And section VI discusses the workflow scheduling with active replication. Then the hybrid approach with applying multiple fault tolerance technologies into scheduling is given in section VII. We conclude this chapter in the section VIII, where some major challenge issues and open problems are identified.

BACKGROUND

Workflow Scheduling

Scheduling is one of the core services in distributed systems. It defines a placement policy, following which the tasks are allocated to the processors. Mapping tasks to processors comes with various performance metrics, e.g. execution time, economic cost, load balance, system throughput, etc., which have been richly studied in the literature (Benoit, Hakem & Robert, 2009; Blythe et al. 2005; Topcuoglu et al. 2002; Wieczorek et al., 2009; Yu & Buyya, 2006a). Generally, a static workflow scheduling algorithm follows three steps: (1) deciding the task scheduling order, (2) mapping task to processors, and (3) task submission.

In step (1), all the tasks in a workflow are ordered into a certain sequence, and the tasks will be scheduled on processors one by one. Apparently, there is a disparity among different sequences on the scheduling performances. An appropriate sequence is supposed to be chosen with considering the scheduling criteria. Anyhow, the task ordering methods must share a common constraint that is ensuring the precedence relationship among tasks. To our knowledge, two approaches on task priority computing are particularly well known: the bottom level (bl) and the top+bottom level (tl+bl) (Topcuoglu et al. 2002). Let t(x) be the execution time of a task x, and c(x,y) be the communication time from a task x to a task y, then the top level is computed as:

$$tl(x) = \max_{z \in parent(x)} (tl(z) + t(z) + c(z,x)),$$

And the bottom level is computed as:

$$bl(x) = t(x) + \max_{y \in child(x)} (c(x,y) + bl(y))$$

Where $z \in parent(x)$ means task z is one parent of task x, and $y \in child(x)$ represents task y is one child of task x.

To tell the difference between the bl-based and the (tl + bl)-based task ordering, we evaluate their impacts on execution time through experiments. We apply both two task priority approaches into the FTSA (Fault Tolerant Scheduling Algorithm) algorithm (Benoit, A., Hakem, M., & Robert, Y. 2008), named as FTSA(bl) and FTSA(tl+bl) respectively. All the job configurations and other scheduling parameters are consistent with the ones in paper (Zhao et al., 2011). From the experiments (Figure 1), we know that the bl-based FTSA's output schedule averagely takes less execution time than (tl + bl)-based FTSA algorithm. And the difference widens along with the increasing number of tasks.

After the tasks are sorted into order, the second step of workflow scheduling, mapping tasks to processors, is the central part of a workflow scheduling algorithm. In this process, the design of the mapping policy heavily relies on the scheduling criteria. For instance, the HEFT algorithm (Heterogeneous Earliest Finish Time) tries to minimize the execution time (Benoit et al. 2009). FTSA extends the HEFT algorithm by applying the fault tolerance while minimizing the execution time. Yu and Buyya (2006a) schedules the work-

flow with the aim of minimizing execution time and economic cost. Oozie, a hadoop workflow management tool that activates a task scheduling when the data and time are ready, depends on the underlying scheduling algorithm to make a mapping, and usually takes the locality and fairness as the scheduling criteria.

After output a schedule through the second step, the scheduler submits the tasks to the system and the job monitoring function deals with failures and collects the final results. Now, we would like to illustrate the first two steps of workflow scheduling with an example: HEFT algorithm (Topcuoglu et al. 2002).

HEFT algorithm:
1. Compute task priority
    a. Set the computation costs of tasks and communication costs of edges with mean values.
    b. Compute bottom level for all tasks by traversing graph upward, starting from the exit task.
    c. Sort the tasks in a scheduling list by non-increasing order of bottom levels.
2. Mapping task to processors
    a. while there are unscheduled task in the list do
        i. Select the first task from the list for scheduling.
        ii. Compute the earliest finish time by simulating the task to each processor.
        iii. Assign the task to the processor that can finish it in the earliest time.

As shown above, in the first step, the HEFT algorithm makes use of bottom level rank for the task ordering. And all the bottom levels are calculated by traversing the job graph upward. After getting the scheduling order, in the second step, HEFT algorithm schedules each task to a proces-

Figure 1. The comparison on execution time between FTSA(bl) and FTSA(tl+bl)

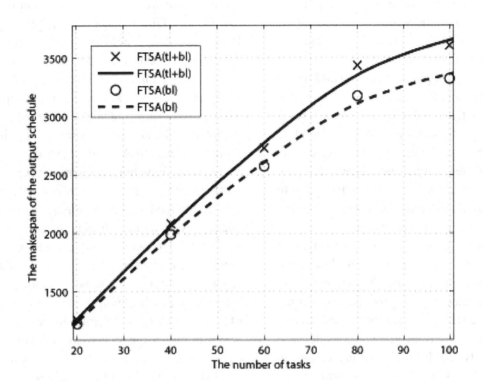

sor, which can complete the task in the earliest finish time (EFT), to minimize the job makespan.

HEFT algorithm facilitated the development of workflow scheduling. And a great number of workflow scheduling algorithms are sprung up thereafter, including the fault tolerant workflow scheduling algorithms.

FAILURES AND FAULT TOLERANCE

As discussed by Selic (2004), a principal engineer at IBM working on rational software tools: "A failure occurs when an actual running system deviates from this specified standard state. The cause of a failure is called an error. An error represents an invalid system state, one that is not allowed by the system behavior specification. The error itself is the result of a defect in the system or fault. In other words, a fault is the root cause of

a failure. That means that an error is merely the symptom of a fault. A fault may not necessarily result in an error, but the same fault may result in multiple errors. Similarly, a single error may lead to multiple failures" (Selic, 2004,p.2).

Failures fall into a variety of categories within different classifications. According to the duration, failures could be transient or permanent. Based on their underlying cause, failures could be design failures and operational failures. Moreover, based on how a failed component behaves once it has failed, Cristian (1991) classifies failures as: crash faults (the component either completely stops operating or never returns to a valid state), Omission faults (the component completely fails to perform its service), Timing faults (the component does not complete its service on time), and response faults (these are faults of an arbitrary nature). While Selic (2004), puts forward the byzantine failures instead of response failures. Balazinska, Hwang, and Shah (2009) differentiate between the fail-stop failure and crash failures, where fail-stop failure is understood as processing nodes fail by stopping execution and losing their internal volatile state, and crash failure is understood that, a failed processing node forever stops sending messages and stops responding to any requests. As implied by Balazinska et al. (2009), the difference between them is fail-stop failure could be easily detected by other nodes. In addition, they also identify the byzantine failure, and communication channel failures.

Indeed, we think that timing failure is kind of QoS requirement of an application, thus is not counted as a type of failure. Response failure, which is identified as wrong responds: either the value of its output is incorrect or the state transition that takes place is incorrect, is considered to belong to the type of byzantine failure. Omission failure, which is defined as a server omits to respond to an input, performs the similar behavior with crash failure, even though they may have different fault sources. Therefore, we only differentiate the crash failure and byzantine failure in the chapter. And some examples of crash failures are as follows: operating system halted, power outages, hardware failure, communication data lost, network interruption, etc. And byzantine failures can be found as: the incorrect behaviors caused by communication noise, program bug, hacker attack, etc.

Distributed system is generally employed to speed up the complex job execution and improve efficiency. Due to the large entities of a distributed system, fault tolerance technologies are critically imperative to tolerate failures in order to reduce the wasted work. Based on the existing fault tolerant technologies, the basic idea for fault tolerance is making use of redundancy, namely, time redundancy and resource redundancy. For instance, primary/backup scheme, which schedules a backup processor for each running task in case of a failure of the primary, tolerates failures through extending the overall execution time. Whenever a failure occurs on the primary task, the backup task is activated to take place of it. The active replication scheme, also known as state machine replication, schedules multiple copies on different processors. All copies run in parallel to tolerate fixed number of failures. The task could be completed with at least one successfully finished replica (Guerraoui & Schiper, 1996).

Derived from both primary/backup scheme (PB) and active replication scheme (AR), a number of variants have emerged (Figure 2), including backup overloading, checkpoint (C), primary/backup scheme with multiple backups (PBM), dynamic rescheduling (R), and active replication scheme with dynamic number of replicas (ARD) etc. Briefly, the checkpoint technology makes use of time redundancy to tolerate failures. And it also tries to minimize the wasted execution by periodically saving the processor state into another place, e.g. external memory. Once a failure occurs, the task does not need to resume its execution from the very beginning, but from the last checkpoint. There is a trade-off between the checkpoint frequency and I/O latency. A high frequency reduces the amount of re-execution works, however, leads to a lot of I/O operations, so that reduces the system performance and vice versa. Primary/backup with overloading backups, requests less replication cost to provide fault tolerance. Much free processor time could be reserved by setting backups overloading with each other. And it is a big challenge to constrain the overloading conditions on primary-backup overloading, backup-backup overloading, and a hybrid between them. Primary/backup scheme with multiple backups extends the original primary/backup to multiple backup replicas, where each task is associated with a primary replica and multiple backups. In case of more than one failure occurring in one task execution process, the job can still be completed successfully. Dynamic rescheduling is quite similar with the primary/backup scheme: it assigns a new processor for the task once a failure occurs in the task. The difference between them is that primary/backup statically arranges a primary and a backup processor in advance, and can only tolerate one failure, while dynamic rescheduling assigns the backup processor in real time, and can tolerate a number of failures. Active replication scheme with dynamic number of replicas is somewhat different with the traditional active replication, because it does not employ the same number of replicas for each task. The goal is to minimize the resource usage while providing the comparable reliability.

As discussed above, both the primary/backup and active replication approaches have their specific shortcomings. The major drawback of the primary/backup or rescheduling scheme is that they are sensitive to the execution time: if a task encounters several failures during the execution, then the makespan will be extended to a much longer time. The checkpoint technology alleviates this problem at a cost of I/O latency for saving checkpoint data. Conversely, the active replication scheme is more sensitive to resource usage: if the system is designed to tolerate t failures, each task has to be assigned with t+1 replicas. This could severely reduce the system throughput. Therefore, primary/backup or rescheduling scheme is suitable during periods of resource competition, and active replication scheme is appropriate for time critical system with rich resources.

FAULT TOLERANT WORKFLOW SCHEDULING

Table 1 surveyed the existing works on fault tolerant scheduling algorithms, and classified them into six categories, with corresponding to the six fault tolerant technologies in Figure 2. Every fault tolerant scheduling algorithm is designed with a comprehensive study on the target job model, system model, fault model and scheduling criteria.

The jobs are studied from three aspects: (1) considering requirements on response time, jobs could be classified as real time or non-real time jobs; (2) considering the job submission pattern, they can be defined as aperiodic or periodic jobs, (3) considering the internal job structure, they could be understood as independent or dependent jobs. In particular, a job is defined as a real time job, if it has to be executed immediately after the submission. There is a hard time restrict on the response for real time job. Non-real time jobs relax the response time of a job, and could be associated with a generous deadline. Aperiodic or periodic represents the arriving pattern of jobs, where aperiodic jobs are randomly submitted to the system, while periodic jobs are submitted at every fixed work period. Independent or dependent illustrates the major point of this work. There is no relationship among independent tasks. And in dependent jobs, results from a parent task are the input of his child tasks, which start running as

Figure 2. The taxonomy on fault tolerant technologies

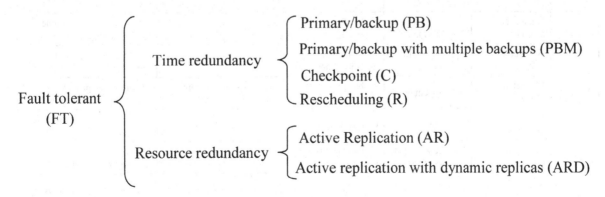

Table 1. A survey on fault tolerant scheduling

FT	Scheme	Task model	System model	Failure	NO. of failures	Scheduling constraints
PB	Ghosh et al. (1994), (1997)	Aperiodic, independent tasks	Real time multi-processor systems	Permanent or transient failure	1	Backup overloading, backup deallocation
	Manimaran and Murthy, (1997), (1998)	Aperiodic, independent tasks	Real time multi-processor systems	Permanent or transient failure	1	Distance based scheduling, Resource Reclaiming, processor grouping
	Naedele (1999)	Aperiodic independent tasks	Real time homogeneous system	Permanent or transient failure	1	Backup overloading with decision deadline
	Alomari, et al. (2004)	Aperiodic, independent tasks	Homogeneous system	Permanent or transient failure	1	Primary-backup overloading (PB), dynamic grouping
	Qin and Jiang (2006)	DAG represented dependent tasks	Heterogeneous system	Fail-silent	1	Reliability driven, BB overlapping conditions for dependent tasks.
	Sun et al. (2007b)	Aperiodic, independent tasks	Homogeneous system	Permanent or transient failure	1	Hybrid overloading (PB overloading, BB overloading)
	Zheng et al. (2009)	DAG represented dependent tasks	Grid system	Permanent or transient failure	1	BB overloading
PBM	Balasubramanian et al. (2009)	Periodic, soft real time independent tasks	Real time and embedded system	Fail-stop	t	t faults tolerant guarantee.
R	Sun et al. (2007a)	DAG represented dependent tasks	Grid system	Crash failures	Multiple	Schedule the task to processor with less execution time
	Hadoop, Condor etc	DAG, or independent tasks	Cloud system	Crash failures	Multiple	Rescheduling with locality or time consideration.
AR	Hashimoto (2000)	DAG represented dependent tasks	Homogeneous system	Crash failures	1	Reduce communication overheads
	Girault et al. (2001) (2003)	DAG represented dependent tasks	Real time and embedded system	Crash failures	t	Scheduling based on scheduling pressure
	Abawajy (2004)	A tasks set comprise a job	Grid system	Fail stop	t	Scheduling based on possible replica reservation
	Benoit et al. (2008)	DAG represented dependent tasks	Heterogeneous system	Crash failures	t	Minimizing execution time.
	Benoit et al. (2009)	DAG represented dependent tasks	Heterogeneous system	Crash failures	t	Minimizing communication cost.
ARD	Dima et al. (2001)	DAG represented dependent tasks	Embedded distributed system	Fail-silent, omission	t	Aggregating all plain scheduling into a single one
	Wang et al. (1995)	Aperiodic independent tasks	Real time Homogeneous system	Fail-stop	Dynamic	Maximizing the performance index
	Litke et al. (2007)	Independent tasks	Mobile Grid system	Crash, omission failures	t- comparable	Maximize the profit with ensuring the fault tolerance
	Kandaswamy et al. (2008)	Workflow	Grid system	Crash failures	Dynamic	Scheduling with considering the deadline and reliability
	Zhao et al. (2011)	DAG represented dependent tasks	Heterogeneous system	Crash failures	t- comparable	Minimizing resource usage, meeting the deadline

continued on following page

Table 1. Continued

FT	Scheme	Task model	System model	Failure	NO. of failures	Scheduling constraints
PB&AR	Bertossi et al. (1999)	Independent periodic tasks	Real time and homogeneous system	Fail-stop	t	Preferring passive replication whenever possible
	Luo et al. (2006)	Periodic, independent tasks	Heterogeneous system	Fail-stop	t	Minimizing execution time, preferring passive replication whenever possible
	Kim et al. (2010)	Independent tasks	Real time and homogeneous system	Fail-stop	t	Consider hot standby and cold standby respectively.

long as the parent tasks finish. By convention, we denote the dependent tasks by the terminology "workflow".

The target systems are introduced in terms of heterogeneous or homogeneous, and real time or non-real time. A heterogeneous system is composed of many different kinds of hardware and software working cooperatively to solve problems, while the software and hardware configurations are all the same for homogeneous systems. In recent years, the notions of Grid and Cloud have become popular. Grid computing system is a representative heterogeneous system. With the new deployed machines and old, slow machines are replaced with new, fast ones continuously, cloud computing is also believed to become more heterogeneous in the future.

From Table 1, we know that the failure that follows a fail-stop property, are commonly addressed in the existing scheduling algorithms, and incorporating byzantine failure into scheduling is still an open problem.

At last, scheduling criteria in Table 1 could be summarized into: execution time, economic cost, reliability, communication cost, and computation cost. For more information on scheduling criteria, a good study on the scheduling criteria has been addressed in the literature (Wieczorek et al., 2009; Yu & Buyya, 2006b).

Learning from the Table 1, five subjects are specifically identified as the major directions for future research.

(1) DAG Represented Dependent Tasks

Concerning the task model in terms of independent or dependent, task scheduling are paying more attention to the DAG represented dependent tasks in recent years. As shown in Table 1, primary/backup based scheduling algorithms mostly concern the independent tasks before the year of 2004, while three approaches proposed after the year of 2006, focus more on DAG represented dependent tasks. With more and more applications coming from sophisticated science, the workflow represented dependent tasks are supposed to be equally important with independent tasks.

(2) Byzantine Failures

Crash failures, following the fail-stop manner, are much easier to identify than byzantine failures. And the byzantine fault tolerance consumes more replicas to tolerant failures. Typically, 3t+1 replicas are employed to tolerant t failures (Castro & Liskov, 2002). Therefore, most real systems do not consider byzantine fault tolerance in their implementation (Driscoll, Hall, Sivencrona &

Zumsteg, 2003; Clement, Marchetti, Wong, Alvisi & Dahlin, 2008; Reiser & Kapitza, 2007). However, byzantine failures occur with a much higher frequency than crash failures in real systems. For instance, a regular personal computer may experience one crash failure in several months, yet many software bugs a day. Therefore, it is significant to apply the byzantine fault tolerance into real systems. Furthermore, the design of an advanced workflow scheduling algorithm in the context of byzantine fault tolerance is also a challenge that should be explored in the future.

(3) Heterogeneous System

Heterogeneous system has become a significant platform since the emergence of Grid computing. Grid computing, emerging in the 1990s, aims to combine the computer resources from multiple administrative domains to reach a common goal. The computer resources in Grid show a high heterogeneity. Likewise, cloud computing appeared thereafter in 2000s, and has been a hot topic on research and engineering. Although many cloud systems are constructed on homogeneous computers, we still think that heterogeneous is the future direction of distributed computing. As shown in Table. 1, the literature published in recent years (Abawajy, 2004; Benoit et al. 2008, 2009; Kandaswamy, Mandal & Reed, 2008; Litke, Skoutas, Tserpes & Varvarigou, 2007; Luo, Yang, Pang & Qin, 2006; Qin & Jiang, 2006; Sun, Guo, Jin, Sun & Hu, 2007a; Zheng, Veeravalli and Tham, 2009; Zhao et al., 2011) are all focusing on the heterogeneous system.

(4) Primary-Backup Overloading

Backup overloading comprises backup-backup (BB) overloading, primary-backup (PB) overloading and the hybrid approach. As shown in Table 1, backup-backup overloading, primary-backup

overloading and the hybrid approach have been well studied in scheduling independent tasks. Moreover, workflow scheduling with backup-backup overloading is also studied in Qin and Jiang (2006) and Zheng et al. (2009), which extends the conditions on backup overloading from a task's direct predecessors to all its predecessors. The problem of workflow scheduling with both PB overloading and the hybrid overloading are still open research problems.

(5) PBM or PB&AR

There are some preliminary explorations on the scheduling with the PBM or the hybrid PB&AR approach, for instance, in order to guarantee the reliability and deadline, the proposed algorithms (Bertossi, Mancini & Rossini, 1999; Luo et al., 2006) copy passive replicas with a higher priority, and schedule active replicas only when the passive replicas cannot meet the deadline. Kim, Lakshmanan and Rajkumar (2010) address the problem of guaranteeing reliability requirements with bounded recovery times on fail-stop processors in fault-tolerant multiprocessor real-time systems. The proposed R-BFD and R-BATCH algorithms, which employ both the passive and active replicas, could meet the reliability requirement with less number of processors. However, none of them consider the workflow represented jobs, and workflow scheduling with the PBM or the hybrid PB&AR approach is still an open problem. Some challenges include the backup overloading conditions, timing decision for launching PB or AR, tradeoff among different scheduling criteria etc.

WORKFLOW SCHEDULING WITH PRIMARY BACKUP

In this section, we shall discuss the primary/backup based scheduling in terms of backup overloading.

Backup Overloading for Independent Tasks

In order to tolerate one permanent failure, primary/ backup based scheduling algorithm allocates two replicas for each task to different processors. And the backup copy is activated if its primary copy fails due to the failure of its assigned processor. If it is required to tolerate more failures, primary/ backup could also be extended with more backup replicas (Balasubramanian et al., 2009). A big advantage of primary/backup technology is that, it is able to tolerate failures without consuming many additional resources, so that improve the system throughput. Moreover, a number of technologies, such as resource reclaiming, and backup overloading, could further improve the workflow schedulability. Resource reclaiming means that, a backup is deleted when its primary finishes execution successfully. Reserved time slots for backups could be released for newly arrived tasks.

There are three forms of backup overloading: backup-backup overloading (BB), primary-backup overloading (PB), and the hybrid overloading. Backup-backup overloading allows the backups of two tasks to overload with each other, while primary-backup overloading allows a task's primary to overload with another task's backup. The hybrid overloading approach is a combination between them. A BB or PB overloading could also be extended to backup-backup overloading chain or primary-backup overloading chain, respectively. In the following, we will show the overloading conditions allowed in primary/backup based scheduling, especially in the workflow scheduling.

As discussed in Ghosh, Melhem and Mosse, (1994), (1997), the schedule for primary and backup copies of an independent task is based on the following conditions:

C1. Both primary and backup should be scheduled between the ready time and deadline.

C2. The beginning time of backup has to be greater than the end time of primary so that backup can execute if a fault is detected in the processor where the primary is executing.

C3. Primary and backup for a task have to be scheduled on different processors to allow any single fault to be tolerated.

C4. (BB overloading). If two primary tasks that are scheduled on the same processor, their backups must not overlap, otherwise it will not be possible to reschedule two primaries from the same processor onto the backup slot if the primary fails.

Condition C1 applies the deadline requirement of a job into the scheduling process. Condition C2 and C3 state the guarantee that a backup will take over the execution failed by a primary from both time and space views. Condition C4 restricts the backup overloading by not allowing backup overloading between two backups whose primaries are scheduled on the same processor. As shown in Figure 3, this is obviously proven by the fact that, backup overloading can only be launched when two backups, B1 and B2, is impossibly executed at the same time. Conversely, if the two primaries, P1 and P2, are scheduled on the same processor, the processor's failure will results in the execution of both two backups, which is not allowed.

Through Condition C1-C4, we can safely schedule the primaries and backups of any independent tasks, with the goal of deadline guarantee, 1-failure tolerance, and schedulability improvement. If setting the scheduling criterion as minimum replication cost, we could overload as many backups as possible provided they keep to the conditions C1-C4. The schedulability could be further improved if each task is associated with a decision deadline, which confines the latest time of deciding a task schedule (Naedele, 1999). A primary (or a backup) is scheduled firstly according to the above rules. If we cannot find any available slots for it, check if it can overload with any backup, whose primary can finish before the

Figure 3. BB overloading and PB overloading

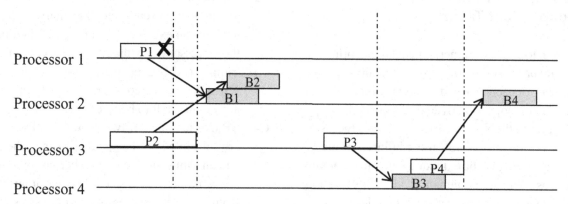

decision deadline. If any, overload the primary (or the backup) to the corresponding backup after its primary finish. Therefore, we get the following condition C4-1 that extends the C4 with the notion of decision deadline.

C4-1. After a primary is executed successfully, its backup could be released using the resource reclaiming, or overloaded with any new primary/backup copies, which is still within the decision deadline.

Different with the original condition C4, condition C4-1 allows conditional primary-backup or backup-backup overloading (Even their primaries are on the same processor) by checking their primary could be completed before the decision deadline or not. Therefore, condition C4-1 could further improve the system throughput and schedulability.

Derived from C4-1, we now consider the possible primary-backup overloading (PB) for independent tasks. The reason for introducing PB overloading is quite obviously that, for a primary, PB-overloading can assign an earlier start time than that of BB-overloading, because the primary can be overloaded on an already scheduled backup. This, in turn, helps its backup to find an earlier start time, thus resulting in a better chance of meeting the task deadline. As discussed in Alomari,

Somani, and Manimaran (2004), the condition for PB overloading could be stated as in rule C5:

C5. (PB overloading). Assuming there are two arbitrary independent tasks t1 and t2, if a task t1's primary and another task t2's backup that are both scheduled on the same processor, then t1's backup and t2's primary must not overlap.

Through condition C5 (Figure 3), we can launch a PB overloading for two independent tasks B3 and P4, where the two tasks will be executed even one processor fails. However, C5 cannot guarantee the successful execution of a bag of independent tasks, when the number of tasks is not less than three. As discussed in Sun, Zhang, Yu, Defago and Inoguchi (2007b), Sun, Yu and Inoguchi (2008), a looped PB overloading chain, which is denoted as an overloading chain that involves a same processor repeatedly, may fail task execution even if only one failure occurs and it follows the restrictions of C5. As shown in Figure 4, due to the failure of P1, B1 will take over the execution of task 1. Because B1 and P2 are overloaded with each other, B2 has to take over the execution of P2, followed by B3 taking over P3. However, B3 cannot be executed because of the failure of processor 1 during its execution for P1. Therefore, task t3 will not be executed in such cases. And the backup overloading constraints of C5 cannot guarantee 1-fault tolerance in the case of a bag of tasks.

Therefore, we extend C5 to C5-1 for PB overloading as follows:

C5-1. Looped chain is not allowed in PB overloading.

Until now, we have summarized the independent conditions for launching either BB overloading or PB overloading. A hybrid overloading is a combination between PB and BB overloading. Sun et al. (2007) applies the hybrid overloading into scheduling, and all rules or advantages for hybrid overloading are inherited from BB and PB overloading.

Backup Overloading for Workflow

Backup overloading for a Directed Acyclic Graph (DAG) represented workflow has to consider the precedence constraints between tasks. Otherwise, the task execution could possibly fail even with only one failure. As illustrated in Figure 5, a job comprises two tasks: t1 and t2, and t2 depends on t1. Task t2 can start only after receiving the results from task t1. Both primaries and backups of the task t1 and t2 are scheduled to three processors, where P1 and B2 are scheduled on the same processor 1, P2 is scheduled on processor 2 and B1 is scheduled on processor 3. If processor 1 fails during P1 execution, B1 is going to take over the task of P1. However, since the precedence constraint between t1 and t2, P2 has to wait for the result from B1, which is impossible here because the start of reserved time slot for P2 is earlier than the finish of B1. Therefore, the precedence constraint among tasks should be incorporated into the backup overloading for DAG represented workflow.

Before giving the constraints on backup overloading for workflow, we firstly introduce the notion of "strong copy". Given a task t, its primary is a strong primary copy, if and only if the execution of its backup implies the failure of the processor that the primary locates before finish. Two dependent tasks are in a strong relationship if the child primary is a strong copy. Otherwise, they are in a non-strong relationship. As shown in Figure 6, if processor1 encounters a failure, P2 will not execute because he cannot receive the results from B1 at the start, so B2 will execute instead. P3 can successfully execute because its start time is later than B2. In this example, P2 is not a strong primary, and P1 and P3 are strong primaries. P1 and P2 are in a non-strong relationship, while P2 and P3 are in a strong relationship. Considering a primary and its direct predecessors, the conditions for BB overloading in workflow scheduling are hold as follows (Qin & Jiang, 2006). It inherits all the conditions stated in C1-C4, and also another two new constraints on backup overloading are added:

C6. The two tasks are independent with each other.
C7. The two primaries are strong primary copies.

According to Condition C6, the BB overloading is not allowed between any two tasks with direct precedence relationships. This can be proven by a contradiction: suppose two backups are overloaded with each other, the failure of the parent task's primary results in the execution of its backup. Because two backups are overloaded with each other, the backup of the child task will not execute anymore, and then its primary must be successfully executed. However, since a primary should be scheduled earlier than its backup, the primary of the child task has to start before the finish of the backup of the parent task, which is impossible because if so, he cannot receive the result from the parent task.

However, condition C6 cannot guarantee the successful execution of a workflow. For instance, the workflow as shown in Figure 7, task t3 is independent with the task t1 and t2. In the schedule,

Figure 4. A looped PB overloading chain

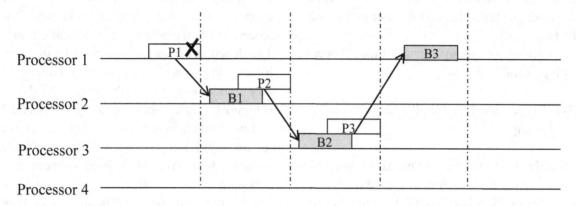

P1 and P3 are two strong primaries, while P2 is not. Following the condition C1-C4, B2 and B3 can overload with each other. Suppose processor 1 encounters a failure, in the case of the schedule in Figure 7, task t3 will also fails. Because P2 is not a strong primary, B1 and B2 are executed when P1 encounter a failure. P3 also fails for the same

location with P1, and B3 cannot execute when B2 is in execution. Therefore, we added condition C7 for workflow scheduling. And in summary, backup overloading is only allowed when two tasks are independent and both two primaries are strong.

We have summarized the conditions in backup overloading for two tasks with direct prece-

Figure 5. Scheduling two tasks with precedence constraints to the distributed system

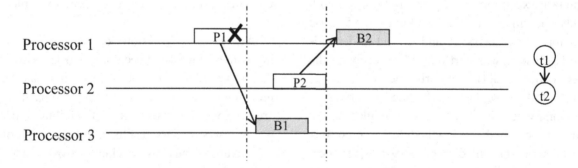

Figure 6. The strong and non-strong primary for workflow scheduling

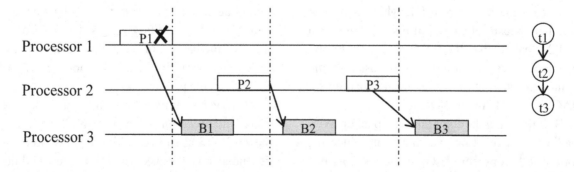

Figure 7. Backup overloading for tasks with a strong primary and a non-strong primary

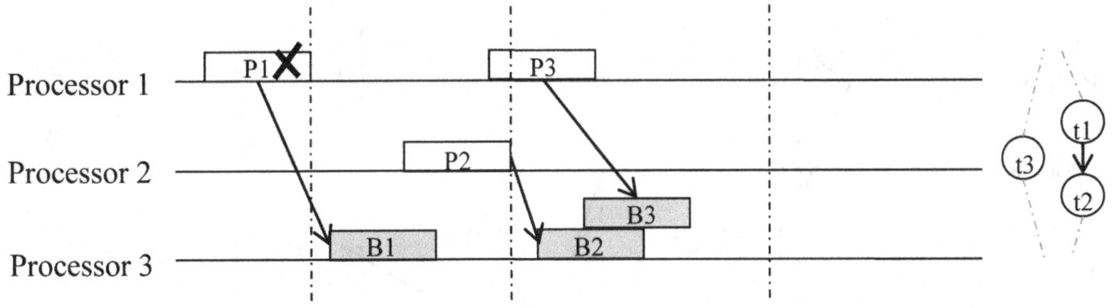

dence relationship. The next, we will extend it to consider not only direct precedence relationship but also all predecessors. We, firstly, discuss the two problems of when and where to schedule a backup in the context of precedence relationship, then we will restrict the extended backup overloading conditions.

Derived from the condition C1, both primary and backup of an independent task should be scheduled between the ready time and deadline, the problem for workflow scheduling is when to schedule a backup in the context of workflow. Condition C6 already reminds us the backup overloading is not allowed between two tasks with direct precedence relationship. Thus it left us two choices for scheduling a new backup: before or after the direct predecessors' backup. Obviously, a new backup cannot be scheduled before the start of its predecessor's backup for the same reason as C6. And a new backup could be scheduled only after the finish of its predecessors' backups (Zheng et al., 2009).

The second question is where a backup can be scheduled? Backup of a task t must not be scheduled on processors that the non-strong primaries of predecessors are located. As shown in Figure 8, both P2 and P3 are non-strong primaries, B3 cannot be scheduled on processor 4 because P3 is on processor 4. B3 also cannot be scheduled on processor 1 and 2, because the failure of P1 or P2 could result in the failure of both P3 and B3. Therefore, the conclusion is held. Let $P_{dp}^{ns}(j)$ denotes the direct predecessors set, which satisfies

a non-strong relationship with j, and u is a task in $P_{dp}^{ns}(j)$. Zheng et al. (2009) state that the processors that belong to set

$$P_p^{ns}(j) = \left\{ P_{dp}^{ns}(j) \right\} \bigcup \left\{ \bigcup_{u \in S_{dp}^{ns}(j)} \left\{ P_p^{ns}(u) \right\} \right\}$$ are suf-

ficient to determine the set of processors that backup of a task cannot be scheduled on.

Having determined the processors that a backup can be scheduled on, we now restrict the conditions of backup overloading on the remaining schedulable processors. The backup overloading condition is extended to the following C6-1 (Zheng et al., 2009),

C6-1. Backup overloading is not allowed among tasks with precedence relationships.

From the condition C6, we know that the BB overloading is not allowed between any two tasks with direct precedence relationships. Similarly, backup of a task will never be able to overload with other predecessors as their backups finish even before direct predecessors of this task. Therefore, a task's backup cannot overlap with any of its predecessors.

Primary/Backup Based Workflow Scheduling

Conditions C1-C7 with the extended conditions C4-1, C5-1, and C6-1 constrain the backup overloading for primary/backup based scheduling. Ap-

Figure 8. Schedule a backup with precedence constraints

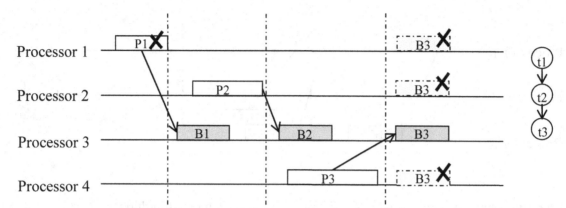

plying them into scheduling process, a workflow execution could be granted with 1-fault tolerance, schedulability improvement and deadline guarantee. In this section, workflow scheduling algorithms are designed with incorporating the above conditions (Qin & Jiang, 2006; Zheng et al. 2009). Specifically, reliability, execution time, and replication cost are set as the scheduling criteria in the scheduling process.

The eFRD (efficient fault-tolerant reliability-driven algorithm) inherits the backup overloading conditions into scheduling, and moreover, takes the reliability maximization as the scheduling criterion.

In the eFRD algorithm, each processor or communication link is associated with the assumption that their failure distribution follows a Poisson process. When scheduling a new task to the processor, the reliability provided by the previous schedule is calculated for the new task, then within the constraints of backup overloading conditions and deadline, the primary and backup are assigned on the processor that provides the maximum reliability. The eFRD description is as follows.

eFRD algorithm:
1. Sort all tasks by their deadlines.
2. Schedule the primary copy

a. Assign each primary to a processor, which provides the maximum reliability and meets the deadline.
3. Schedule the backup copy
a. Find the available processor that place the backup.
b. Find the available time intervals, either the unoccupied time intervals or overloading with existing backups.
c. Compute the reliability provided by such available time intervals.
d. Assign the backup to an available interval, which provides the maximum reliability.

As shown above, after a submission of a new workflow, all tasks are sorted by their deadlines (step I). Then the next step is to schedule all primaries of these tasks. If the deadline for the task is satisfied, we calculate the corresponding reliability provided by these processors. The processor that provides the maximum reliability is selected for each primary (step II). After all primaries are scheduled, the last step is to schedule backups. Processors are selected based on the condition C4, C6 and C7. Then available time intervals on these processors, either the unoccupied time intervals or overloading with existing backups, are checked for each backup. The time interval that provides the maximum reliability will be assigned to this backup.

Unlike the eFRD, Minimum Replication Cost with Early Completion Time (MRC-ECT) algorithm tries to minimize the replication cost, which is formally defined as $C(j) = \dfrac{t(j) - t^o(j)}{t(j)}$, where $t(j)$ denotes the execution time of the task j, and $t^o(j)$ indicates the amount of time that backup of task j can overload with other backups on the same processor (Q. Zheng et al. 2009). Without specifying the exact scheduling algorithm for primaries, MRC-ECT only illustrates the steps for scheduling backups.

MRC-ECT algorithm:
1. Sort all tasks using certain algorithms.
2. Schedule the primary copy using certain algorithms.
3. Schedule the backup copies.
    a. Find the available processors.
    b. Find the available time slots on these processors, either the unoccupied time intervals or overloading with existing backups.
    c. Assign the backup to a time slot, which provides the minimum replication cost.

As shown above, when scheduling a new backup, we firstly find the processors that it can be scheduled on (using condition C4, C6-1, C7). Then for each such processor, estimate its earliest possible start time and execution time, if the backup is schedulable on this processor, check all the available time slots, including both overloadable existing schedules and the time gap between non-overloadable schedules. If find any scheduling slot with less replication cost or the same replication cost but earlier finish time, remember this slot. The backup is scheduled to the slot with minimum replication cost.

MCT-LRC algorithm:
1. Sort all tasks using certain algorithms.
2. Schedule the primary copy using certain algorithms.
3. Schedule the backup copies.
    a. Find the available processors.
    b. Find the available time on these processors, either the unoccupied time intervals or overloading with existing backups.
    c. Assign the backup to a time slot, which can finish the backup in the earliest time.

Minimum Completion Time with Less Replication Cost (MCT-LRC) is quite similar with MRC-ECT, except that it takes the completion time minimization as the scheduling criterion. As shown above, in step III.a, find all the available processors for current backup using the condition C4, C6-1, and C7. Then the earliest possible finish time for current backup is checked on each processor. The checking procedure is as follows: firstly, estimate the earliest possible start time on the current processor. If the backup can be scheduled on this processor, set the backup start time as the earliest possible start time. Secondly, if the earliest possible start time does not work, find the available time slot from both overloadable existing schedules and the time gap between non-overloadable schedules. Thirdly, if still cannot find any possible slot for current backup, set the $deadline - t(j)$ as the backup start time. Through the above three steps, we have found the possible earliest start time for current backup. Finally, calculate the replication cost, and the current backup will be scheduled on the processor with earliest finish time. Alternatively, if several processors provide the same earliest finish time, the backup is scheduled on the one with minimum replication cost.

In this section, we have surveyed the backup overloading conditions in primary/backup based workflow scheduling. With the knowledge of backup overloading conditions, we could make use of fewer resources for 1-fault tolerance, so that improve the system schedulability and throughput.

WORKFLOW SCHEDULING WITH ROLLBACK-RECOVERY OR RESCHEDULING

Workflow Scheduling with Checkpoint

Rollback-recovery and rescheduling are both making use of the time redundancy for fault tolerance. And different with primary/backup, rollback-recovery tries to minimize the wasted execution by periodically saving the processor state or the logging of nondeterministic events into external storage, i.e. checkpoint. Rescheduling is quite similar with the primary/backup scheme. However, it is a kind of dynamic behavior, and quite popular applied in real-time systems. Informally, rescheduling can tolerant any number of failures.

As summarized in the literature (Maloney and Goscinski, 2009), the rollback-recovery approaches can be classified into checkpoint-based and log-based, where checkpoint-based protocols rely solely on periodically preserving the system state for restoration, and log-based protocols combine checkpointing with logging of nondeterministic events, which is often a natural choice for applications that frequently interact with the outside world. One major challenge in checkpointing is the coordination among processors so that they could establish a stable recovery state. And a number of excellent works (Elnozahy, Alvisi, Wang & Johnson, 2002; Maloney and Goscinski, 2009) have addressed this problem. However, checkpoint coordination is not the main point of this chapter. Instead, we focus on the combination research on workflow scheduling and checkpoint. Nurmi, Barbara, Wolski and Brevik, (2004) address the checkpoint scheduling problem from the view of checkpoint frequency, where an optimized checkpoint frequency is computed based on the history failure data. Unfortunately, to our best knowledge, the existing works are barely working on the problem of which processor should be scheduled for the recovery operation after a checkpoint is launched. Approaches that directly come into mind, such as randomly selection, token ring, voting, could assist the recovery scheduling. And the availability or reliability of processors within a distributed system has a direct impact on the scheduling performance.

Workflow Scheduling with Rescheduling

Due to the reason of easy implementation, dynamic rescheduling has been commonly implemented in some real systems, such as Hadoop, Condor. Taking Hadoop as an example, the default FIFO scheduler maintains a job queue for non-running jobs. When a job is interrupted due to the failure of a processor (named as tasktracker in Hadoop), the affected running tasks are removed from the running queue and put into the non-running cache. By this way, the tasks in non-running cache will be submitted to the scheduler again, and rescheduled to another tasktracker. Rescheduling could be associated with various criteria, such as execution time, reliability, and economic cost. Correspondingly, different scheduling algorithms can be designed based on the trade-off of such criteria.

Rescheduling algorithm:
1. Schedule a workflow using certain workflow scheduling algorithm. (e.g HEFT).
2. If a failure occurs
   a. Assign the affected tasks to another processor with the minimum finish time.

A rescheduling algorithm for workflow is illustrated as above (Sun et al. 2007). It does not specify the exact scheduling algorithm for a workflow. Any algorithm, e.g. HEFT, could be applied. After a failure occurs on a processor, all the affected tasks are rescheduled on another processor, which can provide the minimum finish time. If the scheduling criterion is set with reliability (or economic cost), the rescheduled processor, that is with maximum reliability (or minimum economic cost), will be selected for the failed tasks, correspondingly.

WORKFLOW SCHEDULING WITH ACTIVE REPLICATION

The Criteria in Workflow Scheduling with Active Replication

In this section, we will discuss the other fault tolerant workflow scheduling approach: workflow scheduling with active replication. We classify the active replication into two categories: traditional active replication (AR) and active replication with dynamic number of replicas (ARD). The traditional active replication always makes use of t+1 replicas for each task to tolerate t failures. However, the ARD approach assigns a different number of replicas for different tasks to provide a comparable reliability with t-fault tolerance. Obviously, with using fewer number of replicas, ARD could dynamically handle the failures, and save many computation resources than the traditional active replication.

A combination between scheduling and active replication is a strategy design following which replicas are assigned to different processors at the same time. In a simple way, multiple replicas could be assigned to processors randomly, or following a token ring strategy. However, these simple algorithms cannot satisfy the various requirements from different systems. In this section, we are trying to classify these requirements. And based on

them, we would like to introduce the scheduling algorithms corresponding to the classification.

As shown in Table. 1, the problem of scheduling with active replication is studied in the literature (Abawajy, 2004; Beitollahi & Deconinck, 2006; Benoit et al. 2008, 2009; Girault et al., 2001, 2003; Hashimoto, 2000; Ramamritham & Stankovic, 1995). Girault et al. (2003) apply the software redundancy for computation tasks, and time redundancy for communication tasks. In their FTBAR algorithm, they compute the schedule pressure for each task, and select the one with greatest schedule pressure for next scheduling step. The selected task is assigned to t+1 processors with minimum schedule pressure for the current task. The schedule pressure for a task i is defined as,

$$\sigma(i) = t_{start}(i) + t_{exe}(i, p) + t_{end}(i) - R$$

Where $t_{start}(i)$ is the earliest start time computed from the very beginning, $t_{exe}(i, p)$ is the execution time on a processor p, and $t_{end}(i)$ is the latest end time computed from the end of the workflow, and R is the total time length of the critical path. The schedule pressure measures that how much the schedule of the task lengths the critical path of the workflow (Girault et al., 2003). Therefore, essentially speaking, the FTBAR algorithm is also trying to minimize the time length of workflow execution.

Similarly with the FTBAR algorithm, FTSA algorithm (Benoit et al., 2008) also tries to minimize the execution time with applying the active replication scheme. FTSA algorithm employs the tl+bl based priority for ordering tasks. And at each scheduling step, it places the highest priority task to t+1 processors that could complete the task in the shortest time. From a study of both FTBAR and FTSA algorithms, execution time is the first critical common criterion in workflow scheduling with active replication.

In the current distributed system, communication speed among processors is much slower than the CPU accesses memory speed. Communication cost, defined as the communication time among processors, is one of the major reasons for delaying the execution time. Furthermore, a large amount of communications would cause network congestion and slower the internet speed. In order to improve the scheduling efficiency and reduce the communication cost, the simple idea is scheduling the corresponding task to the processor that holds the input data, which is denoted as locality in Hadoop. And most existing scheduling algorithms in Hadoop, e.g. FIFO, FAIR (Zaharia, Borthakur, Sarma, Elmeleegy, Shenker & Stoica, 2009), are all taking the locality as a critical criterion for scheduling. However, they make use of dynamic rescheduling for fault tolerance as introduced in last section.

Benoit et al. (2009) consider the communication cost in the scheduling process, and propose the CAFT algorithm (Contention-Aware Fault-Tolerant) to orchestrate all the intermediate communications. During each scheduling step, a task replica is placed on the non-locked processor which either currently contains the most predecessor replicas (high degree of locality), or can finish it at the earliest time. Furthermore, as observed by Hashimoto (2000) and Hashimoto, Tsuchita and Kikuno (2002), task duplication is an effective solution for both fault tolerance and communication cost reduction. In Hashimoto (2000), every task is assigned to at least two processors for 1-fault tolerance. And more replicas are assigned in the available time gaps among existing schedules, so that a child task is more likely to receive the intermediate results from the local processor. The big drawback of their approach is only tolerating one failure, which deviates from the basic idea of the active replication scheme. Although multiple replicas could reduce the communication cost, it also significantly increases the computation cost, so that decrease the schedulability and system throughput.

Beitollahi and Deconinck (2006) evaluate the performance of rate-monotonic scheduling algorithms, and also incorporate the active replication into the scheduling process. However, it is not related with workflow. Abawajy (2004) simply applies the active replication into Grid computing environment, and does not specifically discuss the scheduling criterion. Therefore, a summary from all these literatures is that, execution time and communication cost are specifically addressed in the existing workflow scheduling algorithms. In the next we will introduce the corresponding scheduling algorithms.

Workflow Scheduling with AR Scheme

In this section, we will discuss the workflow scheduling algorithms, with the objective of minimizing execution and minimizing communication cost, respectively. Two typical algorithms, FTSA (Benoit et al. 2008) and CAFT (Benoit et al. 2009) are specifically introduced here.

FTSA algorithm:

1. Computing the bottom level (bl) for each task, and set top level (tl) as 0 for each entry task.
2. For each ready task
   a. Select the free task with highest tl+bl priority.
   b. Assign the task to the first t+1 processors that allow for the earliest finish time
   c. Update the top level.

FTSA algorithm (Benoit et al. 2008) is a fault tolerant version of the classic HEFT algorithm (Topcuoglu et al. 2002). It employs the tl+bl (top level + bottom level) method for computing the task priority. At each scheduling step, the task with the highest priority is selected. And provided that t failures are requested to tolerate, the task is scheduled on the t+1 processors that allow for minimum finish time. After scheduling this task, update the top level priority, and enter the next step.

CAFT algorithm:

1. Computing the bottom level (bl) for each task, and set top level (tl) as 0 for each entry task.
2. For each ready task
   a. Select the free task i with highest tl+bl priority.
   b. Assign task i's first replica to the non-locked processor that holds the maximum number of predecessors' replicas.
   c. Add corresponding communications, and lock the related processors (including the scheduled processor and the ones from which communications are added).
   d. Repeat the above process until all t+1 replicas are scheduled, then turn to the next task.

As shown above, CAFT algorithm also sorts tasks based on tl+bl priority. At each step, the task with highest task priority is selected for execution. Each replica is scheduled on a non-locked processor that holds the maximum number of predecessors' replicas. This improves the locality so that reduces the communication cost. Then the least number of necessary communications are added from non-locked predecessors. New scheduled processor and the ones from which communications are added, will get locked. Through this way, communications are orchestrated to avoid useless data transfer. When there is no processor left for the mapping of the remaining replicas if a processor a locked, we add t additional communications and release the processors involved in a communication with a replica of task i.

Workflow Scheduling with ARD Scheme

Scheduling with ARD scheme is studied in the literature (Dima et al. 2001; Kandaswamy et al. 2008; Li, & Mascagni, 2003; Litke et al. 2007; Wang, Ramamritham and Stankovic, 1995; Zhao et al. 2010). They improve the active replication by employing dynamic number of replicas during the scheduling process. Based on the failure prediction methods (Javadi, Kondo, Vincent & Anderson, 2009; Narasimhan et al. 2005; Oliner, Sahoo, Moreira, Gupta & Sivasubramaniam, 2004; Rood & Lewis, 2010; Vilalta & Ma, 2002), replicas would be placed on processors which are more reliable than the others, and also different number of replicas can be assigned while providing a comparable reliability. Through this way, the scheduling algorithm would save a large amount of computation resources, and improves the system throughput by assigning new tasks into the saved time intervals. Dima et al. (2001) study the fault tolerant scheduling based on an understanding of failure pattern. Under different failure patterns, the possible plain schedules are generated by certain scheduling algorithm. Then all the plain schedules are aggregated into an overall schedule. In the overall schedule, different number replicas are possibly assigned.

In Litke et al. (2007), assuming the failures distribution follows a weibull process, we can predict the reliability of the next time interval. Then the minimum number of processors that can provide a higher reliability than a given threshold is scheduled for the task. In Wang, Ramamritham and Stankovic (1995), a performance index (PI) is defined as $PI = VR - PF$, where V is the reward if the task is feasibly scheduled associated with probability R, and P is the penalty from a failure with a probability F. Each task is scheduled with optimized resource redundancy, which can maximize the performance index for the task. Kandaswamy et al. (2008) studied the ARD based scheduling in Grid environment, and also optimized the number of replicas with aggregating minimum processors and deadline constraints. Based on their work, we took the DAG represented workflow into consideration, and studied the scheduling with ARD scheme. We propose the MaxRe (Maximum Reliability) scheduling algorithm with the target of reducing computation cost (Zhao et al. 2010). Moreover, with incorporating both job deadline and computation cost, we extend the MaxRe algorithm to DRR algorithm (Deadline, Reliability, Resources-aware scheduling algorithm), which guarantees that the workflow can be finished within the deadline, yet employing much fewer resources to achieve a higher reliability (Zhao et al, 2011).

MaxRe algorithm:
1. Computing the bottom level (bl) for each task.
2. Computer the reliability requirement for each task using $r = \sqrt[n]{R}$.
3. For each ready task
    a. Select the task with highest bl priority.
    b. Compute the reliability provided by simulating the task onto the processors.
    c. Select the minimum number of processors, whose combined reliability is greater than r.
    d. if no enough processors, due to the subreliability requirement, reject the job.
    e. Assign the task to these processors.

As shown in Figure 1, we find that scheduling based on bottom level averagely takes shorter execution time than tl+bl based scheduling. Therefore, our MaxRe algorithm sorts all tasks based on their bottom level. At each scheduling step, select the task with highest bl priority. Then compute the reliability provided by simulating the task on each processor. The task will be assigned the minimum processors whose combined reliability

is greater than the task reliability requirement. If we cannot find enough processors for the task, we have to reject the job. After getting the placement, assign the task to the corresponding processors.

DRR algorithm:
1. Compute the bottom level (bl) for each task.
2. Computer the reliability requirement for each task using $r = \sqrt[n]{R}$.
3. Assign the subdeadline for each task by recursively calculating from the exit task to top.
4. for each unscheduled task
    a. Select the task with highest bl priority.
    b. Compute the reliability provided by simulating the task onto the processor
    c. Sort the processors according to the reliability.
    d. Select the minimum number of processors, whose combined reliability is greater than r, and moreover the finish time is shorter than subdeadline.
    e. if no available processors satisfy either the subdeadline or subreliability requirement, reject the job.
    f. Assign the task to thes e processors.

The DRR algorithm is extended from the MaxRe algorithm. It incorporates the deadline into the scheduling process, so that satisfies some user requirements on both reliability and deadline. As shown above, DRR algorithm also computes bl as the task priority. Before scheduling, the subdeadline for each task is computed recursively from the exit task to the entry task, where the exit task's subdeadline equals to the overall deadline. During the scheduling process, the minimum number of processors whose combined reliability is greater than r, and the finish time is shorter than subdeadline are selected. If no available processors satisfy either the subdeadline or subreliability requirements, the job is rejected.

The major design objective of DRR algorithm is to ensure both reliability and deadline. Because a workflow consists of a number of tasks, we need to compute the subreliability and subdeadline for each task, while the computed subreliability and subdeadline should not violate the overall reliability and deadline.

The subreliability for a task, denoted as r, is computed using the formula $r = \sqrt[n]{R}$, where R is the overall reliability requirement. This method implies that the subreliabilities for all tasks are equally computed. We have two main reasons for this. Firstly, the tasks in a workflow are dependent on each other. Except the entry tasks, all others have to wait for the results from their parent tasks. Therefore, all the entry tasks and the intermediate task are equally important for their descendant tasks. Otherwise, if these tasks encounter any failures, their descendant tasks could also be failed. Secondly, all exit tasks of a workflow do not have any more descendants. They may have a different impact on the user, which means several of their failures could be accepted by the user, as long as the major result is gotten. However, in such cases, we have to learn the semantics of user's workflow, and identify which one is more important than others. This is quite difficult and complex for a sing workflow scheduling algorithm. Therefore, we simply assign an equal subrealiability to all tasks. The subreliability for each task is satisfied by assigning multiple replicas to the system. And a minimum number of replicas, whose combined reliability is greater than the subrealiability, are selected. It is quite obvious that the overall reliability would be guaranteed as long as the subreliability is satisfied.

The subdeadline for each task is computed using a breadth first search based deadline assignment algorithm. We apply the Breadth-First-Search (BFS) algorithm into the subdeadline assignment process, while the subdeadline of an exit task is set with the overall deadline. Beginning with the exit tasks, we find their parents using the BFS algorithm, and compute their subdeadline as follows,

Parent's subdeadline = child's subdeadline – child's execution time – communication time

In the case of multiple results is gotten for one task, we always select the minimum one as its final value. Through this way, the computed subdeadlines are doomed to be the latest finish time of a task. And it is directly proven that, the workflow cannot be completed within the overall deadline, once a subdeadline is violated by its execution time length. However, even if the subdeadline is not violated by its execution time length, we still cannot ensure that the job will be completed within the overall deadline. The reason is that a processer may be simultaneously accessed by several tasks, which is named as processor contention. We illustrate this by an example (Figure 9): suppose one workflow consists of four tasks: one entry task x and its three children tasks y1, y2 and y3, and suppose the target system has two processors: P1 and P2. Using the above formula, the task y1, y2 and y3's subdeadlines are all set with the overall deadline, and the task x's subdeadline is the minimum one among three results computed from three children, respectively. Suppose the task x's execution time is shorter than this computed subdeadline, then all subdeadlines of the four tasks could be intuitively satisfied. However, because the target system has only two processors, there must be two children tasks (e.g. task y1 and y3) are scheduled on the same processor, and one of them (i.e. task y3) has to wait until the finish of the other. In this case, task y1 and y3's total execution time would possibly violate the deadline constraint. Due to the processor competition, we have optimized the DRR scheduling algorithm by adding the processor available check into scheduling. Once a processor cannot get through the processor check, we will not schedule the replica to it.

Figure 9. Example: deadline violation caused by processor competition

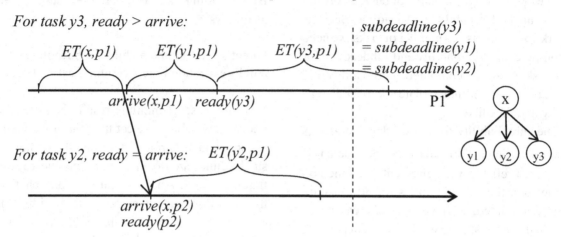

The time complexity of the DRR algorithm is $O(MN\log M + N\log N)$, where M is the number of processors in the system, and N is the number of tasks in the workflow. Through the MaxRe and DRR scheduling algorithm, we find that a significant reduction on both computation and communication resources could be achieved. As the experiments done by Zhao et al. (2011), 50% computation resources and 70% communication resources are averagely saved, compared with the FTSA algorithm.

A HYBRID APPROACH

In the previous sections, we have discussed about the workflow scheduling with the solely independent fault tolerant approaches. Other than that, a hybrid fault tolerance based scheduling is also introduced in the literature (Bertossi et al., 1999; Kim et al., 2010; Luo et al., 2006). In their scheduling algorithms, each backup task is associated with either an active or a passive decision. If the backup is decided to be an active backup, then it will be actively assigned to a processor, and started to work at the same time with others. Conversely, if the backup is determined as a passive backup, then it will be started only after the primary fails.

Both Bertossi et al. (1999) and Luo et al. (2006) focus on independent periodic tasks, and propose solutions for fault tolerant scheduling. Since the hard-real-time system is much more sensitive to the response time than the other systems, their solutions are paying more attention to the response time, that is a passive replica is always preferred except that if a replica cannot finish before the deadline, an active replica will be arranged for the task. Kim et al. (2010) defined the hot standby and cold standby, which correspond to active replica and passive replica, respectively. The proposed R-BFD and R-BATCH algorithms are applied for hot standby and cold standby allocation, respectively.

In summary, the hybrid approach between primary/backup and active replication have been considered in some works. However, few of them have proposed such solutions for workflow represented jobs. We believe that, the hybrid approach is critically important for fault tolerance. And applying it into workflow scheduling is still a challenge that should be explored in the future. And a major challenge of this problem is the decision making policy on which task should be arranged an active replica, or which task should be arranged a passive replica.

CONCLUSION AND FUTURE RESEARCH DIRECTIONS

In this chapter, we have summarized the existing research on the fault tolerant workflow scheduling. We start from the two common fault tolerant technologies: primary/backup and active replication, then introduce the related variants, including: rescheduling, checkpoint, primary/backup with multiple backups, and active replication with dynamic number of replicas. Based on these fault tolerant technologies, we did a survey on the fault tolerant scheduling algorithms.

As we discussed above, the major challenge issue in primary/backup based workflow scheduling is on confining the backup overloading conditions. Existing literature have studied the backup overloading conditions for both independent tasks and dependent tasks. Following the conditions, a backup could be scheduled safely on a processor to ensure the 1-fault tolerance, and improve the schedulability. The major challenge issue in active replication based workflow scheduling, is on improving the scheduling quality, i.e. shortening execution time, reducing communication cost and computation cost. We have introduced the representative scheduling algorithms corresponding to these criteria.

From the survey, we have learned the focus point of existing works, and identified some new research directions for either a combination study or further improvements. In summary, future research directions focus on the following aspects:

1. Backup-Backup overloading, Primary-Backup overloading and the hybrid overloading conditions in primary/backup based workflow scheduling algorithm.
2. The tradeoffs among various scheduling criteria are still a critical challenge that should be explored.
3. Incorporate the scheduling into the checkpoint based fault tolerant system, and design a recovery policy coupled with the scheduling algorithm.
4. With satisfying certain QoS requirements, e.g. execution time, scheduling algorithms need designing with the combined PB&AR approach.
5. Take the byzantine fault tolerance into consideration, and comprehensively consider the byzantine fault tolerance and scheduling algorithm.

In summary, the workflow technology is getting increasingly important for the management of large-scale complex jobs. And with the system scale getting bigger, the underlying distributed hardware environment is also getting more fragile than before. Therefore, fault tolerant workflow scheduling is still on the way for a creative future.

REFERENCES

Abawajy, J. H. (2004). Fault-tolerant scheduling policy for grid computing systems. *Proceedings of 18th International Parallel and Distributed Processing Symposium*, (pp. 238-244). doi: 10.1109/IPDPS.2004.1303290

Alomari, R., Somani, A. K., & Manimaran, G. (2004). Efficient overloading techniques for primary-backup scheduling in real-time systems. *Journal of Parallel and Distributed Computing*, *64*(5), 629–648. doi:10.1016/j.jpdc.2004.03.015

Balasubramanian, J., Gokhale, A., Wolf, F., Dubey, A., Lu, C., Gill, C., & Schmidt, D. C. (2009). *Resource-aware deployment and configuration of fault-tolerant real-time systems*. ISIS Technical Report ISIS-09-109. Retrieved from http://www.isis.vanderbilt.edu/node/4121

Balazinska, M., Hwang, J. H., & Shah, M. A. (2009). Fault-tolerance and high availability in data stream management systems. In Liu, L., & Özsu, M. T. (Eds.), *Encyclopedia of database systems* (pp. 1109–1115). Springer, US.

Beitollahi, H., & Deconinck, G. (2006). Fault-tolerant partitioning scheduling algorithms in real-time multiprocessor systems. *Proceedings of the 12th Pacific Rim International Symposium on Dependable Computing*, (pp. 296-304). doi: 10.1109/PRDC.2006.34.

Benoit, A., Hakem, M., & Robert, Y. (2008). Fault tolerant scheduling of precedence task graphs on heterogeneous platforms. *Proceedings of the 10th Workshop on Advances in Parallel and Distributed Computational Models*, (pp. 1-8). doi: 10.1109/IPDPS.2008.4536133

Benoit, A., Hakem, M., & Robert, Y. (2009). Contention awareness and fault-tolerant scheduling for precedence constrained tasks in heterogeneous systems. *Parallel Computing, 35*(2), 83–108. doi:10.1016/j.parco.2008.11.001

Bertossi, A. A., Mancini, L. V., & Rossini, F. (1999). Fault-tolerant rate-monotonic first-fit scheduling in hard-real-time systems. *IEEE Transactions on Parallel and Distributed Systems, 10*(9), 934–945. doi:10.1109/71.798317

Blythe, J., Jain, S., Deelman, E., Gil, Y., Vahi, K., Mandal, A., & Kennedy, K. (2005). Task scheduling strategies for workflow-based applications in grids. *Proceedings of IEEE International Symposium on Cluster Computing and the Grid*, (pp. 759-767). doi: 10.1109/CCGRID.2005.1558639

Castro, M., & Liskov, B. (2002). Practical Byzantine fault tolerance and proactive recovery. *ACM Transactions on Computer Systems, 20*(4), 398–461. doi:10.1145/571637.571640

Clement, A., Marchetti, M., Wong, E., Alvisi, L., & Dahlin, M. (2008). Position paper: BFT: The time is now. *Proceedings of the 2nd Workshop on Large-Scale Distributed Systems and Middleware*, (pp. 1-4). doi: 10.1145/1529974.1529992

Cristian, F. (1991). Understanding fault-tolerant distributed systems. *Communications of the ACM, 34*(2), 56–78. doi:10.1145/102792.102801

Dima, C., Girault, A., Lavarenne, C., & Sorel, Y. (2001). Off-line real-time fault-tolerant scheduling. *Proceedings 9th Euromicro Workshop on Parallel and Distributed Processing*, (pp. 410-417). doi: 10.1109/EMPDP.2001.905069

Driscoll, K., Hall, B., Sivencrona, H., & Zumsteg, P. (2003). Byzantine fault tolerance, from theory to reality. *Lecture Notes in Computer Science, vol. 2788, Computer Safety, Reliability, and Security* (pp. 235-248). Berlin, Germany: Springer-Verlag. doi: 10.1007/978-3-540-39878-3_19

Elnozahy, E. N., Alvisi, L., Wang, Y. M., & Johnson, D. B. (2002). A survey of rollback-recovery protocols in message-passing systems. *ACM Computing Surveys, 34*(3), 375–408. doi:10.1145/568522.568525

Ghosh, S., Melhem, R., & Mosse, D. (1994). Fault-tolerant scheduling on a hard real-time multiprocessor system. *Proceedings of 8th International Parallel Processing Symposium*, (pp. 775-782). doi: 10.1109/IPPS.1994.288216

Ghosh, S., Melhem, R., & Mosse, D. (1997). Fault-tolerance through scheduling of aperiodic tasks in hard real time multiprocessor systems. *IEEE Transactions on Parallel and Distributed Systems, 8*(3), 272–284. doi:10.1109/71.584093

Girault, A., Kalla, H., Sighireanu, M., & Sorel, Y. (2003). An algorithm for automatically obtaining distributed and fault-tolerant static schedules. *Proceedings of 2003 International Conference on Dependable Systems and Networks*, (pp. 159-168). doi: 10.1109/DSN.2003.1209927.

Girault, A., Lavarenne, C., Sighireanu, M., & Sorel, Y. (2001). Fault-tolerant static scheduling for real-time distributed embedded systems. *Proceedings 21st International Conference on Distributed Computing Systems*, (pp. 695-698). doi: 10.1109/ICDSC.2001.919002

Guerraoui, R., & Schiper, A. (1996). Fault-tolerance by replication in distributed systems. *Proceedings of the 1996 Ada-Europe International Conference on Reliable Software Technologies*, (pp. 38-57). Retrieved from http://portal.acm.org/citation.cfm?id=697290

Hashimoto, K. (2000). A new approach to fault-tolerant scheduling using task duplication in multiprocessor systems. *Journal of Systems and Software, 53*(2), 159–171. doi:10.1016/S0164-1212(99)00105-3

Hashimoto, K., Tsuchita, T., & Kikuno, T. (2002). Effective scheduling of duplicated tasks for fault tolerance in multiprocessor systems. *IEICE Transactions on Information and Systems. E (Norwalk, Conn.), 85-D*(3), 525–534.

Hu, C., Wu, M., Liu, G., & Xie, W. (2007). QoS scheduling algorithm based on hybrid particle swarm optimization strategy for grid workflow. *Proceedings of the 6th International Conference on Grid and Cooperative Computing*, (pp. 330-337). doi:10.1109/GCC.2007.100

Javadi, B., Kondo, D., Vincent, J. M., & Anderson, D. P. (2009). Mining for statistical models of availability in large-scale distributed systems: An empirical study of SETI@home. *Proceedings of the 17th IEEE/ACM International Symposium on Modelling, Analysis and Simulation of Computer and Telecommunication Systems*, (pp. 1-10). doi: 10.1109/MASCOT.2009.5367061

Kandaswamy, G., Mandal, A., & Reed, D. A. (2008). Fault tolerance and recovery of scientific workflows on computational grids. *Proceedings of the 8th Cluster Computing and the Grid*, (pp. 777-782). doi: 10.1109/CCGRID.2008.79

Kim, J., Lakshmanan, K., & Rajkumar, R. R. (2010). R-BATCH: Task partitioning for fault-tolerant multiprocessor real-time systems. *Proceedings of 10th IEEE International Conference on Computer and Information Technology*, (pp. 1872-1879). doi: 10.1109/CIT.2010.321

Li, Y., & Mascagni, M. (2003). Improving performance via computational replication on a large-scale computational grid. *Proceedings of the 3rd IEEE International Symposium on Cluster Computing and the Grid*, (pp. 442-448). Retrieved from http://portal.acm.org/citation.cfm?id=792426

Litke, A., Skoutas, D., Tserpes, K., & Varvarigou, T. (2007). Efficient task replication and management for adaptive fault tolerance in mobile Grid environments. *Future Generation Computer Systems, 23*(2), 163–178. doi:10.1016/j.future.2006.04.014

Luo, W., Yang, F., Pang, L., & Qin, X. (2006). Fault-tolerant scheduling based on periodic tasks for heterogeneous systems. *Lecture Notes in Computer Science, vol. 4158, Autonomic and Trusted Computing* (pp. 571-580). Berlin, Germany: Springer-Verlag. doi: 10.1007/11839569_56

Maloney, A., & Goscinski, A. (2009). A survey and review of the current state of rollback-recovery for cluster. *Journal of Concurrency and Computation: Practice & Experience, 21*(12), 1632–1666. doi:10.1002/cpe.1413

Manimaran, G., & Murthy, C. S. R. (1997). A new scheduling approach supporting different fault-tolerant techniques for real-time multiprocessor systems. *Microprocessors and Microsystems, 21*, 163–173. doi:10.1016/S0141-9331(97)00030-6

Manimaran, G., & Murthy, C. S. R. (1998). A fault-tolerant dynamic scheduling algorithm for multi-processor real-time systems and its analysis. *IEEE Transactions on Parallel and Distributed Systems, 9*(11), 1137–1152. doi:10.1109/71.735960

Naedele, M. (1999). Fault-tolerant real-time scheduling under execution time constraints. *Proceedings of 6th International Conference on Real-Time Computing Systems and Applications*, (pp. 392-395). doi: 10.1109/RTCSA.1999.811286

Narasimhan, P., Dumitras, T. A., Paulos, A. M., Pertet, S. M., Reverte, C. F., Slember, J. G., & Srivastave, D. (2005). MEAD: Support for real-time fault-tolerant CORBA. *Concurrency and Computation, 17*(12), 1527–1545. doi:10.1002/cpe.882

Nurmi, D., Wolski, R., & Brevik, J. (2004). *Model-based checkpoint scheduling for volatile resource environments*. UCSB Technical Report(2004-25). Retrieved from http://vgrads.rice.edu/publications/wolski3/

Oliner, A. J., Sahoo, R. K., Moreira, J. E., Gupta, M., & Sivasubramaniam, A. (2004). Fault-aware job scheduling for BlueGene/L systems. *Proceedings of the 18th International Parallel and Distributed Processing Symposium*, (pp. 64-73). doi: 10.1109/IPDPS.2004.1302991

Qin, X., & Jiang, H. (2006). A novel fault-tolerant scheduling algorithm for precedence constrained tasks in real-time heterogeneous systems. *Parallel Computing, 32*(5-6), 331–356. doi:10.1016/j.parco.2006.06.006

Ramamritham, K., & Stankovic, J. A. (1995). Determining redundancy levels for fault tolerant real-time systems. *IEEE Transactions on Computers, 44*(2), 292–301. doi:10.1109/12.364540

Reiser, H. P., & Kapitza, R. (2007). VM-FIT: Supporting intrusion tolerance with virtualization technology. *Proceedings of the First Workshop on Recent Advances on Intrusion-Tolerant Systems*, (pp. 18-22). Retrieved from http://wraits07.di.fc.ul.pt/9.pdf

Rood, B., & Lewis, M. J. (2010). Availability prediction based replication strategies for grid environments. *Proceedings of the 10th IEEE/ACM International Conference on Cluster, Cloud and Grid Computing*, (pp. 25-33). doi: 10.1109/CCGRID.2010.121

Schroeder, B., & Gibson, G. A. (2006). A large-scale study of failures in high-performance computing systems. *International Conference on Dependable Systems and Networks (DSN06)*, November 2006, (pp. 249-258). doi: 10.1109/DSN.2006.5

Selic, B. (2004). *Fault tolerance techniques for distributed systems*. IBM Technical report. Retrieved July 27, 2004, from http://www.ibm.com/developerworks/rational/library/114.html

Sun, W., Yu, C., & Inoguchi, Y. (2008). Dynamic scheduling real-time task using primary-backup overloading strategy for multiprocessor systems. *IEICE Transactions on Information and Systems. E (Norwalk, Conn.), 91-D*(3), 796–806. doi:doi:10.1093/ietisy/e91

Sun, W., Zhang, Y., Yu, C., Defago, X., & Inoguchi, Y. (2007b). Hybrid overloading and stochastic analysis for redundant scheduling in real-time multiprocessor systems. *Proceedings of the 26th IEEE International Symposium on Reliable Distributed Systems*, (pp. 265-274). doi: 10.1109/SRDS.2007.11

Sun, Z., Guo, W., Jin, Y., Sun, W., & Hu, W. (2007a). Rescheduling policy for fault-tolerant optical grid. *Proceedings of SPIE, the International Society for Optical Engineering, 6784*(2), 67841D.1-67841D.8. doi: 10.1117/12.743719

Talukder, A. K. M., Kirley, M., Buyya, R., & Tham, C. K. (2007). Multiobjective differential evolution for workflow execution on grids. *Proceedings of the 5th International Workshop on Middleware for Grid Computing*, (pp. 13-18). doi: 10.1145/1376849.1376852

Topcuoglu, H., Hariri, S., & Wu, M. Y. (2002). Performance effective and low complexity task scheduling for heterogeneous computing. *IEEE Transactions on Parallel and Distributed Systems*, *13*(3), 260–274. doi:10.1109/71.993206

Vilalta, R., & Ma, S. (2002). Predicting rare events in temporal domains. In *Proceedings of the 2002 IEEE International Conference on Data Mining* (pp. 474-481). doi: 10.1109/ICDM.2002.1183991

Wang, F., Ramamritham, K., & Stankovic, J. A. (1995). Determining redundancy levels for fault tolerant real-time systems. *IEEE Transactions on Computers*, *44*(2), 292–301. doi:10.1109/12.364540

Wieczorek, M., Hoheisel, A., & Prodan, R. (2009). Towards a general model of the multi-criteria workflow scheduling on the grid. *Future Generation Computer Systems*, *25*(3), 237–256. doi:10.1016/j.future.2008.09.002

Wieczorek, M., Podlipnig, S., Prodan, R., & Fahringer, T. (2008). Bi-criteria scheduling of scientific workflows for the grid. *Proceedings of the 8th IEEE International Symposium on Cluster Computing and the Grid*, (pp. 9-16). doi: 10.1109/CCGRID.2008.21

Wu, B., Chi, C., Chen, Z., Gu, M., & Sun, J. (2009). Workflow-based resource allocation to optimize overall performance of composite services. *Future Generation Computer Systems*, *25*(3), 199–212. doi:10.1016/j.future.2008.06.003

Yu, J., & Buyya, R. (2006a). Scheduling scientific workflow applications with deadline and budget constraints using genetic algorithms. *Science Progress*, *14*(3), 217–230.

Yu, J., & Buyya, R. (2006b). A taxonomy of workflow management systems for grid computing. *Journal of Grid Computing*, *3*(3-4), 171–200. doi:10.1007/s10723-005-9010-8

Yu, J., Buyya, R., & Tham, C. K. (2005). Cost-based scheduling of scientific workflow applications on utility grids. *Proceedings of the 1st International Conference on e-Science and Grid Computing*, (pp. 140-147). doi: 10.1109/E-SCIENCE.2005.26

Zaharia, M., Borthakur, D., Sarma, J. S., Elmeleegy, K., Shenker, S., & Stoica, I. (2009). *Job scheduling for multi-user MapReduce clusters*. University of California at Berkeley, Technical Report No. UCB/EECS-2009-55. Retrieved from http://www.eecs.berkeley.edu/Pubs/TechRpts/2009/EECS-2009-55.html

Zhao, L., Ren, Y., & Sakurai, K. (2011). A resource minimizing scheduling algorithm with ensuring the deadline and reliability in heterogeneous systems. *Proceedings of the 25th International Conference on Advanced Information Networking and Applications*. IEEE Computer Society Press.

Zhao, L., Ren, Y., Xiang, Y., & Sakurai, K. (2010). Fault tolerant scheduling with dynamic number of replicas in heterogeneous system. *Proceedings of 12th IEEE International Conference on High Performance Computing and Communications*, (pp. 434-441).

Zheng, Q., Veeravalli, B., & Tham, C. K. (2009). On the design of fault-tolerant scheduling strategies using primary-backup approach for computational grids with low replication costs. *IEEE Transactions on Computers*, *58*(3), 380–393. doi:10.1109/TC.2008.172

ADDITIONAL READING

Babu, S. (2010). Towards automatic optimization of MapReduce programs. *Proceedings of the 1st ACM Symposium on Cloud Computing*, (pp. 137-142). ACM Press. doi: 10.1145/1807128.1807150

Baker, J., Bond, C., Corbett, J. C., Furman, J. J., Khorlin, A., Larson, J., et al. (2011). Megastore: Providing scalable. *The 5th Biennial Conference on Innovative Data Systems Research*, (pp. 223-234).

Bessani, A. N., Correia, M., da Silva Fraga, J., & Lung, L. C. (2009). An efficient Byzantine-resilient Tuple space. *IEEE Transactions on Computers, 58*(8). doi:10.1109/TC.2009.71

Chtepen, M. (2009). Adaptive task checkpointing and replication: Toward efficient fault-tolerant grids. *IEEE Transactions on Parallel and Distributed Systems, 20*(2), 180–190. doi:10.1109/TPDS.2008.93

Clement, A., Marchetti, M., Wong, E., Alvisi, L., & Dahlin, M. (2009). Making Byzantine fault tolerant systems tolerate Byzantine failures. *Proceedings of the 6th USENIX Symposium on Networked Systems Design and Implementation* (pp. 153-168). USENIX.

Comput, J. P. D., Vengerov, D., Mastroleon, L., Murphy, D., & Bambos, N. (2010). Adaptive data-aware utility-based scheduling in resource-constrained systems. *Journal of Parallel and Distributed Computing, 70*(9), 871-879. Elsevier Inc. doi: 10.1016/j.jpdc.2009.08.006

Fei, X., Lu, S., & Lin, C. (2009). A MapReduce-enabled scientific workflow composition framework. *2009 IEEE International Conference on Web Services* (pp. 663-670). IEEE. doi: 10.1109/ICWS.2009.90

Garg, S. K., Buyya, R., & Siegel, H. J. (2010). Time and cost trade-off management for scheduling parallel applications on utility Grids. *Future Generation Computer Systems, 26*(8), 1344-1355. Elsevier B.V. doi: 10.1016/j.future.2009.07.003

Gomez, L. A. B., Maruyama, N., Cappello, F., & Matsuoka, S. (2010). Distributed diskless checkpoint for large scale systems. *The 10th IEEE/ACM International Conference on Cluster, Cloud and Grid Computing*, (pp. 63-72). IEEE. doi: 10.1109/CCGRID.2010.40

Gu, X., Papadimitriou, S., Yu, P. S., & Chang, S.-P. (2008). Toward predictive failure management for distributed stream. *Processing Systems. The 28th International Conference on Distributed Computing Systems* (pp. 825-832). IEEE. doi: 10.1109/ICDCS.2008.34

Guerraoui, R., & Vukolić, M. (2010). Refined quorum systems. *Distributed Computing, 23*(1), 1–42. doi:10.1007/s00446-010-0103-7

Isard, M., Prabhakaran, V., Currey, J., Wieder, U., Talwar, K., & Goldberg, A. (2009). Quincy: Fair scheduling for distributed computing clusters. *Proceedings of the ACM SIGOPS 22nd Symposium on Operating Systems Principles*, (pp. 261-276). doi:10.1145/1629575.1629601

Jarvis, S. A., Saini, S., & Nudd, G. R. (2003). GridFlow: Workflow management for grid computing. *The 3rd IEEE/ACM International Symposium on Cluster Computing and the Grid*, (pp. 198-205). IEEE. doi: 10.1109/CCGRID.2003.1199369

Kc, K., & Anyanwu, K. (2010). Scheduling Hadoop Jobs to Meet Deadlines. *IEEE Second International Conference on Cloud Computing Technology and Science* (pp. 388-392). doi:10.1109/CloudCom.2010.97

Ko, S. Y., Hoque, I., Cho, B., & Gupta, I. (2010). Making cloud intermediate data fault-tolerant. *Proceedings of the 1st ACM Symposium on Cloud Computing*, (pp. 181-192). ACM. doi:10.1145/1807128.1807160

Lamport, L., Malkhi, D., & Zhou, L. (2009). Vertical paxos and primary-backup replication. *Proceedings of the 28th ACM Symposium on Principles of Distributed Computing* (pp. 312-313). ACM. doi:10.1145/1582716.1582783

Liu, K. (2010). A compromised-time-cost scheduling algorithm in SwinDeW-C for instance-intensive cost-constrained workflows on a cloud computing platform. *International Journal of High Performance Computing Applications, 24*(4), 445–456. doi:10.1177/1094342010369114

Pineau, J.-F., Robert, Y., & Vivien, F. (2011). Energy-aware scheduling of bag-of-tasks applications on master-worker platforms. *Concurrency and Computation: Practice & Experience, 23*(2), 145-157. John Wilcy and Sons Ltd. doi: 10.1002/cpe.1634

Rood, B. (2009). Grid resource availability prediction-based scheduling and task replication. *Journal of Grid Computing, 15*(2), 757–500. doi:doi:10.1007/s10723-009-9135-2

Saito, Y., & Shapiro, M. (2005). Optimistic replication. *ACM Computing Surveys, 37*(1), 42–81. doi:10.1145/1057977.1057980

Sashi, K., & Selvadoss, A. (2011). Dynamic replication in a data grid using a modified BHR region based algorithm. *Future Generation Computer Systems, 27*(2), 202-210. Elsevier B.V. doi:10.1016/j.future.2010.08.011

Stavrinides, G. L., & Karatza, H. D. (2010). Scheduling multiple task graphs with end-to-end deadlines in distributed real-time systems utilizing imprecise computations. *Journal of Systems and Software, 83*(6), 1004-1014. Elsevier Inc. doi:10.1016/j.jss.2009.12.025

Tu, M. (2010). Secure data objects replication in data grid. *IEEE Transactions on Dependable and Secure Computing, 7*(1), 50–64. doi:10.1109/TDSC.2008.19

Tu, M. (2010). Secure data objects replication in data grid. *IEEE Transactions on Dependable and Secure Computing, 7*(1), 50–64. doi:10.1109/TDSC.2008.19

Zaharia, M., Borthakur, D., & Sarma, J. S. Elmeleegy, K., Shenker, S., & Stoica, I. (2010). Delay scheduling: A simple technique for achieving locality and fairness in cluster scheduling. *Proceedings of the 5th European Conference on Computer Systems*, (pp. 265-278). doi: 10.1145/1755913.1755940

Zhao, W. (2009). Design and implementation of a Byzantine fault tolerance framework for Web services. *Journal of Systems and Software, 82*(6), 1004–1015. doi:10.1016/j.jss.2008.12.037

KEY TERMS AND DEFINITIONS

Active Replication: Active replication scheme, also known as state machine replication, schedules multiple copies on different processors.

Backup Overloading: Backup overloading comprises backup-backup (BB) overloading, primary-backup (PB) overloading and the hybrid approach.

Fault Tolerance: Measure of the ability of the system to sustain in the face of failures.

Primay/Backup: A replicated copy of resource or data that are used to recover from failures.

Rescheduling: Rescheduling is quite similar with the primary/backup scheme. However, it is a kind of dynamic behavior, and quite popular applied in real-time systems. Informally, rescheduling can tolerant any number of failures.

Workflow: Workflow technologies are proposed to facilitate and automate the execution of these scientific applications. It is defined as a series of operational steps that are scheduled for execution on computing infrastructure.

Chapter 6
Privacy in Participatory Sensing Systems

Tishna Sabrina
Monash University, Australia

Manzur Murshed
Monash University, Australia

ABSTRACT

Participatory sensing is a revolutionary new paradigm where ordinary citizens voluntarily sense their environment using readily available sensor devices such as mobile phones and systematically study, and then reflect on and share this information using existing wireless networks. It provides data collection, processing, and dissemination opportunities for socially-responsible applications spanning environmental monitoring, intelligent transportation, and public health, which are often not cost-viable using dedicated sensing infrastructure. The uniqueness of the participatory sensing system lies in its data communication infrastructure which is constituted by the deliberate participation of community people. However, the potential lack of privacy of the participants in such system makes it harder to ensure their voluntary contribution. Thus preserving privacy of the individuals contributing data has introduced a key challenge in this area. On the other hand, data integrity is desired imperatively to make the service trustworthy and user-friendly. Different interesting approaches have been proposed so far to protect privacy that will encourage participation of the owners of data sources in turn.

INTRODUCTION

The participatory sensing system is a system providing cost-effective, reliable, and impartial data collection, processing and dissemination.

DOI: 10.4018/978-1-4666-1888-6.ch006

Here the data communication is initiated by the ordinary citizens using their sensor-equipped mobile devices to collectively measure, contribute and thus develop database for the desired service by sharing information of mutual interest. The concept has become very popular lately with the massive boost in the usage of mobile devices capable of capturing, classifying and transmitting image, sound, location and other data, interactively or autonomously (Burke *et al.*, 2006). However, thinking practically none would be tolerant enough to contribute voluntarily if her privacy is not protected. The right against unsanctioned invasion of privacy by the government, corporations or individuals is part of many countries' privacy laws, and in some cases, constitutions. To work within the scope of privacy laws and meet the specific privacy requirements of the contributors is a must to run the system effectively. At the same time, the data of interest should maintain its credibility and the quality of service should meet the users' need in order to keep the service dependable and attractive to the users.

This chapter will introduce and explicate the system of participatory sensing as an emerging system with the intrinsic challenges of meeting privacy requirements and maintaining data integrity and the comparative study of various solutions approached so far. It will enlighten various sectors of privacy issues in participatory sensing system and possible approaches to face the privacy attack while maintaining the data integrity at the same time. It will discuss the pros and cons of various existing privacy preserving approaches. Among which some are computationally less expensive and real-time in operation while some may be more applicable in practical scenarios. Some concentrate on preserving privacy regardless the cost it has to pay by compromising the data integrity, while some overcome the dependency on a centrally trusted node to be more realistic.

BACKGROUND

The concept of participatory sensing system was proposed a few years back as a system that facilitates community people share data for mutual benefit. It is initiated by ordinary citizens using their privately-owned sensors to collectively measure and contribute by sharing information of mutual interest from the environment. Unlike web applications, here data is likely to be sensed from different places people visit in course of their daily life using ad hoc sensing devices mounted on cell phones, vehicles, etc. Then the data are sent to servers via some inexpensive wireless communication architecture. The server is able to generate aggregate results using the data received from all participating users. Accordingly it replies to the queries made by the users at any time. In short, it is a system by the people and for the people.

The interactive participatory sensing network is formed by mobile devices deployed to enable public and professional users gathering, analyzing and sharing specific information. Moreover, participatory sensing can easily scale up by attracting more volunteers among the ever-increasing mobile phone users. Devices connected to the Internet of Things will engage in many participatory sensing systems, most through automatic risk assessment without directly asking for user consent. As for example microphones and image-capturers attached with the mobile devices can record environmental data. Cell tower localization, GPS and other technologies can provide location and time-synchronization data. Wireless radios and on-

Figure 1. Basic concept of a participatory sensing system

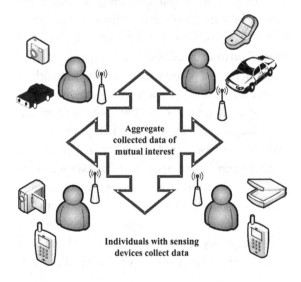

board processing equipments enable interaction with both local data processing and remote servers. Examples of participatory sensing system include documenting invasive plants and insects in national parks, monitoring heavy duty trucks idling or stopped in the neighborhood, reporting noise level, roughness, variation in elevation along bike routes, reporting garbage in the beaches, monitoring gasoline or grocery prices, monitoring the effectiveness of diet programs, reporting accidents or hazards etc. Unlike sensors of wireless sensor network, these sensors are always under their owners' control which implies battery backup is not a major concern as that in a wireless sensor network. The mobility of users carrying the sensor nodes makes it distinctive from the static feature of wireless sensor networks and incorporates dynamicity in it. With all these capabilities, participatory sensing is now considered as one of the most emerging research areas.

Different application areas have motivated the revolutionary concept of participatory sensing system among which some are public health, urban planning, natural resource management, etc.(Burke *et al.*, 2006). A participatory sensing approach can be used to gather real world acoustic data for noise planning tool for a community. An example application in the public health sector may be a system helping chronic patients and their doctors by autonomously capturing and selectively sharing information to link environmental factors with symptoms. Sehgal *et al.* (2008) demonstrated *MobiShop* to share consumer pricing information implementing a participatory sensing network of mobile phones. This application scheme is enhanced by Deng & Cox (2009) as they proposed *LiveCompare* for improving inter store grocery price comparison by utilizing individual price tags instead of error-prone parsing of docket information and by introducing incentive to encourage participation. Thus mobile camera phones network to track market dispersion has introduced the role of participatory sensing in commerce (Bulusu *et al.*, 2008) by addressing the challenge of collect-

ing offline non-structured information and thus enabling users to share market information and make decisions thereby.

PARTICIPATORY SENSING SYSTEMS

Participatory sensing system is also referred as urban sensing or people-centric sensing or sometimes opportunistic sensing. With participatory sensing the mobile user consciously opts to meet an application request out of personal or financial interest. A participatory approach incorporates people into significant decision stages of the sensing system, such as deciding what data is shared and to what extent privacy mechanisms should be allowed to impact data fidelity. Therefore, a participatory system design mainly focuses on tools and mechanisms that assist people to share, publish, search, interpret and verify information collected using mobile devices, as well as social techniques like reward schemes to encourage the involvement of the public. To put it in a very simple way, based on the active number of contributions made by a user she may get some service from the service provider for free of cost as asked for it in the form of reward.

With opportunistic sensing, the mobile node may not be aware of active applications. Instead a mobile device is utilized whenever its state matches the requirements of an application. This state is automatically detected; the owner of the device does not knowingly change the device state for the purpose of meeting the application request. To support symbiosis between the custodian and the system, sensor sampling occurs only if the privacy and transparency needs of the custodian are met. The main privacy concern here is the potential leak of personally sensitive information indirectly when providing sensor data (e. g., the custodian's location). To maintain transparency, opportunistic use of a device should not noticeably impact the normal user experience of the custodian as she uses it for her own needs. Thus, the primary challenges in opportunistic sensing are determining when the state of the sensing device matches the requirements of applications, and sampling when the device state and custodian requirements (i.e., privacy and transparency) are met.

The very basic architecture of a participatory sensing network consists of a collection of Mobile Nodes (MNs), some Points of Interest (POIs), and an Application Server (ApS) which is most of the time found to be a location-based service provider. The individual MNs that constitute the mobile sensing infrastructure are devices with sensing, computation, data storage, and wireless communication capabilities. These MNs are mostly carried by humans or attached to other moving objects such as vehicles. The POIs are the objects whose specific attribute information is to be captured by the MNs. The MNs collect and report the particular attributes of the POIs to the ApS. The ApS is the server that receives reports from MNs and based on that it makes the service available for the users e.g., informs users about the price of petrol pumps in their vicinity. The ApS is tasked to provide the attribute information on demand from the users.

A very common application of participatory sensing system is *PetrolWatch* (Dong *et al.*, 2008). In that participatory sensing application, the users automatically collect, contribute, and share fuel pricing information using camera enabled mobile phones mounted on the car dashboard. Whenever the vehicle approaches a service station, the *PetrolWatch* knows it through the use of GPS and GIS and the camera is automatically triggered to take snaps of fuel pricing billboards. These pictures are processed by computer vision algorithms to extract fuel prices. The fuel prices are annotated with location coordinates of the service station and time at which the capture took place and sent to ApS. Users can query the ApS to locate the cheapest petrol station in their vicinity. ApS responds to the query based on the database developed with the data contributed.

Figure 2. Basic architecture of a participatory sensing network

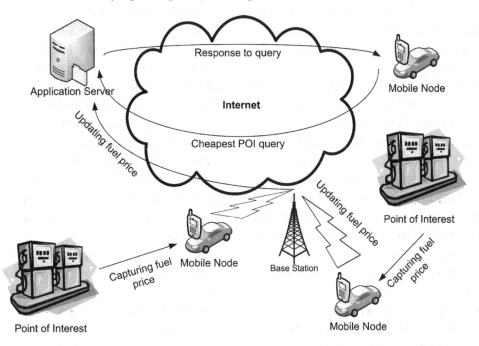

RESEARCH CHALLENGES

As the name of the system indicates, the communication infrastructure of this system is constituted by the participation of general mass of people which makes it unique in nature. But the potential lack of privacy of the participants in such systems makes it harder to ensure voluntary participation. While reporting about a hospital's AIDS treatment unit, if someone's HIV infection gets exposed, this would be the last choice for her. Similarly, while discussing some interesting aspects of a tourist spot, few people would risk unveiling her presence in a casino, especially if she comes from a conservative community. Thus the inherent challenge of preserving privacy in a participatory sensing system has attracted researchers in this field as soon as basic communication architecture for this application is proposed.

The people-centric network of participatory sensing approach offers not only enormous prospects of beneficial services but also some core challenges to face in order to make it useful and applicable in practical scenario. Ruzzelli *et al.* (2007) highlight some technical, commercial, and user acceptance issues related to deployment of participatory sensing systems. First and foremost issue is the assurance of privacy and security of the users as they participate in the system. As a basic right of the user, she should be protected against any malicious entity that can compromise the user information. In this practical world, users are generally interested to participate only if they can benefit for themselves or possibly understand the benefits for a wider community. Otherwise the users may gradually lose interest to participate actively and thus appears the challenge of identifying methods to motivate user participation. Then, the power consumption issue comes as users prefer to avoid early battery depletion of their mobile device. A responsible filtering and interpretation of data arriving from the users is a vital issue to ensure data management and usability. Choice of transmission standard is an issue which should consider aspects such as service cost, network scalability, expected data traffic, and power consumption of the device.

MobiSense (Reddy *et al.*, 2009) identifies and addresses some basic challenges like network coordination, data integrity, attestation, and privacy. One of the obvious reasons behind the huge potential of participatory sensing system is that it makes use of the existing technology and infrastructure. Then again this is the main cause evoking the challenge of coordinating systems designed for other purposes and provoking the use of models to infer about what cannot be directly measured or sensed. It faces the challenges of data control and user participation by verifying participant context, validity of samples, human contributions, and providing reputation scores for participants. It also identifies the concern of establishing data integrity while allowing participants to regulate their own privacy and participation. To address this challenge MobiSense proposes using end-to-end data pipeline from collection to analysis. All these underscoring factors involved in participatory sensing system drew the attention of many researchers in this area.

It is not unusual that the participants may start finding no interest to remain active in the system due to lack of any proper incentive scheme (Lee & Hoh, 2010). In absence of proper evaluation of the contribution, it is quite unavoidable for the system to start suffering from inadequate participation. As the system depends on people participating voluntarily to contribute data, insufficient contribution may cause degradation in the quality of service. That is why the concept of reward system is proposed to keep user participation up to the expected level and ensure ample data aggregation thereby.

It is also assumed that all the participants are rational in the sense that they do not want to destroy the system. However in practical scenario, it is not unusual if someone pursues to exploit the system and want to fail the system thereby. Considering this challenge, the concept of reputation scheme is introduced. The trustworthiness of users participating in the system is hence needed to be investigated. Then again, more complicated attack models like conspiracy attack between the server and some malicious users etc. are yet to be investigated.

TAXONOMY OF PRIVACY

Privacy appears to become a major issue for modern people as their daily life may involve many vulnerable exposures to fraud. With advancement of technology, people are getting more dependent on online shopping sites like eBay or more attracted to social networking sites like Facebook than before. But at the same time, frauds are also taking advantage of weak points of modern technology and getting more inventive. Recent growing incidents of credit card frauds, impersonating facebook accounts and even the latest launching of the classified media Wikileaks have impelled people focus on the significance of privacy.

The literature suggests, there exist two main types of privacy concerns: data-oriented and context-oriented. Data-oriented concerns concentrate on the privacy of data collected from or query posted to a participatory sensing system. On the other hand, context-oriented concerns focus on contextual information such as the location of the participant and the timing of the traffic

flow in a participatory sensing network. Another privacy issue of associating the user and the data evolves the concept of ownership privacy as the mobile user may not want to release the ownership information of a controversial contribution.

Balancing all the privacy requirements is a cumbersome job. Thanks to the variety of applications, the priority settings for privacy of the participants may be different. In most cases, location privacy is likely to be the main concern of the participants. While in some others the participants may prioritize their ownership privacy or contributed data privacy. The concept of friend network can address this concern of ownership privacy. The idea is to route the data through the network for a specific hop count before sending it to the application server.

PRIVACY ATTACKS AND ADVERSARY MODELLING

Privacy concerns may be violated by two types of attacks. First, a malicious node of the participatory sensing network may abuse its ability of decrypting data to compromise the payload being transmitted. Secondly, a third party adversary not having the ability to decrypt data payloads may eavesdrop the wirelessly transmitted data and track the traffic flow information hop-by-hop. For instance, when a malicious third party knows

Figure 3. Taxonomy of privacy in participatory sensing

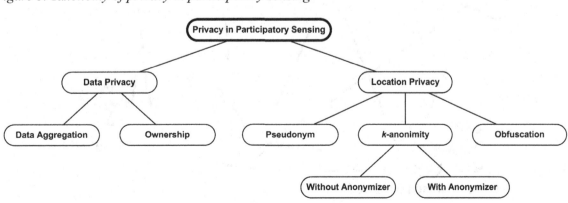

that a person is in a mental hospital, she is able to infer that the victim has a mental problem which is a severe breach in the victim's privacy (Lee *et al.*, 2005). Moreover, in the ubiquitous computing environment, it is easier to intercept the message than wired networks. The attacker can easily acquire the location information without the consent of the user from the intercepting message and then infer the context of the victim by collecting and analyzing the victim's location information within a certain period of time.

The focus of a malicious third party is to reveal the sensitive information included in the data captured however encoded it might be. From these eavesdropped encoded messages, an eavesdropper tries to infer sensitive information using same decoding approach of the ApS and thus reveal the association (e. g., location or data ownership) of the victim. For example, if the POI is in a close proximity of a cancer hospital and the adversary understands it from the eavesdropped messages,

then it may infer that the observer is a potential cancer patient.

Some prior information about the target victim strengthens adversary. It is natural that adversary has close access to victim in real world. So victim's user id is known. Then overhearing partial information beforehand, adversary may decide her strategy, i.e., where to position. For instance, someone overhears from the conversation of her boss that he would visit a doctor on next Friday in the afternoon. Now, if she receives some information from eavesdropped message that her boss was near a particular hospital at that particular time, she may deduce that her boss suffers from a particular disease which is being treated in that hospital.

Four potential privacy risks from adversary can be described as:

1. **Compromising ApS:** If adversary is able to compromise someone having access to ApS, i.e., an employee, which may be possible for

Figure 4. Adversary model

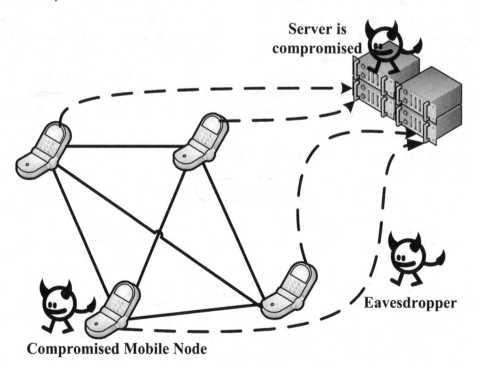

a short duration, it may have access to ApS data recovered. However, the basic security mechanism of ApS such as audit trail and access logs will not allow its compromised employee to continue the undue activity for long. Hence data captured in this way is limited in size and is likely to reveal little information.

2. **Eavesdropping user report within friend network:** It is highly likely that adversary is a member of friend network. Thus adversary will receive a certain amount of messages.

3. **Compromising the trusted third party:** An Anonymization Server (AS) is a trusted third party introduced to do the anonymization for the users. An adversary compromising the AS can eavesdrop the unanonymized POI-attribute and thus reveal the user's association straight away.

4. **Eavesdropping report towards ApS:** Residing near the ApS adversary can receive quite a good number of reports towards ApS. Having equipped with the same decoding application as ApS, it is likely to infer significant user-POI association.

PRESERVING DATA PRIVACY

If we talk about privacy in data communication, the first thing to come into our mind is encryption. In cryptography, encryption is the process of converting information using an algorithm to make it unreadable to anyone except those possessing special knowledge, usually referred to as a key. But the fact is that encryption is not viable in participatory sensing systems as in these cases the sensed dataset is usually small and predictable to defeat public key cryptography. Moreover, law enforcement agencies require public network dataflow remain unencrypted to mitigate national security threats.

Reddy *et al.* (2009) suggest that participatory sensing system can support several types of data collection:

1. **Top-down** data gathering, in which participants collect data to aid some expert designed experiments or investigations e. g. studies of environmental exposure, transportation usage pattern etc.

2. **Bottom-up** data gathering, in which people participate in same type of studies as in "top-down", but this time triggered from a need perceived within the community.

3. **Self-reflective** data gathering, in which data is sensed and collected from the system in a self-discovering way e. g. exploring one's dietary habit, regular driving patterns, social interactions etc.

Data oriented privacy is another side of researchers' interest which is true for all of the data collection types while being more evident in cases like self-reflective ones. Here, the main challenge is to allow individuals to share data for computing community statistics with privacy assurances. Because they may be interested in the statistics, but do not trust to share their private data with the third party. For example, as recording her weight periodically a weight watcher is expected to be interested to find efficacy of a diet chart regardless of her preference to hide her true weight and/or average weight and/or trend of weight i. e. loss or gain. It may be desired to find the average weight loss trend as well as the distribution of weight loss as a function of time on the diet from which individual's weight and/or weight trend should not be extractable.

Ganti *et al.* has (2008) developed mathematical foundations and architectural components for providing privacy guarantees on stream data in grassroots participatory sensing applications. They name their privacy-preserving architecture *PoolView*. It relies on data perturbation at the data source to allow users to ensure privacy of their individual data as they use tools that perturb such data prior to sharing for aggregation purposes. Then it uses community-wide reconstruction techniques to compute the aggregate information of the interest. Thus user privacy is preserved against traditional attacks e.g., filtering and specialized attacks e.g., MMSE at the same time community information both average and distribution are successfully recovered. It is best suited for a closed community with a known empirical data distribution. Context privacy is not addressed in this work; rather the focus is on data management privacy.

Pham *et al.* (2010) has enhanced the previous privacy preservation model ensuring correct reconstruction of community statistics in the case of correlated multidimensional time-series data. It also proposes perturbation-based approach of addressing data privacy in participatory sensing. The system is applied to construct accurate traffic speed maps in a small campus town from shared GPS data of participating vehicles, where the individual vehicle are allowed to "lie" about their actual location and speed at all times.

Privacy preserving data aggregation has been gaining popularity mainly in the field of sensor networks. But they differ from participatory sensing system in a way that those sensors are deployed with a single authority and their static topology conflict the dynamic property of mobile users that constitute the data infrastructure of a participatory sensing system. Being inspired from this big portion of work in sensor networks, Shi *et al.* (2010) propose PriSense to support user privacy in data aggregation. This technique is mainly based on data-slicing and mixing. Their initial idea is very close to PDA of He *et al.* (2007). However, the main difference lies in their application scenario and how the cover nodes are selected. Moreover, it supports a wide range of statistical additive and non-additive aggregation functions such as Sum, Average, Variance, Count, Max/Min, Median, Histogram, and Percentile with accurate aggregation results.

There is a variant of this problem named ownership privacy which is actually defined at client side and achieved at server side while receiving some data from a user. It mainly concentrates on associating the user and data. Due to some political reason or safety assurance, a user may not want to relate her with some controversial issue which she wants to share anonymously. Some classified media like WikiLeaks will be more than happy to deal with such controversial issues at a good cost. Thus evokes the requirement of privacy protection in such scenarios. Hu & Shahabi (2010) address this concern in their hot-potato-privacy-protection algorithm which is actually based on data routing through a friend network. Their main idea is to rout the data through a friend network before sending it to the destined server in a way that at the end the server will not be able to relate the data to the contributor. However it lacked highlight on how to ensure trustworthiness of the data contributed. At the same time, no reward scheme can be applied here as the users are not associated.

PRESERVING LOCATION PRIVACY

Location privacy preservation in the context of participatory sensing has some similarity with the same problem in ubiquitous computing and ad hoc computing areas. All user reports in a participatory sensing system contain user id to facilitate reputation history of contributors and reward eligibility measure for future service. Thus it exposes user's presence near the reported POI. But who will risk exposing her cancer treatment or casino night while contributing to community? Existing techniques to deal with it are based on *k*-anonymity, pseudonym or obfuscation concepts. The concept of *k*-anonymity states that a data or query collected by an application is *k*-anonymous if it is indistinguishable, with respect to some chosen attributes, among $k - 1$ other data or query received by the same application. Spatial cloaking is mostly used in *k*-anonymity schemes, although it suffers from lack of data integrity. The main idea of *k*-anonymity via spatial cloaking states that instead of sending the exact location information, the whole region of all the *k* nodes including the actual one is sent as the location tag of the data or query.

Creating Confusion

In one of the initial approaches, diffusion method has been employed by Lee *et al.* (2005) that scatters the users' location information to confuse the attacker. In addition, the base station or the access point transmits dummy messages that would look like real traffic but had no actual meaning. However, the diffusion has not been applied to multiple packets, and the dummy user has not been made more like a real user.

Beresford & Stajano (2003) concentrate on the class of location-aware applications that accept pseudonyms, and thus ensure anonymization of location information. A long-term pseudonym for each user does not provide much privacy. Hence the framework is based on frequently changing pseudonyms and thus users avoid being identified by the locations they visit. This framework is further developed by introducing the concept of mix zones as a connected spatial region of maximum size in which none of the users has registered any application call-back. In other words, mix zone (Beresford & Stajano, 2003) concept occurs in the scene whenever two users occupy the same place at the same time. Thus it provides unlinkability between users coming in and going out of the zone. However, a powerful adversary may use historical data to de-anonymize pseudonyms more accurately. Then again, smaller mix zone may not solve the anonymization problem in practical situations. It is also demonstrated that even with a relatively large mix zone, location privacy can be low due to the high temporal and spatial resolution of the location data generated by their applied system.

The model for CliqueCloak (Gedik *et al.*, 2005) accommodates different *k*-anonymity requirement for each user, but actually compromises real time operation as it waits until *k* different queries have been sent from a particular region. Path Confusion (Hoh *et al.*, 2007) incorporates a delay in the anonymization and just like CliqueCloak it compromises real time operation. In CacheCloak (Meyerowitz & Choudhury, 2009) mobility prediction is made to enable prospective path confusion while using potentially not-trusted A participatory sensing system. Mobility predictions are entirely based on previously observed user-movements and so prevent predictions from absurdities such as passing through impassible structures or going the wrong way on one-way streets.

Duckham & Kulik (2005) introduces obfuscation as a new technique to safeguard location privacy. It aims to achieve location privacy by providing imperfect spatial information. To degrade the quality of information about a person's location, instead of providing the single actual location, a set of locations is sent to the location based service provider. However, too much imperfection of information eventually degrades the quality of location-based service. This limitation is addressed here by introducing the idea of automated negotiation to achieve desired balance between the level of privacy and the quality of service. Nevertheless, selecting an appropriate obfuscation set is a difficult task. On the other hand, as a cloaked region the obfuscation set is a discrete one which incurs high communication cost to send it to the server.

Ardagna *et al.* (2007) enhances this obfuscation by introducing composition of various obfuscation techniques. It establishes the concept of relevance as a general functional metric for location accuracy that qualifies a location with respect to either accuracy or privacy requirements. As a cloaked region the obfuscation set is assumed to be planar and circular. Henceforth, the three possible variety of obfuscating a circular set are obfuscation by enlarging the radius, by shifting the center and by reducing the radius. To satisfy users privacy preferences, any one among the three or composition of any two techniques can be applied.

Another option for preserving location privacy when requesting a location-based service is pseudonym-based communication by the user. Zhong & Hengartner (2009) propose this interesting idea along with the introduction of multiple servers to trade off between centralized and distributed systems. The multiple servers are owned by different organizations that deploy location brokers to keep track of the current location of users. At the same time, secure comparison servers are there to interact with the user to confirm her current cell of having at least k users registered to it. Thus k-anonymity is achieved in a distributed manner to maintain user's location privacy. For scenarios where locations are public and visited by many people this pseudonym-based method is more appropriate. Because anonymization approaches will greatly decrease the data quality in these cases. On the other hand, space cloaking technique is not a preferable solution here as data with more geographical information is needed.

Shankar *et al.* (2009) has presented a fully decentralized and autonomous k-anonymity based client-side system, SybilQuery for preserving privacy of location-based queries. The basic framework has demonstrated that for each query by the client it would generate $k-1$ Sybil queries and thereby ensuring k-anonymity. It address the limitation of most of the spatial cloaking approaches for depending on a trusted third party anonymizer. Peer-to-peer techniques (e. g. Friend Network) on the other hand, rely on the participation of k peers and thus restrict the autonomy of such systems. The approach proposed here requires no change in the server side and only requires minor modifications to the querying clients. In the implementation, it takes as input a path to be followed by a vehicle along which a vehicle may issue several queries to the ApS. It will then output $k-1$ Sybil paths that statistically will resemble the input path. To make it more ap-

propriate in practical situations, the basic design can accommodate some extensions like randomizing path selection, handling active adversaries, endpoint caching, providing path continuity and adding GPS sensor noise. Thus the efficiently generated queries are indistinguishable from the real ones. The computational cost of this system mainly consists of handling different databases involved in its different steps.

The problem of query privacy is addressed in *SpaceTwist* (Yiu *et al.,* 2008) by applying obfuscation to generate an anchor and retrieve information on k nearest points of interest from the location based service provider. This scheme needs neither of any trusted third party nor any communication between other users to form groups. It maintains a good balance between privacy of the user and the success rate of finding closest point of interest as a reply of the query. Nevertheless it has not dealt with the dynamicity of any user's privacy preference and only concentrates on obtaining k nearest neighbour replies successfully.

Creating Anonymities with a Trusted Third Party

The very basic approach to address location privacy is k-anonymization which can be achieved with or without the help of a trusted third party. In cryptography, a trusted third party is defined as an entity which facilitates interactions between two parties who both trust the third party while the third party reviews all critical transaction communications between those parties, based on the ease of creating fraudulent digital content.

Xu & Cai (2009) focus on spatial cloaking and partition domain into number of safe subdomains as small as possible ensuring each subdomain contains k users and finally each node takes the subdomain it resides as its cloaking box. They provide analytical model of communication overhead to find this cloaking area. However, their approach is not compared in terms of cost or size of the cloaking area with similar works in literature.

This subdomain concept is somehow similar to Tessellation (Kapadia *et al.,* 2007), which is basically *k*-anonymity by generalization. It involves partitioning the geographic area into a collection of cells and merged neighboring cells to form tiles that users could use to mask their true locations. Kapadia *et al.* (2007) introduce this concept of tessellation, a novel blurring mechanism and propose a framework for nodes to receive tasks anonymously. It involves clustering to protect users' privacy against the system while reporting context, and *k*-anonymous report aggregation to improve the users' privacy against application receiving the context. *k*-anonymity requires that at least *k* reports are combined together before being revealed.

Almost at the same time, Machanavajjhala *et al.* (2007) has introduced the concept of *l*-diversity in order to address the limitations of *k*-anonymity based techniques while handling some specialized attacks. They have showed two types of attacks with which a k-anonymized dataset may encounter severe privacy problems. First, they show that an attacker can discover the values of sensitive attributes when there is little diversity in those sensitive attributes. Second, attackers often have background knowledge, and then k-anonymity does not guarantee privacy against attackers using background knowledge. They give a detailed analysis of these two attacks and propose a novel and powerful privacy definition called *l*-diversity. To ensure *l*-diversity, every group of tuples that share the same non-sensitive information should be associated with at least roughly equally distributed sensitive values.

Huang *et al.* (2009) has enhanced the concept of Tessellation for preserving spatial and temporal privacy in the context of participatory sensing. To protect identity disclosure of the transmitting user information, they adopt *k*-anonymization and to guard against attribute disclosure, they implement *l*-diversity. They have made an important contribution in identifying the significant problem of protecting participatory user's location privacy,

which is supposed to be important from user's viewpoint although her association with the reported POI needs to be revealed to ensure data integrity. However, this work does not consider the potential damage of data integrity by their proposed solution where users from different points of interest report the centre of a tile consisting of *k* points of interest or alternatively their mean location as location of all those different points. The receiving server will associate this reported point with the nearest point of interest and thus suffer from false association of *k*-1 other points within the tile. Data integrity is orthogonal to security/privacy. Hence finding an acceptable trade-off is a challenging task. Moreover, for the anonymization purpose they depend on third party entity, the AS which may suffer from the limitation of a single point of failure and being compromised.

Mokbel *et al.* (2006) has proposed a new framework named Casper that consists of two main components, the location anonymizer and the privacy-aware query processor. It provides location privacy for a query source accommodating user specific anonymity preference. Here the location anonymizer blurs the location information by spatial cloaking. Then the privacy-aware query processor which is embedded in the ApS gives a candidate answer list that is inclusive and minimal. It can be applied to a large number of mobile users. However it suffers from the dependency on a trusted third party.

Kalnis *et al.* (2007) has focused on anonymizing location of the query source and processing the transformed spatial queries. It discards Clique Cloak for compromising real time operation. The limitation of Huang's naive algorithm is also addressed here as they named it center-of-ASR attack. Two approaches of k-anonymization by spatial cloaking are proposed here-Nearest Neighbour Cloak (NNC) and Hilbert Cloak (HC). NNC addresses the center-of-ASR attack, but may compromise spatial anonymity in the presence of outliers. Then a theorem is established that a spatial cloaking algorithm will guarantee spatial k-anonymity if every tile satisfies the reciprocity property. HC satisfies the reciprocity property which states that a tile should contain the user and at least additional k-1 user and every user in that tile also will generate the same tile for the given k. It is achieved by utilizing Hilbert space-filling curve to transfer multi-dimensional data onto one-dimensional space. The adversary model states that ApS might be compromised or it might reside in between AS and ApS. But the weakness of this work is that the AS was assumed to be a trusted server which is not very practical and also may cause a single point of failure.

Bamba *et al.* (2008) give another dimension to spatial cloaking by introducing l-diversity along with k-anonymity and incorporating temporal cloaking functionality into its location perturbation process. At the same time, it maintains the user preference for privacy while accommodating its inherent dynamicity. One shortcoming of this approach is the communication overhead that incurs for every mobile user participating in the process. However, this factor can be balanced out considering the anonymization success rate and desired service achieved. Then again its dependency on a central trusted server makes it vulnerable in practical scenarios.

Creating Anonymities without any Trusted Third Party

To address the bottleneck of centralized trusted third party Chow *et al.* (2006) introduce a distributed system architecture and propose the first peer-to-peer (P2P) spatial cloaking algorithm to protect location privacy of mobile users. In this algorithm the user achieves k-anonymity by collaborating as a group with other k-1 nearby peers. Thus it approaches the dynamic behavior of the user. Then one of the peers from the group acts as the agent and forwards the query on behalf of the originator. As the query is based on the cloaked spatial region, the location based service provider provides the agent a list of candidate answer which

is readily forwarded to the originator. The query originator then acquires the actual answer filtering out the other false candidates. Here k-anonymity is a user specified privacy requirement which is a key aspect of this algorithm. Nonetheless this approach lacks highlighting how to deal with potentially compromised peers.

In the field of ad-hoc network, Hashem & Kulik (2007) contribute the same interesting idea of using one of the k-1 other mobile nodes to act as the query requestor to protect the identity of the query initiator and thus maintain the location privacy of the user. At the same time it addresses the short-coming of the previous work by coping with no trust among peers. It enhances the previous idea of Chow *et al.* (2006) by combining anonymity and obfuscation, thus addressing the potential security threat of trusting large number of group members. At first obfuscation is employed by each mobile user to hide her actual location in a locally cloaked area (LCA) both from the service provider and her peers as well. Then anonymity is achieved by combining its LCA with the LCAs of k-1 other peers. Finally that k-anonymized globally cloaked area (GCA) is sent as the location information while requesting a location based service from the service provider. Thus this approach is totally free from trusting any of the involved parties, neither the peers nor the service provider. However the communication among the neighbors and the service provider may increase the overall communication cost of this technique.

Takabi *et al.* (2009) introduces a cryptographic scheme to adopt the distributed collaborative approach to achieve location privacy based on k-anonymity. It requires neither a trusted third party nor the users to trust each other. Cryptography is used to learn the presence of minimum k users in the query area including the query originator. Thus it replaces the need of location broker from Zhong's (2008) solution. Though both the methods exhibit efficient implementation, a comparative study of their performance could have made it more worthwhile.

Hu & Shahabi (2010) has removed the dependency on a trusted third party by introducing the concept of friend network on which data travels. This is also more applicable for applications where data with more geographical information is needed and hence rejects spatial cloaking methods. Thus this approach aims to design a Privacy Assurance system for Mobile Sensing Networks (PA-MSN) to protect both location privacy and ownership privacy. Here they have designed a Hot-Potato-Privacy-Protection (HP³) algorithm in which the user sends the data to one of the friends and that friend will choose another friend to deliver the data to the next hop. The last user sends the data to the server when the pre-defined hopping threshold is reached. The possible adversary may be a malicious server or a compromised peer mobile user. To address malicious users the image data is encrypted using the server's public key and the communications between friends are secured by some pre-negotiated shared secret between each pair of them. However this can be risky for friends as being unaware of the content they may be transferring data of anti-social activities. Due to the limited number of hops everyone becomes a suspect for a malicious server and it cannot make an attack on the user privacy with a probability greater than $1/n$ even with the full knowledge of the network. To address the problem of interception by compromised nodes, they have extended their algorithm and introduced image splitting and redundancy, where each piece takes individual path to reach the server. The strength of their work lies in addressing two privacy issues- location and ownership at the same time, considering two attack models- malicious server and corrupted user. However they have not showed any study on cost of redundancy and image splitting. Moreover they have not mentioned anything about the optimum number of friends, since vulnerability may arise from very few numbers of friends.

Hashem *et al.* (2010) further investigates it in the context of group of users. Group queries offer a new dimension of privacy challenge as here

location of all group members are vital to find out their nearest neighbour while at the same time any group member can be compromised. A novel framework based on a decentralized architecture for privacy preserving group nearest queries is introduced by Hashem *et al.* (2010). The concept of private filter is developed to determine the actual group nearest neighbour without revealing user location to any involved party, against the queries from a spread out group of users providing their locations as regions instead of exact points to the service provider. However, this approach does not work for group of size 2. This is an interesting problem with similar issues of participatory sensing applications.

LOCATION PRIVACY AND DATA INTEGRITY TRADE-OFF

While privacy requirement of the participants is needed to be ensured, in contrast data integrity is also desired undeniably to make the service dependable and intelligible. However, it is found that data integrity and user privacy are somehow orthogonal. Database literatures also support this concept in the Bell-La Padula model and Biba model where the former ensures security at the expense of integrity and the latter ensures integrity at the expense of security. So there should be a wise trade-off of data integrity and user privacy depending on the application of the particular participatory sensing system and the user's requirements. To simultaneously protect privacy and encourage participation of the owners of data sources, different approaches have been proposed so far. But, very few of them have focused on achieving data integrity while preserving privacy which is an indispensable requirement of participatory sensing. The spatial cloaking approach gives very good solution for maintaining location privacy. But it somehow ignored the part of data integrity which is met by the method of subset coding. Recently we have addressed this problem by developing a subset coding scheme, which aims to control the balance between location privacy and data integrity by exploiting the volume of information available.

Murshed *et al.* (2010) address this highly significant problem of location anonymization with subset coding without major loss of data integrity and proposed a greedy anonymization scheme to make participatory sensing an acceptable technology to the community. In their approach an MN sends report about an observed POI to AS via a friend network. The AS returns the anonymized version of the report, in the form of a carefully selected subset of POIs along with the observed attribute, to the MN using the reverse friend-chain. The MN forwards the anonymized report to the application server (ApS). In the threat model, the adversary eavesdrops messages for a short time close to the base station of its region of interest and uses the same decoding technique as ApS.

They propose to report location anonymously as a subset of locations where subsets will be formulated in such a way that the receiving server may achieve high data integrity, but the adversary receiving a limited amount of transmitted reports would fail to do so. Decoding is performed on majority association. At each observation, a subset with the maximum match is selected to expand with next level rule. The proposed scheme enables the application server to retain complete data integrity as no privacy is expected to be preserved at this level. On the contrary, privacy is preserved significantly at adversary level where degradation of data integrity is an added benefit; not a liability.

The proposed subset coding technique was presented in naive form in 2010 for a simplified system model with trusted AS and naive adversary. In 2011 the same research group has enhanced the idea to achieve almost lossless data integrity while rendering protections against a significantly hostile adversary model. Robust system architecture is proposed by them to safeguard against different types of adversaries including the colluding ones. It introduces the concept of friend network in the

field of privacy in participatory sensing system to deal with communication through insecure channel. It also enhances the previous greedy anonymization algorithm by considering a number of alternative heuristics to finally achieve almost lossless data integrity.

Success of any participatory sensing system depends on its ability to guarantee contributor's location privacy from potential adversaries. The proposed subset rule-based k-anonymization technique offers agreed level of location privacy from the potential adversaries while retaining very high data integrity at the application server end. Success of the Internet of Things depends on such robust privacy aware communication protocols.

It identifies that traditional k-anonymization by spatial cloaking can achieve only $1/k$ data integrity which for reasonable high anonymity is significantly poor performance. Then again, most of them initially focus on trusted AS which is a hard assumption. Some later models relax the assumption adding some Gaussian noise to user reports. However, a reasonably strong adversary should be able to infer actual data from this type of noise.

FUTURE RESEARCH DIRECTIONS

Whereas traditional wireless sensor network is usually deployed in large unattended areas to monitor specific data, participatory sensing system has completely ad hoc topology with high mobility and here sensed data has very significant real world implication. That is why it is believed to become a very popular system in near future. Huge popularity of Wikipedia and Facebook/Twitter and also numerous blogs where contribution from general people develop the contents indicate the potentiality of such system very soon. The participatory sensing system, its applications and limitations offer a new era of research.

With many prospective application scenarios, it worth investigating its prospect to replace the expensive, traditional and dedicated sensor network infrastructure. Some issues are there regarding communication protocols which have to be cost effective. Another important point to note here is that, contributors to participatory sensing system have to provide their user identifications while reporting so that undue attempt to feed false data into system can be filtered along with blacklisting their senders. This will facilitate building up a reputation scheme that is required for some applications. Moreover, this will allow the system develop a reward-based service provision when users will request for information. Those who have contributed more, may access more significant data. This policy will encourage users participate more and eventually increase the usability of the system to a great extent. Participation is rewarded in many other systems such as credit card payment system with the same motive. The underlying fact is that, the reports to the server cannot be anonymous; it has to contain a registered user's identification.

More realistic system model with far stronger adversary that positions in multiple areas to capitalize weakness of wireless communication needs to be sorted out. These realistic assumptions have brought new philosophical research areas and also made the problem significantly more complex. To increase data integrity significantly all possible modifications in the anonymization scheme needs to be explored.

To enhance the acceptance of the system it needs to be more close to reality and so dynamicity of human nature for privacy preference needs to be incorporated. Researchers from field of social science are still exploring the distinctiveness of human nature. As a result people from a same community can vary extensively in their preference for privacy. Sometimes age group or economy group can vaguely represent people's concern about privacy. Incorporating this variation in preference for privacy of the mass participating in the system offers a new research area.

The introduction of motivating schemes for participation is considered to be very effective in recent time. Without proper inspiration people may drop off participation which will make the system a failure in course of time. Keeping that in mind, reward policies for active participation are proposed recently. Different variations of this reward methodology considering different application scenarios and different target people is another worth investigating field in this field of study. Rewards in cash or in the form of service may be offered to users based on the degree of their respective participation. Naturally, importance of data varies according to time of arrival, source of data, etc. The incentive mechanism should consider all these. On the other hand, if the mechanism deprives some users initially based on the importance, eventually the unsatisfied user may cease to participate in future and number of users will decrease consequently. An appropriate user behaviour model needs to be developed to mitigate this risk.

With introduction of the incentive scheme, malicious party may exploit it for personal benefit. Since reward will be higher for observation about remote places, some people may send fabricated report about remote areas without going there. Detecting such attempt by checking inconsistency of reports is a non-trivial research challenge. Again, data is likely to change periodically in many application scenarios such as price of commodities. This has to be distinguishable from any malicious attempt to inject fabricated data. For example, real estate people may want to have less noise level reported about a certain area where their clients have houses to sell and therefore feed some false noise monitoring report into system. Designing a system intelligent enough to distinguish between false data and real fluctuation of data is a researcher's job.

Privacy of users actually goes beyond the concept of location privacy in the context of PSS. For example, in consumer price sharing application scenario, a user may not care about presence in a super-store, but will be very sensitive about purchase of a particular item such as alcohol or a particular medicine. In this case, product-level privacy may be incorporated with spatial privacy. Moreover, adversary inference often depends heavily on temporal correlation of spatial occurrence. Hence, incorporating these additional dimensions to the location privacy scheme poses another research issue.

DISCUSSION

The prospect of participatory sensing systems and their applications are manifold. It is necessary to identify and address the issues that may work against the success of this system. The popularity of Wikileaks is directly linked up to its will and ability to keep the sources anonymous. Similar factor will prevail behind the success of participatory sensing system. Hence, user's privacy must be protected to bring this concept into reality. On the other hand, along with ensuring privacy, integrity of data also needs to be maintained. Here data integrity is the main quality of service and it implies the correct association of point of interest with the reported attributes. For example, reported price of a particular store needs to be associated correctly, otherwise user will end up in purchasing at higher price from different store which diminishes the main purpose of such system. This privacy-integrity trade-off poses a significant research challenge which is indispensable to be solved satisfactorily to ensure voluntary participation of large number of users. So far the researchers have proposed different methods like obfuscation, pseudonym and *k*-anonymity based techniques among which some are offering good privacy protection while some other may balance it with the data integrity. It is important to choose the proper scheme considering the main application purpose of the system.

CONCLUSION

Participatory sensing system is one of the most flourishing systems of recent days. However the concept has to face the challenges of smart processing of inputs from ubiquitous devices such as mobile phones, handling of collected information in a secured and privacy preserving way, and ensuring user-friendly and timely delivery of data maintaining desired integrity. We addressed the highly significant problem of location anonymization without major loss of data integrity and proposed a greedy anonymization scheme to make participatory sensing an acceptable technology to the community.

As Gadzheva (2008) suggested that protecting privacy in an increasingly transparent society would only be possible with the development of an intelligent interplay between technological design and legal regulation that would reflect the great expansion of ubiquitous data processing and surveillance capabilities. Failure to address the legitimate concerns of users could have a negative impact on businesses, network operators and service providers and seriously impact the deployment of those beneficial services.

REFERENCES

Ardagna, C. A., Cremonini, M., Damiani, E., Vimercati, S. D. C., & Samarati, P. (2007). *Location privacy protection through obfuscation-based techniques*. In IFIP WG 11.3 Working Conference on Data and Applications Security.

Bamba, B., Liu, L., Pesti, P., & Wang, T. (2008). *Supporting anonymous location queries in mobile environments with PrivacyGrid*. In World Wide Web Conference.

Beresford, A. R., & Stajano, F. (2003). Location privacy in pervasive computing. *IEEE Pervasive Computing / IEEE Computer Society and IEEE Communications Society*, 2(1), 46–55. doi:10.1109/MPRV.2003.1186725

Bulusu, N., Chou, C. T., Kanhere, S., Dong, Y., Sehgal, S., Sullivan, D., & Blazeski, L. (2008). *Participatory sensing in commerce: using mobile camera phones to track market price dispersion.* In UrbanSense Workshop Program at ACM Conference on Embedded Networked Sensor Systems.

Burke, J., Estrin, D., Hansen, M., Parker, A., Ramanathan, N., Reddy, S., & Srivastava, M. B. (2006). *Participatory sensing.* In ACM Conference on Embedded Networked Sensor Systems.

Chow, C. Y., Mokbel, M., F., & Liu, X. (2006). A peer-to-peer spatial cloaking algorithm for anonymous location-based services. In *Proceedings of the 14th annual ACM International Symposium on Advances in Geographic Information Systems*, 2006.

Deng, L., & Cox, L. P. (2009). Grocery bargain hunting through participatory sensing. In *Mobile Computing Systems and Applications*. Livecompare.

Dong, Y. F., Blazeski, L., Sullivan, D., Kanhare, S. S., Chou, C. T., & Bulusu, N. (2009). *PetrolWatch: Using mobile phones for sharing petrol prices.* In International Conference on Mobile Systems, Applications and Services.

Dong, Y. F., Kanhare, S. S., Chou, C. T., & Bulusu, N. (2008, June). *Automatic collection of fuel prices from a network of mobile cameras.* In IEEE International Conference on Distributed Computing in Sensor Systems.

Duckham, M., & Kulik, L. (2005). Lecture Notes in Computer Science: *Vol. 3693. Simulation of obfuscation and negotiation for location privacy* (pp. 31–48).

Gadzheva, M. (2008). Location privacy in a ubiquitous computing society. *International Journal of Electronic Business, 6*(5). doi:10.1504/IJEB.2008.021181

Ganti, R. K., Pham, N., Tsai, Y., & Abdelzaher, T. F. (2008). *Poolview: Stream privacy for grassroots participatory sensing.* In ACM Conference on Embedded Networked Sensor Systems.

Gedik, B., & Liu, L. (2005). *Location privacy in mobile systems: A personalized anonymization model.* In IEEE International Conference on Distributed Computing Systems.

Hashem, T., & Kulik, L. (2007). *Safeguarding location privacy in wireless ad-hoc networks.* In International Conference on Ubiquitous Computing.

Hashem, T., Kulik, L., & Zhang, R. (2010) *Privacy preserving group nearest neighbour queries.* In International Conference on Extending Database Technology.

He, W., Liu, X., Nguyen, H., Nahrstedt, K., & Abdelzaher, T. F. (2007). *PDA: Privacy-preserving data aggregation in wireless sensor networks.* In IEEE Conference on Computer Communications.

Hoh, B., Gruteser, M., Xiong, H., & Alrabady, A. (2007). *Preserving privacy in GPS traces via uncertainty-aware path cloaking.* In ACM Conference on Computer and Communications Security.

Hu, L., & Shahabi, C. (2010). *Privacy assurance in mobile sensing networks: Go beyond trusted servers.* In IEEE Pervasive Computing and Communication.

Huang, K. L., Kanhare, S. S., & Lu, W. (2010). Preserving privacy in participatory sensing systems. *Computer Communications, 33*(11). doi:10.1016/j.comcom.2009.08.012

Kalnis, P., Ghinita, G., Mopuratidis, K., & Papadias, D. (2007). Preventing location-based identity inference in anonymous spatial queries. *IEEE Transactions on Knowledge and Data Engineering, 9*(12), 1719–1733. doi:10.1109/TKDE.2007.190662

Kapadia, A., Triandopoulos, N., Cornelius, C., Peebles, D., & Kotz, D. (2007). *AnonySense: Opportunistic and privacy-preserving context collection*. In International Conference on Pervasive Computing.

Lee, G., Kim, W., & Kim, D. (2005). *An effective method for location privacy in ubiquitous computing*. In Embedded and Ubiquitous Computing workshops.

Lee, J. S., & Hoh, B. (2010). *Sell your experiences: a market mechanism based incentive for participatory sensing*. In IEEE International Conference on Pervasive Computing and Communications.

Machanavajjhala, A., Kifer, D., Gehrke, J., & Venkitasubramaniam, M. (2007). L-diversity: privacy beyond k-anonymity. *ACM Transactions on Knowledge Discovery from Data, 1*(1), 3. doi:10.1145/1217299.1217302

Meyerowitz, J., & Choudhury, R. R. (2009). *Hiding stars with fireworks: Location privacy through camouflage*. In International Conference on Mobile Computing and Networking.

Mokbel, M. F., Chow, C. Y., & Aref, W. G. (2006). The new Casper: Query processing for location services without compromising privacy. In *Proceedings of the 32nd International Conference on Very Large Data Bases*.

Murshed, M., Iqbal, A., Sabrina, T., & Alam, K. H. (2011). *A subset coding based k-anonymization technique to trade-off location privacy and data integrity in participatory sensing systems*. In IEEE International Symposium on Network Computing and Applications.

Murshed, M., Sabrina, T., Iqbal, A., & Alam, K. H. (2010). *A novel anonymization technique to trade-off location privacy and data integrity in participatory sensing systems*. In International Conference on Network and System Security.

Pham, N., Ganti, R. K., Uddin, Y. S., Nath, S., & Abdelzaher, T. F. (2010). *Privacy-preserving reconstruction of multidimensional data maps in vehicular participatory sensing*. In European Conference on Wireless Sensor Networks.

Reddy, S., Samanta, V., Burke, J., Estrin, D., Hansen, M., & Srivastava, M. (2009). *MobiSense – Mobile network services for coordinated participatory sensing*. In International Symposium on Autonomous Decentralized Systems.

Ruzzelli, A., Jurdak, R., & O'Hare, G. (2007). *Managing mobile-based participatory sensing communities*. In Participatory Research Workshop at ACM Conference on Embedded Networked Sensor Systems.

Sehgal, S., Kanhere, S. S., & Chou, C. T. (2008). *Mobishop: Using mobile phones for sharing consumer pricing information*. In IEEE International Conference on Distributed Computing in Sensor Systems.

Shankar, P., Ganapathy, V., & Iftode, L. (2009). *Privately querying location-based services with SybilQuery*. In ACM International Conference on Ubiquitous Computing.

Shi, J., Zhang, R., Liu, Y., & Zhang, Y. (2010). *Prisense: Privacy-preserving data aggregation in people-centric urban sensing systems*. In IEEE Conference on Computer Communications.

Takabi, H., & Joshi, J. B. D., & Karimi, H. A. (2009). *A collaborative k-anonymity approach for location privacy in location-based services*. In International Conference on Collaborative Computing: Networking, Applications and Worksharing.

Xu, T., & Cai, Y. (2009). *Location cloaking for safety protection of ad hoc networks*. In IEEE International Conference on Computer Communications.

Zhong, G., & Hengartner, U. (2009). *A distributed k-anonymity protocol for location privacy.* In IEEE International Conference on Pervasive Computing and Communications.

ADDITIONAL READING

Beresford, A. R., & Stajano, F. (2003). Location privacy in pervasive computing. *IEEE Pervasive Computing / IEEE Computer Society and IEEE Communications Society, 2*(1), 46–55. doi:10.1109/MPRV.2003.1186725

Hashem, T., Kulik, L., & Zhang, R. (2010). *Privacy preserving group nearest neighbour queries.* In International Conference on Extending Database Technology.

Hu, L., & Shahabi, C. (2010). *Privacy assurance in mobile sensing networks: Go beyond trusted servers.* In IEEE Pervasive Computing and Communication.

Huang, K. L., Kanhare, S. S., & Lu, W. (2010). Preserving privacy in participatory sensing systems. *Computer Communications, 33*(11). doi:10.1016/j.comcom.2009.08.012

Lee, J. S., & Hoh, B. (2010). *Sell your experiences: A market mechanism based incentive for participatory sensing.* In IEEE International Conference on Pervasive Computing and Communications.

Murshed, M., Sabrina, T., Iqbal, A., & Alam, K. H. (2010). *A novel anonymization technique to trade-off location privacy and data integrity in participatory sensing systems.* In International Conference on Network and System Security.

KEY TERMS AND DEFINITIONS

Adversary: A rival entity interested enough to gather sensitive information to victimize someone from the background.

Data Integrity: Ability to infer information with reliability.

Data Privacy: Preference of maintaining confidentiality of personal information or possession of some controversial records.

Friend Network: Basically a social network established by the mobile users. Through personal contact any two users can add each other as friend. Alternatively, a new user may ask the server to provide a list of users who are willing to be added by others.

k-Anonymity: Being undistinguishable among $k - 1$ other similar entities.

Location Privacy: Preference of maintaining confidentiality of personal whereabouts.

Participatory Sensing: People participating actively to sense attributes of social or commercial interest in order to facilitate enriching and sharing the information derived in time of need.

Trusted Third Party: An entity which facilitates interactions between two parties who both trust the third party while the third party reviews all critical transaction communications between those parties.

Section 2
Emerging Technologies and Advanced Platforms

Chapter 7
A Computation Migration Approach to Elasticity of Cloud Computing

Cho-Li Wang
The University of Hong Kong, Hong Kong

King Tin Lam
The University of Hong Kong, Hong Kong

Ricky Ka Kui Ma
The University of Hong Kong, Hong Kong

ABSTRACT

Code mobility is the capability to dynamically change the bindings between code fragments and the location where they are executed. While it is not a new concept, code mobility has reentered the limelight because of its potential uses for cloud computing—a megatrend in recent years. The strongest form of mobility allows the execution state of a computational component to be captured and restored on another node where execution is seamlessly continued. Computation migration can achieve dynamic load balancing, improve data access locality, and serve as the enabling mechanism for auto-provisioning of cloud computing resources. Therefore, it is worthwhile to study the concepts behind computation migration and its performance in a multi-instance cloud platform. This chapter introduces a handful of migration techniques working at diverse granularities for use in cloud computing. In particular, this chapter highlights an innovative idea termed stack-on-demand (SOD), which enables ultra-lightweight computation migrations and delivers a flexible execution model for mobile cloud applications.

INTRODUCTION

Cloud computing is emerging as an important paradigm shift in how computing demands are being met in future. It is at an all-time high and actively transforming the role of IT in businesses in recent years. Different people may have different understanding and definitions on cloud computing. But in essence, it can be seen as a model for Internet-wide access to a shared pool of hardware (processors, storage, etc) and software that are configurable on demand and presented as pay-per-use utility services, primarily *Software-as-*

DOI: 10.4018/978-1-4666-1888-6.ch007

a-Service (SaaS), Platform-as-a-Service (PaaS) and Infrastructure-as-a-Service (IaaS). Cloud computing poses both opportunities and challenges. Opportunities center on whatever savings (in upfront expenditure, running costs, energy, etc) coming from improved resource utilization and deployment ease.

Enterprises face the problem of high management cost when running their own data centers. It is difficult to estimate the adequate scale of servers—underestimation leads to overloaded conditions while over-provisioning just means wasted investment. On-demand scalability or elasticity is an essential attribute of cloud computing that eases this trouble and reduces the total cost of ownership. With cloud architecture, computing resources can be rapidly provisioned (scale-out) and released (scale-in) with minimal management effort or service provider interaction (Mell & Grance, 2009). Such an elastic infrastructure marks the beauty of cloud computing for enhancing IT delivery's efficiency and cost-effectiveness. Challenges however include issues of data privacy, security, performance, availability and interoperability. Despite the compelling benefits of cost and flexibility, these areas need significant improvement for cloud computing to go beyond being a fledgling technology.

While enterprises, especially SMBs, are getting on the cloud bandwagon, many may still dread to become a cloud convert. Performance is increasingly becoming their paramount concern ahead of deploying their applications on clouds because it may have direct impact on quality of service and revenue. When applications move from an on-premises platform to a cloud platform, the possible increased latency could overshadow the great promise of clouds. The effect of latency on revenue has been evidenced by various key websites' analyses: Amazon found every 100 ms delay cost them 1% drop in sales; Google and Yahoo! got 20% and 5-9% fewer traffic from an extra load time of 500 ms and 400 ms respectively (Stefanov,

2009). The impact on latency-sensitive applications can be even more dramatic. TABB Group estimates that if a broker's e-trading platform is 5 ms behind the competition, it could lose at least 1% of its flow, analogous to a revenue loss of $4 million per millisecond (Willy, 2008). Todd Hoff listed nine sources of latency in his article (Hoff, 2009); and among them, service dependency and geographical distribution tend to be the aggravated factors adding to extra latency when applications go hosted on clouds.

This is an expected aftereffect of adopting the cloud model which abstracts away network infrastructure details. While the abstraction can be a useful concept, it tends to weaken relationships between software components and their associated data. For example, when scaling out, or if compute cycles and storage are to be bought at their preferential rates from different cloud providers, an application may go distributed and involve more hops over the Internet for interaction, resulting in higher user-perceived latency. Therefore, any techniques that can effectively trim latency down are an important contribution to cloud computing. Collocation of computation and data access is one approach, and can be dynamically achieved by *computation migration (CM)*—an umbrella term of all the concepts behind moving an active computational component from one node to another with its execution state preserved. Besides improving data access locality, CM can also facilitate dynamic load distribution, fault resilience (migrating processes out of nodes with partial failures), and improved system administration (e.g. for server consolidation, graceful shutdown of nodes). It is a useful approach to on-demand cloud provisioning. With virtual machine (VM) migration technology, for instance, one can pool or shrink computing resources as desired by moving VM instances in or out over a cluster of nodes or even a wide area network.

The importance of mobility to cloud computing is well-established and evidenced by substantial work on VM migration, e.g. VMware vMotion (Nelson, Lim, & Hutchins, 2005) and Xen (Clark et al., 2005). However VM migration applies at the infrastructure level only and is too monolithic to serve purposes like offering rapid elasticity and improving locality that only lightweight CM mechanisms may fit. In this chapter, we will demonstrate the use of *multi-level mobility*, ranging from as coarse as a VM instance to as fine as a runtime stack frame, to build an elastic computing infrastructure. We will study and compare several CM projects, namely WAVNet (Xu, 2010), G-JavaMPI (Chen, Ma, Wang, Lau, & Li, 2006), JESSICA2 (Zhu, Wang, & Lau, 2002) and SODEE (Ma, Lam, Wang, & Zhang, 2010), which have been launched to the HKU Grid Point of the China National Grid (CNGrid). WAVNet (Wide-Area Virtual Network) is designed for Internet-wide live VM migration and dynamic IaaS provisioning. G-JavaMPI is a Java-based grid middleware system with transparent MPI process migration. JESSICA2 is a cluster-wide Java virtual machine (JVM) which supports dynamic thread migration across cluster nodes. In SODEE ("SOD execution engine"), we highlight a novel concept, *stack-on-demand (SOD)*, whose essence is to export *just-enough* execution states of a stack machine for agile mobility. We will also see how these systems can collectively form an elastic cloud ecosystem where computational components can move around efficiently.

The rest of this chapter is organized as follows. First, a review of the evolution of CM techniques and approaches to on-demand scaling are given in the background section. Next, we present our developed CM systems and their integration into a multi-level mobility-driven cloud architecture. The performance characteristics of the various CM systems are then evaluated and compared on a Xen-based multi-instance cloud platform. Finally, we outline some future research directions and conclude this chapter.

BACKGROUND

Evolution of Computation Migration Techniques

Mobility support has been a hot research topic over the last two decades. Table 1 shows a comprehensive listing, sorted by year of publication or system release, of all the major work done in this area. Several surveys and publications of latest work classified as follows have covered most of the projects whose original references can be found there by searching their project names: process migration and object migration (Nuttall, 1994; Milojičić, Douglis, Paindaveine, Wheeler, & Zhou, 2000), mobile agents (Fuggetta, Picco, & Vigna, 1998; Braun & Rossak, 2004), thread migration (Meza & Ruz, 2007), Java thread migration (Bouchenak & Hagimont, 2002; Quitadamo, Cabri, & Leonardi, 2008), and VM migration (Hines, Deshpande, & Gopalan, 2009; Riteau, Morin, & Priol, 2010). *Process migration* and *object migration* (a.k.a. *mobile objects*) have been intensively studied since 1980s, so we would skip their details which can be found in the aforesaid surveys. Below we would highlight the core ideas, possible issues and recent trends for the rest of the migration techniques.

Mobile code paradigms like code shipping (a.k.a. *remote evaluation*) and code fetching (a.k.a. *code-on-demand*, e.g. Java applets) can help reduce network traffic by moving the code towards the execution site. *Mobile agents (MAs)* are the next milestone, extending the paradigms with two important properties: (1) the program is developed as an *autonomous* software agent that can halt and ship itself to another computer, and continue execution there; (2) the execution state is maintained along the whole migration itinerary, i.e. the MA does not restart execution from the beginning but continues where it left off. MAs can capture state, either programmatically (*weak mobility*) or transparently (*strong mobility*) via the underlying runtime support, and migrate state

Table 1. List of computation mobility projects

Process migration at kernel level *Monolithic kernels*: Accent (1981), Locus (1983), Mosix (1985), Charlotte (1987), Sprite (1988), V (1988), Kerrighed (1998), OpenSSI (2001), openMosix (2002), Bproc (2002) *Microkernels*: Mach (1986), Arcade (1989), Amoeba (1990), Chorus (1991), RHODOS (1991)
Process migration at user level *Checkpoint libraries*: Condor (1988), LSF (1994), libckpt (1994), MPVM (1995), CoCheck (1996), CosMiC (1997) *Java middleware*: Merpati (2000), M-JavaMPI (2002), G-JavaMPI (2006)
Object migration (mobile objects) *C/C++/Misc.*: Emerald (1987), SOS (1989), Amber (1989), COOL (1990), Davies* (1992), Olsen* (1992), Dome (1995) *Java-based*: JavaParty (1997), Ajents (1999), AdJava (2002)
Mobile agents *C/Tcl/Misc.*: Tacoma (1995), Telescript/Odyssey (1996), Agent TCL/D'Agents (1997), ARA (1997) *Java-based*: Concordia (1997), Mole (1998), Aglets (1998), Voyager (1998), MOA (1998), Grasshopper (1999), ADK (1999), Ajanta (1999), Tracy (2001)
Thread migration Amber (1989), Cronk* (1996), Nomadic Threads (1996), Ariadne (1996), Arachne (1998), NOMAD (1998), Millipede (1998), PM2 (1999), D-CVM (1999), MigThread (2002), Oz (2005), DSM-PEPE (2007)
Java thread migration *App-level*: *source preprocessor*: Wasp (1998), JavaGo (1999); *bytecode preprocessor*: JavaGoX (2000), Brakes (2000) *JVM-level*: *interpreter-based*: Sumatra (1997), ITS (2000), JESSICA (2000); *JIT-compliant*: CTS (2002), JESSICA2 (2002) *Midway*: CIA (2002), Mobile JikesRVM (2008)
Virtual machine migration *Non-live*: Collective (2002), Zap (2002), Denali (2002) *Live*: *pre-copy*: VMware vMotion (2003), Xen (2005), KVM (2007), OpenVZ (2007); *post-copy*: Hines* (2009) *Wide-area live*: VM Turntable (2006), Bradford* (2007), Shrinker (2010)
* Surname of the publication's 1st author for absence of system/project names

along with the code (class files) at its chosen point of runtime. However, most Java-based MA toolkits, such as IBM Aglets, do not provide means of capturing of the execution stack and program counters of the threads owned by the agent, due to some limitations of the JVM. They can only capture object state from the heap via Java serialization. Thus, developers must write MA codes in a way using the heap as the sole repository of all the execution state to avoid loss of state sitting on the stacks for any thread.

Research on transparent *thread migration* patches the above loophole and gives rise to strong-mobility MAs. Thread migration is however very challenging due to tangled relationship among threads sharing and locking objects on the heap and pointer incompatibility that earlier approaches (Cronk, Haines, & Mehrotra, 1996) to migrating user threads in DSMs have to struggle through. On top of Java, its increasingly powerful features have shed some light on this issue for heterogeneous machine architectures. Java thread migration techniques can be classified into application-level and JVM-level approaches. The former works by preprocessing the application source code or bytecode where migration support statements are added. This addresses non-portability of multiple JVM environments, but at the price of severe slowdown. JVM-level approaches can capture more complete state with lower overheads than application-level but entail arduous modification of the underlying JVM kernel including the interpreter or just-in-time (JIT) compiler. Pioneered by the CIA project (Illmann, Krueger, Kargl, & Weber, 2002), some midway approaches arise—the Java Platform Debugger

Architecture (JPDA), now replaced by JVM TI (Oracle, 2007), has enabled a relatively easy way for capturing Java stack information for migration purposes. As long as the JVM implementations follow the JPDA standards, this approach is generally portable despite the fact that it still needs some code preprocessing effort to address the loss of operand stacks. Finally, Mobile JikesRVM (Quitadamo et al., 2008) worked out another midway approach to thread migration by extending the functionalities of a famous *meta-circular* JVM, the IBM JikesRVM, with a 100% Java package (keeping the JVM internal core unchanged).

We have seen some evolution patterns on mobility support research: from coarse (processes) to fine granularities (objects, threads) for efficiency; from lower levels (hacking the OS kernel, JVM internal, native code) to higher levels (user-space, middleware-based, instrumenting bytecode, using debugger interface or meta-circular JVMs) for higher portability and reduced complexity. Somehow, we observe the recent trend seems going reverse and the history repeats itself--- several years ago, the research was going back to an even more coarse-grained migration unit and then drifting towards more lightweight, fine-grained mobility again. Nowadays, virtualization technology (VT) has been indispensable to the IT industry. VMs are extensively used to ease software testing and evaluation, run legacy applications, and enable isolation and consolidation of computing resources. Along the rise of VT, migration of VM instances has gained the most of the research focus. On one hand, VM migration uprooted most of the thorny residual dependency issues (especially the I/O state left behind) that all previous migration mechanisms have not resolved; on the other hand, it intensified the cost of migration for transferring the entire physical memory of the guest OS gets much more costly, particularly in the realm of data-intensive applications. Most VM systems implement *live migration* which moves the memory while the VM is still running to minimize the downtime, using various

strategies like *pre-copy* (as in Xen and vMotion) and *post-copy* (Hines et al., 2009). Using live migration for load balancing is beneficial only if the application runs long enough to compensate the migration cost, and is ill-suited to achieve swift enough on-demand scaling. In fact, the overheads of migrating the virtual local disk have not yet been included. Migrating it (typically in range of GBs) as well will be prohibitively expensive. Common solutions assume the disk image is accessible to all hosts by means of some shared networked storage (SAN/NAS). VM migration also assumes that the hosts are in a common network segment for seamless migration of network connections (via layer-2 redirection). Thus, VM migration's usage has been largely restricted to local area networks. Nevertheless, *wide-area VM migration*, which is parallel to the vision of global resource scheduling and disaster recovery, is an important research direction. Several projects, including Shrinker (Riteau et al., 2010), VM Turntable (Travostino et al., 2006) and a WAN-based modified Xen (Bradford, Kotsovinos, Feldmann, & Schiöberg, 2007), have been steering towards this goal.

Meanwhile, we observe a fast-growing branch of VT for enabling swift wide-area live mobility—that is to eschew the use and migration of bulky VMs and build an application framework or container that can move freely. Given a term *"application mobility"* in the cloud industry, this approach targets at enterprise server-side applications, and is driven by the industry's need for fine-grained scalability and rapid on-demand provisioning that VMs alone could hardly achieve. Virtual Application Appliance (VAA) (AppZero, 2010) and Monterey (Cloudsoft, 2010) are two commercial packages epitomizing this approach. Monterey advocates developing the application as a set of *mobile segments* which can be dynamically moved across multiple resources without interruption to service. AppZero VAA's core idea is to completely decouple an application from the underlying OS (so-called "zero OS") and to encapsulate it with its dependencies (executable

149

libraries, registry entries, configuration files, etc) within a VAA object which can freely move across different OSes. VAA, essentially another (but upper) virtualization layer, attains zero OS footprint, near-native performance and lighter mobility than a classic VM. Echoed with our saying above: "the history repeats itself", the mobility support is going finer-grained and upper-level again after the VM migration wave.

Auto-Provisioning Approaches

Auto-provisioning of computing environments is one key notion that distinguishes cloud computing from other computing paradigms. Being able to schedule shared resources between users, and to support flexible scale-up or scale-down (in response to load changes) are two building blocks for auto-provisioning in clouds. By virtue of virtualization and *auto-scaling* techniques, both the capabilities are being realized. Current paradigmatic cloud offerings commonly adopt an "instance-on-demand (IOD)" approach to auto-scaling. For example, Amazon Elastic Compute Cloud (EC2) provisions IaaS with auto-scaling for customers to ensure the number of EC2 instances (essentially VMs) for their applications increases seamlessly during demand spikes to maintain performance, and decreases automatically during demand lulls to minimize costs. Microsoft's Windows Azure offers cloud services, primarily in the PaaS realm and lately in the big league of IaaS as well by its VM Role support. Azure's auto-scaling option rests on changing the instance count in the service configuration or making use of third-party tools like AzureWatch. Google App Engine (GAE) follows a purely PaaS, container-based architecture. Users write and deploy their apps (in Java Servlet or Python) on GAE; auto-scaling is provided for free and is built-in (beyond user control). If GAE determines that the incoming request demand has outgrown an app's eligible capacity, it will replicate the app across multiple servers, spawn new server instances if needed, and update load balancer's routing to meet the demand.

There are, however, some possible issues with a pure IOD approach. The first issue is related to the adaptability to demand variation, and happens to VM-based platforms such as Amazon EC2 and Azure (VM Role). Spawning new VMs takes minutes, not seconds (Reese, 2008). While users expect *just-in-time* provisioning, the fact that VM-based CPU is not so "burstable" would suggest that having "VM-instances-on-demand" is not responsive enough to meteoric demand surges. Furthermore, since the guest OSes per se consume resources, the more frequent auto-scaling brings VMs up/down, the more the OS footprint customers are billed for, aside from what their apps actually consumed. On the other hand, GAE is good for near real-time auto-scaling and fine billing granularity. GAE responds very fast to demand rise and drop because hunting existing app server instances on Google clusters or spawning new ones are both lightweight. However, GAE poses many restrictions and hard limits on the app design and APIs to use. For example, requests elapsed for over 30 seconds will be killed automatically. Therefore, GAE is not suitable to support long-running apps such as scientific computing. As another matter, the IOD approach might force each instance to be effectively *stateless*. Otherwise, the need for state maintenance will require extra persistent data layer (RDBMSs, Google's BigTable, etc) and complicate auto-scaling.

Working by another principle, *mobility-based* approaches to on-demand scaling, as exemplified by Monterey, AppZero and our CM systems, target at finer-grained scalability, swift adaptability and stateful applications. With strong mobility support, workload can be reconfigured without concerns about app state loss or data inconsistency. Load balancing is performed by moving a portion of an application to infrastructure with spare capacity. Scale-up is performed by requesting additional hardware resources, then load-balancing across them. Scale-down is performed by moving an application off parts of the infrastructure and releasing them. The immediate benefit with this approach is rapid elasticity. Taking our JESSICA2 as an example, it supports dynamic transparent Java thread migration across cluster-wide JVM instances. Auto-scaling of a multithreaded Java application can be easily done by moving its threads around the JVMs. Sufficient scale is obtained by ensuring enough threads "parked" ahead of time or spawned on the fly. Thread migrations cause only little extra resource consumption, so maintaining fair enough bills. Table 2 summarizes and compares all the above solutions in various aspects.

ELASTIC INFRASTRUCTURE WITH MULTI-LEVEL MOBILITY

Overview and Motivations

While making live application mobility a core component of cloud services is well underway, we propose a *multi-level* mobile cloud infrastructure for meeting most kinds of mobility requirements. In the ultimate form, such infrastructure can choose the right level and granularity of mobility in an adaptive and goal-driven manner. Figure 1 shows the taxonomy of our designed migration techniques and their usable system implementations that we have experimented on our campus and the CNGrid-wide computing facilities. The implementation level and the unit of migration

(ranging from VM instances, processes, threads, and stack frames) determine the scope and size of system state for movement. The scope implies whether residual dependency may exist while the size decides the migration cost and also the granularity of adaptation to workload fluctuation in a load balancing event. The top three levels of migration are built into or above the JVM to support transparent mobility of computational components in Java. In view of Java's popularity and portability, this methodology is widely applicable. The use of various migration techniques can facilitate local and global resource scheduling across diverse distributed computing systems in response to changing workloads, resource availability, performance criteria, and costs.

Manifold interesting migration policies can be designed to fulfill the different goals, such as:

- *Demand-driven* ("*follow-the-sun*"): dynamically move processing to the location(s) where the greatest demand is being generated; the movement follows the locus of active users so that the majority of users perceive better responsiveness than if the application had to remain in a single, fixed location.
- *Cost-driven* ("*follow-the-moon*"): set up daily schedules to migrate services back and forth between cross-continent data centers to confine computing to local night-time hours during which power and

Table 2. Comparison of auto-scaling solutions

	Amazon EC2	Microsoft Azure	Google App Engine	JESSICA2
Unit of scale-up/down	VM instance		App/Server instance	Java thread
Resource consumption	Large		Small	Small
Billing granularity	Coarse		Fine	Fine
Adaptability to load changes	Slow		Fast	Fast
Domain of targeted apps	Wide		Narrow	Wide
Long-running app support	Yes		No	Yes

Figure 1. Taxonomy of computation migration techniques

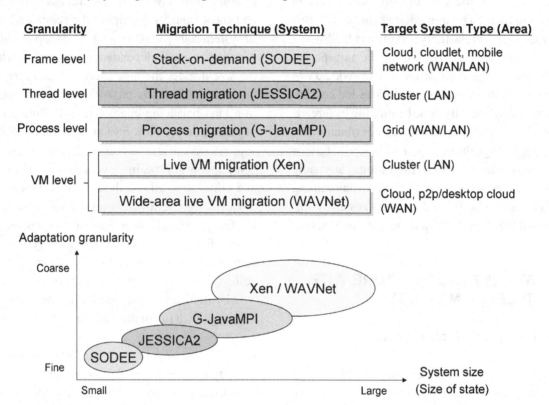

cooling costs are typically lower. This can save electricity costs. Users can exploit the most cost-effective computing resources, survive best in "cloud price wars" by migrating processing on the fly to clouds offering the best spot-prices.

- *Locality-driven* or *compliance-driven* (*"follow-the-data"*): move execution of a software component close to its associated data source for shorter access latency or due to data regulatory requirements.
- *Constraint-driven*: offload a task to clouds if the desktop or mobile device has insufficient CPU/ memory capacity to carry out the computation.
- *Energy-driven*: offload processing to clouds to save energy consumption of a mobile device (especially when it is running out of battery).

More insights into *globalized clouds* and relocatable computing strategies (follow-the-sun, -the-moon, etc) can be found among cloud technologists' discussions (Perry, 2008; Urquhart, 2008; Higginbotham, 2009). In the subsections to come, the migration system support per each level, followed by their integrated use to provide an elastic execution model, will be explained.

WAVNet-Based Desktop Cloud

Desktop Cloud is a new paradigm of cloud computing. It utilizes Internet-wide distributed home desktops and workstations to form a virtualized resource-sharing platform. Such a platform augments standard data-center infrastructures with enormous P2P resources. The Desktop Cloud makes dynamic provision of IaaS for users by pooling idle resources on the edge of Internet. We observe initiatives for such a Cloud philosophy are actively taking place. Cloud@Home (Cunsolo, Distefano, Puliafito, & Scarpa, 2009) is a latest example in point to denote the marriage of Volunteer and Cloud computing. In this new paradigm, client hosts are no longer solely passive interface to Cloud services, but can interact (free or by charge) with other Clouds such that computing resources of single users can be shared with or sold to the others.

The envisioned usage of P2P Desktop Cloud is as easy as connecting to a Virtual Private Network (VPN). Users can join and leave anytime. Just like P2P file sharing, the more the users joining the virtual network, the bigger the resource pool that can be provided. When new resources are discovered, tasks could be offloaded from those overloaded resources for increased throughput and balanced utilization. When resources leave, the running jobs are seamlessly relocated to other available resources. This requires the execution environment to be able to travel transparently across multiple sites. VM live migration is a useful tool to support such mobility. However the current VM migration technology is designed for LANs only. Overlay-based virtual networking approaches shed some light on tackling the connectivity issues across NAT/firewalls. Yet current implementation does not provide a complete network infrastructure to adapt to IaaS, which requires close-to-native network performance and seamless support for VM live migration over WAN.

We propose a performance-oriented network virtualization model called Wide-Area Virtual Network (WAVNet) (Xu, 2010) to achieve the Desktop Cloud vision. WAVNet can well adapt to dynamic provisioning of IaaS over the large-scale WANs. WAVNet provides a *link-layer* virtual network that tunnels application packets for any Internet-connected hosts even behind NATs/firewalls. Direct *host-to-host* connection among discovered resources allows users to utilize the available physical bandwidth with minimal cost. On top of WAVNet, users can also build their own

virtual clusters that could expand or shrink according to resource availability. Seamless WAN-based VM live migration is supported by WAVNet. For quickly looking for the best-fit resources on behalf of user requests from anywhere, we designed an index-based multi-dimensional range-query protocol for resource discovery.

Figure 2 shows the conceptual view of WAVNet. The top and bottom planes represent the virtual and physical networks respectively, which are glued by the *WAVNet overlay*. Each physical host is mapped to a virtual node after joining the WAVNet overlay as a resource. The overlay is organized by a distributed hash table (DHT), which also provides the service of resource discovery. When resource requests from users are settled by the DHT, direct connections (arrows in Figure 2) between relevant virtual nodes are established via WAVNet's connection setup procedures. This process connects the resources as if they were connected to the same Ethernet switch. By explicitly bridging to the hosts' WAVNet interfaces, VMs are also plugged into the same link-layer virtual network (virtual LANs in Figure 2). In this way, IaaS provisioning can be carried out by either requesting VM instantiation on remote hosts, or migrating customized VMs towards them. In WAVNet, all host-to-host connections are built based on the combination of *STUN protocol* and *UDP hole punching* techniques. Previous research (Ford, Srisuresh, & Kegel, 2005) has proved that such techniques could traverse most real-life NATs. By leveraging WAVNet as the virtual networking infrastructure, VMs over the same virtual LAN can be migrated freely without interrupting the task execution and network connection states, despite the fact that the underlying hosts are indeed under multiple Internet domains.

Current Virtual Machine Monitors (VMMs) support live migration over LAN by adopting the *bridging mode* for VM networking. Figure 3(top) shows the bridging mode implemented by Xen. VMs have frontend network drivers (eth0, eth1) that interface with users and back-end drivers

Figure 2. WAVNet virtual network infrastructure for the desktop cloud

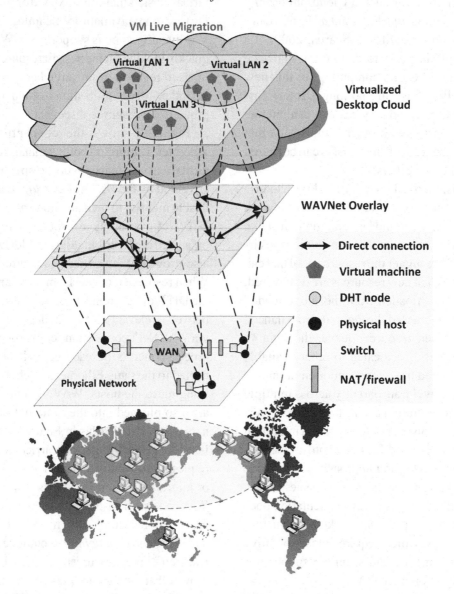

(vif1.0, vif2.0) in the driver domain (Dom0), with peth0 being the physical network interface. To make VMs stay on the same link layer as other hosts in LAN, a software bridge is created, with VMs' back-end drivers and physical host's external network devices as software ports. The key to supporting seamless live migration lies in the link layer network: when live migration finishes and the VM is brought up on the destination host, the VMM will inject an unsolicited ARP broadcast into the software bridge on behalf of the VM; all physical hosts and VMs in the same LAN will receive the ARP frame and update the location of the migrated VM in their local caches. Since applications are usually based on IP protocol, the update of link-layer address does not disrupt the consistency of connection. The ongoing IP packets will be sent to the new location of the VM. Nevertheless, such seamless live migration cannot be applied to WANs because of the connectivity problem caused by NATs.

Figure 3(bottom) shows a simplified architecture of WAVNet. For seamless network connections to a migrated VM instance despite its changed IP address, WAVNet is able to tunnel the link-layer ARP frames through the underlying physical network devices. WAVNet replaces the original software bridge created by the VMM with a customized bridge that uses *tap*, a layer-2 virtual network device, as the external port. The *Packet Assembler (PA)* is in charge of the encapsulation and de-capsulation of data traffic and connection messages. The *WAV-Switch* keeps track of the connections that have been established. It functions like a hardware Ethernet switch, which inspects the link layer address of ingress Ethernet frames, and forward them through the selected egress port according to its cached MAC address table. Instead of keeping MAC address to hardware port mapping, WAV-Switch keeps the soft mapping of MAC address to *connection URI* (i.e. IP:port pair). When an Ethernet frame needs to be forwarded to a certain MAC address, WAV-Switch will look up the local mapping table and determine the connection URI. Suppose link-layer connection is established between host 1 and host 2, as mentioned above. Link layer frames injected by VM instances and VMM will be extracted by WAVNet and tunneled to the other end. When VM live migration is performed, the ARP broadcast will be forwarded by WAVNet to all connected hosts. As a result, existing open connections and ongoing data streams to the migrated VM will not be disrupted due to its location change.

G-JavaMPI: Grid Middleware with Process Migration

G-JavaMPI (Chen et al., 2006) supports parallel execution of MPI (Message Passing Interface) programs written in Java, and location-transparent computations in a grid. Different from traditional MPI implementations, G-JavaMPI supports transparent Java process migration with message redirection between mobile distributed Java processes. This feature facilitates more flexible task scheduling and more effective resource sharing. Our implementation of the migration mechanism exploits the JVM Debugger Interface (JVMDI) functions and minor bytecode modification. This method is portable and does not require modification of the JVM. JVMDI enables a convenient way to control the execution and capture the runtime states of Java process. The destination JVM restores the process states through an exception handler which is inserted in the Java source code at the preprocessing time. The bytecode is also slightly rewritten to safeguard the operand stack state against loss at the legal migration points. To guarantee continuous MPI communication during process migration, a message redirection mechanism is employed. This mechanism makes the physical locations of the processes transparent to the user by supporting *logical ranks* in the program and redirects buffered messages to updated location of the migrating process during process migration.

As a process could be moved multiple times across grid points that are under different control policies for cross-organization resource sharing, we develop an *instance-oriented delegation* mechanism that can provide strict protection on multi-hop delegations. With this feature, the user grants his/her privileges via a security instance instead of the hosts. The security instance contains the description of the resource access operations, the conditions under which the process can perform these operations, as well as a signature of the user to certify the above contents. Permission to access the resource in the destination host can then be granted by simply checking the signature in the security instance and the validity of the specified resource access operations. Whereas in existing delegation mechanisms, the destination host has to verify all the signatures recorded in the delegation document which were

Figure 3. Virtual networking of Xen (LAN) versus WAVNet (WAN)

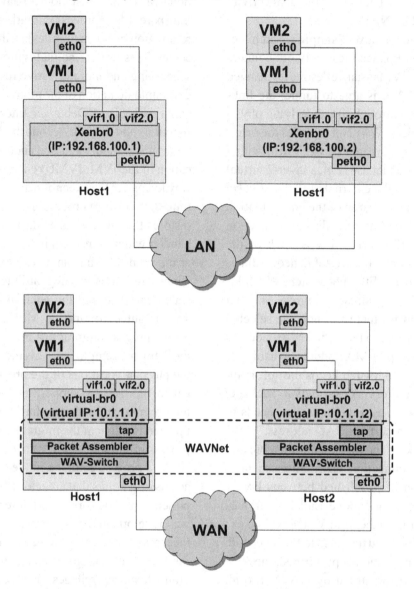

created during migration of the process through a series of hosts. With these supports, a process can be migrated transparently and safely between grid points to avoid running hotspots, to utilize available resource or to move closer to the data source. The process migration feature also gives the administrator certain flexibility in managing and deploying execution resources in response to load imbalances and fluctuations.

JESSICA2: Clustered JVM with Thread Migration

JESSICA2 (Zhu et al., 2002), which stands for Java-Enabled Single-System-Image Computing Architecture (version 2), is a distributed JVM runtime developed for supporting transparent parallel execution of a threaded Java program over a cluster of compute nodes. The system features a low-cost dynamic thread migration which allows

Java threads to move around the cluster while the execution can go full-speed with JIT-compiled code. To support thread migration, we need some mechanisms to capture the thread's execution state and restore it onto the target machine. In a JIT-enabled environment, Java threads are running in a native context---what we call it a *raw thread context (RTC)* is generally unrecognizable on another machine. For portable thread migration, JESSICA2 derives the *bytecode-oriented thread context (BTC)* from the migrant thread's RTC and sends it to the target node for restoration. RTC-BTC transformation however faces two challenges: (1) the native PC in the RTC may situate at the middle of the native code block compiled from a bytecode instruction; (2) the types of stack variables can only be known at runtime. JESSICA2 employs two mechanisms to overcome them:

- **Dynamic Native Code Instrumentation (DNCI)** (Zhu, Wang, & Lau, 2003): instrument native code to help the RTC-BTC transformation when a Java method is first compiled by the JIT compiler during execution. These native codes will spill type information and the latest values of stack variables from registers onto the main memory at some bytecode boundaries chosen by heuristics, e.g. before a method call or a loop. DNCI is suitable for irregular applications which make frequent migrations.
- **JIT Recompilation (JITR)** (Zhu, Fang, Wang, & Lau, 2004): rerun the JIT compiler, trace the steps of the compiler to the thread stop points, and collect the bytecode PC, the stack pointer, the operand types and values during the recompilation. The complete process of this mechanism consists of totally seven steps: stack walk, frame segmentation, bytecode PC positioning, breakpoint selection, type derivation, translation, and native code patching. Their details can be found in our original publication (Zhu et al., 2004). JESSICA2

adopts JITR by default because it charges instrumentation cost only when migration does occur, so the JVMs can run at full speed most of the time during execution.

When threads move to remote nodes, they see different memory spaces. JESSICA2 leverages a software DSM-like service, namely *Global Object Space (GOS)* (Fang, Wang, & Lau, 2003), to support remote object accesses across all nodes. The GOS implements a home-based coherence protocol to guarantee memory consistency across the cluster-wide heap spaces holding cache copies of shared objects. A lazy release consistent view and happens-before ordering are maintained across Java synchronizations. By exploiting the runtime information (e.g. object references) available in the JVM kernel, the GOS service also implements various optimization techniques—*adaptive home migration, connectivity-based object prefetching*, and *synchronized method shipping*—to minimize message round trips. Recently, we arrive at a *profile-guided* version of JESSICA2—lightweight dynamic profiling techniques (Lam, Luo, & Wang, 2010) are employed to detect correlations between thread pairs and the working set of a migrant thread, to make better migration policies with respect to data access locality.

SODEE: Stack-on-Demand Execution Engine

People's desire for mobility and data ubiquity has quickened the fusion of mobile technology and cloud computing—the "mobile cloud computing" trend (Hickey, 2010). Nowadays people carry mobile devices like iPhone and Android with "mobile apps" installed, which may access cloud storage services for application data. Mobile apps can also offload compute-intensive operations to cloud compute services for speedup and expanded functionality. Mobile computing requires more agility of migration because the network is relatively unstable and poor in bandwidth. So the captured state must be as small as possible for speedy transport. Live VM migration is ill-suited to such environments. We propose a *Stack-on-Demand (SOD)* approach (Ma et al., 2010) to mobile cloud computing. The essence is to implement an ultra-lightweight computation migration in which only the top portion of the runtime stack is being migrated. This design exploits the temporal locality of stack-based execution—the most recent execution state always sits on the top segment of a stack. By a partial stack migration, this speculative approach can reduce the migration cost of a bulky stack pointing to many objects. In addition, mobile agent solutions, which allow autonomous components to move around a heterogeneous network, seem best to survive in highly dynamic and unpredictable environments. So the SOD design also incorporates this notion.

Composable Execution Paths

SOD is based on a stack machine, specifically JVM in our case. Unlike traditionally process migration which performs full-rigged state migration (including code, stack, heap and program counter), SOD only migrates the top segment of stack frames (sometimes only the top frame), while the required code and heap data are brought in on demand subsequently. Besides, the execution flow of SOD upon completion of a task at the destination site is not necessarily restricted to returning home. By pushing the residual stack frames off the home in time, the execution can continue on the current site, or transferred to another site to realize *task roaming*. In this way, SOD exhibits some generalized form of distributed computing. Figure 4 illustrates three possible scenarios. Figure 4(a) shows a simple case that the control returns to Node 1 after frame 1 is migrated and finishes execution on Node 2. This execution flow degenerates into the case of Remote Method Invocation (RMI). In Figure 4(b), after frame 1 is migrated and starts executing, frame 2 and 3 are concurrently pushed to Node 2 as well. The

subsequent tasks would all be executed on Node 2. This is essentially a thread migration except that two "migration pipelines" are active concurrently. This scenario is also similar to a post-copy strategy by which the downtime is minimized by migrating and resuming the just-enough state first (the top frame in our case). In Figure 4(c), tasks are distributed in a multi-domain workflow style. While frame 1 is moved to Node 2 and being executed, the segment of frames 2 and 3 is moved to Node 3 in parallel. The control is transferred from Node 1 to Node 2, then to Node 3. This case is like a mobile agent roaming over the network. For instance, the two stack segments may be migrated to their associated data sources for reaping locality benefits. Although the execution still needs to follow a workflow-dictated order, the migration latency of the bottom stack segment is effectively hidden by the on-site execution time of the top frame. With such flexible or *composable* execution paths, SOD enables agile and elastic exploitation of distributed resources. As an illustrative scenario, one may develop a photo sharing website in a way that we call it a "mobile spider" (analogous to a Web spider), which can crawl into mobile devices for image files found there. Now the Java program is a web app server. When it receives requests from client browsers, it searches for images in specific directories, generates HTML pages with links to the photos found, and sends them back to the clients. We suppose this app server is hosted on a user's long-running desktop (or even on a cloud). The user may store photos on the PC as well as on an iPhone device, especially those newly taken. If the app server is granted SOD-style mobility, methods for searching photos could go to the user's iPhone, sharing the on-device photos with other clients. The SOD approach realizes this transparently without the need of ridiculously installing a web/FTP server on the iPhone or manual upload of photos to the desktop beforehand.

Figure 4. Flexible execution paths constructed based on SOD migration

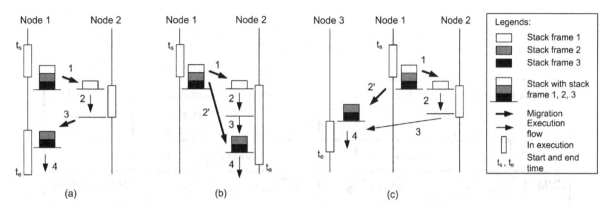

System Implementation

The SOD model is implemented into a Java distributed runtime called the *SOD Execution Engine (SODEE)*. Figure 5 shows the system architecture. SODEE consists of three key modules.

- **Class preprocessor:** Transforms the Java application bytecode before it is loaded into the JVM such that it is able to migrate and run seamlessly on a remote node.
- **Migration manager:** Serves migration requests and communicates with other migration managers to perform code and state migration.
- **Object manager:** Handles requests to fetch data from the heap of the home and writes execution result of migrated frames back home.

We adopted a highly portable design so that the system does not depend on a specific version of JVM, nor requires tricky hacking into the JVM kernel. Codes for distributed execution semantics are incorporated into the Java executable ahead of class loading time through the class preprocessor that employs a bytecode engineering library, specifically BCEL (Apache, 2001), to do so. Class preprocessing is automatic, one-off and performed offline, needing no user intervention

or source code modification. During preprocessing, the bytecode is rearranged to facilitate safe migration and augmented with helper functions for state restoration and remote object access. Since execution state is totally inside the JVM, we use the JVM Tool Interface (JVMTI) to expose them. Most modern JVMs support mixed-mode execution: program will run in interpreted mode, experiencing degraded execution performance, if some debugging functions are enabled; and while it is not the case, the program runs in JIT mode. All debugging functions are disabled before and after a migration event, so this approach is of reasonably slight overheads.

Migration manager is implemented as a JVMTI agent in C and enabled at JVM startup time as a command line option. It interacts with the JVMTI layer to access the JVM internal runtime data for capturing the state, essentially the partial stack of the migrant thread. It manages code movement towards the destination as well. We assume a worker JVM is prestarted on the destination node for receiving the current class of the top frame. Subsequent classes are transferred and loaded on demand in an event-driven manner. After class loading, the agent invokes the current method through the Java Native Interface (JNI). Execution then resumes at the last execution point restored by a special technique using the restoration exception handler injected into the code. Object

Figure 5. SODEE system architecture

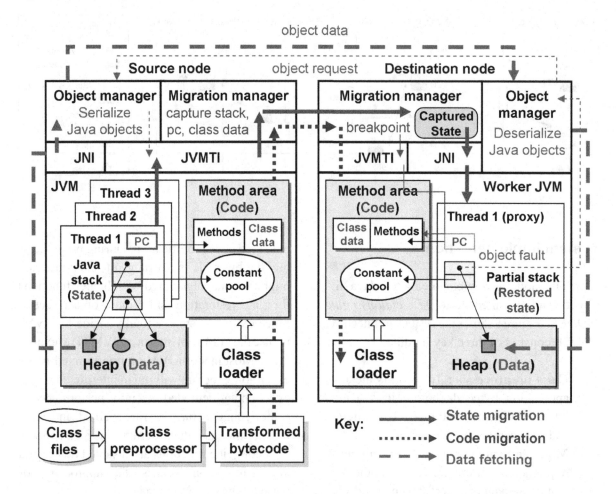

manager is implemented in both C and Java. On the destination side, object manager refers to the Java methods that handle sending of object requests and flushing of execution results to the home. On the source side, it refers to the agent thread that listens to object requests, retrieves object references needed via JVMTI and invokes Java serialization via JNI to send the object to the requester. When the active frame encounters object misses, the execution will jump to the object fault handler for the frame (inserted during preprocessing), calling the object manager to fetch the missed object from the source node. Upon reaching the last frame, its return value and updated objects are handed to the local JVMTI client which in turn sends them back home. The home JVMTI client

will pop the outdated frame off the stack using the ForceEarlyReturn<type> functions, supplied with the received return value. Execution will then resume seamlessly on the residual stack.

State Capturing and Restoration Mechanisms

The usual execution state includes program counter (pc), stack, heap and static data. In Java, pc is managed per thread and refers to the bytecode index (bci) in the current method. Each frame has an array of local variables, an operand stack (storing intermediate computing results), a reference to the runtime constant pool of the current class, and the return location back to the caller, or pc if it is the last frame. In our design, most of the heap and the lower part of the stack are left behind, and they are fetched on demand. Upon receiving a migration request, the migration manager suspends the execution and captures the topmost consecutive stack frames of the thread being migrated. For each frame, the current class name, method signature, pc and local variables are serialized and sent to the destination node while referenced objects are left behind and being fetched on demand. JVMTI does not provide interfaces to access the operand stack of each frame, nor does it provide functions to reestablish execution contexts such as the pc. Moreover, when the execution point lies inside a native method, data in the frame are machine-dependent. These data are difficult to capture and restore. Our solution is to restrict migrations to happen only at specific points where the operand stacks of all frames are empty and the execution is right outside a native method. These so-called *migration-safe points (MSPs)* are essentially located at the first bytecode instruction of a source code line where the operand stack of the current frame is always empty. If the execution is suspended at locations other than MSPs, it will be resumed immediately until hitting an upcoming one. To make sure other frames' operand stacks are all empty upon migration, bytecode rearrangement is done at preprocessing stage to introduce new local variables to store intermediate values on the operand stacks.

For state restoration, class static fields are restored by calling JNI functions; stack frames are restored by JVMTI functions and the restoration handlers embedded in each method during preprocessing. The handler would be activated if a specific exception is thrown. Local variables are restored to their captured values, and pc is restored by jumping to the bci where the execution was suspended previously. Figure 6 outlines the procedure of reestablishing the stack frames one by one. The migration manager begins by setting a breakpoint at the start of the entry function of the program, i.e. the main() method. The program

is then started, and the breakpoint is reached immediately just after method entry; the breakpoint event is captured, passing control to the JVMTI callback function, cbBreakpoint (1). The migration manager then sets another breakpoint at the start of the next invoked method (frame), if any. Next, it throws a specific exception in the current method. The exception is caught immediately, jumping to the restoration handler (2). The local variables and pc of the current method are then restored. The control jumps to the suspension point where the execution was suspended previously (3); then the next method, i.e. method2, is executed, creating the second frame (4). The above steps are repeated until the last frame gets restored (5) (6) (7).

Elastic Execution Model

Integrating the various migration systems into a universal mobile cloud infrastructure has yet a handful of challenges to solve. Now there are four levels of migration: VM, process, thread, and stack frame. The key question is which of them should be picked adaptively for different scenarios. Here we would provide some hints to the answer as follows: VM live migration is good for administrative purposes like resource consolidation. It is suitable for I/O-centric applications for existing network connections can be migrated seamlessly while all above-VM migration solutions rely on message redirection mechanisms at software level. In terms of on-demand scaling or load balancing, fine-grained computation migrations are more preferred to live migration of bulky VMs. Thread migration is good for near-instant provisioning and sharing resources on the same machine or cluster. Thread migration between two grid points is not recommended because threads usually have stronger coupling than processes; grid-wide distributed threads sharing a single logical heap are too inefficient. In this regard, Java process migration, which carries the entire heap along the travel, is more suitable for grids.

Figure 6. State restoration logic

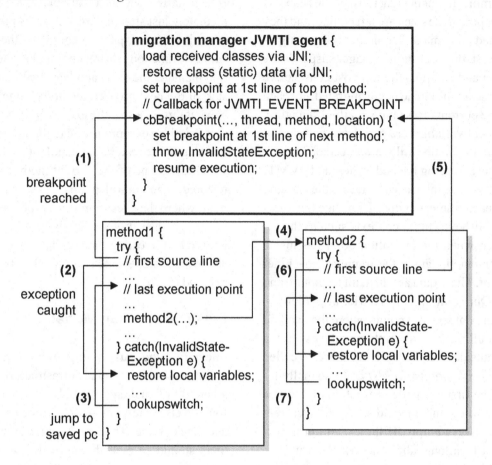

SOD, emphasizing agility and low freeze time, is good for interactive and mobile applications. As another challenge, implementing a clean unified scheduling policy for driving the different layers of migration is needed to cope with the possible conflicts between them. For example, with JESSICA2 and Xen, suppose a distributed Java environment of *jvm-a* and *jvm-b* is created atop two respective guest OSes *vm-a* and *vm-b* on the same cluster. If JESSICA2 decides to migrate a thread from *jvm-a* to *jvm-b* for locality benefit, and meanwhile the lower layer schedules *vm-a* to relocate to a new cluster by its own policy, the net effect (on locality) can be negative as long-haul interaction with the thread left behind in the old cluster is resulted. Possible solutions to these conflicts rest on synchronizing the migration events across the layers (say, via some shared status files), setting up priority configurations (e.g. let upper-layer decisions always suppress the lower), and triggering group-based migration (e.g. migrating *vm-a* and *vm-b* together to the new cluster can preserve the wholeness of the clustered JVM runtime). This chapter focuses on the mechanism and performance aspects of mobility and leaves the policy issues as future work.

Figure 7 depicts an overview of the multi-level mobility infrastructure and illustrates how the various migration techniques might be applied. Suppose an e-Science researcher has a parallel Java application comprising both intra-node and inter-node parallelism by means of multiple threads and multiple MPI processes respectively. He is running it on a Xen virtual cluster hosted on his desktop PC. Later on, the application is found to overload his PC and run slowly. With a hypervisor-level load balancer and wide-area live migration facility such as our WAVNet, all or part of his virtual cluster can be offloaded to a compute cloud service. The live migrants are seamlessly restored on the cloud. Auto-scaling can be swiftly done at JVM level: with JESSICA2, new JVM instances are spawned on the cloud-provisioned VMs, the overall workload is then evened out by migrating a proportional count of Java threads from the boarded JVMs to the spawned JVMs. In the midst of execution, the application may need to access some big data files held in another e-Science grid. JESSICA2 does not serve this wide-area scenario well. Live migration of VM instances won't fit too because hypervisors may

be absent on grids which are more HPC-oriented and performance-savvy. In this case, transparent Java process migration enabled by G-JavaMPI is an effective choice for collocating the MPI processes with their associated data sources in the grid. Finally, the application could have another kind of threads not for computation but presentation. The scientific computing results are to be formatted as reports and displayed on the researcher's iPhone, but there involves user interaction, say parameter input, report type selection, data sorting and searching. To improve user-perceived latency, the report conversion task could be migrated with the computation results as state to the mobile device, and execute there.

Figure 7. An elastic cloud ecosystem with multi-level mobility

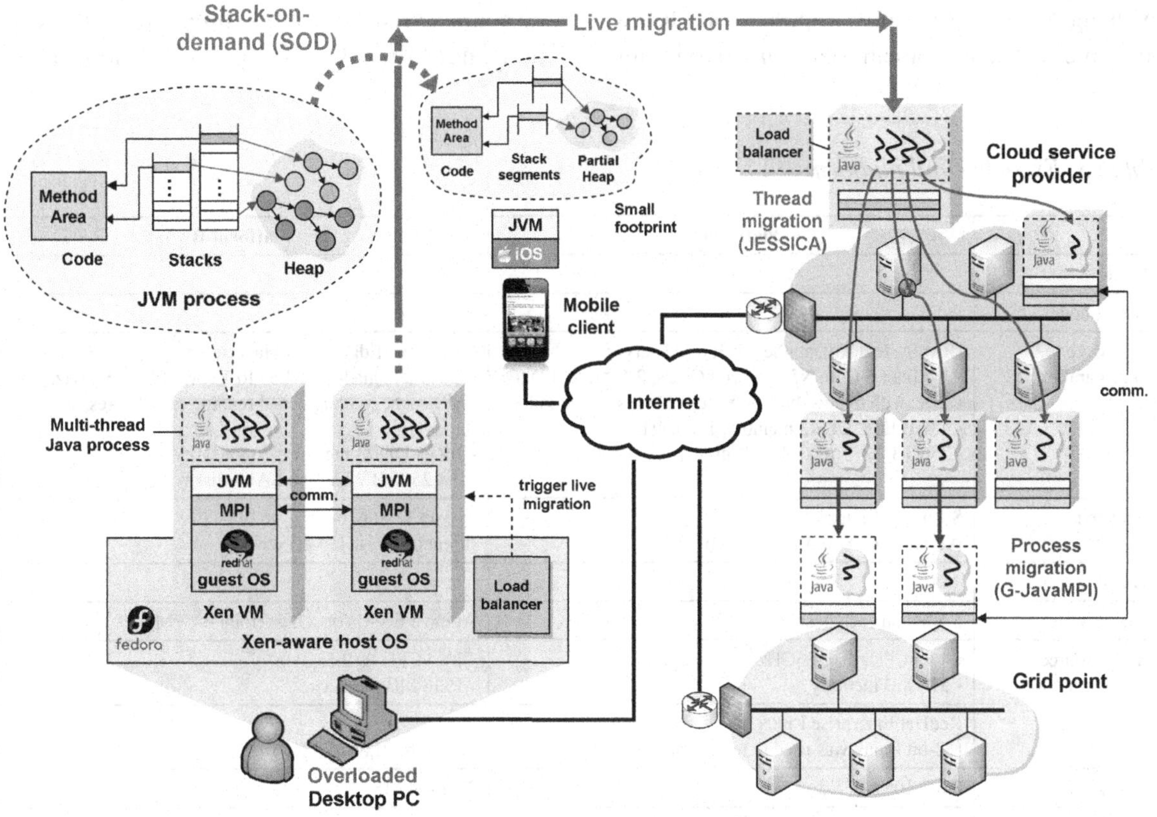

PERFORMANCE EVALUATION

The various CM mechanisms have been evaluated on a Xen virtual cluster emulating a multi-instance cloud infrastructure. The virtual cluster is created on top of a physical cluster with enough CPU cores given to each VM instance. All hosts are connected through Gigabit networks. Table 3 shows the configurations of our experimental platforms. We will specify in each subsection which platform was being used for each experiment. In particular, WAVNet and SODEE require wide-area and mobile networking environments respectively; these specific set-ups will be detailed in their subsections accordingly.

Overhead Analysis

This part of evaluation aims to characterize and compare the overheads of different migration mechanisms. We did the experiment on Platform A using a suite of scientific applications listed in Table 4; their problem sizes (n), maximum

heights (h) of Java stacks and accumulated sizes (F) of all local/static fields are also shown for reference. We ran each program atop SODEE, G-JavaMPI, JESSICA2 and JDK in order to measure the overhead of stack segment migration, thread migration, process migration and VM live migration respectively. SODEE and G-JavaMPI need an underlying JVM (JDK 1.6) to execute. To emulate a cloud computing environment, all the execution is encapsulated in Xen VM instances.

We measure the *migration overhead (MO)* by the difference of execution time with and without activating migration. This should have covered all direct and indirect overheads due to migration. The experimental results are shown in Table 5. The columns headed "w/ mig" and "w/o mig" refer to the execution time with and without migration. The "w/o mig" readings of SODEE, G-JavaMPI and JDK are about the same, showing that without migration, the debugger interface and minor bytecode modification have virtually no penalty on the execution time. The raw execution time of JESSICA2 is significantly longer than

Table 3. Experimental platform

	Platform A	Platform B
Host		
No. of nodes	2	12
Hardware configuration	IBM System X iDataPlex dx360 M3 server - 2 × Intel 6-Core X5650 Xeon CPUs, 2.66GHz, 12MB cache, with hyper- threading (i.e. 12 cores, 24 threads) - 48GB ECC DDR3 memory, 1333MHz - 250GB 7.2K rpm SATA II disk	Dell PowerEdge M610 blade server - 2 × Intel Quad-Core E5540 Xeon CPU, 2.53GHz, 8MB cache, with hyper- threading (i.e. 8 cores, 16 threads) - 16GB DDR3 memory, 1066MHz - 2 × 250GB 7.2K rpm SATA disks
OS version	Scientific Linux 5.5 x86_64 (kernel: 2.6.18-194.26.1.el5xen)	Fedora 11 x86_64 (kernel: 2.6.18-164.el5xen)
Guest		
No. of VMs	5 VMs on each host	At most 6 VMs on a host (total 64 VMs)
VM resource configuration	- 4 × vCPUs @ 2.66GHz - 512 MB memory	- 1 × vCPU @ 2.53GHz - 1536 MB memory
OS version	RedHat Enterprise Linux AS 4.6 i686 (32-bit Linux was used to resolve subtle compatibility issues seen by JESSICA2)	
Xen version	3.0.3-105.el5_5.2	3.0.3-94.e15
Java version	Oracle JDK 1.6.0_20-b02 (32-bit) server mode	

Table 4. Application benchmark programs

App	Description	n	h	F (byte)
Fib	Calculate the n-th Fibonacci number recursively	46	46	< 10
NQ	Solve the n-queens problem recursively	14	16	< 10
TSP	Solve the traveling salesman problem of n cities	12	4	~ 2500
FFT	Compute an n-point 2D Fast Fourier Transform	256	4	> 64M

others for its implementation is based on Kaffe JVM 1.0.6 whose JIT compiler is not as optimized as JDK. MO in each test case is derived by subtracting readings of "w/o mig" from "w/ mig". We can see that SODEE induces the least MO for all benchmarks. This suggests that the SOD approach—skipping transfer of the lower part of stack and the entire heap—can benefit most applications. JESSICA2 (thread migration) belongs to a lightweight kind, next to SOD. As an exceptional case, FFT's MO is significantly larger since the application involves restoration of a big static array (64MB) and every access to this array involves some state checks and consistency protocol overheads. G-JavaMPI and VM live migration belong to heavyweight kinds; their average MOs among all cases are over 1 sec. G-JavaMPI captures heap memory state using JVM TI functions and object serializations, and stores the states in the file system. In contrast, states in SOD are transferred directly through sockets. So in some cases, the overhead of G-JavaMPI may even exceed the coarser live migration mechanism which migrates in unit of memory pages.

We use the term *migration latency (ML)* to denote the time gap between receiving a migration request and getting the execution resumed at the destination. ML can be broken down into three parts. *Capture time* means the interval between a migration request being received and the state data being ready to transfer. *Transfer time* is the time needed for the state data, upon being ready for transfer, to reach the destination. *Restore time* counts from the moment of state data being available at the destination to the point of execution

resumption. Besides the state, code also needs to be shipped. The time for sending and loading application classes into the destination JVM would be counted under the restore time. The state data for different systems may be defined differently. For SODEE and JESSICA2, it covers mostly the stack areas; for G-JavaMPI, it includes also the heap; for Xen, it means the entire OS memory. For SODEE, G-JavaMPI and JESSICA2, ML is equivalent to downtime during which the execution is frozen. For Xen, ML equals the *total migration time (TMT)* rather than downtime because page pre-copying initiated well ahead of execution stoppage is counted as part of state capturing. Though Xen's downtime is relatively short (in range of hundreds ms), its TMT—the elapsed time between migration request arrival and execution resumption—is a long time (at least several seconds). Xen's MO, which measures the degradation of execution, is somewhere between ML and TMT.

The results are shown in Table 6. We do not have breakdown of Xen's live migration latency but show its TMT and downtime. "Cap", "Tran", "Res" denote the capture, transfer and restore time respectively. For JESSICA2, there is an extra column "JITR" denoting the time for re-running the JIT compiler for deriving bytecode-level pc and stack variable types, etc. These steps are required before being able to capture stack frame content, so their overheads are counted into ML as well. JESSICA2 sees a much longer restore time in FFT due to time-consuming allocation of a big static array. This array also increased all components of G-JavaMPI's ML considerably. However,

Table 5. Migration overhead

Sys App	SODEE on Xen (Stack seg. mig.)			JESSICA2 on Xen (Thread mig.)			G-JavaMPI on Xen (Process mig.)			JDK on Xen (VM live mig.)		
	Exec. time (sec)		MO (ms)	Exec. time (sec)		MO (ms)	Exec. time (sec)		MO (ms)	Exec. time (sec)		MO (ms)
	w/ mig	w/o mig		w/ mig	w/o mig		w/ mig	w/o mig		w/ mig	w/o mig	
Fib	12.776	12.693	83	47.311	47.215	96	16.452	12.682	3770	13.37	12.28	1090
NQ	7.722	7.673	49	37.493	37.300	193	7.937	7.638	299	8.36	7.15	1210
TSP	3.599	3.586	13	19.544	19.448	96	3.674	3.590	84	4.76	3.54	1220
FFT	10.799	10.605	194	253.633	250.197	3436	15.131	10.752	4379	12.94	10.15	2790

SODEE's timings were not affected because the migration was taken place in a method which did not operate on the array. By SOD, only the top stack frame was captured and restored. As heap data was not transferred during migration, the data size does not affect SOD's ML. Therefore, SOD attains a very short downtime (suitable for latency-sensitive apps). On the contrary, in G-JavaMPI, the whole process data is serialized in an eager-copy manner. For Fib and NQ, G-JavaMPI needs to deal with around 46 and 16 stack frames (see Table 4) respectively, due to recursive calls, thus resulting in a longer downtime. Ignoring FFT, one can perceive a coarse ratio of the downtime across the various migration units—*frame*: *thread*: *process*: $VM \approx 1: 3: 10: 150$.

Effect of Virtualization on Mobility Performance

This part of experiment studies the effect of virtualization on the performance of computation migration. While using VMs as containers of applications help isolate the computing resources of a single host, our experiments show that the isolation is imperfect. When multiple VM instances, representing multiple tenants' applications, are running on the same host, there is still some interference between the VM instances even though sufficient CPU cores are provided. The degree of interference is also found dependent on the underlying vCPU pinning scheme. This experiment

was done on two hosts of Platform A. We placed five VMs on each host which consists of 12 cores (24 hyper-threads); each VM was assigned four vCPUs (occupying four hyper-threads).

In one scheme, the vCPUs were pinned in a sequential manner such that the processor id 0,1,2,3 were assigned to Dom0 (host), processor id 4,5,6,7 were given to Dom1 (VM1), and so on for VM2 to VM5. We ran a busy while loop in each of Dom2, Dom3, etc and performed application benchmarking in Dom1. The measured execution time of the applications in Dom1 was found degraded quite significantly: Fib (-56.58%), NQ (-16.99%), FFT (-32.93%), TSP (-29.60%). The degradation is due to interference between the while loops and the testing applications—one vCPU of the neighboring domains occupied a hyper-thread belonged to the physical core servicing a vCPU of Dom1. Such coupling leads to cache contamination and poor isolation. In the second scheme, we avoid such coupling by ensuring each domain is using the four hardware threads belonging to two cores of the same processor. The migration latencies of Fib, NQ, TSP and FFT atop SODEE, JESSICA2 and G-JavaMPI were measured to assess the impact of active jobs in other VM instances on the mobility performance in terms of capture, transfer and restore time. We took the readings under four cases: idle/idle, busy/idle, idle/busy, busy/busy. For example, busy/idle means the source node is busy while the destination node is idle (note: "busy" means all tenants, Dom2 to Dom5, are

Table 6. Migration latency

App	SODEE			JESSICA2				G-JavaMPI			Xen	
	ML (ms)			ML (ms)				ML (ms)			TMT (sec)	Downtime (ms)
	Cap	Tran	Res	JITR	Cap	Tran	Res	Cap	Tran	Res		
Fib	6.31			19.15				89.73			6.17	1007.60
	0.25	2.71	3.36	6.40	0.20	10.29	2.26	42.47	2.44	44.83		
NQ	6.80			11.10				69.25			6.06	1010.26
	0.32	2.89	3.59	3.04	0.11	1.73	6.23	35.49	2.81	30.94		
TSP	8.08			20.58				78.34			5.87	1020.67
	0.30	2.80	4.97	1.18	0.050	10.60	8.74	31.95	4.46	41.94		
FFT	19.39			60.80				3659.56			7.17	1291.26
	0.35	14.90	4.14	1.72	0.080	2.40	56.60	742.21	2440.38	476.97		

running the while loops; whereas "idle" means all tenants have 0% CPU utilization). The evaluation results are shown in Figure 8. In general, we can see two things: (1) the deviations in capture/restore/jitr readings across the four cases are relatively small, showing computational performance consistency is possible in a multi-instance environment with proper vCPU pinning; (2) there is negative effect on the transfer time despite best-effort isolation through vCPU pinning. This reveals that the busy loops in Dom2–5 have put a modest load on the VMM and degraded the networking performance.

Scaling out by Wide-Area Live Migration

In this part, the performance of wide-area live migration over WAVNet is evaluated. The experimental setup consists of computers leased from three sites forming a WAN setting: The University of Hong Kong (HKU), Providence University (PU) in Taiwan and Shenzhen Institutes of Advanced Technology (SIAT) in mainland China. The machines in SIAT and HKU have Intel Pentium 4 2.8GHz CPUs, and the machines in PU are equipped with Intel Xeon 5130 2.00GHz CPUs. All hosts are running Linux (kernel version 2.6) and Xen hypervisor 3.0. For evaluating the physi-

cal network performance among sites, one host with public IP address was configured in each site.

By using the *netperf* tool, we compare network throughput of WAVNet of the privileged domain (WAV-Dom0), the guest domain (WAV-VM), and the guest domain during VM live migration (WAV-VM-Mig). We run the netperf test on a host in HKU, and the VM is initially on a host in SIAT, and then migrated to HKU. Figure 9 shows that all three cases have similar performance. For WAV-VM-Mig, since the VM finally relocates to HKU, the netperf gives result similar to LAN performance, as reflected by the sudden hike in the curve. Next, we evaluate the effectiveness of migrating http server for better request/response throughput and shorter waiting time. This is one possible real-life application of live migration. We set up an http server on a VM located in SIAT, and use the *ApacheBench* stress test tool to evaluate the request processing throughput for the underlying network. Table 7 shows the results obtained from HKU and PU. Before live migration, the http throughput from PU to the VM on SIAT is around 1.5 requests/sec, while that from HKU is around 3 request/sec. The difference is due to higher network latency between PU and SIAT. After the http server is migrated from SIAT to a host in HKU over WAVNet, the http throughput from PU and HKU greatly increases to 5 requests/

Figure 8. Migration latency breakdown under a multi-VM environment

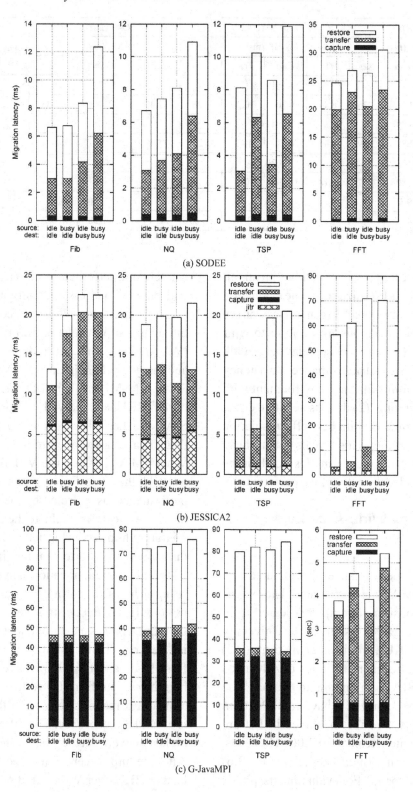

(a) SODEE

(b) JESSICA2

(c) G-JavaMPI

Figure 9. NetPerf TCP stream test

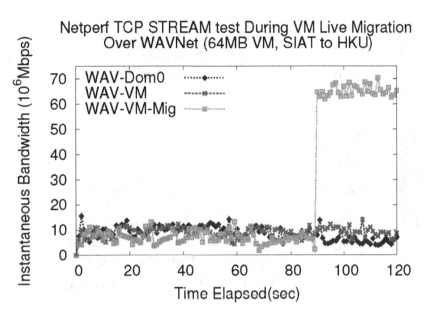

sec and over 320 requests/sec respectively. This reflects that when http server can be migrated to a nearby host, users of the http service perceive quicker responses from the server.

The performance benefit that VM live migration could bring to parallel applications over WAN is also evaluated. We use an MPI program solving the heat distribution problem for evaluation. Four VMs are brought up to run the MPI processes. Three of them are located in HKU machines, and the other in SIAT; their underlying physical hosts form a WAVNet virtual network. We measure the execution time for problem sizes of 64×64, 128×128 and 256×256. As shown in Figure 10, if none of the VMs is migrated, the MPI program

for the above problem sizes lasts for 397 sec, 1214 sec and 3798 sec respectively. In another test, the VM in SIAT is migrated to another host in HKU. The program execution times then become 121 sec, 179 sec and 365 sec, respectively, which are 30.5%, 14.7% and 4.7% of the results without VM migration. The time reduction is because of improved locality or localized communications (removing the communication bottleneck with the SIAT VM). The result also reveals that for long-running applications, VM migration overhead is relatively fixed despite the increasing problem size.

Table 7. ApacheBench performance result

	Req/sec	Avg Resp Time (msec)	Connection Time (msec)		
			Min	Mean	Max
From PU (before migration)	1.51	661.278	661	664	888
From PU (after migration)	5	199.979	156	200	296
From HKU (before migration)	3.12	320.266	226	320	620
From HKU (after migration)	322.73	3.099	3	3	5

Figure 10. MPICH heat distribution

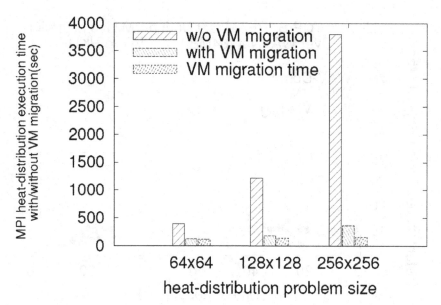

Scaling out by Java Thread Migration

In this experiment, we testify the use of multi-level mobility for an application scenario similar to what we depict in Figure 7. For demonstration's sake, the experiment covers only two levels: Xen's live migration and JESSICA2's thread migration. We evaluate how their combined use can achieve task offloading from a desktop to the Cloud for speedup. We use 12 hosts of Platform B for the evaluation. For simplicity, one of the hosts picks the role of the desktop PC and the other 11 hosts serve as the cloud infrastructure. There are 63 Xen VMs prestarted on the 11 hosts. Our benchmark program is a multithreaded Java program that renders a 3D image in parallel using the ray tracing algorithm. The image has 720×550 pixels and 132 objects; the rendering process uses anti-aliasing, a ray tracing level of 10, and 64 Java threads. Once a horizontal line of image is rendered, the buffer will be sent back to another desktop outside Platform B for real-time display. As shown in Figure 11, in the beginning, the program runs on a single JVM instance (the master JVM) encapsulated in a Xen VM hosted on the desktop, and the average throughput is 673.9 pixels/sec. At the 22nd second, live migration is triggered, moving the VM seamlessly to the cloud platform. The total migration time takes 43.67 seconds while the downtime lasts about 1.8 seconds. After boarding the cloud platform, scale-out takes place by calling a script to add 63 worker JVMs to the JESSICA2 runtime. The runtime will dynamically and transparently migrate one thread from the master JVM to each of the joining worker JVMs. Throughout the course of execution, the instantaneous throughput may be penalized during memory page pre-copying (for live migration), mark-sweep GC cycles and JIT recompilations. After the thread migration phase, the whole rendering process gets utilizing the abundant vCPU resources of all the Xen VMs, growing the average throughput to 4349.9 pixels/sec. Although the speedup (about 6.5) is not very impressive, this experiment has demonstrated the possible use of multi-level mobility for on-demand auto-scaling.

Effectiveness of SOD Execution Model

In the last experiment, we evaluate how much SOD can help save resources while stateful migration takes place by simulating the "mobile spider" application scenario. We perform the experiment using an iPhone 4 handset with an Apple A4 CPU (800MHz), 512MB RAM, and 16GB storage. JamVM 1.5.1b2-3 (JVM) and GNU Classpath 0.96.1-3 (Java class library) are installed on the iPhone. It is connected through Wi-Fi connection to the network of Platform B. We run the application server program on Dom0 directly. There are 5 directories, holding 100 image files each. There is another empty directory named "ip4". When the server program tries to read from this directory, a migration request is channeled to SODEE, mov-

ing the task (directory scanning) to the iPhone, and what actually being read from becomes the directory of the same name on the device. After the on-device search process completes, the execution returns to the host program with the information of the image files found captured as state. The host replies the requesting client with the aggregated search results in HTML format. Here are the testing results:

- **Memory consumption:** The memory footprint of the server process on the host is 31,907,096 bytes (about 30MB). When migrated to the iPhone via SOD, memory consumption measured on iPhone is 842,544 bytes. That means the memory footprint has dropped 38 times, implying a significant level of memory savings (up

Figure 11. Live migration followed by thread migration for scaling out

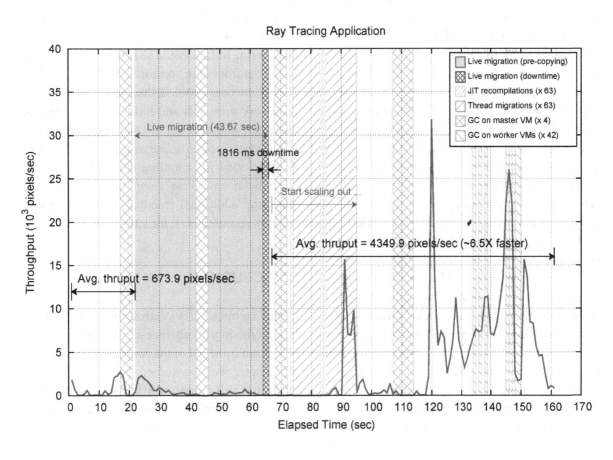

to 97.36%) achieved by SOD migration, compared to process migration.

- **Bandwidth consumption:** If the whole process state is migrated, the bandwidth required is 147,610 bytes. With SOD, bandwidth required is 21,695 bytes. The percentage bandwidth saving obtained by SOD than process migration is up to 85%.

The savings in memory and bandwidth of SOD compared with other migration mechanisms come from skipping the state in lower parts of the stack and the heap content (possibly up to 5×100 file objects) during the round trip between the host and device. This confirms the agility of SOD migration.

FUTURE RESEARCH DIRECTIONS

Below we would outline two more directions to drive the research forward in the future.

While the SOD migration mechanism has been established to address agility, the next step of maturing it to a holistic approach is to investigate automatic stack analysis techniques and strategic migration policies. The purpose of stack analysis is to find out which stack frames are worth migrating, thus having an appropriate migrant stack segment size determined at runtime. Ontology-based task description or other semantic technologies may help this process. Based on the analysis output including a map of Java classes used, working set sizes, object connectivity plus user-specified constraints and platform information, migration decisions can be made effectively. The system could also *pin down* specific stack frames, preventing them from being migrated for reasons like data security and locality. Another possible enhancement of the SOD execution model is to make it *speculate* on local resources before offloading processing to priced cloud computing services. By wrapping method bodies in try-catch constructs via bytecode instrumentation, exception

handlers are appended for handling exceptions like ClassNotFoundException and OutOfMemoryException via a migration approach. The execution state is captured and rocketed into the Cloud which has a sufficient class library base and memory capacity for retrying the execution. Such an *exception-driven* mobility model glues mobile platforms and cloud platforms seamlessly without the need to develop and maintain two-sided (client and server) application code.

Our research effort on the P2P Desktop Cloud is still being elementary. The implementation of WAVNet can be enhanced in several aspects. First, UDP hole punching does not traverse all NAT/firewalls, particularly for symmetric NAT/firewall. In the future, protocols such as ICE (Rosenberg, 2010) and TURN (Mahy, Matthews, & Rosenberg, 2010) can be integrated into the system. Second, virtual networks built atop virtual network devices require copying to and from the memory assigned to socket buffers, constituting a major overhead in the transmission process. To reduce the overhead, memory referencing techniques such as ring buffers could be applied. Third, when resources from both home user desktops and data centers are being pooled, the underlying resource discovery protocols and billing policies will be a non-trivial matter. As a *hybrid cloud* approach, a P2P version of *cloudbursting* (Barr, 2008) can be developed for handling demand spikes that overwhelm enterprise computing resources by acquiring additional resources from the public desktop resource pool for a transient period.

CONCLUSION

Cloud computing, virtualization and mobility have come to a confluence and stimulated a top-to-bottom overhaul of the computing industry. In this chapter, we have studied various computation migration techniques which function at different implementation levels, from coarse to fine granularities. The use of virtual machines and live migration has provided coarse resource isolation and execution mobility at the infrastructure level for cloud computing. Higher-level fine-grained computation mobility mechanisms such as Java thread migration can facilitate efficient auto-provisioning of cloud computing resources for quick adaptation to workload changes. Our proposed stack-on-demand (SOD) execution model allows part of a runtime stack to move across virtually any Java platforms at low cost and high agility. SOD-style mobility enables bidirectional migration of stateful computations between mobile devices and the cloud infrastructure, improves their interfacing and eases the design of sophisticated mobile cloud applications. We believe that with multi-level mobility, computing can float freely across cluster nodes, grids and clouds, as well as mobile devices to fulfill diverse goals like rapid elasticity, enhanced data locality and global resource scheduling. Developing an integrated conflict-free migration policy that adaptively decides on the best migration technique to use for an application scenario is a challenging but vital piece of future work for a fully elastic cloud ecosystem to materialize.

ACKNOWLEDGMENT

This work is supported by Hong Kong RGC grant HKU 7179/09E and Hong Kong UGC Special Equipment Grant (SEG HKU09).

REFERENCES

Apache. (2001). *Byte code engineering library*. Retrieved March, 1, 2011, from http://jakarta.apache.org/bcel/

AppZero. (2010). *AppZero virtual application appliances (VAA)*. Retrieved March, 1, 2011, from http://www.appzero.com/

Barr, J. (2008). *Cloudbursting - Hybrid application hosting*. Amazon Web Services Blog. Retrieved March, 1, 2011, from http://aws.typepad.com/aws/2008/08/cloudbursting-.html

Bouchenak, S., & Hagimont, D. (2002). *Zero overhead Java thread migration* (Research Report No. RT-0261). INRIA. Retrieved March, 1, 2011, from http://hal.inria.fr/inria-00069913/en/

Bradford, R., Kotsovinos, E., Feldmann, A., & Schiöberg, H. (2007). Live wide-area migration of virtual machines including local persistent state. In *Proceedings of the 3rd International Conference on Virtual Execution Environments* (pp. 169–179). New York, NY: ACM.

Braun, P., & Rossak, W. (2004). *Mobile agents: Basic concepts, mobility models, and the Tracy toolkit*. San Francisco, CA: Morgan Kaufmann Publishers Inc.

Chen, L., Ma, T., Wang, C.-L., Lau, F. C. M., & Li, S. (2006). G-JavaMPI: A grid middleware for transparent MPI task migration. In di Martino, B., Dongarra, J., Hoisie, A., Yang, L. T., & Zima, H. (Eds.), *Engineering the Grid: Status and perspective*. Nova Science.

China National Grid (CNGrid). (2002). *Website*. Retrieved March, 1, 2011, from http://www.cngrid.org

Clark, C., Fraser, K., Hand, S., Hansen, J. G., Jul, E., Limpach, C., et al. (2005). Live migration of virtual machines. In *Proceedings of the 2nd Conference on Symposium on Networked Systems Design & Implementation* - Vol. 2 (pp. 273–286). Berkeley, CA: USENIX Association.

Cloudsoft. (2010). *Cloudsoft Monterey middleware for application mobility*. Retrieved March, 1, 2011, from http://www.cloudsoftcorp.com/

Cronk, D., Haines, M., & Mehrotra, P. (1996). *Thread migration in the presence of pointers* (Tech. Rep.).

Cunsolo, V. D., Distefano, S., Puliafito, A., & Scarpa, M. (2009). Volunteer computing and desktop cloud: The cloud@home paradigm. In *Proceedings of the 8th IEEE International Symposium on Network Computing and Applications* (pp. 134–139).

Fang, W., Wang, C.-L., & Lau, F. C. M. (2003, November). On the design of global object space for efficient multi-threading Java computing on clusters. *Parallel Computing, 29*, 1563–1587. doi:10.1016/j.parco.2003.05.007

Ford, B., Srisuresh, P., & Kegel, D. (2005). Peer-to-peer communication across network address translators. In *Proceedings of USENIX 2005 Annual Technical Conference* (pp. 172–192). Berkeley, CA: USENIX Association.

Fuggetta, A., Picco, G. P., & Vigna, G. (1998, May). Understanding code mobility. *IEEE Transactions on Software Engineering, 24*, 342–361. doi:10.1109/32.685258

Grid Point, H. K. U. (2010). *The HKU grid point for systems research and applications in multiple disciplines*. Retrieved March, 1, 2011, from http://www.hku.hk/cc/events/gridpoint/en/about/about.htm

Hickey, A. R. (2010). *Report: Mobile cloud computing a $5 billion opportunity*. Retrieved March, 1, 2011, from http://www.crn.com/mobile/222300633

Higginbotham, S. (2009, July). *Google gets shifty with its data center operations*. Retrieved March, 1, 2011, from http://gigaom.com/2009/07/16/google-gets-shifty-with-its-data-center-operations

Hines, M. R., Deshpande, U., & Gopalan, K. (2009, July). Post-copy live migration of virtual machines. *SIGOPS Operating Systems Review, 43*, 14–26. doi:10.1145/1618525.1618528

Hoff, T. (2009). *Latency is everywhere and it costs you sales - How to crush it*. Retrieved March, 1, 2011, from http://highscalability.com/latency-everywhere-and-it-costs-you-sales-how-crush-it

Illmann, T., Krueger, T., Kargl, F., & Weber, M. (2002). Transparent migration of mobile agents using the java platform debugger architecture. In *Proceedings of the 5th International Conference on Mobile Agents* (pp. 198–212). London, UK: Springer-Verlag.

Lam, K. T., Luo, Y., & Wang, C.-L. (2010). Adaptive sampling-based profiling techniques for optimizing the distributed JVM runtime. In *Proceedings of the 24th IEEE International Symposium on Parallel & Distributed Processing*.

Ma, R., Lam, K. T., Wang, C.-L., & Zhang, C. (2010). A stack-on-demand execution model for elastic computing. In *Proceedings of the 39th International Conference on Parallel Processing* (pp. 208–217).

Mahy, R., Matthews, P., & Rosenberg, J. (2010, April). *Traversal using relays around NAT (TURN): Relay extensions to session traversal utilities for NAT (STUN)* (RFC No. 5766). RFC Editor. Internet Requests for Comments. Retrieved March, 1, 2011, from http://tools.ietf.org/html/rfc5766

Mell, P., & Grance, T. (2009). *The NIST definition of cloud computing* (Tech. Rep.). National Institute of Standards and Technology, Information Technology Laboratory. Retrieved March, 1, 2011, from http://csrc.nist.gov/groups/SNS/cloud-computing/cloud-def-v15.doc

Meza, F., & Ruz, C. (2007). The thread migration mechanism of DSMPEPE. In *Proceedings of the 7th International Conference on Algorithms and Architectures for Parallel Processing* (pp. 177–187). Berlin, Germany: Springer-Verlag.

Milojičić, D. S., Douglis, F., Paindaveine, Y., Wheeler, R., & Zhou, S. (2000, September). Process migration. *ACM Computing Surveys, 32,* 241–299. doi:10.1145/367701.367728

Nelson, M., Lim, B.-H., & Hutchins, G. (2005). Fast transparent migration for virtual machines. In *Proceedings of the USENIX Annual Technical Conference* (pp. 391–394). Berkeley, CA: USENIX Association.

Nuttall, M. (1994, October). A brief survey of systems providing process or object migration facilities. *SIGOPS Operating Systems Review, 28,* 64–80. doi:10.1145/191525.191541

Oracle. (2007). *Java virtual machine tool interface (JVM TI).* Retrieved March, 1, 2011, from http://download.oracle.com/javase/6/docs/technotes/guides/jvmti/

Perry, G. (2008, June). *On clouds, the sun and the moon.* Retrieved March, 1, 2011, from http://gigaom.com/2008/06/21/on-clouds-the-sun-and-the-moon/

Quitadamo, R., Cabri, G., & Leonardi, L. (2008, February). Mobile JikesRVM: A framework to support transparent Java thread migration. *Science of Computer Programming, 70,* 221–240. doi:10.1016/j.scico.2007.07.009

Reese, G. (2008). *On why I don't like auto-scaling in the Cloud.* O'Reilly Media. Retrieved March, 1, 2011, from http://broadcast.oreilly.com/2008/12/why-i-dont-like-cloud-auto-scaling.html

Riteau, P., Morin, C., & Priol, T. (2010, February). *Shrinker: Efficient wide-area live virtual machine migration using distributed content-based addressing* (Tech. Rep.). Rennes, France: INRIA Rennes. Retrieved March, 1, 2011, from http://hal.inria.fr/inria-00454727/en/

Rosenberg, J. (2010, April). *Interactive connectivity establishment (ICE): A protocol for network address translator (NAT) traversal for offer/answer protocols* (RFC No. 5245). RFC Editor. Internet Requests for Comments. Retrieved March, 1, 2011, from http://tools.ietf.org/html/rfc5245

Stefanov, S. (2009). *Don't make me wait! Or building high-performance web applications.* Tech talk at eBay. Retrieved March, 1, 2011, from http://www.slideshare.net/stoyan/dont-make-me-wait-or-building-highperformance-web-applications

Travostino, F., Daspit, P., Gommans, L., Jog, C., de Laat, C., & Mambretti, J. (2006, October). Seamless live migration of virtual machines over the MAN/WAN. *Future Generation Computer Systems, 22,* 901–907. doi:10.1016/j.future.2006.03.007

Urquhart, J. (2008, June). *"Follow the law" meme hits the big time.* Retrieved March, 1, 2011, from http://blog.jamesurquhart.com/2008/06/follow-law-meme-hits-big-time.html

Willy, V. (2008). *The value of a millisecond: Finding the optimal speed of a trading infrastructure.* Retrieved March, 1, 2011, from http://www.tabbgroup.com/PublicationDetail.aspx?PublicationID=346

Xu, Z. (2010). *WAVNet: Wide-area virtual networks for dynamic provisioning of IaaS.* Unpublished Master's thesis, The University of Hong Kong, Pokfulum Road, Hong Kong.

Zhu, W., Fang, W., Wang, C.-L., & Lau, F. C. M. (2004). A new transparent Java thread migration system using just-in-time recompilation. In *Proceedings of the 16th IASTED International Conference on Parallel and Distributed Computing and Systems* (pp. 766–771). ACTA Press.

Zhu, W., Wang, C.-L., & Lau, F. C. M. (2002). JESSICA2: A distributed Java virtual machine with transparent thread migration support. In *Proceedings of the 4th IEEE International Conference on Cluster Computing* (pp. 381–388).

Zhu, W., Wang, C.-L., & Lau, F. C. M. (2003). Lightweight transparent Java thread migration for distributed JVM. In *Proceedings of the 32nd International Conference on Parallel Processing* (pp. 465–472).

ADDITIONAL READING

Armbrust, M., Fox, A., Grith, R., Joseph, A. D., Katz, R. H., Konwinski, A., et al. (2009, February). *Above the clouds: A Berkeley view of cloud computing* (Tech. Rep. No. UCB/EECS-2009-28). EECS Department, University of California, Berkeley. Retrieved March 1, 2011, from http://www.eecs.berkeley.edu/Pubs/TechRpts/2009/EECS-2009-28.html

Chen, P.-C., Lin, C.-I., Huang, S.-W., Chang, J.-B., Shieh, C.-K., & Liang, T.-Y. (2008). A performance study of virtual machine migration vs. thread migration for grid systems. In *Proceedings of the 22nd International Conference on Advanced Information Networking and Applications – Workshops* (pp. 86–91). Washington, DC, USA: IEEE Computer Society.

Chieu, T. C., Mohindra, A., Karve, A. A., & Segal, A. (2009). Dynamic scaling of web applications in a virtualized cloud computing environment. In *Proceedings of the 2009 IEEE International Conference on e-Business Engineering* (pp. 281–286). Washington, DC: IEEE Computer Society.

Coalition, V. C. E. (2010, June). *Enhanced business continuity with application mobility across data centers*. Retrieved March, 1, 2011, from http://www.vce.com/pdf/solutions/VCE_External_Whitepaper_Application_Mobility_June_7_2010.pdf

Crandell, M. (2011). *Top ten cloud computing and virtualization myths*. Cloud Expo. Retrieved March, 1, 2011, from http://cloudcomputing.sys-con.com/node/1682883

Lagar-Cavilla, H. A., Whitney, J. A., Scannell, A. M., Patchin, P., Rumble, S. M., de Lara, E., et al. (2009). Snowflock: Rapid virtual machine cloning for cloud computing. In *Proceedings of the 4th ACM European Conference on Computer Systems* (pp. 1–12). New York, NY: ACM.

Menon, A., Santos, J. R., Turner, Y., Janakiraman, G. J., & Zwaenepoel, W. (2005). Diagnosing performance overheads in the Xen virtual machine environment. In *Proceedings of the 1st ACM/USENIX International Conference on Virtual Execution Environments* (pp. 13–23). New York, NY: ACM.

Orenstein, G. (2010). *Forecast for 2010: The rise of hybrid clouds*. Retrieved March, 1, 2011, from http://gigaom.com/2010/01/01/on-the-rise-of-hybrid-clouds

Rajan, S. S. (2010). *Dynamic scaling and elasticity - Windows Azure vs. Amazon EC2*. Cloud Expo.

Retrieved March. 1, 2011, from http://cloudcomputing.sys-con.com/node/1626508

Satyanarayanan, M., Bahl, P., Caceres, R., & Davies, N. (2009). The case for VM-based cloudlets in mobile computing. *IEEE Pervasive Computing / IEEE Computer Society [and] IEEE Communications Society, 8*, 14–23. doi:10.1109/MPRV.2009.82

Sonnek, J., Greensky, J., Reutiman, R., & Chandra, A. (2010). Starling: Minimizing communication overhead in virtualized computing platforms using decentralized affinity-aware migration. In *Proceedings of the 39th International Conference on Parallel Processing* (pp. 228–237).

Triebes, K. (2010). *On-demand cloud bursting made possible by architecture*. Retrieved March, 1, 2011, from http://virtualizationreview.com/blogs/app-delivery-ondemand/2010/09/on-demand-cloud-bursting-via-architecture.aspx

Tuppeny, D. (2010, October). *Google App Engine (GAE) vs Amazon Elastic Computing (EC2) vs Microsoft Azure*. Retrieved March, 1, 2011, from http://blog.dantup.com/2010/10/google-app-engine-gae-vs-amazon-elastic-computing-ec2-vs-microsoft-azure

Vaquero, L. M., Rodero-Merino, L., & Buyya, R. (2011, January). Dynamically scaling applications in the cloud. *SIGCOMM Computer Communication Review, 41*, 45–52. doi:10.1145/1925861.1925869

Voorsluys, W., Broberg, J., Venugopal, S., & Buyya, R. (2009). Cost of virtual machine live migration in clouds: A performance evaluation. In *Proceedings of the 1st International Conference on Cloud Computing* (pp. 254–265). Berlin, Germany: Springer-Verlag.

Zhang, X., Jeong, S., Gibbs, S., & Kunjithapatham, A. (2010, July). Towards an elastic application model for augmenting computing capabilities of mobile platforms. In *Proceedings of the 3rd International ICST Conference on Mobile Wireless Middleware, Operating Systems, and Applications* (pp. 161–174).

Zhou, Y., Cao, J., Raychoudhury, V., Siebert, J., & Lu, J. (2007). A middleware support for agent-based application mobility in pervasive environments. In *Proceedings of the 27th International Conference on Distributed Computing Systems Workshops*. Washington, DC: IEEE Computer Society.

KEY TERMS AND DEFINITIONS

Auto-Scaling: A feature that allows a cloud computing service to automatically expand or diminish the scale of computing resources in order to react to changing workload conditions.

Desktop Cloud: An emerging type of P2P-based distributed computing architecture integrating compute and storage resources of Internet-wide desktop PCs into a single, dynamic and virtualized resource pool for sharing among Internet users.

Distributed JVM: A set of interconnected Java virtual machine (JVM) instances spanning multiple computing nodes, typically of the same cluster, that enable parallel execution of a multi-threaded Java application as if it was running on a single powerful machine. Such a JVM-level clustering solution is designed with rich transparent runtime support including single address space and cluster-wide thread scheduling to make parallel programming much easier.

Live Migration: The movement of a running virtual machine (VM) between different physical machines without disrupting any active network connections. Despite a small downtime, there is no noticeable impact of live migration against end users. Live migration seeks to improve manageability, performance and fault tolerance of distributed computing systems.

Multi-Level Mobility: An adaptive computation mobility concept in which a computational component (e.g. a stack frame, a thread, a process or a VM instance), can migrate from one execution site to another using a migration mechanism (e.g. partial stack migration, thread migration, process migration or live VM migration), whose granularity and implementation level along the software stack are well suited to the specific goal of the migration (e.g. load balancing, locality optimization and resource consolidation).

Stack-On-Demand (SOD): A new concept of lightweight execution migration in which only the top portion (topmost activation records or stack frames) of the runtime stack of a thread is being migrated.

Task Roaming: A mobile agent concept that an autonomous software component (implementing a task) can travel across a series of computing platforms to carry out some operations per stop. A typical use case is to reduce the data access latency seen by the component with respect to multiple data sources distributed geographically. With the SOD mechanism, task roaming can be done more efficiently.

Chapter 8
Managing Network Quality of Service in Current and Future Internet

Mark Yampolskiy
Leibniz Supercomputing Centre (LRZ), Germany

Wolfgang Fritz
Leibniz Supercomputing Centre (LRZ), Germany

Wolfgang Hommel
Leibniz Supercomputing Centre (LRZ), Germany

ABSTRACT

In this chapter, the authors discuss the motivation, challenges, and solutions for network and Internet quality of service management. While network and Internet service providers traditionally ensured sufficient quality by simply overprovisioning their internal infrastructure, more economic solutions are required to adapt the network infrastructures and their backbones to current and upcoming traffic characteristics and quality requirements with sustained success. The chapter outlines real-world scenarios to analyze both the requirements and the related research challenges, discusses the limitations of existing solutions, and goes into the details of practitioners' current best practices, promising research results, and the upcoming paradigm of service level management aware network connections. Special emphasis is put on the presentation of the various facets of the quality assurance problem and of the alternative solutions elaborated with respect to the technical heterogeneity, restrictive information sharing policies, and legal obligations encountered in international service provider cooperation.

MOTIVATION

Referring to the Internet as information superhighway is an old and outworn, but still valid metaphor. If we need to drive from A to B, we expect a road in good shape, do not want to make any major detour and try to avoid any traffic jams. Most drivers will prefer roads that can be used free of charges, motorcyclists typically prefer a nice scenery, and fleet managers want to make sure that all of the cargo that is split among several trucks arrives in time. Commuters drive to their workplace, families go on holidays, truck drivers feel at home on the streets, and some people just

DOI: 10.4018/978-1-4666-1888-6.ch008

drive for fun. Sometimes we are in a hurry, sometimes it feels OK to be a bit late, and sometimes there are accidents.

The situation on the Internet is quite similar: We need to get emails, files, or any other types of data packets from A to B. No matter whether we use the Internet as a part of our professional or our private life, we expect our Internet connection to be of "high quality". But what does quality mean in this context? While most users would use characteristics like fast and reliable, research and industry have agreed on quite a large set of so-called *quality-of-service* (QoS) parameters in the past decades, including *bandwidth*, *delay*, *jitter* (delay variation), *packet loss rate*, etc. Then, with the professionalization of network and Internet service providers, the demand for contracts and *service level agreements* (SLAs) has risen: It no longer was only important which characteristics a working connection had, but also which network availability a provider could guarantee, how fast any technical failures could be repaired, and how long planned downtimes and maintenance windows would take. To avoid that customers and providers start to dispute about discrepancies in how each of them thought those SLAs were met by the provider, neutral and objective measurement and monitoring criteria and systems became necessary. It only took a few years until a previously technical-level-only issue turned into a complicated multi-billion dollar business that depends on comprehensive network QoS management concepts and tools.

However, there is only one Internet, and just like the same road that is used by motorcycles, cars, busses, and trucks with 50 tons of cargo, the Internet uplink we have at home must be used for all types of data, whether it is a short email, a huge file upload, or a feature-length video-on-demand movie download. Yet, unlike the road we would drive on, we want to finish the file upload to Australia during watching the live news-feed from the United States, all the while sitting in front of a PC somewhere in Europe. With multiple services providers in various countries involved, both the heterogeneity of the involved technical components and the complexity of legal and organizational constraints explode. The lack of contracts – and therefore of some type of trust – between all involved parties, as well as the risk of abuse, e.g., by users claiming that a huge file upload is an important voice-over-IP phone call in order to obtain a better quality connection, Internet QoS management is a very hard to achieve and challenging task.

One of the major challenges thus is that requirements differ a lot depending on the actual use case or application the Internet is used for. In the consumer area, applications like telephony and on-line gaming have quite low traffic and bandwidth demands, but require very good availability and latency / jitter characteristics; on the other hand, video-on-demand traffic, which requires considerably higher bandwidth, is currently expected to raise by about 500% within the next three years. In industry and research, however, we have even further increased demands for bandwidth and availability. For example, the large hadron collider at CERN in Geneva, Switzerland, conducts physics experiments that produce about 15 petabytes (i.e., thousands of terabytes) of raw data each year. This data must be processed and analyzed by physicists around the globe and is thus being split and transported to several dozens of higher education, academic, and research institutions worldwide. While a larger delay is perfectly fine for those connections, their throughput and availability are crucial for the overall success of this huge long-term project.

In this chapter, we take a four-step approach to investigate network QoS management for both the current and the future Internet as shown in Figure 1. We first discuss network QoS management solutions that already exist beyond the Internet, for example in phone networks and managed backbone connections. They provide valuable ideas and suggestions of how Internet QoS management should work like, but so far any attempt to apply these techniques has failed. Second, we analyze the requirements and constraints for Internet QoS management in detail based on various real-world scenarios and aspects including triple play connectivity for home users and Internet neutrality issues. The result of this evaluation is the benchmark for all the solutions and approaches we discuss. Third, we look at the big picture of network QoS management and delve into the scientific challenges that are associated with all these practical troubles. One of the obvious issues we discuss is the limitation of traditional routing algorithms to a single QoS parameter, such as the currently available bandwidth or the expected delay. However, among several other topics we also discuss the burden that is imposed on new ideas and solutions, which stem from the scientific community, by real-world constraints including the limited amount of information that is exchanged between network service providers for legal and competitive reasons. Fourth, we present a selection of solutions for QoS guarantees in multi-domain network connections including the Internet, based on real-world best practices, recent and promising research projects, and upcoming trends. For example, we analyze the concepts behind the rapid link provisioning that is offered by the Internet2-lead DCN collaboration, discuss the I-SHARe tool that can be used to plan new dedicated end-to-end links, and the E2Emon application that is used in the pan-European research network Géant in order to monitor the QoS across organizations' and countries' borders. We also discuss the new paradigm of service level management aware routing, which explicitly deals with the planning of connections under end-to-end constraints and provides management functionality for the handling of multiple QoS parameters in parallel. We investigate its three building blocks – a novel inter-domain routing algorithm, a complete management information model, and a generic function schema – in detail.

After this thorough discussion we present our vision of the future and how Internet QoS management will look like in the near future. Deriving from where we are today and which direction further developments should take, we outline a series of open research issues. They are intended to sensitize young as well as experienced researchers to this important and highly practically relevant area of research and to foster individual and larger research projects therein. We conclude this chapter with a short summary of the key issues.

THE STATE OF THE ART

In order to start from a common base, we now give an overview of the established approaches to cope with quality assurance. To guarantee that, there are several possibilities today, depending on the actual purpose and intended use. These evolved beyond pure research proposals already years ago, while the Internet evolved as well. We go briefly through the most widely used techniques, beginning with an overview of how QoS can be done within a single domain and then describe other aspects like backbone or telephone networks.

Techniques and Technologies for QoS-Assurance within a Single Domain

Independent from the particular use case, quality assurance is possible as long as QoS is done within a single domain. In order to classify the traffic in packet switched networks, different types were introduced: "real time traffic", "streaming traffic", and "regular traffic". Each of them has certain requirements regarding delay, jitter, packet loss, availability, and data rate. Several techniques have been elaborated that can assure the compliance with the requirements specified for the particular types of communication. In the following we present two solutions, DiffServ and IntServ, that have evolved beyond the state of being pure research proposals and even managed to become Internet standards.

Figure 1. This chapter's structure

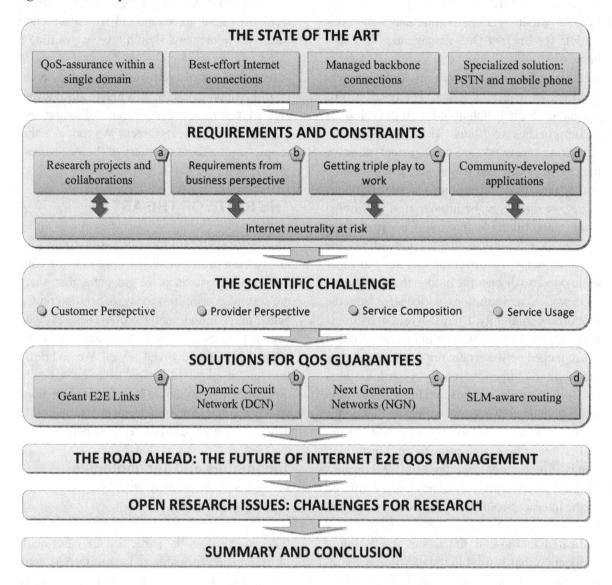

The *Differentiated Services* (DiffServ) enables the classification of IP packets based on the content they transport. The IP header's so-called *Type-of-Service* (TOS) field indicates how the particular packet should be handled, e.g., whether a regular treatment is acceptable or the delay has to be minimized (Information Sciences Intitute, 1981) (Network Working Group, RFC 249 - Coordination of Equipment and Supplies Purchase, 1971). Referring to the highway metaphor, ambulances could be treated with higher priority than normal cars. The clear advantages of DiffServ are its simplicity, scalability regarding multiple connections between various peers, and its robustness against route changes. However, there are several major drawbacks: Probably the most intuitive one is that this mechanism can be easily misused. By encoding the requirements in the IP header, users can take advantage of this and simply classify their whole own traffic with the highest and best possible quality. This in turn would inevitably lead to an increase of the concurrence among high-quality communication flows and consequently to the same problems we can see without using this technique at all. Secondly, DiffServ does not support a definition of thresholds for different QoS parameters that should be met. Finally, every so-called *Autonomous System* (AS), through which the traffic is routed, is free to support or ignore TOS flags and even if the AS do support it, the way they treat the same values may vary between different AS.

In contrast, the *Integrated Services* (IntServ) tackle the core cause of a bad and often also unpredictable network quality – the concurrence of various communication flows for the same limited resource. For signaling among network infrastructure components, IntServ uses the RSVP protocol. The *Resource Reservation Protocol* (RSVP) (Network Working Group, RFC 2205 - Resource ReSerVation Protocol (RSVP), 1997) supports a fine-grained resource reservation along the path between two communicating peers. In our example, this leads to the reservation of an exclusive street or road along the whole path. But even if all AS along the path support this resource reservation (which is not guaranteed in the Internet), this technique still faces two major drawbacks: First of all, it does not scale very well considering the amount of communication flows in the Internet. Furthermore, in the Internet it is not guaranteed that all IP packets will follow the same path between two communicating peers. Instead, different IP packets might take different routes, arrive at the destination from different paths that may not have been reserved and thus compete against other communication flows.

In the last few years, traffic engineering via MPLS (*Multiprotocol Label Switching*) became more and more popular. MPLS can establish fixed communication paths in packet switched networks. If MPLS is combined with RSVP, an integral part of the previously mentioned IntServ, it can therefore actively guarantee the communication flows' quality.

Best-Effort Internet Connections

The Internet consists of a collaboration of (independent) network providers, also referred to as AS. Customers can connect to the Internet using their local *Internet Service Provider* (ISP) that focuses on delivering Internet access to the people. Referring to the Internet as an information superhighway, an ISP can be seen as the owner and maintainer of a road network within a city. Every ISP guarantees certain connection characteristics to its customers, e.g., from their homes to the ISP's network (or road). However, the connection to other communication partners is provided using a so-called best-effort strategy. Best-effort means that there may be traffic jams if there are too many customers on the road/in the network, for example.

As long as the communication takes place between two customers within the same network, the SP can relatively easy guarantee a certain connection. It is rather difficult when they reside in the networks of different ASs. Referring to the road network, you may imagine that travelling through the country sometimes means that you have to pay for certain roads or streets, and that their quality and topology might differ, as they belong to other owners. This principle also applies to the Internet, but it usually remains hidden from the end users. AS often have so-called peering or transit agreements with their neighboring AS. As the AS usually are not limited to a sole and exclusive area, i.e., their networks can overlap geographically, any two or more AS may make such agreements, as long as they can be physically connected to each other. These contracts define rules and conditions to clarify when traffic from these AS may be exchanged or forwarded and what has to be paid by the AS from which the traffic originates.

The costs defined in these agreements heavily influence the particular route an AS uses to forward its traffic, as it usually selects one of the cheapest ones. Therefore, the SPs do not consider the connection quality besides the pure connectivity. This has not been a major drawback, since the Internet has been used for data transfers only for a long time. But with the increasing amount and diversity of multimedia content, the connection quality became an important factor and was subject to the users' interest as well.

The easiest, most obvious, and most broadly used technique is overprovisioning – providing such large resources that even in busy periods they do not run out. As a rule of thumb, many AS oversize their resources by 500% (so that only 20% of the available capacity is used) in order to handle concurrent communication flows properly without influencing each other. The most probable reason for this preference is the fact that up to 75% of a network's *Total Cost of Ownership* are related to *Operational Expenditure* (OPEX) rather than *Capital Expenditure* (CAPEX) on new equipment (TPACK, 2007). Furthermore, it is more difficult to manage complex equipment than to manage "simple" equipment, what in turn influences operational expenditures again. Even though overprovisioning provides statistically good results for all communication flows, for a single communication flow it does not provide the real quality assurance, as it does not consider any user specific requirements at all.

Managed Backbone Connections

Whereas the previously mentioned ISPs (also called *Tier 3* networks) are specialized on connecting users to the Internet, other AS specialize on the inter-network (*Tier 2*) or even global (*Tier 1*) connectivity. In the three-tier Internet model, ISPs are customers of Tier 2, and Tier 2 AS are customers of Tier 1 for transit services. This does not exclude peering agreements between Tier 2 and between Tier 1 ASs.

In order to provide transit services, Tier 1 and Tier 2 realize so-called *backbone* networks. As we recall, the contracts between end-users and ISPs include only access properties to the ISP's network.

Even though the contracts between the AS are generally subject to a *non-disclosure agreement* (NDA), it is commonly known that SLAs between AS contain a detailed specification of quality parameters as well as penalties in case if one AS violates the agreement. However, these SLAs do not cover a single end-user communication flow, but rather the aggregated traffic of various flows.

Most of today's backbone networks demanding outstanding high availability, reliability, and quality use the so-called *Synchronous Digital Hierarchy* (SDH) (Willis, 2001), as it features several key factors. For example, SDH is able to cope with a high utilization of the available bandwidth and to transport data with constant delay and jitter. Furthermore, it supports OAM (*Operation, Administration, and Maintenance*) functionality, thus the permanent monitoring in order to detect, localize, and correct outages that might occur. If it is not possible to correct the detected error, SDH supports automatically switching to a protection path. All these features account for high quality connections.

On the other hand, using SDH in backbone networks does not necessarily guarantee such high quality to the end-user connections, because multiple communication flows have to be multiplexed into STM-n (*Synchronous Transport Mode n*) containers. Therefore, the streams compete against the limited resources with all the resulting implications. Assigning an own STM-n container to every customer is not quite feasible as the "slowest" mode is specified for a transmission rate of 51.84 Mbit/s. Also the duration it takes to establish an SDH connection is not short enough for the most end-user applications.

A Specialized Solution for a Special Case: PSTN and Mobile Phone

In contrast to backbone networks, telephone networks are networks that are able to assign dedicated circuits to their users. In addition, it provides an excellent example for service-tailored quality assurance. The excellent service quality the end users are used to is based on two essential characteristics: low noise and low jitter. Low noise was especially important in the former *Public Switched Telephone Network* (PSTN) – every new connection meant that a new physical line had to be switched. As the voice signal started to be transferred digitally, low jitter became another issue. In order to establish new, monitor active, and release circuits that are not needed anymore, the *Signaling System No 7* (SS7) is used (Russell, 2006). It is a protocol family that takes care of communication among components responsible for managing (different) communication paths that may cross multiple providers, technologies and different kinds of networks (PSTN, mobile, and so on). In case of ISDN (*Integrated Services Digital Network*), the PSTN providers are able to assign exclusive channels of 56 kbit/s (USA and some other countries) respectively 64 kbit/s (Europe) for every new connection. Only the combination of a fixed path and the reservation of bandwidth that is sufficient for real-time transmission of voice signals leads to the good quality we all experience with telephone connections. Referring to our highway metaphor, a customer could call a gatekeeper and ask it for a dedicated road or lane to the desired destination. The gatekeeper then checks with other gatekeepers, whether or not the request can be realized, and takes care of assigning a lane on the road so that the customer can travel to his destination without any traffic jams.

Guaranteeing quality in mobile networks is slightly more complicated. Apart from aspects like accounting visitors from other networks, supporting a change of the base station or cope with inter cell interference, the connections' quality heavily depends on the radio links' quality. Therefore, a number of error correction methods have been applied, like the *Forward Error Correction* (FEC) or the *Radio Link Protocol* (RLP) that are technical measures for the correction of bit errors that occur during the signal's transmis-

sion and for the detection and re-requesting of damaged blocks (the latter is only reasonable for data connections, of course). Apart from the radio links, the *Global System for Mobile* communication (GSM) is also based on resource reservation and assigns dedicated 13 kbit/s channels for voice connections (the payload data rate depends on the particular codecs) to every new connection. Even though the data rate is significantly lower than the one in ISDN, GSM is able to deliver a similar connection quality due to highly sophisticated coding techniques. But as these are highly optimized for voice communications, these networks are still not able to deliver connections of such high data rate we are used to from our computers, laptops, etc.

PLANNING FUTURE NETWORK INFRASTRUCTURES: REQUIREMENTS AND CONSTRAINTS

Unfortunately, the concepts outlined above are not always sufficient to cope with today's requirements. In this section, we present several scenarios that exemplify such requirements and constraints for upcoming solutions for QoS assurance. We start with the demands raised in international research projects like the *Large Hadron Collider* (LHC), then analyze both the customer and provider perspectives in business applications, and discuss the challenges of triple play. As the Internet is not only imposed, but also lives by the means it is used for, we describe some applications developed within the community and their impact on networks. This depicts the myriad of (sometimes different) perceptions and requirements originated in real world scenarios (see Figure 2). In order to provide an unbiased big picture, we will also present the concerns raised by the possibility of losing Internet neutrality.

Research Projects and Collaborations

The *Large Hadron Collider* (LHC) is one of the most prominent and complex of today's research projects in particle physics. The data every experiment produces is always stored in CERN's own so-called Tier 0 (T0) computing centre for the long-time storage on tapes. Additionally, the limited amount of experimental data from recent few days is stored on the fast access devices. The later is used for forwarding of all experimental data from CERN to 11 Tier 1 (T1) supercomputing centres spread mostly across Europe and North America. The T1 centres are not only in charge for data permanent storage, but also for providing high-speed access to it for the Tier 2 (T2) centres. The actual data processing analysis is then performed in 160 T2 centres spread across the entire world. As the experiments take place day and night, the connections between CERN and the T1 centres have to be available day and night, too. In this model, the network connections between T0, T1, and T2 centres become to be a critical factor for the success of the whole experiment. Therefore LHC project demands high available permanent connections with exceedingly high bandwidth (currently 10Gbit/s pro connection, upgrade to 40Gbit/s is planned). Thus, in order to fulfill the high availability requirement, maintenance windows that prejudice the connections' quality have to be agreed on with the responsible persons at CERN as well. Another well-known

example is the recently started GRID initiative PRACE (*Partnership for Advanced Computing in Europe*). Its structure is very similar – there are again different Tiers (currently two T0 centres and a variety of T1 and T2 centres). These are distributed all over Europe and presently span twenty participating countries. The T2 computing centres run mostly jobs that can be executed sequentially. Therefore, the results do not have to be transferred to other computing centres in real time so that the requirements already sketched for the LHC are sufficient. In contrast, the case is different with T1 and T0. As they are used to execute jobs in parallel, they have to collaborate and exchange their results. Thus they depend on network connections that are not only highly reliable, but also do not suffer from noteworthy delay, jitter or bit error rate.

Both, LHC as well as PRACE ask for the autarchy of their connections (which is a common requirement of such large research projects). That means the particular link must not interfere with other traffic – for example by not using it for other purposes than the project ones.

QoS Guarantees from the Business Perspective

Having outlined these practical examples of advanced network infrastructures, we now focus on the business perspective first. Concluding the above mentioned LHC and PRACE, the requirements of such projects can be characterized as

Figure 2. Scenarios for requirements elicitation

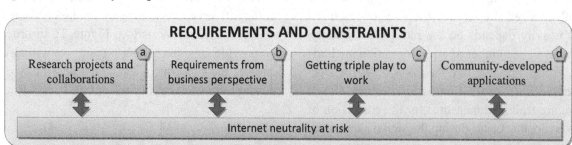

(a) long term permanent connections, which (b) should satisfy exceedingly high project-specific end-to-end quality requirements. Despite the prominence and importance of such projects, there are not many scenarios with that kind of requirements. For the multitude of business and research applications it is typical to have long-term requirements on Internet connections, which are, however, significantly less challenging than those of LHC and PRACE.

Even though end-users only consider the applications they can access through or use in the Internet, multiple service providers are involved in the realization of those services. It is common to classify these providers based on the focus of their activities in the vertical supply chain (see Figure 3). In this architectural concept, the so-called *carrier* providers provide and maintain the physical infrastructure, such as optical fibers. Carriers lease this infrastructure to ISPs. ISPs realize the logical layer on top of the leased and/ or own infrastructure, which allows the transmission of IP packets between communicating peers. The relations between carriers and ISPs are of a contractual nature with the exact QoS requirements, measurement methods, and penalties for the violation of agreed thresholds specified in the SLAs. These are two layers commonly associated with the way the Internet works.

With the evolution of the Internet into a business platform, two additional layers have been established. The so-called *Internet Application Providers* (IAPs) and *Internet Content Providers* (ICPs) are using the logical layer provided by ISPs for the delivery of their services to the customers. The difference between these two can be easily explained using the video-on-demand example: in this example, IAPs would provide the technique for the delivery of the video-stream from an ICP to the end-users. ICPs are in charge of the provisioning of the requested movie as video-stream and for managing all legal issues. It is obvious that in this example, the end-users' experience with the service accessed using the ICP's portal must be good and directly depends on the quality of the point-to-point connection provided by IAP, which in turn directly depends on the quality of the network connection realized by ISPs. As the later are realized by ISPs with the *best effort* strategy, the delivery of the requested content cannot be always guaranteed.

The outlined video-on-demand scenario is not the only one, in which the quality of the IAPs' and/or ICPs' services relies on the network connection. For instance, meanwhile it is common to have multiple portals to search and book flights as well as hotels. Accessing information and booking, however, requires some formal credentials from the airlines and hotels. Alone due to the multiplicity of such portals, airline companies, and hotels an establishment of direct contracts between the involved parties would become an organizational nightmare. Instead it is common to build service supply chains, in which companies specialized in different tasks, e.g., in the booking of requested tickets, act as an intermediary between airlines/ hotels and web-portals. Also here the quality of various services delivered in the chain among the SPs provided to a high extent depend on the quality of the established network connections.

Furthermore, with so-called *Cloud* providers offering the on-demand adjustment of available resources, it is now possible to host business applications in Clouds for the cost-efficient handling of user requests' fluctuations. In this case, the elasticity requirement, i.e., the on-demand adjustment of relevant parameters, should also be applied to the network connections. Consequently, in order to provide high quality services to the end-users and among each other, IAPs and ICPs should be able to request connections with the specified quality. Later in this chapter we present the *Digital Circuit Network* (DCN) project aiming to cope with these requirements. In this project techniques for the on-demand establishment of the multi-domain network connections with dedicated bandwidth are elaborated.

Figure 3. Layered architecture of an all-IP network according to (Renda, 2008)

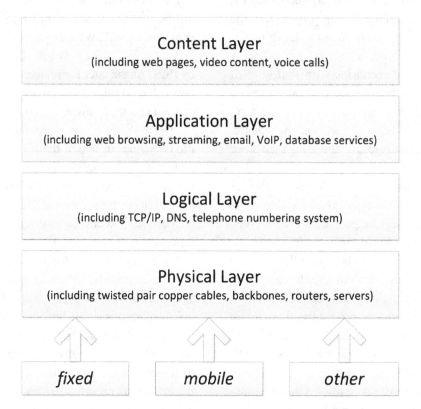

Business-to-Customer Challenges: Getting Triple Play to Work

But the business perspective is not the only one we have to consider. From the customer perspective, we are consuming three kinds of services. For meanwhile over 100 years people spread around the world can communicate with each other via telephone, about 70 years ago television has made its first steps and since the 1990ies we can exchange data and content via the Internet. Usually, all three kinds of services are provided by different provider classes, which in turn use service-tailored equipment for the delivery of the specific kind of data.

Telecommunication companies have originally provided an on-demand established audio communication between two communication partners, i.e., point-to-point, using analogous signals via physically switched wires. The high

noise level frequently experienced by end-users and difficulties of infrastructure management and maintenance faced by providers have led, however, to a paradigm switch. Telephone communication is currently delivered as digitally encoded signal over virtual circuit with the physical resources, i.e., bandwidth, reserved end-to-end for the particular communication channel. Especially resource reservation is important, as the audio signal should be transmitted in real-time with low delay and very low jitter.

In order to deliver the TV content, cable providers have to fulfill different requirements. First of all, it is a unidirectional point-to-multipoint communication. In opposite to telephone communication, no connection establishment is needed, as the TV signal is continuously broadcasted. Also there is no need for delay minimization. However, the TV broadcast has to be transmitted in real-time and with high quality. The first requirement originates from the fact that in original concepts TV receivers were not supposed to buffer the received signal; instead they were designed to display the received signal in real-time. The quality constraint originates from user experience, as one will be annoyed by noisy video- or audio- signals or if synchronization between these two is lost. Consequently, also for cable providers it is common to reserve bandwidth for different channels and keep unused frequency areas between channels as a buffer preventing interferences among them. It is obvious that the bandwidth of the channel must be selected according to the quality of the delivered content.

Finally, the Internet was not originally supposed to provide multimedia content. Instead it was the platform for textual communication, e.g., via *email*, and for file transfers, e.g., via *ftp*. As the Internet evolved from the DARPA research project, i.e., the requirements were strongly influenced by the U.S. military, its main quality criterion was the robustness of the network against all kinds of equipment outages. The basis for the interconnecting networks was (and still is) the IP protocol and the packet routing principle. As in the Internet no resources are typically assigned to the user connection, a better utilization of available bandwidth is possible, which is not the case especially for telephone connections. From the user perspective, the fast delivery of the requested content, e.g., a file or webpage, is important, but quality parameters like delay and jitter during the data transfer often are completely irrelevant.

Opposed to these networks specialized in the fulfillment of particular requirements, the idea arose to deliver all three kinds of content through the same network infrastructure (so-called *triple play,* introduced around 2005). The envisaged service consolidation will allow a single provider to offer the whole coverage package to its users. As more providers will have to compete with each other, the end-users will benefit from the cost reduction. On the other hand, outages in the

underlying network infrastructure might lead to a simultaneous failure of all services. Also the removal of service borders enforce providers, previously specialized in the delivery of a single service, to look for a cost-effective extension of the existing infrastructure to support a triple play service. This, however, leads to the development of alternative solutions. Later we present the concept of *Next Generation Networks* (NGN) – a solution developed by ITU-T for telecommunication service providers. This solution is especially interesting, as it breaks with the concepts of the ISO/OSI reference model, which is used in the Internet as a structure for the protocol stack and for the definition of goals for the protocol layers.

Community-Developed Applications and their Impact on Networks

Whereas the evolution of triple play is driven by network providers and vendors of network equipment, one can also see very strong movements in the user community. Meanwhile, the Internet and increasingly also mobile communication becomes a platform, where many users seek to increase their social state, popularity grade, or simple use it as a business platform. Motivated by these and other reasons, users tend to develop new applications. Opposed to the development of triple play, community-developed applications show an extremely high grade of diversity, and the basic ideas are often unpredicted by others until they are revealed and become public and popular. The social networking platforms *Facebook* and *Twitter* can be seen as two – meanwhile very well known – examples of this trend. Furthermore, not only the user community, but also big companies are very present in the development of novel applications, as it can be seen, e.g., at *Google Maps* and *YouTube*.

In this chapter we intentionally omit the discussion about trends and techniques on the server side, which are needed in order to cope with the demands of such community-developed applications. Instead, we focus on the QoS aspects in network connections. Even though the mentioned social networking applications do not really fit in the triple play concept, they do not produce new requirements for network connections needed, e.g., for the broadcasting of a news post. However, a completely different situation is faced in *peer-to-peer networks*. These are not physical networks, but rather dynamically built and steadily reconfigured overlay networks operated on top of the existing physical infrastructure. Originally predominantly used for sharing of various sort of content, this community-developed technology is increasingly used in various user-faced applications. Probably the most prominent examples are the content-sharing program *BitTorrent* and the communication program *Skype*. As Skype offers some of its services for free, they may incorporate the exchange of triple play content for personal conversations and for conferencing among multiple users. As the quality of any overlay network directly depends on the quality of the underlying physical network connections, outages of the physical networks can inflict damage to the quality of the user-faced service. For instance, whereas the telephony via Skype between Europe and North America provides very good quality, during the communication with somebody outside of these highly internetworked areas one can occasionally experience very high delays and delay variations in the transmission of voice.

Meanwhile, it is probably impossible to even simply list all community-developed applications. To summarize the existing trends, common for such applications is their very rapid development time, high diversity, and often the unpredictability of application scenarios, and variety of the quality parameters they depend on. This raises the necessity for any quality assurance technique to be highly adaptive and extendible, as we will see in the SLM-aware Routing approach later on.

Internet Neutrality at Risk: Staying at the Edge of the Abyss?

Despite the variety of all the services, applications and requirements explained in the previous sections the data has to be managed and transferred equally – regardless of its content or origin. This is not only mandatory for today's, but also for tomorrow's networks – what further challenges they ever may face. For example, an ISP must not forbid its customers to use certain services just because they do not fit into the ISP's portfolio. Neither may it treat data originating from its own network with preference. Such regulations violate the so-called network neutrality.

The debate about this neutrality, especially the Internet *neutrality,* is a very controversial topic with the discussion ongoing meanwhile for over 10 years. The difficulty of this discussion is that both opponent parties have very good arguments for and against it. The whole scale debate is performed in multiple dimensions, among others:

1. The *technical* dimension, covering features needed for traffic shaping;
2. The *competitive* dimension, covering competition among providers at the various layers of the supply chain; and
3. The *consumerist* dimension, covering the influence of different decisions on the end-users (Renda, 2008).

The examples discussed in this chapter up to now present use cases in which the equal treatment of IP packets belonging to different communication flows and services would prevent the realization of high quality user-faced services. In some cases this is fully inacceptable. For example, the bad quality of network connections used in telemedicine might endanger human lives.

On the other hand, the defenders of the Internet neutrality have outlined several scary Pandora-box scenarios. From the *technical* perspective, traffic shaping would allow ISPs to treat various kinds of traffic differently. In the simplest case, ISPs will be able to block various applications, e.g., via port blocking or deep packet inspection. Also a more hidden differentiated treatment is possible. For instance, IAPs might face the situation when the packets used for the quality testing of the connection between two communicating peers are treated by ISPs differently than the actual data traffic. In this case, the quality of the connections might become hardly predictable and therefore barely manageable.

One of the most common arguments discussed from the *competition* perspective is that the loss of the Internet neutrality will allow ISPs to intentionally degrade the connection quality for competing providers and/or services. This argument is especially sound in conjunction with the possibility that the ISP extends its services in the vertical supply chain to those, which are classically provided by IAPs/ICPs. For instance, if an ISP provides VoIP as its own service, it can block or significantly reduce the performance of similar services, e.g., Skype. Further, such situations will force IAPs/ICPs to seek arrangements with ISPs in order to get a better connection quality for their services. This in turn might endanger the innovation potential of the Internet, as the newcomers will face harder competition with the already established providers. However, the potential loss of the Internet neutrality is not only the providers' problem. The possibility for traffic shaping will allow ISPs to introduce *customer-tiering*, by which customers will be requested to pay not only for the access to the internet, but also for having access to different quality levels. Also the misbehavior among SPs might diminish the multitude of the applications and content available to the end-users.

These are just some of the reasons and examples frequently used by the defenders of the Internet neutrality concept. Even though this chapter is dedicated to the evolvement in the Internet, we have included the view of the opponents in order to present a broader picture. Despite the outlined almost apocalyptical prognoses, so far we – as

end-users – cannot see significant drawbacks in the services provided to us, which are caused by the development and the ongoing deployment of the new technologies opposing the network neutrality. We further would like to finalize this section with the words of Tim Berners-Lee, the inventor of the World Wide Web, who stated in his blog "Net Neutrality is NOT saying that one shouldn't pay more money for high quality of service. We always have, and we always will." (Berners-Lee, 2006)

THE SCIENTIFIC CHALLENGES

Before we continue with actual solutions to these outlined requirements and constraints, we want to introduce the relevant scientific challenges in the following section. They are mostly derived from operational experiences within the outlined scenarios. First, the term "scientific challenges" can be described as a gap between our goals (i.e., what we want to achieve) and our abilities to achieve (i.e., what we are able to based on already elaborated concepts) under consideration of all accompanying requirements and constraints (i.e., what is acceptable and what is not). Often the difficulty to reach this goal is caused by the combination of requirements and constraints. Therefore, in practice often solutions are elaborated, which fulfill only parts of the known requirements.

The goal we are speaking about in this chapter can be described as *multi-domain network connections with guaranteed end-to-end quality for customer-specific parameters*. Our abilities have been outlined in the previous sections and can be summarized as either

1. Single-domain connections with guaranteed quality,
2. Multi-domain connection with best-effort quality, or
3. Multi-domain connection with highly service-specific QoS parameters.

Consequently we can assume that the difficulty to reach our goal is based on the unique combination of requirements and constraints, which have to be considered. In scientific research it is common to use a systematical approach in order to derive those requirements and constraints. For the requirements analysis we can survey the problem from the following perspectives:

1. The user-/customer-requirements;
2. The service provider restrictions and constraints;
3. The service composition; and
4. The dynamics of the service usage.

In the following we will present challenges identified by such a survey and discuss the difficulties of their realization.

Simultaneous Support of Multiple Customer-Specific Properties

The necessity to support multiple customer-specific properties at the same time has dramatic and manifold consequences. Most dramatically it affects the routing, i.e., the process of path finding under consideration of the specified conditions. The routing algorithms established in Internet, in PSTN-, as well as in LAN- and WAN-networks operate on a single parameter. One of the most prominent examples is OSPF (*Open Shortest Path First*), which is based on Dijkstra's algorithm (Dijkstra, 1959). The high performance of those algorithms is based on the Bellman's optimality principle (Bellman, 1952), which in turn depends on the distinct order of values. If, for instance, the cost of a connection segment is used as the single parameter, which has to be considered by routing, a path with a minimal cost can be relatively easy found. When routing is done with a single parameter, just the one with smallest cost is chosen from all alternative segments. With more than one parameter, such a selection cannot always be made. This can be illustrated using an example with two equally important connection parameters, which have to be considered at the same time: cost and delay. If we have two alternatives, the first one (10 Cents, 20ms) and the second one (20 Cents, 10ms), then it is impossible to decide which of them is the more preferable one. The problem of path finding with multiple constraints is known since mid of the 1980ies (Jaffe, 1984). Various related problems have been analyzed, e.g., in (Ziegelmann, 2007). Among others it has been shown that the transformation from multiple parameters to a single one can only provide an approximate solution, but not necessarily guarantees the fulfillment of all requirements. Also several algorithms have been elaborated, for instance SAMCRA (Kuipers, 2004), which operate on multiple parameters at the same time. Besides remaining performance issues, these algorithms generally require complete knowledge about the whole network and all the properties of all network segments. However, the dependence on the complete global knowledge makes routing algorithms inapplicable for multi-domain routing, as it would violate SP-policies to share this much information with third parties (see below).

A further big issue of the customer-specific connection properties is the diversity of the ways how they should be treated. During the routing the values of connection segments considered for the path have to be aggregated in order to compute the expected property of the path. Furthermore, if end-to-end constraints have to be considered, the calculated value has to be compared with those constraints. The typical procedure in existing routing algorithms is the summation of values and the selection of the alternative with the smallest value as most preferable one. This procedure is very well applicable to QoS parameters like costs and delay. However, it is not necessarily the case for other connection properties. For instance, if we consider bandwidth, the smallest value of all involved connection segments defines the maximal available bandwidth of the end-to-end connection. In other words, an aggregation function for bandwidth should be defined as the *minimum*-function. Also, regarding the comparison with the end-to-end requirements, the calculated bandwidth should be not smaller than the defined value. Dependent on the quality parameter, the aggregation and comparison functions can become even much more complex. Up to now, only service specific solutions have been implemented for a limited amount of quality parameters. The support of customer-specific parameters would, however, require a semantic-aware treatment of those properties, which cannot be easily implemented in existing solutions.

Service Providers' Concerns and Preferences

But the customer is not the only one, whose interests have to be considered. To motivate the SPs' view, we have to remark that there are various routing strategies and paradigms (Tanenbaum, 2003). Regardless of the routing strategy, an intelligent routing procedure always depends on the information about available connections or connectivity possibilities. If the route has to fulfill constraints or be optimized for some parameter(s), also the information about properties of these connections is needed. Whereas the intra-domain routing can rely on the complete information about network topology and connection properties, an inter-domain routing has to cope with various constraints caused by the participation of multiple SPs.

At first we have to mention in this context the very restrictive SP-policies, which are usually applied on information. Information about network topology, available capacities, all kinds of statistics, and many others is usually considered as very sensitive. The reasons for these restrictions are also manifold. For instance, the information about the network topology can be used by hackers for various attacks. The information about available capacities and network utilization might provide an economical advantage to other

SPs competing for some contract. Furthermore, these information policies are probably the main reason, why inter-domain routing in Internet and in PSTN networks operates only on information about connectivity, i.e., the accessibility of a distant endpoint through a particular interface. On the other hand, in order to guarantee the end-to-end requirements also information about the quality of the involved connection segments has to be considered. Consequently, an information-gap between the necessary and the available information has to be overcome.

A further very important aspect is the SP's route preferences. This means that if multiple alternative routes exist, some of them are more preferable than others. The reasons for this behavior are manifold. Most important in multi-domain environment are contractual relationships between SPs, which result in the amount of money transferred between them. There could be various strategic or also purely technical reasons, e.g., load balancing or better utilization of the installed infrastructure. Regardless of the reasons, it is essential for SP acceptance that their preferences are considered during the routing. At the same time, if end-to-end customer requirements have to be considered, such preferences cannot always be followed. Consequently, a balance between SP preferences and customer requirements has to be found.

Multi-Domain Heterogeneity

The independence of SPs has not only influence on their preferences regarding the route. Various factors like different financial situations, contractual relationships with hardware vendors, diverse heritages from the past as well as other factors might influence the choice of network technologies and hardware used by SP in its own network. Heterogeneity of hardware and network technologies inevitably results in the heterogeneity of the available network state information. As long as only the pure connectivity between two endpoints counts, this cannot be seen as a big issue. If, however, customer requirements have to be considered, the heterogeneity of the state information becomes a very big issue. For instance, when monitoring the network infrastructure, which is necessary for outage detection, some technologies can report Error Bits, others only can provide Error Seconds. But even if the same technology and hardware of the same vendors is used, configuration parameters can build a semantic wall. For example, the influence of irreparable frames (at ISO/OSI layer 2) on the overall performance degradation depends on the configured size of frames transported on layer 2. Therefore, the solution has to cope with the multi-dimensional heterogeneity presented by SPs.

Crossing Domain Boundaries

Due to the above-mentioned heterogeneity of the applied hardware and network technologies as well as the organizational boundaries, connecting neighboring domains or SPs is another challenging area. Even though such connections are comparatively very short (we speak about a couple of meters/feet), their influence on the overall connection quality should not be underestimated. For instance, for a connection with a fixed path and without local repair functionality, an outage of a short *inter-domain* connection immediately leads to an outage of the overall end-to-end connection, exactly as it would be the case with significantly longer connections within domains.

Regarding the solutions considering only connectivity, like PSTN or the current Internet, the connectivity state of an inter-domain connection can be easily determined. If, however, the quality of the inter-domain connection has to be determined, it becomes a bigger issue. Even though the trust relations between neighboring SPs are usually very good, getting management access to the network infrastructure of the neighbor SP can be seen as very unrealistic assumption, as it would violate the SP's policies. On the other hand, without information about the quality of

the inter-domain connection, the planning of a connection compliant with end-to-end customer requirements can be barely done. This raises the necessity to find a way to determine the quality of Inter-Domain connections without violating the SPs' policies.

Managing Composed Multi-Domain Service Instance

The experience gained from PSTN and backbone networks has shown that for the quality assurance a thorough planning of the needed resources is necessary. However, the planning and assignment of resources to a connection alone is not sufficient to seriously guarantee end-to-end requirements. In addition, these decisions have to be supported by the management procedures. The management aspects become indispensible in the case of quality guarantees for long-lasting network connections.

Multi-domain network connections are realized via the so-called *horizontal supply chain*, in which all involved SPs are independent autonomous organizational domains with equal rights. Such a service instance composition is typical for Internet- and telephone-connections. In opposite to horizontal supply chains, in which management and quality assurance aspects are very well understood, the management of service instances realized via vertical supply chains remains a very big issue. In the Internet there is no integrated support for multi-domain connection management at all. Telephone connections management aspects are mostly limited to signal the establishment and the teardown of a connection as well as the monitoring of connection persistence.

The difficulty of the management of multi-domain network connections can be backtracked to the restrictive policies of the involved SPs. Similar to information policies, management access to their own network infrastructure is generally seen as a very sensitive task, which is allowed to be performed only by a limited amount of approved tools and persons residing within one's own organizational boundaries. An external domain interface can be seen as an intuitive and simple solution for this problem. Through this interface the management functionality of the connection segment(s) provided by a single SP should be accessible. However, the roles, their responsibility areas, communication ways between the involved SPs, and – most important – the integration of a single-domain management functionality of the involved segments into a multi-domain management functionality of the whole service instance still have to be defined for a new and provided for an established multi-domain network connection. But even if such a multi-domain management functionality is in place, there are still other (dynamic) influences that have to be considered.

Cope with Dynamics of Service Change and Service Usage

Meanwhile, many firms and private persons see the Internet as an opportunity to become a piece of the steadily growing IT marketplace. Motivated by economical, strategically, or other reasons, the Internet became a showplace for multiple emerging services. An observation of the recent development shows the steadily growing amount and diversity of these emerging services. Also the portion of services relying on the connection quality increases. Such a tendency will inevitably lead to the development of applications, which demand connection properties, which have not been considered in the past. To provide an example, *energy-efficient* (also referred to as "green") connections are currently a very important topic of research, which have not been considered at all only few years ago. Consequently, every solution we are looking for has to be easily extendible to support new connection properties, which have not been considered in the past. Otherwise the solution can become obsolete or – which is much worse – a slowing factor for the development of novel customer-facing services.

The other aspect is the dynamics of the service usage. This means the amount of simultaneous requests for new service instances, the average service time of one connection, and the amount of SPs which can be involved into connection ordering and provisioning. The scalability of a solution regarding these and other aspects can become a limiting factor for its application areas. For instance, mass-services like telephony have to cope with thousands of simultaneous connection requests and established connections provided to millions of users.

Similar to scalability, also the robustness of the solution can be a limiting factor for an application area. This means robustness against various outages by all involved roles and components. For instance, IP routing in Internet is very robust against infrastructure failures, which makes it very viable for data transfer.

Having to Build Everything from Scratch

Up to now all discussion in this paragraph has presumed that only pre-installed and pre-configured infrastructure can be considered for the planning of the new network connection. However, there are cases where infrastructure needed to interconnect two endpoints is either not available or is not sufficient to fulfill of all customer requirements. This situation is often faced by the providers of backbone network connections. Usually, a multi-domain aspect is removed from the equation, so that only technical aspects can be considered. For instance, transatlantic telecommunication cables are provided by a consortium of multiple telecommunication companies (TAT-14 Cable System Homepage, 2007). On the other hand, if multiple SPs participate in the provisioning of a backbone connection in a fully independent manner, the inter-domain communication and negotiation of technical parameters among the involved SPs become very critical and challenging additional factors, which we discuss next.

SOLUTIONS FOR QOS GUARANTEES IN MULTI-DOMAIN NETWORK CONNECTIONS

As we now know the challenges that come with multi-domain network connections, we want to have a look at the currently ongoing work aiming to cope with the requirements discussed above. We start with the presentation of E2E Links – a novel service offered within the Géant project. E2E Links provide to international research projects the possibility for the establishment of permanent connections with customer tailored quality parameters. After that, we go on with a description of the research project DCN led by Internet2. The focus of this project lays on the dynamic provisioning of network connections with dedicated bandwidth. Then we present concepts elaborated for the Next Generation Networks (NGN). These are efforts done in the telecommunication industry as a means for triple-play support. Finally, we present the modern concept of service level management aware routing; it aims to cope with the variety and frequency of changes to relevant QoS parameters. The map of the parallel ongoing developments together with their short descriptions is depicted in Figure 4.

Real World Practice: Géant E2E Links

Géant (GÉANT Project Home, 2011) is a pan-European collaboration of more than 30 *national research and education networks* (NRENs) including the *German Research Network* (DFN), the *Italian Consortium GARR*, and many others. Whereas the focus of these NRENs is to deliver high quality network infrastructure to national research and education institutions, the collaboration aims at interconnecting these NRENs and therefore provide a highly reliable, high performance network infrastructure for international research projects like the LHC at CERN. We

already outlined the requirements of them in the previous sections.

As already mentioned, such large research projects often ask for specific requirements regarding the connections' quality, which is why the "shared" infrastructure is not always suitable and has to be adjusted to the customer's needs. As such connections do not vanish or institute very frequently, putting effort in satisfying these requirements is an acceptable burden.

In order to meet the outlined requirements, at the end of 2005 in Géant a novel service called *End-to-End Links* (E2E Links) was introduced. E2E Links are long-term dedicated end-to-end connections between two endpoints. This service is provided to a rather limited number of users. Long-term in this context means life times of typically at least a few months up to several years. The provisioning of shorter living connections is seen as out-of-scope of this service, as the duration of planning and establishment of E2E Links might vary between few weeks and several months. Such big time variations are caused by the frequent necessity to procure and to install new network equipment, which is necessary for the fulfillment of customer requirements.

From the technical point of view, E2E Links are dedicated optical point-to-point connections realized on ISO/OSI layers 1 and 2 that are delivered by one or more NRENs (see Figure 5). Usually, two or more NRENs are involved in the realization of an E2E Link. As NRENs are independent organizations, various network technologies are frequently used for the realization of different segments of the same E2E Links.

The planning and installation of E2E Links is done manually. This means that interconnection points of involved connection segments (in the project referred to as *Demarcation Points*, DP) have to be agreed upon between two neighboring NRENs. Further, as the physical network infrastructure might have to be installed, the parameters of the network infrastructure and of the used network technologies have to be negotiated and

Figure 4. Solution building blocks for the presented challenges

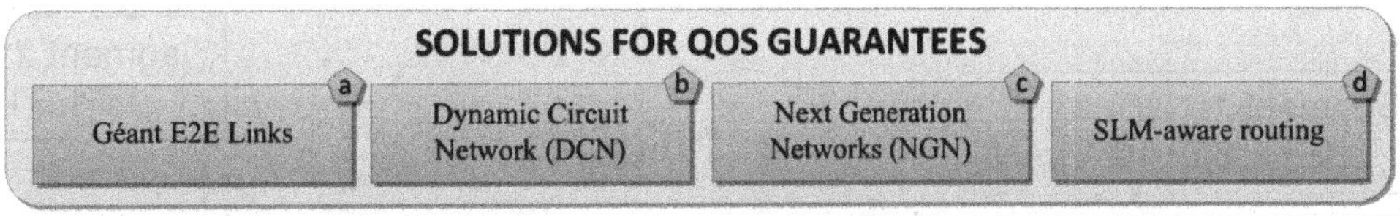

| | **SOLUTIONS FOR QOS GUARANTEES** | | | |
	(a) Géant E2E Links	(b) Dynamic Circuit Network (DCN)	(c) Next Generation Networks (NGN)	(d) SLM-aware routing
Start	2005	2007	1999	2009
Type	Novel service	Research project	Standardized technology	Research proposal
Focus and special features	Long term connections. Manual planning, installation, and maintenance. No pre-installed infrastructure is required.	Short term connections. Pre-installed and pre-configured infrastructure is required.	Short term connections. Pre-installed and pre-configured infrastructure is required.	Short and long term connections. Requires quality assurance in single domain. Adaptive selection and configuration of management functionalities.
Supported QoS	*Bandwidth*, constant *delay*, low *jitter*, high *availability*	*Bandwidth*, in the future also *delay*	Service specific *QoS classes*	User-defined combinations
Countries	European Union	United States, European Union	Worldwide	Germany

agreed upon among the connection planning teams. All these and other tasks require some high density information exchange and coordination efforts among employers of different organizations. In the case of connections leaving the same geographical region, e.g., connections between Europe and U.S., the time difference increase the difficulty of the communication tasks.

As outages of the network equipment cannot always be avoided, a steady monitoring of E2E Links is needed. Such a monitoring system should not only detect an outage, but also help with the localization of the problem area. Further, if an alarm is raised, the multi-domain *Incident & Problem Management* processes are required in order to fix the recognized problem. Similar to the connection planning task, these processes are done manually and therefore require information exchange among involved teams from different

NRENs. Later in this section we will describe the tool support for information exchange among NRENs.

The customers of E2E Links are big international research projects and collaborations like the ones mentioned above, LHC and PRACE. An example for such an E2E connection is a connection from CERN to another Tier1 supercomputing centre in Germany and thus usually crosses multiple NRENs. "Dedicated" means that these links are set up for this particular purpose only. When we speak about users in the context of Géant, we do not think of the particular researcher or employee but of the actual project, for example LHC, PRACE, and so on. These projects have got several end points distributed over Europe that need to be connected by the mentioned E2E links. But simply connecting a few end sites is not the only requirement such projects' demands.

Figure 5. Typical structure of an E2E link

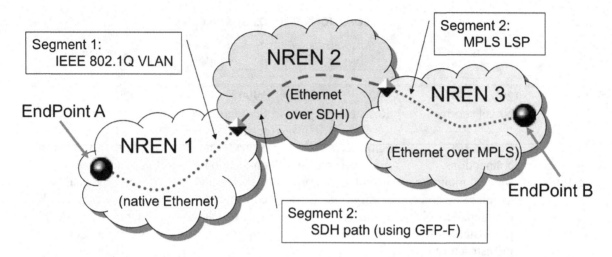

The connections' autonomy can be implicitly guaranteed by these E2E links, as they are set up for these projects only and therefore are not used to route regular Internet or other projects' traffic. When research projects order such an E2E link, they can choose between different options, for example, just ask for a certain amount of bandwidth (typically 1 Gbit/s or 10 Gbit/s) or even go for a whole dedicated wavelength.

Realization and Tool Support

In order to foster not only the planning, but also to guarantee an efficient monitoring of such high quality E2E links over multiple domains, some tools have been created that support the NRENs' network engineers in these tasks. We now describe how experts can gain from these when they (still manually) plan a new E2E link with the I-SHARe tool (Information Sharing across Heterogeneous Administrative Regions) and how monitoring concepts like the E2E Monitoring System (E2Emon) or measurement points like HADES Active Delay Evaluation System (HADES) support them in keeping track of the link's properties.

Supporting Tools: Planning a New Link with I-SHARe

Before we can describe the actual planning process we want to give a brief overview of I-SHARe's design and purpose. A lot of different people (from various network planning teams) have to coordinate their work during an E2E link set up. To foster all operational procedures and processes among different administrative groups, I-SHARe was created (Information Sharing across Heterogeneous Administrative Regions, 2011). I-SHARe is a shared information and tracking tool that helps the domains' experts to do their work more easily, more efficiently, more seamlessly, and more quickly: It takes care of storing the customer requests' details as well as the domains' essential information, such as experts' contact information, operational groups responsible for certain kinds of action (e.g., link planning, link maintenance, etc.) or technical details about *user to network interfaces* (UNIs) or *network to network interfaces* (NNIs). Furthermore, experts can use it to store information about the progress of their planned and set up E2E links. In order to achieve all these goals, I-SHARe provides two primary architectural component classes:

- The **domain part** is being used by every NREN to insert and manage its own (single-domain) key information, e.g., contact information of operational groups responsible for particular tasks, and make it available to other partners (see Figure 6).
- The **central server** takes care of receiving all information from the domain parts and incorporating it in relevant multi-domain processes. Further, the central server provides the platform for the insertion and management of information relevant for the multi-domain view. For example, when experts plan a new link, they use the central server to look up other domains' information or connection points' technical details, coordinate their work and keep track of the link's progress.

I-SHARe does not take any actions automatically (people still have to take decisions and do the actual work themselves), but it supports them in finding the right information at the right time and place.

After all NRENs have published their key data the experts can use the central server to plan a new link. Every link cycles through certain phases during its instantiation and operation:

- **Ordered**: This phase contains all links that have been requested, acknowledged, and planned to realize.
- **Set Up**: When the actual set up (and negotiation between all involved partners) is being started, the link is put into this phase.
- **Operational**: All currently established and working links belong to this phase.

Figure 6. Interaction of I-SHARe's domain part and central server (Cesaroni, et al., 2008)

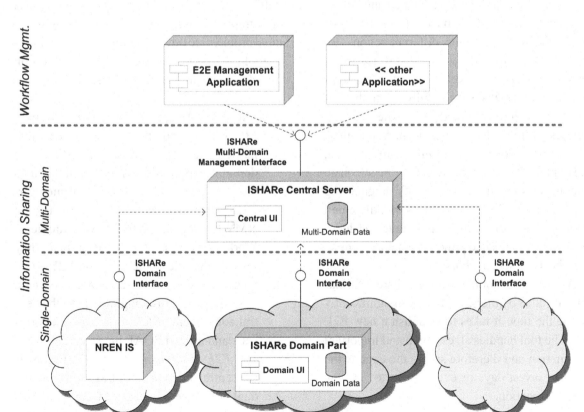

- **Decommissioned**: All former operational, now released connections are listed here.

Usually, one of the connecting domains' customers – for example, a research project – requests a new link from its own to another location. If the contacted partner approved the particular request, one of the domain's experts needs to login to I-SHARe and open a new link request. After he identified the end points (usually given by the request), filled in the mandatory request information (requested bandwidth, ...), and selected a possible route through the NRENs, the link appears in the ordered list. This list contains a checklist that indicates the current state of the link request and covers actions like route finding, NNI negotiation (agree on technical details), offer to the end site, etc., and may be edited in the link's detailed view. After all preliminary steps have been completed successfully, the link can be put to the setup phase that is similarly designed and covers the actual infrastructure installation. Of course, the check list now contains different actions, for example, E2E link ID assigned, infrastructure ready, or connection tested. After all these steps have been completed successfully again, the link may be put to the operational phase, where the link remains until it is decommissioned. At all times, experts may look up the required information, like contact addresses, by selecting the adequate domains or sites. In order to notify neighboring domains, I-SHARe provides user-friendly email functionalities, too. At any time, notes or documents may be uploaded to the system, for example, data sheets or screen shots.

Although the domains need to share information with other partners, I-SHARe can significantly reduce the time it takes to establish a new E2E link. The tool handles all essential and important information and therefore spares the experts the effort to invest days or even weeks to find the right information.

Supporting Tools: Monitoring with E2Emon and HADES/BWCTL

After a new link has been set up and become operational, it needs to be monitored. This is rather simple if the institution that wants to monitor also operates the hardware that has to be monitored. It becomes quite complex, if different domains operate a link together and want to monitor the link as a whole. We described the SPs' concerns about management access in the previous sections. To satisfy the demand of such an E2E monitoring anyway, we present the solutions that have been found in Géant. We start with a holistic, abstract monitoring of the whole E2E link using the *E2E Link Monitoring System* (E2Emon) and then continue with monitoring systems HADES and BWCTL measuring more detailed parameters, such as delay or jitter.

E2Emon was designed to provide a general health information of the monitored links in a semi-graphical user interface and methods to signal problems to other monitoring/troubleshooting tools. To gather the necessary data, E2Emon consists of two architectural parts:

- The *E2E Measurement Point* (E2Emon MP) is deployed once at every NREN that participates in the service realization. The domains export information about the links they are part of from their local monitoring system into an XML file (using the NMWG schema (Network Measurements Working Group, 2006)). After that, they provide that file to the E2Emon MP, which then acts a standalone server and takes care of on-request delivering the file to the central component of E2Emon via in the project standardized SOAP interface.

- The *E2E Monitoring System* (E2Emon) is the central component of E2Emon and only deployed once – in case of Géant, the *E2E Coordination Unit* (E2ECU) is responsible for operating it. As the E2ECU also supports the operation of E2E links operating E2Emon there, too, is very handy. The central component is the part of E2Emon the whole "intelligence" is located at. It takes care of putting the information together and displays them vividly.

E2Emon fetches the domains' abstract data (they only define whether their link segment state is *up*, *down*, *degraded*, or *unknown*) and stitches them together according to their demarcation points, thus transition points to other domains. According to the segments' states, the central component then computes the overall health information (the aggregated state is only "up", if all domains report their segments as "up", for example) and displays it semi-graphically. In case E2Emon recognizes errors among the path, it supports e-mail notification as well as SNMP traps to inform the responsible domains. They can then take further actions and ask their local monitoring system for more detailed data in order to be able to restore the link's quality. Therefore, E2Emon is well suited to keep track of the links' health states. The experts can use it to be informed about link failures and start their troubleshooting based on these information.

The success of E2Emon, which is operational since 2006 and has gained a broad acceptance in the project, is based on two very important properties. On the one hand, the tool has convinced by its simplicity. On the other hand, it has proven to be able to solve one of the organizational key issues in multi-domain collaborations: It preserves the domains' autonomy when it comes to monitoring information. The NRENs can keep their detailed data locally and are only asked to provide an abstracted state of their segment. Therefore, no access to the domains' hardware is necessary.

But the link's health state is not the only parameter NRENs and customers are interested in. As many customers also request delay or jitter values, these metrics have to be monitored as well. Depending on the particular metric, two

possible *Measurement Archives* (MAs) come into consideration. HADES is responsible for measuring the *one-way packet delay* (OWD), *one-way packet loss* (OWPL) and *one way delay variation* (OWDV). The *Bandwidth Controller* (BWCTL), was developed by Internet2 on the other hand to measure the available bandwidth between to end points. BWCTL is co-located with the HADES boxes that are applied once at every end point within the Géant network. Each of them uses an own network interface to perform the particular measurements. HADES performs so-called active measurement – it generates test packets and takes care of sending and receiving them. BWCTL produces large data streams that are intended to measure the actual available bandwidth between the two end points. As all of these measurements highly depend on synchronized clocks, the measurement boxes contain a GPS antenna. Géant uses these boxes to perform regular measurements of all of its connections. Applying all of these within the network enables the collaboration to deliver an holistic monitoring approach for these sensitive E2E connections.

Géant Challenges Solved

As Géant aims to deliver its infrastructure to research projects, it first and foremost addresses their wishes and demands. The project has proven to be able to deliver highly reliable and high performance dedicated network connections by applying the discussed methods and tools. On the contrary, considering the cost aspect in routing or combining different technologies (like in triple play) is not a primary point of significance.

Research Project: The Internet2-lead DCN Collaboration

A similiar project is the *Dynamic Circuit Network* (DCN[1]) that is led by Internet2. Multiple regional and national grade research organizations, e.g., ESnet in the U.S. and Géant in Europe, collaborate with Internet2 in this project. In this chapter, we first outline the goals of the project, and then present and discuss the developed architecture aiming for enabling these goals.

Goal: Short-Term On-Demand Connections with Guaranteed Bandwidth

As discussed above, the ongoing discussion about expected network demands of upcoming applications is quite controversial. The common understanding is, however, that the quality of upcoming applications highly depends on the available bandwidth between communicating peers. Therefore, the main goal of DCN is to develop technology, which enables an establishment of network connections with dedicated capacity, i.e., bandwidth. As for now, considering other QoS parameters during the establishment of new connections is seen as out-of-scope of this project. The targeted customers of the service are research collaborations involving participants from different countries. In order to enable researchers spread around the world to exchange data on-demand, DCN aims to be able to establish connections on short notice, which is one of the major differences to the previously discussed Géant E2E-Links service.

Besides the main goal also several secondary goals can be identified within DCN. The first one is the evaluation of the proposed multi-domain architecture, which will be described in the next section. The evaluation of aspects like scalability and robustness are essential for the selection of application areas for the developed technology. Application areas can also be influenced by the time needed for the establishment of a new connection, as well as the supported granularity of bandwidth reservation. A further aspect is the definition and evaluation of interfaces, which will allow unambiguous signaling among participating domains. As many collaboration partners apply different techniques for bandwidth reservation,

DCN can also be seen as a platform for the evaluation of the interoperability between these techniques. Last but not least, the network service providers' acceptance of the technique should also be evaluated, as it can be seen as one of the most critical success factors.

As for now, DCN has advanced beyond the pure concepts and several successful demonstrations for the provisioning of multi-domain connections have been performed. DCN's multi-domain architecture is outlined below.

Multi-Layer Hierarchical Management Architecture

In networks it is common to distinguish between *in-band* and *out-of-band* signaling. In the first case, signaling between network management systems is performed through the same communication channel as the user data. A classic example of in-band signaling is DiffServ in IP networks. For out-of-band signaling, communication between management systems is performed through a separate channel. This type of signaling is used, for example, in PSTN networks. Comparing the two signaling types, one can say that in-band signaling provides better utilization of the available bandwidth. The out-of-band signaling on the other side provides true separation between user-data and management communication channels, which in turn prevents interferences between them as well as allows a simplified handling of both of them.

As DCN is focused on the assurance of bandwidth for user data, its management is performed via an out-of-band channel. Furthermore, it is also typical to separate network management and communication tasks in so-called *planes*. In DCN, tasks related to transmission of user data are referred to as *data plane*. The so-called *control plane* is responsible for all kinds of management decisions and signaling among involved management systems. Please note that this separation schema in data and control planes is only one of commonly used structures of a network system.[2]

The bandwidth reservation for end-user network connections, which is the main goal of DCN, is performed in the data plane. The DCN data plane operates on packet switched networks, as they are common in Internet. During the discussion about IntServ in Internet, we have seen that possible changes of a data flow's route neglect the effect of resource reservation. Therefore, in DCN, any connection provided to the end-users has a fixed route.[3] As the participating collaboration partners are independent organizations, determining a static route is only possible at the domain abstraction level, i.e., by specifying the equipment at the edges of involved domains. The fixation of the route within a single domain is not explicitly required as long as the provider of the particular part of the overall connection can guarantee the bandwidth of its part. The techniques for bandwidth assurance can vary between the involved collaboration partners, as they are independent organizations. The quality assurance techniques described in the previous sections are used by different participants, for example, the reservation of an SDH channel or combination of MPLS and IntServ. This means in turn that the heterogeneity of network technologies and quality assurance techniques is vivid in the DCN collaboration. The bridging between various network technologies is very well understood and broadly used, e.g., in Internet. As, from the perspective of DCN users, not the used network technique but rather only the connection bandwidth is important, technical heterogeneity does not have any negative influence on the main goal.

All communication between the involved network service providers for the negotiation of communication path and connection parameters is done via the control plane. In DCN, control plane means the networking infrastructure, which is used to share information between entities capable of configuring and managing network equipment (Lake, et al., 2008). In other words, the control plane controls and manages the data plane. The DCN architecture of the control plane defines that each participating domain must have a so-called *Domain Controller* (DC) and may have an *Inter Domain Controller* (IDC). The purpose of the DC is the actual management of the domain infrastructure in a local domain, i.e., communication with and configuration of switches and routers in the own network. This is a component, which is responsible for resource reservation and – if needed for a particular used in domain quality assurance technique – path definition within the particular single domain. The IDC's purpose on the other hand is the coordination of activities with other domains in order to provide a multi-domain service with the requested characteristics.

Communication among IDCs is done via an IDC Protocol. The IDC protocol supports two models for communication among IDCs: the *daisy-chain model* and the *meta-scheduling model*.

The daisy-chain model is graphically represented in Figure 7. The communication in this model is similar to the one established in PSTN networks. If an end user connected to Domain 1 needs a connection to an end-user connected to Domain 3, she sends a particular request to the IDC of Domain 1. This IDC can in turn decide through which domain the requested connection should go. If it is Domain 2, as it is depicted in Figure 7, the IDC of Domain 1 forwards the connection request to the IDC of Domain 2. Consequently, all communication is performed in the chain of IDCs responsible for domains along the path between two end points in this model.

The meta-scheduling model depicted in Figure 8 is an example of classical hierarchical management (Hegering, Abeck, & Neumair, 1999) applied to multi-domain infrastructures. In this model, a meta-scheduler takes a central place in all kinds of communications and multi-domain decisions. The end-user sends a request for the new connection to the meta-scheduler. The meta-scheduler in turn decides through which domains the connection can go and then directly contacts IDCs

Figure 7. DCN daisy-chain model according to (Lake, et al., 2008)

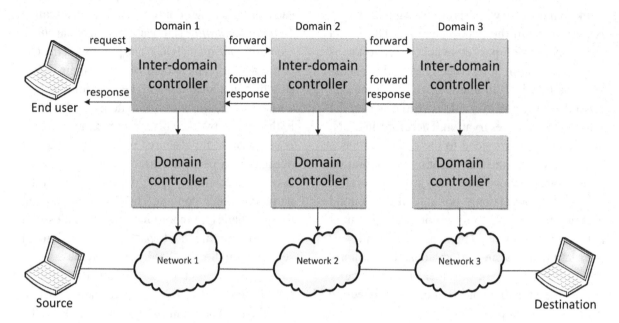

of relevant domains, i.e., the meta-scheduler is in charge of all kinds of signaling to and from all IDCs. In this model no direct communication among IDCs is needed.

The two models supported in DCN have different advantages and disadvantages. The biggest advantage of the daisy-chain model is its distributed character, which makes it very robust to failures of individual IDCs. On the other hand the distributed manner inevitably leads to concurrence among different requests for limited resources. Further, this model generally generates longer communication chains, which can influence the reaction time in the case of outages of already productive service instances. The meta-scheduling model on the contrary avoids any concurrence for resources and can further be used for global (i.e., multi-domain) optimizations, for instance, in order to increase the maximal amount of simultaneously possible service instances. The second model is however significantly less scalable and leaks robustness against a failure of meta-scheduler.

Regardless of which model is used, resource reservation for new service instances is needed in order to guarantee its bandwidth. In DCN, the communication among IDCs is used first to find and reserve an end-to-end route. Only if such a path with the available necessary resources could be successfully found, resource reservation is signaled over the control plane. The purpose of this two-stage procedure is the minimization of the time needed for resource reservation. Whereas such a two-stage reservation procedure has no conflicts in the meta-scheduler model, this approach can lead to failures due to an overbooking of resources in the daisy-chain model.

As for now, several successful demonstrations for the switching of dynamic circuits over multiple domains have been performed. These demonstrations have shown that bandwidth reservation can be successfully done despite the heterogeneity of the data plane. The basis for a successful collaboration among multiple domains is the interoperability among IDCs from different domains, which stems from the common IDC

Figure 8. DCN meta-scheduler model (Lake, et al., 2008)

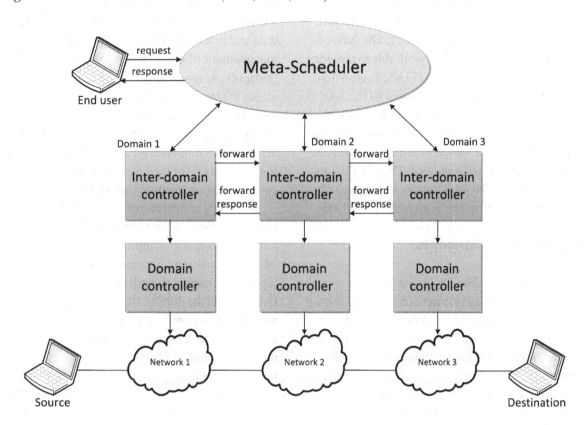

protocol to a high extent. Nevertheless, DCN is not yet ready to become a fully productive service. For instance, for true quality assurance also the permanent monitoring of the connection quality is needed as the means for the recognition of service outages. In this context, the newly established DICE collaboration project of the research networks DANTE, Internet2, Canarie, and ESnet should be mentioned. The purpose of this project is the establishment of a multi-domain multi-layer monitoring of dynamic circuits (How to connect: Internet2's Dynamic Circuit Network, 2008). In opposite to the DCN project, which focused only on bandwidth, DICE will cover the monitoring of multiple QoS parameters of established connections, such as bandwidth, one-way delay, packet loss, and link state.

The Telecommunication Providers' Step to the Future: Next Generation Networks (NGN)

Having discussed more practical examples, let us have a look at upcoming approaches to deal with *Next Generation Networks* (NGN). The architectures of networks currently used are typically service-bound and designed for dedicated services, e.g., data, phone, and video transmission. As mentioned in the section about triple-play, the goal of NGN is the establishment of a convergent platform, which should allow the realization of all three kinds of services on the same network infrastructure. The development of NGN is driven by the telecommunication industry as a reaction to the factors such as open competition among operators due to deregulation of markets, explosion of digital traffic, increasing demand for new multimedia services, convergence of networks and services, etc. (ITU-T, Recommendation Y.2001: General overview of NGN, 2001). The NGN is defined as a packed based network able to provide telecommunication services (ITU-T, Recommendation Y.2001: General overview of NGN, 2001) (ITU-T, ITU-T's Definition of NGN, 2008). It is commonly assumed that NGN will operate on the IP networks, but the concepts are applicable also to other network technologies. One of the key characteristics of NGN is the capability to establish network connections with end-to-end QoS.

Architectural Concepts

Whereas projects like DCN can be seen as an evolution of existing Internet concepts and infrastructure, the NGN concept is rather a revolution. In order to explain this, we have to take a brief look at the ISO/OSI reference model. This model consists of seven layers, with different functionalities associated. In case of the Internet, these seven layers are "collapsed" to only four layers with joint (but the same) functionality. In this model, both DCN planes, i.e., control and data, reside on the application layer.

However, the designers of the NGN see the ISO/OSI reference model as not flexible enough to cope with the challenges of modern applications: "Whilst the stated scope of OSI BRM[4] could be construed to be totally generic for all open systems standards development, in practice the OSI BRM has become synonymous with the rigidity associated with the seven layers defined therein, specific characteristics of each layer so defined, and the specific OSI layer protocols that were developed to match these characteristics." (ITU-T, Recommendation Y.2011: General principles and general reference model for Next Generation Networks, 2004). Instead, the key cornerstone of NGN is the mandatory decoupling of the service-related functions from the underlying transport-related technologies. This separation is reflected in two principal architectural layers – *service stratum* and

transport stratum (see Figure 9). The purpose of the service stratum is to transfer service-related data and to provide functions for controlling and management of network service to the user. The transport stratum realizes and provides functionalities to transfer data to the service stratum, i.e., user data and signaling messages, between communicating peers. Further, the transport stratum also provides functions for controlling and managing transport resources, which in turn define the communication channel's properties.

The NGN architecture foresees that each stratum comprises one or more layers, i.e., the stratum's functionality is implemented by a recursion of multiple layers. Especially for the transport layer it is common to realize the additional functionality on the top of the functionality of the underlying network layer, e.g., the TCP/IP connection can be realized on the top of functionality provided by Ethernet or SONET/SDH. However, the same procedure for building specialized layers can also be applied to the service stratum. For example, a video-on-demand service might be realized based on the separate services for video and for audio transmission.

In the NGN architecture, each layer in both stratums contains *User* (also called *Data*), *Control*, and *Management planes*. The purpose of the user (or *data*) plane is to transfer the data in the particular stratum or layer within the stratum. The control and management planes provide the set of functions needed respectively for controlling the operation of entities and for the management of the entities in the particular stratum or layer. The management plane has to provide functions needed for the support of management processes as described in (ITU-T, Recommendation M.3400: TMN Management functions, 2000). Classically, to the management functional areas belong *Fault, Configuration, Accounting, Performance* and *Security Management* (FCAPS). But it can include other management processes, like customer administration, or traffic and routing management (ITU-T, Recommendation Y.2001: General

Figure 9. NGN basic reference model adopted from (NGN BRM)

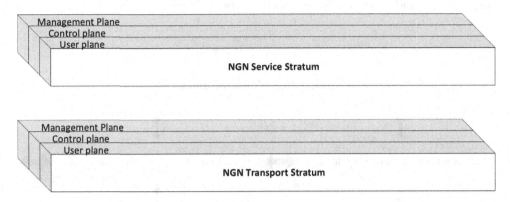

overview of NGN, 2001). From an architectural perspective, all three planes are always present for each stratum and for each layer within it. However, in practice, only the data (or user) plane should always exist. Therefore, the control and management planes may be null for a particular layer.

Another distinction is made between functions and services. The same functions can be used for the realization of different services. At the same time multiple functions might be needed for building one service. In order to consider the functional inter-relationships it is convenient to group them within the same stratum and within the same functional group, i.e., control and management. The relationships between function groups and resources needed for their realization are depicted in Figure 10.

Supporting Connection QoS whenever it is Needed

The ambitious goal of NGN is to support a wide range of QoS enabled services, which can be delivered to the end-users in unicast, multicast, and broadcast modes. The variety of services, however, inevitably means the variety of their quality requirements. The conceptual separation of service and transport strata in the NGN architecture allows to focus only on the transport strata. Instead of considering a particular service's

demands, the transport strata should provide functions needed for the signaling of QoS-related tasks and mechanisms for QoS controlling. NGN foresees three main control mechanisms, how the needed connection quality can be determined and requested from transport strata:

1. **Service-requested QoS**: The end-user's *Terminal Equipment* (TE) requests an application-specific service. Based on the user request, the *service controller* should determine the network connection's quality parameters, which should be sufficient for fulfilling the user demand. The service controller is then in charge of authorizing the requested service and of signaling a corresponding request to the transport stratum.

2. **User-requested QoS with prior authorization**: The end-user's TE is capable of signaling its explicit needs to the network. The service controller is in charge of authorizing the TE for the particular task and of the direct request and management of QoS resources.

3. **User-requested QoS without prior authorization**: The end-user TE is capable of signaling and can send its requests directly to the *network resource controller* without prior authorization.

Figure 10. General functional model according to (ITU-T, Recommendation Y.2011: General principles and general reference model for Next Generation Networks, 2004)

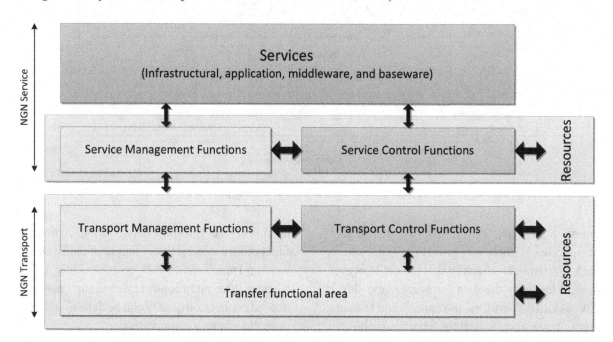

The biggest advantage of the first scenario is that the end-user's TE (or application) does not have to implement the signaling capabilities. Therefore, it remains fully independent from the underlying layers, which can implement different signaling protocols. On the other hand, the TE is then always forced to go through a service controller for any kinds of service requests. Further, only services supported by the service controller can be requested. The advantages and disadvantages of the remaining two models are inverse.

In all outlined scenarios the mapping from the service-specific user requirements to the corresponding transport-network specific QoS parameters and their thresholds is needed. In the first scenario it should be done by the service controller, in the remaining two by the end-user's TE. Especially in the telecommunication area multiple studies have been performed in order to determine the tolerance values from the end-user perspective. The results of such studies for the

most common multimedia services are depicted in Figure 11. Each rectangle shows the boundaries of still-acceptable values of *delay* and *packet loss* for services like audio conversation, video messaging and streaming, email access, etc. The values represent the end-user perception and therefore are independent of the network technology. Please note that in this study the *jitter* parameter is not considered, as it is assumed that the TE is able to perform jitter correction via packet buffering.

Quality parameters and corresponding thresholds for different services identified in such studies are the basis for the definition of *QoS classes*. In other words, each QoS class specifies a set of requirements, whose fulfillment is sufficient for a good end-user experience of the service belonging to this particular class. The relevant QoS parameters and thresholds are in turn the basis for the development of recommendations for how the outlined requirements should be implemented with the particular network technology. An ex-

Figure 11. Mapping of user-centric QoS requirements according to (ITU-T, Recommendation G.1010: End-user multimedia QoS categories, 2001)

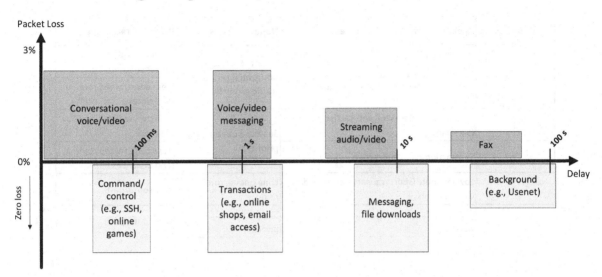

ample for such guidance for IP QoS classes in NGN is depicted in Figure 12. For instance, the recommendation for "constrained routing" (listed in column "Network techniques") means that the QoS class specific thresholds should be considered during the path finding process.

One of the biggest advantages of QoS classes is the possibility to optimize the infrastructure supporting them. It allows the solutions to be significantly more scalable then the general-purpose solutions. Moreover, it reduces the complexity of the signaling protocols. On the other hand, such solutions are only optimized for the needs of considered services, or of services with similar demands. If, for example, community-developed application demands other combinations of thresholds or – what is even more challenging from the QoS management perspective – the support of a less common QoS parameter, the introduction of a new QoS class supporting such demands might take a very long time. This, of course, is a big limitation factor of QoS classes in a highly dynamic and innovative environment of the Internet.

Deployment of the NGN Infrastructure

The process of the NGN infrastructure deployment is currently undertaken by the telecommunication companies around the world (ITU-T, ITU's ICT Eye, 2011). However, this is a very long-lasting and complex process, which might take several years till completion. The speed of the transition is dictated by the enormous investments required to a high extent. Alone for the EU the operators' investments costs are estimated at €300 billion (Kroes, 2009).

The consideration of networks commonly uses the clear distinction between core and access networks. This distinction is also very important for the transition to the NGN technology, as the development of *NGN core* and *NGN access* networks require different time spans, different amounts of investments and different strategies (ITU-T, Deployments of Next Generation Networks (NGN): country case studies, 2009):

- *NGN core network deployment* is commonly defined as the replacement of the

Figure 12. Guidance for IP QoS classes according to (ITU-T, Recommendation Y.1541: Network performance objectives for IP-based services, 2006)

QoS class	Application types and examples	Node mechanisms	Network techniques
0	Real-time, jitter sensitive, high interaction (VoIP, VTC)	Separate queue with preferntial servicing, traffic grooming	Constrained routing and distance
1	Real-time, jitter sensitive, interactive (VoIP, VTC)		Less constrained routing and distances
2	Transaction data, highly interactive (Signalling)	Separate queue, drop priority	Constrained routing and distance
3	Transaction data, interactive		Less constrained routing and distances
4	Low loss only (short transactions, bulk data, video streaming)	Long queue, drop priority	Any route/path
5	Traditional applications of default IP networks	Separate queue (lowest priority)	Any route/path

legacy equipment, such as telephony switches, with routers and other required equipment. The migration from traditional to NGN core networks is often seen as the opportunity for the core network reorganization by the network operators. This is a very important aspect, as from the provider's perspective the expected cost savings compared to the operation of an IP core network are a key driver for investment to upgrade their network (Commission, 2008).

• The upgrade of the connections from the core network to the end-users is typically referred to as *NGN access networks development*. The definition of NGN networks foresees that the end-user access can be realized with different technologies, over different transmission medias, e.g., fiber, copper, or wireless. Further, for the so called *last mile* to the end-user the distinction between *Fiber to the cabinet* (FTTC), *Fiber to the building* (FTTB), and *Fiber to the home* (FTTH) is made (see Figure 13).

The high investment costs and the level of the development of the old-fashioned infrastructure cause the very big difference of the deployment among different countries and telecommunication operators within. For instance, in Europe many telecommunication operators have already migrated to NGN core networks; the rollout of the FTTH is going rather slowly, compared to the Asian countries, such as New Zealand and Singapore (ITU-T, Trends in Telecommunication Reform 2009: Hands-on or Hands-off? Stimulating growth through effective ICT regulation, 2009). Among countries, the estimated time to a full-scale deployment of NGN mostly varies from 5 to 10 years (ITU-T, Deployments of Next Generation Networks (NGN): country case studies, 2009).

Upcoming Trend: Service Level Management Aware Routing

Based on the principles of *IT Service Management* (ITSM), contracts between SPs and their customers are called SLAs. Various standards, such as *ISO/IEC 20000-1*, and best practices, e.g., the *IT Infrastructure Library* (ITILv3), specify so-called management processes that serve as a blueprint for how operations such as weekly routine maintenance should be handled on both

Figure 13. Options for fiber access (ITU-T, Deployments of Next Generation Networks (NGN): country case studies, 2009)

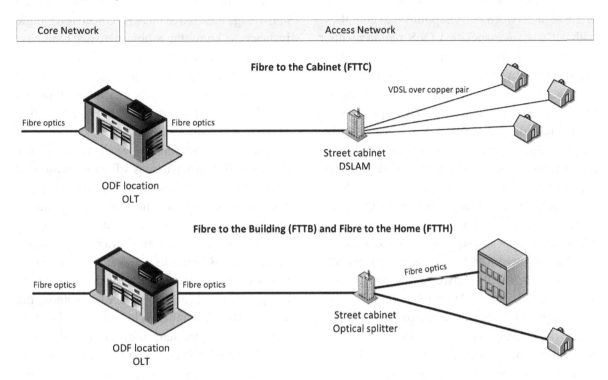

sides. SLAs include service parameters on both the organizational level, such as guaranteed reaction times to customer incident reports, and the technical level, such as guaranteed bandwidth and maximum delay of network links.

Traditionally, the "management world" has been strictly separated from the "technology world", just like the people usually driving cars there are usually not the ones who built a highway themselves. Thus, not too far in the past, at Internet SPs, we found technicians on the one hand and customer relationship managers who sold the services on the other hand. Mapping the QoS criteria that had been specified in an SLA onto the technology layer and vice versa has always been a major issue: If, for example, a customer calls and reports an incident regarding the service she pays for, how could the SP find out whether and which hardware components were affected? Or, if hardware monitoring reported a failure of a

network component, how could the SP determine whether and which customers were affected? If there were multiple incident reports at the same time, how should they be prioritized?

Subsequently, we describe SLM-aware Routing in more details; it is a recent approach motivated by challenges and experiences in national research and education networks in Europe as we already discussed them related to the Géant project. It has been designed with the scientific challenges discussed above in mind, and thus supports multiple customer-specified QoS parameters in parallel, respects SPs' information policy constraints, scales up to large numbers of involved domains, and has a good performance that makes it attractive for use in many scenarios. It should, however, be noted that the *routing* performed by this approach is – similar to DCN and NGNs – static: It does not determine a new route for each IP packet sent, like a classic layer-3 router does;

instead, routing in this context is line switching, i.e., the *a priori* determination of the most appropriate path between two endpoints that complies with all customer-specified QoS requirements, and this path is then being used for all the traffic exchanged between those two endpoints.

The rationale behind that kind of routing is that user- and customer-tailored requirements for connection services can currently be only truly fulfilled when already considered during the ordering process. The SLM-aware Routing approach is a routing process, consisting of three conceptual parts: a *routing procedure*, a *generic function scheme*, and an *information model*. It takes into account all known existing connections with their properties and end-to-end requirements when finding a path between two end-points. Therefore, it can be used in combination with the other approaches described above, for example within the management plane of the NGN transport stratum, on the logical layer above I-SHARe for E2E-Links, or as a part of the IDC in DCN.

SLM-Aware Routing Procedure

The primary duty of any routing is path selection. The SLM-aware Routing algorithm operates on *semi-global* knowledge about available connections. This information is represented at the abstraction level of an SP's organizational domain. Thus, one has to look at the connections between network equipment installed at the administrative edges of provider networks. In general, all connections that can be realized either within a single SP's domain or interconnecting two neighboring SPs are potential connection segments of an end-to-end connection. Because, from an SP's point of view, each realized connection segment is a provided service, the concept refers to an endpoint of a segment as *Service Connection Point* (SCP). This abstraction allows to map SCPs to various real-world edge-components, from logical UNI/NNI interfaces when looking at paths through the

Internet, up to *Points of Presence* (POP) when planning backbone connections. Semi-global knowledge means that there is no need for a single instance to know the whole network topology; instead, locally available information can be enriched by requesting additional data from selected other SPs on demand, and the total information that is gathered is sufficient to find the path fulfilling multiple E2E constraints.

Due to various factors, such as the steady ordering and provisioning of new end-to-end connections as well as the decommissioning of no longer required connections, the available resources are subject to a continuous change and must be treated dynamically. As a prerequisite for SLM-aware Routing to work, each involved SP must have exact knowledge about its own network equipment and available capacities, without the need to share details of this knowledge with other SPs. In general, one starts the routing algorithm at the SP from which a customer has requested a new end-to-end connection. Following a *source routing* strategy, this SP is responsible for the overall success of the path finding and shall select the path segments *en route* to the destination endpoint as far as possible. Only if certain other SPs refuse to give the source SP the required information, selecting the remainder of the connection segments may be delegated to another SP. This is based on the practical experience that SPs are more likely to trust topologically closer SPs and especially immediately neighboring SPs than providers that are far away, and is directly related to the challenge of restrictive SP information policies.

The SLM-aware routing procedure thus is not only responsible for selecting the next connection segment during each step, but also for the communication between the potentially involved SPs. Figure 14 shows how the routing procedure works as a state-machine: The connection planning phases are the states and the outcomes are the transitions. At the beginning (state A1), an intermediate SCP that is at the end of the path considered so far must determine the next connection segment, which is a transition into state A3. However, if required information is missing, the planner has to enter the information-retrieval state A2, which, if a sufficient answer is received, also leads to state A3. After calculating the properties of the entire path, including the new next segment, these properties are evaluated against the end-to-end customer requirements within state A4. If the requirements are fulfilled, the planner returns to the starting state A1 and the distant SCP of the new segment is considered as a new intermediate SCP. However, if an information request was rejected in state A2, the routing task is delegated to the last SP in the considered path, leading to state A5 that sends a "findroute" request to the other SP, which includes all the relevant information this SP requires in order to plan the remaining part of the route. The algorithm terminates either when the desired endpoint is reached (*success*) or no more alternative connection segments are available (*failure*).

The algorithm itself obviously works very similar to a depth-first-search, and thus can be implemented quite efficiently with a high result-

ing performance. However, its quality depends less on how long it takes to find an appropriate end-to-end connection, but on whether all the customer-specified QoS requirements can be fulfilled in a cost-effective way. This algorithm provides the solution for the so-called *multi-constrained path finding* (MCP) problem. For this purpose, the calculations performed within state A4 are essential for the result. They require operations on QoS parameters, and due to the variety of existing QoS parameters and the goal of flexibly supporting additional QoS parameters in the future, a generic function schema is required, which is discussed in the next section.

SLM-Aware Generic Function Scheme

During the routing algorithm that we discussed in the previous section, two types of operations on QoS parameters are required:

1. The values of the QoS parameters of the connection segments must be aggregated, and

Figure 14. State-machine of the SLM-aware routing algorithm according to (Yampolskiy, Hommel, Danciu, Metzker, & Hamm, 2011)

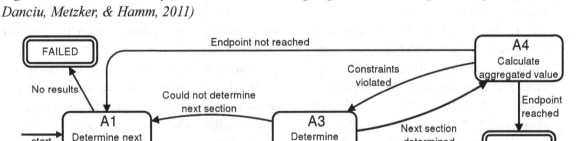

2. The resulting overall values must be compared to the customer's QoS requirements.

The issue addressed by the SLM-aware *Generic Function Scheme* is that different QoS parameters have different aggregation and comparison functions: For example, the *delay* induced by the connection segments must be *added* to each other, while the *bandwidth* of an end-to-end connection equals the *minimum* bandwidth of all involved segments. Similarly, a smaller jitter is *better* than a higher jitter, whereas a higher availability is *better* than a *smaller availability*. In general, there may be arbitrarily complex aggregation and comparison functions, and the function scheme defined for SLM-aware Routing provides a kind of abstraction layer that makes it easy to include any kind of QoS parameters as long as the handful of functions defined in this scheme for each specific type of QoS parameter are implemented.

The generic function scheme consists of five operations:

- An *AggregateLinks*() function enables to accumulate a QoS parameter across multiple links. For example, this could be implemented as *min*(A,B) for two links A and B concerning bandwidth, or as *add*(A,B) concerning delay.
- The *AggregateLinkParts*() function is a prerequisite for *AggregateLinks*() to work. It computes the QoS properties for segments that interconnect two neighboring SPs; thus, it performs the calculation of link properties by assembling the information that is available despite the SPs' restrictive information sharing policies.
- The *OrderCompare*() function determines the better of two values of a single QoS parameter. For example, concerning bandwidth, it should choose the link with the higher bandwidth, while regarding delay, it should choose the smaller one.

- An function called *SelectBest*() is similar to *OrderCompare*(), but has to work with value ranges. For example, a customer could state that a delay of max. 40 ms is fine with her, and one SP might offer a link with a guaranteed delay of 20-25 ms, while another SP may be able to provide a link with a guaranteed delay of 15-35 ms. In this case, 15 ms would be used in the subsequent routing process.
- The function *SelectWorst*() complements *SelectBest*() by choosing the worst link properties in the given value range. This reflects the fact that in most practical situations, we are not interested in finding the absolutely best technical solution for an end-to-end connection, but for the most cost-effective solution that is still guaranteed to fulfill the customer's QoS requirements. Thus, sometimes, not the best, but the still acceptable worst solution for an end-to-end connection or a couple of link segments is also interesting for the optimization of the finally resulting connection under real-world conditions.

As shown in Figure 15, the definition of these functions should be organized within a global registration tree for QoS parameters in order to avoid multiple redundant or even inconsistent implementations.

Furthermore, all these functions operate on single QoS parameters only and thus are easy to implement. However, in order to operate on all of the multiple QoS parameters specified by the customer in parallel, SLM-aware Routing defines the following rules for the aggregation and comparison function on QoS combinations (cf. Figure 16):

It ensures that one vector is better than another vector if and only if all elements of the one vector are better or equal than the corresponding elements of the other vector. This determines that resulting connections fulfill all of the customer's

Figure 15. A registration tree for QoS parameters and their associated functions

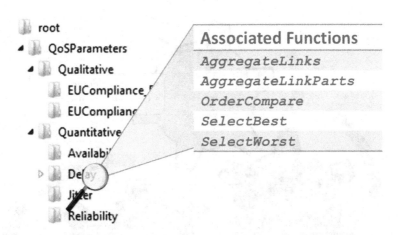

QoS demands. The use of this generic function scheme is not limited to SLM-aware route planning; it can also be applied to, for example, continuous connection monitoring. Its easy extensibility allows for the efficient adaption to new types of QoS parameters.

SLM-Aware Information Model

The basis for each kind of routing obviously is knowledge about available connection segments and their properties. In SLM-aware Routing, due to the semi-global knowledge approach, this kind of information has also to be exchanged between

SPs, so that we need an information model that can be used by the routing algorithm as well as for the protocol that is used to exchange information between SPs.

Figure 18 shows the UML diagram of the part of the information model that represents connections and properties of a single SP when applying SLM-aware Routing. This internally used information model also can be used to describe topological properties. Whenever an external SP requests information about a link, usually only the *LinkProperties* class, its components and the *TimePeriod* are sent back to the requester because the SP may be unwilling to share any more detailed

Figure 16. Aggregation and comparison function on QoS combinations algorithm according to (Yampolskiy, Hommel, Danciu, Metzker, & Hamm, 2011)

$$
\overrightarrow{Compare}(\overrightarrow{U}, \overrightarrow{V}) ::= \begin{cases} =, & \text{if} \quad \forall 1 \le i \le m : u_i = v_i \\ \prec, & \text{if} \quad \forall 1 \le i \le m : (u_i \prec v_i \\ & \qquad \vee u_i = v_i) \wedge \\ & \qquad \exists 1 \le j \le m : u_j \prec v_j \\ \succ, & \text{if} \quad \forall 1 \le i \le m : (u_i \succ v_i \\ & \qquad \vee u_i = v_i) \wedge \\ & \qquad \exists 1 \le j \le m : u_j \succ v_j \\ \ne, & \text{if} \quad \exists 1 \le i \le m : u_i \prec v_i \wedge \\ & \qquad \exists 1 \le j \le m : u_j \succ v_j \end{cases}
$$

Figure 17. How the three parts of SLM-aware routing work together

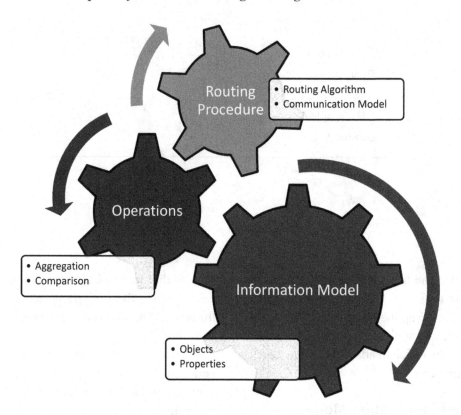

information with other SPs. Avoiding any clashes with very restrictive SP information sharing policies is one of the main reasons why SLM-aware Routing operates on the abstraction level of an SP's organizational domain.

In the information model, *CompoundLinks* are used as wrappers for multiple alternative connection segments that connect the same two SCPs; they reflect the hardware redundancy typically found in SP networks. But while they are hidden from anyone outside the SP, they still can result in connection segments with different properties. The *ComponentLinks*, which represent connection segments, are associated with the *LinkProperties*, which specify all of the segment's QoS properties. Finally, the *ComponentLinkParts* represent the SP's view at inter-domain links. This is necessary because each SP only has information about the quality guarantees that can be given regarding the

SP-facing side of an inter-domain connection. Therefore, the whole quality of such connections has to be calculated from both SPs' views. This makes use of the *AggregateLinkParts*() function specified within the generic function scheme described above.

Each of these three connection classes interconnects two SCPs, which therefore must provide some sort of globally unique identifier. Furthermore, each SCP is associated with the SP domain in which it is located physically. This is necessary because this information must be included in answers to information requests sent by other providers; otherwise, each logical information request would result in two actual information requests to the SPs on both ends of the link.

As shown in Figure 17, these three parts of the SLM-aware Routing process must work together very closely: The information model provides

Figure 18. Information model for available connections and QoS parameters within a single SP (Yampolskiy, Hommel, Marcu, & Hamm, 2010)

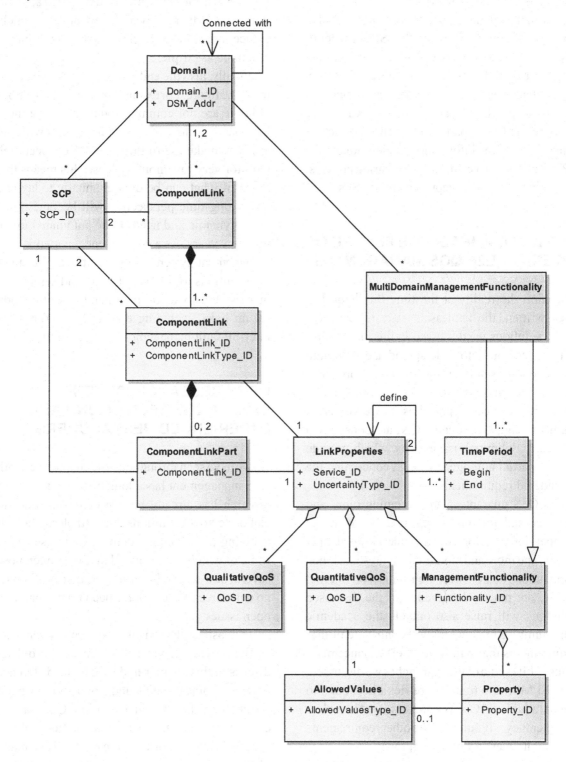

the information that is required by the routing procedure itself, which requires it for evaluating the currently planned connection parts and also for the communication with other SPs in order to plan the remainder of the end-to-end connection. Aggregating and comparing the values of the QoS parameters specified in the information model is handled by parameter-specific functions that have been defined as a part of the generic function scheme. Thus, the information models honors the SP's very restrictive information sharing policies, which increases its acceptance among SPs.

THE ROAD AHEAD: THE FUTURE OF INTERNET E2E QOS MANAGEMENT

Checking the reality at the time this book has been written, the unpleasant state is that most of the solutions we discussed in this chapter has not yet been put into wide-spread use. Although we have the usually sufficient best-effort Internet and managed backbone connections, all of the more advanced approaches, as we discussed them for, e.g., Géant and DCN, are constrained to clearly delimited usage areas, which provide at least partial homogeneity, e.g., concerning the considered requirements.

As QoS guarantees are becoming more and more crucial for businesses already today, the competition in sectors such as triple-play is already strong, and more and more community-developed applications demonstrate their impact on Internet traffic, the practical relevance of the discussed solutions will raise also outside the academic community, which in turn will contribute further requirements that will foster their enhancement. Thus, while some of the approaches we discussed, e.g., SLM-aware routing, are flexible enough to handle additional QoS parameters, it yet is unclear whether they will fulfill all the other requirements that might even not be known today.

The younger history of network-based services also makes it likely that triple play is by far not

the end of the rope: Based on novel and integrated services, various community-developed applications, and further innovations, we are more likely to face some kind of X-play, where X is no longer as simple as "triple".

Finally, also the end-user demands will be rising in the future: For example, 1 Gbit/s connections at home are not common today, but once these high bandwidths will be standard, users will find a way to make use of them and will expect high QoS for very low monthly fees. This means that much of what can be done manually today and has a long-time perspective will become much more dynamic and needs to be automated in the next few years. As a consequence, network QoS management systems will, additionally to their contributions to link negotiation and setup, also increasingly focus on the operations of already set up links, including efficient workflows for inter-SP fault management and accounting.

OPEN RESEARCH ISSUES: CHALLENGES FOR YOUNG AND EXPERIENCED RESEARCHERS

As we have seen throughout this chapter, network QoS management has a long history and a lot of research has already been invested in order to elaborate novel solutions. Nevertheless, the still evolving and changing demands and use cases, some of which we discussed in this chapter, pose several new research challenges, and as of today, no definitive solutions have been found for many open issues yet.

One aspect that has not yet been covered by sufficient research yet, and which we also did not discuss in this chapter in detail, is the difference between point-to-point and point-to-multipoint connections that consider multiple QoS parameters in parallel. Due to the much larger problem space, efficient algorithms are required and many of the traditional approaches cannot be applied anymore; similar to many point-to-point solutions, protocols like the *Distance Vector Multicast Routing Protocol* (DVMRP) depend on well-suited network topologies and do not consider all of the requirements and constraints in parallel. Thus, there still is a high demand for "real" multicast Internet routing, which will also be a key to network traffic reduction by data de-duplication, e.g., for efficient X-play.

Similarly, network QoS must also be addressed in overlay and access networks. For example, peer-to-peer networks, e.g., based on BitTorrent, already greatly enhance bandwidth utilization by choosing not only a single source for the delivery of content, but letting the recipient download the content from various sources in parallel. Currently, this does only work on a best-effort basis, but with the increasing number of commercial peer-to-peer applications, including the distribution of software patches and online game content delivery, also QoS guarantees are of increasing importance. Similarly, mobile ad-hoc networks, which share a single uplink gateway, e.g., in planes and on cruisers, will need to address QoS management in order to provide, for instance, adequate Internet connections for SCADA communication, paying customers, and freebies.

Also, most of the approaches we discussed in this chapter were based on a single party that is primarily responsible for QoS management, e.g., the SP at the end-point of the customer who ordered a link; while it could use delegation mechanisms to have other similar parties perform subtasks for the negotiation and setup of links, in the future we will need to support intelligent networks that have QoS-driven self-organizing and self-adapting characteristics. Autarchy and self-management are keys to success for those networks, and thus processes and algorithms need to be defined in order to manage also the QoS parameters decentralized, but in an orchestrated manner.

Finally, network QoS management does not only need to support the customers' requirements, but must also honor SP-specific policies. Therefore, one major topic is the support of

energy-efficient routing with QoS guarantees, because as a contribution to the Green IT movements, multiple research projects with impressive industry involvement have recently been started both in the United States and Europe. Turning off, for example, the less intensely used links based on current bandwidth utilization or fixed time schedules, has the potential to greatly reduce energy consumption, but may also impact QoS guarantees heavily.

SUMMARY AND CONCLUSION

This chapter explored the heterogeneous and often complex world of network quality of service management in today's and our future Internet. Initially, we investigated what network QoS means from an end user's point of view and discussed the discrepancies with the currently predominant solution attempts that are in use for best-effort Internet connections and managed backbone connections. We then had a look at the requirements and constraints that need to be kept in mind when planning future network infrastructures. We considered the business perspective, application areas such as research networks and triple play for home users, and discussed the impact of community-developed applications on networks. After analysing the relationship with Internet neutrality, we presented several major scientific challenges that need to be overcome in order to create successful solutions: For example, multiple customer-specified QoS parameters need to be fulfilled in parallel, and the involved service providers' security and information sharing policies must be considered. Combined with the multi-domain nature of the task and its high dynamics, there unfortunately are no easy solutions available.

In the second part of this chapter, we then presented several solutions for providing multi-domain network connections with guaranteed QoS based on various real-world examples. First, we studied Géant E2E-Links as they are commonly used across the European research community; for example, the Large Hadron Collider at CERN in Geneva uses these E2E Links to transfer huge amounts of data to several scientific supercomputing centres. Second, we discussed the DCN collaboration led by Internet2; this international collaboration provides short-term connections with guaranteed bandwidth on demand. Finally, we had a look at upcoming technologies and approaches, including the so-called new generation networks and service level management aware routing. Going into the details of SLM-aware routing, we analysed the three building blocks of modern network QoS approaches: A routing algorithm for path selection, a generic function scheme that supports arbitrary QoS parameters in an extensible manner, and an information model, which not only supports the routing algorithm itself, but also the management of the set up link by the involved service providers.

We concluded this chapter with a cautious look into the future by outlining some aspects of future Internet QoS, as well as with a discussion of open research issues that pose as challenges for both the young and the experienced researchers. All things considered, these network QoS management approaches show their feasibility when the end users do not have to think about QoS at all, but for both research and practice there still is a lot to do to ensure the sustainability and efficiency of the future Internet.

ACKNOWLEDGMENT

The authors wish to thank the members of the Munich Network Management Team (MNM-Team) for helpful discussions and valuable comments on previous versions of this chapter. The MNM-Team, directed by Prof. Dr. Dieter Kranzlmüller and Prof. Dr. Heinz-Gerd Hegering, is a group of researchers at Ludwig-Maximilians-Universität München, Technische Universität München, the University of the Federal Armed Forces and the Leibniz Supercomputing Centre of the Bavarian Academy of Sciences and Humanities. See http://www.mnm-team.org/.

REFERENCES

Bellman, R. (1952). The theory of dynamic programming. *Proceedings of the National Academy of Sciences of the United States of America*, (pp. 716-719).

Berners-Lee, T. (2006, June 26). *Net neutrality: This is serious.* Retrieved March 9, 2011, from http://dig.csail.mit.edu/breadcrumbs/node/144

Cesaroni, G., Hamm, M., Simon, F., Vuagnin, G., Yampolskiy, M., Labedzki, M., & Wolski, M. (2008). *ISHARe: Prototype specification.* Géant Technical Report.

Commerce Commission. (2008, December). *Discussion paper on next generation networks.* New Zealand.

Dijkstra, E. (1959). *A note on two problems in connexion with graphs* (pp. 269–271). Numerische Mathematik.

Hegering, H.-G., Abeck, S., & Neumair, B. (1999). *Integrated management of networked systems: Concepts, architectures and their operational application.* Morgan Kaufmann Series in Networking.

Information Sciences Intitute. (1981, September). *RFC 791 - Internet protocol.* Southern California, USA: Author.

Internet2. (2008, July). *How to connect: Internet2's Dynamic Circuit Network.* Retrieved March 07, 2011, from http://www.internet2.edu/pubs/DCN-howto.pdf

ITU-T. (1994, July). *Recommendation X.200: Information Technology - Open Systems Interconnection - Basic Reference Model: The basic model.* ITU-T, USA.

ITU-T. (2000, February). *Recommendation M.3400: TMN management functions.*

ITU-T. (2001, November). *Recommendation G.1010: End-user multimedia QoS categories.* USA.

ITU-T. (2001). *Recommendation Y.2001: General overview of NGN.* USA.

ITU-T. (2006, February). *Recommendation Y.1541: Network performance abjoectives for IP-based services.* USA.

ITU-T. (2008). *ITU-T's definition of NGN.* Retrieved March 7, 2011, from http://www.itu.int/en/ITU-T/gsi/ngn/Pages/definition.aspx

ITU-T. (2009). *Deployments of next generation networks (NGN): Country case studies.* Retrieved March 7, 2011, from http://www.itu.int/ITU-D/treg/Documentation/ITU-NGN09.pdf

ITU-T. (2009). *Trends in telecommunication reform 2009: Hands-on or hands-off? Stimulating growth through effective ICT regulation* (10th edition ed.).

ITU-T. (2004, October). *Recommendation Y.2011: General principles and general reference model for next generation networks.* USA.

ITU-T. (2011). *ITU's ICT eye.* Retrieved March 07, 2011, from http://www.itu.int/ITU-D/icteye/

Jaffe, J. (1984). Algorithms for finding paths with multiple constraints. *Networks, 14,* 95–116. doi:10.1002/net.3230140109

Kroes, N. (2009). Commission guidelines for broadband networks. *Introductory remarks at press conference,* (p. 3). Brussels.

Kuipers, F. (2004). *Quality of service routing in the internet: Theory, complexity and algorithms.*

Lake, A., Vollbrecht, J., Brown, A. Z., Robertson, D., Thompson, M., Guok, C., et al. (2008, May). *Inter-domain controller (IDC) protocol specification.* USA.

Network Measurements Working Group. (2006, August). Retrieved March 07, 2011, from http://nmwg.internet2.edu

Network Working Group. (1971, October). *RFC 249 - Coordination of equipment and supplies purchase.* Illinois, USA.

Network Working Group. (1997, September). RFC 2205 - *Resource reservation protocol (RSVP).* Michigan, USA.

Project, G. É. A. N. T. (2011). *Home.* Retrieved March 07, 2011, from http://www.geant.net

Project, G. É. A. N. T. (2011). *Information sharing across heterogeneous administrative regions.* Retrieved March 07, 2011, from http://forge.geant.net/ishare

Renda, A. (2008). I own the pipes, you call the tune: The net neutrality debate and its (ir)relevance for Europe. In *Regulatory Policy* (p. 36). CEPS Special Reports.

Russell, T. (2006). *Signaling system 7* (5th ed.). Mcgraw-Hill Professional Communication Series.

Tanenbaum, A. (2003). *Computer networks* (4th ed.). Pearson Education Inc. TAT-14 Cable System. (2007). *Homepage.* Retrieved March 07, 2011, from https://www.tat-14.com/tat14

TPACK. (2007, June). *PBB-TE, PBT: Carrier grade Ethernet transport.* Retrieved March 7, 2011, from http://www.tpack.com/resources/tpack-white-papers/pbb-te-pbt.html

Willis, P. (2001). *Carrier scale IP networks: Designing and operating internet networks* (1 ed.). Institution of Engineering and Technology.

Yampolskiy, M., Hommel, W., Danciu, V. A., Metzker, M. G., & Hamm, M. (2011). Management-aware inter-domain routing for end-to-end quality of service. *International Journal on Advances in Internet Technology, 4*(2).

Yampolskiy, M., Hommel, W., Marcu, P., & Hamm, M. (2010). An information model for the provisioning of network connections enabling customer-specific end-to-end QoS guarantees. *Proceedings of the 7th International Conference on Services Computing (SCC 2010)*, (pp. 138-145).

Ziegelmann, M. (2007). *Constrained shortest paths and related problems*. VDM.

KEY TERMS AND DEFINITIONS

Domain: The term *domain* is used in order to emphasize the organizational boundary of all companies involved in the delivery of various services in the Internet. In the Internet, all network provider domains are commonly referred to as *Autonomous Systems* (AS). Further, regarding network service provider, the terms *single-domain*, *intra-domain*, *inter-domain*, and *multi-domain* are used. The terms single domain and intra-domain are synonyms used for the description of aspects, e.g., processes, within a single organization. The term inter-domain is used to refer to aspects of interactions between two domains. Finally, the term multi-domain emphasizes the environment in which multiple domains are involved. The Internet is a multi-domain environment realized via an interconnection of AS networks.

ISP, IAP, ICP: An ISP or *Internet Service Provider* is an *Autonomous Systems* (AS) that focuses on delivering Internet access to the customers and end users. *Internet Application Providers* (IAPs) and *Internet Content Providers* (ICPs) are using the logical layer provided by ISPs for the delivery of their services to the customers. IAPs are providing various platforms, e.g., for *video-on-demand*. ICPs are focusing on the provisioning of the content, e.g., of movies.

Network Neutrality: *It* is commonly used as a term for the non-discriminating or equal treatment of IP packets belonging to different communication flows and transporting different services. The necessity of network neutrality is often discussed very controversial. Often network neutrality is seen as opposing to the differential treatment of IP packets and communication flows, which are a prerequisite for quality assurance.

NGN: Next Generation Networks (NGNs) is a solution developed by ITU-T for telecommunication service providers. NGNs by design support *triple play* and consequently different strategies for quality assurance.

QoS: Quality-of-service (QoS) parameters are network characteristics, which define whether the network connection is suitable for a particular service or not. Different services depend on the specific combination of QoS parameters and their thresholds. Most frequently, the QoS parameters *bandwidth*, *delay*, and *jitter* are used.

SLA: Service Level Agreements (SLAs) are contracts in which relevant QoS parameters, their thresholds, and the quality measurement methods are specified. Especially in the case of long-lasting contracts it is not only important which characteristics a working connection had, but also its *availability* and *reliability*, as well as how fast any technical failures shall be repaired.

Triple Play: It means support for tree types of services over a single physical connection: Internet access, television, and telephony. Originally, all these services were provided using dedicated infrastructures, each of which was designed to support a different service-specific combination of QoS parameters. Triple play is supported in NGNs by design.

ENDNOTES

[1] Please note that this abbreviation is also used in other contexts, which are out of scope of the current discussion, e.g., for Datacenter Communication Network or Digital Content Networks.

[2] It is also common to further separate the control plane in control and management

planes, where the control plane is only responsible for communication with the managed object, whereas the management plane is responsible for all kinds of management decisions.

3 This is a concept broadly discussed under the topic of *Next Generation Networks* (NGN) – the establishment of connection oriented communication paths over packet switched networks.

4 Basic Reference Model, defined in (ITU-T, Recommendation X.200: Information Technology - Open Systems Interconnection - Basic Reference Model: The basic model, 1994)

Chapter 9
Enabling Frameworks for Autonomic Adaptation of Protocols in Future Internet Systems

Vangelis Gazis
University of Athens, Greece

Eleni Patouni
University of Athens, Greece

Nancy Alonistioti
University of Athens, Greece

ABSTRACT

The emergence of several networking standards has been continuous over the last decade. Engineering creativity spawned a wide gamut of innovative technologies for wireless and wireline communications. This increase in technological portfolios, in combination with the requirement to migrate legacy systems and to maximize the use of large investments in network installations, resulted in the design of multiple network evolution paths. Combined with the increasing sophistication of networking technologies, this variety of choice in design has run counter to the simplification – and the efficiency – of management procedures. The task of managing network infrastructures is confronted with an increasingly dishar-monious Babel of standards involving interfaces, protocols, topologies, and versions. As a result, there has been a turn of research interest towards an autonomous mode of management where the elements of the managed system display individualistic proactive behavior that strives to maintain their modus operandi within specific bounds. The umbrella term autonomic computing and communications refers to a capability set that includes a system's ability to monitor selected aspects of its own operation, collect, and record any data resulting from these observations, evaluate its performance under the light of its own operational history, possibly also identifying trends and recurring patterns in the process, and, in the case of subpar performance, undertaking corrective actions targeted to achieve a satisfactory level of performance. To this end, dynamically adaptable protocol stack offer a systemic capacity for change during runtime according to current operational requirements, thus providing an essential framework feature of autonomic systems.

DOI: 10.4018/978-1-4666-1888-6.ch009

INTRODUCTION

The continuous development of telecommunication standards over the last decade has produced a wide gamut of networking technologies. This includes wireless access systems, such as cellular systems (e.g., GSM, GPRS, GERAN, EDGE, UMTS, cdma2000, 3GPP HSPA, etc), broadband WLAN type systems (e.g., IEEE 802.11a/b/g), fixed wireless access systems (e.g., IEEE 802.16d/e), broadcast systems (e.g., DAB, DVB-T/S/C/H, DMB) and short-range wireless systems (e.g., Bluetooth, IEEE 802.15.3a, IEEE 802.15.4) while new ones are being developed rapidly (e.g., 3GPP LTE). Similar developments characterize landline and carrier networking, where several innovative technologies (e.g., Gigabit Ethernet, ADSL/VDSL, IP over SONET, Ethernet over SDH, MPLS/GMPLS, etc) have emerged and/or are being intensively developed.

The intensification of standardization activity has spawned several new protocols and brought on a wave of revisions to existing ones. The fierce rate of standardization promotes a 'mix-and-match' approach to the definition of protocol stack standards that challenges the traditional – so-called 'silo' – approach to the design of a protocol stack. The latter suffers from extreme vertical integration and lack of flexibility in horizontal tasks (i.e., that involve different protocol stacks) related primarily to resource management and cross-standard coordination. The increase brought on by standardization in the number of protocols, aggravated further by the definition of multiple releases and versions, has further perplexed network management tasks. Large-scale network systems like the 3GPP one provide a rich set of options with regard to the interfaces and protocols supported in network deployment. This increase in technological portfolios, in combination with the requirement to migrate legacy systems and to maximize the use of large investments in network installations, resulted in the design of multiple network evolution paths. Combined with the increasing sophistication of networking technologies, this variety of choice in design has run counter to the simplification – and the efficiency – of management procedures. As a result, the task of managing the network infrastructure is confronted with a disharmonious Babel of standards, interfaces, protocols, topologies, and versions.

In addition, the increasing adoption of wireless technologies to access Internet content runs against fundamental design assumptions imprinted in the IETF protocol stacks. These performance limitations are attributed to the black-box principle in protocol stack architecture. To address this issue, the introduction of cross-layer information exchange and the dynamic adaptation of protocol stacks during runtime have been proposed and investigated. Several approaches are now being currently considered to support the autonomic management paradigm where individual network systems can take proactive and/or reactive management actions upon themselves.

Albeit relatively young, the vision of autonomic communications is being pursued intensely by several research activities in both industry and academia. These activities involve the definition, design and deployment of 'self-x' features in emerging communication systems and devices. Following the model proposed by IBM (Kephart & Chess, 2003), an autonomic system should at least incorporate four attributes: self-configuring, self-healing, self-optimizing and self-protecting, commonly referred to as self-CHOP features. Additional novel features for autonomic networking that are exploited in recent research efforts include self-organization, the latter being defined as the system's ability to manifest coherent behavior at the macroscopic scale as the aggregate result of peer-to-peer interactions among system constituents at the microscopic scale.

This vision lays the ground for the deployment of advanced concepts in the Future Internet architecture, including those involving a device agnostic and protocol independent approach to the definition of systems with self-configuring and self-managing properties. To this end, dynamically adaptable protocol stacks found in network elements serve as valuable enablers. The ability to dynamically compose and configure and entire protocol out of distinct functional components provides a powerful vehicle that can be used by an architecture offering a self-x capacity. This chapter presents design blueprints for self-configuration and self-optimization capacities on the basis of protocol frameworks offering dynamic adaptation features (to a lesser or greater degree).

DESIGN CONSIDERATIONS FOR ADAPTABLE PROTOCOL STACKS

Technological Options and Design Classification

Design principles characteristic of concurrent asynchronous operation are imprinted in all the adaptable protocol stack frameworks encountered in the literature.

Design Principles

From a software engineering viewpoint, the particular organization of a protocol stack's software elements is a determinant factor of the runtime flexibility supported by instances of the protocol stack (Bass, Clements, & Kazman, 1998). Thus, the software architecture of a protocol stack determines the level and extent of adaptations applicable to it. As a result, adaptation may be a feasible and, therefore, realistic option for a particular subset of the protocol stack's elements but impossible for other subsets. Whether adaptation takes place during bootstrap time or runtime, is an issue largely determined by the protocol stacks' execution environment. Runtime adaptations that involve the dynamic replacement of protocol code during the protocol's operation may affect the continuous operation of particular protocol layers. The severity and extent of the effect may

range from a slight delay in data processing functions within a single protocol layer to a cascading interruption of the entire protocol stack.

The traditional so-called 'silo' design approach presents a significant obstacle to the development of efficient protocol stacks. Its major shortcomings are a) a tight coupling between the hardware capabilities and the software utilizing them, and, b) insufficient level of interaction among software constructs related to different protocol stacks. Based on rigid integration, this inflexible approach has been historically perceived as an engineering instrument to achieve optimum performance at the level of protocol operation. Modern design approaches and programming methodologies are mature enough to accommodate and support a broad spectrum of adaptation options without excessive impact in the operational performance of protocol products (Bertrand, Cruz, Majkrzak, & Rossano, 2002). Several engineering approaches to design and develop adaptable protocol stacks have been introduced and researched over the last couple of decades. Besides the purely architectural and prototypical body of work, adaptable protocol stack frameworks have also successfully undergone trial and validation in realistic network settings involving conventional (with regard to adaptation) protocol stacks.

Classes of Adaptable Protocol Stacks

Generally, there are three different modular design approaches to the engineering of protocol stacks that support adaptation and some form of cross-layer interaction: adaptable protocols, composable protocols, and, reconfigurable protocols (Tuttlebee, 2002).

Adaptable protocols facilitate large-scale reuse of protocol software code by grouping common protocol functions (e.g., segmentation and reassembly) into a generic layer. This generic layer provides a common subset of functions encountered in multiple protocols, organized into appropriate software constructs (e.g., classes, interfaces, etc). For each protocol, an extension layer complements the generic layer with any additional functions required to meet the particular protocol's specification. Adaptable protocols are instrumented as protocol stack software frameworks and involve object libraries and an Application Programming Interfaces (API) specification.

Composable protocols are based on the analysis of a protocol's operation into elementary functions. The latter provide the building blocks for the development of a complete protocol and entire protocol stacks. Depending on the analysis granularity and the associations manifesting among the elementary protocol functions, the composition procedure may follow either a flat or a hierarchical model.

Customizable protocols are based on an object-oriented architecture for the protocol stack software. The use of object-oriented design techniques renders the introduction of a dynamic adaptation capacity straightforward. The latter typically manifests as the ability to dynamically change the software components involved in a protocol's operation during runtime.

TOWARDS AN AUTONOMOUSLY MANAGED PROTOCOL STACK

Design Considerations

Categories of Protocol Adaptation

In general, a protocol layer may be adapted by two different approaches:

1. By changing the values of selected variables that affect the operation of its internal functions, i.e., by fine-tuning the parameters it consults during runtime.
2. By changing the object code that corresponds to its internal functions, i.e., by swapping the current implementation of the protocol with another one.

From a control perspective, both approaches require that one or more types of interfaces are provided to an external – to the protocol – entity. In the former approach, a single interface that enables one to set the values of selected protocol parameters during runtime is necessary. In the latter approach, three interfaces are necessary; one that provides control over the computational progress (i.e., the ability to start/suspend/resume/stop) of functions associated to the protocol during runtime, one that enables import/export of critical protocol state (i.e., internal state variables), and, one that enables switching the protocol's object code with a given version.

Protocol Adaptation for Performance Optimization

Consequently, from a viewpoint concerned with performance optimization, three distinct cases are possible:

1. The desired level of performance can be attained by changing the values of selected variables of the current implementation of the protocol.
2. The desired level of performance can be attained by switching the current implementation of the protocol with another one.
3. An appropriate combination of a) and b) above.

Figure 1 presents these options graphically. Let line (a) denote the level of performance attainable by the current implementation of the protocol over the value range (i.e., the cartesian product) of its parameters. Let line (b) denote the level of performance attainable by a different implementation of the protocol over the value range of its parameters.

Figure 1. Deciding what kind of adaptation to apply based on performance and change options

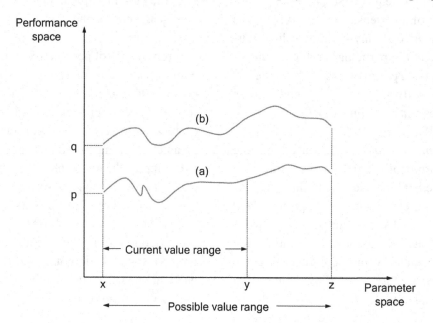

Assuming that the current level of performance is a point in the line (a) in the value range [x, y] we will identify the adaptation that must be applied according to the desirable minimum level of performance.

1. If the latter is less than or equal to the current level of line (a), no adaptation is necessary.
2. If the latter is more than the current level of line (a) but less than or equal to the maximum level of line (a), the desired adaptation is realized by changing the values of selected variables that affect the operation of the protocol.
3. If the latter is more than the maximum level of line (a), the desired is realized adaptation by changing the object code of the protocol. Assuming that the desired level of performance is less than the maximum level of line (b), the protocol implementation associated to line (b) may provide the substitute object code.

Key Protocol Design Issues

The case where the entire protocol behavior is swapped for a different one is not, in fact, uncommon practice; it is what standardization has typically prescribed as part of maintaining and evolving protocol specifications. The Internet protocol suite provides an excellent example of this practice. Having evolved significantly over the years through a sequence of revisions in its specification, TCP can serve our discussion herein as a slow motion window into protocol adaptation in action as played out by decades of standardization. The original TCP version displayed poor performance with regard to its ability to detect and react properly to the emergence of congestion in the Internet. To address this shortcoming, IETF revised the TCP specification to include a capacity for congestion control and avoidance. These revisions extended the TCP state associated to each TCP connection by introducing additional variables. The latter support an additive increase multiplicative decrease algorithm that continuously probes the network's availability with regard to bandwidth and throttles TCP throughput accordingly to avoid contributing to the escalation of congestion phenomena in the Internet (Floyd, 2000).

These revised TCP versions were rolled out in a monolithic manner where the new version replaced the previous one in its entirety. However, given an adaptable protocol stack framework, the incremental update of installed TCP versions with new ones becomes feasible. This requires appropriate design of the TCP protocol software, taking into account the architectural building blocks of the adaptable protocol stack framework. However, at a design level, we can identify three pivotal design patterns (Gamma, Helm, Johnson, & Vlissides, 1995) that support this capacity in a generic way:

1. **State:** The State design pattern factor outs essential object attributes and enables the dynamic adaptation of an object's behavior based on its current state. This is effectively realized by defining an abstract interface for the invocation of the object's behavior. The actual implementation of this interface is accessed through the instance currently embodying the object's state.
2. **Observer:** The Observer pattern enables the decoupled asynchronous interaction among consumers and producers of information. In the context of a protocol's event-based mode of operation, it provides the pivotal capacity of defining events of interest, registering event handlers to appropriate events, and, invoking event handlers registered to a particular event.
3. **Strategy:** The Strategy patterns enables the introduction of variants in an object's behavior by accessing the latter through an abstract interface. Different behaviors are factored out into different classes that realize this interface.

Applying these key design patterns in the context of adaptable protocol stacks is relatively straightforward. The State pattern enables the dynamic update of the set of variables that collectively realize a protocol's state information through an abstract interface. The Observer pattern enables the coupling of computational entities (e.g., processes, threads) factored as Strategy classes to an event of interest, such as the change of state information in a protocol.

Architectural Blueprint

Autonomic systems are founded upon a feedback loop (Figure 2) where sensor information is collected, interpreted and exploited, possibly in combination with historical knowledge, by an intelligent process chartered to manage specific operational aspects (e.g., performance). The intelligent process determines whether these aspects fall within the value regions acceptable by the administrative policies and, if not, identifies and executes appropriate remedial actions using a set of actuators (Denko, Yang, & Zhang, 2009). In the context of self-managing systems, key operational aspects include:

*   **Self-configuration:** The ability of a system to automatically assemble and configure itself from startup.
*   **Self-protection:** The ability of a system to detect an attempt to compromise its operation and swiftly react by taking measures to safeguard its continuity of operation.
*   **Self-healing:** The ability of a system to detect failure in its parts and take recovery actions to resume normal operation.
*   **Self-optimization:** The ability of a system to evaluate itself over a period of time and make decisions as to how it can better optimize its operation.

Figure 1 presents the blueprints of a self-managing adaptable protocol stack. The latter

Figure 2. The architectural blueprint of a self-managing adaptable protocol stack

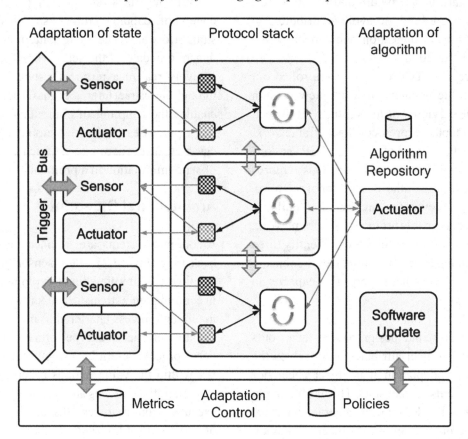

lies at the center of a feedback loop like the one prescribed for autonomic systems. We assume a thread-per-layer processing model applies and, for reasons of simplicity, include just three protocol layers in the illustration.

Each protocol layer comprises three elements: a) a processing resource (e.g., thread) that progresses the computational tasks of the protocol, b) state variables that are immutable to an external – to the protocol – actuator (black and white checker box in Figure 1, and, c) state variables whose values can be modified by an external – to the protocol – actuator during runtime (grey and white checker box in Figure 1. Each protocol layer is accompanied by an external sensor and a pair of external actuators, one for the state variables referenced in c) above and one for the processing resource referenced in a) above. Because control of

computational tasks may need to be exerted over multiple protocol layers in a coordinated manner, a single actuator for the processing resources of all procotol layers is shown is Figure 1. The sensors and the actuators related to protocol state variables are linked to a common bus over which trigger events can flow. The latter are emitted by sensors in response to the value of a monitored variable in a particular protocol layer crossing a particular threshold. Sensors are provisioned with the set of protocol layer variables to monitor and the associated threshold values, if any, by the adaptation control layer in accordance to performance metrics and management policies. The latter jointly determine what type of adaptation is in order by taking into account the overall sensor feedback for the entire protocol stack. When in order, the switching of the object code of one or more protocol layers takes place through a software update function and in coordination to the actuator that controls the processing resources progressing the computational functions of protocol layers (Bass, Clements, & Kazman, 1998).

The next section introduces adaptable protocol stack frameworks and presents their architectural details enabling adaptation. Their capacity for adaptation is classified and evaluated from the viewpoint of a self-managing system with specific requirements in regard to adaptation.

ADAPTABLE PROTOCOL STACKS

Protocol Stack Software Frameworks

With regard to the execution environment chosen for the protocol stack, software frameworks for protocol stacks are classified into the following categories:

Native – The protocol stack software is written in a programming language (e.g., C, C++) and subsequently compiled into native code for a particular execution platform (e.g., operating system). A (non-exhaustive) list of such frameworks is presented and discussed next:

- Among the first efforts in the development of protocol stacks based on generic software constructs, the x-kernel (Peterson, Hutchinson, O'Malley, & Rao, 1990) supported the flexible configuration of communication protocols according to a protocol graph.
- The maximization of reusability of protocol software across different protocols is addressed by the Conduit+ framework for protocol software (Bengt Sahlin Supervisor Prof, 1997). In the Conduit+ framework, the conduit class serves as the basic class, while the so-called information chunk class models all data exchanged among conduit instances.

- Appia (Miranda, Pinto, & Rodrigues, 2001) is another software framework supporting the decomposition of protocol function into modules and their subsequent stratification as a protocol stack (Rosa, Lopes, & Rodrigues, 2006). The interaction of modules is based on events where each protocol module defines the set of events required by it and the set of events provided by it. Protocol state information is organized into so-called session objects, which also feature the set of event handlers for each particular protocol.

Interpreted – The protocol software is written in a programming language (e.g., Java, Ruby) and subsequently executed into an overlay execution environment (e.g., a virtual machine). Traditionally, protocol software has been implemented in native (to the operating system) object code to realize the best possible performance given the available platform resources (e.g., CPU, etc). Requiring compilation for each target execution platform, this approach does not lend nicely to the portability of protocol code. Therefore, recent efforts have studied the development of protocol software in an interpreted language to execute in a virtual machine (e.g., a Java platform). This approach simplifies the portability of protocol code across different execution platforms. A (non-exhaustive) list of such frameworks is presented and discussed next:

- In the HotLava (Krupczak, K L Calvert, & M. Ammar, 1998) approach a protocol is realized as a particular Java class that extends HotLava framework classes providing common protocol behaviour. The latter concerns the management of data structures (e.g., buffers) involved in protocol operations and the management of data connections to other protocol instances according to the applicable protocol graph. A thread pool provides concurrency by assigning a distinct thread that undertakes handling of tasks inherent to each protocol instance (e.g., timer management).

- Jgroup/ARM (Meling, 2006) introduced a framework for protocol composition using protocol modules that interact loosely through an event-based mechanism. Protocol modules provide and require specific sets of services to and from higher and lower protocol modules, respectively. A specific to the module interface provides access to such services while an event listener interface supports the registration to and notification of events of interest.

- Based on the Java platfrom, the JChannels (Jung, Biersack, & Pilger, 1999) architecture defines classes for protocol modules, the protocol stack comprising them and the data conveyed between them. Each protocol module adopts an event-based model of interaction while data processing is carried out under a thread-per-message model. A protocol graph specifies the desired structure of the protocol stack as a pair of unidirectional (with regard to data transfer) sequences of protocol modules.

Compilable – The structure of the protocol stack's software is specified in a platform-independent notation and subsequently employed in formal model transformation procedures that map to a particular programming language and generate code for a particular execution platform (e.g., the operating system). A (non-exhaustive) list of such frameworks is presented and discussed next.

- In the United States, the Software Defined Radio (SDR) Forum has developed the Software Radio Architecture (SRA) focusing on the specification of a common framework for building, configuring, connecting and tearing down distributed, embedded radio (i.e., waveform) applications within a (software radio) device

(Bickle, 2000). SRA is founded upon the OMG CORBA Components (CCM) standard and defines the configuration of the Physical (PHY), Medium Access Control (MAC) and Network (NET) layers of the protocol stack in an XML profile. SRA so-called Core Framework (CF) services use the CORBA middleware and its facilities (e.g., CORBA Naming service) to manage and schedule resources of the underlying POSIX operating system for realizing software radio applications.

- Building upon the SRA standard, the OMG Software-Based Communications (SBC) Special Interest Group (SIG) has published a Platform-Independent Model (PIM) and a Platform-Specific Model (PSM) for software radio systems and components (OMG, 2005). The PIM/PSM architecture covers protocol functions mostly in the radio front-end (e.g., FFT/IFFT, spreading/dispreading, modulation/demodulation) and a selected subset of common protocol stack functions dealing with data exchange. PIM/PSM has been developed according to the OMG Model-Driven Architecture (MDA) approach to abstract all dependencies upon a particular platform (e.g., technology) and thus support the development of truly portable software radio applications.

Addressing largely an implementation viewpoint, these frameworks for protocol software focus on programming abstractions and software development concerns (e.g., maximization of software use) and pay little or no attention to management concerns such as configuration or optimization of performance. Hence this class of adaptable protocol stacks offers little, if any, ground in regard to our discussion on self-x capacities.

Composable Protocol Stacks

This section presents and analyzes different frameworks falling under the category of composable protocol stacks. The latter are founded on the component-based design paradigm where reusable blocks of functionality are packaged in self-contained units of installable software code. A (non-exhaustive) list of such frameworks is presented and discussed next:

- Coyote (Bhatti, Matti A Hiltunen, Richard D Schlichting, & Chiu, 1998) describes a single integrated framework, which provides support for configurable communication services and protocols targeted for mobile communication systems. The basic functional entity in Coyote is the micro-protocol. The latter is an orthogonal function of the entire protocol functionality and forms a fine-grain software module. The custom service configuration is done by configuring the micro-protocols with a standard runtime system, and more specifically by altering the dynamic binding of their event-handlers to specific events. In addition, Coyote provides filtering functionality for processing upstream and/or downstream protocol information by selected micro-protocols.
- Cactus (M A Hiltunen, R D Schlichting, Ugarte, & Wong, 2000) forms a framework for constructing configurable and adaptive distributed service and network protocols. It offers fine-grain customization and dynamic adaptation functionalities using the following mechanisms: a) activation and de-activation of micro-protocols through event handler binding and b) dynamic code loading.
- Horus (R Friedman & R van Renesse, 1996; Robbert van Renesse, Birman, Roy Friedman, Hayden, & Karr, 1995) sup-

ports a communication architecture that implements each protocol layer as micro-protocols. The proposed framework is used for protocol development and experimentation, introducing a methodology for increasing the robustness of the protocol development process. In Horus, protocol stacks are dynamically composed during runtime out of layers of micro-protocols using a graph-based approach that fulfils given group communication requirements and additional features (e.g., flow control, causal order, total order, etc). The Horus system provides an object-oriented framework for communication endpoints, messages and protocol composition.

- Role-Based Architecture (RBA) (Braden, Faber, & Handley, 2002) investigates alternative non-layered approaches to the design and implementation of network protocols as more suitable for the gradual migration to new functionalities. This work introduces a Role-Based Architecture (RBA) with a graph-based organization of roles – the basic constituent of protocols, which can be also extended to address new features. RBA can be realized by different ways: by implementing roles in the entire architecture, above a specific protocol layer or by dividing the functionality in major protocol units. Each role processes and may output payloads and their associated metadata. This approach offers great flexibility, significant capacity for customization and control operations with less interaction problems.
- Da CaPo (Plagemann & Plattner, 1993; Plagemann, Waclawczyk, & Plattner, 1994) provides an environment to overcome the throughput bottleneck by configuring end system protocols, according to available system resources, application requirements and offered network servic-

es. Protocol configuration targets the provision of services with minimal necessary functionality for each request, aiming at optimal performance. Da CaPo employs a three-layer model comprising the application (A) layer, the communication (C) layer and the transport (T) layer. This model is responsible for the dynamic configuration of lightweight protocols and provides the following operations: a) selection of the most suitable protocols, done by the configuration process, b) dynamic negotiation of the protocol configuration (undertaken by a connection manager) and c) provision of a suitable run-time environment (undertaken by a resource manager).

- Dynamically Reconfigurable Architecture for Protocol Stacks (DRAPS) introduces a component-based framework and respective architecture for dynamic reconfigurable protocol stacks (Niamanesh & Jalili, 2007; Niamanesh, Sabetghadam, Yousefzadeh Rahaghi, & Jalili, 2007). DRAPS employs a phased-approach for dynamic protocol stack reconfiguration including the following operations: a) freezing (i.e., to stop the current execution of the component), changing (i.e., addition/removal of components), state transfer and execution (i.e., resuming execution from latest instance). The framework consists from a core framework, which deals with the synchronous dynamic reconfiguration and the associated plug-in components.
- The Distributed Protocol Stacks (DPS) framework (Kliazovich & Granelli, 2008) aims at providing novel networking design, operation and management functionalities targeting performance optimization of data transfer and improved QoS provisioning. The DPS framework combines the concepts of layering, cross-layering and agent-based networking and proposing an evolved protocol stack design, where

a set of protocol can be moved to another network element (node, router, or base station).

Customisable Protocol Stacks

Customizable protocol stacks typically introduce some additional signaling for purposes of protocol reconfiguration procedures. These include dynamic component binding and replacement operations, state management actions and overall coordination signalling. For instance, GFPR (Nancy Alonistioti, E. Patouni, & Gazis, 2006) presents the signalling exchange for end-to-end dynamic binding and replacement of protocol components. A (non-exhaustive) list of such frameworks is presented and discussed next:

- In (Schmidt, Box, & Suda, 1993) an integrated environment termed ADAPTIVE supporting the automatic composition of reusable protocol building-blocks in lightweight, adaptive protocols is proposed. A key aspect of ADAPTIVE is the support of session reconfiguration during runtime. Using the performance measurement tools available in the ADAPTIVE suite, the protocol system can adapt to the combination of network metrics, transport system resources and application/QoS requirements. The metrics considered include throughput, average end-to-end delay as well as jitter, PDU loss and retransmission and connection establishment delay. In ADAPTIVE, a protocol module is responsible for both protocol-dependent processing functions and contextual information management (e.g., timers, sequence numbers, etc) according to its interaction with a peer PM. Two process architecture models are supported, namely task-based and message-based.
- The COMSCRIPT approach (Muhugusa, Marzo, Tschudin, & Harms, 1994) pro-

vides a language designed for network programming. The language is accompanied by an execution environment for the dynamic interpretation of protocol functionality. The COMSCRIPT approach enables the protocol dynamic configuration offering two main advantages: a) it provides solutions to inter-networking problems since applications can realize the requirements-based transparent reconfiguration of an arrangement of COMSCRIPT processes (i.e., a protocol stack), and, b) maximum separation of the protocol logic from the application. It should be noted that a COMSCRIPT process can implement either a single protocol layer or a full protocol stack. COMSCRIPT employs an event-based programming model using a first-class connector object for transparent process reconfiguration as well as for inter-process communication.

- In GRPSFMT (L Berlemann, R Pabst, Schinnenburg, & B Walke, 2005; Lars Berlemann, Ralf Pabst, & Bernhard Walke, 2005) the functionality of an individual protocol layer is composed of a generic part and a specific part that jointly support the particular protocol layer's purpose. The generic part is common to all protocol layers, regardless of their purpose, while the specific part is unique to each protocol layer and effectively complements the generic part to jointly realize the intended protocol functionality.

- In (Clark, M. H. Ammar, & Kenneth L Calvert, 1997) the authors address the problem of determining the proper protocol out of a set of given protocols, given a particular communication requirement. To this end, they consider protocol discovery mechanisms based on protocol feedback and identify their essential features. Their approach exploits distinct features of protocol layers to determine which protocol

graphs (or protocol paths) can support a given communication task.

- In GFPR (Nancy Alonistioti, E. Patouni, & Gazis, 2006) a unified approach for the dynamic stratification and adaptation of protocol stacks is investigated from two main viewpoints: a) consistency assurance by considering the dependencies between different protocol layers due to the different stratification patterns of multiple system standards (e.g., 3GPP), and, b) semantic-based dynamic composition and replacement of protocol components based on queuing facilities. The latter are associated to each component during runtime and subsequently configured to support the exchange of information between adjacent protocol layers. This framework meets the flexibility and adaptation requirements in NGN systems thereby enabling the convergence of heterogeneous systems. Dynamic adaptation is achieved by switching between interchangeable protocol components and modifying the respective protocol layer structure, if necessary (e.g., to meet additional implementation dependencies introduced by the new component).

- DRoPS (Fish, Graham, & Loader, 1998) is a software framework that provides the construction of a modular data transport system and supports runtime adaptation. It includes mechanisms for the initialization of the protocol stack, the establishment of information exchange links among protocol instances, the management of the protocol stack's configuration on the basis of elementary 'add' and 'remove' operations applied at the level of individual protocols, and, the maintenance of a consistent configuration at all times.

The table below categorizes the adaptable protocol stack frameworks and provides a brief summary of their main properties.

Assessment and Evaluation

Herein we assess the adaptation capacity offered by each protocol stack framework from the viewpoint of self-optimization as entailed in the self-management paradigm. To this end, we present the invariant and variant aspects of a protocol's operation as prescribed by each protocol stack framework. Furthermore, we describe the design approach to instrumenting self-configuration and self-optimization through the associated protocol stack framework and detail the associated requirements with regard to software development tasks.

Coyote/Cactus – An uncluttered yet powerful capacity for dynamic protocol adaptation is the one realized in the Coyote/Cactus approach. The use of events and event handlers as the building blocks of protocol composition opens a design route down to the core of the protocol state machine for purposes of orchestrating adaptation during runtime. Coyote/Cactus supports the registration of user-defined event handlers that can execute asynchronously or synchronously to other event handlers in the associated micro-protocol. In the latter case, a user-defined event handler will block until all other event handlers in the associated micro-protocol have completed execution. This mode of invocation meets the functional requirements of dynamic change management in software architectures and, thus, readily supports the dynamic switching of a protocol's algorithm during runtime. However, to realize this capacity, the protocol's software architecture must provide a first-class abstraction for the protocol's algorithm as a self-contained element. From a design perspective, this is a rather trivial task that can be carried out relatively easy by applying the Strategy design pattern in the context of the thread-per-layer processing model. It is, of course, also possible to provide a functionally equivalent capacity in the context of the thread-per-message processing model, yet with comparatively more effort and somewhat less elegancy in design. To provide a self-x capacity, such as self-optimization, an appropriate user-defined event handler can be designed and introduced into a micro-protocol. The subset of the aggregate protocol state that must be evaluated for purposes of self-optimization can be accessed either via direct information exchange among the event-handlers and the event handler undertaking self-optimization, or, indirectly, by using an event-handler that mediates access to the aggregate protocol state according to the Façade design pattern.

Horus/Ensemble – The introduction of self-x capacities in the Horus/Ensemble system is far from straightforward. Because Horus/Ensemble treats each protocol layer as a software module and realizes protocol layering on the basis of nested function and/or procedure calls. To introduce function and/or procedure hooks for purposes of self-optimization, some form of mediating proxy function is required to provide a type-safe interface for protocol chaining. The latter facilitates an inspecting process to reason about and possibly infer the instant state of the protocol before dispatching the method and/or procedure invocation to the next in sequence protocol. This approach supports a degree of self-optimization; however, this design option is inherently cluttered with dependencies upon the type of protocol that is being optimized and, therefore, does not scale efficiently.

RBA – Role-Based Architecture (RBA) is based on a graph-like configuration of the protocol stack that eases the support of self-x capacities such as self-optimization through the definition of appropriate roles. To be applicable to any combination of roles in an RBA protocol configuration, the latter must be implemented as part of the RBA framework. This also requires that the software architecture of an RBA role provide an interface that enables self-x roles to inspect the associated protocol state enclosed therein.

DRAPS – The DRAPS architecture is further aligned to support self-optimization through the adaptation of a protocol's algorithm. It defines a Reconfiguration Manager (RM) that supports

Table 1. Adaptable protocol stack framework properties

Framework	Class		Distinctive feature
	Composable	Customisable	
DiPS/CuPS	■		Provide component-based frameworks for the deployment and multithreaded protocol stacks. DiPS allows the design and implementation of component-based protocol stacks whereas CuPS forms an extension of DiPS to support non-anticipated customizations.
COM-SCRIPT			Provides powerful Finite State Machine (FSM) abstractions in terms of events and event handlers as the building blocks of protocol construction.
x-kernel	■		The x-kernel is an operating system kernel with configuration capabilities as regards its basic functional unit, the communication protocol, defined in terms of microprotocols.
Coyote/ Cactus	■		Builds on the x-kernel model and employs messages for inter-protocol communication. Internally, each protocol is built from fine-grain modules termed micro-protocols. A micro-protocol implements a well-defined property or function of a (composite) protocol. Each micro-protocol comprises a collection of event handlers that undertake processing of particular events of interest to the function realized by the micro-protocol.
Appia	■		Support for QoS through the so-called channel concept and minimization of context switching overhead through a dedicated (i.e., per-channel) processing thread.
Ensemble	■		Provides a formal specification of the protocol services and software layers using modular design and enables the automatic generation of code for the protocol stack's configuration.
THINK		■	Forms an implementation of the FRACTAL framework enabling the specification of components with various granularity levels and different types of binding. In addition, it provides for representations of the system configuration by means of component graphs.
FRACTAL		■	Introduces a generic recursive component model that facilitates the design and deployment of various operating systems (including protocol stacks) and at the same time enables the introduction of dynamic adaptation and reconfiguration capabilities.
Horus	■		Treats each protocol, regardless of its particular function, as an abstract data type with a pair of specific interfaces: a) an interface used by clients of the protocol for issuing requests to it, and, b) an interface used by the Horus runtime system to deliver incoming messages to a particular protocol, as well as other event of interest to it (e.g., for the case of a mobility management protocol, disconnection of an underling link).
RBA	■		RBA realizes protocol functionality through so-called role objects. The latter are organized into graphs of arbitrary complexity that enforce particular sequences of payload processing by roles based on a set of rules.
Da CaPo	■		Da CaPo forms a modular framework that supports the dynamic configuration of protocols to meet application requirements by exploiting the composition of appropriate modules per layer.
ADAPTIVE	■		ADAPTIVE provides a fine-grained composition capacity based on the reuse of elementary functions that are common to a group of protocols. In addition, its rich gamut of process allocation schemes contributes significantly to the achievement of performance objectives.
GRPSFMT		■	Supports the development of protocol stack software through an object-oriented library of prefabricated common protocol functions. Dynamic protocol reconfiguration is supported according to software architecture principles for dynamic change management.
DRAPS		■	Provides an extensible object-oriented middleware framework for the development of reconfigurable protocol layers. The functionality necessitated by reconfiguration signaling and the associated functional support at the protocol level are organized and prefabricated in the middleware framework.
GFPR		■	Proposes a framework for dynamic protocol stack reconfiguration addressing the introduction of flexibility and appropriate management schemes in the stratifications of protocol layers to meet specific service objectives.
JChannels			Provides an extensible object-oriented software framework for the development of protocol stacks on the Java platform.
DRoPS	■		Leverages the microprotocols concept in a modular framework that enables the implementation and dynamic adaptation of protocol while ensuring the configuration consistency,

the switching of protocols between peer layers of the protocol stack. Hence, algorithm switching for the purposes of performance optimization is functionally feasible; all that is required is that RM be infused with logic that monitors performance and decides when to adapt the protocol stack and what kind of adaptation to effect. Inspection of internal state is supported by the DRAPS framework architecture through the associated import/export interface. Consequently, the RM entity of DRAPS can be extended with self-optimization logic and readily support the performance-oriented aspects of autonomic operation.

DPS – Performance optimization is among the design objective of DPS that supports the swapping of protocol functions during runtime. Like DRAPS, to enable self-optimization, the DPS framework must include some kind of performance optimizing logic based on feedback from sensors monitoring the performance metrics.

ADAPTIVE – Targeting the realization of performance efficiency and the accommodation of formal QoS specification, the ADAPTIVE framework is fully streamlined to the functional requirements of self-optimization. In ADAPTIVE, the algorithm embedded in protocol operation is abstracted and managed as a Protocol Machine (PM). Performance is optimized at the PM level by properly choosing the process architecture and the degree of parallelism in protocol functions. However, real time – or at least recent – data regarding performance are not considered in choosing an appropriate PM. Hence, the criteria and the algorithm used in choosing a PM must be extended to include performance data along with assessment metrics and administration policies (Figure 2).

FRACTAL/THINK – The FRACTAL and THINK component frameworks are primarily striving to ease the development of operating system elements, including the protocol stack of course. However, their design focus is on development tasks rather than management tasks that take place during runtime. As a result, supporting

self-optimization is not precluded by their framework's architecture, albeit at the cost of significant development effort.

COMSCRIPT – COMSCRIPT provides powerful Finite State Machine (FSM) abstractions in terms of events and event handlers as the building blocks of protocol construction. Hence a wide spectrum of protocol functions can be defined using the COMSCRIPT model. To provide a self-optimization capacity, a class of event handlers can be defined. The latter will undertake the monitoring of sensor information regarding the performance level of the associated protocol, the detection of situations requiring the adaptation of the protocol stack, and, the enactment of the appropriate changes to the set of event handlers comprising the associated protocol. From a software engineering viewpoint, this incurs considerable effort by requiring that:

1. Event handlers provide a monitoring interface to access state information internal to the event handlers during runtime.
2. An event handler is included that uses the interface referenced in a) to monitor protocol information associated to a set of event handlers and carry out any adaptation actions necessary.

In the following section we illustrate scenarios involving the attainment of a self-x capacity through the application of an adaptable protocol stack framework. We consider CuPS and DRoPS as our instrumentation vehicles for these scenarios.

SCENARIOS AND APPLICATIONS

The aim of this section is to provide concrete links between the concepts of dynamic adaptation and customization of protocol stacks and real life technical problems. To this end, two real-life scenarios are introduced, which provide a bridge between theory and practice. This ensures the investigation of open, real-life and fundamental technical problems for current and future networks, paying special focus on the concepts of protocol self-configuration. Building upon the descriptions of scenarios, we demonstrate how selected frameworks can be utilized for protocol adaptation procedures.

Scenario 1: Mobile Terminal Self-Configuration and Autonomic Network Management

Two groups of multi-RAT (Radio Access Technology) mobile terminals are considered; simultaneous communication is possible both inside and outside the group, by utilizing different RATs. The first group is located at an exhibition centre, while the other group travels by bus towards the exhibition. The first group can achieve communication with other users through a connection to a UMTS network and can download data related to the exhibition through a WLAN network. The second group is connected to a WiFi network available through WiMAX relaying. In this scenario, Flexible Base Station (FBS) failure, increased network traffic and user mobility are considered as triggers for various operations requiring dynamic configuration of both the network side and mobile devices. Examples of such operations include the redistribution of the users' mobile terminals, mobile terminal reconfiguration as regards the application layer and protocol stack, inter-RAT handover and spectrum resource management related operations. In regard to the dynamic protocol stack reconfiguration procedure, this involves the dynamic specification of the protocol stack reconfiguration, the downloading and installation of protocol components and the dynamic switching from the existing to the new components (Bogenfeld & Gaspard, 2008; E. Patouni, 2006).

Scenario 2: Autonomic Decision Making Mechanisms and Self-Governance

In a multi-operator and multi-RAT area, an operator installs (plug-n-play installation) a local area (LA) Base Station (BS) under Wide area (WA) cell in order to meet the user requirements (e.g., increased QoS level). After this operation, part of the devices will attach to the new BS. This is realized with the use of autonomic decision making mechanisms and self-governance algorithms and capabilities that exist in both the user devices and the base stations. If required, the devices protocol stack is dynamically adapted to the new environment and conditions. This includes the dynamic configuration and evolution of operating protocols in the user device (Bogenfeld & Gaspard, 2008; E. Patouni, 2006).

The analysis below describes the use of different customizable frameworks to implement the above analyzed self-configuration and adaptation actions. We consider the case where the implementation of self-configuration actions concerns the dynamic replacement of component X with component Y. Specifically, the CuPS and DRoPS frameworks were investigated and message sequence charts were defined in detail following the architectural specification of these frameworks. The novelty of this work lies in the detailed specification of the required interactions among the functional entities within each framework to support the dynamic switching of protocol components. As regards CuPS, this framework supports the unanticipated customization of protocol stacks during runtime, posing the requirement that the components under replacement (termed hot-swappable components) are inactive. This requirement refers to the lack of internal packet processing activity during the configuration procedure, to avoid packet loss. The figure below illustrates the key steps to achieve the dynamic replacement of component X with component Y using CuPS.

Figure 3. Specification of interactions for dynamic replacement of ComponentX with ComponentY in CuPS

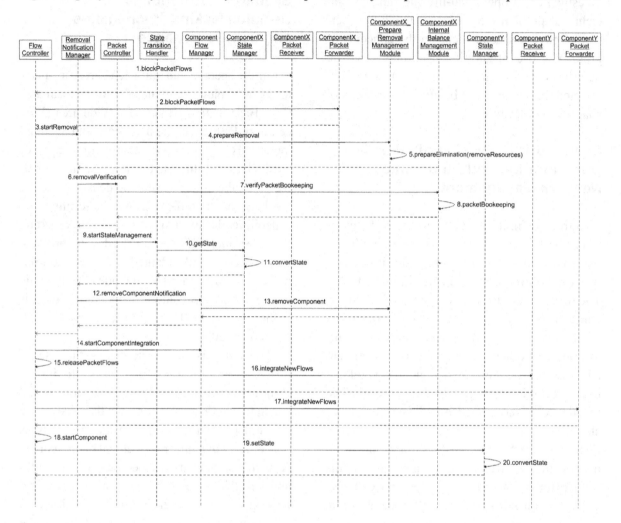

The first phase concerns the dynamic deactivation of existing protocol components. In order to successfully realize the dynamic component replacement within DRoPS, it is necessary that the components under replacement reach an inactive state. This is realized by the Flow Controller (FC) which is responsible for blocking the packet flows of the components under replacement. Specifically the Flow Controller interacts with the Packet Receiver (PR) and Packet Forwarder (PF) management entities residing within ComponentX (under replacement), dispatching the respective message (messages 1, 2). At this point, we should note that the Packet Receiver and Packet Forwarder management entities are responsible for the administration of the data plane packet flows. Once the flows have been blocked, the Flow Controller informs the Removal Notification Manager on the successful flow deactivation and triggers the component removal (message 3). The latter dispatches a "prepare removal" message to the respective management entity residing within ComponentX, namely the ComponentX Prepare Removal Management Module (message 4). The latter takes over the elimination of the component from the runtime system and the release of its allocated resources (message 5).

It should be noted that the successful deactivation of a component entails no loss of packet data; this is achieved by introducing an internal bookkeeping mechanism in the customizable area. This mechanism is integrated locally within the components, being embedded in their Internal Balance Management Module. To this end, the Removal Notification Manager informs the Packet Controller on the component replacement, to verify the removal procedure (message 6). The latter communicates with the Internal Balance Management module of ComponentX which is responsible for the packet bookkeeping (messages 7, 8).

The next phase is related to state management. Specifically, the State Transition Handler is responsible for state transition between the components under replacement. Once notified to start this procedure (message 9), the State Transition Handler interacts with the State Manager residing within Component X to retrieve the state – the latter is responsible for converting state information using defined representation structures (messages 10, 11). Thereafter, the Removal Notification Manager triggers the component removal, which is realized by the Prepare Removal Management Module of ComponentX (message 13).

The last phase deals with the activation of the new component. Specifically, the Flow controller triggers the Component Flow Manager to start the integration of the new component (message 14). Next, the Flow Controller releases the packet flows and communicates with the Packet Receiver and Packet Forwarder management entities, for the successful integration of the new component (ComponentY). Such interactions are illustrated in messages 16 and 17. Finally, the Flow Manager is responsible for starting the new component and properly configuring its state, communicating with ComponentY State Manager (messages 18, 19). The latter is also responsible for realizing the transformation of state representation to the appropriate structures (message 20).

The DRoPS system provides a supporting framework and architecture for the implemen-

tation, operation and reconfiguration of different transport systems, also including runtime adaptable protocols. The key unit in DRoPS is the microprotocol, which implements specific protocol processing operations. In addition, there exists a supporting structure, namely the Sub Protocol Controller (SPC) which incorporates unique attributes per connection. SPC incorporates configuration and activation fields, which are used to achieve the exclusion or inclusion of microprotocols from the current protocol stack configuration and to define which microprotocols are active, respectively. In addition, we should point out the introduction of adaptation agents, which form threads responsible for the execution of adaptation policies for creating new stacks. In the analysis below we consider a custom protocol, the Reading Adaptable Protocol (RAP), which is used to demonstrate the key features of DRoPS framework during the replacement of two microprotocols. An example of the dynamic replacement of microprotocols is the functionality exchange of the microprotocol responsible for the fragmentation and reassembly functions. Specifically we may consider that an existing message oriented implementation is replaced with a stream-oriented implementation. Another example is the dynamic replacement of the microprotocol that realizes the acknowledgement scheme. Thus, the dynamic switching between the IRQ, ARQ, per message ACK and negative ACK only implementations can be implemented.

The message sequence chart in Figure 4 presents the key steps for the dynamic exchange of MicroprotocolX with MicroprotocolY within DRoPS. The SPC Adaptation Agent handles this procedure by forming threads responsible for the creation of new protocol stacks and the optimization of existing ones. At first, the SPC Adaptation Agent will define the new protocol stack configuration and execute the adaptation policies, which implement the optimization of the protocol stack configuration. In addition, it will update the SPC configuration field, based on the new protocol stack configuration. Next, the SPC Adaptation Agent excludes the existing microprotocol and includes the new one. Finally, it initializes the Segment Redirector. The latter is used to allow existing applications to continue using their services, by enabling new connections to use legacy or adaptable implementations.

DIRECTIONS FOR FUTURE RESEARCH

Looking back to the Internet evolution up to the emerging concepts of Future Internet, we trace the challenge of continuous incorporation of new technologies, services and functionalities, to enable the evolution of networking systems. To this end, Future Internet emerged as a holistic solution

that facilitates the seamless integration of legacy and emerging networking paradigms, by:

1. Dealing simultaneously with various requirements regarding innovative network and service technologies,
2. Introducing adaptation capabilities in the mobile devices and network nodes, and,
3. Mastering complexity and scalability issues in the integration of self-management capabilities (L. Patouni, N Alonistioti, & Merakos, 2010).

Among other concerns, Future Internet deals with the incorporation of dynamic configuration and adaptation capabilities of the new nodes – the latter may span from the application and services layer to the physical layer of the protocol stack.

Figure 4. Specification of interactions for dynamic replacement of MicroProtocolX with MicroProtocolY in DRoPS

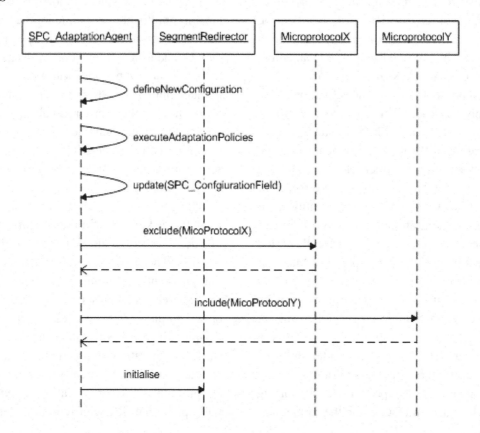

For example the dynamic configuration and activation of services and protocols (protocol self-configuration) is seen as a solution for the interworking between different wireless systems. In such an environment where a variety of options are available regarding supported applications, services and access types, and the operation of mobile devices is characterized by a significant number of parameters; the availability of an adaptable protocol stack provides a valuable capacity for dynamically adapting the operation of a networking system during runtime. It is worth noting that, quite frequently, the facilitation of cross-layer interactions is a side-effect of their architectural decomposition of protocol stack functions as a graph of entities linked through interactions. As a result, the level of support of self-x features that each adaptable protocol stack framework provides varies significantly. It remains, however, their salient characteristic that a subset of self-x properties is either enabled, or, additionally, offered by any adaptable protocol stack framework. Self-configuration is probably the most common feature enabled by an adaptable protocol stack, with self-optimization being the runner up. Self-healing and self-protection are rather uncommon capacities in this design space; this is primarily because, from a functional analysis viewpoint, these self-x properties stem from reliability requirements and, therefore, are orthogonal to the core functions included by design in a protocol while as self-configuration and self-optimization are not.

CONCLUSION

Dynamically adaptable protocol stacks have been investigated rigorously by numerous R & D efforts over the last decade. By capitalizing on developments in operating system technologies and software engineering practice, adaptable protocol stacks now present a theoretically sound, technologically feasible and economically realistic path to the introduction of a powerful capacity for adaptation during runtime in networking systems. To this end, the ongoing initiatives that shape the architecture of the Future Internet have so far included adaptable protocol stacks in their research agenda. A greater capacity for dynamic customization during runtime in an autonomous manner seems to be a commonly agreed and desired feature of Future Internet systems. To this end, we have presented in detail the blueprint of an architecture framework for an adaptable protocol stack supporting autonomic functions.

REFERENCES

Alonistioti, N. Patouni, E., & Gazis, V. (2006). Generic architecture and mechanisms for protocol reconfiguration. *Mobile Network Applications, 11*(6), 917-934. doi: http://dx.doi.org/10.1007/s11036-006-0058-x

Bass, L., Clements, P., & Kazman, R. (1998). *Software architecture in practice.* Boston, MA: Addison-Wesley Longman Publishing Co., Inc.

Bengt, S. (1997). *A Conduits+ and Java implementation of internet protocol security and internet protocol, version 6.* Retrieved from http://citeseer.ist.psu.edu/286786.html

Berlemann, L., Pabst, R., Schinnenburg, M., & Walke, B. (2005). Reconfigurable multi-mode protocol reference model for optimized mode convergence. *Proceedings of European Wireless Conference 2005* (Vol. 1, pp. 280-286). Nicosia, Cyprus. Retrieved from http://www.comnets.rwth-aachen.de

Berlemann, L., Pabst, R., & Walke, B. (2005). Multimode communication protocols enabling reconfigurable radios. *EURASIP Journal on Wireless Communications and Networking, 5*(3), 390–400.

Bertrand, J., Cruz, J. W., Majkrzak, B., & Rossano, T. (2002). CORBA delays in a software-defined radio. *IEEE Communications Magazine, 40*(2), 152–155. doi:10.1109/35.983922

Bhatti, N. T., Hiltunen, M. A., Schlichting, R. D., & Chiu, W. (1998). Coyote: A system for constructing fine-grain configurable communication services. *ACM Transactions on Computer Systems, 16*(4), 321–366. Retrieved from citeseer.ist.psu.edu/article/bhatti98coyote.html doi:10.1145/292523.292524

Bickle, J. (2000, December). *Software radio architecture (SRA) 2.0 technical overview.* Retrieved from http://www.sdrforum.org/

Bogenfeld, E., & Gaspard, I. (2008). *Self-x in radio access networks.*

Braden, R., Faber, T., & Handley, M. (2002). *From protocol stack to protocol heap - Role-based architecture.* Retrieved from citeseer.ist.psu.edu/braden02from.html

Clark, R. J., Ammar, M. H., & Calvert, K. L. (1997). Protocol discovery in multiprotocol networks. *Mobile Networks and Applications, 2*(3), 271-284. doi: http://dx.doi.org/10.1023/A:1013645019693

Denko, M. K., Yang, L. T., & Zhang, Y. (2009). *Autonomic computing and networking* (pp. 239–260). Springer.

Fish, R. S., Graham, J. M., & Loader, R. J. (1998). DRoPS: Kernel support for runtime adaptable protocols. *EUROMICRO Conference, 2,* (pp. 210-29). Los Alamitos, CA: IEEE Computer Society. doi: http://doi.ieeecomputersociety.org/10.1109/EURMIC.1998.708137

Floyd, S. (2000). *RFC 2914 - Congestion control principle.* Retrieved from http://datatracker.ietf.org/doc/rfc2914/

Friedman, R., & van Renesse, R. (1996). Strong and weak virtual synchrony in Horus. In R. van Renesse (Ed.), *Proceedings of the Symposium on Reliable Distributed Systems* (pp. 140-149). doi: 10.1109/RELDIS.1996.559711

Gamma, E., Helm, R., Johnson, R., & Vlissides, J. (1995). *Design patterns: Elements of reusable object-oriented software.* Boston, MA: Addison-Wesley Longman Publishing Co., Inc.

Hiltunen, M. A., Schlichting, R. D., Ugarte, C. A., & Wong, G. T. (2000). Survivability through customization and adaptability: The Cactus approach. In R. D. Schlichting (Ed.), *Proceedings of DARPA Information Survivability Conference and Exposition DISCEX '00* (Vol. 1, pp. 294-307). doi: 10.1109/DISCEX.2000.825033

Jung, M., Biersack, E., & Pilger, A. (1999). Implementing network protocols in Java-A framework for rapid prototyping. *International Conference on Enterprise Information Systems* (pp. 649-656). Retrieved from citeseer.ist.psu.edu/jung99implementing.html

Kephart, J. O., & Chess, D. M. (2003). The vision of autonomic computing. *Computer, 36*(1), 41–50. doi:10.1109/MC.2003.1160055

Kliazovich, D., & Granelli, F. (2008). Distributed protocol stacks: A framework for balancing interoperability and optimization. *IEEE International Conference on Communications, ICC Workshops '08,* (pp. 241-245). doi: 10.1109/ICCW.2008.51

Krupczak, B., Calvert, K. L., & Ammar, M. (1998). Implementing protocols in Java: The price of portability. *Proceedings Seventeenth Annual Joint Conference of the IEEE Computer and Communications Societies INFOCOM '98,* Vol. 2, (pp. 765-773). doi: 10.1109/INFCOM.1998.665099

Meling, H. (2006). *Non-hierarchical dynamic protocol composition in Jgroup/ARM. Proceedings of Norsk Informatikkonferanse*. Molde, Norway: NIK.

Miranda, H., Pinto, A., & Rodrigues, L. (2001). Appia, a flexible protocol kernel supporting multiple coordinated channels. *Proceedings of 21st International Conference on Distributed Computing Systems* (pp. 707-710). doi: 10.1109/ICDSC.2001.919005

Muhugusa, M., Marzo, G. D., Tschudin, C. F., & Harms, J. (1994). *ComScript: An environment for the implementation of protocol stacks and their dynamic reconfiguration*. International Symposium on Applied Corporate Computing {ISACC} 94. Retrieved from citeseer.ist.psu.edu/muhugusa94comscript.html

Niamanesh, M., & Jalili, R. (2007). A dynamic-reconfigurable architecture for protocol stacks of networked systems. *COMPSAC '07: Proceedings of the 31st Annual International Computer Software and Applications Conference (COMPSAC 2007)*, Vol. 1 (pp. 609-612). Washington, DC: IEEE Computer Society. doi: http://dx.doi.org/10.1109/COMPSAC.2007.19

Niamanesh, M., Sabetghadam, S., Yousefzadeh Rahaghi, R., & Jalili, R. (2007). Design and implementation of a dynamic-reconfigurable architecture for protocol stack. *International Symposium on Fundamentals of Software Engineering* (pp. 396-403). doi: http://dx.doi.org/10.1007/978-3-540-75698-9

OMG. (2005). *Platform independent model (PIM) and platform specific model (PSM) for software radio components*. Retrieved from http://sbc.omg.org/

Patouni, E. (2006). *E2R II scenario on autonomic communication systems for seamless experience*. Retrieved from http://e2r2.motlabs.com/dissemination/whitepapers

Patouni, L., Alonistioti, N., & Merakos, L. (2010). Modeling and performance evaluation of reconfiguration decision making in heterogeneous radio network environments. *IEEE Transactions on Vehicular Technology*, *59*(4), 1887–1900. Retrieved from http://www.scopus.com/inward/record.url?eid=2-s2.0-77952257483&partnerID=40&md5=5a0d5ef96671d820675d61a47b541784 doi:10.1109/TVT.2009.2039504

Peterson, L., & Hutchinson, N., O'Malley, S., & Rao, H. (1990). The x-kernel: A platform for accessing internet resources. *Computer*, *23*(5), 23–33. doi:10.1109/2.53352

Plagemann, T., & Plattner, B. (1993). Modules as building blocks for protocol configuration. *Proceedings International Conference on Network Protocols (ICNP '93)*. Retrieved from citeseer.ist.psu.edu/plagemann93module.html

Plagemann, T., Waclawczyk, J., & Plattner, B. (1994). Management of configurable protocols for multimedia applications. *Proceedings of {ISMM} International Conference Distributed Multimedia Systems and Applications* (pp. 78-81). Retrieved from citeseer.ist.psu.edu/plagemann94management.html

Rosa, L., Lopes, A., & Rodrigues, L. (2006). Policy-driven adaptation of protocol stacks. *Proceedings of the International Conference on Autonomic and Autonomous Systems ICAS '06* (p. 5). doi: 10.1109/ICAS.2006.43

Schmidt, D. C., Box, D. F., & Suda, T. (1993). ADAPTIVE - A dynamically assembled protocol transformation, integration and evaluation environment. *Concurrency (Chichester, England)*, 5(4), 269–286. Retrieved from citeseer.ist.psu.edu/article/schmidt93adaptive.html doi:10.1002/cpe.4330050405

Tuttlebee, W. H. W. (Ed.). (2002). *Software defined radio: Enabling technologies*. Chichester, UK: John Wiley & Sons.

van Renesse, R. Birman, K. P., Friedman, Roy, Hayden, M., & Karr, D. A. (1995). A framework for protocol composition in Horus. *PODC '95: Proceedings of the Fourteenth Annual ACM Symposium on Principles of Distributed Computing* (pp. 80-89). New York, NY: ACM. doi: http://doi.acm.org/10.1145/224964.224974

KEY TERMS AND DEFINITIONS

Adaptable Protocols: These protocols facilitate large-scale reuse of protocol software code by grouping common protocol functions (e.g., segmentation and reassembly) into a generic layer.

Composable Protocols: They are based on the analysis of a protocol's operation into elementary functions. Depending on the analysis granularity and the associations manifesting among the elementary protocol functions, the composition procedure for these protocols may follow either a flat or a hierarchical model.

Customizable Protocols: They are based on an object-oriented architecture for the protocol stack software. The use of object-oriented design techniques renders the introduction of a dynamic adaptation capacity straightforward.

Chapter 10
Mobility Management Issues for Next Generation Wireless Networks

Sajal Saha
Narula Institute of Technology, India

Asish K Mukhopadhyay
Dr. B.C. Roy Engineering College, India

ABSTRACT

The next generation networks must support mobility for ubiquitous communication between any two nodes irrespective of their locations. Mobile IP was the first protocol to support mobility. The process of registration in Mobile IP protocol requires large number of location updates, excessive signaling traffic and service delay. This problem is solved by Hierarchical Mobile IP (HMIP) using the concept of hierarchy of Foreign Agent (FA) and the Gateway Foreign Agent (GFA), Mobility Anchor Point (MAP) to localize the registration information. The performance depends upon the selection of GFA or MAP and some key parameters. This chapter discusses several HMIP based mobility management schemes with a comparative analysis of those protocols and proposes an efficient mobility management scheme.

INTRODUCTION

The future generation of networks is expected to be all-IP-based with the ability of seamless inter-working using Internet as the backbone. Users' expectation demands transparent accessibility from any one network to any other globally irre-

DOI: 10.4018/978-1-4666-1888-6.ch010

spective of location. There has been a tremendous growth in the deployment of network systems with the dramatic increase in the usage of different wireless technologies coexisting around us. These different systems usually have different characteristics in terms of mobility, bandwidth, latency, frequency and cost. To support mobility, a major task in mobile communication system is to maintain continuity of communication when a mobile user/device migrates from a cell of one physical network to another cell of the same or different physical network. This is accomplished by changing the communication channel and control from the old to the new base station and the process is known as call handoff or handover. Each handoff requires network resources to reroute the call to the new base station and adds load to the switching processor. It is even critical to manage the handoffs when a roaming user moves into a dissimilar network with different type of the communication channels and mobility characteristics. Minimizing the number of handoffs during a communication session and minimizing delay in handoff execution are the main tasks in handoff process. Mobility protocols are designed to manage the handoffs efficiently with optimized call handoff strategies so that the perceived quality of service (QoS) does not degrade in mobile communication system.

User mobility is one of the most important criteria that mark impact on the in internetworking and QoS, a key parameter in the design of future networks. Mobility in general, can be classified into three categories, - micro mobility, macro mobility and global mobility. Micro mobility is the movement of the mobile node (MN) within the Base Stations (BS) in a subnet which occurs very frequently. Macro mobility is the intra-domain mobility of the MNs among different subnets in a single domain or region. Global mobility refers to the movement of MN from one network domain to another that may be heterogeneous in nature. Micro-mobility protocols may be classified based on some key parameters such as protocol name, hand off type, paging support, traffic inside the network, load balancing, scalability, robustness, QoS support, and traffic direction. Mobility management protocols based on IPv6 show superior performance over IPv4 based protocols. Among the existing protocols, Hierarchical MobileIPv6 (HMIPv6) is the most robust and scalable supporting both macro and micro mobility. Route optimization, a built-in feature of MIPv6, is a common

technique to overcome the problem of triangular routing which is responsible for the increases in handoff latency. HMIPv6 protocol reduces this overload and improves handoff delay by separating the local mobility from global mobility. Along with the standard HMIP protocols, we consider some advanced micro-mobility protocols such as PHMIP(2003), RHMIP(2003),MBBU(2003), DHMIP(2004), MHMIP(2004), FFH-MIP(2004), MIFA(2004), SIGMA(2004), HMIP-MPLS(2007), SHMIP(2007) etc. for our analysis. Extensive analysis has been carried on the issues such as handoff latency and signaling overhead. The analysis compares the merits and demerits of various schemes and recommends the need of a scheme which may accumulate the merits of most of the existing schemes. In this process, analysis of the two mobility models- Free flow model and Random walk model are pertinent. The over all study proposes a network with a new mobility model which may yield a better result than any other existing scheme by removing the binding update with the HA.

BACKGROUND

The fundamental problem for a mobile host (David, 1999) is to have seamless connectivity and continuous reachability and therefore, it must retain its identifier while changing its location. The network addresses are associated with a fixed network location. If a packet's destination is a mobile node, then each new point of attachment made by the node is associated with a new network corresponding to a new IP address, making transparent mobility impossible. Mobility is not supported in the IP layer by traditional IP. Mobile IP enables mobility transparent to applications and higher level protocols such as TCP.

Mobile IP (RFC 2002), a standard proposed by a working group within the Internet Engineering Task Force, was designed to solve this problem by allowing the mobile node to use two IP addresses:

a fixed home address and a care-of address that change at each new point of attachment. Mobile IP introduces of two network entities – Home Agent (HA) and Foreign Agent (FA) in addition to normal IP protocol. A subnet other than a mobile's home subnet (HS) is known as foreign subnet (FS). A mobile node (MN) when moves away from its HS, and enters into a FS, acquires a temporary address of the FA within the FS known as Care-of-Address (CoA). The MN then sends a registration request (RR) message to it's HA informing about its current location (CoA). The HA then captures all the incoming IP addressed to the MN packets coming from the corresponding node (CN). It encapsulates the packets with a new IP header having a destination addresses that of the COA and then transmits over the channel. This process is known as tunneling. The FA decapsulates the packets and submits the original IP packets to the MN. For outbound data, the MN can either send the packets to the CN through direct route using normal IP protocol (triangular routing) or take reverse route through the HA (reverse/backward tunneling). When the MN leaves the current FA (oFA) to enter into a new FA (nFA) under another FS, it requires hand-off before acquiring a new CoA (nCoA). There is a time delay or latency between the MN sends RR message for new registration to the HA and HA receives that. During this period, the MN will be out of the old FS (oFS) and any packet received by the HA will be forwarded to the old COA (oCoA) and may be dropped. If the latency is significant to the order of a bit period, the connection may be disrupted. In this case, latency or hand-off delay may cause loss of packets and becomes a crucial issue for Mobile IP. The hand-off delay is significant when the MN moves to a different network particularly from a LAN to WAN or vice-versa. So any protocol designed for mobile IP must take note of this consideration. The basic principles of mobile IP were first documented by C.Perkins (Perkins, 1998). Many Internet drafts and other sponsored researches (KIRCI, 2006;

Reinbold, 2001; Campbell, 2000) are standardizing the applications of mobile IP based on IPv4. On the other hand, IPv6 is ready to phase out IPv4 with its added advantages of robustness and flexibility, towards seamless communication among the heterogeneous wired and wireless networks.

MICRO MOBILITY PROTOCOLS

Mobile IP exhibits several problems regarding the duration of handoff and the scalability of the registration procedure. As large number of mobile devices change networks quite frequently, a high load on the Home Agent as well as on the networks is generated by registration and binding update messages. IP micro-mobility protocols can complement Mobile IP by offering fast and almost seamless handoff control in limited geographic areas.

The basic idea of all (Ghassemian, 2002) micro-mobility protocols is to keep the frequent updates generated by local changes of the points of attachment away from the home network and only inform the Home Agent about major changes, i.e., changes of a region.

The primary role of micro-mobility protocols is to ensure that packets arriving from the Internet and addressed to Mobile Node are forwarded to the appropriate wireless access point in an efficient manner. To do this, micro-mobility protocols maintain a location database that maps Mobile Node identifiers to location information. There are some examples of micro-mobility protocols.

Cellular IP

Cellular IP (CIP) (Wisely, 2000; Das, 2002; Misra, 2000; David, 1999; Lee, 2003) as depicted in Figure 1, is a micro-mobility protocol based on Mobile IP for macro-mobility management. A specialized Mobility Agent (MA) that acts as a Gateway in the internet. CIP replaces IP inside the wireless access network. In CIP routing is based on the routes established and routes updated by the MN while connected to the network. Each base station maintains a route cache that helps to forward packets from gateway to the MN or from MN to the gateway. Routes are established by hop-by-hop transmission of special control packets by the stations to update their route cache. A beacon is periodically sent by the gateway and it is flooded across the network. By this mechanism the received beacon station know its interface to forward packets towards the gateway. On the other hand MN sends a route update packet when it connects to a new network and it changes its point of attachment i.e. handoff. The handoff is managed in two different ways: hard handoff and soft handoff. Hard handoff provides no guarantee of packet loss but soft handoff ensures that the packet loss will be reduced. CIP have support for the paging mechanism and some stations maintain paging caches that are used in case of paging requests.

CIP supports local mobility and handoff for moving hosts. Figure 1 consists of several wireless access networks. These networks are connected to the Internet over Gateways (GW). When a packet is sent to a Mobile Node (MN), at first the packet reaches at the Gateway. And the Gateway forwards the packet to the MN by the help of the host-specific-routing path. In CIP, for location management and routing, distributed paging cache and distributed routed cache is used. Distributed paging cache finds an idle MN's place not exactly but coarsely. By the way the distributed routed cache finds an active MN's place up to its subnet.

Figure 1. Structure of cellular IP

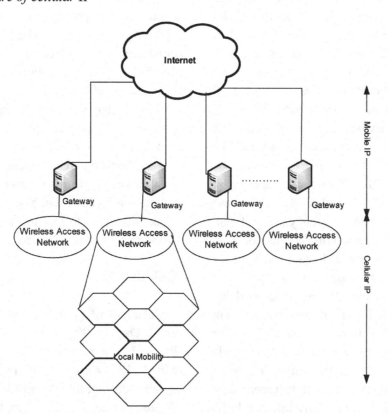

Hawaii

Handoff Aware Wireless Internet Infrastructure (Hawaii) (Wisely, 2000; Das, 2002; Misra, 2000; David, 1999; Lee, 2003) is a micro-mobility protocol based on Mobile IP from Lucent Technologies and this protocol handles intra-domain mobility. Hawaii relies on Mobile IP to provide wide-area inter-domain mobility. Nodes in a Hawaii network execute a generic IP routing protocol and it maintain mobility specific routing information as per host routes in routing tables so it uses host based routing (HBR) (Baek, 2004; Yi). Thus Hawaii nodes can be considered as enhanced IP routers in which existing packet forwarding function is reused. Location information (i.e., mobile specific routing entries) is created, updated and modified by explicit signaling messages sent by mobile nodes. Hawaii uses IP multicasting to page mobile nodes when incoming data packets arrive at an access network and no recent routing information is available. As HAWAII exchanges messages between routers hence the MNs do not require other protocol stacks except Mobile IP for mobility support. It also provides many forwarding schemes for a smooth handoff and packet loss during handoff like non-forwarding scheme and forwarding scheme.

In a domain in Hawaii mobility related works are done by gateways which are called as domain root router. The architecture of Hawaii is illustrated in the Figure 2. The coming packets are routed by IP routing, when the MN is in its own domain. But if the MN is in a foreign domain then the coming packets are firstly taken by the HA. Then they are sent to the domain root router which forwards the packets by the host-based-routing entries to the MN.

Hierarchical Mobile IPv4 (HMIPv4)

Hierarchical Mobile IPv4 (HMIPv4) is a micro-mobility management protocol that reduces the signaling overhead of the Correspondent Node (CN) and the Home Agent (HA) and also improves the handoff performance in Mobile

Figure 2. Structure of Hawaii

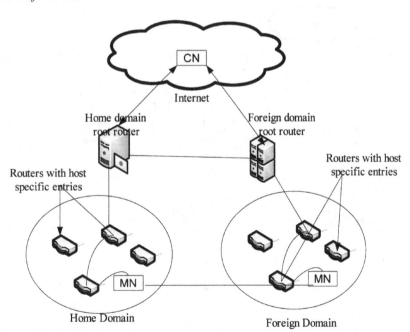

IP. HMIPv4 protocol is based on the hierarchy of *Gateway Foreign Agent* (GFA) and *Foreign Agent* (FA). A mobile node (MN) entering in to the GFA domain receives router advertisements containing information on local GFA. The MN updates the home agent (HA) with an address called the *regional care of address* (RCoA) as its current location. All packets destined for MN are intercepted by GFA, which encapsulates it and sends to the MN's current address. If the MN changes its current point of attachment within its domain, it gets a new address called *local care of address* (LCoA) from the foreign agent serving it. The MN needs to register the LCoA to the GFA and it's mobility is transparent to the HA. HA is updated with the new RCoA whenever the MN moves from one GFA to another. Architecture of HMIPv4 is shown in Figure 3.

Tele-MIP

TeleMIP (Misra, 2000; Gwon, 2004; Reinbold, 2001) is a micro-mobility management protocol and it manages user's movements inside a domain and uses Mobile IP for the inter domain mobility. It defines a two levels Mobile IP hierarchy in wireless access network. Tele-MIP introduces a new entity called the Tele-MIP Mobility Agent (TMA). The TeleMIP network as figured in Figure 4 is composed of routers and base stations with switching capabilities. The network is divided into many subnets in which each subnet is composed of a set of base stations with at least one router that works as FA. Each FA is able to connect with at least one TMA in the network as there may be more than one TMA. A TeleMIP subnet can be viewed as a classical CDMA RAN with

Figure 3. Structure of multi-level HMIPv4

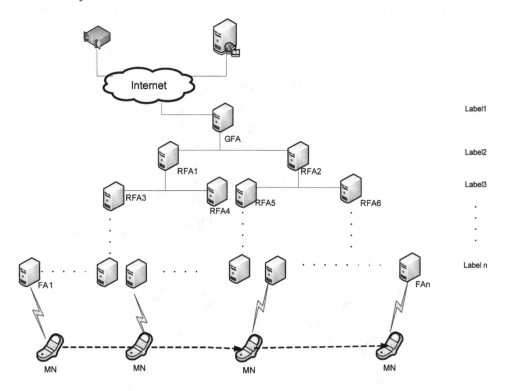

Figure 4. TeleMIP functional layout

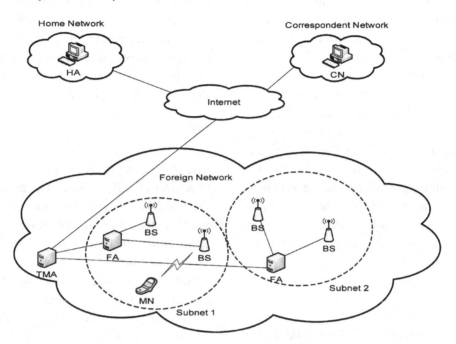

the base station controller performing extended routing tasks.

EMA

The Edge Mobility Architecture (EMA) (Das, 2002; Misra, 2002; Saha, 2004; Reinbold, 2001; O'Neill, 2000; Campbell, 2000, 2002) is proposed by British Telecom, Ansible-Systems and the University of Maryland. This architecture presents a general framework that supports host mobility in wireless access networks. EMA is a micro-mobility management proposal which works over IP and can work with various radio access networks like TDMA, CDMA. The architecture of EMA is shown in Figure 5. It is composed of

Figure 5. EMA domain and routed handoff

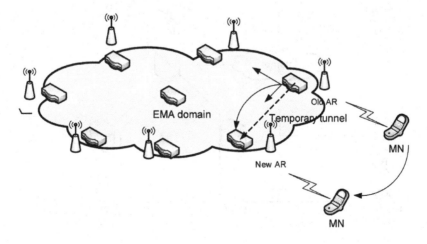

two parts – a generic mobile routing architecture and an effective use of these principles with the TORA routing protocol which is a routing protocol designed for ad-hoc networks.

The edge based routing protocols are needed to be much responsive to the host mobility and further conjecture that exist routing protocols are developed for highly dynamic environments (e.g., mobile ad hoc networks) are applicable. This approach reveals a generic framework in which other fast routing algorithms could support micro mobility. The Edge mobility supports transparent handoff between ARs by using different wireless technologies through information exchange between access routers.

HMIPv6

MIPv4 (Figure 3) is enhanced by the HMIP protocol as HMIPv6 (Soliman, 2005) (Figure 6). In HMIPv6, the GFA is replaced by the new entity called *Mobility Anchor Point* (MAP) (Figure 6) with minor extensions to the Mobile Node operations. This will not affect the operations of the CN and HA. The main idea is that the MN registers the MAP's RCoA with its HA. Therefore, when the mobile node moves locally (that is its MAP

does not change), it only needs to register its new location with its MAP. By using this method, signaling is contained within a smaller area without requiring propagation through the core network and the location update time is reduced. Timing diagram of HMIP protocol is shown in Figure 7.

BRAIN

The Broadband Radio Access for IP Networks (BRAIN) (Eardley, 2002; Gunasundari, 2007; Hancock, 2000) network provides an all IP based wireless network that accumulates the terminal and the infrastructure both of access network. The main aim of the BRAIN network is to build a IP network that provides mobile users QoS support for real time multimedia applications. It merges two networks like the fixed IP network and mobile network by an access network (AN) to provide mobility and QoS support. Its scope provides – In the terminal consists of an internet protocol stack that is compatible with mobile applications and a lower converging layer interfacing the selected radio technology. In the access network it provides support for local mobility that optimizes the transport of IP application data and interconnected to the fixed IP network with router interface. The

Figure 6. Structure of HMIPv6

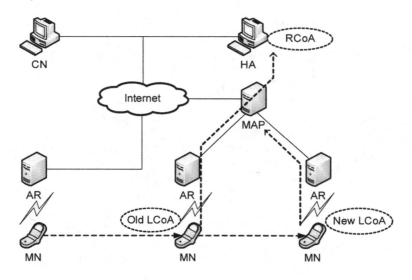

architecture and operation of BRAIN is shown in Figure 8 and Figure 9.

IDMP

Intra Domain Mobility Management Protocol (IDMP) (Das, 2002; Chakrabarty, 2003; Aust, 2004; Diab, 2004, 2005; Campbell, 2000, 2002; Wisely, 2000; Misra, 2000) is a multi-CoA intra domain mobility protocol. It is used in the wireless cellular network to reduce the latency of intra-domain location updates and mobility signaling traffic. IDMP (Figure 10) uses two level hierarchies to provide MN mobility with a special node called mobility agent (MA) to provide a mobile node (MN) with a stable point of packet forwarding. MA is similar to the Mobile IP Regional Registration (MIP-RR) GFA that works as a packet redirector and subnet agent (SA). The SA is similar to the MIP foreign agent that pro-

Figure 7. Timing diagram of HMIPv4 / HMIPv6

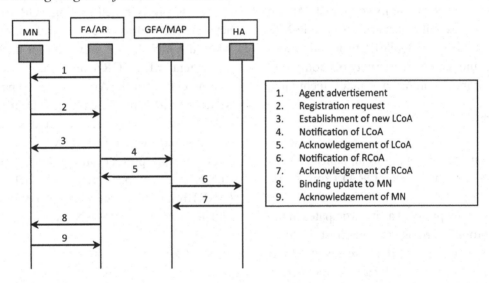

1. Agent advertisement
2. Registration request
3. Establishment of new LCoA
4. Notification of LCoA
5. Acknowledgement of LCoA
6. Notification of RCoA
7. Acknowledgement of RCoA
8. Binding update to MN
9. Acknowledgement of MN

Figure 8. BRAIN network layer scope

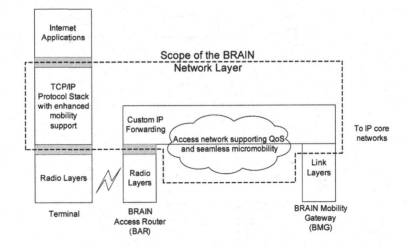

Figure 9. Access network and address assignment

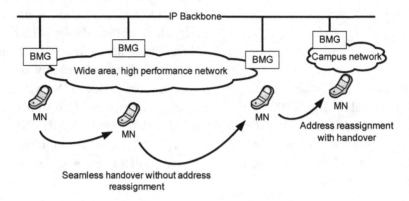

vides subnet specific mobility service. IDMP can also be combined with other protocols (Tele-MIP combines IDMP with Mobile IP) to provide seamless packet movement. It uses network controlled (network or mobile initiated) handoff technique.

MER-TORA

Mobility Enhanced Routing – Temporally Ordered Routing Algorithm (MER-TORA) (You, 2003; Ma, 2004; Pack, 2004; David, 1999; Eardley, 2002) is per host based protocol as it participates in the mobility protocol arranged by per host. Here an AR has its own block of IP addresses and from these address the CoA is allocated to the MN.

To use prefix based routing TORA protocol acts on ARs address prefix to route the packets when the MN do not move, but at the time of movement MER-TORA have the host specific routing entries of the AR to route the packets to MN. When MN movement occurs frequently per host state will occur in routers and to minimize this MN may have a fresh CoA from the current AR to reuse the prefix routing again. In the Figure 11 MN have host specific entries in anchor routers (ANR) from anchor gateway (ANG) with the path update messages as the MN moves.

Figure 10. Structure of IDMP and logical elements

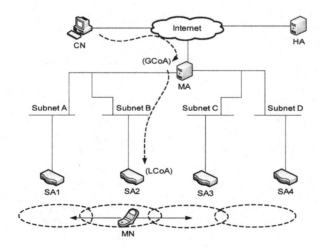

Figure 11. MER-TORA operations

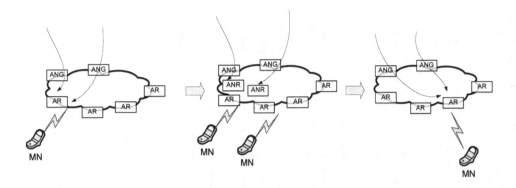

Micro-Mobility Classification

In the Figure 12 the classification of different mobility protocols (Hancock, 2000; Chakrabarty, 2003; Saha, 2004) are given. Cellular IP is supports micro-mobility and macro-mobility, TeleMIP is a macro-mobility protocol. The protocols that support micro-mobility as well as global-mobility are HMIPv4, TR45.6, HAWAII, DMA, EMA, BRAIN, IDMP, MER-TORA, and HMIPV6. MIPv4 and MIPv6 support global mobility. Comparative analysis of various micromobilty protocols is shown in Table 1 and Table 2.

ADVANCE MICRO-MOBILITY PROTOCOLS

PHMIP (Lee, 2003) is the protocol that enables paging service to reduce signaling overhead for local mobility management in the MAP domain of HMIPv6 network. Robust HMIPv6 (RHMIP) (You, 2003) is the protocol which provides robustness and fault tolerance to reduce the failure recovery time. It is 60% faster than the normal recovery time. In Mobility Based Binding Update(MBBU) scheme (Yi et. el.) of HMIPv6 provides a lifetime value for binding update and it can also adjusted to minimum to the maximum value according to the movement of MN as higher binding request and update provides higher signaling overhead.

Figure 12. Classification of different mobility protocols

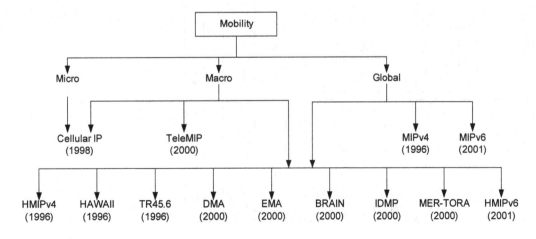

Table 1. Difference between various micro-mobility protocols

Protocol Name	Hand off type	Paging Support	Traffic inside the network	Load balancing	Hand off Delay	Scalability	Robustness	QoS support	Outgoing / incoming traffic
Cellular IP(1998)	Semi-soft/ Hard	√	Low	No	Low	Low	Tree like	X	Symmetric routing
HAWAII (1999)	Forwarding scheme, Multiple Stream Forwarding(FSM)	√	Low	Yes	Low	Low	Tree like	X	Symmetric routing
TeleMIP (2000)	Fast/ Hard	X	Low	Yes	Low	Low	Depends on MN & FA	X	Symmetric routing
EMA (2000)	Make before break/ Break before make	Yes	Low	Yes	Low	High	Tree like topology but support mesh	X	Asymmetric routing by TORA
HMIPv4(1996)	Hard/Fast	√	High	Yes	High	High	Tree like	X	Symmetric routing
BRAIN (2000)	Soft/ Hard	X	High	No	High	High	Tree like topology but support mesh	√	Symmetric routing
IDMP (2000)	Fast	√	Low	No	Low	High	Tree like	Yes	Symmetric routing
MER-TORA (2000)	Forwarding/Non-for-warding	√	Low	--	Low	High	Tree like topology but support mesh	X	Interface based forwarding
Wireless IP (TR45.6) (1996)	Hard	X	High	--	Low		--	X	--
DMA (2000)	Hard	√	Low	Yes	Low	High	Tree like	√	
HMIPv6(2001)	Hard	√	High	Yes	High	High	Tree like	X	Symmetric routing

Table 2. Difference between various micro-mobility protocols

Protocol name	Tunneling	Means of update	Hand off layer	Global Mobility Support	Packet loss	AAA and security support	Optimized route support	Mobility classification
Cellular IP (1998)	X	Data packet	L3	√	Low	X	X	Per host forwarding
HAWAII (1999)	X	Signaling message	L3	√	Low	X	X	Per host forwarding
TeleMIP (2000)	√	Signaling message	L3	√	Low	X	√ (not optimal)	Proxy agent
EMA (2000)	√ (temp)	Signaling message	L3	√	Low	√	√	
HMIPv4 (1996)	√	Signaling message	L3.5	√	High	X	X	Proxy agent
BRAIN (2000)	X	Signaling message	L3	√	Low	Only security support	√	Broadband IP based
IDMP (2000)	√	Signaling message	L2.5	√	Low	X	√	
MER-TORA (2000)	√ (temp)	Signaling message	L3	√	Low	X	√	MANET based
Wireless IP(TR45.6) (1996)	--	Signaling message	L3	√	Low	√	√	--
DMA (2000)	√	Binding update	L3	√	Low	X	X	Proxy agent
HMIPv6 (2001)	√	Signaling message	L3	√	High	√	X	Proxy agent

Dynamic HMIP (DHMIP) (Ma, 2004) provides the technique that it dynamically maintains the hierarchy for the MN and distributes the signaling overhead evenly in the network and by this it reduces the overall signaling cost. The multilevel hierarchy of HMIPv6 (MHMIP) introduces (Pack, 2004) a tree structure hierarchy to provide scalable services in the network. But it encounters additional packet processing overhead. We therefore need to find the optimum level that minimizes the overall cost. Analysis of different protocols shows better result for Fast MIP (FMIP) (Gwon, 2004) in terms of scalability and robustness. It has best handoff performance and provides less signaling overhead compared to HMIP. NS-2(Aust, 2004) extensions for Mobile ad hoc networks provide support for simulation of HMIP NS-2

environment. This extension allows the multilevel hierarchies to provide scalability and reduce the handoff latency by minimizing the packet loss. Analysis based on handoff latency shows that Mobile IP Fast Authentication protocol (MIFA) protocol (Diab, 2004, 2005) minimizes handoff latency. In addition, it does not use any network element beyond the FA or HA causing reduction of signaling cost. Dynamic Authentication, Authorization and Accounting (AAA) protocol required for handoff in the network, reduces the disruption time in AAA (Baek, 2006). This scheme provides faster AAA resolution. HMIP over MPLS (HMIP-MPLS) (Vassiliou et. el.) is an overlay protocol that provides mobility in the network. It also examines the handoffs in the overlay environment. It does not require any change in the existing protocol but enhance it to provide internetworking based on HMIPv6.

COMPARATIVE ANALYSIS OF SOME SIGNIFICANT HMIP PROTOCOLS

We consider a set of significant HMIP based mobility protocols such as HMIP, PHMIP, RHMIP, DHMIP, FFHMIP, MIFA etc. which are supposed to play an important role in IP based mobility management. We analyze the advantages and disadvantages of theses protocols in the context of handoff latency and signaling overhead. The comparative analysis is summarized in Table 3. The timing diagram of HMIPv4 and HMIPv6 are shown in Figure 7, which may be useful while analyzing the various protocols.

It has been shown by the authors that PHMIP (Lee, 2003) reduces mobility management traffic by paging service in MAP domain. PHMIP converts the mobile node into inactive mode when it has no active communication session. In inactive mode, the mobile node configures a new LCoA without performing binding update although it moves to another access router (AR) of that domain. Thus, exact location of mobile node is not known to MAP but it knows that the mobile node is in the paging area. A packet destined for the mobile node, reaches at the MAP. Then MAP sends paging request to all the routers in the paging area to know the exact location of the mobile node. It also buffers the packet to be delivered to the mobile node in inactive mode. It changes the state of the MN to active mode and registers its exact location with MAP. By using PHMIP, the signaling overhead and power consumption is reduced.

In RHMIP (You, 2003), a Mobile Node (MN) uses a *Primary Regional Care-of-address* (P-RCoA) and a *Secondary Regional Care-of-address* (S-RCoA) to register with two different MAPs called P-MAP and S-MAP simultaneously. When MN or CN detects the failure of P-MAP, it

changes its attachment from P-MAP to S-MAP. This recovery procedure reduces the failure recovery time but increase significant amount of signaling overhead. The frequent transmission of binding requests and updates would result in high signaling overhead (Yi et. el.), so determination of the lifetime value of binding cache is the most important issue in HMIP. The MBBU scheme (Yi et. el.) introduces location update concept for dynamic allocation of lifetime to reduce the signaling cost of Binding Update (BU) and Binding Request (BR) in HMIPv6.The number of binding update and binding request messages can be reduced by dynamic allocation of binding update lifetime. In DHMIP (Ma, 2004) location update massage is reduced by introducing hierarchy of FA instead of HA. Incoming packets to the MN are forwarded along with the hierarchy of FA. But during this process, a service delay occurs and to overcome this, a threshold value is used. The threshold value is calculated according to the information of mobile user's traffic load and mobility. Suppose a MN is moving from one subnet S_i to another subnet S_{i+1} under the jurisdiction of a common FA with the threshold value of three. The MN updates the new CoAs to the previous FAs (i.e. S_i). As the previous FAs are close to the new ones, the cost of the update is lower than the cost of the update to the HAs. As soon as the user reaches the subnet S_{i+1} 1, the MN sets up a new hierarchy as the threshold level reached at three. Then the update process is done with the HA. DHMIP reduces the location update message that moves to the HA but the path established from FA to FA along the hierarchy of FA may not be the shortest path. Mobility protocols based on IPv6 are classified in tree structure as shown in Figure 12. In (Pack, 2004), HMIPv6 uses multilevel hierarchy of MAP. A BU message is send to the root MAP (RMAP) by the way of different intermediate MAPs (IMAP). The RMAP checks the BU message with its mapping table to see that MN is registered or not. If MN is registered, the local binding update is completed at the MAP.

Table 3. A comparison of some significant HMIP protocols

Protocol/ Methodology	Assumption	Ref Node	Advantage/ Contribution	Drawback/ Shortcomings	Mobility			Signaling Overhead	Mobile IP version
					Micro	Macro	Global		
PHMIP [Lee] (2003)	MAP knows the paging area	Yes	Reduce signaling overhead and power consumption within MAP domain.	Frequent inter domain movement increase handoff latency.	√	√	√	Low under restricted mobility.	MIPv6
RHMIP [You] (2003)	A MAP can exist in any level in a hierarchy	Yes	Provides fault tolerance, survivability and robustness.	Multiple registrations increase signaling overhead.	√	√	√	High	MIPv6
MBBU [Yi] (2003)	MN sends BU to its HA & other CN to inform current CoA	No	MN's lifetime can be adjusted according to MN's mobility pattern to reduce signaling overhead.	Frequent inter domain movement leads to the normal binding update and same signaling cost.	√	√	√	Low under restricted mobility.	MIPv6
HMIP-B [Ma] (2003)	MAP tunnels packets to the CoA of the MR or buffers them during the MR handoff	Yes	Buffering of packets in MAP during handoff.	Extra BU requires for prefix notification.	√	√	√	High	MIPv6
DHMIP [Pack] (2004)	MIP require the MH to update its location to HA whenever it moves to a new subnet	Yes	Reduce location update messages using hierarchy of FAs.	Not supports traffic engineering.	√	√	√	Low	MIPv4
MHMIP [Gwon] (2004)	RCoA does not change as long as the MN moves within the same MAP domain	Yes	Supports scalability with multi level hierarchical structure.	Additional packet processing overhead increases traffic and signaling overhead.	√	√	√	High	MIPv6
FF-HMIP [Aust] (2004)	100,000 mobile users in 100 X 100 km² area capable of WWAN and hotspot WLAN accesses	No	Better handoff performance and improves signaling overhead.	Cannot remove tunneling overhead.	√	√	√	Low	MIPv6
MIFA [Diab] (2004)	Security association between the FAs in each L3-FHR	Yes	Suitable and cost effective for real-time application with respect to signaling cost, packet forwarding cost and performance.	Additional tunnels are needed if smooth handoff is supported.	√	X	√	High	MIPv4
HMIP-MPLS [Vassiliou] (2007)	Only point-to-point LSPs are considered.	Yes	Supports MPLS and HMIPv6 simultaneously.	Additional signaling overhead.	√	√	√	High	MIPv6
SIGMA [Ma'en] (2004)	MH need to send binding update to CN and LM during handoff	Yes	Decreases Location and Binding Update costs	After the equilibrium point, the signaling cost is higher.	√	√	X	Low	MIPv6
SHMIP [Alrashdan] (2007)	All the networks as well as all the MAPs are identical	Yes	Tunnel traffic registration information at each HA lessen and the traffic overhead is reduced	BU is required to adjacent all MAP's during handoff.	√	√	√	High	MIPv6

The MAP generates a BU reply and sends it to the lower-level MAP (LMAP) in the hierarchy otherwise it forwards the BU message to the next higher level MAP. It is repeated in each MAP until the MN is not registered in the mapping table. Thus the first binding update message in the foreign network is forwarded to the HA and the RMAP in foreign network. The frequent transmission of binding requests and updates

Therefore, determining the lifetime value of binding cache is an important issue in Mobile IP., A good analysis of scalability and robustness for a range of protocols Simple MIPv6 (SMIPv6), Fast MIPv6 (FMIPv6), HMIPv6, Fast HMIPv6 (FHMIPv6) for simulating user mobility and data traffic in large scale IPv6 mobile network is given in (Gwon, 2004). A new hybrid protocol FFHMIPv6 based on HMIP and FMIP is also introduced in that paper.

Simulation results show that SMIP produces high handoff latency, data loss and global signaling. FMIP reduces handoff latency and prevent data loss creating a bi-directional tunnel between MN's previous subnet's access router (pAR) and next subnet's access router (nAR). HMIP incurs considerably less per-handoff signaling overhead than FMIP but HMIP data traffic has a fixed and permanent overhead even after handoff. FFHMIPv6 achieves FMIP-like handoff performance and improve handoff signaling overhead but cannot remove tunneling overhead. The packet loss of FMIP and FF-HMIP is 6 times less than SMIP and 2.5 times less than HMIP and 1.5 times less than F-HMIP. The additional network elements GFA affect HMIPv4 for its wide use in the internet. MIFA (Diab, 2004, 2005) reduces the handoff latency without using any additional network elements other than HA and FA. MIFA's basic idea is that the HA delegates the authentication to the FA and there is no requirement of distribution of shared secret between HA and the MN to FA. An FA acts as an Anchor FA (AFA) when the shared secret between MN and FA s established during registration.

This new technique uses local authentication with the new FA independent of the re-authentication with the HA. In this approach, some functions that are previously implemented by the HA are additional supported by the FA and there is no need of forwarding the Registration Request by the MN beyond the FA to the HA, since this is done by the FA. Thus, the MN quickly transmits data after a handoff. MIFA protocol reduces the re-authentication and re-registration latency. It also enables the FA to authenticate the MN accurately in the network implementing no loss of security and enabling MN quickly to start uplink and downlink transmission. Hence the handoff latency is reduced. MPLS protocol (Vassiliou) merged Radio Access Network (RAN) and HMIP protocol together to provide multimedia service and localized mobility simultaneously in an overlay framework. This architecture requires additional signaling overhead for additional interaction between two merged architecture to achieve the same result.

MOBILITY MODELS

We analyze the mobility pattern of the users with a suitable mobility model. Mobility models help us to design a mobility management scheme. We consider here two specific mobility models- *random walk model* and *fluid flow model* for our analysis.

Random Walk Model

In memory less Random walk model, user's next cell location does not depend on its previous cell location. A ring cellular topology consists of cells such that cell i & $i+1$ are neighboring cells. Mobile user in cell i move to the cell $i+1$ or $i-1$ or remain in cell i. This movement of mobile users assumed to be stochastic and independent of other users. Three update strategies are taken: (a). Time based strategy, (b) Movement based strategy and (c) Distance based strategy

In time-based update strategy, each user transmits an update message every T slots, while in movement-based update, each mobile user transmits an update message whenever it completes M movements between cells. In distance based update, each user transmits an update message whenever the distance, in terms of cells, between its current cell and the cell in which it last reported is D. The act of a user sending an update message is referred to as reporting. There are Hexagonal dimensional random walk mobile terminal in cell for time period then move to neighbor with equally probability 1/6.

Fluid Flow Model

Fluid flow is a model describes the macroscopic movement of mobility user. In this model Mobile user's traffic flow is fluid flow. The model formulates the amount of traffic flowing out of a Region to be proportional to the population density within the region, the average velocity, and the length of the region of boundary. Fluid flow neglects the behavior of individual vehicle (user), but it is capable of capturing the overall dynamic of system calling and non-calling vehicles are two types of continuous fluid.

In this model each mobile user's movement is uniformly distributed in the range $\{0, 2\pi\}$.

For region with length L and population density ρ, average number of user moving out of area per unit time.

$$N = \rho \, V \, l / \pi$$

Because the fluid flow model defines macroscopic movement, it is not suitable in case of individual user's mobility pattern. Another limitation is that this model is more accurate only for the regions containing a large population since average population density and average velocity are used.

Fluid flow model is widely used to analyze cell boundary crossing.

The perimeter of cell l, perimeter of paging area L
$$L = l\sqrt{n}$$
MN moves at avg. velocity $= v$ and Cell boundary crossing rate $r_c = \rho \, v \, l / \pi$
Paging area boundary crossing rate $r_p = \rho \, v \, L / \pi$

We deduce the mathematical model of the architecture to calculate location update cost and packet deliver cost using fluid flow model. Fluid flow model (Soliman, 2005) conceptualizes traffic flow as the flow of a fluid. The model formulates the amount of traffic flowing out of a region to be proportional to the population density within the region, the average velocity and the length of the region boundary.

Let N be the total no. of AR.
If m(k) is the no. of leaf MAP and N(k) is no. of AR under each leaf MAP.
Then, $N(K) = N/m(k)$
L_k is the perimeter of each K level MAP and L_c is the perimeter of each AR.
Then, $L_k = 4\sqrt{(N(k(L_c / 4)^2)*)} = L_c \sqrt{(N/m(k))}$
Let R_k be the MN crossing rate along the cell boundary, $\rho = $MN density per cell and $v = $Average velocity of the MN, then, $R_k = (Áv \, L_k / \pi) = (Áv / \pi) L_c \sqrt{(N/m(k))}$

Location Update Cost

The location update cost based on user mobility can be divided into following factors:

1. Cost of HA for moving out the foreign network area
2. The location update cost while crossing the different levels
3. The location updates cost by a cell while crossing mobile nodes

Factor 1: If the unit location update cost is C^U_L then the cost of HA for moving out the foreign network area $R_{MAP} \, C^U_L$ (i)

Factor 2: Let the number of levels in MAP domain be k, then the crossing rate at k_{th} level is $R_k * 2^k$

And similarly for $(k-1)^{th}$ level, the crossing rate is $R_{k-1} * 2^{k-1}$. If C^k is the unit location update cost for crossing the two k-level MAP domains, then the cost for crossing will be

$$\sum_{k=1}^{D} (R_k * 2^k - R_{k-1} * 2^{k-1}) C_L^k$$

Considering three level mobility management above equation reduces to $= \sum_{k=1}^{3} (8R_3 - 4R_2) C_L^k \dots$ (ii)

Factor 3: If r_c is the number of cells in a level and n be the number of location traversed and r_d is the leaf level with 2^d possibilities and c_1^c is the unit location update cost for crossing cells then the total cost will be

$$(R_C * N - R_D * 2^D) * C_L^C$$

Considering three level mobility management above equation reduces to $(R_C * N - R_3 * 2^3) * C_L^C$

$$= (NR_C - 8 R_3) * C_L^C \dots \dots \text{(iii)}$$

Adding (i), (ii) & (iii) we get the total location update cost per unit

$$C_L / \text{Unit} = R_I C_L^U + \sum_{k=1}^{3} [(8R_3 - 4R_2) C_L^k + (NR_C - 8 R_3) * C_L^C]$$

Considering the number of traversed location as L, we get

$$C_L = L [R_I C_L^U + \sum_{k=1}^{3} [(8R_3 - 4R_2) C_L^k + (NR_C - 8 R_3) * C_L^C]]$$

Packet Delivery Cost

The packet delivery cost based on user population can be divided into following factor

1. The packet operating cost between CN and MAP1
2. The packet operating cost between the two layers of MAP - MAP1 and MAP2 and between MAP2 and Access Router (AR)
3. The packet operating cost between AR and Mobile Node (MN)

Let the number of users sending/receiving packets is X.

Factor 1: The packet operating cost between CN and MAP1 is CN-MAP1

Factor 2: The packet operating cost between the two layers of MAP - MAP_1 and MAP_2 and between MAP_2 and AR are $C_P^{MAP_1 - MAP_2} + C_P^{MAP_2 - AR}$

Factor 3: The packet operating cost between AR and MN is C_P^{AR-MN}

Adding constituents 1, 2, 3 we get the packet delivery cost for a user as

$$C_P / \text{user} = C_P^{CN-MAP_1} + C_P^{MAP_1 - MAP_2} + C_P^{MAP_2 - AR} + C_P^{AR-MN}$$

Total packet delivery cost $C_P = N (C_P^{CN-MAP_1} + C_P^{MAP_1 - MAP_2} + C_P^{MAP_2 - AR} + C_P^{AR-MN})$

THMIP: A NEW MOBILITY MANAGEMENT SCHEME

In this section, we propose a mobility management scheme of multilevel hierarchy with Previous MAP BU, in which different hierarchies of MAPs are set up and the AR is situated at the leaf node as shown in Figure 13. This new technique known as THMIP (Three level Hierarchical Mobile IP)

Figure 13. Proposed architecture of THMIP

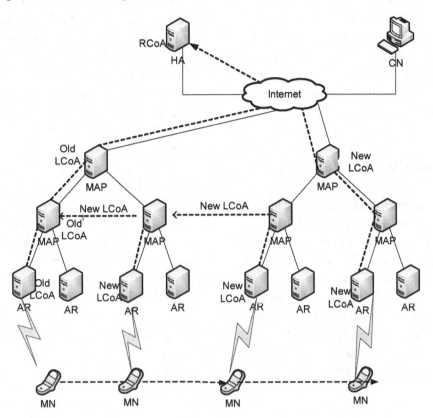

uses local authentication with the new MAP (Mobility Anchor Point) independent of the re-authentication with the HA. It updates the CoA to the previous MAP instead of HA so that BU is done locally. In this way, location update process remain transparent to the HA. For frequent inter-MAP domain movement, multiple location update to previous MAP increase the service delay. To get out of this problem, location update to previous AR is permitted up to two times. In the third time, movement of the MN updates CoA to HA again with RCoA(Regional Care of Address). We simulate its performance in OPNET simulator. The simulation results shows that our proposed mechanism (red colored) achieved better performance (Sajal, 2009, 2011) compared to each of the other protocols.

For simulation purpose we used OPNET simulator and we consider three levels of hierar-chy and introduce MAP to deploy two level of hierarchy. When a MN enters into a MAP domain, it receives a router advertisement message containing the information about the MAP. MN updates the HA with an address assigned by the MAP named RCoA and updates the local AR, MAP with the same address named LCoA. When the MN moves from one MAP domain to another, the MN gets a new CoA from the AR. It updates this CoA to the previous MAP instead of HA so that BU is done locally. In this way, location update process remain transparent to the HA. For frequent inter-MAP domain movement, multiple location update to previous MAP increase the service delay. To get out of this problem, location update to previous AR is permitted up to two times. in the third time, movement of the MN updates CoA to HA again with RCoA. A tunnel is to be established previous MAP and current

MAP to reduce packet loss. Hence the signaling burden is evenly distributed among the network and signaling overhead is reduced drastically. The timing diagram (Figure 16) shows the two scenarios of single inter MAP domain movement and 3m times inter MAP domain movement where m is any positive integer.

PERFORMANCE ANALYSIS

We consider some parameters to derive handoff latency in each protocol as listed in Table 4 and the cost function of handoff latency is listed in Table 5. Based on the analysis of the existing protocols, we propose an improved scheme by simulation with OPNET. Certain assumptions are taken in carrying out the simulation. Among these, two important assumptions are: (1) Three level hierarchy of MAP. And (2) Multiple inter MAP domain movement of MN.

Let T2 is the time required for passing registration message from FA to HA in case of HMIPv4. Let T8 is the time required for registration of MAP to HA in HMIPv6. Let both the values are equivalent and vary from 10 to 100 ms depending on the distance from foreign network to home network. We assume the number of levels n = 3 and the total registration time without signaling is given by,

$$\Delta1 = T3 + T4 + T5$$

In MIFA (Diab, 2004, 2005) protocol, uplink time (T_{uplink}) and downlink time ($T_{downlink}$) are considered different and given by,

$$T_{uplink} = T1 + T3 + T4 \text{ and}$$

$$T_{downlink} = T1 + T3 + T4 + T7$$

so that, Total time,

Table 4. Description of different parameters

Parameter	Description
T1	Time required for Passing registration message from MN to FA.
T2	Time required for Passing registration message from FA to HA.
T3	Time required for MN to process registration.
T4	Time required for FA to process registration.
T5	Time required for HA to process registration.
T6	Time required for Passing message between two adjacent nodes.
T7	Time required for processing previous FA registration.
T8	Time required for registration message from MAP to HA.
T2a	Time required for paging agent's address registered as MN's CoA to the MN's HA.
T9	Time required for router advertisement for paging area information.
Ts	Time required for registration of secondary RCoA.
TPBU	Time required for BU to previous MAP.
TL	Time required for level edge router path request and acknowledgement.
TBU	Time required for binding update and acknowledgement from MN to CN.
TQoS	Time required for QoS setup request and reply.
TBU1-MN	Time to send binding update with buffering flag set to MAP.
TBU2-MN	Time to send binding update with buffering flag reset to MAP.

T=2(T1+ T3+ T4) + T7

In (Vassiliou), time required for level edge router path request and acknowledgement (TL), time required for binding update and acknowledgement from MN to CN (TBU) and time required for QoS setup request and reply (TQoS) are the excess time components apart from the usual operation. Simulation is done considering route optimization. Figure 14 shows the comparative analysis of handoff delay of different architectures and our proposed architecture. The delay shows minimum for our proposed architecture. Figure 15 shows the variation of handoff latency with respect to the change of distance from foreign network to home network. The graph shows that our proposed architecture achieves better handoff performance compared to DHMIP and MBBU. Figure 16 shows the timing diagram of THMIP protocol.

Table 5. Handoff latency of different architecture

Protocol	Handoff Latency
HMIP[Soliman]	2T1+ Δ1+T6 +2T8+ TBU
PHMIP[Lee]	2T1+ Δ1+ T6 + T2a + T9+2T8
RHMIP[You]	2T1 + Δ1+ 2Ts + T6 + 2T8
MBBU[Yi]	2T1 + Δ1+ T6 + 2T8+ TBU
HMIP-B [OMAE]	2(T1+T2)+Δ1+T6+TBU1-MN +TBU2-MN
DHMIP[Ma]	2(T1 + T2)+ Δ1+ 4T7
MHMIP[Pack]	2T1+ T3+ nT4+ T5+ nT6+2T8
FFHMIP[Gwon]	2T1 + Δ1+ T6 + 2TPBU+2T8
MIFA[Diab]	2(T1+ T3+ T4) + T7
HMIP-MPLS[Vassiliou]	2T1+ Δ1+ T6 +3 TL+ TBU+ TQoS+2T8
THMIP[Sajal]	2T1 + Δ1 + T6 + 2(T7 + T8)

Figure 14. Comparative analysis of handoff delay

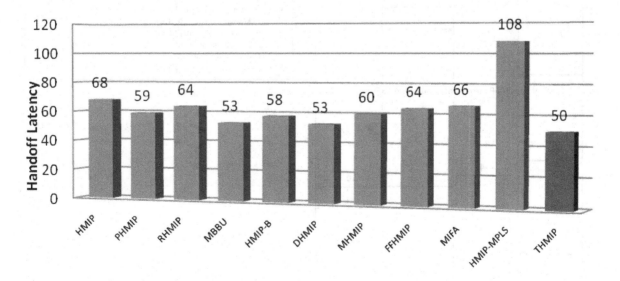

Figure 15. Variation of handoff latency with respect to changed distance between HA and FA

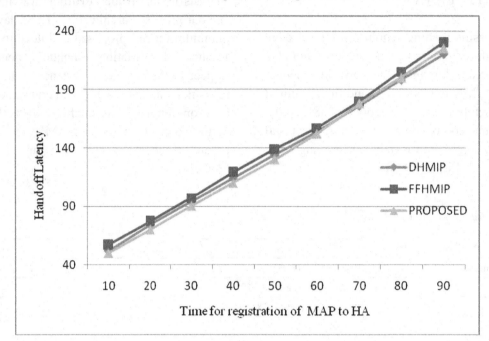

Figure 16. Timing diagram of proposed architecture

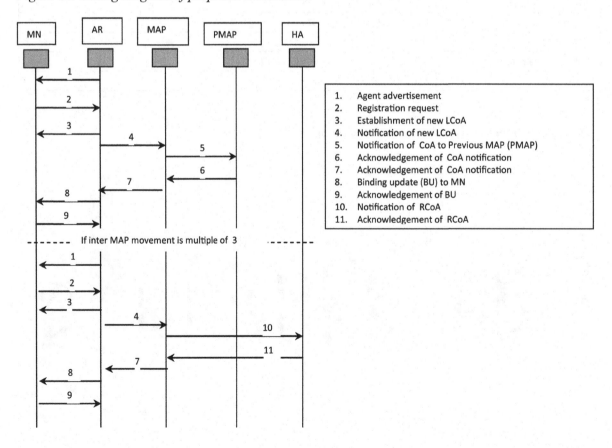

1. Agent advertisement
2. Registration request
3. Establishment of new LCoA
4. Notification of new LCoA
5. Notification of CoA to Previous MAP (PMAP)
6. Acknowledgement of CoA notification
7. Acknowledgement of CoA notification
8. Binding update (BU) to MN
9. Acknowledgement of BU
10. Notification of RCoA
11. Acknowledgement of RCoA

Table 6. Some initial parameters taken in simulation

Max MN velocity	50m/sec
User density	200MN/cell
Maximum buffer size Binding update lifetime	50 bytes 1800sec
MN registration retry maximum	40 msec
Registration request interval	4 msec
Minimum retransmission timeout	10 msec
Maximum retransmission timeout	120 msec
CN data rate	1 Mbps
RC	10
CLC for crossing cells)	2
CUL unit location update cost	1
MN,CN transmitter power	0.5 Watt
MN,CN packet reception power threshold	0.95 dBm
Base station transmitting power	20 watt

Some initial parameters have been considered which is shown in Table 6. THMIP support macro mobility, micro mobility and global mobility. Cellular macro systems have an average perimeter cell size of 4000 meters, maximum mobile node velocity of 100 mph (i.e., 50 meters/second), user density 200 users/cell. Cellular micro systems have an average cell perimeter of 400 meters, maximum velocity is 20 mph (i.e., 8.9 meters/second), and user density is 20 users/cell. Pico-cellular systems have an average cell perimeter size of 40 meters, maximum velocity is 5 mph (i.e., 2.2 meters/second), and a user density of 2 users/cell. We assume that the active mobile node percentage and data session rate are same for all cell sizes. Figure 17 shows the performance comparison of the total cost incurred by THMIP, MIFA, and PMIP. Figures 18, 19, and 20 shows the location update cost, packet delivery cost and total cost incurred by THMIP, MIFA and PMIP respectively by changing the no of cell boundary traversed by the MN

CONCLUSION

Significant mobility management schemes have been analyzed in this chapter. Each scheme has its own merits and demerits. Analysis through OPNET simulation shows that MAP introduces

Figure 17. Comparison of total cost (no. of location traversed is10)

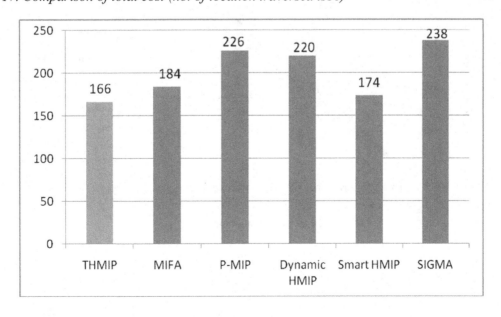

Figure 18. Comparison of packet delivery cost

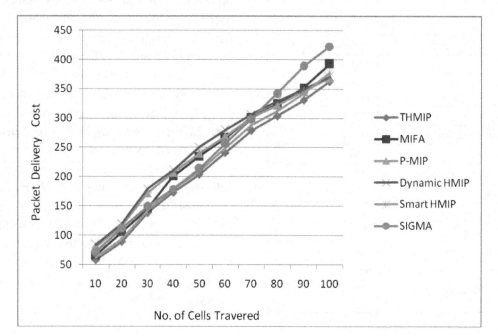

Figure 19. Comparison of location update cost

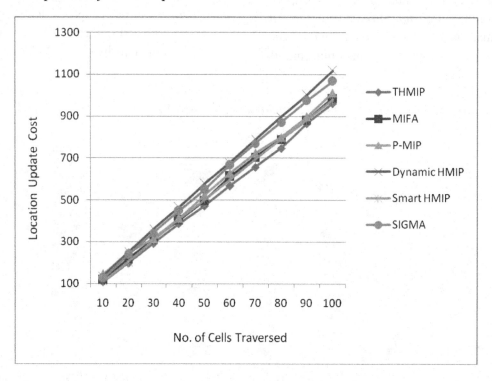

Figure 20. Comparison of total cost

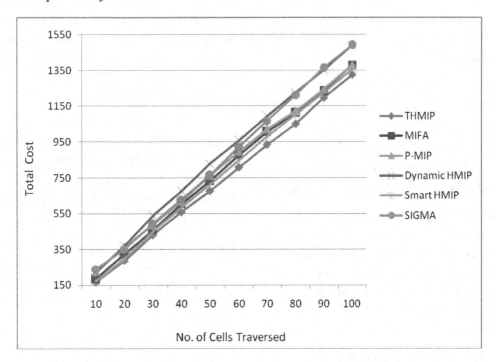

buffer to reduce packet loss during handoff but simultaneously increases handoff latency. Another important observation is that in MBBU, BU lifetime value increases but in frequent movement it will act as HMIPv6 depending upon the stability of the MN. HMIP-MPLS supports multimedia services in HMIPv6 environment but incurs very high signaling overhead. We evaluate handoff latency performance of the existing protocols. THMIP scheme seems to support frequent movement to the user and perform the binding update to the HA with minimum cost as well as with minimum handoff latency. Based on the analysis, we proposed an efficient mobility scheme. We simulate THMIP using both fluid flow model and random walk model. The simulation results show that the proposed scheme THMIP has the minimum handoff latency for multiple inter-domain movement of MN with three levels of hierarchy and fluid flow model.

ACKNOWLEDGMENT

Authors are thankful to AICTE for the financial support of this research work under AICTE, RPS scheme (file no: 8023/BOR/RID/RPS-72/2009-10), India.

REFERENCES

Aust, S., Fikouras, N. A., Sessinghaus, M., & Pampu, C. (2004). *Hierarchical mobile IP NS-2 extensions for mobile ad hoc networks.* 4th IASTED International Multi-Conference on Wireless Networks and Emerging Technologies (WNET 2004).

Baek, J., & Lee, E. (2006). A dynamic authentication, authorization, and accounting (AAA) resolution for hierarchical mobile IPv6 network. *IJCSNS International Journal of Computer Science and Network Security, 6*(7B)

Baek, S.-J., & Park, J.-T. (2004). *Efficient micro-mobility support for wireless network using improved host-based routing.* Berlin, Germany: Springer-Verlag.

Campbell, A. T., & Castellanos, J. G. (2000). *IP micro-mobility protocols.* ACM.

Campbell, A. T., Castellanos, J. G., Kim, S., & Wan, C.-Y. (2002). Comparison of IP micro-mobility protocols. *IEEE Wireless Communications, 9*(1), 72–82. doi:10.1109/MWC.2002.986462

Chakrabarty, M., Misra, I., Saha, D., & Mukherjee, A. (2003). A comparative study of existing protocols supporting IP mobility. *Proceedings of the 4th World Wireless Congress (WWC 2003),* San Francisco, USA, May 27-30, 2003. Retrieved from http://www.cse.unsw.edu.au/~nr/pub/papers/wwc03.pdf

Das, S., McAuley, A., Dutta, A., Misra, A., Chakraborty, K., & Das Sajal, K. (2002). IDMP: An intra-domain mobility management protocol for next generation wireless networks. *Wireless Communications, 9*(3). doi:10.1109/MWC.2002.1016709

David, K., Eardley, P., Hetzer, D., Mihailovic, A., Suihko, T., & Wagner, M. (1999). *First evaluation of IP based network architectures.* Second International Workshop on Broadband Radio Access for IP Based Network.

Diab, A., & Mitschele-Thiel, A. (2004). *Minimizing mobile IP handoff latency* (p. 48). HET-NET.

Diab, A., Mitschele-Thiel, A., & Böringer, R. (2005). Comparison of signaling and packet forwarding overhead for HMIP and MIFA. *WWIC 2005. LNCS, 3510,* 12–21.

Diab, A., Thiel, A. M., & Böringer, R. (2005). Evaluation of mobile IP fast authentication protocol compared to hierarchical mobile IP. *IEEE International Conference on Wireless and Mobile Computing, Networking and Communications,* (pp. 9-16).

Eardley, P., Georganopoulos, N., & West, M. A. (2002). On the scalability of micro-mobility management protocols. *4th International Workshop on Mobile and Wireless Communications Network,* (pp. 470 – 474). DOI: 10.1109/MWCN.2002.1045809

Eardley, P., Mihailovic, A., & Suihko, T. (2002). A framework for the evaluation of IP mobility protocols. *The 11th IEEE International Symposium on Personal, Indoor and Mobile Radio Communications, PIMRC 2000* (pp. 451 - 457). DOI:10.1109/PIMRC.2000.881465

Ghassemian, M., & Aghvami, A. H. (2002). *Comparing different handoff schemes in IP based micro-mobility protocols.* IST Mobile & Wireless Telecommunications Summit 2002. Thessaloniki. Greece.

Gunasundari, R., & Shanmugavel, S. (2007). Influence of topology on micro mobility protocols for wireless networks. *ANSI Information Technology Journal, 6*(7), 966-977. ISSN 1812-5638

Gwon, Y., Kempf, J., & Yegin, A. (2004). *Scalability and robustness analysis of mobile IPv6, fast mobile IPv6, hierarchical mobile IPv6, and hybrid IPv6 mobility protocols using a large-scale simulation* (pp. 4087–4091).

Hancock, R., Aghvami, H., Kojo, M., & Liljeberg, M. (2000). *The architecture of the BRAIN network layer.*

Kirci, P., & Zaim, A. H. (2006). *Mobility management strategies of mobile IP networks.*

Koji, O., Inoue, M., Okajima, I., & Umeda, N. (2003). Handoff performance of mobile host and mobile router employing HMIP extension. *IEEE WCNC 2003,* (Vol. 2, pp. 1218-1223).

Lee, J.-S., Min, J.-H., Park, K.-S., & Kim, S.-H. (2003). Paging extension for hierarchical mobile IPv6: P-HMIPv6. *IEEE ICON, 2003,* 245–248.

Ma, W., & Fang, Y. (2004). Dynamic hierarchical mobility management strategy for mobile IP networks. *IEEE Journal on Selected Areas in Communications, 22*(4), 664–666. doi:10.1109/JSAC.2004.825968

Ma'en, A., Mahamod, I., & Kasmiron, J. (2007). A study on effective transfer rate over smart hierarchical mobile IPv6. *IJCSNS International Journal of Computer Science and Network Security, 7*(5).

Misra, A., Das, S., Das, S. K., Mcauley, A., & Dutta, A. (2000). *Integrating QoS support in TeleMIP's mobility architecture*. Hyderabad, India: ICPWC.

Misra, A., Das, S., Dutta, A., Mcauley, A., & Das, S. K. (2002). IDMP-based fast handoffs and paging in IP-based cellular networks. *IEEE Communications Magazine, 40*(3), 138–145. doi:10.1109/35.989774

O'Neill, A. W., & Tsirtsis, G. (2000). *Edge mobility architecture - Routing and hand-off.* ACM SIGMOBILE.

Pack, S., Nam, M., & Choi, Y. (2004). A study on optimal hierarchy in multi-level hierarchical mobile IPv6 networks. *IEEE GLOBECOM 2004,* (Vol. 2, pp. 1290-1294).

Perkins, C. E. (1998). *Mobile IP*. Addison-Wesley.

Reinbold, P., & Bonaventure, O. (2001). *A comparison of IP mobility protocols*. Retrieved from http://www.infonet.fundp.ac.be

Saha, D., Mukherjee, A., Misra, I. S., & Chakraborty, M. (2004). Mobility support in IP: A survey of related protocols. *IEEE Network Magazine, 18*(6), 34–40. doi:10.1109/MNET.2004.1355033

Sajal, S., et el. (2011). *THMIP- A novel mobility management scheme using fluid flow model*. 2nd International Conference on Emerging Trends and Applications in Computer Science, (NCETACS - 2011), Shillong, India, 4th- 6th March, 2011.

Sajal, S., et el. (2009). Analysis of hierarchical mobile IP based mobility management schemes. *International Conference on Networks & Communications (NetCoM 2009)*, Chennai, 27th -29th December 2009, (pp. 338-343). Retrieved from http://ieeexplore.ieee.org/search/srchabstract.jsp?tp=&arnumber=5383965

Soliman, H., Castelluccia, C., El Malki, K., & Bellier, L. (2005). Hierarchical mobile IPv6 mobility management (HMIPv6). *RFC 4140.*

Vassiliou, V., & Andreas, P. (2007). Supporting mobility events within a hierarchical mobile IP-over-MPLS network. *The Journal of Communication, 2*(2), 61–70.

Wisely, W., & Mohr, J. U. (2000). Broadband radio access for IP networks (BRAIN). *The 11th IEEE International Symposium on Personal, Indoor and Mobile Radio Communications, PIMRC 2000* (Vol. 1, pp. 431-436). DOI: 10.1109/PIMRC.2000.881462

Yi, M.-K., & Hwang, C.-S. (2003). A mobility-based binding update strategy in hierarchical mobile Ipv6. Retrieved from dpnm.postech.ac.kr/papers/DSOM/03/118-yunmnmayuy.pdf

You, T., Sangheon, P., & Yanghee, C. (2003). Robust hierarchical mobile IPv6 (RH-MIPv6). *IEEE VTC 2003,* (Vol. 3, pp. 2014-2018).

KEY TERMS AND DEFINITIONS

AAA: In mobile communication network security, AAA commonly stands for Authentication, Authorization and Accounting. Authentication refers to the process where an MN's identity is authenticated. The authorization function determines whether a MN is authorized to perform a given activity. Accounting refers to the tracking of network resource consumption by users for the purpose of capacity and trend analysis, cost allocation, billing.

Access Network: An access network is that part of a communications network which connects subscribers to their immediate service provider. It is contrasted with the core network, for example the Network Switching Subsystem in GSM.

Access Router (AR): In HMIPv6 protocol AR is an access device with built-in basic routing protocol support used to track, register and assign CoA to the visitor MN. In HMIv4 it is termed as FA.

Gateway Foreign Agent (GFA): A Foreign Agent (FA) that acts as the single point of contact with HA is called GFA in HMIv4. GFA supports local registration when the MN changes its point of Attachment to some other FA of the same administrative Domain of the GFA.

Host-Based Routing (HBR): Host-based routing is useful for those configurations where we need to route from one domain to another domain and want to use an existing system to do the routing rather than using a dedicated router. HBR is not intended for use in network configurations that have high-throughput requirements. HAWAII uses this architecture.

Mobility Anchor Point (MAP): A new node in HMIPv6 called the Mobility Anchor Point (MAP) serves as a local entity to aid in MN handoffs. The MAP, which replaces MIPv4's GFA (Gateway foreign agent), can be located anywhere within a hierarchy of routers.

On-Link CoA (LCoA): The LCoA is the on-link CoA configured on an MN's interface based on the prefix advertised by its default router. In some of the architechture this is simply referred to as the CoA.

Radio Access Network (RAN): A radio access network (RAN) is part of a mobile communication system. Conceptually, it resides between the MN, and the core network (CN). There are two types of RAN: a) GSM radio access network (GRAN) and b) UMTS radio access network (UTRAN).

Regional Care-of Address (RCoA): An RCoA is an address obtained by the MN from the visited network. In HMIPv6 this RCoA remains transparent to the HA and only known to MAP.

Chapter 11
Energy Efficient Data Query, Processing and Routing Techniques for Green Wireless Sensor Networks

Afshin Behzadan
Ryerson University, Canada

Alagan Anpalagan
Ryerson University, Canada

ABSTRACT

While wireless sensor networking plays a critical role in many important applications, it also contributes to the energy footprint - which continues to increase with the proliferation of wireless devices and networks worldwide. Energy-efficiency becomes a major concern in the development of next generation sensor systems and networks. This chapter discusses data management techniques from energy efficiency point of view for green wireless sensor networks.

INTRODUCTION

Wireless sensor networks (WSNs) usually contain power-constraint nodes that require energy-efficient (a.k.a. green) transmission techniques, resource sharing algorithms and networking protocols. Each WNS node consists of one or more sensors for sensing the surrounding environ-

ment. Sensors are small and usually inexpensive, and have limited processing resources. Sensors sense and gather information from the environment, based on the decision guidelines provided by users in forms of queries. Acquired data are transmitted, via embedded radio in nodes, among nodes in a multi-hop way and finally reach the root, i.e., the base station (Estrin, Girod, Pottie, & Srivastava, May 2001).

DOI: 10.4018/978-1-4666-1888-6.ch011

Usually, a WSN has no infrastructure and has an ad-hoc topology. This topology is due to the fact that sensor networks are typically deployed in hard-to-access environment. Obstructions in the environment can limit the wireless communication between nodes, affecting the network connectivity. These networks have many applications, such as military target tracking and surveillance, natural disaster relief, biomedical health monitoring and hazardous environment exploration and sensing.

Data Query, Processing, and Routing

Data sensing and transmitting consume a considerable portion of nodes' energy which is limited and vital (Potdar, Sharif, & Chang, May 2009). The main goal of *query processing* is to answer queries posed by users, while decreasing the energy consumption and prolonging network lifetime are also considered (Gehrke & Madden, March 2004). Queries are declared by users to the network and the network returns the required data by using the query processing engine (Madden, Franklin, Hellerstein, & Hong, Tinydb, An acquisitional query processing system for sensor

Figure 1. A wireless sensor network scheme

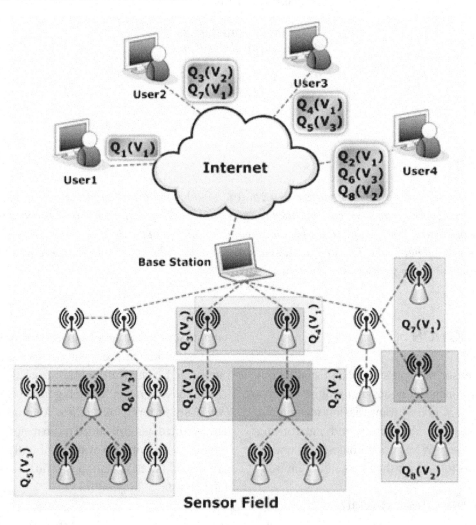

networks, March 2005). A single query processing scheme assumes one active query in the network. However, in reality, different users may connect to the base station and query various data. In many cases, although different users may have different requests, their requests are somewhat similar. Thus, assigning a network to a single query and running queries sequentially not only lead to undesirable delays in responding to user requests, but also results in a vast energy wasting by doing redundant operations corresponding to different queries. Therefore, *multi-query processing* has been considered in which multiple queries run in the network simultaneously (Trigoni, Yao, Demers, Gehrke, & Rajaraman, June 2005).

Severe energy constraints and consequently communication and processing limitations of sensor nodes make centralized methods not suitable for these networks, as their execution involves noticeable processing overhead and needs a global view of the network. Generating this global view especially when the network is large will lead to a quick energy drain of nodes. Therefore, distributed and lightweight methods which are executable by low-powered sensor nodes and that need only local information to run properly, are required (Akyildiz, Su, Sankarasubramaniam, & Cayirci, March 2002).

Multi-hop data routing, driven by the above mentioned limitations, is typically used in a tree topology for data delivery, where intermediate nodes (as parents) receive data from their beneath nodes (i.e., child nodes), apply aggregation functions on them and their local data, and send the aggregated data to the next hop towards the base station (Yao & Gehrke, January 2003). This topology is formed by issuing a "flood" from the base station towards the network, through which nodes are assigned to different levels. Due to flooding and the location of nodes, each node might receive multiple flooding messages from some other nodes which can be its candidate parents. Thus, each node can have some candidate parents. However, at the end of flooding process, each node selects a parent in one level lower than its level, to which it will send the acquired data. Higher amount of traffic leads to faster energy depletion and the nodes suffering this problem have a shorter lifetime compared to nodes dealing with a less amount of traffic. Thus, uneven distribution of children among parents implies uneven drain of energy and lifetimes for nodes. As the nature of sensor networks is ad-hoc and randomly distributed, the connectivity of the network highly depends on the lifetime of nodes.

STATE-OF-THE-ART: FROM ENERGY EFFICIENCY POINT OF VIEW

Load balancing can be used to reduce the overall energy consumption of the wireless sensor networks. Generally, the load balancing problem in wireless sensor network can be considered from the routing and query processing point of view, since one of the main purposes of load balancing in such networks is the data delivery in an energy efficient way. The main areas for this purpose are routing and query processing. Routing aims to route the data in the network with the least cost, mostly based on the energy and least number of hops. On the other side, query processing tries to decrease the amount of data which travels through the network. Both of the mentioned areas try to decrease the energy consumption of individual nodes, and have many related concepts associated with each other.

Load balancing also tries to decrease the energy consumption not only for individual nodes, but also for the whole network. Approaches which rely on load balancing adjust the load. The load is usually defined from the energy point of view and as the energy consumption due to data communication among nodes. However, the inseparable part of load balancing is routing, since it benefits from the routing concepts and techniques, but in a balanced way. Therefore, three areas should be reviewed and investigated for proposing a solution for the load balancing problem.

When the concept of "utility" is considered for nodes in sensor networks, utility based approaches will be a relevant area. Also, sensor nodes can be considered as independent agents as they have local information. A utility based approach which models nodes as independent agents having their own local knowledge, implies using a game theoretical approach with nodes as players. Game theory approaches have recently received attention in different areas of sensor networks such as routing, load balancing and security, as the nature of these networks encourages this tendency. As our work considers a utility-based approach based on game theory concepts, a section of this chapter is dedicated to reviewing the use of game theory in sensor networks.

Query Processing in Sensor Networks

Many works have been proposed in the area of query processing and energy conservation techniques in wireless sensor networks. The authors in (Rosemark, Lee, & Urgaonkar, May 2007) present some fundamentals for processing of queries and discuss some optimization techniques for data gathering. TAG (Madden, Franklin, Hellerstein, & Hong, December 2002) introduces in-network aggregation to conserve energy.

The following works propose various techniques to increase energy efficiency. The authors in (Gehrke & Madden, March 2004) moot some fundamentals for query processing systems and mention some optimization techniques for query plan generation. The proposed work in (Munteanu, Beaver, Labrinidis, & Chrysanthis, February 2005) partitions the network among multiple routing trees to run a single query, to increase performance and fault tolerance. In (Muller & Alonso, October 2006), the authors propose some multi-query processing fundamentals and use a framework to support it. In their work, base station (BS) batches and aggregates queries together and injects a new query resulted from them to the network. In the run time if any new query arrives, it will be aggregated by the previous queries, but the new resulted query will be sent as the second query to the network. This is a transient state in which two combined queries run in the network. The transient state continues until the first query finishes, and then only the second query continues to run. However, the proposed solution aggregates all the received queries together and, in cases that queries are not compatible with each other their aggregation will not be beneficial.

In (Trigoni, Yao, Demers, Gehrke, & Rajaraman, June 2005) the idea of dividing the network into multiple zones and processing of results inside each zone is investigated. Results from each zone are collected and aggregated by nodes inside the zone, and finally only one aggregated data will be sent out. This way, the amount of outgoing traffic from each zone decreases, which leads to a considerable energy conservation. The authors in (Trigoni, Guitton, & Skordylis, 2006) propose some routing techniques for optimum result transition to BS in multi-query environments. The authors in (Lee, Lee, Zheng, & Winter, April 2006) use some pre-computed partial results, called materialized in-network views, to decrease energy consumption and share network among multiple queries. In their work, some partial aggregation results are computed before running of queries and they are kept in nodes. When the queries run, if a node has the desired value, it returns its partial aggregation value and does not send the query further to its beneath nodes. This way a, decrease in communication and computation overhead can be gained. However, computation of materialized views at first can impose a considerable energy overhead, and also in time dependent applications, after a while views are spoiled and cannot be used anymore. The proposed work in (Zhang, Yu, & Chen, September 2005) supports concurrent run of queries; however in that work each node has to aggregate received queries and run aggregated query which can impose considerable computation overhead on it and energy consumption.

Load Balancing in Sensor Networks

Several authors studied balanced data gathering in sensor networks. Harvey et al. (Harvey, Ladner, Lovasz, & Tamir, July 2003) propose an optimum centralized method for making an optimal semi-matching which minimizes the variance of the load among nodes. Considering a bipartite graph, a semi-matching is a balanced assignment of vertices in one part to vertices in another part. The graph can be represented as a set of tasks in one part and a set of machines in another part, each is able to process a subset of tasks. Then, an edge exists between a node from tasks part and another node in machines part, if and only if that machine is able to perform the task. Loads on machines are determined by the number of tasks they run. Thus, the goal is to assign tasks to machines in a fair way, so at the end, machines run as equal number of tasks as possible. Their method produces optimum load balanced assignments in all cases. To avoid unbalanced assignments, formation of a kind of path, called *alternating path* in the graph is prevented, as it is a sign of unbalancing.

Due to the limitations of sensor nodes and their autonomous mode, most of the proposed works in the literature tend to be distributed. Sadagopan et al. in (Sadagopan, Singh, & Krishnamachari, 2006) propose a decentralized utility based method for making the balanced data gathering tree. They use a game theoretic approach, where nodes are the selfish players of a tree construction game. Their method is suitable where in-network aggregation can be applied as they consider nodes with similar amount of data. In-network aggregation gives the opportunity to interpret the whole game as a number of games per level of tree. Thus in each level, the game is the balanced joining of children to possible parents in one level higher. However, this technique may cause a number of switchings by children among parents when different parents increase their bids resulting in considerable communication overhead.

In (Sadagopan, Singh, & Krishnamachari, 2006) the authors also discussed the construction of a spanning tree where no in-network aggregation is applied. They assume each sensor node samples and transmits one unit of data per epoch. With this situation, each leaf node transmits one unit of data, while every intermediate node transmits its local data plus data from nodes in the sub-tree for which it is the root. Assuming each data unit transmission consumes one unit of energy, each leaf node dissipates one unit of data and each intermediate node dissipates energy proportional to size of its sub-tree. The goal is to construct a spanning tree such that all the sensor nodes are fairly utilized on the average. If s^i shows the size of sub-tree rooted at node i, and e^i shows its current energy, then the fractional remaining energy of node i is defined as $\dfrac{e^i - s^i}{e^i}$. To ensure fair utilization of energy resources the goal is the construction of a spanning tree which maximizes the summation of the fractional remaining energy of all nodes. If the network is modeled by graph $G=(V,E)$, the strategy space of s_k^i of each node i in iteration k is

$$s_k^i = \left\{ j \mid (i,j) \in E \right\} \tag{1}$$

Then, the utility function of each node is defined as follows:

$$u_k^i = \min_{j \in s_k^i} \left\{ \frac{1}{e^i} + Q_k^j \right\} = \min_{j=s_k^i} Q_k^j, \tag{2}$$

where Q_k^j is the length of the shortest path from sensor node j to the BS at iteration k. $\forall k : Q_{BS} = 0$. Thus, at each iteration, a sensor node i chooses a node j that offers it the shortest path to BS, by using $\dfrac{1}{e^z}$ as the metric of edge length for any edge $(z,w) \in E$, where $z, w \in V$. This mechanism can be implemented by a distributed distance vector algorithm. Thus, the energy balanced tree construction terminates when the distance vector algorithm terminates.

As mentioned earlier, different characteristics can be considered for classification of the literature in the context of load balancing and energy conservation. First, the proposed works are either centralized and decentralized (or distributed). The latter is preferred for sensor environment since it is scalable and provides light weight solutions. Next, existing works can be investigated from the heterogeneity aspect. Heterogeneity includes some criteria such as different power, communication range, the amount of traffic from each node, transmission range and etc. Considering the current literature, most of works can be divided into two major groups. The first group considers homogenous nodes, and the second one considers two different types of nodes. One type includes more powerful nodes having more capabilities which are deployed in a fewer number. The other group includes a higher number of nodes with lower power and fewer capabilities. While consideration of homogenous nodes suggests flat network structure, heterogeneity in the mentioned form suggests a hierarchy for the network structure formed by clustering in which and powerful nodes act as cluster heads and the rest constitutes nodes inside clusters. In the following, based on this brief discussion, some related works are briefly discussed.

Chu et al. (Chu, et al., October 2009) proposed a centralized approach for dynamic monitoring of nodes' energy to determine if changing the parent of a node is necessary. The process includes two procedures in the gateway. In the first procedure, priority of each node is determined. It starts from the node with heaviest nodes and repeats for every node. The number of parents is used for breaking ties, meaning that the node with the least parents is the winner. The energy of selected node's parent is compared to the energy of other nodes from lower layer in its communication range. The link among node and its parent is remains intact unless the energy of parent is less than the other nodes from the lower layer in its communication range. In that case, the second procedure starts and a new parent with the least load is selected. The least number of neighbours is used for breaking ties in this procedure.

Application of Game Theory in Sensor Networks

Game theory is a discipline aiming to model situations in which decision makers have to make specific actions that have mutual, possibly conflicting, consequences (Fudenberg & Tirole, 1991). It has been used primarily in economics, in order to model the competition between companies. In the area of wireless networks, game theory is often used as a tool for making cooperation between nodes, terminals or various authorities. Game theory is applied to help solving problems in routing, resource allocation and power management (Niyato & Hossain, 2007).

Game theory is related to the actions of decision makers who know that their actions affect each other. A game includes a set of players $i=\{1, 2,..., N\}$, each of which selects a strategy $s \in S_i$, where S_i is a strategy space including all possible strategies for i. Player i has the objective of maximizing its utility u_i. A game can be modeled by a set of players, a set of available resources in the game, all possible choices for each player made possible from the set of resources, and the payoffs assigned to each player after choosing a specific resource.

Two types of games can be considered: in *noncooperative* games, each player selects strategies without coordination with others. On the other hand, in a *cooperative* game, the players have the choice and try to cooperate with each other, so that they can gain a maximum benefit which is higher than what they could have obtained by playing the game without cooperation (Uliman,

Pomalaza, Oppernann, & Lehtomaki, August 2004). The objective is to allocate the resources so that the total utility is maximized. In wireless networks, the formation of coalitions involves the sharing of certain resources. However, when the costs of such resource sharing are more than the benefits gained by the nodes, they are less likely to participate.

Nash equilibrium: The equilibrium strategies are chosen by the players in order to maximize their individual payoffs. In game theory, the Nash equilibrium is a solution concept of a game involving two or more players, in which no player has anything to gain by changing only his own strategy unilaterally (Charilas & Panagopoulos, 2010). If each player has chosen a strategy and no player can benefit by changing his strategy while the other players keep their selected strategy unchanged, then the current set of strategy choices and the corresponding payoffs constitute a Nash equilibrium.

Repeated games: In strategic games, the players make their decisions simultaneously at the beginning of the game. On the contrary, the model of an extensive game defines the possible orders of the events. In repeated games, players can make decisions during the game and react to other players' decisions. In this case, a game is played many times and the players can check the outcome of the previous game before playing in the next repetition.

A game theoretic approach is suitable for this purpose, since it considers independent players with local knowledge. This feature supports the nature of sensor environments, in that nodes have only local information due to their limitations. In proposing such an approach, nodes are considered as players of the game trying to reach a higher benefit according to their individual utility functions. On the top level, a global utility function also should be defined in a way that when each player tries to gain more individual utility, it implicitly helps in maximizing the global benefit defined by the global utility function. As each game should

have a termination at the end, Nash equilibrium can be used to show that the game will stop at some point. However, Nash equilibrium proves the termination of the game, and not necessarily the optimum outcome resulted by playing the game.

When a rational interaction is considered between nodes, the forwarding nodes can be encouraged to cooperate in data routing. Then, based on a price-based scheme nodes try to benefit other nodes to receive more benefits from them in a corporation scheme. In this section, the discussion of game theory in wireless sensor networks is provided by surveying recent work on routing among nodes, which relies on price-based or utility-based approaches and use concepts of the game theory.

Non-Cooperative Games: The authors in (Han & Liu, 2007) use game theory to analyze the outcome of a game, in which the deployed sensors belong to different authorities and can receive incentives for cooperative forwarding for routing, data storage and aggregation. When sensors request a service from another sensor belonging to a different authority, the other sensor may choose to cooperate or decline based on its resources. In this game, where none of nodes from different domains decline to cooperate with nodes from another domain, the Nash equilibrium results in non-cooperation of nodes belonging to different sponsors. To avoid this situation, the authors propose the use of tokens as incentives to encourage cooperation between sensors which belong to different sponsors.

In (Suris, DaSilva, Han, & MacKenzie, 2007), the authors consider the problem of packet forwarding in wireless sensor networks using game theory. In classical game theory, players choose a particular strategy in response to strategies of other players and this strategy does not change over time. However, in (Suris, DaSilva, Han, & MacKenzie, 2007) the frequency with which a player chooses a given strategy varies over the time in response to the strategies chosen by other players. This allows players to choose from a set of actions and strategies and use of only local information. The authors assume a heterogeneous sensor network from different classes, where any two non-neighbouring classes communicate via multi-hop routing. Nodes can be selfish. They consider inter-class relaying, when a class can cooperate and forward packets or decline to relay. They model the game as that of non-cooperative repeated N-player game between classes of nodes, where nodes participate repeatedly in games with other nodes. In repeated games, a node's action in a given round is influenced by the actions of other nodes and corresponding payoffs in previous rounds. Thus, a repeated game offers ways to punish nodes that do not cooperate by decreasing their payoffs at the end of the game. This can be done by making bad reputation or decrease in incentives resulting in reduced payoffs at the end of the game. Cooperation is similarly rewarded, by examining the payoffs after repeated rounds of the game. Nodes with richer history of cooperation have better reputation, accumulate incentives faster and are included in routes. In transmitting or forwarding a packet, classes spend battery energy b and gain an incentive c. If classes refuse to retransmit, they gain nothing and there is no cost to them. They show that for packet forwarding between stationary classes, Nash equilibrium is achieved if each player plays the Patient Grim strategy (Suris, DaSilva, Han, & MacKenzie, 2007) and the discount factor is approximately close to unity.

The proposed work in (Frattasi, Fathi, & Fitzek, 2006) can be also considered in the set of approaches that use the game theory in sensor networks, as it models the load balancing problem by using techniques from game theory to make a routing tree in sensor network by a decentralized way. The authors design the utility functions of individual nodes such that the network objectives are met when the sensors maximize their individual utility functions. The problem here is to construct a routing tree rooted at the base station. Every node has a level in the network which is the number

of hops from the sink node. A node must find and attach to a parent with fewer children than the current one. The decisions taken by a node at every level are independent of the decisions taken by nodes located at other levels. They describe a distributed algorithm to design the utility functions of individual nodes, such that when these utility functions are optimized by the sensor nodes, the overall objective of the network is met.

Cooperative Games: A reliable query routing scheme is proposed in (Wang, Xue, & Schulz, 2006), where it is suggested that the number of sensors working simultaneously to collaborate on aggregation should be chosen such that global objectives are achieved. The global objectives are defined as increasing network utilization, communication efficiency and energy consumption. For this purpose the authors use a game-theoretic approach. In this approach, sensors are modeled as intelligent agents cooperating to find optimal network architectures that maximize their payoffs. Payoff for a sensor is defined as benefits resulted from its action minus its individual costs. The problem is modeled as a reliable routing, in which a set of sensors are the players of the routing game. When the base station sends a query to the nodes, it is checked for a match with the attributes of the data sensed by the node. They model this idea by a value v_i that represents the closeness of the match. If $v_i = 0$, it implies that the query does not match any attributes. Data is routed to the sink node through an optimally chosen set of sensors. They call this game as the reliable query routing (RQR) game. Each sensor node is modeled as relaying a received data packet to only one neighbour and hence forms only one link between any pair of source and destination nodes. The strategy space of a sensor node is modeled in the form of a binary vector, $\{l_{i1}, l_{i2}, ..., l_{in}\}$, where $l_{ij} = 1 / 0$ represents decision of a sensor node s_i to send or not to send a packet to sensor node s_j. Each node's payoff is a function of the reliability of the path between it and the base station and the expected value of information at that node. This results in a routing tree that is optimal, since if a sensor node decides to choose a different neighbour on another tree, it results in reduced payoffs to/from other nodes. Hence, this also forms the Nash equilibrium for PQR game. Since the network is unreliable, they use a path metric called the *path weakness* to evaluate various suboptimal paths. The path weakness determines how much the node would have gained by switching from its current path to an optimal one. A negative switching suggests that a node s_i is benefiting more from its given strategy, but at the expense of some other sensor. A positive switching indicates that the sensor node could have performed better.

Directions to Node Heterogeneity

In general, the investigation of node heterogeneity in the literature is mostly limited to two aspects such as nodes with different load, or two kinds of deployed nodes in the network with different capabilities like different communication ranges for each type. Considering two different types of sensor nodes in the network is a big help towards network clustering and localization of data processing and communicating in most of nodes. However, uniform distribution of powerful nodes acting as cluster heads among other normal nodes is a challenging problem in practice, especially in situations where human interference in not possible. In such cases some cluster heads may have larger number of nodes in their clusters, while other have less, and the existing load balancing algorithms cannot achieve a good performance. Even, it is possible that a collection of nodes cannot find a nearby cluster head, and have to connect in multi hop way to the closest cluster head. Increasing number of cluster heads relative to number of normal nodes is a solution, but it inevitably ends up with more expensive outcome. Thus, considering load balancing among all nodes

looks important. This is also true in large clusters which may be considered as small networks.

Also, it looks very interesting if an algorithm can adapt itself according to different application needs. While some applications are more sensitive to delay, for some others more quality even with the cost of more delay is preferred. Thus, just consideration of prolonging the lifetime of the network is not enough and a proper solution should consider application needs too. In the next section, a decentralized utility-based approach for the load balanced data routing is presented. The main goal of the algorithm is to prolong the network lifetime by balancing load among nodes.

LOAD BALANCING ALGORITHM: GAME THEORETICAL APPROACH

In this section the algorithm for balanced data routing in wireless sensor networks is explained in details. The approach is based on game theoretic concepts by defining of utility functions for nodes as players of the games. Nodes' actions are based on utility function so that they gain more benefits according to utility function. The most important of advantage of using game theory, is that nodes are viewed as independent entities having their local knowledge, which facilitates the distributed implementations of algorithms.

Network Model and Problem Formulation

System Model: Wireless sensor networks are usually modeled via a graph $G = (V, E)$ with set of nodes (G) and their adjacency (E). As mentioned before, each node has a level equal to its distance to the base station in terms of number of hops. Data routing tree is a tree topology $T = (V_T, E_T)$, $V_T \subseteq E_T$ and $E_T \subseteq E$ built on a graph G. Using this tree, the acquired data from the network are streamed to the base station. The routing tree is formed when each node selects a closer node to the base station as its parent to send its data. Different policies can be considered for parent selection such as random selection, selection based on distance, or selection based on the quality of the link. However, as the network becomes denser, consideration of load on nodes looks more important, since nodes with higher load have a faster energy depletion and failure. Here, load is defined as the required energy for receiving, processing and transmitting of data.

Data Aggregation: One of the advantages of sensor nodes is their processing ability (Madden, Franklin, Hellerstein, & Hong, March 2005). Although this ability is limited, it gives the opportunity of moving some of the data processing operations into the network. As the energy resources are restricted in sensor nodes, the main goal of in-network data processing is to decrease the amount of communication overhead among nodes. In-network aggregation (Madden, Franklin, Hellerstein, & Hong, December 2002) is the most common case of such processing, where each node aggregates its acquired data with the received data from other nodes, and sends the aggregated data to its parent in the routing tree. Aggregation functions can be divided into two main groups: perfect and imperfect (Sadagopan, Singh, & Krishnamachari, 2006). For perfect aggregations, the number of output data items is constant and independent of the number of input data items. Examples of these kinds of aggregations are maximum and average functions. The former causes one data item to be sent out from each node, and the latter leads to two output data items from each node, i.e. the sum and the number of values. Perfect aggregations can be completely performed in the network. On the other hand, the number of output data items for imperfect aggregation is variable and depends on the number of input data items. Median function is an example of such kind of aggregations. For the computation of a median function, all data should be available. This requirement forces nodes to send all raw

data to the base station, where the result can be determined, after these data has been gathered.

While in-network aggregations decrease processing and communication overheads on nodes, load balancing techniques try to distribute them evenly among nodes (Bouabdallah, Bouabdallah, & Boutaba, 2009). Load balancing tends to distribute excessive loads on nodes among other possible nodes in a fair manner to prolong their lifetime (Bouabdallah, Bouabdallah, & Boutaba, 2009) and maintain network connectivity as a global objective. Most of the proposed works in the context of load balancing are accompanied by aggregation techniques. Existing works in the literature which use aggregation along with load balancing, can be divided into two groups. The first group considers perfect aggregation (Sadagopan, Singh, & Krishnamachari, 2006). The main feature of this consideration is the equal load sent out from each node. In the second group, different loads from nodes are assumed (Sadagopan, Singh, & Krishnamachari, 2006). This assumption makes the load balancing problem more complicated when dealing with the second group compared to the first group, but it is more practical. In this case, in addition to perfect aggregations, imperfect aggregations can be included, where the load sent out from each node can be different due to the fact that complete in-network aggregations cannot be performed. A perfect solution for heterogeneous case should also work for homogenous case as load homogeneity is a specific case of load heterogeneity when the output loads of nodes are equal.

Node heterogeneity is not limited to various amounts of produced data. Nodes may also differ in the amount of power supply, total amount of data which they can transmit in a time slot, or the total bandwidth that they can allocate for data transmission to their children. Besides the energy issue, time and bandwidth are two important factors in the quality of data delivery. Thus, the importance of load balancing can mainly be discussed from three aspects: nodes energy consumption, delay and link quality in terms of available bandwidth, all of which are critical for applications in sensor networks, and it would be more realistic if they are considered in the proposed solutions.

Terminology: For a better description of the algorithms, some definitions and system model are provided in this section.

$G = (V,E)$: a graph which models the network and includes a set of nodes V and their adjacency (set E).

$T = (V_T, E_T)$: a tree that models the routing tree, where $V_T \subseteq V$ is the set of its constitutive nodes with their adjacency set (E_T) where $E_T \subseteq E$.

Node Level: Level of node $v \in V$ in graph G is its distance to the root in number of hops.

P_v^p: Set of potential parents for node v in graph G, including nodes from which v accepts flooding message during the construction process of graph G.

P_v^c: Set of potential children for node v in graph G, including nodes that receive flooding message from v during the construction process of graph G.

N_v^u: Set of nodes which are located in the same level as v and are two hops away from it with the intermediate node u between v and them.

N_v: Set $N_v^u \; \forall u \in P_v^c$, i.e. all two hops away nodes from v which are located in the same level as of v.

E_V: Set of children for node v in tree T, called v's existing children.

$P(v)$: v's parent in tree T.

The construction of tree T is implemented on graph G. The construction of graph G itself is explained in the next section. By the end of construction of graph G each node v knows sets P_v^p and P_v^c.

Nodes are considered heterogeneous in terms of their initial energy, data transmission rate, the amount of their produced data, and the total bandwidth which they can provide their children with, to transmit their data. The presented solution to the mentioned problems consider Stackelberg model for the game. With this model nodes playing parent role are leaders of the game and nodes with child role are followers. Parents have cooperative behaviour, while children have selfish behaviour. Leaders make decisions before followers, since they can predict decision of followers. The behaviour of parents influences the behaviour of their children, so that even with selfish actions of children as followers, they still help to the global benefit of the game.

A wireless sensor network can be modeled as a graph $G=(V,E)$ where sets V and E correspond to nodes in the network and the connections between them respectively. An edge $e_{ij} \in E$ exists between nodes $v_i, v_j \in V$, if they are located within each other communication range. Due to similar communication ranges, edge e_{ij} is considered as a bidirectional link which can be used for both transmitting and receiving purposes. Streaming of data from nodes towards the base station is supported by a routing infrastructure made by flooding mechanism starting from the base station. During this flooding, each node may accept several flooding messages from other forwarding nodes in its adjacency. However, based on an adopted parent selection policy, it finally selects only one of the sender nodes as its parent. At the end of the parent selection process a topology is formed which can usually be stated by a spanning tree $T = (V, E_T)$ where $E_T \subseteq E$ denotes parent-child} relationship among nodes. The root of this tree is the base station. There is a variety of policies for parent selection in the literature. However, taking the energy constraint of nodes into account is highly critical for network longevity. From the energy consumption point of view, as sensor networks are deployed in an ad hoc manner, their connectivity is highly dependent on node lifetimes.

As mentioned before, using aggregation functions is highly considered in sensor networks as it decreases the data traffic in the network. Two major groups of aggregation functions are perfect and imperfect aggregations. A high percentage of applications rely on perfect aggregations. However, in some other applications, queries impose the use of imperfect aggregations, where in-network aggregation cannot be applied on the acquired data.

Heterogeneous Load Balancing Formulation: Since for the imperfect aggregation case, different amounts of outgoing traffic from nodes are considered, heterogeneity on load would cover perfect aggregation case which implies homogeneity of load. Thus, in the following explanations load variety of nodes is assumed. Let $E(v)$ show the initial energy of a node v. A portion of this energy is consumed for sensing and processing purposes and the rest will be used for communication. Again, as the energy required to sense and process data is negligible comparing to communication energy consumption, it is omitted in the computations. A simple and well-known model is used to model radio communication between sensor nodes. Let E_{elec} is the energy needed to operate transmitter and receiver circuit, and ε_{amp} is the required energy to amplify transmission for achieving an acceptable signal to noise ratio. Then, energy required for sending k bits to distance d, and the energy required to receive these k bit can be determined through (3) and (4).

$$E_{Tx}(k,d) = E_{elec}k + \varepsilon_{amp}kd^2 \qquad (3)$$

$$E_{Rx}(k) = E_{elec}k \qquad (4)$$

To find out the value of k, consider C_v as the set of v's children with $|C_v|$ members, and each

node $u \epsilon C_v$ sends $L(u)$ bits. Then, $\varepsilon_{R(v)}$ shows the consumed energy for reception of all data units by v from its children, and can be determined by (5).

$$\varepsilon_{R(v)} = E_{elec}\sum_{i=0}^{|C_v|-1}L(u_i). \qquad (5)$$

After receiving data, v performs aggregation function on its local data and the received data. Aggregation functions on k, bits of data can be modeled by

$$Agg(\lambda_1,\lambda_2) = \lambda_1 k + \lambda_2, \qquad (6)$$

where $0 \leq \lambda_1 \leq 1$ is the *compression factor* and $\lambda_2 \geq 0$ is the *overhead factor*. Compression factor shows the average amount of compression obtained by applying the aggregation function, and the overhead factor shows the amount of data imposed by applying aggregation function, regardless of the input data amount. For example maximum or minimum functions can be shown by $Agg(0,1)$, average by $Agg(0,2)$, and median by $Agg(0,1)$.

Now, if v's local sensed data is $S(v)$ bits, and it has $|C_v|$ children, the amount of data after applying aggregation function, $L(v)$, which will be sent by v is

$$L(v) = \lambda_1(S(v) + \sum_{i=0}^{|C_v|-1}L(u_i)) + \lambda_2 \qquad (7)$$

Thus, the energy required to transmit the received data along with its local data is shown by $\varepsilon_{S(v)}$ and defined as:

$$\varepsilon_{S(v)} = E_{Tx}(L(v),r) = E_{elec}L(v) + \varepsilon_{amp}L(v)r^2, \qquad (8)$$

where r is the v's communication range. Considering (5) and (8), the energy that v spends to receive, process and transmit data is determined by (9):

$$\varepsilon\left(v\right) = \varepsilon_{R(v)} + \varepsilon_{S(v)} \qquad (9)$$

Then, the remaining energy of v is

$$\varepsilon'(v) = E\left(v\right) - \varepsilon(v) \qquad (10)$$

Also, v's lifetime can be defined as

$$\Delta(v) = \frac{E(v)}{\varepsilon(v)} \qquad (11)$$

Network lifetime is defined as the time to the first node failure. By this definition, the longer node lifetimes are, the longer network lifetime is.

From the delay point of view, if node v can receive and transmit with rate $R(v)$ data units, the time required to receive data from its children is shown by $T_{R(v)}$ and computed by

$$T_{R(v)} = \frac{1}{R(v)} \sum_{i=0}^{|C_v|-1} L(u_i) \qquad (12)$$

Then, v processes the received data and aggregates them with its local data. Assuming that the processing time is negligible, the time in terms of epochs, required to transmit v's data can be determined by

$$T_{S(v)} = \frac{L(v)}{R(v)} \qquad (13)$$

Thus, the total delay that v incurs to receive, process and transmit all data is defined by:

$$T\left(v\right) = T_{R(v)} + T_{S(v)} \qquad (14)$$

The delay amount should be specifically considered for applications that are real-time and delay is important for them, such as safety or security monitoring systems. A special case can be obtained when each node v has the communication rate of one data unit, $R(v)=1$, and produces one data unit per time slot, $L(v)=1$, and the aggregation function is perfect, with function $Agg(0,1)$. In this case $T_{R(v)} = |C_v|$ and $T_{S(v)} = 1$ leading to the total delay $T\left(v\right) = |C_v| + 1$ imposed by v.

On the other hand, when the reliability is more important and some delays can be tolerated by the application, then a proper utilization of bandwidth should be considered. The most common way suggests the division of available bandwidth among children relative to the amount of their sent data. Thus, the available bandwidth for data transmission gained by node u with parent v, shown by $B_{T(u)}$, is:

$$B_T\left(u\right) = L\left(u\right) \frac{B_R\left(v\right)}{\sum_{i=0}^{|C_v|} L\left(u_i\right)}, \qquad (15)$$

where $B_R\left(v\right)$ is the total bandwidth that v can allocate to its children for data transmission. In the special case, as mentioned before, and when $B_R\left(v\right)$ is considered with unit of one, $B_T\left(u\right)$ equals to $|C_v|^{-1}$.

A combination of delay and bandwidth functions forms the utility function for nodes when they play child role. This combination is able to support different kinds of application needs for delay and reliability where response time and bandwidth have specific importance based on the application. Utility function for child u with parent v is defined through

$$\Gamma\left(v, \varepsilon'(v), |C_v|\right) = U_C(u) =$$

$$\varepsilon'(v)\left[F_t \frac{R(v)}{\lambda_1(L(v) + \sum_{i=0}^{|C_v|} L(u_i)) + \lambda_2} + F_f \frac{B_R(v)}{\sum_{i=0}^{|C_v|} L(u_i)}\right],$$

$$0 \le F_t \le 1, 0 \le F_f \le 1 , \qquad (16)$$

where F_t and F_f are time and frequency coefficients correspondingly and indicate the importance of them. Γ shows the bid generated and sent by the parent v, with remaining energy $\varepsilon'(v)$ and $|C_v|$ children. Each child in a selfish manner tends to join a parent by which it obtains the highest possible utility.

Load factor corresponding to an arbitrary set S consisting of $|S|$ nodes is defined as the standard deviation of loads on nodes $v \in S$, and formulated as follows:

$$\sigma_S = \sqrt{\frac{\sum_{i=0}^{|S|} (\varepsilon(v_i) - \varepsilon(v_i))^2}{|S|}} , \qquad (17)$$

where $|S|$ is the number of $v \in |S|$ and $\varepsilon(v_i)$ is the average of loads on them. For a node v when it plays parent role, the utility function can be defined as

$$U_P(v) = \frac{1}{\sigma_{N_v}} , \qquad (18)$$

where N_v is the set of nodes two hops away in the same level as of v in the graph G including v, or in other words, the set of connected parents to v including v. Minimizing σ_{N_v} leads to maximizing the output of $U_{P(v)}$ which is the individual benefit for node v in parent role.

As nodes may have both child and parent roles based on their location in the network, the utility function for an arbitrary node v is defined by

$$U(v) = U_C(v) + U_P(v) , \qquad (19)$$

At a top level, minimizing load factor with a set equal to the set of all nodes in the network can be considered as the global goal in construction of routing tree. In this case, no extra load is imposed on any node and all of them have as closest as possible lifetime to each other. Although in this case the lifetime for all nodes is not the maximum possible lifetime, no node suffers from extra load imposed by other nodes. Because the maximum life time for a node can be achieved when it behaves selfishly and does not accept children to join itself. However, this behaviour has the cost of joining its possible children to other parents resulting in an extra load on them and shortening their and network lifetimes. For simplicity of explanation V_T is considered equal to V, though it does not limit the generality of the solution. Thus, the game is to create a routing tree for which U_V, defined by (20), is maximum.

$$U_V = \frac{1}{\sigma_V} \qquad (20)$$

The difference between various nodes in terms of their lifetime, imposed delay and offered bandwidth to their children arises from the number of children. If some parents have extra number of children or loads and some others have less, then based on the mentioned definitions, the delay imposed by them in data transmission and the bandwidth offered by them to their children for data transmission are also uneven. This unbalancing leads to a longer delay and poorer quality for children of nodes with higher load, but less delay and richer quality and even unused resources like energy or bandwidth for children of nodes with lighter load. Thus, adjusting loads among parents is also a critical problem for quality of service guarantee.

Construction of Communication Infrastructure: As mentioned in the previous section, it is assumed that the graph $G = (V,E)$ exists. Thus, before going through the details of algorithms, the construction process of this graph or in other words infrastructure of both algorithms is explained in this section. Algorithm 1 shows the construction process of communication infrastructure which is modeled by graph $G = (V,E)$.

The construction is based on the node distances to the base station, and starts with broadcasting a flooding message from this point as the *root* in level 0 of the tree. Receiving nodes of this message set their level to 1, their potential parent to the root, inform the root about their setting and re-broadcast the flooding message. Upon receiving the flooding message by other nodes in the network, each receiver node goes through a series of investigations. Firstly, it accepts the flooding message if its level is not determined yet. By accepting this message, the node sets its level one more than the sender's level, adds the sender to its potential parents set, and informs the sender of this new setting. When a sender of flooding message receives a related setting message from another node, it adds the sender of the setting message to its potential children set. If a node accepts the flooding message for the first time, it re-broadcasts that message. Due to flooding nature, it is generally possible that a node receives multiple flooding messages from different nodes. Thus, a node may receive a flooding message after determination of its level raising one of the following cases: (i) The sender has a higher level than the level of node's potential parents. In this case, receiving node ignores the received message. (ii) The sender has a level equal to the level of node's potential parents. In this case, receiving node accepts the sender as another

potential parent for itself and notifies it by sending a state acknowledgment message. (iii) The sender has a lower level than the level corresponding to potential parents of the node. In this case, receiving node removes all previous parents from its potential parents set and informs them about this action, so they remove the node's ID from their potential children set. Then, it adds the sender ID to its potential parents set as its new potential parent, sets its level one more than the sender's level, informs the sender of this new setting, and re-broadcasts the flooding message. The flooding process continues until all nodes receive this request and do not broadcast it anymore. Eventually, each node $v \in V$ has a set of potential parents P_v^p and a set of potential children P_v^c.

Heterogeneous Balanced Data Routing Algorithm

In this section, details of heterogeneous balanced data routing (HDBR) is explained. The presented algorithm is not only suited for the case that imperfect aggregation functions are used and nodes are heterogonous, but also works for homogenous case as well where perfect aggregation functions are used. HBDR algorithm includes a series of games, each is played in one level of graph G. These games are played in a sequential order. The first game is the game in the highest level among leaf nodes and their parents. As soon as this game terminates, the second game starts in one level lower, and after its termination, next game corresponding to one level lower can start. This procedure continues until the termination of game in the lowest level, among nodes in the first level and the root that is base station. In fact, playing order follows a bottom-up model from leaves towards root.

Each game includes a number of rounds. In each round some children join parents. The first round of the games is called *initial round*. Gen-

Algorithm 1. Graph G construction, run in each node $v \in V$

---

if v is root **then**

   $v.level \leftarrow 0$

     broadcast *floodingMsg*

else

  if $v.level = null$ **and** $receive(floodingMsg)$ **then**

    $v.level \leftarrow floodingMsg.sender.level + 1$

                    $P_v^p \leftarrow floodingMsg.sender$

     send *stateAck*

     broadcast *floodingMsg*

  else if $v.level \neq null$ \$ **and** $receive(floodingMsg)$ **then**

    if $floodingMsg.sender.level \geq v.level$ **then**

      discard *floodingMsg*

    else if $floodingMsg.sender.level = v.level - 1$

      $P_v^p \leftarrow floodingMsg.sender$

     send *stateAck*

    else if $floodingMsg.sender.level < v.level - 1$

      remove all members in P_v^p

     send *updateAck*

     $v.level \leftarrow floodingMsg.sender.level + 1$

                    $P_v^p \leftarrow floodingMsg.sender$

     send *stateAck*

     broadcast *floodingMsg*

    end if

  end if

end if

if $receive(stateAck)$ **then**

  $P_v^c \leftarrow stateAck.sender$

end if

if $receive(updateAck)$

  remove *stateAck.sender* from P_v^c

end if

---

erally, in this round, nodes gather information about their one-hop neighbours. In the following rounds, referred as *subsequent rounds*, children gradually join parents in a load balanced way. Algorithm 2 and Algorithm 3 show the process of tree construction.

The first game starts from leaves. Based on the information obtained through flooding, each node knows the set of its potential parent and potential children. If a node has just one potential parent, it immediately joins that parent, since the joined parent is its only option. On the other hand, if a node has some potential parents, it sends a join request (*joinReq*) message indicating it is a common children among some potential parents. Each *joinReq* message contains three areas. First field indicates the data amount which was sent by the sender of message. Two other fields, which will be discussed later in this section, do not have any value or in other words are *null* in the first round. Therefore, the *joinReq* message in the initial round is referred as *null joinReq*, and is used to inform potential parents about their potential children status.

Each parent $v \in V$, updates its load ($\varepsilon(v)$) and potential load ($\varepsilon_p(v)$) based on joining nodes and received *joinReq* messages respectively, using (9). In the computation of $C_v = E_v$, and in the computation of $\varepsilon_p(v)$, $C_v = E_v \bigcup P_v^c$. In fact, $\varepsilon_p(v)$ shows the load on v when all its potential children join it, in the worst case. After determining the remaining energy and potentially remaining energy, v computes its bid, i.e. $bid(v) = \Gamma(v, \varepsilon(v), E_v)$ and potential bid, i.e. $bid_p(v) = \Gamma(v, \varepsilon_p(v), E_v \bigcup P_v^c)$, which it can offer to its children. These bids are broadcasted to its potential children in the form of $\{bid(v), bid_p(v)\}$ pairs, called *bid pair*.

Each child node can receive some bid pairs according to the number of its potential parents. By receiving these pairs, child node $u \in V$ selects parent $v \in P_u^p$ which offers the highest benefit or bid. Based on the formula for bid, the highest bid from a node implies better quality of service in longer time meaning more stability of the offer than others. If for some parents the offered bids are the same, their potential bids are used for breaking ties. This means from parents with equal offered bids, those are chosen which have the maximum the potential bid. Thus, in the worst case when all potential children join that parent it still has better benefit for u. The chosen parents after these two steps investigation are the best choice for children. Child u shows its willingness for joining those parents by sending *joinReq* mes-

sages to them. As mentioned before, a *joinReq* from node u to node v contains three fields. The first field includes the amount of data which u will send to v in each time unit. The second and third fields indicate the maximum and minimum bids respectively among the received bids by u from its parents except v.

A *joinReq* from child u to parent v is an indication about the load on other parent in N_v^u. Based on the third field in the received *joinReq* messages, v chooses a child which has a parent with minimum offered bid indicating a combination of high load and short lifetime for that parent. This cooperative behaviour relaxes the load on the second parent and helps it to have a longer lifetime. After choosing u, based on its *joinReq* message, v adds the amount of data indicated as the first field in *joinReq* to its current amount data, and computes the benefit based on this new amount of data showing the benefit in the case that u finally joins v. This predicted bid is called $nextBid$. Also, v sends an acceptance message to u to inform it. Each accept message contains the $nextBid$ value. Then, v compares *nextBid* to the second fields of received *joinReq* messages which show maximum bids of other potential parents. If the *nextBid* is larger than all other maximum bids, v continues with child acceptance in a same way as before and re-computes the *nextBid*. Child acceptance continues unless one maximum bid larger than *nextBid* can be found. In that case, v stops child acceptance and sends the reject message to the rest of potential children which request joining.

A child may receive some acceptance messages. By receiving acceptance messages, child u chooses a parent with maximum included *nextBid* in its acceptance message. When u joins a parent, it broadcasts a join acknowledge message to not only inform the joined parent, but also to inform other parents about leaving them.

Let child u joins parent v. Then, u is added to E_v and also removed from $P_w^c, \forall w \in P_u^p$. By re-

Algorithm 2. Node $v \in V$ in parent role

---

while $\left| P_v^c \right| > 0$ do the following steps

if initial round **then**

  wait for all $u \in P_v^c$

  update $\varepsilon(v)$

$$\varepsilon'(v) \leftarrow E(v) - \varepsilon(v)$$

  if receive $(joinReq)$

    update $(\varepsilon_p(v))$

$$\varepsilon_p'(v) \leftarrow E(v) - \varepsilon_p(v)$$

  end if

  generate $bid(v)$ and $bid_p(v)$

$$bidPair(v) \leftarrow bid(v), bid_p(v)$$

  broadcast $bidPair(v)$

else

  wait for $joinReq\,timeout$

  if receive $(joinReq)$ **then**

    $nextbid(v) \leftarrow bid(v)$

    $oldMinParent \leftarrow null$

    boolean $skipFlag \leftarrow$ **false**

    while $nextbid(v) > bid(w)$, $\forall w$ of received bid s **and** $skipFlag \leftarrow$ **false**

      $minBid \leftarrow$ **minimum** $(received\,bid_{Min} \in joinReq)$

      $selectedChild \leftarrow joinReq.sender$

      $minParent \leftarrow$ the parent which sent $minBid$ to $selectedChild$

      if $minParent = oldMinParent$ **then**

        $skipFlag \leftarrow$ **true**

      else

        $oldMinParent \leftarrow minParent$

        compute $Nextbid(v)$ based on new load

        $acceptMsg(v, selectedChild) \leftarrow bid(v)$

        send $acceptMsg(v, selectedChild)$ to $selectedChild$

      end if

    end while

    send $rejectMsg$ to the rest requesters

    wait for $joinAck$ timeout

    for all received $joinAck(u, w)$ **do**

      $P_v^c \leftarrow P_v^c - \{u\}$

      if $v = w$ **then**

        update $\varepsilon(v), \varepsilon_p(v), \varepsilon'(v), \varepsilon_p'(v)$

      else

        update $\varepsilon_p(v), \varepsilon_p'(v)$

      end if

Algorithm 3. Node $u \in V$ in child role

---

while $p(u) = \varnothing$ do the following steps

if *initial round* and v is *leaf* **then**

  if $P_v \mid = 1$

| **then**

    join $(P(v))$

  else if $P_v \mid > 1$

| **then**

    send $\left(joinReq, P_v^p \right)$

  end if

else if receive $(bidPair)$ **then**

  wait for all $v \in P_v^p$

  BestBids set $\leftarrow \varnothing$

  BestParents set $\leftarrow \varnothing$

  BestBids $\leftarrow$ received bids with maximum *bid*

  BestBids $\leftarrow$ *bids* $\in$ *BestBids* set with maximum bid_p

  BestParents $\leftarrow$ *bid.sender*, $\forall bid \in BestBids$ set

  for all $w \in BestParents$ set **do**

    $bid_{max} \leftarrow$ **maximum** $\left(bid(v) \right), \forall v \in P_v^p - \{w\}$

    $bid_{min} \leftarrow$ **minimum** $\left(bid(v) \right), \forall v \in P_v^p - \{w\}$

    $joinReq(u,w) \leftarrow \{L(u), bid_{max}, bid_{min}\}$

    send $(joinReq(u,w), w)$

  end for

else if receive $(acceptMsg)$

  wait for all involved parents

  bestChoice $\leftarrow$ **minimum** $(bid(v))$ in all received *acceptMsg* s

  bestParent $\leftarrow$ *bestChoice.sender*

  join *bestParent*

()   **broadcast** $(JoinAck(u, bestParent))$

else if *receive*$(rejectMsg)$

  wait until next round

end if

---

ception of every *joinAck* message which is destined for *v*, *v* re-computes its remaining energy, bid and potential bid, and re-broadcasts the bid pair. From this point and by broadcasting the new bid pair to the its potential children, the next round begins with similar steps mentioned above.

When a child joins a parent the game terminates for it. For a parent *v*, when $\mid P_v^c \mid = 0$ the games ends. As mentioned before, games are played in a sequence from leaf nodes towards the base station. An intermediate node has two roles: parent for its children in one level higher and child role for its potential parents in one level lower. Thus, it plays two games. Because the sequence of games is from higher level to lower levels, such nodes first play a game in parent role with nodes in one level higher, and after its termination they start playing another game in child role with nodes in one level lower. This way may affect synchronization among nodes in different levels of the graph, as some nodes may finish their first game faster than others, and start the second game sooner. Thus, in the initial round of each game a node in parent role waits to receive null *joinReq* from all its potential children and then each child node waits to receive *bidPair* from all its potential parents. Considering such scheduling helps to synchronization of related nodes to each other and guarantees when a node continues the game it has received all necessary data. Let node v_1 waits for v_2. To make sure that v_2 has not failed and is waiting for reception of data from some other nodes, v_1 and v_2 can exchange a Hello messages on some certain intervals to differentiate between node failure and waiting status.

Algorithm terminates when the last games ends, i.e. when nodes in the second level join the parent in the first level.

SIMULATION RESULTS

In this section the performance of the algorithm, referred to as HBDR, is investigated and discussed. A network with size $500m \times 500m$ is considered. The performance of the algorithm is compared to the proposed algorithm in the (Sadagopan, Singh, & Krishnamachari, 2006) which we refer to it as cumulative algorithm, since it considers cumulative cost based the residual energy of nodes on the path from each node to the base station.

Table 1 includes default values of various parameters in simulations. Scenario-specific changes in this default values is mentioned in the corresponding section of each scenario. The following are explanations of different scenarios.

Network Lifetime

Network lifetime is defined as the time from the start of running the network until the first node failure. Network lifetime is an important factor, since as mentioned earlier, sensor networks have ad-hoc topology and consequently network connectivity depends on aliveness and data forwarding of nodes. In this scenario the effect of changes in number of nodes and node communication ranges on network lifetime is investigated. Generally, increase in number of nodes or node communication range leads to higher adjacency among them which gives more chance of load balancing.

In one scenario, number of nodes increase from 50 nodes to 300 nodes in steps of 50 and the communication ranges is fixed on 150 meters. In the other, communication range increases from $50m$ to $350\ m$ in the steps of $50\ m$ and the number of nodes is fixed on 150 nodes. Figure 2 and

Table 1. Node $u \in V$ in child role

Parameter	Value
Network Dimension	500(m)×500(m)
Number of Nodes	150
Node Communication Range	150(m)
Aggregation Function (λ_1, λ_2)	(1,0)
()(Time Coefficient, Frequency Coefficient)	(1,1)
E_{elec}	50 nj
E_{Amp}	100 pj
Initial Energy	10 joule
Data Amount	128 bits
Data Rate	3 kbps
Bandwidth	30 KBuad (BPSK modulation is used)

Figure 3 depict the results of these two scenarios respectively.

As shown in the figures, HBDR method has a better performance than cumulative method in both cases. The reason is that cumulative method run proactive distance vector algorithm updating and regenerating routing tree periodically. Since it is implemented in a distributed way, and the flooding mechanism is used and during this flooding nodes choose a parent with minimum cost to join. Thus, it is probable that a bunch of potential children joins a specific potential parent because it has the best cost among others. Although the algorithms is able to update, the routing tree joining of number of nodes to one parent because of its appropriate offer results in faster energy drain of that node. This fast energy drain forces a sooner regenerating process of routing tree. However, for HBDR the balanced assignment of potential children based on their load and also the cost of the parent is considered.

For the scenario in which communication range is considered variable when the communication range is short because of less amount of adjacency among nodes, the strategy space of nodes for parent selection is limited. Thus, two methods have similar performance. While the communication range increases, the chance of selection among different parents also increases. This increases the chance of more load balancing specifically for HDBR algorithm, resulting in longer network lifetime. When the communication range becomes larger than 200 meters, since the network dimension is $500m \times 500m$, more nodes can directly connect to base station, and this decreases the impact of load balancing, resulting in the same performance for both methods.

Standard Deviation of Node Lifetime

As mentioned before, standard deviation from the average node lifetime is an indication of load balance efficiency of the methods. Higher variation

Figure 2. Number of nodes vs. network lifetime

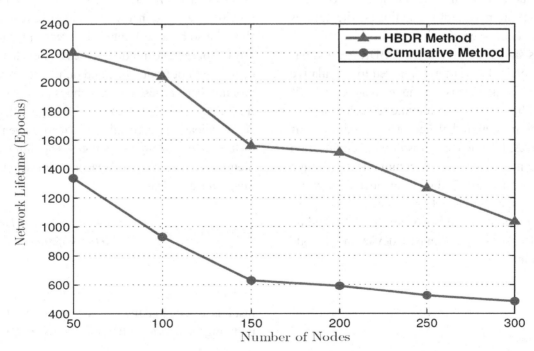

Figure 3. Node communication range vs. network lifetime

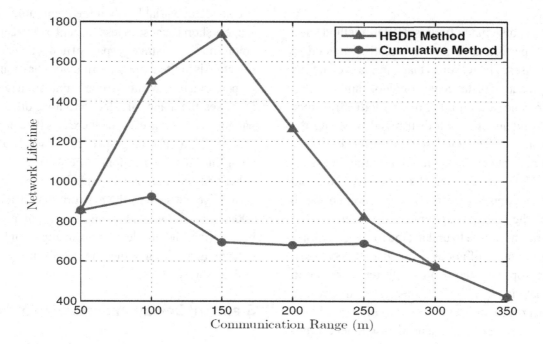

to the average implies shorter lifetime for some nodes leading to shorter network lifetime. Figure 4 and Figure 5 shows the standard deviation of network lifetimes, when number of nodes and node communication range are variable respectively. All the parameters for simulation are the same as the previous scenario.

As shown in the figures, HBDR method has less standard deviation compared to cumulative method. This means that nodes that run HDBR algorithm have closer lifetime to each other, resulting from more balanced assignment of loads to nodes. For the case in which communication range is variable, when communication range relative to network dimension increases, more nodes are able to attach base station directly. As a result, both methods have close node lifetime leading to similar standard deviation of node lifetime.

Updating Factor

Although the total number of message exchanges is important, it is not a precise factor for communication overhead of algorithms. For more precise investigation, the frequency of exchanges should also be investigated. The reason is that it is probable a large number of message exchanges occurs but not frequently, and on the other hand less number of message exchanges occurs more frequently. The latter case may impose larger communication overhead, specifically when the difference of message exchanges is not high. The mentioned point is a good reason to define *updating factor* as below:

$$updating\,factor = \frac{total\,number\,of\,message\,exchange}{network\,lifetime}$$

(21)

Network lifetime is a good indication of how fast it is needed that the tree is regenerated. Thus, updating factor is an indication of what amount of

Figure 4. Number of nodes vs. standard deviation node lifetime

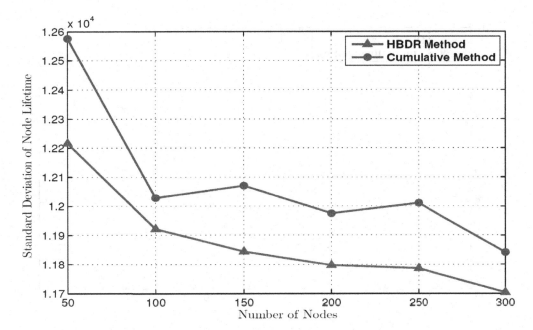

Figure 5. Node communication range vs. standard deviation node lifetime

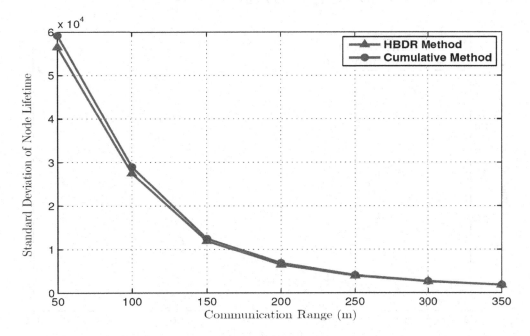

message exchanges is required in each epoch to keep the tree up-to-date and network connected. The less the updating factor is, the less communication overhead per epoch is imposed. Again, simulation results are reflected under the condition of different number of nodes, and different node communication range respectively.

As it can be seen in figures, HDBR method mostly outperforms cumulative method. This is because, although cumulative method imposes

Figure 6. Number of nodes vs. updating factor

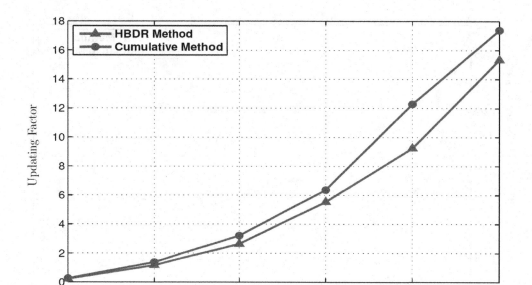

Figure 7. Node communication range vs. updating factor

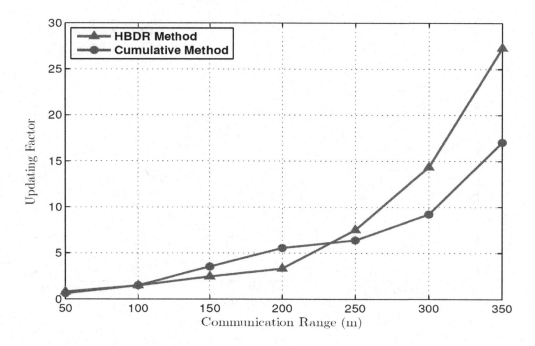

fewer amounts of message exchange, it is not a more balanced algorithm than HDBR algorithm. Thus, over-used nodes have faster energy depletion and updating of the tree have to occur more often than HBDR method, resulting in a higher updating factor than HBDR method. However, as indicated in Figure 7, when the communication range is variable and it becomes close to the network dimension, more nodes can directly connect to base station. This direct connection causes fewer loads on nodes in both approaches. Thus, both approaches update trees less frequently. However, because the number of message exchanges needed in each construction of tree using cumulative method is less than the number of message exchanges required in each construction of tree using HBDR method, it outperforms HBDR method in this case.

CONCLUSION AND FUTURE RESEARCH DIRECTIONS

This chapter introduced an algorithm based on game theoretic approach for load balanced data routing in wireless sensor networks. Load is defined as the amount of energy required to receive, process and transmit information by nodes. Load balancing is critical for sensor networks as the only energy resource for sensor nodes is their limited battery supplies resulting in computation and communication limitations. The presented algorithm specifically aimed to solve the problem of constructing a load balanced tree for data routing. The game theoretic approach implies designing of games in that, nodes as players have two roles as child and parent. In a child role, nodes are selfish players trying to gain more possible available bandwidth, while in parent role they act as cooperative nodes trying to decrease the load on their connected parents which are two-hop away nodes in the same level. Each parent is connected to its connected parents via nodes in one lower level.

Considering load heterogeneity of nodes opens a challenging area. Accordingly, taking heterogeneous nodes in terms of the amount of sending data into account is a solution for applications for which in-network aggregation is not possible. As this case is more general than the homogenous case, solving this problem will lead to a solution for all kinds of queries. Considering a few mobile nodes in the network will add some challenging dynamics to the problem, where some nodes move from one communication area to another. This will cause different load for both nodes which are located in the communication range of the mobile node and mobile node itself, when it goes through communication range of different nodes.

Although the presented algorithm is discussed for construction of routing tree, they can easily be adapted to support updating a portion of trees, i.e. sub-trees during runtime. Because in a long duration of query running, it is probable from a certain time, initial conditions based on which the construction is conducted change and consequently the current tree topology becomes non-optimum. However, reconstruction of the whole tree may not be beneficial, and fixing the problem in a sub-tree of the whole tree solves the problem. Also, nodes can have different communication ranges as another heterogeneity criterion. This difference may rise from different levels of residual energy, or deploying nodes with different cases. In both cases, importing different range of communication in the formulas looks practical.

REFERENCES

Akyildiz, I., Su, W., Sankarasubramaniam, Y., & Cayirci, E. (2002, March). Wireless sensor networks: A survey. *Computer Networks*, *38*, 393–422. doi:10.1016/S1389-1286(01)00302-4

Bouabdallah, F., Bouabdallah, N., & Boutaba, R. (2009). On balancing energy consumption in wireless sensor networks. *IEEE Transactions on Vehicular Technology*, 58.

Charilas, D., & Panagopoulos, A. (2010). A survey on game theory applications in wireless networks. *Computer Networks*, *54*(18). doi:10.1016/j.comnet.2010.06.020

Chu, Y., Tseng, C., Hung, C., Liao, K., Ouyang, C., Yen, C., et al. (October 2009). Application of load-balanced tree routing algorithm with dynamic modi□cation to centralized wireless sensor networks. *IEEE Sensors*, (pp. 1392–1395). New Zealand.

Estrin, D., Girod, L., Pottie, G., & Srivastava, M. (May 2001). Instrumenting the world with wireless sensor networks. *International Conference on Acoustics, Speech, and Signal Processing (ICASSP)*, (pp. 2033–2036).

Frattasi, S., Fathi, H., & Fitzek, F. (2006). 4g: A user-centric system. *Special Issue on Advances in Wireless Communications: Enabling Technologies for 4G*.

Fudenberg, D., & Tirole, J. (1991). *Game theory*. MIT Press.

Gehrke, J., & Madden, S. (March 2004). Query processing in sensor networks. *Pervasive Computing, 3*.

Han, Z., & Liu, R. (2007). Non-cooperative resource competition game by virtual referee in multi-cell OFDMA networks. *IEEE Journal on Selected Areas in Communications, 25*, 1079–1090. doi:10.1109/JSAC.2007.070803

Harvey, N., Ladner, R., Lovasz, L., & Tamir, T. (July 2003). *Semi-matchings for bipartite graphs and load balancing*. Workshop on Algorithms and Data Structures (WADS 2003), Canada.

Lee, K., Lee, W., Zheng, B., & Winter, J. (April 2006). *Processing multiple aggregation queries in geo-sensor networks*. The 11th International Conference on Database Systems for Advanced Applications (DAS-FAA06). Singapore.

Madden, S., Franklin, M., Hellerstein, J., & Hong, W. (December 2002). Tag a tiny aggregation service for ad-hoc sensor networks. 5th Symposium on Operating Systems Design and Implementation. Boston, Massachusetts, USA.

Madden, S., Franklin, M., Hellerstein, J., & Hong, W. (2005, March). Tinydb, An acquisitional query processing system for sensor networks. *ACM Transactions on Database Systems, 30*, 122–173. doi:10.1145/1061318.1061322

Muller, R., & Alonso, G. (October 2006). *Efficient sharing of sensor networks*. IEEE International Conference on Mobile Adhoc and Sensor Systems. Vancouver, BC, Canada.

Munteanu, A., Beaver, J., Labrinidis, A., & Chrysanthis, P. (February 2005). Multiple query routing trees in sensor networks. *The IASTED International Conference on Databases and Applications (DBA05)*, (pp. 145–150). Innsbruck, Austria.

Niyato, D., & Hossain, E. (2007). Radio resource management games in wireless networks: An approach to bandwidth allocation and admission control for polling service in IEEE 802.16. *Wireless Communications, 14*, 27–35. doi:10.1109/MWC.2007.314548

Potdar, V., Sharif, A., & Chang, E. (2009, May). Wireless sensor networks: A survey. *WAINA, 09*, 636–641.

Rosemark, R., Lee, W., & Urgaonkar, B. (May 2007). *Optimizing energy-efficient query processing in wireless sensor networks*. International Conference on Mobile Data Management, Mannheim, Germany.

Sadagopan, N., Singh, M., & Krishnamachari, B. (2006). Decentralized utility-based design of sensor networks. *Mobile Networks and Applications, 11*, 341–350. doi:10.1007/s11036-006-5187-8

Suris, J., DaSilva, L., Han, Z., & MacKenzie, A. (2007). *Cooperative game theory for distributed spectrum sharing*. IEEE International Conference on Communications.

Trigoni, N., Guitton, A., & Skordylis, A. (2006). Routing and processing multiple aggregate queries in sensor networks. *The 4th International Conference on Embedded Networked Sensor Systems*, (pp. 391–392). Colorado, USA.

Trigoni, N., Yao, Y., Demers, A., Gehrke, J., & Rajaraman, R. (June 2005). *Multi-query optimization for sensor networks*. The First IEEE International Conference on Distributed Computing in Sensor Systems (DCOSS 2005). Marina del Rey, CA: IEEE.

Uliman, I., Pomalaza, R. C., Oppernann, I., & Lehtomaki, J. (August 2004). *Radio resource allocation in heterogeneous wireless networks using cooperative games*. Nordic Radio Symposium 2004/Finnish Wireless.

Wang, L., Xue, Y., & Schulz, E. (2006). *Resource allocation in multi-cell ofdm systems based on non-cooperative game*. 17th Annual IEEE International Symposium on Personal, Indoor and Mobile Radio Communications.

Yao, Y., & Gehrke, J. (January 2003). *Query processing in sensor networks*. The First Biennial Conference on Innovative Data Systems Research (CIDR). Asilomar, California.

Zhang, X., Yu, X., & Chen, X. (September 2005). *Inter-query data aggregation in wireless sensor networks*. International Conference on Wireless Communications, Networking and Mobile Computing (WCNM 2005). Wuhan, China.

KEY TERMS AND DEFINITIONS

Data Aggregation: Data aggregation is any process in which information is gathered and expressed in a summary form, for purposes such as statistical analysis.

Load Balancing: A technique to distribute network or computational load among multiple resources.

Network Lifetime: The time duration for a network to be operational.

Query Processing: A method to execute query on a dataset.

Chapter 12
SCAMSTOP:
A Platform for Mitigating Fraud in VoIP Environments

Yacine Rebahi
Fraunhofer Fokus, Germany

Reinhard Ruppelt
Fraunhofer Fokus, Germany

Mohamed Nassar
INRIA Research Center Nancy – Grand Est, France

Olivier Festor
INRIA Research Center Nancy – Grand Est, France

ABSTRACT

In traditional telecommunication networks, fraud accounts for significant annual losses at an average up of 5% of the operators' revenue and still increasing. The current shift towards Voice-over-IP (VoIP) networks increases to exposure to fraud due to the lack of strong built-in security mechanisms and the full usage of the open Internet. In this book chapter, the authors discuss an anti-fraud framework they are currently developing within the SCAMSTOP project. Although a short description of the framework is provided, the focus of this chapter is mainly on the methods used to detect fraudulent activity. In particular the authors focus on unsupervised methods including signature and clustering based techniques. Preliminary testing results are also discussed.

INTRODUCTION

The openness, innovative services and low cost structure of Voice-over-IP services has helped providers to attract large numbers of subscribers over the past few years. These same reasons have, unfortunately, also attracted attackers and malicious users who find in these new packet-based networks an opportunity to earn money in a fraudulent way. In traditional telecommunication networks, various experts estimate that fraud accounts for annual losses at an average of 3% to 5% of the operators' revenue. This portion is even

DOI: 10.4018/978-1-4666-1888-6.ch012

still increasing at a rate of more than 10% yearly. Hence, with the openness of the VoIP technology an even higher threat of fraud and higher losses of revenue are expected.

In this chapter, we are interested in investigating the fraud and service misuse problem in VoIP environments. For instance, we study,

- Under which forms does this problem appear in such networks,
- How difficult is VoIP fraud to be detected,
- What can we reuse / adapt from the existing techniques and algorithms in the fight against fraud, and
- Which kind of data do we need to explore to look for fraud patterns?

The mentioned issues and some others are being discussed in the SCAMSTOP project, an FP7 funded collaborative project[1]. The latter aims at designing and implementing innovative and adaptive algorithms for misuse and fraud detection in the VoIP domain. By designing these algorithms, we are not only aiming at achieving a high detection rate but also targeting a scalable architecture ensuring low processing and limited memory usage so as to ensure the applicability of these algorithms in large scale VoIP deployments.

BACKGROUND

Fraud can be defined as any activity that leads to the obtaining of financial advantage or causing of loss by implicit or explicit deception. It is the mechanism through which the fraudster gains an unlawful advantage or causes unlawful loss. This can be as simple as telling a lie to obtain some compensation benefits. Fraud losses keep impacting every business enterprise. The costs of fraud are passed on to the society in the form of increased customer inconvenience, opportunity costs, increased prices for goods and services,

and even additional criminal activities funded by the fraudulent gains.

Although Fraud (or scam) is a problem that spans most areas of our daily life (e. g., telecommunications, banking and finance, insurance, e-commerce), we will be more concerned in this document with the fraudulent activities that might occur in VoIP environments.

FRAUD CLASSIFICATION

The classification of fraud can be achieved in different ways according to the point of view from which these activities are observed. However, the categorization that is generally cited in the literature (Bolton & Hand, 2002) is the following,

Subscription fraud: this occurs from obtaining an account or service, often with false identity details, without the intention of paying. The account is usually used for call selling or intensive self-usage.

Superimposed fraud: this type of fraud occurs when a fraudster uses a service or an account without having the necessary authority. In other words, a fraud is said to be superimposed when a fraudster illegally gets resources from legitimate users by gaining access to their phone accounts. The fraudster is said to be an insider when the corresponding activity is committed by an employee of the telecommunication operator. This type of fraud is said to be external if it is committed by a member of the general public. With other respects, this kind of fraud can be detected by the appearance of unknown calls on a bill.

A SHORT STATE OF THE ART

The common techniques used for fraud detection are: rule-based techniques, data-mining as well as both supervised and unsupervised machine learning.

Rule-based is one of the main techniques used so far for fraud detection. The rule-based approach defines fraud patterns as rules (Verrelst, Lerouge, Moreau, Vandewalle, Störmann, & Burge, 1996). The rules might consist of one or more conditions. If all the conditions are met, an alarm is produced. To define the rules, different types of data are needed (Gopal & Meher, 2007), for instance, call detail records (CDRs) and customers data (e.g., age, balance). Unfortunately, this technique presents severe drawbacks (Verrelst, Lerouge, Moreau, Vandewalle, Störmann, & Burge, 1996) related to false alarms, rules management and the choice of thresholds.

Data mining is another set of techniques used in fraud detection. It can be divided into two categories: supervised and unsupervised learning. In the former, extensive training using labeled data classes of both fraudulent and non-fraudulent cases are used. This training data will be utilized to develop a model which will be in charge of discovering new cases that can be classified as legitimate or fraudulent (Abbott, Matkovsky, & Elder, 1998).

In the context of supervised methods for fraud detection, different techniques were suggested including neural networks (Lee & Heinbuch, 2001), decision trees (Li, Huang, Jin, & Shi, 2008), fuzzy logic (Sanver & Karahoca, 2007), and Bayesian networks (Abbott, Matkovsky, & Elder, 1998). Within this category, the most popular technique is neural networks. Unfortunately this technique suffers from some drawbacks such as the heavy dependence on the accurate training of the system. As a consequence, a large amount of data is required in the learning phase in order to ensure that the results are statistically accurate. Also, the individual relations between the input variables and the output variables are not developed by engineering judgment so that the model tends to be a black box or input/output table without any analytical basis.

Contrary to the supervised methods, unsupervised methods can be used in the case where we are not aware of which transactions in the database are fraudulent and which are legal. These techniques are based on what is called "profile / signature" (Hollmén, 2000) or "normal behavior" (Li, Huang, Jin, & Shi, 2008) (Hilas & Sahalos, 2005). Here, the past behavior of the user is cumulated in order to build a profile that will be used to predict the user's future behavior. As this profile describes the habitual usage pattern of the user (called "normal behavior"), any significant deviation from the "normal behavior" has to be reported because it might hide some fraudulent activities. The idea behind signatures is the fact that a CDR is not enough by itself for detecting fraud and it has to be enhanced by investigating the user behavior (Edge, 2009) (Ferreira P., Alves, Belo, & Cortesão, 2006). A signature can be seen as a statistical description or a set of features that captures the typical behavior of the user, including the average number of calls, time of the calls, area where the calls are made, number of calls at working times, number of calls by night, etc. (Cortes & Pregibon, 2001). Unfortunately, the current use of this method does not take into account the customer data nor the price plans of the VoIP providers as it will be discussed later on.

In the SCAMSTOP platform, we combine the rule-based technique with the unsupervised method. The latter will be evolved to take into account the customers data, and the price plans of the VoIP providers. Also, a special focus will be on the smooth cooperation with other VoIP Subsystems such as IDS and Firewall.

MAIN FOCUS OF THE CHAPTER

The Session Initiation Protocol (SIP)

There are many protocols that may be employed to provide VoIP communication services. Among them, the Session Initiation Protocol (SIP) (Rosenberg & Schulzrinne, 2002) has been rapidly gaining widespread acceptance as the signaling protocol of choice for fixed and mobile Internet multimedia and telephony services.

SIP is an application-layer control protocol that allows users to create, modify, and terminate sessions with one or more participants. It can be used to create two-party, multiparty, or multicast sessions that include Internet telephone calls, multimedia distribution, and multimedia conferences.

In SIP, a user is identified through a SIP Uniform Resource Identifier (URI) in the form of "sip:user@domain". This identifier can be resolved to a SIP proxy that is responsible for the user's domain. To identify the actual location of the user in terms of an IP address, the user needs to register at a SIP registrar responsible for his domain. Thereby when inviting a user, the caller sends his invitation to the SIP proxy responsible for the user's domain, which checks in the registrar's database the location of the user and forwards the invitation to the callee. The callee can either accept or reject the invitation. The session initiation is then finalized by having the caller acknowledging the reception of the callee's answer. During this message exchange, the caller and callee exchange the addresses at which they would like to receive the media and what kind of media they can accept. After finishing the session establishment, the end systems can exchange data directly without the involvement of the SIP proxy.

The VoIP Fraud is Harder

Although, the current telecommunication fraud is a billions-dollar business, it seems that the related operators' losses, when VoIP is deployed, will be much higher. This can be argued as follows,

- The infrastructure of VoIP networks is packet-based, distributed between different components, and some of these components are connected to the public Internet. As a consequence, VoIP networks will inherit IP related vulnerabilities. For instance, the use of IP spoofing, eavesdrop-

ping, and botnets will be of great benefits for the fraudsters to carry out their attacks;
- The services in VoIP are multilayered and usually provided through different entities and actors, namely, network provider, service provider, and content provider. Each of these actors, is a potential candidate for fraud, and these multi-entities based services make fraud investigation harder in IP based networks;
- VoIP networks are based on open interfaces and protocols. Despite the fact that this is an asset for VoIP networks since it greatly facilitates interaction between different operators and providers, this openness can also lead to misuse especially that mentioned protocols and interfaces are well documented and available for whoever wants to read them. In addition, tools, scripts, and detailed hacking instructions are publicly available on the Internet. As a consequence, this can be a major source for perpetrating fraud;
- VoIP technologies are recent and a limited set of experts have enough knowledge about the corresponding environments. This situation is worsened by the fact that these technologies are very complex, so fraud detection in this kind of environment is a very challenging task.

Tools and Methods Used in VoIP Fraud Activities

The tools and methods that fraudsters usually use include,

- **Scanning:** This involves the use of a computer and a sequential number dial-out program to obtain the PIN.
- **Use of viruses:** Fraudsters can use viruses and Trojan horses to get private data stored in computers and / or smartphones

- **Phishing:** impersonate a trusted organization or a VoIP provider and ask customers for some private information in order to fix a pretended problem.

- **Spam:** most of spam activities require you to take advantage of the good deals they are offering. If some personal data is given to them, this information will be used for carrying out attacks.

- **Social networks:** browsing into social networks, for instance web sites of public domains where personal data is posted can reveal information useful to take over some of the user's assets.

- **Equipment stealing or hacking**.

It is common that these techniques are combined together in order to maximize the profits.

Fraud Scenarios in VoIP Networks

In (Rebahi, Fiedler, & Gouveia, D2.1, 2010), we described in details the shapes that traditional telecommunication fraud could take. We discussed cases such as subscription fraud, roaming fraud, technical fraud, premium rate fraud, and some others. While all of these fraud use cases can be seen as direct threats to VoIP networks, the VoIP technologies add some other risks as well. These are:

1. **Service plan misuse:** In general VoIP services are offered as flat rate services. Operators calculate these plans based on average usage scenarios. While such services are intended for personal use only, some subscribers offer this service to other people –family and friends- as well resulting in high usage and high losses to the operator.

2. **Credit Card fraud:** In this case, fraudsters use the toll free service of a VoIP provider to find out the PIN numbers of a stolen credit card. That is, while sitting in Nigeria for example, the fraudster would call a premium service in the USA that would require the credit card and PIN number and keep trying this until the right number was found.

3. **Identity theft:** While the access control scheme of the VoIP protocols (based on MD5 hash technology (Rivest, 1992)) is fairly robust it can be attacked. This would result in revealing a user's password to the attacker which would then misuse the user's service.

4. **Viruses and malicious code:** As most, if not all VoIP components will be connected to the public Internet, it might be possible that a virus or a malicious code that was downloaded by a customer can call premium numbers or deliver unwanted content. Unfortunately, the customer will be charged for these services that he did not intend to use.

Problems Facing Fraud Detection in VoIP

When developing fraud detection mechanisms, we need to be aware of the following obstacles:

Limitation in fraud detection knowledge: Fraud detection is usually not discussed in public domains because the persons who work on developing related techniques think that disclosing more details about the developed mechanisms will give fraudsters the information that they require to evade detection. As a consequence, data is not made available and results are not disclosed, so making the evaluation of the developed techniques often difficult if not impossible.

Non-suitability of the existing anti-fraud solutions: Telecom operators and VoIP providers may have millions of subscribers and customers. This leads of course to huge data sets (millions of transactions every day) to be investigated in order to detect fraud. Processing these huge databases for detecting scam in transactions or calls requires more appropriate statistical models, and also fast and efficient algorithms.

Data Collection for Fraud Detection

In this paragraph, we give an overview of the main types of data that need to be collected in order to achieve a successful detection framework in VoIP environments.

Call Detail Record (CDRs)

Every time a call is placed on a telecommunications network, descriptive information about the call is saved as a call detail record. The number of Call Detail Records (CDRs) that are generated every day and stored is huge. At a minimum, each Call Detail Record has to include the originating and terminating phone numbers, the start date and time as well as the duration of the call.

The CDRs might also include some additional data which is not necessarily required for billing, for instance, the identifier of the telephone exchange writing the record, a sequence number identifying the record, the result of the call (whether it was answered, busy etc), the route by which the call entered the exchange, any fault condition encountered, and any facilities used during the call, such as call waiting.

Customer Data

Telecommunication companies need also to maintain databases of information related to their customers. This information is huge especially if the company has millions of subscribers. The customer data typically includes name and address information and may include other information such as service plan and contract information, credit score, family income and payment history. This information is often used in conjunction with other data in order to improve the detection results.

Calendars and Holidays Data

A change in the user behavior does not necessarily induce a fraud activity. In fact, the behavior changes in function of contexts: social context, holidays, travel, etc. The contexts can be divided into two groups: personal (e.g., going abroad) and global (e.g., holiday season) even if they are often related. Integrating a degree of context awareness into the fraud management system, like connecting the system to a calendar, will help in correctly defining the user behavior and prevent false alarms.

Solutions and Recommendations

In this section, we first provide a brief description of the architecture adopted in the SCAMSTOP project. Then, we discuss in more details how the unsupervised methods such as the signature / profile-based technique as well as clustering-based approaches are being used within the framework. The methodology we followed to build the SCAMSTOP framework is the following:

- **Problem statement:** This part deals with answering questions such as: what does fraud mean in our context, how does it appear in VoIP environments, what are the different categories, and which kind of solutions can be used in fighting it? This was already discussed in the "background" section of this chapter;

- **Assessment of the existing solutions and algorithms:** Fraud and service misuse is a problem that has been investigated to some extend in the literature, not in the context of VoIP but in some other context like: telecom fraud, insurance fraud, credit cards fraud, etc. Our goal here was to assess the existing solutions from the technical point of view as well as to evaluate their applicability to this project. This was also already investigated in the "background" section;

- **Collecting requirements:** requirements are needed to build a platform that has to meet in particular the expectations of the

SCAMSTOP VoIP partners. This will be discussed in this section;

- **SCAMSTOP architecture specification:** Based on the requirements, the architectural building blocks are defined as well as the interfaces in between the different components. This is also described in this section.

The SCAMSTOP Framework Requirements

The requirements were collected mainly from two sources: (1) the related literature, and (2) the SCAMSTOP VoIP providers. General requirements related to fraud management systems deal in particular with: flexibility, scalability, and transparency. The requirements set by the VoIP partners were in particular related to the ease to use, the combination of online and offline detection, and the expectation that the developed platform has to fit in the existing VoIP infrastructures. The main requirements devised in the context of SCAMSTOP are the following:

1. The Fraud Detection System (FDS) needs to smoothly cooperate with other VoIP Subsystems such as Intrusion Detection Systems (IDS) and Firewalls. In case a fraud alert is generated by the FDS, all other systems including the IDS, the Firewall and the SBCs (Session Border Controller) should be informed about this alert.

2. In case a fraud activity is detected, the user should be penalized. This penalty can take various forms (e.g., adapting the quota of a specific account), adjust the premium rate charge, block specific international numbers, activate blocking forwarding etc.

3. The FDS must also be flexible by allowing the addition, removal and update of fraud detection algorithms to accommodate changing fraud scenarios and yield to fewer false positives.

4. The FDS needs to analyze all the data flowing through all the different elements in a VoIP Network.

5. The FDS must be scalable in the sense that additional fraud rules will have to be added to the detection module. This means that the number of billing records to inspect will also increase with the new services offered.

6. The FDS should also perform real-time and non real-time detection.

7. The FDS must operate transparently. A good solution does not require traffic to be rerouted or detoured, but rather forms an independent layer on top of the existing system.

8. The FDS must be scalable and support a huge number of users in order to satisfy the SMEs' requirements.

9. The FDS must fit in the VoIP solutions being offered by the VoIP providers.

10. The FDS must be easy to deploy and maintain.

An Overview on the SCAMSTOP Architecture

Based on the collected requirements, we have designed the SCAMSTOP functional architecture and coupled it with SIP security and intrusion detection functional blocks. The specifications of the SCAMSTOP architecture are based on Figure 1.

Profiling (or signature based technique) is one of the main components in the SCAMSTOP architecture. The idea behind profiling is to build a model or a signature for each subscriber that describes his normal behavior. The profile can be considered as a list of some statistical features that keep track of the user normal behavior. This profile will probably change over time, and if a significant deviation from the normal behavior is detected, an alarm is generated. The use of profiling is very important especially in cases where we do not have enough information about fraud scenarios, which is the most probable case in VoIP fraud. In SCAMSTOP, the signature (or profile)

Figure 1. SCAMSTOP architecture

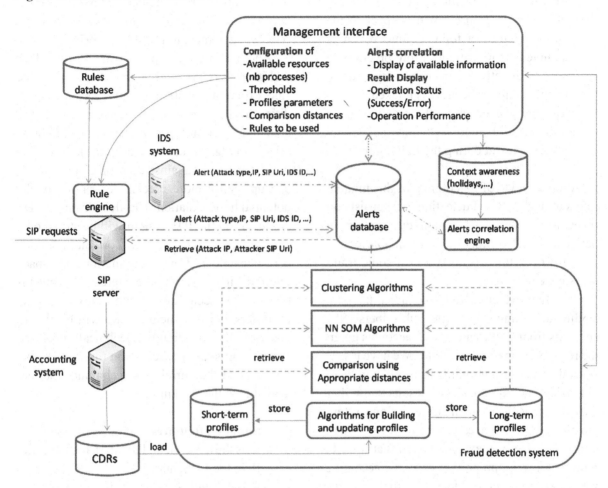

is composed from 3 prototypes (working days, working days by night, weekends and holidays). We identified the features to be used and the way they are computed (e.g., number of calls per day, mean duration of calls, top longest calls, top frequent destinations, etc). To be more precise, we have specified two types of profiles: long-term and short term profiles. Both profiles are the same except the fact that the long-term one is computed for sufficiently long period of time (one month or more); the short-term one is computed every day. We have also specified how the long-term and short-term profiles are compared based on the Hellinger distance (Ferreira P., Alves, Belo, & Cortesão, 2006).

It is worth to mention that in defining the users profiles, the VoIP providers' service plans were taken into account. For instance, most VoIP providers are offering flat rate options and they do not expect fraud activities to be carried out from this side. However, the computed statistical parameters are related to services that are both free and non-free. This allows the SMEs to assess whether they flat rate offers are beneficial.

The goal of the clustering module is to separate the subscribers in two or multiple clusters (or groups) based on their call activities or profiles. When a user changes its behavior, because of a fraud or a stolen account, this can lead to its migration from one group to another. That is, this module has two tasks:

- **Training:** we monitor the membership of the different users with respect to the clusters during a training time which is assumed clean of fraud. More precisely, a clustering activity runs every day and the membership of the users is tracked.
- **Testing:** we check if the behavior of a user is compliant to the "normality" model which is learnt during the training time.

Another mode of functioning of this module refers to unsupervised detection and consists on revealing the abnormal situations during a certain period of time. No information is available for this period if everything is normal or if some fraud cases have occurred.

As a first exercise, we have studied the possibility to distinguish Single Subscribers (SS) accounts from Call Centers (CC) accounts given the records of one VoIP provider. We have tested several clustering algorithms such as hierarchical clustering and K-means. The results show that the call centers form small clusters of one or few members. The SS accounts form few clusters but of big size of members. Given that the CC represent a small proportion of all the accounts, we proposed one-class Support Vector Machines (SVM) (Vapnik, Statistical Learning Theory, 1998) to efficiently encompass SS and consider outliers as CC.

Neural Networks (NNs) are inspired by the neural connections in the human brain. They are used across a large number of applications confronting various classifications and clustering problems. Several types of NNs can be identified: Feed Forward, Radial Basis Function, Self Organizing, Recurrent, etc. NNs have been used as a fraud detection mechanism mainly in credit card fraud detection. Based on the recent bibliography and some preliminary tests, the different types of NNs were tested on a subset of user behavior data and the Self Organized Map (SOM) type was chosen for the VoIP fraud detection problem because of its characteristics: SOM is not based on previous

observations of fraud incidents, it has good clustering capabilities and it converges relatively fast (He, Wang, Graco, & Hawkins, 1997).

Another important part in the SCAMSTOP architecture is the alerts correlation. From one side, different detection modules are used in addition to the IDS systems. These modules will generate different types of alarms that might be related to a given use case or not. These alarms will be matched against each other in order to end up with a more precise description of the potential fraud situation. The alerts from the FDS modules and the IDS system will be stored on a common database. The alert correlation engine is responsible of discovering the time and space relationships between the alerts. This means that in some scenarios we don't only detect the fraudsters and stop them but we will be able to understand how the fraud has technically occurred and prevent similar cases in the future. We have investigated the correlation techniques that are available in the literature:

- **Similar attributes:** for example the same IP is the target of an IDS alert and the caller IP in the FDS alert
- **Pre-defined scenarios:** for example, an ARP spoofing alert followed by high-price calls.
- **Pre and post conditions of an attack:** if the pre-condition of the fraud alert is the post condition of an intrusion alert.
- **Statistical causality analysis:** Determines by statistical tests if an alert X is the cause of an alert Y.

In SCAMSTOP, we focus on rule-based correlation by investigating similar attributes over a common range of time. This technique does not require the operator to write scenarios and compensate the need for large data-sets in order as it is required for applying statistical tests.

Privacy Issues in SCAMSTOP

In the SCAMSTOP project, we also dealt with privacy issues. In fact, the issues rose at two levels:

- Using the CDRs for testing purposes within the SCAMSTOP project,
- Integrating the signature / profile based technique into the VoIP platforms deployed by the SMEs in their premises. The signature / profile based technique is used to generate some statistical parameters describing the service usage by a certain customer as discussed before.

In order for the CDRs used in the project to be realistic, they were taken from the real production networks representing actual call patterns from customers. To protect the customers' privacy, these CDRs have been anonymized. All telephone numbers and IP addresses have been replaced by random strings. To preserve call patterns, each number and IP address is replaced by the same random string throughout the entire process. This, however, was not enough for telephone numbers as the fraud detection systems relies on additional information derived from those numbers, namely the country and the type of service within this country. Therefore, the number was split into two parts, a prefix and a number within that prefix. Each prefix represented a certain group of numbers, for instance, mobile numbers in Norway. However, the prefix was chosen randomly, too, so that no actual information can be derived from it. Together with the anonymized CDRs, a list is being provided that marks the rate group this prefix belongs to.

It is worth to mention that fraud cannot be addressed without data processing. In SCAMSTOP, we limited this data to the minimum. In fact, we did not need to investigate the CDRs in detail; however, we generated some statistical features that were describing the overall user behavior. On the other side, the SME partners have also checked with the appropriate authorities the limits for using the users' related data. It turns out that the use of such statistics did not lead to any problem from the legal point of view.

Call Detail Records

In the "Main Focus of the chapter" section, we started already discussing the Call Detail Records (CDRS) which are the main source for looking for fraud patterns. In this part, we go deeper and describe how the CDRs received from the VoIP providers look like and which related features are being used in our investigation. The CDRs were collected from two VoIP providers that are member of the SCAMSTOP consortium. In fact this step is necessary as the CDRs are encoded in different ways and a preparation phase is needed to develop a framework that fits for both providers.

The CDRs received from the first VoIP provider contains the following fields (Time: start time of call, SIP Response Code: 2xx, 3xx, 4xx, 5xx or 6xx, SIP Method: INVITE –mainly–, User-name, From URI, To URI, To-Tag, From-Tag, User-Agent, Source IP, RPID: Remote Party ID, Duration).

The CDRs received from the second VoIP provider contain the following fields (number: destination number, user ID –caller–, IP address –caller–, user ID –callee–, IP address –callee–: VoIP provider knows the IP addresses of all the PSTN gateways they are using and through this determine whether the call was to the PSTN or not, start time, duration, SIP status, flags –"missed", "hidden", "forwarded"–, rating and correlation info: e.g., SIP messages that belong to the same call).

The VoIP providers offered to the project a data corpus of anonymized CDRs. Examples of anonymized CDRs from both providers are given in

The common fields between the CDRs from both VoIP providers are caller *(a_number)*, callee *(b_number)*, start time of the call *(start_time)*, duration of the call in seconds *(duration)*, end SIP status or response *(status)*, IP address of the

Table 1. Examples of anonymized CDRs

CDR fields	VoIP provider #1		VoIP provider #2	
	CDR #1	CDR #2	CDR #3	CDR #4
a_number	14664:73909677	14664:35511746	03775:07996615	37389:33035557
b_number	29287:74189354	29287:23520414	56009:66349831	37389:11757486
start_time	01/04/2010 00:00:11	01/04/2010 00:00:08	01/07/2010 00:00:04	30/09/2010 23:57:12
duration	0	3	8	0
status	487	200	200	487
a_ip	20.54.97.249	1.24.45.148	243.22.64.32	254.144.194.199
b_ip	115.231.248.209	222.36.97.253	228.182.97.252	148.45.153.19
group	int	int	int	int
flags	missed, hidden, outgoing	outgoing	-	-

caller *(a_ip)*, IP address of the callee *(b_ip)*, and finally the group of the destination *(group)*.

There are two differences between the two groups of CDRs:

1. All the CDRs from the first VoIP provider represent outgoing calls. (VoIP provider uses additional flags to annotate the CDRs, e. g., "incoming", "outgoing", "missed", "hidden")
2. The second VoIP provider and the first VoIP provider use different destination groups. The second VoIP provider has "int", "mob", "local", "free-pstn", and "pay" groups. The first VoIP provider has "nationalfixed", "nationalmobile", "national free", "national" and "int" groups.

All numbers and IP addresses are anonymized. Our investigations are based on the common fields mentioned above.

Signatures and Profiles Generation

In this section, the definition of a signature or a profile for each subscriber is addressed. The signature can be composed of a number of prototypes (e.g., weekday vs. weekend prototypes). We need to determine the features to be used and

the way they are computed (e.g., number of calls per day, mean duration of calls, top longest calls, top frequent destinations, etc.). This requires a memory vs. processing analysis, especially when the profiling of a large number ranging from thousands to millions of subscribers is envisioned.

The signatures can be built using one of the common following modes: event-driven (e.g., a given number of transactions / calls is committed: for instance, a new signature is generated for each 50 call transactions) and time-driven (e.g., a new signature is generated after a given time window has elapsed, for instance, each day). A discussion of the limitations of these two computation modes is found in (Cortes & Pregibon, 2001). For the SCAMSTOP framework, we will use the time-driven mode instead of the event-driven mode because the latter depends on when and how often the event is triggered which might lead to unexpected overhead.

It is of particular importance to select the features that are more suitable for detection. The categorization of features will take into account the price plan of the VoIP providers as mentioned earlier. For example, instead of using a local / national / international categorization for the destination of a call, we opt for a free / non-free one, especially since VoIP providers nowadays offer free calls towards a large number of fix and mobile international destinations. Moreover, we need to know how much each service / call destination really costs to the provider, since in many scenarios free service plans are abused (e.g., excessively shared with friends and family).

Other issues include context awareness, signature updating, signature initialization when new subscribers enter the system, and subscriber clustering into groups (e.g., personal vs. professional profiles).

Signature Definition and Features

We define the signature of a subscriber as composed of three prototypes,

- Working days
- Working days by night
- Weekends (and holidays)

For each prototype we compute the following features

- The K most frequently called numbers (e.g., K=10). This parameter will help in detecting sudden changes in the called numbers or used SIP URIs. This feature can be used later to socially cluster profiles into groups. Here, we will need dynamic storage for this feature such as lists since we do not know a priori how many different numbers are called by one subscriber. We can also add a rule to limit the dimension of the list to a threshold number (e.g., 100 extensions a day), that is to generate an alarm if this threshold is bypassed. After filling the list, we sort it out and store only the K-top couples (extension, frequency).
- Number of calls per period of time: We segment the whole day into 4 intervals
  - **Night:** [00am-06am]
  - **Morning:** [06am-12am]
  - **Afternoon:** [12pm-06pm]
  - **Evening:** [06pm-00am]

We compute the number of calls starting within each interval. 4 values are computed for the weekend prototype, 2 for the working day and 2 for the night. The values are divided by the total number of calls. Furthermore, we compute the mean number of calls, the mean duration and the mean inter-arrival time for each interval.

Example: Let us compute this feature for the prototype "working days" for a duration of 2 days: user A has 4 calls in the morning and 8 calls in the afternoon of day 1 and has 6 calls in the morning and 10 calls in afternoon of day 2. The resulting feature is:

Morning: $(4+6)/(4+6+10+8)=10/28$
Afternoon: $18/28$

- Percentage of called destination numbers: This is a categorical feature since destination numbers are grouped into categories. In traditional telephony, there was only one operator that covered one country. The used categories are: local, national and international. After the emergence of the mobile telephony followed by broadband providers, the peering topology should be better expressed in the categorization scheme, for example by using local (within the same operator's network), national fixed (towards other operators), national mobile, international fixed, international mobile, toll free, and premium numbers. In the most general case of VoIP (where we have PC-to-PC calls as well as PC-to-phone ones), we suggest that the categorization scheme reflects the price plan of both the operator and the subscribers. In fact, there are (at least) two faces of the price plan: what the subscribers pay to the operator and what the operator pays to the other provider peers. Let's assume there are two kinds of the superimposed fraud: positive and negative: in the first, the fraudster tries to augment his own gain; in the second, he tries to augment the loss of the provider (i.e., by abusing the flat rate offer). The fraud detection has two goals as well: reduce the amount of fraud paid by the operator, and also reduce the superimposed fraud on the subscribers. For instance, we propose the following categories:

○ Totally free calls (including SIP-2-SIP, calls to operator, emergency and free SIP-2-PSTN),
○ Free calls but paid by the operator,
○ Paid calls (range one: mostly fixed destinations). This can be further categorized to calls within Europe, calls to North America, calls to other destinations (Asia, Africa, etc.) and calls to high risk destinations.
○ Paid calls (range two: mostly mobile destinations),
○ Premium (over-charged) calls.

Here, we will also distinguish in calls between weekday daytime, weekday nighttime, and weekends

- Number of calls towards suspected or blacklisted destinations/countries based on previous fraud cases. For each category we compute the number of calls divided by the total number of calls;
- Number of calls to premium numbers,
- Call duration: This is a continuous variable. We divide the range of this variable to the following intervals:
  ○ less than 1 min
  ○ between 1 and 2 min
  ○ between 2 and 4 min
  ○ between 4 and 7 min
  ○ beyond 7 min

We compute the number of calls belonging to each interval and we divide it by the total number of calls for each destination category above. We can also reduce the signature by computing only 5 values over all the calls.

- Mean and standard deviation of call duration: for each of the destination categories above.

Signature Updating and Decay Factors

Signatures updating requires two sliding windows: one describing long-term behavior (e.g., one week or one month) and a second one describing a short-term behavior (one day, for instance). The signatures (long and short term) will be compared over time using appropriate distances. The update of these signatures is made in a regular way (for instance every day).

Updating a signature consists of setting a scheme for updating the different feature values. Most of the features we have chosen are scalar (number of calls having their start-time in a specific time frame, number of calls having their destinations in a specific category, number of calls having their durations in a specific interval, mean and standard deviation of call duration) except the K-most frequent destinations. Scalar features are updated based on the comparison of the short and long term signatures. If an outlier (i.e, a suspicious behavior) is met, the features are not updated which means we keep the values of the previous long-term signature. If no outlier is met, the new long-term signature is just a weighted combination of the previous long-term signature and the current short term signature.

To update a categorical view, we use the probabilistic bumping algorithm proposed in (Cortes & Pregibon, 2001): At each moment in time, we have an item to move from the list of the top frequent destinations.

This item is chosen based on frequency and recency (i.e., an item that is added recently is not chosen). This is represented by a probability value. When we have to add a new item to the list (e.g., after a new signature is computed, one new destination is in the top K list), we choose a random number and compare it to the probability associated with the chosen item. If the random number is greater, we proceed with the replacement.

Signature Initialization and Subscription Fraud Detection

The signature initialization can be straightforward: we compute a signature with the first set of transactions, and then we start to update it periodically (time-based). The problem is that in the subscription fraud, the subscriber creates an account and starts to abuse the service directly because he has no intention to pay. There will not be a large shift in behavior while updating the signature since the subscriber will start an abnormal behavior from the beginning on and will stay in this behavior. Therefore, we need to verify the initial signature using a rule-based approach or by comparing it to known fraudsters profiles. If the subscriber is residential (private) we compare its signature to a set of normal profiles of residential users; if it is business (professional, enterprise with many employees using the service) we compare its signature to a set of normal business profiles. A deeper verification is to compare the signature of the new subscriber to a group of profiles based on customer data such as age, family situation and location. An alarm is raised if the initialized signature doesn't belong to any of the normal groups.

Detecting Deviation in Users' Signatures

A detection algorithm has for mission to compare the long-term and the short-term signatures for each subscriber based on the computed signatures. If any deviation is met, an alarm is generated. As different algorithms related to the different features within a signature might be applied, the corresponding results will be correlated and combined in order to avoid conflicts and false alarms.

Distances

In order to compare two signatures, a distance metric is required. The following formula is used to aggregate the distances between individual features into an overall distance metric,

$$d\left(S,C\right) = \alpha_1 f_1\left(Sa,Ca\right) + \alpha_2 f_2\left(Sb,Cb\right) \\ + \alpha_3 f_3\left(Sc,Cc\right) + \alpha_4 f_4\left(Sd,Cd\right)$$

(1)

where S represents the long term signature and C the short term one where the individual features are denoted as Sa, Sb.. and Ca, Cb... The α coefficients are used for weighting and normalization (e.g., we can give more weight to the mean call duration over a number of calls. Similarly we can give more weight to the number of calls towards premium telephone numbers over number of calls towards free destinations). The f_i are distance functions for individual features. An alarm is raised if $d\left(S,C\right) >$ *threshold*. Still, choosing good coefficients makes the use of this scheme a challenge.

Different distances are proposed in the literature to compute different kinds of features related distances, however, in this context, we will only describe the Hellinger distance,

Hellinger Distance

In probability and statistics, the Hellinger distance is used to quantify the similarity between two probability distributions. In our context, the distance is defined between vectors (or tuples) having only positive or zero elements denoting the different features. Here we consider features as probability distributions. This distance is suitable for scalar features computed over different bins or intervals (e.g., distribution of destination numbers, distribution of start-time, and distribution of call duration).

Other probabilistic distances can also be used (e.g., Mahalonobis, Patrick-Fisher, Matusita, Divergence (Jain & Dubes, 1988) (Kittler, 1986)).

Clustering

The user accounts are naturally divided into different groups based on their account type (residential, professional) or on their social activities. Users belonging to the same group may have the same response for a set of context changes (e.g., holidays, weekend). This response is reflected in the calls activities (e.g., a rise in the number of calls and the average call duration, or inversely). By using clustering techniques, we aim to discover these groups and track users that appear to abnormally change their groups. For example, a residential profile that moves towards a professional profile may reveal a service plan misuse. A profile that suddenly changes its social clique may reveal that the account has been compromised. The advantage of the clustering techniques is to provide the variations of other users as a baseline, thus eliminating the bias caused by special contexts.

We distinguish two types of clustering analysis: static clustering is applied to determine clusters characteristics, and dynamic clustering is provided to identify changes on cluster membership over time.

Basically the clustering techniques map the callers into a n-dimensional feature space where each feature represents a call activity variable, as shown in Figure 2. A clustering algorithm is then applied in order to assign the callers to different groups. The clustering module in SCAMSTOP provides a framework to test different static and dynamic clustering techniques. Next we mention some interesting approaches that we intend to test in our framework.

In (Ferreira P. G., Alves, Belo, & Ribeiro, 2007), the authors address dynamic clustering of user profiles or signatures. Their approach is based on a number of fixed centroids or anchors. Signatures are assigned to the nearest centroid's cluster. The authors highlight that not every migration should be reported as an anomaly. Instead, they consider that a signature S is anomalous when its variation over a time period t, is outside the range $[M - 2 \partial; M + 2 \partial]$. M and ∂ are respectively the average and the standard deviation for the variations of all the signatures belonging to the same cluster.

Since one of the requirements of SCAMSTOP is to be able to handle large multi-dimensional datasets while minimizing the needed resources in terms of memory and I/O processing, we consider applying scalable clustering algorithms such as BIRCH (Zhang, Ramakrishnan, & Livny, 1996). BIRCH has the advantage to proceed on cluster-

Figure 2. Clustering concept

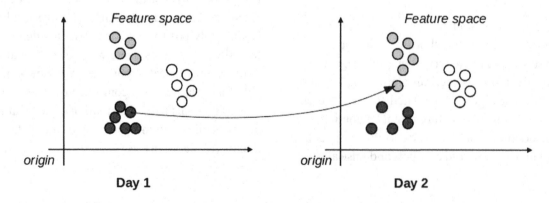

ing in an incrementally and dynamically manner. The algorithm produces a best-effort clustering with respect to the available resources and time constraints. The results are then improved when new resources are available.

Preliminary Tests

In this part, we will provide some early results related to some testing activities that we carried out when implementing both signature-based and clustering techniques.

Signature-Based Technique Performance

In these experiments, we analyze only one feature, namely the number of calls. This feature is calculated for all the callers of one VoIP provider during a month. We start by showing the overall activities in terms of the number of calls for this provider during this month. This activity is depicted in Figure 3. It is worth to mention that the data used here come from a VoIP provider that is a member of the SCAMSTOP consortium.

We see in this figure that the weekend traffic is negligible compared to the weekday one, hence the necessity to separate the behavior of callers in weekends from their behavior in weekdays.

We calculate the number of calls for each caller and for each day during one month. We have identified about 3645 different callers. In order to automatically filter out the most suspicious cases, we have defined two heuristics:

1. The caller has two different behaviors during the month.
2. The two behaviors occur in two separate periods of time (e.g., the first behavior occurs in the first half of the month while the second behavior occurs during the second half).

We took into account only the workdays because as mentioned earlier, the weekdays have completely different patterns.

The first heuristic is based on a one-class support vector machines (SVM) using the linear and hyperplane formulation (Chang & Lin, 2001). The SVM labels the days as belonging to class (-1) (high activities) and class (+1) (low activities).

We represent the first heuristic by a score (s1). We calculate s1 as the absolute sum of labels of all the days. Obviously, s1 is smaller when the two classes are of nearly equal sizes.

The second heuristic is represented by a score (s2) based on the number of days in intersection between the period of the first behavior and the period of the second behavior. The period of a behavior is defined by the time between the first day and the last day belonging to this behavior class. For example, if the first behavior takes place

Figure 3. Analysis related to the number of calls

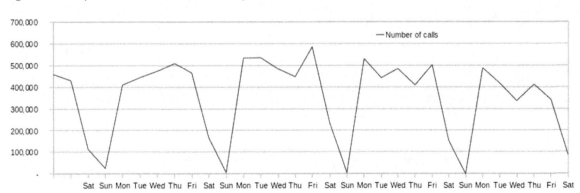

between the 2nd and the 31st of the month and the second behavior occurs between the 1st and the 5th of the month. The two behaviors have 4 days of intersection. Note that the weekend days are not taken into account. Obviously, s2 is smaller when the two behaviors occur during two different periods of time.

Since s1 and s2 have the same order of magnitude (number of weekdays during the month), we merge the two heuristics into one score s = s1 + s2. The suspicious callers are the ones having a low score s.

Next, we comment the 4 top suspicious cases in terms of our heuristics.

We show in Figure 4 a churn case.

In the case of Figure 5 the caller disappears completely. The user has probably gone in holidays or moved to another operator.

In the case of Figure 6, the activities of the caller increase. This can be a fraud case or a mere increase in the activities of the caller. Notice that there are no calls during weekends. This is typical for professional users.

In Figure 7 the caller passes from no calls at all to a small amount of calls and then to a more significant activities. Probably this is a merely new caller.

Still, if we have an unexpected number of new callers, this may indicate some fraud types (e.g., cloning accounts).

Clustering-Based Technique Performance

In the following, we show preliminary tests of static clustering using the K-means algorithm. For our tests, we use the WEKA Java library (Hall, Frank, Holmes, Pfahringer, Reutemann, & Witten, 2009).

As a first experiment, we test one-dimensional clustering using only the number of calls feature. This statistic is calculated for all the callers over a month period. The histogram in Figure 8 shows the results of 10-means clustering (using the Euclidian distance, and minimizing the in-cluster sum of squared errors). Each bar represents the number of members for a cluster. The clusters are ordered from the nearest to the farthest from the origin and are represented at the x-labels by their respective centroids. The histogram shows that the

Figure 4. Case of churn

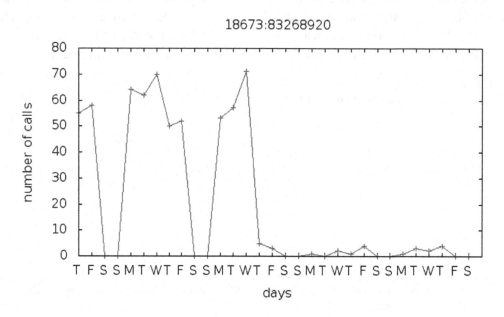

Figure 5. Case of a lost caller

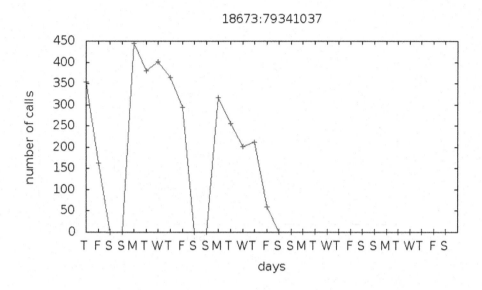

Figure 6. Case of increase in call activities

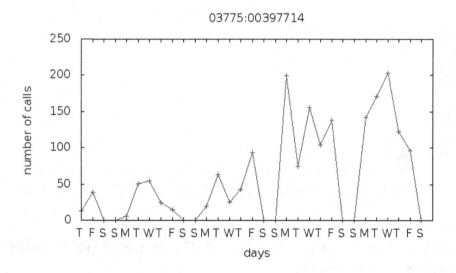

majority of the users are naturally clustered into the two clusters near the origin (more than 92% of the callers). The other clusters are formed by few call centers having large numbers of calls.

We have also tested the K-means algorithm in a 3dimensional space composed of the following features:

1. The number of calls
2. The success rate of the calls
3. The average duration of the calls.

These three statistics are calculated over a month period. The 3 facets of 3-Means clustering (using the Euclidian Distance with normalization, and minimizing the within cluster sum of squared

Figure 7. Case of a new caller

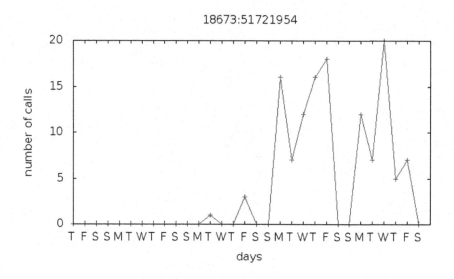

Figure 8. Histogram of 10-Means clustering of the number of calls for one month data

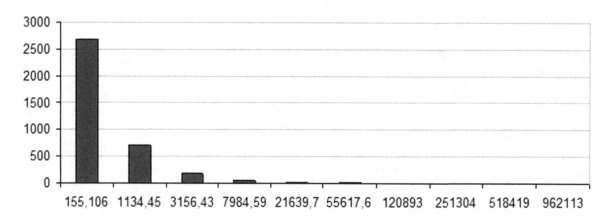

errors) is shown in Figures 9, 10 and 11. The cluster 1 ('triangles' pointing down) (9% of the callers) contains the member having the largest number of calls but it is more characterized by small success ratio and average duration. The cluster 2 ('triangles' pointing to the right) (41% of the callers) has medium success ratio and average duration. The cluster 3 ('squares') (50% of the callers) contains the members having small number of calls with high success rate and high average duration.

FUTURE RESEARCH DIRECTIONS

The framework discussed in this book chapter is being developed in the context of the European FP7 project SCAMSTOP (contract number: 232458, website: www.sme-scamstop.eu). The architecture is already specified and some related features were discussed in this document. The development phase just started, however some early results were also included in previous sections. The implementation issues we are currently addressing can be summarized as follows:

Figure 9. Number of calls vs. average duration of 3-D clustering over one month data

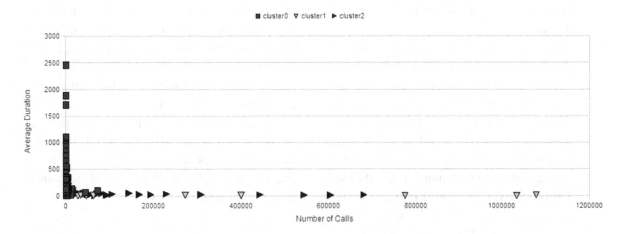

Figure 10. Number of calls vs. success ratio of 3-D clustering over one month data

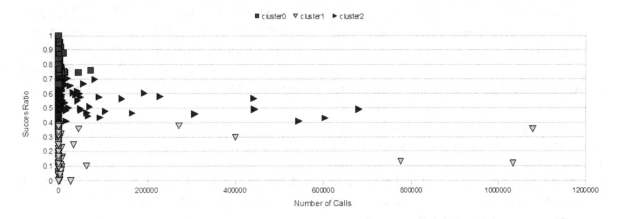

Figure 11. Success ratio vs. average duration of 3-D clustering over one month data

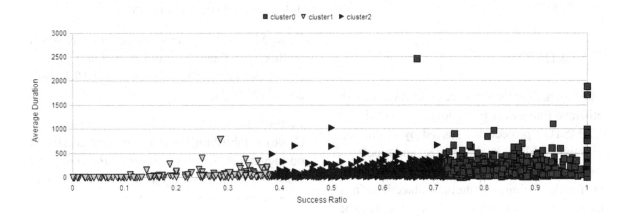

- How to make the platform scalable to process a huge amount of data in a short period of time
- How to test the signature-based and the clustering techniques without some prior knowledge about concrete fraud scenarios
- How to build efficient and scalable dynamic clustering in order to detect abnormal migrations caused by fraud scenarios. One approach is to identify callers that have similar call activities under two different contexts (for instance workdays and weekends) and assign them to the same cluster. For instance, the K-Nearest Neighbors (K-NN) algorithm can be used to assign for each caller a set of neighbors who share similar variations. However, the scalability of the K-NN over a large data-set is in question.

Another problem is to define when cluster migration would be malicious. We expect that by monitoring the clustering membership over a long period time, we can identify callers that are stable (i.e. always stay in the same cluster) from callers that alternates between 2 or 3 clusters. In both cases, moving to a merely new cluster should be remarked. Another approach is to compare the variation of the call activities of a caller with respect to the variations of all the members of the same cluster.

CONCLUSION

In this book chapter, we gave an overview of an anti-fraud framework being developed within the SCAMSTOP project. We started by discussing the fraud problem, its scope, size, and typology. After that, we have shorty assessed the existing anti-fraud techniques. As the main objective of this chapter is to give an overview of how fraud can be addressed in the context of VoIP networks, we put more light on the VoIP technologies, the difficulties to fight against fraud in such environments, the tools that can be used to carry out fraud activities, and the problems that might be a handicap in detecting such threats. We also listed the types of data needed for an efficient detection. After giving an overview of the SCAMSTOP framework, we investigated in more details how unsupervised methods such as signature-based and clustering-based techniques are being implemented in our framework. Finally, some conducted preliminary tests were discussed.

REFERENCES

Abbott, D. W., Matkovsky, I. P., & Elder, J. F. (1998). An evaluation of high-end data mining tools for fraud detection. *Proceedings of IEEE International Conference on Systems, Man, and Cybernetics*, Vol. 3, (pp. 2836 -2841). San Diego, CA.

Bolton, R. J., & Hand, D. J. (2002). *Statistical fraud detection: A review.*

Chang, C., & Lin, C. (2001). *LIBSVM: A library for support vector machines.*

Cortes, C., & Pregibon, D. (2001, July). Signature-based methods for data streams. *Data Mining and Knowledge Discovery*, 5(3), 167–182. doi:10.1023/A:1011464915332

Edge, M. E. (2009). A survey of signature based methods for financial fraud detection. *Computers & Security*, 28, 381–394. doi:10.1016/j.cose.2009.02.001

Ferreira, P., Alves, R., Belo, O., & Cortesão, L. (2006). Establishing fraud detection patterns based on signatures. In *Proceedings of the Industrial Conference on Data Mining, Lecture Notes in Computer Science, Vol. 4065*, (pp. 526-538).

Ferreira, P. G., Alves, R., Belo, O., & Ribeiro, J. (2007). Detecting telecommunications fraud based on signature clustering analysis. *Proceedings of Business Intelligence Workshop of 13th Portugese Conference on Artificial Intelligence.*

Gopal, R. K., & Meher, S. K. (2007). A rule-based approach for anomaly detection in subscriber usage pattern. *Proceedings of World Academy of Science, Engineering and Technology,* (p. 25).

Hall, M., Frank, E., Holmes, G., Pfahringer, B., Reutemann, P., & Witten, I. H. (2009, November). The WEKA data mining software: An update. *SIGKDD Explorations Newsletter, 11*(1), 10–18. doi:10.1145/1656274.1656278

He, H., Wang, J., Graco, W., & Hawkins, S. (1997). Application of neural networks to detection of medical fraud. *Expert Systems with Applications, 13,* 329–336. doi:10.1016/S0957-4174(97)00045-6

Hilas, C. S., & Sahalos, J. N. (2005). User profiling for fraud detection in telecommunication networks. *Fifth International Conference on Technology and Automation,* (pp. 382-387).

Hollmén, J. (2000, December). *User profiling and classification for fraud detection in mobile communications networks.* Dissertation for the degree of Doctor of Science in Technology, Helsinki University of Technology, Department of Computer Science and Engineering.

Jain, A. K., & Dubes, R. C. (1988). *Algorithms for clustering data.* Prentice-Hall, Inc.

Kittler, J. (1986). Feature selection and extraction. In Young, T. Y., & Fu, K. S. (Eds.), *Handbook of pattern recognition* (pp. 59–83). New York, NY: Academic Press.

Lee, S. C., & Heinbuch, D. V. (2001, July). Training a neural-network based intrusion detector to recognize novel attacks. *IEEE Transactions on Systems, Man, and Cybernetics. Part A, Systems and Humans, 31,* 294–299. doi:10.1109/3468.935046

Li, J., Huang, K.-Y., Jin, J., & Shi, J. (2008). A survey on statistical methods for health care fraud detection. *Health Care Management Science, 11*(3), 275–287. doi:10.1007/s10729-007-9045-4

Rebahi, Y., Fiedler, J., & Gouveia, F. (2010). *Fraud in VoIP networks: Size and scope.* Project Deliverable. http://www.sme-scamstop.eu/contributions/SCAMSTOP_D2.1.public.pdf

Rivest, R. (1992, April). The MD5 message-digest algorithm. *IETF RFC 1321.*

Rosenberg, J., & Schulzrinne, H. (2002, June). SIP: Session initiation protocol. *IETF RFC 3261.*

Sanver, M., & Karahoca, A. (2007, July 18-24). Fraud detection using an adaptive neuro-fuzzy inference system in mobile telecommunication networks. *Proceedings of the 10th Joint Conference on Information Science,* (pp. 1440-1446). Utah, USA.

Vapnik, V. (1998). *Statistical learning theory.* John Wiley and Sons.

Verrelst, H., Lerouge, E., Moreau, E., Vandewalle, J., Störmann, C., & Burge, P. (1996). *A rule based and neural network system for fraud detection in mobile communications. ACTS PROJECT AC095 ASPeCT.* European Commission.

Zhang, T., Ramakrishnan, R., & Livny, M. (1996). BIRCH: An efficient data clustering method for very large databases. *Proceedings of the 1996 ACM SIGMOD International Conference on Management of Data* (pp. 103-114). ACM.

ADDITIONAL READING

Bella, B., Eloff, J. P., & Olivier, M. S. (2009). *A fraud management system architecture for next-generation networks*. Forensic Science International.

Boukerche, A., & Notare, M. S. (2000). *Neural fraud detection in mobile phone operations* (pp. 636–644). Springer-Verlag.

Fawcett, T., & Provost, F. (1997, January). Adaptive fraud detection. *Data Mining and Knowledge Discovery*, *1*(3), 291–316. doi:10.1023/A:1009700419189

He, H., Wang, J., Graco, W., & Hawkins, S. (1997). Application of neural networks to detection of medical fraud. *Expert Systems with Applications*, *13*, 329–336. doi:10.1016/S0957-4174(97)00045-6

Jing-Xin, W., Zhi-Ying, W., & Kui, D. (2004). *A network intrusion detection system based on the artificial neural networks* (pp. 166–170). ACM.

Kou, Y., Lu, C.-T., Sirwongwattana, S., & Huang, Y.-P. (2004). Survey of fraud detection techniques. *2004 IEEE International Conference on Networking, Sensing and Control,* (Vol. 2, pp. 749—754).

Krenker, A., Volk, M., Sedlar, U., Bešter, J., & Kos, A. (2009, Feb). Bidirectional artificial neural networks for mobile-phone fraud detection. *ETRI Journal*, *31*(1), 92–94. doi:10.4218/etrij.09.0208.0245

McGibney, J., & Hearne, S. (2003). *An approach to rules based fraud management in emerging converged networks. Waterford Institute of Technology.* Ireland: Telecommunications Software & Systems Group.

Moradi, M., & Zulkernine, M. (2003). *A neural network based system for intrusion detection and classification of attacks*. Retrieved from http://research.cs.queensu.ca/~moradi/148-04-MM-MZ.pdf

Moreau, Y., Stoermann, C., & Ag, S. (1996). *Novel techniques for fraud detection in mobile telecommunication networks*.

Murad, U., & Pinkas, G. (1999). *Unsupervised profiling for identifying superimposed fraud* (pp. 251–261). Springer-Verlag.

Olusegun, O. I. (May 2005). *Telecommunication fraud detection using Bayesian networks*. Thesis, Muizenberg, Cape Town, South Africa: African Institute for Mathematical Sciences.

Quinlan, J. R. (1986, March). Induction of decision trees. *Machine Learning*, *1*(1), 81–106. doi:10.1007/BF00116251

Quinlan, J. R. (1993). *C4.5: Programs for machine learning*. Morgan Kaufmann Publishers Inc.

Rosset, S., Murad, U., Neumann, E., Idan, Y., & Pinkas, G. (1999). *Discovery of fraud rules for telecommunications - Challenges and solutions* (pp. 409–413). ACM Press.

Williams, G. J., & Huang, Z. (1997). *Mining the knowledge mine: The hot spots methodology for mining large real world databases* (pp. 340–348). Springer-Verlag.

KEY TERMS AND DEFINITIONS

CDR: A Call Data Record is simply the information describing a call. A CDR includes for instance information like the originating and terminating phone numbers, the start date and time as well as the duration of the call.

Clustering: Clustering starts by mapping the users to an n-dimensional feature space where each feature represents a call activity variable. A clustering algorithm is then applied in order to assign the users to different groups.

FDS: A Fraud Detection System is in general a comprehensive solution for organizations to mitigate risks from frauds concerning identity and service usage.

Fraud: Fraud is any activity leading to the obtaining of financial advantages or causing of losses by implicit or explicit deception. *Signature*: A signature is a data structure capturing the typical behavior of a service user in terms of type of use, length of use, and frequently of use.

SIP: The session Initiation protocol (SIP) is an application-layer control protocol that allows to create, modify, and terminate sessions with one or more participants.

VoIP: Voice over IP (VoIP) is the technology allowing telephone calls to be made over computer networks like the Internet.

ENDNOTE

[1]   http://www.sme-scamstop.eu/

Compilation of References

3 GPP WG. (2006). *IP multimedia subsystem Cx and Dx interfaces: Signaling flows and message contents.* 3GPP TS 29.228, Release 7, v7.6.0.

3 GPP WG. (2011). *3rd generation partnership project.* Retrieved from http://www.3gpp.org

Abawajy, J. H. (2004). Fault-tolerant scheduling policy for grid computing systems. *Proceedings of 18th International Parallel and Distributed Processing Symposium*, (pp. 238-244). doi: 10.1109/IPDPS.2004.1303290

Abbott, D. W., Matkovsky, I. P., & Elder, J. F. (1998). An evaluation of high-end data mining tools for fraud detection. *Proceedings of IEEE International Conference on Systems, Man, and Cybernetics*, Vol. 3, (pp. 2836 -2841). San Diego, CA.

Abdelal, A., & Matragi, W. (2010). Signal-based overload control for SIP servers. In *Proceedings of IEEE CCNC*, Las Vegas, NV.

Akyildiz, I., Su, W., Sankarasubramaniam, Y., & Cayirci, E. (2002, March). Wireless sensor networks: A survey. *Computer Networks, 38*, 393–422. doi:10.1016/S1389-1286(01)00302-4

Al-Jaljouli, R., & Abawajy, J. (2007). Secure mobile agent-based e-negotiation for online trading. *Proceedings of the 7th IEEE International Symposium on Signal Processing and Information Technology (ISSPIT 2007)*, (pp. 610-615).

Al-Jaljouli, R., & Abawajy, J. (2007). *Electronic negotiation and security of exchanged information in e-commerce. Technical Report TR C07/12.* Deakin University, School of Engineering and Information Technology.

Al-Jaljouli, R., & Abawajy, J. (2010). *Negotiation strategy for agent-based E-negotiation. Proceedings of Principles and Practice of Multi-Agent Sytems*. PRIMA.

Alomari, R., Somani, A. K., & Manimaran, G. (2004). Efficient overloading techniques for primary-backup scheduling in real-time systems. *Journal of Parallel and Distributed Computing, 64*(5), 629–648. doi:10.1016/j.jpdc.2004.03.015

Alonistioti, N. Patouni, E., & Gazis, V. (2006). Generic architecture and mechanisms for protocol reconfiguration. *Mobile Network Applications, 11*(6), 917-934. doi: http://dx.doi.org/10.1007/s11036-006-0058-x

Amooee, A. M., & Falahati, A. (2009). Overcoming overload in IMS by employment of multiserver nodes and priority queues. In *Proceedings of International Conference on Signal Processing Systems*, (pp. 348-352).

Ando, R. (2010, December 22). Internet phone and video service Skype went down in a global service outage. *Reuters News*. Retrieved from http://www.reuters.com/article/idUSTRE6BL47520101222

Apache. (2001). *Byte code engineering library*. Retrieved March, 1, 2011, from http://jakarta.apache.org/bcel/

AppZero. (2010). *AppZero virtual application appliances (VAA)*. Retrieved March, 1, 2011, from http://www.appzero.com/

Ardagna, C. A., Cremonini, M., Damiani, E., Vimercati, S. D. C., & Samarati, P. (2007). *Location privacy protection through obfuscation-based techniques*. In IFIP WG 11.3 Working Conference on Data and Applications Security.

Aust, S., Fikouras, N. A., Sessinghaus, M., & Pampu, C. (2004). *Hierarchical mobile IP NS-2 extensions for mobile ad hoc networks*. 4th IASTED International Multi-Conference on Wireless Networks and Emerging Technologies (WNET 2004).

Baek, J., & Lee, E. (2006). A dynamic authentication, authorization, and accounting (AAA) resolution for hierarchical mobile IPv6 network. *IJCSNS International Journal of Computer Science and Network Security, 6*(7B)

Baek, S.-J., & Park, J.-T. (2004). *Efficient micro-mobility support for wireless network using improved host-based routing*. Berlin, Germany: Springer-Verlag.

Balakrishnan, P., & Somasundaram, T. (2011). SLA enabled CARE resource broker. *Future Generation Computer Systems, 27*(3), 265–279. doi:10.1016/j.future.2010.09.006

Balasubramanian, J., Gokhale, A., Wolf, F., Dubey, A., Lu, C., Gill, C., & Schmidt, D. C. (2009). *Resource-aware deployment and configuration of fault-tolerant real-time systems*. ISIS Technical Report ISIS-09-109. Retrieved from http://www.isis.vanderbilt.edu/node/4121

Balazinska, M., Hwang, J. H., & Shah, M. A. (2009). Fault-tolerance and high availability in data stream management systems. In Liu, L., & Özsu, M. T. (Eds.), *Encyclopedia of database systems* (pp. 1109–1115). Springer, US.

Bamba, B., Liu, L., Pesti, P., & Wang, T. (2008). *Supporting anonymous location queries in mobile environments with PrivacyGrid*. In World Wide Web Conference.

Barr, J. (2008). *Cloudbursting - Hybrid application hosting*. Amazon Web Services Blog. Retrieved March, 1, 2011, from http://aws.typepad.com/aws/2008/08/cloudbursting-.html

Bass, L., Clements, P., & Kazman, R. (1998). *Software architecture in practice*. Boston, MA: Addison-Wesley Longman Publishing Co., Inc.

Beitollahi, H., & Deconinck, G. (2006). Fault-tolerant partitioning scheduling algorithms in real-time multiprocessor systems. *Proceedings of the 12th Pacific Rim International Symposium on Dependable Computing*, (pp. 296-304). doi: 10.1109/PRDC.2006.34.

Bellman, R. (1952). The theory of dynamic programming. *Proceedings of the National Academy of Sciences of the United States of America*, (pp. 716-719).

Bellman, R., & Zadeh, L. A. (1970). Decision making in fuzzy environment. *Journal of Management Science, 17*(4), 141–164. doi:10.1287/mnsc.17.4.B141

Bengt, S. (1997). *A Conduits+ and Java implementation of internet protocol security and internet protocol, version 6*. Retrieved from http://citeseer.ist.psu.edu/286786.html

Benoit, A., Hakem, M., & Robert, Y. (2008). Fault tolerant scheduling of precedence task graphs on heterogeneous platforms. *Proceedings of the 10th Workshop on Advances in Parallel and Distributed Computational Models*, (pp. 1-8). doi: 10.1109/IPDPS.2008.4536133

Benoit, A., Hakem, M., & Robert, Y. (2009). Contention awareness and fault-tolerant scheduling for precedence constrained tasks in heterogeneous systems. *Parallel Computing, 35*(2), 83–108. doi:10.1016/j.parco.2008.11.001

Beresford, A. R., & Stajano, F. (2003). Location privacy in pervasive computing. *IEEE Pervasive Computing / IEEE Computer Society and IEEE Communications Society, 2*(1), 46–55. doi:10.1109/MPRV.2003.1186725

Berhe, G., Brunie, L., & Pierson, J.-M. (2005). Content adaptation in distributed multimedia systems. *Journal of Digital Information Management: Special Issue on Distributed Data Management, 3*(2), 96–100.

Berlemann, L., Pabst, R., Schinnenburg, M., & Walke, B. (2005). Reconfigurable multi-mode protocol reference model for optimized mode convergence. *Proceedings of European Wireless Conference 2005* (Vol. 1, pp. 280-286). Nicosia, Cyprus. Retrieved from http://www.comnets.rwth-aachen.de

Berlemann, L., Pabst, R., & Walke, B. (2005). Multimode communication protocols enabling reconfigurable radios. *EURASIP Journal on Wireless Communications and Networking, 5*(3), 390–400.

Berners-Lee, T. (2006, June 26). *Net neutrality: This is serious*. Retrieved March 9, 2011, from http://dig.csail.mit.edu/breadcrumbs/node/144

Bertossi, A. A., Mancini, L. V., & Rossini, F. (1999). Fault-tolerant rate-monotonic first-fit scheduling in hard-real-time systems. *IEEE Transactions on Parallel and Distributed Systems, 10*(9), 934–945. doi:10.1109/71.798317

Bertrand, J., Cruz, J. W., Majkrzak, B., & Rossano, T. (2002). CORBA delays in a software-defined radio. *IEEE Communications Magazine, 40*(2), 152–155. doi:10.1109/35.983922

Bhatti, N. T., Hiltunen, M. A., Schlichting, R. D., & Chiu, W. (1998). Coyote: A system for constructing fine-grain configurable communication services. *ACM Transactions on Computer Systems, 16*(4), 321–366. Retrieved from citeseer.ist.psu.edu/article/bhatti98coyote.htmldoi:10.1145/292523.292524

Bhoj, P., Singhal, S., & Chutani, S. (2001). SLA management in federated environment. *Journal of Computer Networks, 35*, 5–24. doi:10.1016/S1389-1286(00)00149-3

Bickle, J. (2000, December). *Software radio architecture (SRA) 2.0 technical overview*. Retrieved from http://www.sdrforum.org/

Blythe, J., Jain, S., Deelman, E., Gil, Y., Vahi, K., Mandal, A., & Kennedy, K. (2005). Task scheduling strategies for workflow-based applications in grids. *Proceedings of IEEE International Symposium on Cluster Computing and the Grid*, (pp. 759-767). doi: 10.1109/CCGRID.2005.1558639

Bogenfeld, E., & Gaspard, I. (2008). *Self-x in radio access networks*.

Bolton, R. J., & Hand, D. J. (2002). *Statistical fraud detection: A review*.

Bouabdallah, F., Bouabdallah, N., & Boutaba, R. (2009). On balancing energy consumption in wireless sensor networks. *IEEE Transactions on Vehicular Technology, 58*.

Bouchenak, S., & Hagimont, D. (2002). *Zero overhead Java thread migration* (Research Report No. RT-0261). INRIA. Retrieved March, 1, 2011, from http://hal.inria.fr/inria-00069913/en/

Braden, R., Faber, T., & Handley, M. (2002). *From protocol stack to protocol heap - Role-based architecture*. Retrieved from citeseer.ist.psu.edu/braden02from.html

Bradford, R., Kotsovinos, E., Feldmann, A., & Schiöberg, H. (2007). Live wide-area migration of virtual machines including local persistent state. In *Proceedings of the 3rd International Conference on Virtual Execution Environments* (pp. 169–179). New York, NY: ACM.

Brandic, I., Music, D., Leitner, P., & Dustdar, S. (2009). VieSLAF framework: enabling adaptive and versatile SLA-management. *Lecture Notes on Computer System, 5745*, 60–73. doi:10.1007/978-3-642-03864-8_5

Braun, P., Brzostowski, J., Kersten, G., Kim, J., Kowalczyk, R., Strecker, S., & Vahidov, R. (2006). E-negotiation systems and software agents: methods, models, and applications. In Gupta, J. N. D., Forgionne, G. A., & Mora, M. (Eds.), *Intelligent decision-making support systems: Foundation, applications, and challenges*. Heidelberg, Germany: Springer Decision Engineering Series. doi:10.1007/1-84628-231-4_15

Braun, P., & Rossak, W. (2004). *Mobile agents: Basic concepts, mobility models, and the Tracy toolkit*. San Francisco, CA: Morgan Kaufmann Publishers Inc.

Bulusu, N., Chou, C. T., Kanhere, S., Dong, Y., Sehgal, S., Sullivan, D., & Blazeski, L. (2008). *Participatory sensing in commerce: using mobile camera phones to track market price dispersion*. In UrbanSense Workshop Program at ACM Conference on Embedded Networked Sensor Systems.

Burke, J., Estrin, D., Hansen, M., Parker, A., Ramanathan, N., Reddy, S., & Srivastava, M. B. (2006). *Participatory sensing*. In ACM Conference on Embedded Networked Sensor Systems.

Busch, L., & Horstmann, I. (1997). A comment on issue-by-issue negotiation. *Journal of Games and Economic Behaviour, 19*, 144–148. doi:10.1006/game.1997.0543

Buyukkokten, O. (2002). Efficient web browsing on handheld devices using page and form summarization. *ACM Transactions on Information Systems, 20*(1), 82–115. doi:10.1145/503104.503109

Calisti, M. (2002). Constraint satisfaction techniques for negotiating agents. *Proceedings of AAMAS Workshop*.

Campbell, A. T., & Castellanos, J. G. (2000). *IP micromobility protocols*. ACM.

Campbell, A. T., Castellanos, J. G., Kim, S., & Wan, C.-Y. (2002). Comparison of IP micro-mobility protocols. *IEEE Wireless Communications, 9*(1), 72–82. doi:10.1109/MWC.2002.986462

Carvalho, M., Ekel, P., Martins, C., & Pereira, Jr. (2005). Fuzzy set-based multi objective allocation of resources: Solution algorithms and applications. *Invited talk from the 4th Congress of nonlinear analysis (WCNA 2004), 63*(5-7), 715-724.

Castro, M., & Liskov, B. (2002). Practical Byzantine fault tolerance and proactive recovery. *ACM Transactions on Computer Systems, 20*(4), 398–461. doi:10.1145/571637.571640

Cesaroni, G., Hamm, M., Simon, F., Vuagnin, G., Yampolskiy, M., Labedzki, M., & Wolski, M. (2008). *ISHARe: Prototype specification*. Géant Technical Report.

Chakrabarty, M., Misra, I., Saha, D., & Mukherjee, A. (2003). A comparative study of existing protocols supporting IP mobility. *Proceedings of the 4th World Wireless Congress (WWC 2003)*, San Francisco, USA, May 27-30, 2003. Retrieved from http://www.cse.unsw.edu.au/~nr/pub/papers/wwc03.pdf

Chang, C., & Lin, C. (2001). *LIBSVM: A library for support vector machines*.

Charilas, D., & Panagopoulos, A. (2010). A survey on game theory applications in wireless networks. *Computer Networks, 54*(18). doi:10.1016/j.comnet.2010.06.020

Chavez, A., Dreilinger, D., Guttman, R., & Maes, P. (1997). A real-life experiment in creating an agent marketplace. *Software Agents and Soft Computing*, 160-179.

Chen, L., Ma, T., Wang, C.-L., Lau, F. C. M., & Li, S. (2006). G-JavaMPI: A grid middleware for transparent MPI task migration. In di Martino, B., Dongarra, J., Hoisie, A., Yang, L. T., & Zima, H. (Eds.), *Engineering the Grid: Status and perspective*. Nova Science.

Chin, Y. Y., Lui, J. C., & Chen, S. (2008). A customer privacy protection protocol on agent-based electtronic commerce transaction. *Proceeding of 8th International Conference on Intelligent Systems Design and Applications (ISDA)*, Vol. 3, (pp. 6-10).

China National Grid (CNGrid). (2002). *Website*. Retrieved March, 1, 2011, from http://www.cngrid.org

Chow, C. Y., Mokbel, M., F., & Liu, X. (2006). A peer-to-peer spatial cloaking algorithm for anonymous location-based services. In *Proceedings of the 14th annual ACM International Symposium on Advances in Geographic Information Systems*, 2006.

Chu, Y., Tseng, C., Hung, C., Liao, K., Ouyang, C., Yen, C., et al. (October 2009). Application of load-balanced tree routing algorithm with dynamic modication to centralized wireless sensor networks. *IEEE Sensors*, (pp. 1392–1395). New Zealand.

Clark, C., Fraser, K., Hand, S., Hansen, J. G., Jul, E., Limpach, C., et al. (2005). Live migration of virtual machines. In *Proceedings of the 2nd Conference on Symposium on Networked Systems Design & Implementation* - Vol. 2 (pp. 273–286). Berkeley, CA: USENIX Association.

Clark, R. J., Ammar, M. H., & Calvert, K. L. (1997). Protocol discovery in multiprotocol networks. *Mobile Networks and Applications, 2*(3), 271-284. doi: http://dx.doi.org/10.1023/A:1013645019693

Clement, A., Marchetti, M., Wong, E., Alvisi, L., & Dahlin, M. (2008). Position paper: BFT: The time is now. *Proceedings of the 2nd Workshop on Large-Scale Distributed Systems and Middleware*, (pp. 1-4). doi: 10.1145/1529974.1529992

Cloudsoft. (2010). *Cloudsoft Monterey middleware for application mobility*. Retrieved March, 1, 2011, from http://www.cloudsoftcorp.com/

Commerce Commission. (2008, December). *Discussion paper on next generation networks*. New Zealand.

Cortes, C., & Pregibon, D. (2001, July). Signature-based methods for data streams. *Data Mining and Knowledge Discovery, 5*(3), 167–182. doi:10.1023/A:1011464915332

Cortes, M., Ensor, J. R., & Esteban, J. O. (2004). On SIP performance. *Bell Labs Technical Journal, 9*(3), 155–172. doi:10.1002/bltj.20048

Cristian, F. (1991). Understanding fault-tolerant distributed systems. *Communications of the ACM, 34*(2), 56–78. doi:10.1145/102792.102801

Cronk, D., Haines, M., & Mehrotra, P. (1996). *Thread migration in the presence of pointers* (Tech. Rep.).

Cunsolo, V. D., Distefano, S., Puliafito, A., & Scarpa, M. (2009). Volunteer computing and desktop cloud: The cloud@home paradigm. In *Proceedings of the 8th IEEE International Symposium on Network Computing and Applications* (pp. 134–139).

Dacosta, I., & Traynor, P. (2010). Proxychain: Developing a robust and efficient authentication infrastructure for carrier-scale VoIP networks. In *Proceedings of the USENIX Annual Technical Conference*, Boston, MA.

Dacosta, I., Balasubramaniyan, V., Ahamad, M., & Traynor, P. (2009). Improving authentication performance of distributed SIP proxies. In *Proceedings of IPTComm*, Atlanta, GA.

Damianou, N., Dulay, N., Lupu, E., & Sloman, M. (2001). The Ponder policy specification language. *International Workshop on Policies for Distributed Systems and Network, LNCS 1995*, (pp. 18-38).

Das, S., McAuley, A., Dutta, A., Misra, A., Chakraborty, K., & Das Sajal, K. (2002). IDMP: An intra-domain mobility management protocol for next generation wireless networks. *Wireless Communications, 9*(3). doi:10.1109/MWC.2002.1016709

Dastjerdi, A., Tabatabaei, S., & Buyya, R. (2010). An effective architecture for automated appliance management system applying ontology-based cloud discovery. *10ᵗʰ IEEE/ACM International Conference onCluster, Cloud and Grid Computing* (pp.104-112). New York, NY: IEEE Press.

David, K., Eardley, P., Hetzer, D., Mihailovic, A., Suihko, T., & Wagner, M. (1999). *First evaluation of IP based network architectures.* Second International Workshop on Broadband Radio Access for IP Based Network.

Deng, L., & Cox, L. P. (2009). Grocery bargain hunting through participatory sensing. In *Mobile Computing Systems and Applications*. Livecompare.

Denko, M. K., Yang, L. T., & Zhang, Y. (2009). *Autonomic computing and networking* (pp. 239–260). Springer.

Diab, A., Thiel, A. M., & Böringer, R. (2005). Evaluation of mobile IP fast authentication protocol compared to hierarchical mobile IP. *IEEE International Conference on Wireless and Mobile Computing, Networking and Communications,* (pp. 9-16).

Diab, A., & Mitschele-Thiel, A. (2004). *Minimizing mobile IP handoff latency* (p. 48). HET-NET.

Diab, A., Mitschele-Thiel, A., & Böringer, R. (2005). Comparison of signaling and packet forwarding overhead for HMIP and MIFA. *WWIC 2005. LNCS, 3510*, 12–21.

Dijkstra, E. (1959). *A note on two problems in connexion with graphs* (pp. 269–271). Numerische Mathematik.

Dima, C., Girault, A., Lavarenne, C., & Sorel, Y. (2001). Off-line real-time fault-tolerant scheduling. *Proceedings 9th Euromicro Workshop on Parallel and Distributed Processing,* (pp. 410-417). doi: 10.1109/EMPDP.2001.905069

Distributed Management Task Force. (2011). *DMTF standards.* Retrieved from http://www.dmtf.org/standards

DMTF Policy Working Group. (2009). *CIM simplified policy language (CIM-SPL), v1.0.0.0.* Retrieved from http://www.dmtf.org/sites/default/files/standards/documents/DSP0231_1.0.0.pdf

Dong, Y. F., Blazeski, L., Sullivan, D., Kanhare, S. S., Chou, C. T., & Bulusu, N. (2009). *PetrolWatch: Using mobile phones for sharing petrol prices.* In International Conference on Mobile Systems, Applications and Services.

Dong, Y. F., Kanhare, S. S., Chou, C. T., & Bulusu, N. (2008, June). *Automatic collection of fuel prices from a network of mobile cameras.* In IEEE International Conference on Distributed Computing in Sensor Systems.

Driscoll, K., Hall, B., Sivencrona, H., & Zumsteg, P. (2003). Byzantine fault tolerance, from theory to reality. *Lecture Notes in Computer Science, vol. 2788, Computer Safety, Reliability, and Security* (pp. 235-248). Berlin, Germany: Springer-Verlag. doi: 10.1007/978-3-540-39878-3_19

Duckham, M., & Kulik, L. (2005). Lecture Notes in Computer Science: *Vol. 3693. Simulation of obfuscation and negotiation for location privacy* (pp. 31–48).

Eardley, P., Georganopoulos, N., & West, M. A. (2002). On the scalability of micro-mobility management protocols. *4th International Workshop on Mobile and Wireless Communications Network,* (pp. 470–474). DOI: 10.1109/MWCN.2002.1045809

Eardley, P., Mihailovic, A., & Suihko, T. (2002). A framework for the evaluation of IP mobility protocols. *The 11th IEEE International Symposium on Personal, Indoor and Mobile Radio Communications, PIMRC 2000* (pp. 451 - 457). DOI:10.1109/PIMRC.2000.881465

Edge, M. E. (2009). A survey of signature based methods for financial fraud detection. *Computers & Security, 28*, 381–394. doi:10.1016/j.cose.2009.02.001

Ejzak, R. P., Florkey, C. K., & Hemmeter, R. W. (2004). Network overload and congestion: A comparison of ISUP and SIP. *Bell Labs Technical Journal, 9*(3), 173–182. doi:10.1002/bltj.20049

Elnozahy, E. N., Alvisi, L., Wang, Y. M., & Johnson, D. B. (2002). A survey of rollback-recovery protocols in message-passing systems. *ACM Computing Surveys, 34*(3), 375–408. doi:10.1145/568522.568525

Estrin, D., Girod, L., Pottie, G., & Srivastava, M. (May 2001). Instrumenting the world with wireless sensor networks. *International Conference on Acoustics, Speech, and Signal Processing (ICASSP)*, (pp. 2033–2036).

Faccin, S. M., Lalwaney, P., & Patil, B. (2004). IP multimedia services: Analysis of mobile IP and SIP interactions in 3G networks. *IEEE Communications Magazine, 42*(1), 113–120. doi:10.1109/MCOM.2004.1262170

Fang, W., Wang, C.-L., & Lau, F. C. M. (2003, November). On the design of global object space for efficient multithreading Java computing on clusters. *Parallel Computing, 29*, 1563–1587. doi:10.1016/j.parco.2003.05.007

Faratin, P., & Rodríguez-Aguilar, J. (2005). Agent-mediated electronic commerce VI, theories for and engineering of distributed mechanisms and systems. *Proceedings of AMEC- Revised Selected Papers, LNCS 3435*. Springer.

Faratin, P., Sierra, C., & Jennings, N. R. (1998). Negotiation decision functions for autonomous agents. *Journal of Robotics and Autonomous Systems, 24*(3-4), 159–182. doi:10.1016/S0921-8890(98)00029-3

Fatima, S., Wooldridge, M., & Jennings, N. (2002). Optimal negotiation strategies for agents with incomplete information. In J. J. Meyer & M. Tambe (Eds.), *Intelligent Agents VIII. Agent Theories, Architectures and Languages, Springer-Verlag, LNAI, Vol. 2333*, (pp. 377-392).

Fatima, S., Wooldridge, M., & Jennings, N. (2003). Optimal agendas for multi-issue negotiation. *Proceedings of the Second International Joint Conference on Autonomous Agents and Multi-agent Systems (AAMAS '03)*, (pp. 129-136).

Fatima, S., Wooldridge, M., & Jennings, N. (2004). An agenda based framework for multi-issue negotiation. *Journal of Artificial Intelligence, 152*(1), 1–45. doi:10.1016/S0004-3702(03)00115-2

Fatima, S., Wooldridge, M., & Jennings, N. (2006). Multi-issue negotiation with deadlines. *Journal of Artificial Intelligence Research, 6*, 381–417.

Fawaz, Y., Berhe, G., Brunie, L., Scuturici, V.-M., & Coquil, D. (2008). Efficient execution of service composition for content adaptation in pervasive computing. *International Journal of Digital Multimedia Broadcasting, 2008*, 1–10. doi:10.1155/2008/851628

Ferreira, P. G., Alves, R., Belo, O., & Ribeiro, J. (2007). Detecting telecommunications fraud based on signature clustering analysis. *Proceedings of Business Intelligence Workshop of 13th Portugese Conference on Artificial Intelligence.*

Ferreira, P., Alves, R., Belo, O., & Cortesão, L. (2006). Establishing fraud detection patterns based on signatures. In *Proceedings of the Industrial Conference on Data Mining, Lecture Notes in Computer Science, Vol. 4065*, (pp. 526-538).

Fershtman, C. (2000). A note on multi-issue two-sided bargaining: Bilateral procedures. *Journal of Games and Economic Behavior, 30*, 216–227. doi:10.1006/game.1999.0727

Fish, R. S., Graham, J. M., & Loader, R. J. (1998). DRoPS: Kernel support for runtime adaptable protocols. *EUROMICRO Conference, 2*, (pp. 210-29). Los Alamitos, CA: IEEE Computer Society. doi: http://doi.ieeecomputersociety.org/10.1109/EURMIC.1998.708137

Floyd, S. (2000). *RFC 2914 - Congestion control principle.* Retrieved from http://datatracker.ietf.org/doc/rfc2914/

Ford, B., Srisuresh, P., & Kegel, D. (2005). Peer-to-peer communication across network address translators. In *Proceedings of USENIX 2005 Annual Technical Conference* (pp. 172–192). Berkeley, CA: USENIX Association.

Frattasi, S., Fathi, H., & Fitzek, F. (2006). 4g: A user-centric system. *Special Issue on Advances in Wireless Communications: Enabling Technologies for 4G.*

Friedman, R., & van Renesse, R. (1996). Strong and weak virtual synchrony in Horus. In R. van Renesse (Ed.), *Proceedings of the Symposium on Reliable Distributed Systems* (pp. 140-149). doi: 10.1109/RELDIS.1996.559711

Fudenberg, D., & Tirole, J. (1991). *Game theory.* MIT Press.

Fuggetta, A., Picco, G. P., & Vigna, G. (1998, May). Understanding code mobility. *IEEE Transactions on Software Engineering, 24,* 342–361. doi:10.1109/32.685258

Gadzheva, M. (2008). Location privacy in a ubiquitous computing society. *International Journal of Electronic Business, 6*(5). doi:10.1504/IJEB.2008.021181

Gamma, E., Helm, R., Johnson, R., & Vlissides, J. (1995). *Design patterns: Elements of reusable object-oriented software.* Boston, MA: Addison-Wesley Longman Publishing Co., Inc.

Ganti, R. K., Pham, N., Tsai, Y., & Abdelzaher, T. F. (2008). *Poolview: Stream privacy for grassroots participatory sensing.* In ACM Conference on Embedded Networked Sensor Systems.

Gantz, J., & Reinsel, D. (2010). *The digital universe decade- Are you ready?* IDC Digital Universe Report May 2010. Retrieved Mac 21, 2011, from http://www.emc.com/digital_universe

Garroppo, R. G., Giordano, S., Spagna, S., & Niccolini, S. (2009). Queueing strategies for local overload control in SIP server. In *Proceedings of IEEE Globecom,* Honolulu, Hawaii.

Ge, X., & Dong, S. (2010). Analysis and research of the negotiation strategies based on time constraint. *Proceedings of the 2nd International Workshop on Intelligent Systems and Applications (ISA),* (pp. 1- 5).

Gedik, B., & Liu, L. (2005). *Location privacy in mobile systems: A personalized anonymization model.* In IEEE International Conference on Distributed Computing Systems.

Gehrke, J., & Madden, S. (March 2004). Query processing in sensor networks. *Pervasive Computing, 3.*

Geng, F., Wang, J., Zhao, L., & Wang, G. (2006). A SIP message overload transfer scheme. In *Proceedings of ChinaCom.*

Ghassemian, M., & Aghvami, A. H. (2002). *Comparing different handoff schemes in IP based micro- mobility protocols.* IST Mobile & Wireless Telecommunications Summit 2002. Thessaloniki. Greece.

Ghosh, S., Melhem, R., & Mosse, D. (1994). Fault-tolerant scheduling on a hard real-time multiprocessor system. *Proceedings of 8th International Parallel Processing Symposium,* (pp. 775-782). doi: 10.1109/IPPS.1994.288216

Ghosh, S., Melhem, R., & Mosse, D. (1997). Fault-tolerance through scheduling of aperiodic tasks in hard real time multiprocessor systems. *IEEE Transactions on Parallel and Distributed Systems, 8*(3), 272–284. doi:10.1109/71.584093

Gil Iranzo, R. (2005). *Agents negotiating in semantic web architecture* (SWA). Ph.D. Thesis. Technology Department, University Pompeu Fabra.

Girault, A., Kalla, H., Sighireanu, M., & Sorel, Y. (2003). An algorithm for automatically obtaining distributed and fault-tolerant static schedules. *Proceedings of 2003 International Conference on Dependable Systems and Networks,* (pp. 159-168). doi: 10.1109/DSN.2003.1209927.

Girault, A., Lavarenne, C., Sighireanu, M., & Sorel, Y. (2001). Fault-tolerant static scheduling for real-time distributed embedded systems. *Proceedings 21st International Conference on Distributed Computing Systems,* (pp. 695-698). doi: 10.1109/ICDSC.2001.919002

Gopal, R. K., & Meher, S. K. (2007). A rule-based approach for anomaly detection in subscriber usage pattern. *Proceedings of World Academy of Science, Engineering and Technology,* (p. 25).

Govind, M., Sundaragopalan, S., Binu, K. S., & Saha, S. (2003). Retransmission in SIP over UDP - Traffic engineering issues. In *Proceedings of International Conference on Communication and Broadband Networking,* Bangalore, India.

Grid Point, H. K. U. (2010). *The HKU grid point for systems research and applications in multiple disciplines.* Retrieved March, 1, 2011, from http://www.hku.hk/cc/events/gridpoint/en/about/about.htm

Guerraoui, R., & Schiper, A. (1996). Fault-tolerance by replication in distributed systems. *Proceedings of the 1996 Ada-Europe International Conference on Reliable Software Technologies*, (pp. 38-57). Retrieved from http://portal.acm.org/citation.cfm?id=697290

Gunasundari, R., & Shanmugavel, S. (2007). Influence of topology on micro mobility protocols for wireless networks. *ANSI Information Technology Journal, 6*(7), 966-977. ISSN 1812-5638

Gurbani, V., Hilt, V., & Schulzrinne, H. (2011). *Session initiation protocol (SIP) overload control*. IETF Internet-Draft, draft-ietf-soc-overload-control-02.

Guttman, R., Moukas, A., & Maes, P. (1998). Agent-mediated electronic commerce: a survey. *Journal of Knowledge Engineering Review, 13*(3).

Gwon, Y., Kempf, J., & Yegin, A. (2004). *Scalability and robustness analysis of mobile IPv6, fast mobile IPv6, hierarchical mobile IPv6, and hybrid IPv6 mobility protocols using a large-scale simulation* (pp. 4087–4091).

Hall, M., Frank, E., Holmes, G., Pfahringer, B., Reutemann, P., & Witten, I. H. (2009, November). The WEKA data mining software: An update. *SIGKDD Explorations Newsletter, 11*(1), 10–18. doi:10.1145/1656274.1656278

Hamed Kebriaei, H., & Majd, V. (2008). A simultaneous multi-attribute soft-bargaining design for bilateral contracts. *Journal of Expert Systems with Applications, 36*(3).

Hancock, R., Aghvami, H., Kojo, M., & Liljeberg, M. (2000). *The architecture of the BRAIN network layer.*

Han, Z., & Liu, R. (2007). Non-cooperative resource competition game by virtual referee in multi-cell OFDMA networks. *IEEE Journal on Selected Areas in Communications, 25*, 1079–1090. doi:10.1109/JSAC.2007.070803

Harvey, N., Ladner, R., Lovasz, L., & Tamir, T. (July 2003). *Semi-matchings for bipartite graphs and load balancing*. Workshop on Algorithms and Data Structures (WADS 2003), Canada.

Hashem, T., & Kulik, L. (2007). *Safeguarding location privacy in wireless ad-hoc networks*. In International Conference on Ubiquitous Computing.

Hashem, T., Kulik, L., & Zhang, R. (2010) *Privacy preserving group nearest neighbour queries*. In International Conference on Extending Database Technology.

Hashimoto, K. (2000). A new approach to fault-tolerant scheduling using task duplication in multiprocessor systems. *Journal of Systems and Software, 53*(2), 159–171. doi:10.1016/S0164-1212(99)00105-3

Hashimoto, K., Tsuchita, T., & Kikuno, T. (2002). Effective scheduling of duplicated tasks for fault tolerance in multiprocessor systems. *IEICE Transactions on Information and Systems. E (Norwalk, Conn.), 85-D*(3), 525–534.

He, W., Liu, X., Nguyen, H., Nahrstedt, K., & Abdelzaher, T. F. (2007). *PDA: Privacy-preserving data aggregation in wireless sensor networks*. In IEEE Conference on Computer Communications.

Hegering, H.-G., Abeck, S., & Neumair, B. (1999). *Integrated management of networked systems: Concepts, architectures and their operational application*. Morgan Kaufmann Series in Networking.

He, H., Wang, J., Graco, W., & Hawkins, S. (1997). Application of neural networks to detection of medical fraud. *Expert Systems with Applications, 13*, 329–336. doi:10.1016/S0957-4174(97)00045-6

He, J., Gao, T., Hao, W., Yen, I., & Bastani, F. (2007). A flexible content adaptation system using a rule-based approach. *IEEE Transactions on Knowledge and Data Engineering, 19*(1), 127–140. doi:10.1109/TKDE.2007.250590

Hickey, A. R. (2010). *Report: Mobile cloud computing a $5 billion opportunity*. Retrieved March, 1, 2011, from http://www.crn.com/mobile/222300633

Higginbotham, S. (2009, July). *Google gets shifty with its data center operations*. Retrieved March, 1, 2011, from http://gigaom.com/2009/07/16/google-gets-shifty-with-its-data-center-operations

Hilas, C. S., & Sahalos, J. N. (2005). User profiling for fraud detection in telecommunication networks. *Fifth International Conference on Technology and Automation*, (pp. 382-387).

Hilt, V., & Widjaja, I. (2008). Controlling overload in networks of SIP servers. In *Proceedings of IEEE ICNP*, Orlando, Florida, (pp. 83-93).

Hiltunen, M. A., Schlichting, R. D., Ugarte, C. A., & Wong, G. T. (2000). Survivability through customization and adaptability: The Cactus approach. In R. D. Schlichting (Ed.), *Proceedings of DARPA Information Survivability Conference and Exposition DISCEX '00* (Vol. 1, pp. 294-307). doi: 10.1109/DISCEX.2000.825033

Hindriks, K., & Tykhonov, D. (2008). Opponent modeling in automated multi-issue negotiation using Bayesian learning. *Proceedings of the 7th International Joint Conference on Autonomous Agents and Multi-Agent Systems, Vol. 1,* (pp. 331-338).

Hines, M. R., Deshpande, U., & Gopalan, K. (2009, July). Post-copy live migration of virtual machines. *SIGOPS Operating Systems Review, 43,* 14–26. doi:10.1145/1618525.1618528

Hoff, T. (2009). *Latency is everywhere and it costs you sales - How to crush it.* Retrieved March, 1, 2011, from http://highscalability.com/latency-everywhere-and-it-costs-you-sales-how-crush-it

Hoh, B., Gruteser, M., Xiong, H., & Alrabady, A. (2007). *Preserving privacy in GPS traces via uncertainty-aware path cloaking.* In ACM Conference on Computer and Communications Security.

Hollmén, J. (2000, December). *User profiling and classification for fraud detection in mobile communications networks.* Dissertation for the degree of Doctor of Science in Technology, Helsinki University of Technology, Department of Computer Science and Engineering.

Homayouni, M., Jahanbakhsh, M., Azhari, V., & Akbari, A. (2010). Controlling overload in SIP proxies: An adaptive window based approach using no explicit feedback. In *Proceedings of IEEE Globecom*, Miami, FL, USA.

Hong, Y., Huang, C., & Yan, J. (2010a). Analysis of SIP retransmission probability using a Markov-modulated Poisson process model. In *Proceedings of IEEE/IFIP Network Operations and Management Symposium*, Osaka, Japan, (pp. 179–186).

Hong, Y., Huang, C., & Yan, J. (2010b). *Modeling chaotic behaviour of SIP retransmission mechanism.* Technical Report 2010-0501, Department of Systems and Computer Engineering, Carleton University. Available upon request.

Hong, Y., Huang, C., & Yan, J. (2010c). Mitigating SIP overload using a control-theoretic approach. In *Proceedings of IEEE Globecom*, Miami, FL, U.S.A.

Hong, Y., Huang, C., & Yan, J. (2011b). Controlling retransmission rate for mitigating SIP overload. In *Proceedings of IEEE ICC*, Kyoto, Japan.

Hong, Y., Huang, C., & Yan, J. (2011c). Design of a PI rate controller for mitigating SIP overload. In *Proceedings of IEEE ICC*, Kyoto, Japan.

Hong, Y., Yang, O. W. W., & Huang, C. (2004). Self-tuning PI TCP flow controller for AQM routers with interval gain and phase margin assignment. In *Proceedings of IEEE Globecom*, Dallas, TX, US, (pp. 1324-1328).

Hong, Y., Huang, C., & Yan, J. (2011a). Modeling and simulation of SIP tandem server with finite buffer. *ACM Transactions on Modeling and Computer Simulation, 21*(2). doi:10.1145/1899396.1899399

Hsiao, J., Hung, H., & Chen, M. (2008). Versatile transcoding proxy for Internet content adaptation. *IEEE Transactions on Multimedia, 10*(4), 646–658. doi:10.1109/TMM.2008.921852

Hu, C., Wu, M., Liu, G., & Xie, W. (2007). QoS scheduling algorithm based on hybrid particle swarm optimization strategy for grid workflow. *Proceedings of the 6th International Conference on Grid and Cooperative Computing,* (pp. 330-337). doi:10.1109/GCC.2007.100

Hu, L., & Shahabi, C. (2010). *Privacy assurance in mobile sensing networks: Go beyond trusted servers.* In IEEE Pervasive Computing and Communication.

Huang, L. (2009). Locating interested subsets of peers for P2PSIP. In *Proceedings of International Conference on New Trends in Information and Service Science,* (pp. 1408-1413).

Huang, K. L., Kanhare, S. S., & Lu, W. (2010). Preserving privacy in participatory sensing systems. *Computer Communications, 33*(11). doi:10.1016/j.comcom.2009.08.012

Illmann, T., Krueger, T., Kargl, F., & Weber, M. (2002). Transparent migration of mobile agents using the java platform debugger architecture. In *Proceedings of the 5th International Conference on Mobile Agents* (pp. 198–212). London, UK: Springer-Verlag.

Imperial College London. (2011). *Ponder2 project*. Retrieved from http://ponder2.net

Information Sciences Intitute. (1981, September). *RFC 791 - Internet protocol*. Southern California, USA: Author.

Internet2. (2008, July). *How to connect: Internet2's Dynamic Circuit Network*. Retrieved March 07, 2011, from http://www.internet2.edu/pubs/DCN-howto.pdf

ITR. (2010). *Internet traffic report*. Retrieved from http://www.internettrafficreport.com/

ITU-T. (2000, February). *Recommendation M.3400: TMN management functions*.

ITU-T. (2001). *Recommendation Y.2001: General overview of NGN*. USA.

ITU-T. (2001, November). *Recommendation G.1010: End-user multimedia QoS categories*. USA.

ITU-T. (2004, October). *Recommendation Y.2011: General principles and general reference model for next generation networks*. USA.

ITU-T. (2006, February). *Recommendation Y.1541: Network performance abjoectives for IP-based services*. USA.

ITU-T. (2008). *ITU-T's definition of NGN*. Retrieved March 7, 2011, from http://www.itu.int/en/ITU-T/gsi/ngn/Pages/definition.aspx

ITU-T. (2009). *Deployments of next generation networks (NGN): Country case studies*. Retrieved March 7, 2011, from http://www.itu.int/ITU-D/treg/Documentation/ITU-NGN09.pdf

ITU-T. (2009). *Trends in telecommunication reform 2009: Hands-on or hands-off? Stimulating growth through effective ICT regulation* (10th edition ed.).

ITU-T. (2011). *ITU's ICT eye*. Retrieved March 07, 2011, from http://www.itu.int/ITU-D/icteye/

Jaffe, J. (1984). Algorithms for finding paths with multiple constraints. *Networks*, *14*, 95–116. doi:10.1002/net.3230140109

Jain, A. K., & Dubes, R. C. (1988). *Algorithms for clustering data*. Prentice-Hall, Inc.

Jiang, H., Iyengar, A., Nahum, E., Segmuller, W., Tantawi, A., & Wright, C. (2009). Load balancing for SIP server clusters. In *Proceedings of IEEE INFOCOM*, (pp. 2286-2294).

Ji, P., Ge, Z., Kurose, J., & Towsley, D. (2007). A comparison of hard-state and soft-state signaling protocols. *IEEE/ACM Transactions on Networking*, *15*(2), 281–294. doi:10.1109/TNET.2007.892849

Jung, M., Biersack, E., & Pilger, A. (1999). Implementing network protocols in Java-A framework for rapid prototyping. *International Conference on Enterprise Information Systems* (pp. 649-656). Retrieved from citeseer.ist.psu.edu/jung99implementing.html

Kalnis, P., Ghinita, G., Mopuratidis, K., & Papadias, D. (2007). Preventing location-based identity inference in anonymous spatial queries. *IEEE Transactions on Knowledge and Data Engineering*, *9*(12), 1719–1733. doi:10.1109/TKDE.2007.190662

Kandaswamy, G., Mandal, A., & Reed, D. A. (2008). Fault tolerance and recovery of scientific workflows on computational grids. *Proceedings of the 8th Cluster Computing and the Grid*, (pp. 777-782). doi: 10.1109/CCGRID.2008.79

Kapadia, A., Triandopoulos, N., Cornelius, C., Peebles, D., & Kotz, D. (2007). *AnonySense: Opportunistic and privacy-preserving context collection*. In International Conference on Pervasive Computing.

Keeney, R., & Raiffa, H. (1976). *Decisions with multiple objectives: Performances and value tradeoffs*. New York, NY: John Wiley.

Keller, A., & Ludwig, H. (2003). The WSLA framework: Specifying and monitoring service level agreements for web services. *Journal of Network and Systems Management*, *11*(1), 57–81. doi:10.1023/A:1022445108617

Kephart, J. O., & Chess, D. M. (2003). The vision of autonomic computing. *Computer*, *36*(1), 41–50. doi:10.1109/MC.2003.1160055

Kersten, G., & Lai, H. (2007). Satisfiability and completeness of protocols for electronic negotiations. *European Journal of Operational Research*, *180*(2), 922–937. doi:10.1016/j.ejor.2005.04.056

Kersten, G., & Noronha, S. (1999). WWW-based negotiation support: Design, implementation. *International Journal of Cooperative Information Systems, 5*(2-3).

Kfir-Dahav, N., Monderer, D., & Tennenholtz, M. (2000). Mechanism design for resource bounded agents. *Proceedings of 4th International Conference on Multi-agent Systems (ICMAS)*, (pp. 309-315).

Kim, J., Lakshmanan, K., & Rajkumar, R. R. (2010). R-BATCH: Task partitioning for fault-tolerant multiprocessor real-time systems. *Proceedings of 10th IEEE International Conference on Computer and Information Technology*, (pp. 1872-1879). doi: 10.1109/CIT.2010.321

Kirci, P., & Zaim, A. H. (2006). *Mobility management strategies of mobile IP networks.*

Kitatsuji, Y., Noishiki, Y., Itou, M., & Yokota, H. (2010). Service initiation procedure with on-demand UE registration for scalable IMS services. In *Proceedings of the Fifth International Conference on Mobile Computing and Ubiquitous Networking*, Seattle, WA.

Kittler, J. (1986). Feature selection and extraction. In Young, T. Y., & Fu, K. S. (Eds.), *Handbook of pattern recognition* (pp. 59–83). New York, NY: Academic Press.

Kliazovich, D., & Granelli, F. (2008). Distributed protocol stacks: A framework for balancing interoperability and optimization. *IEEE International Conference on Communications, ICC Workshops '08*, (pp. 241-245). doi: 10.1109/ICCW.2008.51

Koji, O., Inoue, M., Okajima, I., & Umeda, N. (2003). Handoff performance of mobile host and mobile router employing HMIP extension. *IEEE WCNC 2003*, (Vol. 2, pp. 1218-1223).

Kowalczyk, R., & Bui, V. (2001). Lecture Notes in Computer Science: *Vol. 2003. On constraint-based reasoning in e-negotiation agents. Agent-Mediated Electronic Commerce III* (pp. 31–46).

Kraus, S., Wilkenfeld, J., & Zlotkin, G. (1995). Multiagent negotiation under time constraints. *Journal of Artificial Intelligence, 75*(2), 297–345. doi:10.1016/0004-3702(94)00021-R

Kritikos, K., & Plexousakis, D. (2009). Requirements for QoS-based web service description and discovery. *IEEE Transactions on Service Computing, 2*(4), 320–327. doi:10.1109/TSC.2009.26

Kroes, N. (2009). Commission guidelines for broadband networks. *Introductory remarks at press conference*, (p. 3). Brussels.

Krovi, R., Graesser, A., & Pracht, W. (1999). Agent behaviors in virtual negotiation environments. *IEEE Transactions on Systems, Man, and Cybernetics, 29*, 15–25. doi:10.1109/5326.740666

Kuipers, F. (2004). *Quality of service routing in the internet: Theory, complexity and algorithms.*

Kumar, V. (1992). Algorithms for constraint-satisfaction problems: A survey. *AI Magazine*, 32–44.

Kurbel, K., & Loutchko, I. (2005). A model for multilateral negotiations on an agent-based job marketplace. *Journal of Electronic Commerce Research and Applications, 4*(3), 87–203.

Lake, A., Vollbrecht, J., Brown, A. Z., Robertson, D., Thompson, M., Guok, C., et al. (2008, May). *Inter-domain controller (IDC) protocol specification.* USA.

Lam, K. T., Luo, Y., & Wang, C.-L. (2010). Adaptive sampling-based profiling techniques for optimizing the distributed JVM runtime. In *Proceedings of the 24th IEEE International Symposium on Parallel & Distributed Processing.*

Lee, G., Kim, W., & Kim, D. (2005). *An effective method for location privacy in ubiquitous computing.* In Embedded and Ubiquitous Computing workshops.

Lee, J. S., & Hoh, B. (2010). *Sell your experiences: a market mechanism based incentive for participatory sensing.* In IEEE International Conference on Pervasive Computing and Communications.

Lee, K., Lee, W., Zheng, B., & Winter, J. (April 2006). *Processing multiple aggregation queries in geo-sensor networks.* The 11th International Conference on Database Systems for Advanced Applications (DAS-FAA06). Singapore.

Lee, J.-S., Min, J.-H., Park, K.-S., & Kim, S.-H. (2003). Paging extension for hierarchical mobile IPv6: P-HMIPv6. *IEEE ICON, 2003*, 245–248.

Lee, S. C., & Heinbuch, D. V. (2001, July). Training a neural-network based intrusion detector to recognize novel attacks. *IEEE Transactions on Systems, Man, and Cybernetics. Part A, Systems and Humans, 31*, 294–299. doi:10.1109/3468.935046

Li, H. (2001). *Automated e-business negotiation: Model, life cycle, and system architecture*. Ph.D. Thesis, Department of Computer and Information Science and Engineering, University of Florida.

Li, Y., & Mascagni, M. (2003). Improving performance via computational replication on a large-scale computational grid. *Proceedings of the 3rd IEEE International Symposium on Cluster Computing and the Grid*, (pp. 442-448). Retrieved from http://portal.acm.org/citation.cfm?id=792426

Li, J., Huang, K.-Y., Jin, J., & Shi, J. (2008). A survey on statistical methods for health care fraud detection. *Health Care Management Science, 11*(3), 275–287. doi:10.1007/s10729-007-9045-4

Litke, A., Skoutas, D., Tserpes, K., & Varvarigou, T. (2007). Efficient task replication and management for adaptive fault tolerance in mobile Grid environments. *Future Generation Computer Systems, 23*(2), 163–178. doi:10.1016/j.future.2006.04.014

Liu, S.-H., Cao, Y., Li, M., Kilaru, P., Smith, T., & Toner, S. (2008). A semantics- and data-driven SOA for biomedical multimedia systems. *10th IEEE International Symposium on Multimedia* (pp. 553-558). New York, NY: IEEE Press.

Liu, Y., Presti, F. L., Misra, V., Towsley, D. F., & Gu, Y. (2003). Scalable fluid models and simulations for large-scale IP networks. In *Proceedings of ACM SIGMETRICS*, (pp. 91-101).

Lomuscio, A., Wooldridge, M., & Jennings, N. (2003). A classification scheme for negotiation in electronic commerce. *International journal of Group Decision and Negotiation, 12*(1), 31-56.

Lui, J. C., Misra, V., & Rubenstein, D. (2004). On the robustness of soft-state protocols. In *Proceedings of IEEE ICNP*, Berlin, Germany, (pp. 50–60).

Lum, W., & Lau, F. (2003). User-centric content negotiation for effective adaptation service in mobile computing. *IEEE Transactions on Software Engineering, 29*(12), 1100–1111. doi:10.1109/TSE.2003.1265524

Luo, W., Yang, F., Pang, L., & Qin, X. (2006). Fault-tolerant scheduling based on periodic tasks for heterogeneous systems. *Lecture Notes in Computer Science, vol. 4158, Autonomic and Trusted Computing* (pp. 571-580). Berlin, Germany: Springer-Verlag. doi: 10.1007/11839569_56

Luo, X., Jennings, N., Shadbolt, N., Leung, H., & Lee, J. (2003). A fuzzy constraint based model for bilateral, multi-issue negotiations in semi-competitive environments. *Journal of Artificial Intelligence, 148*, 53–102. doi:10.1016/S0004-3702(03)00041-9

Ma, R., Lam, K. T., Wang, C.-L., & Zhang, C. (2010). A stack-on-demand execution model for elastic computing. In *Proceedings of the 39th International Conference on Parallel Processing* (pp. 208–217).

Ma'en, A., Mahamod, I., & Kasmiron, J. (2007). A study on effective transfer rate over smart hierarchical mobile IPv6. *IJCSNS International Journal of Computer Science and Network Security, 7*(5).

Machanavajjhala, A., Kifer, D., Gehrke, J., & Venkitasubramaniam, M. (2007). L-diversity: privacy beyond k-anonymity. *ACM Transactions on Knowledge Discovery from Data, 1*(1), 3. doi:10.1145/1217299.1217302

Madden, S., Franklin, M., Hellerstein, J., & Hong, W. (December 2002). Tag a tiny aggregation service for ad-hoc sensor networks. *5th Symposium on Operating Systems Design and Implementation*. Boston, Massachusetts, USA.

Madden, S., Franklin, M., Hellerstein, J., & Hong, W. (2005, March). Tinydb, An acquisitional query processing system for sensor networks. *ACM Transactions on Database Systems, 30*, 122–173. doi:10.1145/1061318.1061322

Mahy, R., Matthews, P., & Rosenberg, J. (2010, April). *Traversal using relays around NAT (TURN): Relay extensions to session traversal utilities for NAT (STUN)* (RFC No. 5766). RFC Editor. Internet Requests for Comments. Retrieved March, 1, 2011, from http://tools.ietf.org/html/rfc5766

Maloney, A., & Goscinski, A. (2009). A survey and review of the current state of rollback-recovery for cluster. *Journal of Concurrency and Computation: Practice & Experience, 21*(12), 1632–1666. doi:10.1002/cpe.1413

Manimaran, G., & Murthy, C. S. R. (1997). A new scheduling approach supporting different fault-tolerant techniques for real-time multiprocessor systems. *Microprocessors and Microsystems, 21*, 163–173. doi:10.1016/S0141-9331(97)00030-6

Manimaran, G., & Murthy, C. S. R. (1998). A fault-tolerant dynamic scheduling algorithm for multiprocessor real-time systems and its analysis. *IEEE Transactions on Parallel and Distributed Systems, 9*(11), 1137–1152. doi:10.1109/71.735960

Materna, B. (2006). Threat mitigation for VoIP. In *Proceedings of Third Annual VoIP Security Workshop*, Berlin, Germany.

Ma, W., & Fang, Y. (2004). Dynamic hierarchical mobility management strategy for mobile IP networks. *IEEE Journal on Selected Areas in Communications, 22*(4), 664–666. doi:10.1109/JSAC.2004.825968

May, M., Bolot, J. C., Jean-Marie, A., & Diot, C. (1999). Simple performance models of differentiated service schemes for the Internet. In *Proceedings of IEEE INFOCOM*, (pp. 1385–1394).

McBurney, P., & Parsons, S. (2003). Dialogue game protocols. *Journal of Communications in Multiagent Systems, LNCS, 2650*, 269–283. doi:10.1007/978-3-540-44972-0_15

Meling, H. (2006). *Non-hierarchical dynamic protocol composition in Jgroup/ARM. Proceedings of Norsk Informatikkonferanse*. Molde, Norway: NIK.

Mell, P., & Grance, T. (2009). *The NIST definition of cloud computing* (Tech. Rep.). National Institute of Standards and Technology, Information Technology Laboratory. Retrieved March, 1, 2011, from http://csrc.nist.gov/groups/SNS/cloud-computing/cloud-def-v15.doc

Menasce, D. (2002). QoS issues in web services. *IEEE Internet Computing, 6*(6), 72–75. doi:10.1109/MIC.2002.1067740

Meyerowitz, J., & Choudhury, R. R. (2009). *Hiding stars with fireworks: Location privacy through camouflage.* In International Conference on Mobile Computing and Networking.

Meza, F., & Ruz, C. (2007). The thread migration mechanism of DSMPEPE. In *Proceedings of the 7th International Conference on Algorithms and Architectures for Parallel Processing* (pp. 177–187). Berlin, Germany: Springer-Verlag.

Milojičić, D. S., Douglis, F., Paindaveine, Y., Wheeler, R., & Zhou, S. (2000, September). Process migration. *ACM Computing Surveys, 32*, 241–299. doi:10.1145/367701.367728

Miranda, H., Pinto, A., & Rodrigues, L. (2001). Appia, a flexible protocol kernel supporting multiple coordinated channels. *Proceedings of 21st International Conference on Distributed Computing Systems* (pp. 707-710). doi:10.1109/ICDSC.2001.919005

Misra, A., Das, S., Das, S. K., Mcauley, A., & Dutta, A. (2000). *Integrating QoS support in TeleMIP's mobility architecture.* Hyderabad, India: ICPWC.

Misra, A., Das, S., Dutta, A., Mcauley, A., & Das, S. K. (2002). IDMP-based fast handoffs and paging in IP-based cellular networks. *IEEE Communications Magazine, 40*(3), 138–145. doi:10.1109/35.989774

Mohan, R., John, S., & Li, C.-S. (1999). Adapting multimedia Internet content for universal access. *IEEE Transactions on Multimedia, 1*(1), 104–114. doi:10.1109/6046.748175

Mokbel, M. F., Chow, C. Y., & Aref, W. G. (2006). The new Casper: Query processing for location services without compromising privacy. In *Proceedings of the 32nd International Conference on Very Large Data Bases*.

Montagna, S., & Pignolo, M. (2010). Comparison between two approaches to overload control in a real server: "Local" or "hybrid" solutions? In *Proceedings of IEEE MELECON*, (pp. 845-849).

Moore, B., Ellesson, E., Strassner, J., & Westerinen, A. (2001). Policy core information model – Version 1 specification. *IETF RFC 3060*. Retrieved October 13, 2010, from http://tools.ietf.org/html/rfc3060

Muhugusa, M., Marzo, G. D., Tschudin, C. F., & Harms, J. (1994). *ComScript: An environment for the implementation of protocol stacks and their dynamic reconfiguration.* International Symposium on Applied Corporate Computing {ISACC} 94. Retrieved from citeseer.ist.psu.edu/muhugusa94comscript.html

Muller, R., & Alonso, G. (October 2006). *Efficient sharing of sensor networks.* IEEE International Conference on Mobile Adhoc and Sensor Systems. Vancouver, BC, Canada.

Munteanu, A., Beaver, J., Labrinidis, A., & Chrysanthis, P. (February 2005). Multiple query routing trees in sensor networks. *The IASTED International Conference on Databases and Applications (DBA05)*, (pp. 145–150). Innsbruck, Austria.

Murshed, M., Iqbal, A., Sabrina, T., & Alam, K. H. (2011). *A subset coding based k-anonymization technique to trade-off location privacy and data integrity in participatory sensing systems.* In IEEE International Symposium on Network Computing and Applications.

Murshed, M., Sabrina, T., Iqbal, A., & Alam, K. H. (2010). *A novel anonymization technique to trade-off location privacy and data integrity in participatory sensing systems.* In International Conference on Network and System Security.

Naedele, M. (1999). Fault-tolerant real-time scheduling under execution time constraints. *Proceedings of 6th International Conference on Real-Time Computing Systems and Applications*, (pp. 392-395). doi: 10.1109/RTCSA.1999.811286

Nahum, E. M., Tracey, J., & Wright, C. P. (2007). Evaluating SIP server performance. In *Proceedings of ACM SIGMETRICS*, San Diego, CA, US, (pp. 349–350).

Narasimhan, P., Dumitras, T. A., Paulos, A. M., Pertet, S. M., Reverte, C. F., Slember, J. G., & Srivastave, D. (2005). MEAD: Support for real-time fault-tolerant CORBA. *Concurrency and Computation, 17*(12), 1527–1545. doi:10.1002/cpe.882

Nelson, M., Lim, B.-H., & Hutchins, G. (2005). Fast transparent migration for virtual machines. In *Proceedings of the USENIX Annual Technical Conference* (pp. 391–394). Berkeley, CA: USENIX Association.

Network Measurements Working Group. (2006, August). Retrieved March 07, 2011, from http://nmwg.internet2.edu

Network Working Group. (1971, October). *RFC 249 - Coordination of equipment and supplies purchase.* Illinois, USA.

Network Working Group. (1997, September). RFC 2205 - *Resource reservation protocol (RSVP).* Michigan, USA.

Neumann, D., Benyoucef, M., Bassil, S., & Vachon, J. (2003). Applying the Montreal taxonomy to state of the art e-negotiation systems. *Journal of Group Decision and Negotiation, 12*, 287–310. doi:10.1023/A:1024871921144

Niamanesh, M., Sabetghadam, S., Yousefzadeh Rahaghi, R., & Jalili, R. (2007). Design and implementation of a dynamic-reconfigurable architecture for protocol stack. *International Symposium on Fundamentals of Software Engineering* (pp. 396-403). doi: http://dx.doi.org/10.1007/978-3-540-75698-9

Niyato, D., & Hossain, E. (2007). Radio resource management games in wireless networks: An approach to bandwidth allocation and admission control for polling service in IEEE 802.16. *Wireless Communications, 14*, 27–35. doi:10.1109/MWC.2007.314548

Noel, E., & Johnson, C. R. (2007). Initial simulation results that analyze SIP based VoIP networks under overload. In *Proceedings of 20th International Teletraffic Congress*, Ottawa, Canada, 2007.

Noel, E., & Johnson, C. R. (2009). Novel overload controls for SIP networks. In *Proceedings of 21st International Teletraffic Congress*, 2009.

Nordin, N. A., Shin, W. H., Ghauth, K. I., & Mohd, M. I. (2007). Using service-based content adaptation platform to enhance mobile user experience. *Proceeding of the 4th International Conference on Mobile Technology and Applications* (pp. 552-557). New York, NY: ACM Press.

Nurmi, D., Wolski, R., & Brevik, J. (2004). *Model-based checkpoint scheduling for volatile resource environments.* UCSB Technical Report(2004-25). Retrieved from http://vgrads.rice.edu/publications/wolski3/

Nuttall, M. (1994, October). A brief survey of systems providing process or object migration facilities. *SIGOPS Operating Systems Review, 28*, 64–80. doi:10.1145/191525.191541

O'Neill, A. W., & Tsirtsis, G. (2000). *Edge mobility architecture - Routing and hand-off.* ACM SIGMOBILE.

OASIS. (2011). *eXtensible access control markup language (XACML) version 3.0.* Retrieved from www.oasis-open.org/committees/xacml/

Ohta, M. (2006a). Overload protection in a SIP signaling network. In *Proceedings of International Conference on Internet Surveillance and Protection.*

Ohta, M. (2006b). Overload control in a SIP signaling network. In *Proceeding of World Academy of Science* (pp. 205–210). Vienna, Austria: Engineering and Technology.

Oliner, A. J., Sahoo, R. K., Moreira, J. E., Gupta, M., & Sivasubramaniam, A. (2004). Fault-aware job scheduling for BlueGene/L systems. *Proceedings of the 18th International Parallel and Distributed Processing Symposium,* (pp. 64-73). doi: 10.1109/IPDPS.2004.1302991

OMG. (2005). *Platform independent model (PIM) and platform specific model (PSM) for software radio components.* Retrieved from http://sbc.omg.org/

Oracle. (2007). *Java virtual machine tool interface (JVM TI).* Retrieved March, 1, 2011, from http://download.oracle.com/javase/6/docs/technotes/guides/jvmti/

Pack, S., Nam, M., & Choi, Y. (2004). A study on optimal hierarchy in multi-level hierarchical mobile IPv6 networks. *IEEE GLOBECOM 2004,* (Vol. 2, pp. 1290-1294).

Park, J., Baek, J., & Hong, J. (2001). Management of service level agreements for multimedia Internet service using a utility model. *IEEE Communications Magazine, 39*(5), 100–106. doi:10.1109/35.920863

Pathan, M., & Buyya, R. (2009a). Resource discovery and request-redirection for dynamic load sharing in multi-provider peering content delivery networks. *Journal of Network and Computer Applications, 32*(5), 976–990. doi:10.1016/j.jnca.2009.03.003

Pathan, M., & Buyya, R. (2009b). Architecture and performance models for QoS-driven effective peering of content delivery network. *Multiagent and Grid System, 5*(2), 1574–1702.

Patouni, E. (2006). *E2R II scenario on autonomic communication systems for seamless experience.* Retrieved from http://e2r2.motlabs.com/dissemination/whitepapers

Perkins, C. E. (1998). *Mobile IP.* Addison-Wesley.

Perry, G. (2008, June). *On clouds, the sun and the moon.* Retrieved March, 1, 2011, from http://gigaom.com/2008/06/21/on-clouds-the-sun-and-the-moon/

Peterson, L., & Hutchinson, N., O'Malley, S., & Rao, H. (1990). The x-kernel: A platform for accessing internet resources. *Computer, 23*(5), 23–33. doi:10.1109/2.53352

Pham, N., Ganti, R. K., Uddin, Y. S., Nath, S., & Abdelzaher, T. F. (2010). *Privacy-preserving reconstruction of multidimensional data maps in vehicular participatory sensing.* In European Conference on Wireless Sensor Networks.

Plagemann, T., & Plattner, B. (1993). Modules as building blocks for protocol configuration. *Proceedings International Conference on Network Protocols (ICNP '93).* Retrieved from citeseer.ist.psu.edu/plagemann93module.html

Plagemann, T., Waclawczyk, J., & Plattner, B. (1994). Management of configurable protocols for multimedia applications. *Proceedings of {ISMM} International Conference Distributed Multimedia Systems and Applications* (pp. 78-81). Retrieved from citeseer.ist.psu.edu/plagemann94management.html

Planat, V., & Kara, N. (2006). SIP signaling retransmission analysis over 3G network. In *Proceedings of MoMM2006,* Yogyakarta, Indonesia.

Potdar, V., Sharif, A., & Chang, E. (2009, May). Wireless sensor networks: A survey. *WAINA, 09,* 636–641.

Project, G. É. A. N. T. (2011). *Home.* Retrieved March 07, 2011, from http://www.geant.net

Project, G. É. A. N. T. (2011). *Information sharing across heterogeneous administrative regions.* Retrieved March 07, 2011, from http://forge.geant.net/ishare

Prokkola, J. (2007, July). *QoS measurement methods and tools.* Paper presented at the Easy Wireless Workshop of 16th IST Mobile and Wireless Communications Summit, Budapest, Hungary.

Pruitt, D. G. (1981). *Negotiation behavior*. Academic Press, Inc. Kowalczyk, R., & Bui, V. (2000). On fuzzy e-negotiation agents: Autonomous negotiation with incomplete and imprecise information (DEXA). *11ᵗʰ International Workshop on Database and Expert Systems Applications* (DEXA'00), Vol. 1034.

Qin, X., & Jiang, H. (2006). A novel fault-tolerant scheduling algorithm for precedence constrained tasks in real-time heterogeneous systems. *Parallel Computing, 32*(5-6), 331–356. doi:10.1016/j.parco.2006.06.006

Quitadamo, R., Cabri, G., & Leonardi, L. (2008, February). Mobile JikesRVM: A framework to support transparent Java thread migration. *Science of Computer Programming, 70*, 221–240. doi:10.1016/j.scico.2007.07.009

Rahwan, I., Kowalczyk, R., & Pham, H. (2002). Intelligent agents for automated one-to-many e-commerce negotiation. *Proceedings of the 25ᵗʰ Australian Conference on Computer Science*, (pp. 197-204). Australian Computer Society Press.

Ramamritham, K., & Stankovic, J. A. (1995). Determining redundancy levels for fault tolerant real-time systems. *IEEE Transactions on Computers, 44*(2), 292–301. doi:10.1109/12.364540

Raman, S., & McCanne, S. (1999). A model, analysis, and protocol framework for soft state-based communication. In *Proceedings of ACM SIGCOMM*, Boston, MA, US.

Rebahi, Y., Fiedler, J., & Gouveia, F. (2010). *Fraud in VoIP networks: Size and scope*. Project Deliverable. http://www.sme-scamstop.eu/contributions/SCAM-STOP_D2.1.public.pdf

Reddy, S., Samanta, V., Burke, J., Estrin, D., Hansen, M., & Srivastava, M. (2009). *MobiSense – Mobile network services for coordinated participatory sensing*. In International Symposium on Autonomous Decentralized Systems.

Reese, G. (2008). *On why I don't like auto-scaling in the Cloud*. O'Reilly Media. Retrieved March, 1, 2011, from http://broadcast.oreilly.com/2008/12/why-i-dont-like-cloud-auto-scaling.html

Reinbold, P., & Bonaventure, O. (2001). *A comparison of IP mobility protocols*. Retrieved from http://www.infonet.fundp.ac.be

Reiser, H. P., & Kapitza, R. (2007). VM-FIT: Supporting intrusion tolerance with virtualization technology. *Proceedings of the First Workshop on Recent Advances on Intrusion-Tolerant Systems,* (pp. 18-22). Retrieved from http://wraits07.di.fc.ul.pt/9.pdf

Renda, A. (2008). I own the pipes, you call the tune: The net neutrality debate and its (ir)relevance for Europe. In *Regulatory Policy* (p. 36). CEPS Special Reports.

Riteau, P., Morin, C., & Priol, T. (2010, February). *Shrinker: Efficient wide-area live virtual machine migration using distributed content-based addressing* (Tech. Rep.). Rennes, France: INRIA Rennes. Retrieved March, 1, 2011, from http://hal.inria.fr/inria-00454727/en/

Rivest, R. (1992, April). The MD5 message-digest algorithm. *IETF RFC 1321*.

Robenstein, A., & Wolinsky, A. (1985). Equilibrium in market with sequential bargaining. *Econometrica: Journal of the Econometric Society, 53*(5).

Robinson, W. N., & Volkov, V. (1998). Supporting the negotiation life cycle. *Communications of the ACM, 41*(5), 95–102. doi:10.1145/274946.274962

Rood, B., & Lewis, M. J. (2010). Availability prediction based replication strategies for grid environments. *Proceedings of the 10th IEEE/ACM International Conference on Cluster, Cloud and Grid Computing*, (pp. 25-33). doi: 10.1109/CCGRID.2010.121

Rosa, L., Lopes, A., & Rodrigues, L. (2006). Policy-driven adaptation of protocol stacks. *Proceedings of the International Conference on Autonomic and Autonomous Systems ICAS '06* (p. 5). doi: 10.1109/ICAS.2006.43

Rosemark, R., Lee, W., & Urgaonkar, B. (May 2007). *Optimizing energy-efficient query processing in wireless sensor networks*. International Conference on Mobile Data Management, Mannheim, Germany.

Rosenberg, J. (2008). *Requirements for management of overload in the session initiation protocol*. IETF RFC 5390.

Rosenberg, J. (2010, April). *Interactive connectivity establishment (ICE): A protocol for network address translator (NAT) traversal for offer/answer protocols* (RFC No. 5245). RFC Editor. Internet Requests for Comments. Retrieved March, 1, 2011, from http://tools.ietf.org/html/rfc5245

Rosenberg, J., & Schulzrinne, H. (2002, June). SIP: Session initiation protocol. *IETF RFC 3261*.

Rosenberg, J., et al. (2002). SIP: Session initiation protocol. *IETF RFC 3261*.

Roussaki, I., & Louta, M. (2003). *Efficient negotiation framework and strategies for the next generation electronic marketplace*. MBA Thesis, National Technical University of Athens, Athens, Greece.

Russell, T. (2006). *Signaling system 7* (5th ed.). Mcgraw-Hill Professional Communication Series.

Ruzzelli, A., Jurdak, R., & O'Hare, G. (2007). *Managing mobile-based participatory sensing communities*. In Participatory Research Workshop at ACM Conference on Embedded Networked Sensor Systems.

Saaty, T. (2008). Decision making with the analytic hierarchy process. *International Journal of Services Sciences*, *1*(1), 83–98. doi:10.1504/IJSSCI.2008.017590

Sadagopan, N., Singh, M., & Krishnamachari, B. (2006). Decentralized utility-based design of sensor networks. *Mobile Networks and Applications*, *11*, 341–350. doi:10.1007/s11036-006-5187-8

Saha, D., Mukherjee, A., Misra, I. S., & Chakraborty, M. (2004). Mobility support in IP: A survey of related protocols. *IEEE Network Magazine*, *18*(6), 34–40. doi:10.1109/MNET.2004.1355033

Sahai, A., Durante, A., & Machiraju, V. (2002). *Towards automated SLA management for web services*. Technical Report HPL-2001-310, Hewlett-Parkard Labs, Palo-Alto, CA.

Sajal, S., et el. (2011). *THMIP- A novel mobility management scheme using fluid flow model*. 2nd International Conference on Emerging Trends and Applications in Computer Science, (NCETACS - 2011), Shillong, India, 4th- 6th March, 2011.

Sandholm, T. (1996). Limitation of the Vickery auction in computational multi agent systems. *Proceedings of the Second International Conference on Multi-agent Systems (ICMAS-96)*, (pp. 299-306).

Sandholm, T., & Vulkan, N. (1999). Bargaining with deadlines. *Proceedings of the National Conference on Artificial Intelligence*. Retrieved from http://www.cs.wustl.edu/cs/techreports/1999/wucs-99-06.tr.ps.Z

Sanver, M., & Karahoca, A. (2007, July 18-24). Fraud detection using an adaptive neuro-fuzzy inference system in mobile telecommunication networks. *Proceedings of the 10th Joint Conference on Information Science*, (pp. 1440-1446). Utah, USA.

Schäfer, R. (2001). Rules for using multi-attribute utility theory for estimating a user's interests. *Proceedings of Workshop on Adaptivity and User Modeling*.

Schmidt, D. C., Box, D. F., & Suda, T. (1993). ADAPTIVE - A dynamically assembled protocol transformation, integration and evaluation environment. *Concurrency (Chichester, England)*, *5*(4), 269–286. Retrieved from citeseer.ist.psu.edu/article/schmidt93adaptive.html-doi:10.1002/cpe.4330050405

Schroeder, B., & Gibson, G. A. (2006). A large-scale study of failures in high-performance computing systems. *International Conference on Dependable Systems and Networks (DSN06)*, November 2006, (pp. 249-258). doi: 10.1109/DSN.2006.5

Sehgal, S., Kanhere, S. S., & Chou, C. T. (2008). *Mobishop: Using mobile phones for sharing consumer pricing information*. In IEEE International Conference on Distributed Computing in Sensor Systems.

Selic, B. (2004). *Fault tolerance techniques for distributed systems*. IBM Technical report. Retrieved July 27, 2004, from http://www.ibm.com/developerworks/rational/library/114.html

Shahidi, M., Attouk, A., & Aghvami, H. (2008). Content adaptation: Requirements and architecture. *Proceedings of the 10th International Conference on Information Integration and Web-based Applications and Services* (pp. 626-629). New York, NY: ACM Press.

Shankar, P., Ganapathy, V., & Iftode, L. (2009). *Privately querying location-based services with SybilQuery*. In ACM International Conference on Ubiquitous Computing.

Shen, C., & Schulzrinne, H. (2010). On TCP-based SIP server overload control. In *Proceedings of IPTComm*, Munich, Germany.

Shen, C., Schulzrinne, H., & Nahum, E. (2008). SIP server overload control: Design and evaluation. In *Proceedings of IPTComm*, Heidelberg, Germany.

Shi, J., Zhang, R., Liu, Y., & Zhang, Y. (2010). *Prisense: Privacy-preserving data aggregation in people-centric urban sensing systems.* In IEEE Conference on Computer Communications.

Shiraz, M., & Barfouroush, A. (2008). Conceptual framework for modeling automated negotiation in multiagent systems. *Negotiation Journal, 24*(1), 45–70. doi:10.1111/j.1571-9979.2007.00166.x

Sim, K., & Wong, E. (2001). Toward market-driven agents for electronic auction. *IEEE Transactions on Systems, Man, and Cybernetics, 3*(6), 474–484.

Si, Y., Edmond, D., Dumas, M., & Hofstede, A. (2007). Specification and execution of composite trading activities. *Journal of Electronic Commerce Research, 7*(3-4), 221–263. doi:10.1007/s10660-007-9005-6

Sloman, M., Luk, W., Lupu, E., & Dulay, N. (2004). *Polyander project.* Retrieved from http://www-dse.doc.ic.ac.uk/Projects/polyander

Soliman, H., Castelluccia, C., El Malki, K., & Bellier, L.(2005). Hierarchical mobile IPv6 mobility management (HMIPv6). *RFC 4140.*

Song, X., & Dou, W. (2011). A workflow framework for intelligent service composition. *Future Generation Computer Systems, 27*(5), 627–636. doi:10.1016/j.future.2010.06.008

Stefanov, S. (2009). *Don't make me wait! Or building high-performance web applications.* Tech talk at eBay. Retrieved March, 1, 2011, from http://www.slideshare.net/stoyan/dont-make-me-wait-or-building-highperformance-web-applications

Stevens, W. R. (1994). *TCP/IP illustrated (Vol. 1).* Boston, MA: Addison-Wesley.

Sun, W., Zhang, Y., Yu, C., Defago, X., & Inoguchi, Y. (2007b). Hybrid overloading and stochastic analysis for redundant scheduling in real-time multiprocessor systems. *Proceedings of the 26th IEEE International Symposium on Reliable Distributed Systems,* (pp. 265-274). doi: 10.1109/SRDS.2007.11

Sun, Z., Guo, W., Jin, Y., Sun, W., & Hu, W. (2007a). Rescheduling policy for fault-tolerant optical grid. *Proceedings of SPIE, the International Society for Optical Engineering, 6784*(2), 67841D.1-67841D.8. doi: 10.1117/12.743719

Sun, J., Tian, R., Hu, J., & Yang, B. (2009). Rate-based SIP flow management for SLA satisfaction. In *Proceedings of IEEE* (pp. 125–128). New York, USA: IFIP IM.

Sun, W., Yu, C., & Inoguchi, Y. (2008). Dynamic scheduling real-time task using primary-backup overloading strategy for multiprocessor systems. *IEICE Transactions on Information and Systems. E (Norwalk, Conn.), 91-D*(3), 796–806. doi:doi:10.1093/ietisy/e91

Suris, J., DaSilva, L., Han, Z., & MacKenzie, A. (2007). *Cooperative game theory for distributed spectrum sharing.* IEEE International Conference on Communications.

Sycara, K., Roth, S., Sadeh, N., & Fox, M. (1991). Distributed constraint heuristic Search. *IEEE Transactions on Systems, Man, and Cybernetics, 21,* 1446–1461. doi:10.1109/21.135688

Takabi, H., & Joshi, J. B. D., & Karimi, H. A. (2009). *A collaborative k-anonymity approach for location privacy in location-based services.* In International Conference on Collaborative Computing: Networking, Applications and Worksharing.

Talukder, A. K. M., Kirley, M., Buyya, R., & Tham, C. K. (2007). Multiobjective differential evolution for workflow execution on grids. *Proceedings of the 5th International Workshop on Middleware for Grid Computing,* (pp. 13-18). doi: 10.1145/1376849.1376852

Tanenbaum, A. (2003). *Computer networks* (4th ed.). Pearson Education Inc. TAT-14 Cable System. (2007). *Homepage.* Retrieved March 07, 2011, from https://www.tat-14.com/tat14

Telecommunications Portal, I. P. (2011). *SIP express router.* Retrieved from http://www.iptel.org/ser/

Tong, M., Yang, Z., & Liu, Q. (2010). A novel model of adaptation decision-taking engine in multimedia adaptation. *Journal of Network and Computer Applications, 33*(1), 43–49. doi:10.1016/j.jnca.2009.06.004

Tonnies, S., Kohncke, B., Hennig, P., & Balke, W.-T. (2009). A service oriented architecture for personalized rich media delivery. *IEEE International Conference on Service Computing* (pp. 340-347). New York, NY: IEEE Press.

Topcuoglu, H., Hariri, S., & Wu, M. Y. (2002). Performance effective and low complexity task scheduling for heterogeneous computing. *IEEE Transactions on Parallel and Distributed Systems, 13*(3), 260–274. doi:10.1109/71.993206

TPACK. (2007, June). *PBB-TE, PBT: Carrier grade Ethernet transport.* Retrieved March 7, 2011, from http://www.tpack.com/resources/tpack-white-papers/pbb-te-pbt.html

Travostino, F., Daspit, P., Gommans, L., Jog, C., de Laat, C., & Mambretti, J. (2006, October). Seamless live migration of virtual machines over the MAN/WAN. *Future Generation Computer Systems, 22*, 901–907. doi:10.1016/j.future.2006.03.007

Trienekens, J., Bouman, J., & Zwan, M. (2004). Specification of service level agreements: Problems, principles and practices. *Software Quality Journal, 12*, 43–57. doi:10.1023/B:SQJO.0000013358.61395.96

Trigoni, N., Guitton, A., & Skordylis, A. (2006). Routing and processing multiple aggregate queries in sensor networks. *The 4th International Conference on Embedded Networked Sensor Systems*, (pp. 391–392). Colorado, USA.

Trigoni, N., Yao, Y., Demers, A., Gehrke, J., & Rajaraman, R. (June 2005). *Multi-query optimization for sensor networks.* The First IEEE International Conference on Distributed Computing in Sensor Systems (DCOSS 2005). Marina del Rey, CA: IEEE.

Tuttlebee, W. H. W. (Ed.). (2002). *Software defined radio: Enabling technologies.* Chichester, UK: John Wiley & Sons.

Uliman, I., Pomalaza, R. C., Oppernann, I., & Lehtomaki, J. (August 2004). *Radio resource allocation in heterogeneous wireless networks using cooperative games.* Nordic Radio Symposium 2004/Finnish Wireless.

University of Murcia. (2011). *Deresec project.* DEpendability and Security by Enhanced REConfigurability. Retrieved from http://www.deserec.eu/

Urquhart, J. (2008, June). *"Follow the law" meme hits the big time.* Retrieved March, 1, 2011, from http://blog.jamesurquhart.com/2008/06/follow-law-meme-hits-big-time.html

Vapnik, V. (1998). *Statistical learning theory.* John Wiley and Sons.

Vassiliou, V., & Andreas, P. (2007). Supporting mobility events within a hierarchical mobile IP-over-MPLS network. *The Journal of Communication, 2*(2), 61–70.

Verrelst, H., Lerouge, E., Moreau, E., Vandewalle, J., Störmann, C., & Burge, P. (1996). *A rule based and neural network system for fraud detection in mobile communications.* ACTS PROJECT AC095 ASPeCT. European Commission.

Vilalta, R., & Ma, S. (2002). Predicting rare events in temporal domains. In *Proceedings of the 2002 IEEE International Conference on Data Mining* (pp. 474-481). doi: 10.1109/ICDM.2002.1183991

Vogler, H., Spriestersbach, A., & Moschgath, M. (1999). *Protecting competitive negotiation of mobile agents.* IEEE Workshop on Future Trends of Distributed Computing Systems (FTDCS).

Wang, L., Xue, Y., & Schulz, E. (2006). *Resource allocation in multi-cell ofdm systems based on non-cooperative game.* 17th Annual IEEE International Symposium on Personal, Indoor and Mobile Radio Communications.

Wang, F., Ramamritham, K., & Stankovic, J. A. (1995). Determining redundancy levels for fault tolerant real-time systems. *IEEE Transactions on Computers, 44*(2), 292–301. doi:10.1109/12.364540

Wang, Y. G. (2010). SIP overload control: A backpressure-based approach. *ACM SIGCOMM Computer Communications Review, 40*(4), 399–400.

Wang, Y., Tan, K., & Ren, J. (2005). *Towards autonomous and automatic evaluation and negotiation in agent-mediated internet marketplaces* (*Vol. 5*, pp. 343–366). Kluwer Academic Publishers.

Warabino, T., Kishi, Y., & Yokota, H. (2009). Session control cooperating core and overlay networks for "minimum core" architecture. In *Proceedings of IEEE Globecom*, Honolulu, Hawaii.

Wieczorek, M., Podlipnig, S., Prodan, R., & Fahringer, T. (2008). Bi-criteria scheduling of scientific workflows for the grid. *Proceedings of the 8th IEEE International Symposium on Cluster Computing and the Grid,* (pp. 9-16). doi: 10.1109/CCGRID.2008.21

Wieczorek, M., Hoheisel, A., & Prodan, R. (2009). Towards a general model of the multi-criteria workflow scheduling on the grid. *Future Generation Computer Systems, 25*(3), 237–256. doi:10.1016/j.future.2008.09.002

Wilkes, J. (2008). *Utility functions, prices, and negotiation.* HP Laboratories.

Willis, P. (2001). *Carrier scale IP networks: Designing and operating internet networks* (1 ed.). Institution of Engineering and Technology.

Willy, V. (2008). *The value of a millisecond: Finding the optimal speed of a trading infrastructure.* Retrieved March, 1, 2011, from http://www.tabbgroup.com/PublicationDetail.aspx?PublicationID=346

Wisely, W., & Mohr, J. U. (2000). Broadband radio access for IP networks (BRAIN). *The 11th IEEE International Symposium on Personal, Indoor and Mobile Radio Communications, PIMRC 2000* (Vol. 1, pp. 431-436). DOI: 10.1109/PIMRC.2000.881462

Wong, T., Fang, F., & Leung, D. (2004). Automating buyer-seller negotiation in supply chain management. *Proceedings of 5th Asia Pacific Industrial Engineering and Management System Conference.*

Wong, W., Zhang, D., & Kara-Ali, M. (2000). Negotiating with experience. *Proceedings of AAAI Workshop on Knowledge-Based Electronic Markets,* (pp. 85–90).

Wu, B., Chi, C., Chen, Z., Gu, M., & Sun, J. (2009). Workflow-based resource allocation to optimize overall performance of composite services. *Future Generation Computer Systems, 25*(3), 199–212. doi:10.1016/j.future.2008.06.003

Xu, L., Huang, C., Yan, J., & Drwiega, T. (2009). De-registration based S-CSCF load balancing in IMS core network. In *Proceedings of IEEE ICC,* Dresden, Germany.

Xu, T., & Cai, Y. (2009). *Location cloaking for safety protection of ad hoc networks.* In IEEE International Conference on Computer Communications.

Xu, Z. (2010). *WAVNet: Wide-area virtual networks for dynamic provisioning of IaaS.* Unpublished Master's thesis, The University of Hong Kong, Pokfulum Road, Hong Kong.

Xu, Z., Martin, P., Powley, W., & Zulkernine, F. (2007). Reputation-enhanced QoS-based web services discovery. *IEEE international Conference on Web Services* (pp. 249-256). New York, NY: IEEE Press.

Yampolskiy, M., Hommel, W., Marcu, P., & Hamm, M. (2010). An information model for the provisioning of network connections enabling customer-specific end-to-end QoS guarantees. *Proceedings of the 7th International Conference on Services Computing (SCC 2010),* (pp. 138-145).

Yampolskiy, M., Hommel, W., Danciu, V. A., Metzker, M. G., & Hamm, M. (2011). Management-aware inter-domain routing for end-to-end quality of service. *International Journal on Advances in Internet Technology, 4*(2).

Yang, J., Huang, F., & Gou, S. Z. (2009). An optimized algorithm for overload control of SIP signaling network. In *Proceedings of 5th International Conference on Wireless Communications, Networking and Mobile Computing.*

Yang, S., & Shao, N. (2007). Enhancing pervasive web accessibility with rule-based adaptation strategy. *Journal of Expert Systems with Applications, 32,* 1154–1167. doi:10.1016/j.eswa.2006.02.008

Yao, Y., & Gehrke, J. (January 2003). *Query processing in sensor networks.* The First Biennial Conference on Innovative Data Systems Research (CIDR). Asilomar, California.

Yi, M.-K., & Hwang, C.-S. (2003). A mobility-based binding update strategy in hierarchical mobile Ipv6. Retrieved from dpnm.postech.ac.kr/papers/DSOM/03/118-yunmnmayuy.pdf

Yokoo, M. (2001). Distributed constraint satisfaction: Foundations of cooperation in multi-agent systems. *IEEE Transactions on Knowledge and Data Engineering,* 143.

You, T., Sangheon, P., & Yanghee, C. (2003). Robust hierarchical mobile IPv6 (RH-MIPv6). *IEEE VTC 2003,* (Vol. 3, pp. 2014-2018).

Yu, J., Buyya, R., & Tham, C. K. (2005). Cost-based scheduling of scientific workflow applications on utility grids. *Proceedings of the 1st International Conference on e-Science and Grid Computing*, (pp. 140-147). doi: 10.1109/E-SCIENCE.2005.26

Yu, J., & Buyya, R. (2006a). Scheduling scientific workflow applications with deadline and budget constraints using genetic algorithms. *Science Progress, 14*(3), 217–230.

Yu, J., & Buyya, R. (2006b). A taxonomy of workflow management systems for grid computing. *Journal of Grid Computing, 3*(3-4), 171–200. doi:10.1007/s10723-005-9010-8

Yunhua, K., Danfeng, Y., & Bertino, E. (2008). Efficient and secure content processing by cooperative intermediaries. *IEEE Transactions on Parallel and Distributed Systems, 19*(5), 615–626. doi:10.1109/TPDS.2007.70758

Zaharia, M., Borthakur, D., Sarma, J. S., Elmeleegy, K., Shenker, S., & Stoica, I. (2009). *Job scheduling for multi-user MapReduce clusters*. University of California at Berkeley, Technical Report No. UCB/EECS-2009-55. Retrieved from http://www.eecs.berkeley.edu/Pubs/TechRpts/2009/EECS-2009-55.html

Zaim, A. H. (2003). JumpStart just-in-time signaling protocol: A formal description using extended finite state machines. *Optical Engineering (Redondo Beach, Calif.), 42*(2), 568–585. doi:10.1117/1.1533795

Zen, Z. (2009). An agent-based online shopping system in e-commerce. *Journal of Computer and Information Science, 2*(4), 14–19.

Zhang, T., Ramakrishnan, R., & Livny, M. (1996). BIRCH: An efficient data clustering method for very large databases. *Proceedings of the 1996 ACM SIGMOD International Conference on Management of Data* (pp. 103-114). ACM.

Zhang, X., Yu, X., & Chen, X. (September 2005). *Inter-query data aggregation in wireless sensor networks*. International Conference on Wireless Communications, Networking and Mobile Computing (WCNM 2005). Wuhan, China.

Zhao, L., Ren, Y., & Sakurai, K. (2011). A resource minimizing scheduling algorithm with ensuring the deadline and reliability in heterogeneous systems. *Proceedings of the 25th International Conference on Advanced Information Networking and Applications*. IEEE Computer Society Press.

Zhao, L., Ren, Y., Xiang, Y., & Sakurai, K. (2010). Fault tolerant scheduling with dynamic number of replicas in heterogeneous system. *Proceedings of 12th IEEE International Conference on High Performance Computing and Communications*, (pp. 434-441).

Zheng, Q., Veeravalli, B., & Tham, C. K. (2009). On the design of fault-tolerant scheduling strategies using primary-backup approach for computational grids with low replication costs. *IEEE Transactions on Computers, 58*(3), 380–393. doi:10.1109/TC.2008.172

Zhong, G., & Hengartner, U. (2009). *A distributed k-anonymity protocol for location privacy*. In IEEE International Conference on Pervasive Computing and Communications.

Zhou, C., Chia, L., & Lee, B. (2004). DAML-QoS ontology for web services. *Proceeding of IEEE International Conference on Web Services* (pp. 472-479). New York, NY: IEEE Press.

Zhou, C., Chia, L., & Lee, B. (2005). Semantics in service discovery and QoS measurement. *IEEE IT Professional, 7*(2), 29–34. doi:10.1109/MITP.2005.41

Zhu, W., Wang, C.-L., & Lau, F. C. M. (2002). JESSICA2: A distributed Java virtual machine with transparent thread migration support. In *Proceedings of the 4th IEEE International Conference on Cluster Computing* (pp. 381–388).

Zhu, W., Wang, C.-L., & Lau, F. C. M. (2003). Lightweight transparent Java thread migration for distributed JVM. In *Proceedings of the 32nd International Conference on Parallel Processing* (pp. 465–472).

Zhuang, Y., Fong, S., & Shi, M. (2008). Knowledge-empowered automated negotiation for e-Commerce. *Journal of Knowledge Information Systems, 17*, 167–191. doi:10.1007/s10115-007-0119-x

Ziegelmann, M. (2007). *Constrained shortest paths and related problems*. VDM.

About the Contributors

Jemal Abawajy is a faculty member at Deakin University and has published more than 100 articles in refereed journals and conferences as well as a number of technical reports. He is on the editorial board of several international journals and edited several international journals and conference proceedings. He has also been a member of the organizing committee for over 60 international conferences and workshops serving in various capacity including best paper award chair, general co-chair, publication chair, vice-chair and program committee. He is actively involved in funded research in building secure, efficient and reliable infrastructures for large-scale distributed systems. Towards this vision, he is working in several areas including: pervasive and networked systems (mobile, wireless network, sensor networks, grid, cluster, and p2p), e-science and e-business technologies and applications, and performance analysis and evaluation.

Mukaddim Pathan is a Research Scientist at CSIRO, the national government body of scientific research in Australia. He also holds the position of an adjunct lecturer at the Australian National University. His research interests include data management, resource allocation, load balancing, and coordination policies in wide-area distributed systems such as content delivery networks, cloud computing, and sensor networks. He is the editor of "Content Delivery Networks" book, published by Springer. He has authored and co-authored a number of research papers in internationally recognized journals and conferences. He is involved in the organization of the UPGRADE-CN and IDCS workshops and is a PC member of several international conferences. He has edited a few research issues in reputed international journals and also serves as a reviewer and editorial board member of several renowned journals. He is a member of IEEE, IEEE Computer Society, and ACM.

Mustafizur Rahman is a Consultant of Business Analytics and Optimization service line at IBM Australia. He also worked as Endeavour Research Fellow at the Institute of High Performance Computing, Agency for Science Technology and Research (A*STAR), Singapore. He received PhD degree from Department of Computer Science and Software Engineering at the University of Melbourne, Australia. His research interests include workflow scheduling and resource management in Grid/Cloud computing systems as well as fault-tolerance and load balancing in P2P and self-managing systems. He has been actively engaged in the research and development projects of CLOUDS Lab at the University of Melbourne and received 2010 Endeavour Research Fellowship Award from Australian Government. He has authored and co-authored several research papers in internationally recognized journals and conferences. He is a member of IEEE, IEEE Computer Society, and ACM. He has been involved in the organization of several international workshops and conferences. He also serves as the reviewer of renowned journals, including *Future Generation Computer Systems* (FGCS) and *Concurrency & Computation: Practice & Experience* (CCPE).

Al-Sakib Khan Pathan received Ph.D. degree in Computer Engineering in 2009 from Kyung Hee University (KHU), South Korea. He received B.Sc. degree in Computer Science and Information Technology from Islamic University of Technology (IUT), Bangladesh in 2003. He is currently an Assistant Professor and FYP Coordinator at Computer Science Department in International Islamic University Malaysia (IIUM), Malaysia. Till June 2010, he served as an Assistant Professor at Computer Science and Engineering department in BRAC University, Bangladesh. Prior to holding this position, he worked as a Researcher at Networking Lab, KHU, South Korea till August 2009. His research interest includes wireless sensor networks, network security, and e-services technologies. He has served as a Chair and a PC member in numerous international conferences/workshops. He is currently serving as the Editor-in-Chief of IJIDCS, an Area Editor of IJCNIS, and editor of several other well-known journals and books. He also serves as a referee of a few renowned journals. He is a member of IEEE, IEEE ComSoc Bangladesh Chapter, and several other international organizations.

Mustafa Mat Deris received Ph.D degree in Computer Science in 2002 from University Putra Malaysia. He is currently a Professor in the faculty of Computer Science and Information Technology, Universiti Tun Hussein Onn Malaysia. He has published more than 150 articles in refereed journals and proceedings. He is on the editorial board of several international journals and conferences and also guest editor of *International Journal of BioMedical Soft Computing and Human Science* for *Special Issue on "Soft Computing Methodologies and Its Applications"* a reviewer of several international journals such as *IEEE Transaction on Parallel and Distributed Computing, Journal of Parallel and Distributed Databases, Journal of Future Generation on Computer Systems,* Elsevier, *Journal of Cluster Computing,* Kluwer, *Journal of Computer Mathematics*, Taylor & Francis, UK, and IEEE Conference on Cluster and Grid Computing. He has served as a program committee member and co-organizer for numerous international conferences/workshops including Grid and Peer-to-Peer Computing, (GP2P 2005, 2006), Autonomic Distributed Data and Storage Systems Management (ADSM 2005, 2006, 2007), and Grid Pervasive Computing Security, organizer for Rough and Soft Sets Theories and Applications (RSAA 2010), Fukuoka, Japan, and Soft Computing and Data Engineering (SCDE 2010), Jeju, Korea. His research interests include distributed databases, data grid, soft computing, and data mining.

* * *

Raja Al-Jaljouli is a Ph.D. student in Science and Technology Faculty at Deakin University and a holder of Masters Degree in Software Engineering, University of New South Wales. She is currently in the stage of submitting Ph.D. thesis. The Masters Degree thesis was on the security of data gathering mobile agents. She has published a number of conference papers, technical reports, and a book chapter. She served as a reviewer of book chapters for publication. Her research interests are in mutli-agent systems, security of mobile agents, security protocols, negotiation strategies, utility function in E-commerce application, E-negotiation, and formal verification methods.

Nancy Alonistioti has a B.Sc. degree and a PhD degree in Informatics and Telecommunications (Dept. of Informatics and Telecommunications, University of Athens). She has working experience as senior researcher and project manager in the Dept. of Informatics and Telecommunications at University of Athens. She has participated in several national and European projects, (CTS, SS#7, ACTS RAINBOW, EURESCOM, MOBIVAS, ANWIRE, E2R, LIAISON, E3, SELFNET, SACRA, CONSERN, UNIVER-SELF etc) and has experience as Project and Technical manager of the IST-MOBIVAS, IST-ANWIRE, ICT-SELFNET projects, which had a focus on reconfigurable mobile systems, cognitive mobile networks, and FI. She has served as PMT member and WP Leader of the FP6 IST E2R project. She is co-editor and author in "Software Defined Radio, Architectures, Systems, and Functions," published by John Wiley in May 2003. She has served as Lecturer in University of Piraeus and she has recently joined the faculty of Dept. Informatics and Telecommunications of Univ. of Athens. She is TPC member in many conferences in the area of mobile communications and mobile applications for systems and networks beyond 3G. She has over 55 publications in the area of mobile communications, reconfigurable, cognitive, and autonomic systems and networks and Future Internet.

Alagan Anpalagan received the B.A.Sc. (H), M.A.Sc. and Ph.D. degrees in Electrical Engineering from the University of Toronto, Canada. He joined the Department of Electrical and Computer Engineering at Ryerson University in 2001 and became Professor in 2010. He served the department as Graduate Program Director (2004-09) and the Interim Electrical Engineering Program Director (2009-10). During his sabbatical (2010-11), he was a Visiting Professor at Asian Institute of Technology and Visiting Researcher at Kyoto University. Dr. Anpalagan's industrial experience includes working at Bell Mobility on 1xRTT system deployment studies (2001), at Nortel Networks on SECORE R&D projects (1997) and at IBM Canada as IIP Intern (1994). Dr. Anpalagan directs a research group working on radio resource management (RRM) and radio access & networking (RAN) areas within the WINCORE Lab. His current research interests include cognitive radio resource allocation and management, wireless cross layer design and optimization, collaborative communication, green communications technologies, and QoE-aware femtocells.

Afshin Behzadan holds a M.A.Sc degree in Electrical and Computer Engineering from Ryerson University, Canada. He was a member of RRM+RAN research group in WINCORE Lab at Ryerson University. He received his B.Sc. degree in Software Engineering from Yazd University, Iran, in 2005. He also holds a M.Sc. degree in Software Engineering from Amirkabir University of Technology, received with honour in 2008. His research focuses on energy efficient routing and clustering strategies and the related techniques in wireless sensor and ad-hoc networks.

Jorge Bernal Bernabé received the Computer Engineering and the MSc in Computer Science from the University of Murcia. Currently, he is a research staff in the Department of Information and Communications Engineering of the University of Murcia. He has been working in several European projects while pursuing his PhD. His scientific activity is mainly devoted to the security and management of distributed systems.

Jose M. Alcaraz Calero received the Computer Engineering, MSc and PhD degrees with honors at the University of Murcia. He has been working at University of Murcia since 2004 in several European and international projects. Currently he is research staff at Hewlett Packard Laboratories.

Felix J. Garcia Clemente is an Assistant Professor of Computer Networks at the Department of Computer Engineering of the University of Murcia. His research interests include security and management of distributed communication networks. He received an MSc and PhD degrees in Computer Science from the University of Murcia.

Olivier Festor is a research director at INRIA Nancy-Grand Est where he leads the MADYNES research team. He has a PhD degree (1994) and a Habilitation degree (2001) from Henri-Poincare University, Nancy, France. He spent 3 years at the IBM European Networking Center in Heidelberg, Germany and one Q4 year at the EURECOM Institute in Nice, France. His research interests are in the design of algorithms and models for automated security management of large scale networks and services. This includes monitoring, fuzzing, and vulnerability assessment. Application domains are IPv6, Voice over IP services, and dynamic ad-hoc networks.

Wolfgang Fritz received Diploma in Information Technology in 2009 from the department of Electrical Engineering at Technische Universität München. In late 2009, he joined the Leibniz Supercomputing Centre in Garching/Munich as a research assistant at the network planning group. His current research focuses on multi-domain circuit management and monitoring, especially within the European Géant project. Of special interest is not only a network structure of static, dedicated links between all participants, but also the aspect of dealing with transatlantic connections of a more dynamic nature. Both technical and organizational aspects are essential to cover management procedures as well as a holistic monitoring of these circuits, covering the whole life cycle from their ordering to their decommissioning.

Mohd Farhan Md Fudzee is a faculty member at Tun Hussein Onn University of Malaysia (UTHM) and Software & Multimedia Research Centre, UTHM. Currently, he is attached to Deakin University, Australia, as a post graduate student/researcher. He has completed Diploma in Computer Science, Bachelor of Science in IT (honours), and Master of Science in IT. He has completed several research grants, won several medals in research and innovation competitions, and awarded a teaching and learning award. He has published a book in IT, book chapters, several papers in reviewed conferences and journals as well as technical reports and contributed to the academic activities as reviewer. He has also been a member of IEEE, ACM, and NAUI Scuba Diver. His research interest includes multimedia computing (content adaptation, performance modelling, and analysis) and e-learning applications.

Vangelis Gazis holds B.Sc., M.Sc., and Ph.D. degrees from the Dept. of Informatics and Telecommunications at the University of Athens, and an M.B.A. degree from the Athens University of Economics and Business. He is a senior researcher at the Communication Networks Laboratory (CNL) group at the Dept. of Informatics and Telecommunications and has participated in national (OTE-DECT, GRNET, GUNet) and European IST projects (MOBIVAS, ANWIRE, GEANT-2, SELFNET). He specializes in mobile service provision, reconfigurable mobile systems, cross-layer design, adaptable protocol stacks, ontology languages for autonomic systems and self-managing cognitive systems and has over 40 publications in these thematic areas.

Wolfgang Hommel has a PhD in Computer Science from Ludwig Maximilians University, Munich, and heads the network services planning group at the Leibniz Supercomputing Centre (LRZ) in Germany. His current research focuses on IT security and privacy management in large distributed systems, including identity federations and Grids. Emphasis is put on a holistic perspective, i.e., the problems and solutions are analyzed from the design phase through software engineering, deployment in heterogeneous infrastructures, and during the operation and change phases according to IT service management process frameworks, such as ISO/IEC 20000-1. Being both a regional computing centre for higher education institutions with more than 100,000 users and a national supercomputing centre, the LRZ offers a plethora of real world scenarios and large projects to apply and refine the research results in practice. Wolfgang Hommel is also a member of the MNM-Team.

Yang Hong received B.S. degree in Electronic Engineering from Shanghai Jiao Tong University, China, M.E. degree in Electrical Engineering from National University of Singapore, Singapore, and Ph.D. degree in Electrical Engineering from University of Ottawa, Canada. His research interests include SIP overload control, Internet congestion control, modeling and performance evaluation of computer networks, and industrial process control.

Changcheng Huang received his B.Eng. in 1985, and M.Eng. in 1988, both in Electronic Engineering from Tsinghua University, Beijing, China. He received a Ph.D. degree in Electrical Engineering from Carleton University, Ottawa, Canada in 1997. From 1996 to 1998, he worked for Nortel Networks, Ottawa, Canada where he was a Systems Engineering Specialist. He was a systems Engineer and Network Architect in the Optical Networking Group of Tellabs, Illinois, USA during the period of 1998 to 2000. Since July 2000, he has been with the Department of Systems and Computer Engineering at Carleton University, Ottawa, Canada where he is currently an Associate Professor. Dr. Huang won the Canada Foundation for Innovation (CFI) new opportunity award for building an optical network laboratory in 2001. He was an Associate Editor of IEEE Communications Letters from 2004 to 2006. He is currently a senior member of IEEE.

King Tin Lam received his B.Eng. degree in Electrical and Electronic Engineering and M.Sc. degree in Computer Science both from the University of Hong Kong in 2001 and 2006, respectively. He worked in the IT Department of the Hong Kong and Shanghai Banking Corporation for five years between graduations of the two degrees. Mr. Lam is currently a full-time Ph.D. candidate in the Department of Computer Science at the University of Hong Kong. His research interests include distributed Java virtual machines for cluster computing, software transactional memory, and server clustering technologies.

Asish K Mukhopadhyay holds a M.Tech (ECE) from Indian Institute of Technology, Kharagpur and PhD(Engg) from Jadavpur University, Kolkata, India. He has long experience in teaching, administration and industry in various academic institutions and industry for more than three decades. His current area of research includes next generation wireless and mobile networks. He has about 50 publications in national/ international journals and conference proceedings. He is a Life Fellow of the Institution of Engineers (I), Sr.Member, IEEE, Sr. Life Member, CSI; Life Member of ISTE, SSI, and IETE.

Manzur Murshed received his BScEng (Hons) degree in Computer Science and Engineering from Bangladesh University of Engineering and Technology (BUET), Dhaka, Bangladesh in 1994, and PhD degree in Computer Science from the Australian National University, Canberra, Australia in 1999. He is currently an Associate Professor and the Head of Gippsland School of Information Technology, the Faculty of Information Technology, Monash University, Australia. He has so far published more than 125 refereed research papers. His ten most-cited publications have more than 1200 citations. He received two Australian Research Council Discovery Project grants in 2006 and 2010. He has been serving as a guest editor of a special issue series of the *Journal of Multimedia* since 2009. He received 2007 Vice-Chancellor's Knowledge Transfer commendation award from the University of Melbourne and 2006 Early Career Research Excellence award from the Faculty of IT, Monash University. He was also awarded 1994 BUET Gold Medal.

Mohamed Nassar works currently as an expert research engineer at the INRIA research center Nancy-Grand Est. His research interests are networks and services security. He holds a PhD diploma in Computer Sciences from Nancy-I University. His PhD research focuses on monitoring and intrusion detection in VoIP networks. He holds a research Master degree from the Nancy-I University and an Engineering diploma from the Lebanese University.

Eleni Patouni received the B.Sc. and M.Sc degrees (with honours, ranked 1st in her class) from the Department of Informatics and Telecommunications, NKUA in 2003 and 2005, respectively. In 2010, she received the PhD degree from the same department. Since October 2004, she has been participating in the European IST-FP6 Integrated Projects "E2R," "E2R II" (End-to-End Reconfigurability phase I and II), IST-FP7 E3 (End-to-End Efficiency), and IST FP7 Self-NET. Currently she is involved in the FP7 EC ICT-2007-216248 Large Scale Integrating Project UniverSelf, as a senior research associate and delegate work package leader for WP4 "Deployment & Impact". Since 2009, she is also a laboratory assistant and adjunct Lecturer in department of Informatics, TEI Athens. She is currently an adjunct Lecturer in department of Statistics and Insurance Science, University of Piraeus. She has more than 30 publications in the thematic areas of beyond 3G, cognitive networks, and autonomic communication systems; she received the best paper award in the IFIP Autonomic Networking Conference, 2006. She has also contributed in OMA. Her main research interests include mobile network and reconfigurable protocols, component-based models, network-management and decision-making aspects as well as cognitive, and autonomic networking issues.

Ricky K.K. Ma received his B.Eng. degree in Computer Engineering and M.Phil. degree in Computer Science both from the University of Hong Kong in 1997 and 2002 respectively. He worked in Hong Kong Productivity Council for more than six years. Mr. Ma is currently a part-time Ph.D. candidate in the Department of Computer Science at the University of Hong Kong. His research interests include cloud computing and task migration techniques.

Gregorio Martínez Pérez is an Associate Professor in the Department of Information and Communications Engineering of the University of Murcia. His research interests include security and management of distributed communication networks. He received an MSc and PhD in Computer Science from the University of Murcia.

Juan M. Marín Pérez is a research staff in the Department of Information and Communications Engineering of the University of Murcia. He received Engineering and MSc degrees in Computer Science from the University of Murcia. He has been working in several European projects while doing his PhD. His research interests include security and management of distributed systems.

Jesus D. Jimenez Re is a research staff member in the Department of Information and Communications Engineering of the University of Murcia. He received Engineering and MSc degrees in Computer Science from the University of Murcia. He has been working in several European projects while doing his PhD. His research interests include security and management of distributed systems.

Yacine Rebahi holds a PhD in Mathematics and a Bachelor degree in Computer Science. Currently he works as a Senior Scientist leading the Reliable Networking Infrastructure (RNI) team at the Fraunhofer FOKUS competence center NGNI. Prior to joining FOKUS in 2002, he worked at Ericsson on Voice-over-IP (VoIP). At FOKUS, he has worked on various European and industry projects. His research activities are mostly dedicated to emergency services in next generation networks, security, and Future Internet. Dr. Rebahi's over 50 publications between journal and conference papers, and chapter books. Dr. Rebahi has been leading several research and industry projects in the following fields of security: Trust in ad-hoc networks, Security and privacy issues in the context of policy making process, DoS attack detection in VoIP networks, spam mitigation in VoIP environments, fraud and service misuse in VoIP networks. In addition Dr. Rebahi is member of the IEEE.

Reinhard Ruppelt received his Diploma in Mathematics in 1979 from the University of Bremen. Since 1981 he worked as a researcher at the Institut für Luft- und Raumfahrt of Technische Universität Berlin before he joined the Hahn-Meitner-Institut Berlin in 1985. From 1987 to 2000 he was with GMD Fokus working on error correction algorithms and network protocol development. Since 2001 he is with Fraunhofer Fokus with primary interests in NGN, IMS, IPv6, and VoIP. His main fields of interests are attack detection in VoIP networks, spam mitigation in VoIP environments, and fraud and service misuse in VoIP networks.

Tishna Sabrina received her BScEng (Hons) degree in Electrical and Electronics Engineering from Bangladesh University of Engineering and Technology, Dhaka, Bangladesh, in 2005. She is currently enrolled as a PhD student at Gippsland School of Information Technology, the Faculty of Information Technology, Monash University, Australia. Her research interests include telecommunications, sensor networks, participatory sensing networks, and security and privacy.

Sajal Saha is an Assistant Professor in the department of Computer Application, Narula Institute of Technology, Kolkata, India since August 2004.He is ME in Information Technology from West Bengal University of Technology (2007), MCA from Sikkim Manipal Institute of Technology, Sikkim (2004) and BSc (Physics) from Calcutta University(2001). Currently he is pursuing PhD from National Institute of Technology, Durgapur, India. He is engaged in research in the area of overlay based heterogeneous networks, and Mobile IP route optimization. He is the recipient of Silver medal for securing 2nd position in ME examination. . He has many publications in international/national journals of repute and various conference proceedings. He is a member of IEEE and member of ACM, as well as a Global member of Internet Society (ISOC).

Kouichi Sakurai received the B.S. degree in mathematics from Faculty of Science, Kyushu University and the M.S. degree in applied science from the Faculty of Engineering, Kyushu University in 1986 and 1988, respectively. He was engaged in research and development on cryptography and information security at the Computer and Information Systems Laboratory of Mitsubishi Electric Corporation from 1988 to 1994. He received his Doctorate in Engineering from the Faculty of Engineering, Kyushu University in 1993. From 1994, he worked for the Department of Computer Science of Kyushu University as an Associate Professor, and became a full Professor in 2002. His current research interests are in cryptography and information security. Dr. Sakurai is a member of the Information Processing Society of Japan, the Mathematical Society of Japan, ACM, IEEE, and the International Association for Cryptologic Research.

Antonio F. Gómez Skarmeta received the MS degree in Computer Science from the University of Granada and BS (Hons.) and the PhD degrees in Computer Science from the University of Murcia Spain. He is a Full Professor in the same Department and University. He has worked on different research projects at regional, national and especially at the European level in areas related to advanced services like multicast, multihoming, security, and adaptive multimedia applications in IP and NGN networks.

Cho-Li Wang received his Ph.D. degree in Computer Engineering from University of Southern California in 1995. He is currently an Associate Professor of the Department of Computer Science at the University of Hong Kong. Dr. Wang's research interests mainly focus on distributed Java virtual machines on clusters, Grid middleware, and software systems for pervasive/mobile computing. Dr. Wang is serving in a number of editorial boards, including *IEEE Transaction on Computers* (TC), *Multiagent and Grid Systems* (MAGS), and the *International Journal of Pervasive Computing and Communications* (JPCC). He is the regional coordinator (Hong Kong) of IEEE Technical Committee on Scalable Computing (TCSC).

Mark Yampolskiy first studied applied mathematics at one of the technical universities in Moscow and later on computer science at the Technical University Munich (TUM). He defended his PhD thesis in the area of computer networks and network management. The focus of his current research is dedicated to quality assurance in multi-domain network connections. Situated at the Leibniz Supercomputing Centre (LRZ), he is working in the Géant research collaboration. Within this collaboration, he is involved in numerous research and service activities tackling network management issues in multi-domain environments. Among other duties, he is in charge for the design and development of the monitoring system for multi-domain backbone connections, Géant E2E Links. Mark Yampolskiy is a member of the Munich Network Management (MNM) team, a team of researchers focusing on various aspects of networking, network management, and collaborative distributed environments.

James Yan is currently an Adjunct Research Professor with the Department of Systems and Computer Engineering, Carleton University, Ottawa, Canada. Dr. Yan received his B.A.Sc., M.A.Sc., and Ph.D. degrees in Electrical Engineering from the University of British Columbia, Vancouver, Canada. From 1976 to 1996 with Bell-Northern Research (BNR) and from 1996 to 2004 with Nortel, he was a telecommunications systems engineering manager responsible for projects in performance analysis of networks and products, advanced technology research and assessment, planning new network services and architectures, development of network design methods and tools, and new product definition. From 1988 to 1990, he participated in an exchange program with the Canadian Federal Government, where he was project prime for the planning of the evolution of the nationwide federal government telecommunications network. Dr. Yan is a member of IEEE and Professional Engineers Ontario.

Laiping Zhao received the B.E. degree and M.E. degree in Software Engineering from Dalian University of Technology in 2007 and 2009, respectively. Now he is a Ph.D. candidate in Kyushu University, supported by China Governmental Scholarship. His research interests include cloud computing, fault tolerance computing, and resource scheduling.

Index